MW01493813

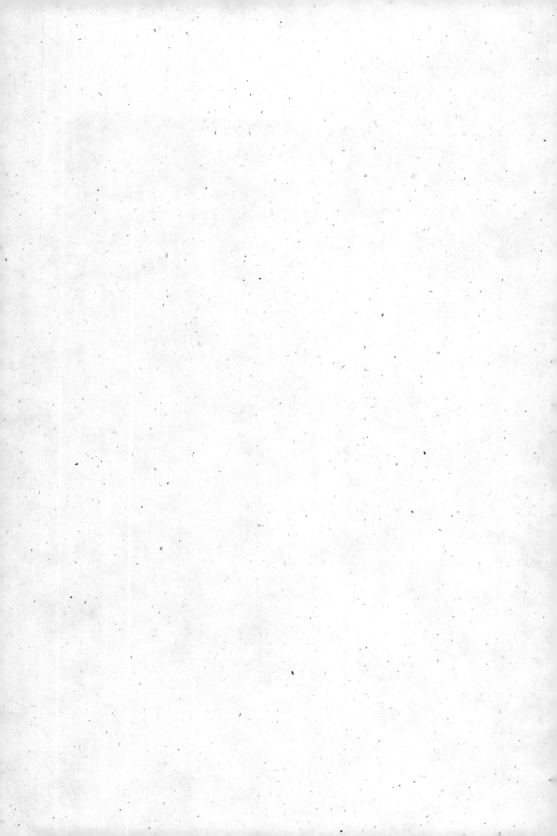

IMPERMISSIBLE PUNISHMENTS

IMPERMISSIBLE PUNISHMENTS

HOW PRISON BECAME A PROBLEM FOR DEMOCRACY

JUDITH RESNIK

THE UNIVERSITY OF CHICAGO PRESS

Chicago and London

The University of Chicago Press, Chicago 60637
The University of Chicago Press, Ltd., London
© 2025 by Judith Resnik
Published 2025
Printed in the United States of America

34 33 32 31 30 29 28 27 26 25   1 2 3 4 5

ISBN-13: 978-0-226-75474-1 (cloth)
ISBN-13: 978-0-226-75491-8 (e-book)
DOI: https://doi.org/10.7208/chicago/9780226754918.001.0001

Library of Congress Cataloging-in-Publication Data

Names: Resnik, Judith, author.
Title: Impermissible punishments : how prison became a
    problem for democracy / Judith Resnik.
Description: Chicago : The University of Chicago Press, 2025. |
    Includes bibliographical references and index.
Identifiers: LCCN 2024047957 | ISBN 9780226754741 (cloth) |
    ISBN 9780226754918 (e-book)
Subjects: LCSH: Punishment—United States—History. |
    Prisoners—Legal status, laws, etc.—United States. | Prisons—
    Law and legislation—United States. | Prison discipline—United
    States. | Democracy—United States. | Punishment—History.
Classification: LCC KF9731.R468 2025 | DDC 365/.6440973—dc23/
    eng/20241010
LC record available at https://lccn.loc.gov/2024047957

♾ This paper meets the requirements of ANSI/NISO Z39.48-1992
(Permanence of Paper).

To Denny Curtis, who tried to keep people out of prison, lessen their sentences, and alter their conditions of confinement. Along the way, he changed the legal academy by being among the inventors of clinical education that links students to clients who illuminate a world in need of change. With love and admiration.

CONTENTS

The transcript of the whipping trial and more materials related to the book can be found at http://impermissiblepunishments.law.yale.edu/.

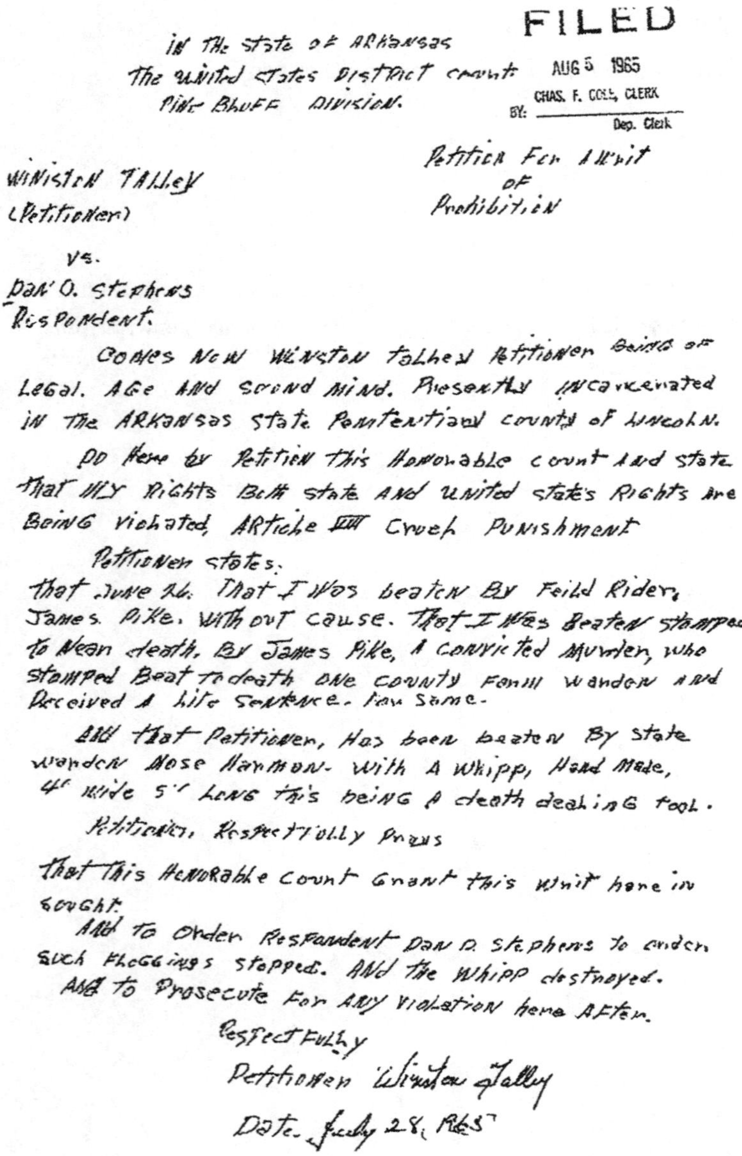

FILED
AUG 5 1965
CHAS. F. COLE, CLERK
BY: ______ Dep. Clerk

in The state of ARkansas
The united states District count
Pine Bluff Division.

Winiston Talley
(Petitioner)

Petition For A writ
of
Prohibition

vs.

Dan O. Stephens
Respondent.

Comes Now Winston talley Petitioner Being of Legal. Age And sound mind. Presently incarcerated in The ARkansas state Penitentiary county of Lincoln.

Do Here by Petition This Honorable count And state that my Rights Both state And united state's Rights are Being violated, ARticle VIII Cruel Punishment

Petitioner states:

that June 26. That I Was beaten By Feild Rider, James. Pike. With out cause. That I Was Beaten stamped to Near death, By James Pike, A convicted Murder, who stamped Beat to death one county Farm warden and Received A life sentence. for same.

And that Petitioner, Has been beaten By state warden Mose Harmon. with A Whipp, Hand Made, 4" wide 5' Long this being A death dealing tool.

Petitioner, Respectfully Prays

that This Honorable count Grant this writ here in sought.

And to Order Respondent Dan D. Stephens to order such Floggings stopped. And the Whipp destroyed.

And to Prosecute For Any violation here After.

Respectfully
Petitioner Winston Talley
Date. July 28, 1965

FIGURE I.1 Winston Talley's petition to federal judges in Arkansas, 1965, National Archives of the United States

"IF WHIPPING WERE TO BE AUTHORIZED"

"[I]f whipping were to be authorized, how does one, or any court, ascertain the point which would distinguish the permissible from that which is cruel and unusual?"

—Judge Harry Blackmun, writing for a federal appellate court banning whipping, *Jackson v. Bishop*, 1968[1]

In the annals of the US Civil Rights Movement, the city of Little Rock, Arkansas is famous. In 1957, Arkansas Governor Orval Faubus sought to defy a federal desegregation order by deploying the state's National Guard to block nine Black students from entering Little Rock's Central High School. After President Dwight Eisenhower sent in troops, Faubus closed the school for a year.[2]

Arkansas has another, less well-known claim to fame. A decade after Black teenagers braved the taunts of white crowds, Chief Judge J. Smith Henley of the federal court in Arkansas read the 1965 petition from Winston Talley, whose handwritten submission, reproduced in figure I.1, begins this book. Talley told the court that, "presently incarcerated," he had been "beaten with a Whipp," which he described as "Hand made" and measuring four inches wide and five feet long. Talley invoked the US Constitution's ban on "cruel and unusual punishment" and asked that "the Honorable Court . . . order . . . such floggings stopped. And the Whipp destroyed."

Unlike many federal judges who summarily dismissed prisoners' filings, Henley appointed prominent lawyers to represent Talley, as well as two other white prisoners seeking relief and, after taking testimony, decided the case. Chief Judge Henley agreed that prisoners had a *right* to get into court but did *not* agree that the US Constitution prohibited whipping. Instead, he set forth minimal constraints (the "*Talley* Rules"), calling for decision-making procedures and limiting lashes to ten at a time.

In 1967, William King Jackson, joined by two more white petitioners, brought new challenges. Federal judges again appointed luminaries of the Arkansas bar who, during the first and only US trial on whipping, established that the state forced prisoners to pick cotton, okra, and cucumbers six days a week, ten or more hours a day. Recorded in the 641-page transcript, witnesses described how staff and prisoners (called "trustys") whipped individuals for not making quotas to net "profits" for Arkansas, which had *no* line in its budget for prisons. After listening for three days, federal judges reiterated that, as long as it was regulated, whipping was not "cruel and unusual punishment."

The following year, Judge Harry Blackmun, writing for an appellate panel before his elevation to the US Supreme Court, reversed that ruling. A first for the country, their decision categorically ruled out a form of "discipline" prison officials said they needed. In private notes, the judges described being appalled at whipping but worried about circumscribing prison officials' powers and not wanting to end solitary confinement. The resulting lengthy opinion did not reference slavery or the trial's evidence of brutal lashings in the "colored section" when Judge Blackmun discussed the challenge of distinguishing "the permissible from" *impermissible punishments* of people convicted of crimes.

That problem has haunted governments for three hundred years, which is why this book exists. To explain past and present delineations of the "permissible/impermissible" in punishment, I integrate and interrogate the history and impact of two social movements— one producing the profession called "corrections" and the other creating a new legal regime named "prisoners' rights." My account draws from both sides of the Atlantic to examine ideologies of punishment; the institutionalization and precepts of the corrections profession; the law that prisoners brought into being; and the shifting, contested understandings of what democratic societies owe to the people they incarcerate.

A brief preview is in order. Beginning in the eighteenth century, a pantheon of famous white European men—Cesare Beccaria, Jeremy Bentham, John Howard, Gustave de Beaumont, Alexis de Tocqueville, and Francis Lieber—put punishment on the map of social inquiry. Probing punishment's utilities, moralities, and aims, these men were pioneering sociologists and activists. They visited prisons, collected data, and railed against punishments common in their day. They called on governments to justify punishments as rationally related to legitimate ends, including (in contemporary terms) retribution, deterrence, incapacitation, and rehabilitation. Again using contemporary nomenclature, they were "abolitionists" in the sense that each called for the end of some punishments then seen to be *normal* exercises of state power. They heralded *penitentiaries* as a great Enlightenment reform to displace the "barbarous" practices of branding, executing, and exiling individuals convicted of crimes.

What did prison entail? That newfangled institution did not come as a prepack but had to be built—not only in terms of constructing facilities but also through developing norms, mores, and purposes. During the first half of the nineteenth century, prisons imposed purposefully rigid, *degrading* punishments justified as *redeeming* and *deterring* criminals. Vivid accounts of prison squalor came with the "invention of the penitentiary"; in response, religious leaders, philanthropists, and newly minted social scientists formed societies seeking to improve prisoners' plights. After the US Civil War, the ideology behind punishment practices shifted from retributive suffering to *reforming* individuals through a "science of penology," proffering expertise in making society safe by institutionalizing people convicted of crimes.

To turn ideas into practice requires an infrastructure. In the 1870s, with Enoch Wines (a minister and educator) and Rutherford

B. Hayes (Ohio's governor en route to the United States presidency) at the helm, a small group launched the US-based National Prison Association, later called the American Correctional Association (ACA). They joined Europeans to form the International Penitentiary Commission (IPC, and by some, called the International Prison Commission), begun in 1872 in London, renamed the International Penal and Penitentiary Commission (IPPC) in 1929, and dissolved in 1951. Governments appointed representatives to what was one of the first transnational government organizations in the world. The IPC convened "congresses" in European capitals where royalty greeted delegates, proceedings were transcribed, and resolutions issued.

Just as US federal judges in the 1960s debated what forms of punishment governments could impose, these corrections officials did so a century earlier. They discussed the utility and morality of whips, chains, dangling people from bars by their thumbs, diets of bread and water, and dark cells. They sought amelioration through classification and individualized treatment, championed lessening the use of prisons through proportionality in punishment, indeterminate sentences, conditional releases on probation or parole, and formation of "patronage societies" to assist "discharged" prisoners. Their playbook turned a variety of ad hoc practices into a system that made stringent control of human activities appear to be normal *in* and definitional *of* prisons.

World War I interrupted what IPC leaders had proclaimed the "march of progress." In the 1920s, new entities—the Howard League (an English prison reform organization) and the League of Nations— threatened to displace the IPC as the font of corrections policy. After attending the first post-war IPC Congress in London in 1925, Margery Fry and Gertrude Eaton of the Howard League called on the world's "conscience" to do something wholly radical. They proposed an international convention to end "torture" in many prisons and to articulate "rights" so as to standardize decent treatment for detainees. After these astute women lobbied the League of Nations in Geneva, the IPC took up the project of delineating permissible from impermissible in-prison punishments. Speaking on behalf of governments but promising not to bind them, the (renamed) IPPC circulated proposed rules. The result was another "first-ever": Standard Minimum Rules for the Treatment of Prisoners, adopted in 1934 by the League of Nations.

Beware. While a victory in bringing prisoners' plight to the international stage to persuade governments to fund improvements, the fifty-five "Standard Rules" were suggestions, crafted from a "humanitarian and social point of view." Nowhere mentioned were the Howard League's terms of "torture" and "rights." The 1934 Rules thus provide one window into the power of corrections officials to shape the contours of normatively permissible punishments. These Rules also shed light on the awful treatment prisoners endured worldwide. The calls for adequate food, water, light, and air, access to visitors, and assistance upon release reflected that those basics were often lacking.

Key to this book is what the Rules *did* allow: In-prison punishments included "corporal punishment," "food reductions," and "dark rooms," with caveats that such deprivations ought to be administered in "accordance with law" and with approval of medical personnel. Thus, long before Judge Blackmun raised the problem of line drawing, correctional officials came down on the side of profound and violent control over human movement. Likewise, long before Winston Talley went to court, prisoners had tried to get relief. Some famously chronicled the disabling and vicious hierarchies of race and class within prisons,[3] and many banded together in what authorities termed "strikes" and "riots" that, from prisoners' perspectives, were "mini revolutions" and "uprisings." At times, those shout-outs prompted a modicum of assistance but imposed no legal constraints on the totalizing power of prison officials.

Talley's 1965 lawsuit exemplified the emergence of a new vocabulary of *rights* and clarified the central political question: whether governments *had* to treat prisoners as persons entitled to respect and legal protection. Until World War II, *rightlessness* was the answer. In 1935, the IPPC made that clear when, instead of abandoning plans to hold its congress in Berlin, the organization went forward, hosted by Nazi leaders lauding their methods of trial and punishment, including concentration camps. Throughout the 1940s, the

IPPC clung to the view that prison management was a "science" for experts untouched by politics. But internment camps and enslavement make plain that political norms are the bases for decisions on who is punished and how.

The experiences in World War II of detention and death that respected no boundaries of class, race, gender, religion, or national affiliation propelled the 1946 founding of the United Nations and its 1948 Declaration of Human Rights. The IPPC's engagement with fascist governments made its continuation untenable, and the United States withdrew support. Although the IPPC closed its doors in 1951, its template of rules and congresses lived on—albeit with important revisions. Democratic obligations of equal treatment can be found in the United Nations 1955 Standard Minimum Rules for the Treatment of Prisoners. While tracking some of the 1934 version, the revisions reflected a new world order in which governments were supposed to protect the "dignity" and "rights" of detainees and ensure they were not walled off from the outside.

The UN Rules did not end the power of corrections, as power resided in each country to comply. Yet to think of prisons as "lawless" is to miss that "law" has always been pivotal. Per statutes, judges sentence people to prisons, and legislatures delegate discretion to people running facilities. Yet until the 1960s, US prisoners who tried to get into court mostly hit a brick wall. State and federal governments—in Arkansas, Alabama, California, Illinois, New York, and elsewhere—routinely argued that the US Constitution had *nothing* to say about how imprisoned people were treated. Judges agreed and kept their "hands off" decisions of prison administrators.

That history means that when in 1965, Talley *lost* his argument that the "Whipp [be] destroyed," he *won* in the sense that, by getting heard on the merits, he broke centuries of hegemonic power. In the wake of the Holocaust and in the midst of the US Civil Rights Movement, and because of the guts of prisoners like Winston Talley and William King Jackson (both were beaten for filing lawsuits), courts became one of many sites of debates about punishment's parameters. These prisoners established a new proposition—that incarcerated people had the *legal* authority to call for limits on sovereign punishment powers and, as a consequence, some punishment practices *had* to change. As of this writing, constitutional law requires prisons to try to keep prisoners safe, provide some health care, create procedural protections when imposing certain in-prison punishments, respect the liberty of worship, and neither discriminate by race nor impede individuals' access to courts.

The incarcerated individuals who pushed beyond punishment theorists of the past did not all have the same profiles. Talley, Jackson, and their co-petitioners initiating Arkansas' whipping cases were lower-middle-class white men with little education, longtime engagements with criminal law enforcement, and no record of connections to the politics of their era. In contrast, other pioneers— Thomas X Cooper in Illinois, Martin Sostre in New York, and Caliph Washington in Alabama—were incarcerated Black political activists who fought racism and segregation in prisons and gained support from organizations including the Nation of Islam, the NAACP Legal Defense and Education Fund, and the ACLU. The imaginative leaps of this mix, some people acting individually and others collectively, transformed US constitutional law and rattled the foundations of punishment practices.

The 1968 whipping ban came in the same year the US Supreme Court decided its first prisoners' class action, with Caliph Washington at the lead challenging Alabama's statutory mandate that "white and colored convicts [not] be chained together or . . . allowed to sleep together." The Supreme Court agreed with the prisoners that racial segregation was unconstitutional, but three justices added a caveat that prison officials retained the power "to take into account racial tensions in maintaining security, discipline, and good order in prisons and jails."[4] The mantra of "security, discipline, and good order" continues to be central in the law governing prisons, which now stems from constitutions, statutes, regulations, and policies at national and transnational levels. Rights are routinely cabined by what corrections officials argue to be situationally demanded; the result is what I term a *prison discount*.

To understand the developments shaping the meaning of "rights" in prison requires widening the lens beyond the whipping and segregation cases. In 1970, Chief Judge Henley—who in 1965 had constrained but tolerated whipping—became the first in the country to conclude that a state's *entire* prison system was unconstitutional ("a dark and evil world"). Henley's painful account of Arkansas' prisons' density, noise, and violence is why I do not use the words "corporal punishment" interchangeably with the term "whipping." Prisons are all-engulfing structures that impose on people's being (staff included) from head to toe. It is the *corporality* of incarceration that is my topic of which Arkansas is an example, and not an outlier.[5]

When attacking the totality of conditions, the Arkansas prisoners argued that endless, forced labor was unconstitutional. Yet, while detailing the oppressiveness of field work on "hoe squads," Henley declined to end it. He cited the Thirteenth Amendment, which prohibited slavery in 1865 "except as a punishment for a crime" after a person had been "duly convicted." That "Punishment Clause" was part of legal traditions on both sides of the Atlantic that prisoners were civilly "dead"—ineligible to enter into employment or other contracts, sell property, or marry. Indeed, soon after the Civil War, judges explained that prisoners were "slaves of the State" who could be forced to work in prisons or "leased out" to the private sector.[6] In the twenty-first century, the Thirteenth Amendment continues to enable prisons to use prisoner labor to sustain large-scale incarceration. In a few systems (Arkansas included), no compensation is provided; in many others, day rates are a fraction of an hourly minimum wage.

The violence, forced labor, and racism of prisons have not been hidden from view. While, as Michel Foucault argued, a myriad of disciplinary structures aiming for control may be hard to grasp, the penitentiary is not invisible.[7] Indeed, I can document the Arkansas litigation in part because the *Arkansas Democrat* and the *Arkansas Gazette* provided front-page coverage of the whippings, filth, and sadistic violence that included criminal trials of prison officials, whose indictments under federal civil rights statutes were proudly announced in 1969 by President Richard Nixon's Attorney General. Many witnesses testified about being subjected to electric shocks and other brutalization; nonetheless, Arkansas juries acquitted. Those verdicts are yet another example of the many venues in which lines are drawn between permissible and impermissible punishments, and they provide chilling reminders of public toleration for leaving prisoners in harm's way.

I use Arkansas as one focal point because of the wealth of materials and trial records that eventually resulted in court orders to end whipping, provide health care, and sanitation. Being first is interesting, but what makes Arkansas *important* is that it was not unusually awful. Although having none of the veneer of the European and American elites running the American and international correctional associations, prison authorities in Arkansas were part of a tradition that took unfettered power for granted. Chief Judge Henley is likewise important because resistance to his directives (Arkansas protested all the way to the Supreme Court) had parallels across the country after other judges found prisons—North, South, East, and West—to be violent, filthy places that warehoused people for decades.

The opening segment of this book provides this history of Enlightenment ideologies of punishment, the penitentiaries that were purpose-built for punishment, and the transatlantic institutional scaffolding of the corrections profession. The second segment pivots on Arkansas in the 1960s and thereafter, when doors opened to rethinking what governments did to prisoners, and state legislators balked at and then provided funds to expand prisons' footprints but not their services. The third segment moves through the last several decades to understand the *resiliency* of prison keepers and of prisoners and to explore answers to the question of line drawing between permissible and impermissible punishments.

Prisons are, in important respects, different institutions than they were when Talley was confined in the 1960s; lawmaking in the name of prisoners' rights imposed new limits on punishment practices. Yet the rate and absolute number of people held in detention has soared, the harm to minority communities intensified, and the "prison-industrial complex" expanded—limiting the import of rights.[8] Moreover, the individualized experiences of incarceration have, because of the scale, become a community assault. That impact is not shared equally, which is why I prefer the term *massive incarceration* (rather than *mass* incarceration) to capture the harder hits on communities of color, where imprisonment has become a familiar facet of many people's life cycle. A 2008 Pew Foundation publication, *One in 100*, referenced the number of Black men *in* prison and hence the loss of so many *to* prison when they would otherwise be in school or the labor market.

The numbers are embedded in economic and social inequalities that lasted long after slavery formally ended. New Deal programs helped white more than Black Americans and men more than women, and the "war on poverty" devolved into a "war on crime" that exacerbated inequality.[9] For decades, federal policies enabled segregated housing and segregated workforces, and left segregated schools untouched.[10] More recent shifts have only begun to dent a geography of intertwining poverty and racial segregation that feeds prison populations in states across the country. The "institutional and individual racism" that Albert Woodfox described in his 2016 memoir of forty years in solitary confinement in Louisiana has long been apparent.[11] Decades earlier, Arthur Liman, who wrote New York State's 1972 official review of the uprising at Attica Prison where forty-three people died after Governor Nelson Rockefeller ordered in troops, concluded that the "process of criminal justice will never fulfill either its promises or its obligations until the entire judicial system is purged of racism."[12] Instead, racial disparities grew.[13]

The directors of many prison systems saw the skyrocketing populations as *their* problem. By 1980, prison officials knew well what federally funded studies documented—density correlated with increased violence and disease. The manuals of the ACA repeatedly called for single celling and adequate space per person. Yet double celling became a commonplace response to crowding. A few lower courts, relying on these standards and data from the US military and health care professionals, held double celling unconstitutional. But in 1981, the US Supreme Court pulled them, the law of prisoners' rights, and corrections standards back. By licensing putting two (or more) people into a cell built for one, the Court enabled prosecutors to ramp up indictments and judges to impose in-prison sentences without governments having to pay the price of providing what professionals had defined to be minimally decent housing in facilities with adequate services.[14] Thereafter, the ACA and the federal government retreated from single-cell standards. Pervasive hyper-density means that thousands of individuals have to endure long-term, intense proximity—including using toilets in front of cellmates.

Crowded facilities exacerbate corrections officials' ever-present worries about losing control; hyper-density has been one justification for expansive use of solitary confinement, sometimes in a "supermax" built to deprive hundreds of people of all sociability or physical movement. In 2019, prison officials reported that between 55,000 and 62,000 people were held fifteen days or more for an average of twenty-two hours or more a day in cells; research from other sources estimated that more than 122,000 people were, on any day of that year, in isolation in jails and prisons around the country.[15] Among them, according to prison officials, were thousands held for more than three years and many "seriously mentally ill," as defined by those prison systems. *Aggressive imprisonment* is the term I use to describe this amalgam of punitive practices.

Prisons are not only noisy, jammed, hyper-dense, and at times radically isolating, they are also *costly*. Because of rulings in Arkansas and elsewhere finding the "totality of conditions" unconstitutional, state legislatures have had to put in money. Legislatures and the executive branch thus became other venues in which the permissible-in-punishment was debated.[16] Contrary to many economic models, requiring taxpayer funding did not lower the demand. Using racist imagery, politicians pressed for long sentences, and supported—through "creative financing"—new construction. Legislative allocations turned correctional agencies into large bureaucracies, spending tens of billions of dollars to press, as of 2024, almost two million people into facilities rated as having a capacity to hold far fewer.[17] Thus "punishment" decisions do not only take place when a person is sentenced; conditions of incarceration and supervision are replete with choices about the quantum of punishment imposed, as are rules on eligibility for housing and employment after release.

In 2020, COVID put a spotlight on the effects of crowded jails and prisons. By June, prisoners were 5.5 times more likely to be infected and three times more likely to die than were people outside of prisons.[18] Staff likewise had a risk higher than did the general population. Some thought that COVID would be the "aha" moment to spark the decarceration movement, yet relatively few people were released to increase safety. Moreover, health care worsened, and many appellate courts pulled back the remedies—such as requiring more soap, social distancing, and some de-densification—that lower court judges had ordered.

The persistence and the toleration of miserable prison conditions bring me to this book's final aim, which is to address Judge Blackmun's hard question about the impermissible in punishment. If Arkansas can no longer whip prisoners, why can governments cut off people from their families, subject them to isolation and to intense, close contact with strangers, and turn normal human movement and desires into in-prison crimes? How could the social order in 2020 tell everyone to be physically distant yet tolerate risks of COVID by holding prisoners in dense, congregate housing? More generally, why do prisons continue to exist when other detention facilities were closed after exposés detailing the conditions in mental hospitals and asylums to which tens of thousands had been consigned? Legislators and executive branch actors shut down facilities, changed admission criteria, enacted statutory rights for people with disabilities, and empowered organizations (including the US Department of Justice) to provide oversight and bring lawsuits.

Criticisms of prisons gained steam *within* the corrections establishment in the twentieth century, when many prison officials advocated for "conditional release" that generated today's probation, parole, or supervised release. The resulting, sprawling legal regime selects people to remain outside prison if compliant with rules and if attending regular meetings with officials employed by government or private companies. One critique is that these conditional statuses are "net widening," expanding state control over people who might otherwise have been left alone; in 2024, more than three and a half million people in the United States were estimated to be subject to such surveillance.[19] Another problem is that requirements—such as "be good," do not drink, and do not associate with felons—give officials discretion that lands many people in prison for "technical" reasons including not reporting on time.[20] Indeed, probation has become a major feeder of prison populations. In 2024, violations of probation or parole were the most common offense of people imprisoned in Connecticut.

Another option in punishment's repertoire is to use money as a penalty. Economic sanctions date back centuries; their exploitive potential is reflected in the Eighth Amendment's specific prohibition of "excessive fines." When people had no funds, states routinely converted a monetary fine into jail time to "work off" dollars owed. Arkansas again provides a terrible example. In 1968, staff murdered an eighteen-year-old Black man after he had been sent to hoe fields at the Pulaski County Penal Farm to pay—at a dollar a day—his $110 fine. Two years later, the US Supreme Court held unconstitutional putting a person in jail without a judge learning if an individual had an ability to and willfully refused to pay.[21]

Although jail is now less likely to be a direct consequence, the widespread use of fines has become the subject of concern as localities fill their coffers by extracting money from people encountering police and courts. Just as Arkansas "benefited" from the labor of its prisoners, some localities have used fines and fees to fund themselves. Those regressive, discriminatory taxes gained notoriety in 2015 after Michael Brown died in the hands of police in Ferguson, Missouri and the US Department of Justice documented that police and judges worked together to target communities of color. Throughout the country, mounds of debt generated through encounters with law enforcement mean that people are at risk of losing driver's licenses, voting rights and, if held in contempt of court orders, of being detained.

The injuries resulting from massive incarceration and its alternatives have contributed to calls for abolition—of prisons, probation, monetary fines, and, for some advocates, state-based punishment itself.[22] Terms such as "harm reduction," "restorative justice," and "reconciliation" capture an ambitious agenda to respond to interpersonal injury without inflicting more. In addition to this advocacy by self-described progressives, fiscal conservatives and religious moralists are critical of long-term incarceration as economically wasteful and interpersonally disabling. One approach is to shrink the authority of governments by decriminalizing many actions; another is to take the state out of the practice of punishment altogether. Were the aegis of law diminished, a host of current infractions could no longer result in either criminal or civil sanctions. Instead, the focus could be on lowering interpersonal conflict and promoting healing.

In this world when deregulation and privatization are in vogue and the project of democratic constitutionalism is wobbling, I have no enthusiasm for internalizing conflicts to the immediate participants or for turning to individual victims and communities as the exclusive sources of judgment. Rather, I want to shore up and invigorate what democratic governance entails, including in its practices of punishment. Instead of turning away from aspirations for collective and egalitarian governance in relationship to crimes, I reframe Judge Blackmun's question in light of more than a half century of struggles with it. Whether called sanctions, punishment, reconciliation, or something else, what is *impermissible* for democratic governments to do when seeking public acknowledgment that an individual has unlawfully intruded on other people? And what *must* governments provide to the people they sanction?

In this book, I lay the groundwork for developing a new constraint on punishment. I argue that governments cannot set out to "ruin" a person, an idea that was discussed in a 2019 US Supreme Court discussion of the Eighth Amendment's prohibition on "excessive fines." Referencing the English Magna Carta and the "draconian fines" of the post–Civil War Black Codes aiming to put Black people back into servitude, the Court explained that governments were not to use their punishment powers for what a concurring opinion described as the economic "ruin of [a] criminal."[23] Thinking about ruin shifts the focus from what governments *aim* to do to the experiences of the people *subjected* to that punishment. Anti-ruination obligations acknowledge that punishment now entails a relationship beyond sheer domination.[24]

A twenty-first-century *anti-ruination* principle ought not be limited to economic sanctions; from both individual and state perspectives, democratic governments cannot set out to diminish individuals' personhood through trying to debilitate them. Indeed, a thin version of anti-ruination explains why courts have ruled out a total lack of medical care, utter filth, and wanton violence in prisons. Moreover, the transnational corrections establishment agrees and has embraced a duty of care and acknowledged that prisoners have rights, even as failures to fulfill those obligations are legion.

The reason I use the term "ruination" rather than "ruin" is to underscore the action governments must take to make good on this premise. Further, the ruination I hope will be avoided is that of individuals and of a social order committed to being a democratic, rather than a totalitarian, regime. That distinction was repeatedly drawn in the 1960s and 1970s as the federal government, understanding itself as the leader of the "free world," sought to distance itself from its "race problem" in part through recognizing criminal defendants' and prisoners' rights.[25] As Justice Byron White explained in 1974 when the Court required some procedural protections before prisons took away good-time credits, "no iron curtain" existed "between the Constitution and the prisons of this country."[26] The recognition that incarcerated people are members of the political community imposes on the state a task different from what governments had in prior centuries. Democratic egalitarianism polities cannot select anyone, including those "duly convicted," to debilitate; the legal relationship between people who are incarcerated and government does not end when law *puts* them into prison because law *follows* them there.

In the third decade of the twenty-first century, the risk of ruination has been exacerbated because the scale of incarceration outstrips staffing, as vacancy rates soar in crumbling facilities on both sides of the Atlantic. Moreover, prisoners' rights are at risk in the United States, where federal judges have called for abandoning "evolving standards of decency" as a metric of "cruel and unusual punishments" and relying instead on what was "barbarous" in the 1790s. Hence, if ruin is going to stop, it will come from an appreciation that punishment is a political act that entails accepting the distinctive and expensive obligations a democratic polity *takes on* if it *takes away* people's liberties. When analyses of permissible punishments occur—in correctional association meetings, legislatures, executive offices, courts, boardrooms, and living rooms—the questions are how governments can express commitments to equality and attend to the impact of deprivations on people punished and maintain well-being and degrees of autonomy. This anti-ruination obligation is distinct from the hierarchical ideology embedded in rehabilitation and can complement commitments to harm reduction and healing. Because it puts a significant burden on government decisions limiting individuals' autonomy, it ought to reduce incentives to do so.

Marshaling the will to end the ruin of people *in* prison requires pressing to stop the ruin of people *outside* of prison. As odd as it sounds, prisons are social service providers. Even under the limited scope of US prisoners' rights, governments have affirmative obligations to supply food, clothing, housing, and health care. People on the streets do not, as of this writing, have federal rights to those services. In contrast, in many countries, subsidies exist as part of government relationships with people, in detention and not. Thus, what makes the United States "exceptional" today is not some characterological, intrinsic punitive stance, but its turn in the last decades away from reckoning with the history of slavery, away from providing minimal safety nets to all persons, and away from the transnational dialogue on punishment that its leaders helped to start more than a century ago.

A consequence of the United States' impoverished approach to social services is that people outside prison could think that incarcerated individuals are getting "more" than government provides to people not "duly convicted." Yet people on the streets have not lost the opportunity to seek food, health care, and housing. Distribution of resources is compelled by the act of taking a person's freedom away. This proposition was put forth by Enlightenment theorist Jeremy Bentham who, while describing prisoners as "less eligible" than the working poor, nonetheless insisted they be provided food, clothing, and health care.[27] The hard truth is that the fates of people in and outside of prisons are linked in terms of the need for social services, the racism that shadows criminal law enforcement and welfarist programs, and the imperative to legitimate exercises of state power. Altering an understanding of what states must provide to incarcerated people entails acceptance of the asymmetrical relationship that a government has with its populations; some need affirmative assistance or merit punishment that others do not.

This new metric of punishment's legitimacy—the burdens of the special relationship that governments have to people they punish—marks the rejection of prison practices reiterating the structure of slavery and concentration camps and embraces propositions advanced by William Talley and others about their status as political equals. Thus far, this encounter between rights and incarceration has not generated a full acceptance of the obligations that flow. I delve into incarceration's practices to make plain how foreign and abnormal they are when compared to ordinary human activities.

The history documents that the construction of this form of captivity was built on a sequence of choices that were neither inevitable nor are irretrievable. Appreciating the weirdness of micro-control of individuals is one route to realizing that prison's current parameters are *abhorrent* when measured against the baseline of reasonable expectations for personal liberty, autonomy, and respect in democratic social orders aiming to lessen racist and class hierarchies. Thus, prisons operating on an anti-ruination principle have to rethink the radical reduction in autonomy that is commonplace in incarceration. Moreover, once democratic orders no longer embrace punishment practices developed and justified by Enlightenment ideology, the accompanying vocabulary drenched in colonial hierarchies of "civilization" that produced goals of "corrections" and "rehabilitation" can be replaced by obligations of respect for all people, including the "duly convicted."

This book is thus an invitation to learn about the people—prisoners, theorists, correctional professionals, judges, and politicians—who shaped prisons and to enter into debates about the results. I show what governments have done, how a corrections bureaucracy gained power, what prisoners succeeded in stopping, as well as the impediments to and the potential for fundamental change.

PART I

FROM THE 1800S TO WORLD WAR II

TRANSATLANTIC EXCHANGES ABOUT LEGITIMATE FORMS OF PUNISHMENT

Winston Talley's 1965 petition did not describe itself as stating a "theory" of punishment, but it had one—that governments were constrained when punishing people for crimes. Talley thus joined a long line of theorists and practitioners who thought that state punishment ought to be bounded, albeit *not* because convicted people were equals protected by law. A trio of eighteenth-century Enlightenment reformers—John Howard, Cesare Beccaria, and Jeremy Bentham—helped make punishment a topic of political and philosophical debate. They insisted that *reason* had to play a role when choosing punishments and called for abolition of some forms of punishment then common while affirming others that today we think are grotesque.

Bringing these eighteenth-century European writers into a book that begins with Arkansas' 1960s prison system is, in one sense, countercultural. Given the entanglement of incarceration with Jim Crow and the perpetuation of the subordination of Black people, accounts in the United States often assume its prisons' "exceptionalism" in being unusually punitive and degrading. Yet US practices—including whips—were also entwined with practices around the globe as criminal law violently enforced hierarchies founded in class, colonialism, race, religion, nationality, and gendered identities. For centuries, sovereigns had power to do as they pleased, be it whipping, executions, branding, confinement, or exile to colonies. The rising reliance on detention reflected that, when facing economic dislocation, population growth, wars, and protests, many countries tried to assert control through confinement of people labeled criminal, poor, or otherwise deviant.[1]

Thus, while Talley's claim of right was novel, Arkansas' defenses were not. The state could rely on its decades of whipping as well as a transatlantic history ratifying the unfettered sovereign authority to do so. Until the middle of the nineteenth century, the US military "flogged" misbehaving members. Through much of the twentieth century, English sentences included lashing ("birching" if under eighteen). Moreover, while atypical by the 1960s in the United States, whipping was then licit elsewhere; in the twenty-first century, "caning" remains in use in some countries as does "paddling" children, including in some US schools today. In this part, I unfold a mix of practices and of political theories valorizing penitentiaries, licensing whipping and, through a transnational enterprise calling itself "corrections," making these punishments commonplace.

1

THE "ENLIGHTENED" PUNISHMENTS OF THE EIGHTEENTH CENTURY

One compendium of corporal punishment "around the world" defined its infliction of "ritualized physical pain or ordeal . . . to bind the recipient or observers to the rules, norms, or customs" of particular social orders. Didier Fassin, who traced the lineage of punishments (a word derived from the Latin *punire*, meaning to chastise or avenge), has argued that Christian theology, committed to suffering for sins, shifted punishment's focus from "a debt to repay" to "a suffering to inflict."[1] The whip, along with other forms of corporal punishment, was one technique that gained a pedigree through its deployment across continents.

Some religions use mortification of the flesh as evidence of devotion, and certain faiths endorse corporal punishment for violation of their laws. Interpersonal hierarchies of many sorts are marked by physical domination. "Masters" whipped enslaved people, servants, and apprentices; traffickers in sex and labor whip today. Inside households, power over women and children sometimes took form in what English law termed "physical chastisement."[2] Parents (generally fathers) used "the strap" to punish disobedient children, husbands beat their wives, and teachers paddled students. For centuries, sovereigns condoned those "private" acts until successful mobilizations against slavery and other forms of "domestic" violence generated law's condemnation. In this chapter, I sketch whipping and other European punishment practices that prompted Enlightenment activist–theorists to argue that governments need to alter and justify the punishments imposed.

VALORIZING WHIPPING IN EIGHTEENTH-CENTURY AMSTERDAM AND BEYOND

Governments forced themselves on people's bodies through enslavement, indentured servitude, and detention. The proud displays of such infliction often entailed public rituals. Examples here come via reproduction of two prints from a once-famous 1783 "Atlas," compiled by an art dealer, Pierre Fouquet, advertising the virtues of Amsterdam, which had been among the first cities in Europe to establish a prison.[3] By the eighteenth century's end, with its population down to about 230,000 inhabitants, the city sought to invite commerce and tourism through promoting its ports, bridges, canals, churches, two synagogues, town hall, markets, homes for the elderly and orphans, and its detention centers.

The imposing Men's House of Correction, shown in figure 1.1 and constructed in the early 1780s, reflected a state-of-the-art effort to curb pauperism, vagrancy, and crime. The "largest structure built in Amsterdam in the eighteenth century," it was designed to hold seven hundred people plus seventy labeled "sick." Amsterdam aimed to contain all sorts of people perceived to be a threat; a fifth of the one hundred prints in *Fouquet's Atlas* displayed various confinement facilities in that city—intent on "fighting poverty with a building."[4]

The Men's House of Correction had an insistent hygiene, with light, ventilation, and sloping floors for easy cleaning that was utterly foreign to the dilapidation and dirt of Arkansas' 1960s prison farms. Yet continents and centuries apart, the punishment systems were parallel. The oversized Dutch facility reflected Amsterdam's expansion of the "net" of social control. In the 1780s, as in the 1960s (and now), minor offenses generated long terms of confinement. A third violation of Amsterdam's ordinance against begging resulted in a sentence of three to five years.[5] In Arkansas, conviction of "grand larceny," defined as theft of $35 or more, put people like Talley in prison for comparable time.

FIGURE 1.1 *Men's House of Correction [Het Rasphuis]*, in Pierre Fouquet, *Nieuwe atlas* (Amsterdam: D. J. Changuion and P. den Hengst, 1783), courtesy of the Beinecke Rare Book and Manuscript Library, Yale University

Moreover, both Amsterdam's and Arkansas' prisons centered on forced labor, albeit explained differently. The first Dutch prison, opened in 1596, was known as the Rasphuis because prisoners were "forced to pulverize ('rasp') dyewood to create powder for colouring textiles." As a Dutch commentator (himself once a political prisoner) explained, idleness was the source of crime and work its antidote. Amsterdam's much-enlarged 1780s facilities aimed to confine "all the beggars of Amsterdam" to generate "repentance and re-integration."[6] Twentieth-century Arkansas espoused no interest—aside from extracting labor—in the people consigned to prison. The word "rehabilitation" did not enter Arkansas' penal statutes until 1968, when the state was losing the whipping case and the press revealed torture and corruption at its facilities.

FIGURE 1.2 *Interior courtyard, Men's House of Correction [Het Rasphuis]*, in Pierre Fouquet, *Nieuwe atlas* (Amsterdam: D. J. Changuion and P. den Hengst, 1783), courtesy of the Beinecke Rare Book and Manuscript Library, Yale University

With these different predicates, authorities inside the two prison systems were desperate to maintain control. One method was whipping. As bizarre as it may seem to twenty-first-century viewers, the *Atlas* promoting Amsterdam's glories included a print reproduced in figure 1.2 of the Men's House of Correction's courtyard, where a prisoner was shown being flogged while spectators, guards, and other detainees watched.

PUNISHMENT AS POLITICAL THEORY

The practices of imposing punishment, expanding as countries were buffeted by waves of civil unrest and revolution, became the life work of John Howard and Cesare Beccaria and a major concern of Jeremy Bentham, whose output extended far beyond the penitentiary. Their commentary influenced decisions about running Amsterdam's House of Correction and continues to shape today's justifications for punishment.[7] Their modes of reasoning illustrate a key facet of my analysis: that *baselines*, by which I mean practices common within a social order, are critical in assessments of the permissibility of particular forms of punishment. Before explaining why each man *cared* about prisons when so few did and what they thought, I sketch their analytic interrelationships and differences.

In England, private jailors charged detainees and held people longer if they could not pay fees for their confinement. That exploitation repelled John Howard, a member of the country's upper class who responded by obsessively chronicling that misery. His report, published in 1777 (the era of the American Revolution), gained the public's eye. Howard campaigned for clean prisons where prisoners were made to do "hard labor." Howard's excursions (today's sociological "field studies") put faces on the critique made famous in intellectual circles by the Italian Marquis Cesare Beccaria, whose 1764 monograph, *On Crimes and Punishments*, was initially published anonymously because he feared prosecution for heretical views. Beccaria, who called for the end of capital punishment ("public murder"), argued that sanctions were necessary to maintain social order and that, to impinge less on people's liberty, punishment ought to be proportionate to a crime's severity. Jeremy Bentham incorporated aspects of Beccaria's analyses into hundreds of pages of a self-proclaimed utilitarian system, aiming to deter individuals by showing them frightening punishments.

Even as Howard was a prompt for Bentham's interest in prison construction and Beccaria and Bentham overlapped, they differed. Howard thought all sinners, criminals included, needed religious *redemption* through degradation, while Bentham was committed to the "universality of reason" rather than *sin*. Aiming to alter individuals' calculations of the costs and benefits of crime, the purpose of degrading punishments was *deterrence*, not personal reform. Beccaria, like Bentham, was a utilitarian but had a broader set of analytic and emotive predicates ("consult the human heart") that mixed social contract, natural rights, and utilitarianism to shape arguments against the death penalty and to lessen punitive measures through a proportionality between an offense and a sanction.

Howard, Beccaria, and Bentham converged when calling on the state to *reason* about why and how it punished. We walk in their footsteps when we insist that governments should *explain* their choices in reference to specified goals. Moreover, an amalgam of these men's goals became canonically legitimate ends: to deter crime; incapacitate individuals to prevent commission of new crimes; reform or rehabilitate people; express societal disapproval; and under the rubric of retribution, impose deserved deprivations, pain, suffering, and extract compensation. Even as divisions remain deep about how to weigh, operationalize, and reconcile (if possible) tensions within this set, state-authorized intrusions on liberty are supposed to have these kinds of purposes, rather than to terrorize or destroy. Those aspirations should not beguile; each man endorsed punishments now seen as repugnant. They exemplify why reasons sourced in the Enlightenment—aiming to act *on* individuals without respect *for* their personhood—do not suffice for social orders aspiring to be egalitarian.

HOWARD'S 1770S EMPIRICAL ZEALOTRY

Born in 1726 into a well-to-do family, Howard's fascination with detention may have been sparked by his own brief confinement when, on a European tour common for men of his class, a French privateer imprisoned the ship's passengers in Brest. Several decades later, when appointed Sheriff of Bedfordshire, Howard learned about people "dragged back to jail" and left in squalid conditions until they paid jailor and court clerk fees.[8] Howard determined to visit every prison in England. He measured (apparently with tape in hand) spaces, assessed conditions, and ventured abroad in search of better systems. That pioneering empiricism resulted in the 1777 *State of the Prisons in England and Wales*, detailing disease-ridden, corrupt, and violent conditions. Howard offered Amsterdam as a model; he had toured the facility that was later replaced by the 1780 House of Correction depicted in figures 1.1 and 1.2.[9]

Armed with "a program and an argument," Howard launched public campaigns to promote individual cells, exercise, adequate food, and religious instruction; to end fee-for-service jails; and to stop prisoners' transportation to colonies.[10] Howard influenced a constellation of reformers as the American Revolution cut off shipping people to that colony and prison populations swelled. Amid the religious, cultural, and political tumult, Howard became popular. English artists glorified him as a savior of the imprisoned, and his statue is in London's St. Paul's Cathedral. A 1790 etching, "Visiting and Relieving the Miseries of a Prison," depicted Howard seeking the release of an impoverished family. In another such scene, reproduced in figure 1.3, the painter George Romney depicted Howard as a "Christ-like figure breaking through the prison's darkness to free the disenfranchised from the misery of their confinement."[11]

FIGURE 1.3 George Romney, *Howard Visiting a Prison*, 1780–1785, courtesy of the Yale Center for British Art

Howard's ameliorative aims should not obscure his commitment to painful punishment. Howard's Protestantism translated into admiration for hard labor as a route to redemption. Taken with the Dutch maxim, "Make them diligent and they will be honest," Howard incorporated aspects of Amsterdam's approach when drafting England's Penitentiary Act of 1779. The goals were separate facilities for men and women that required "well regulated labour, and religious instruction" as the "means under Providence, not only of deterring others from the Commission of the like Crimes, but also of reforming the Individuals, and inuring them to Habits of Industry." In these "hard labor houses," prisoners were to be fed "bread and any coarse meat, or other inferior food" and assigned work of the "most servile kind, in which drudgery is chiefly required" such as "sawing stones, polishing marble, beating hemp, rasping logwood, [and] chopping rags." Although England did not build such prisons, some localities constructed their own versions.[12]

John Howard's name has been carried forward through the Howard League, an English prison reform association that, as explained in this book's introduction, aimed in the twentieth century to stop "torture" and recognize prisoners' "rights." Howard took a different tack. Seeking to abolish filth in prison was, for him, consistent with admiration for cruelties inflicted in the name of redeeming sinners.

"SUPERFLUOUS" SEVERITY: BECCARIA'S PROPORTIONALITY, "HUMAN HEART," AND CAGES OF "IRON"

While Howard was a political activist and a nascent sociologist, Cesare Beccaria was a Milanese intellectual who gained lasting fame from his 1764 monograph, *On Crimes and Punishments*, which made its way rapidly across the continent—translated into French in 1766, English in 1767, and Dutch in 1768, with new editions in later centuries.[13] Beccaria recoiled at the breadth and volume of state punishment. He wrote that being a part of a political community required sacrifice of some liberties, yet sovereigns ought to limit punishments; to obtain the "greatest possible happiness

FIGURE 1.4 Cesare Beccaria, *Dei delitti e delle pene* (Harlem, Paris: Chez Molini Libraire, Quai des Augustins, 1766), courtesy of the Lillian Goldman Law Library, Yale Law School

or . . . the least possible unhappiness," it was "better to prevent crimes than to punish them." A related maxim, "the greatest good [or happiness] for the greatest number," came from Beccaria, while often credited to Jeremy Bentham.[14] While Beccaria is labeled a utilitarian, his writing shows influences of social contract and natural rights theories associated with Rousseau, Montesquieu, and others. To draw lines between permissible and impermissible punishments, Beccaria paired a cost-benefit analysis with taking into account "the rights of man and of unconquerable truth" and "the human heart."[15]

Beccaria's visibility stemmed in part from opposition to capital punishment; Beccaria asserted it was "absurd" for a government in an effort "to deter citizens from murder" to "order a public one." Beccaria argued against the "slaughter" on several grounds, including that it gave men an "example of barbarity."[16] Reproduced in figure 1.4 is a frontispiece, based on a sketch attributed to Beccaria, used in several editions of *On Crimes and Punishments*. Depicted is a seated, clear-sighted image of the Renaissance Virtue Justice, her scales fallen to the floor, her head turned away, and her hands rejecting an executioner's offer of severed heads.

Beccaria's rejection was grounded on what came to be called proportionality: For a punishment to "attain its end, the evil it inflicts has only to exceed the advantage derivable from the crime. . . . All [severity] beyond this is superfluous and for that reason tyrannical." This precept was coupled with another, "promptness in punishment" after a crime's commission. Calling on the legislature to revise its laws, Beccaria ended with the admonitions that punishment had to be "public, prompt, necessary, the least possible in the given circumstances, proportionate to the crimes, dictated by laws."[17]

Beccaria's precepts sound better than the examples of punishments he approved. Radical in his rejection of executions, Beccaria endorsed "penal servitude," complete with "fetters or chains, under the rod, under the yoke, in a cage of iron."[18] Even with an appeal to emotions and mildness ("the least possible"), Beccaria endorsed stomach-churning harshness.

BENTHAM'S EXEMPLARY AND AFFLICTIVE
PUNISHMENTS AND HIS "WHIPPING MACHINE"

Howard and Beccaria influenced Bentham. Howard's attention to prison construction intrigued Bentham, insistent on architecture's role in all facets of governance. Bentham admired Beccaria, whom he called the "first evangelist of Reason." Both men disliked judicial discretion and found solace in the specificity of "codification," a word Bentham coined. Writing a few years after Beccaria's 1764 monograph and referencing it in the Italian original as well as English and French translations, Bentham used "Beccaria's ideas . . . [as his] starting point" and then assimilated, refined, departed from, and broadcast Beccaria's approach. Both pinned punishment's success on its "intensity, duration, certainty, and propinquity."[19] Over time, Bentham came to think (as did others) that some of what Beccaria had said was his own.

Bentham's materials include sixty thousand folios—some one hundred thousand pages—tallied by the Bentham Project at University College London (UCL); the forty-five works range from short pamphlets to the 2,500 pages of his *Rationale of Judicial Evidence*.[20] That output, coupled with Bentham's wish to become an auto-icon, has enhanced his visibility. Contemporary visitors to UCL can see Bentham's wax head and suit-clad skeleton, restuffed in 2018.[21] Bentham's directive to preserve his corporal presence has resonance with his views on punishment. It may have reflected his distaste for religion; the display could be seen to spoof Christian emulation of the body of Jesus. Further, through demonstrating that anyone could become a statue, it jabbed at the aristocracy.[22] Another explanation is that Bentham, a brilliant propagandist, understood that memorialization would bring attention to his efforts to reframe law around the world.

Bentham's early analyses of punishment can be found in the 1778 *A View of the Hard Labor Bill* (supporting draft legislation Howard had shaped) and his 1790s plan for a building he called the "Panopticon" that, while never built, became synonymous with the specter of prison surveillance. Based on an architectural model of workhouses his brother designed in Russia, Bentham hoped that the government would sign a contract he drafted to put him in charge of a Panopticon to house about one thousand people and be sited where one of London's museums now sits. In addition, in lengthy "letters" to English officials and an essay written in the early 1800s, Bentham detailed his opposition to prisoner transportation. Bentham's 1830 treatise *The Rationale of Punishment*—including tracts written decades earlier—offered a sweeping catalogue of many forms of punishment.[23] The caveat to my account is that, as explained by Philip Schofield, Director of UCL's Bentham Project, English versions are often retranslations by Richard Smith of French volumes edited by Étienne Dumont, who distilled and at times embroidered texts, omitted some aspects, and reorganized others. Reconstruction from extant originals is underway; for now, published and online versions are the sources.

Bentham sought punishments calibrated to maximize welfare. Describing punishment as "an evil," Bentham argued that the benefits came from inflictions that were proportionate to the offense, to the offender, and known to the public. "Exemplary" physical punishments and frightening prisons were sources of "general prevention" (today's deterrence) creating incentives to obey the law. Bentham's discussion of whipping in *The Rationale of Punishment* was part of his analysis of a variety of punishments, described in twelve gruesome chapters. Bentham imposed an infrastructure on the ghoulish array that distinguished between "simple afflictive punishments," causing temporary pain, and "complex afflictive punishments," designed to be permanent.[24] Whipping fell into the first category while discoloration, disfigurement, branding, mutilation, and capital punishment exemplified the second.

Because Bentham sought specific time-bound impact, he commended simple afflictive punishments and opposed disfigurements that "render infamous the offender not the offense."[25] He rejected leaving marks on convicted persons who, when returning to the community, ought not be regarded with contempt. (As discussed later, the head of the English prison system took a similar position when drafting what became the League of Nations' 1934 Standard

Minimum Rules for the Treatment of Prisoners; his proposal was that no punishment should leave a "lasting injury" or "result in any permanent marks which will subsequently be visible on ordinary occasions to the eyes of his fellow citizens so as to degrade him in their esteem."[26])

Bentham aimed to build in roles for the public, control government officials, and limit exercises of arbitrary power. He wanted to scare people so their utility calculus would lead them not to commit crimes. For example, Bentham suggested use of a "whipping machine," made of cane and whalebone, to deliver blows evenly. Rather than pain varying with the strength and emotions of the person administering lashes, a judge was to proscribe the "force and rapidity." To amplify the deterrent impact, Bentham suggested putting whipping machines in one place for spectators to observe several people whipped at once. Yet Bentham also recorded hesitations about whipping; such an "acute punishment" left no "leisure for reflection" and produced relief when it ended. In *The Rationale of Punishment*, Bentham wrote that whipping would be more productive if coupled with forced labor, darkness, and solitary confinement. Moreover, in a 1797 discussion of the Poor Laws, Bentham registered qualms when calling for abolition of "[w]hipping and all other punishments at present inflictable for begging and vagrancy."[27]

Over the decades, Bentham became an opponent of capital punishment. In an essay written in 1773 and appended to the 1830 *Rationale of Punishment*, Bentham argued it ought to be reserved for "offenses which in the highest degree shock the public feeling"; murders with aggravating circumstances were his examples; some fifty years later, Bentham wrote that capital punishment ought to, without exception, be abolished.[28]

Bentham also argued for the abolition of another punishment—exiling people to colonies—on which England relied heavily. Before the American Revolution, Britain had sent some fifty thousand people across the Atlantic; between 1788 and the 1860s, England shipped more than 160,000 British and Irish citizens to a penal colony in New South Wales.[29] Bentham explained in *The Rationale of Punishment* that transportation was useless. The "main object or end of penal justice is *example*" to show "bystanders" the pain, while transportation was "hidden" and "abstracted."[30] Bentham made that pitch directly in 1802 and 1803 in open letters to Lord Pelham, the British Home Secretary; shipping people to penal colonies was expensive and made impossible "inspection, the only effective instrument of reformative management." In contrast, putting people into a local penitentiary (such as his Panopticon) would permit "satisfaction" for the injured party and, as long as the labor was "productive," imprisonment could be both frightening and self-supporting.[31]

Bentham is the unusual analyst of the Enlightenment who argued that *law*, as well as policy, imposed a constraint. In his 1802 letter, Bentham asserted that banishment's permanency violated the Magna Carta, which prohibited a man's loss of his country "unless he be exiled according to the law of the land." Parliament had not extended sentences to terms beyond those imposed, nor provided for British citizens to be put into permanent exile, which was "a punishment . . . inflicted, silently and without sentence . . . superadded to a punishment for years."[32] As Bentham wrote in *A Plea for the Constitution*, his 1802 letter had "hints" about "*illegality*" but largely relied on the language of "*policy*" (his italics), while his 1803 letter specified several legal violations. First, because Parliament had not established the Crown's power to govern New South Wales, the Crown had no authority to issue regulations there. Second, England's Habeas Act referenced confinement in a "prison" but New South Wales, larger than England, could not be described as such. Third, given the distance, exile resulted in terms in excess of the sentences imposed. Fourth, no one had been sentenced to death; however, because of filthy transport "hulks," many people died en route.[33] (At this book's conclusion, I return to Bentham, who also relied on legal obligations when explaining that the government had to provide incarcerated people with adequate food, clothing, medical care, and housing.[34])

Even as the late eighteenth century was awash with the "rights talk" of the French and American Revolutions, Bentham is the rare voice I have found before the twentieth century who argued to end a punishment not only as inefficient or immoral but because some forms of punishment violated the *rights* of those subjected to it. That position is not without irony, given that Bentham had called natural law "simple nonsense" and the French Declaration of Rights "nonsense upon stilts."[35] Whether Bentham relied on the Magna Carta and Habeas Corpus Act as positive (rather than natural) rights or aimed to persuade by deploying words evocative for his time, Bentham staked out the claim that people subjected to punishment had rights against its imposition. "Britons, free by law as Britons can be, have been kept in that land of exile in a state of bondage."[36]

Like Howard and Beccaria, Bentham merits no halos. Bentham's analyses assumed one could specify and quantify the "greatest happiness" and make causal connections between certain punitive measures and people's actions. Bentham's assessments have been undermined at both theoretical and empirical levels.[37] His model of rationality has been criticized for failing to understand human psychology, the diversity of people's experiences, and the variables that shape preference formation. Indeed, Bentham largely ignored empirical and normative questions about what to count as "costs" and as "benefits" and how to weigh them. Moreover, Bentham imagined assessments by a single "Tribunal of Public Opinion," rather than the diverse and riven public discourse that has emerged. He likewise missed that public oversight would entail predatory behavior (today's "doxxing").[38] In addition to these internal critiques come views that utilitarianism's narrowness misses a host of concerns located in moral and political philosophy.

Another form of criticism comes from Michel Foucault's 1970s book, *Discipline and Punish*, which linked Bentham to a pernicious surveillance that made less visible the expansion of state control. In his social history of punishment powers and practices, Foucault argued that punishment had become "the most hidden part of the penal process, carried out by officials who had largely unfettered autonomy."[39] Foucault's insightful analyses of the "strange institution" of the prison need to be distinguished from ideas he attributed to Bentham, who sought to make *patent* the practice of state punishments. Bentham promoted surveillance as a technique of oversight for the jailor as well as the jailed. Bentham wanted a watchtower inside prisons to give the public a platform for firsthand inspection of punishment's pains and hence be deterred. Bentham's proposed circular Panopticon was a multipurpose template, with potential use for hospitals, schools, workhouses, and poor houses.[40] Thus, as Anne Brunon-Ernst has explained, Foucault "got it wrong" when positing a single oppressive Panopticon.[41]

Moreover, Bentham's commitment to observation applied to government. "Publicity" (another term he coined) aimed to enable people to see how power operated so as to assess the utilities. Bentham's precept that "the more strictly we are watched, the better we behave" was the basis for his advocacy of open court proceedings; while "presiding at trial," judges were themselves "on trial." If attendance was insufficient, he proposed paying "auditors" to observe.[42] Thus, Bentham not only laid the groundwork for extensive use of incarceration, he also contributed to the presumption of open courts, which meant that, in the 1960s, the press was welcome in Arkansas to record what transpired at the whipping trial.

2

NINETEENTH-CENTURY RATIONALES FOR DELIBERATELY DESPOTIC DEGRADATION

The flogging scene from Amsterdam was not idiosyncratic. Executions were public rituals, and European artists glorified many forms of corporal punishment.[1] Yet on occasion, the plight of a prisoner and the oppressiveness of incarceration took center stage. Illustrative is Thomas Ryder's etching (figure 2.1) of *The Captive*, from a 1774 painting by English artist, Joseph Wright.

FIGURE 2.1 *The Captive*, print by Thomas Ryder, 1746–1810, after Joseph Wright of Derby, 1734–1797, courtesy of the Yale Center for British Arts

Inspiration came from a 1768 English novel of a traveler horrified at the treatment. Depicting this man with a "chain upon his legs" in the Paris Bastille,[2] Wright's illumination echoed images of saints.

The reason to look at images of Amsterdam's House of Correction and the chained prisoner is to see the praise for, concern about, and expanding girth of prisons. This Enlightenment innovation had remarkable *success* in replacing the stocks, branding, and executions and turning penitentiaries into icons of punishment. What *The Captive* also reflects is that with the "birth" of the prison came calls for its reform. While the Amsterdam flogging print is a proud account of spectators watching the whipping of a man strapped to a pedestal topped by a justice-like female statue, the depiction of an emaciated, chained prisoner on straw is about misery. Many people were appalled at conditions and, like John Howard, tried to improve, rather than abolish, this punitive practice. They focused on whether to house people together or separately, to impose silence, demand work, and how to enforce "discipline," including by whipping.

This chapter sketches the entrenchment of authoritarian prison practices that gained widespread acceptance in the nineteenth century, in part through commentary by Gustave de Beaumont, Alexis de Tocqueville, and Francis Lieber. These ambitious men shared interests in government, political theory, and in being taken seriously; they became famous for work on democracy, slavery's abolition, and laws for war.[3] Yet the three took for granted that sovereigns had absolute authority to take all agency away from the people they incarcerated. Beaumont, Tocqueville, and Lieber were committed to punishment regimes that entailed domination through forced labor and solitude. They disagreed somewhat about profound isolation and whipping. What united them was persuading governments that penitentiary practices in New York and Pennsylvania were models for adoption. These men endorsed deprivations that make for hard reading—and that people had to live. Moreover, what they described in the nineteenth century—forced labor enforced by physical punishment—was how Arkansas treated prisoners in the 1960s.

QUESTING FOR MODEL PENITENTIARIES

"The place for convicted criminals in New Orleans cannot be called prison: it is a horrid sink, . . . fit only for those dirty animals found here with the prisoners. It must be observed that those who are detained here are not slaves: it is the prison for persons from the ordinary course of life."

—Gustave de Beaumont and Alexis de Tocqueville,
On the Penitentiary System, 1833[4]

In France, efforts to identify the "'best' system of imprisonment" began in the early nineteenth century with an outpouring of commentary about the chaotic mélange of its prisons.[5] After the founding of a Royal Society for the Improvement of Prisons, an 1819 report called for reforms. A decade later, the Parisian lawyer Charles Lucas published three volumes on the developing "penitentiary science." Paralleling the Italian Cesare Beccaria, Lucas called for an end to capital punishment and, akin to the English Jeremy Bentham, Lucas proffered prisons as a "replacement penalty."[6]

In 1830, Tocqueville, joined by his fellow Frenchman, Beaumont, left a turbulent France after the abdication of Charles X. They persuaded the new King, Louis-Philippe, to authorize (but not pay for) a trip to survey prisons in the United States. Both were young magistrates in the French legal system and critics of French prisons that (as Tocqueville later told the French Parliament) had higher death rates than did US prisons.[7] Prison was also personal for Tocqueville. During the French Revolution, his aristocratic father had been held at the Bastille, which was the exemplar of the oppression depicted in *The Captive*. Beaumont and Tocqueville arrived in the United States in May of 1831 and stayed through February of 1832. The two Frenchmen traveled west to Ohio, north to Canada, and south to Louisiana.[8] Visiting more than a dozen institutions, they devoted ten days to New York's Sing Sing and Auburn penitentiaries and twelve to Philadelphia's Eastern State Penitentiary.[9]

Beaumont and Tocqueville reported back in their monograph *On the Penitentiary System in the United States and Its Application in France*. Published in 1833, the original consisted of more than 220 pages and lengthy appendices. They excluded "Southern states, where slavery still exists" because in "every place where one-half of the community is cruelly oppressed by the other, we must expect to find in the law of the oppressor, a weapon already ready to strike nature which revolts or humanity that complains."[10] In the decade after their US visit, both men worked to end slavery in French colonies.[11] Their notes on US prisons, slavery, Indian tribes, and much else[12] demonstrated that the two were "liberal aristocrats dedicated to defending liberty"[13]—albeit not for the imprisoned.

Through overlapping intellectual circles, Beaumont and Tocqueville met Lieber, who had been born in Germany and moved to the United States in the 1820s. Lieber also had firsthand experiences of detention. He had fought in the Prussian Army against Napoleon and twice been imprisoned as a "nationalistic German liberal." Beaumont and Tocqueville asked Lieber to do an English translation, from which I borrowed this section's opening quote. Lieber added commentary, which prompted Beaumont and Tocqueville to complain that Lieber had "loaded [the translation] down with notes in which, in his capacity as a foreigner, he feels himself obliged to contradict the smallest truths that we utter about America."[14]

Nonetheless, the three men profited from their joint venture. Lieber's translation contributed to his national reputation in the nascent field of political science, of which he was one of its first professors. After years at the University of South Carolina, Lieber moved in the 1860s to Columbia University, where he formulated rules on the law of war (prisoners included) that Abraham Lincoln used during the Civil War. *On the Penitentiary* boosted the profiles of Beaumont and Tocqueville; the book, translated into several languages, won an award from the French Académie des Sciences Morales et Politique, to which the coauthors were admitted.[15] Continuing to work for legislative reforms, Beaumont and Tocqueville submitted a revised monograph to the French Parliament in 1836 and 1843. The two were in the government that came to an end with Louis Napoleon's ascension in 1851. In addition to losing their posts, their opposition to him landed each, briefly, in detention.[16]

Newer translations of *On the Penitentiary* include a 2018 version to restore the original.[17] I use the English 1833 volume because of its currency in that century and because the opinionated Lieber turned it into a dialogue about incarceration's purposes and methods. Their exchange underscores that the treatment of prisoners was *patent* to those who looked and that these nineteenth-century intellectuals endorsed the radical control they observed. They helped legitimate prison practices that remain common in the twenty-first century.

"THE MOST COMPLETE DESPOTISM"

The "American penitentiary system must be regarded as of . . . vital interest to the whole civilized world."

—Francis Lieber's Introduction, *On the Penitentiary System*, 1833[18]

"[T]he penitentiary system in America is severe. While society in the United States gives the example of the most extended liberty, the prisons of the same country offer the spectacle of the most complete despotism."

—Beaumont and Tocqueville, *On the Penitentiary System*, 1833[19]

Lieber's dense, thirty-page introduction was an ode to his new homeland; it should be "a matter of pride to every American, that the new penitentiary system has been first established and successfully practiced in his country." In contrast, Beaumont and Tocqueville recorded US prisons' severity and "despotism." That word triggered (in contemporary parlance) Lieber, who advised readers:

[I]t would be unnecessary to dwell upon the impropriety of calling a system despotic which mainly grew out of the feeling of humanity . . .—a system which, at the most, can appear despotic only at the first glance, but which is truly merciful if compared to the former system of prisons—or to speak more correctly, total want of any system.[20]

Lieber need not have protested. Even as Beaumont and Tocqueville documented horrific conditions, they admired the discipline, including its *despotic* aspects. They were clear-eyed about the control imposed in the two interrelated approaches that they (and many others) detailed—one prison opened in 1818 in Auburn, New York and the other, in 1829, named the Eastern State Penitentiary in Philadelphia, Pennsylvania. In the name of reformation, both institutions insisted on isolation and silence to generate repentance and prevent criminals from learning deviance from others. At its start, Auburn put about eighty prisoners into solitary confinement; within two years, some had died, others tried to kill themselves, and the public uproar prompted a new governor to pardon "survivors." Given that "complete isolation" had sent the "unfortunates, on whom this experiment was made, . . . into a state of depression," Auburn shifted to isolation at night and, during the day, made its prisoners march lockstep, silent and single file, in brutalizing regimented work enforced by whipping.

A decade later and influenced by Quaker theology, Eastern State consigned prisoners to single cells 24/7 where they slept, ate, and worked.[21] The idea was that, to mitigate tedium, prisoners would turn to handicrafts and the Christian Bible. If leaving cells, individuals were hooded and designated by numbers to keep them anonymous. (The notes by Tocqueville and Beaumont used numbers for interviewees.) Yet despite Eastern State's size, shown in Beaumont's drawing (figure 2.2), it sometimes double celled when the population grew.[22]

The virtues and vices of Auburn's and Philadelphia's innovations spawned debates about which to prefer.[23] One factor was money; Auburn cost less. An 1847 estimate was that the smaller cells and leasing of prisoners to private manufacturers garnered Auburn profits of $500 a year, while Eastern State required outputs of about $20,000.[24] Another was culture; Beaumont and Tocqueville told the French Parliament that adopting either model would be hard. They thought the French loquacious and lacking the religious commitments animating the strict US silencing rules.

FIGURE 2.2 Gustave de Beaumont, second sketch book, drawing of Eastern State Penitentiary, 1831–1832, Yale Tocqueville Manuscripts, courtesy of the Beinecke Rare Book and Manuscript Library, Yale University

Their 1833 report, more descriptive than prescriptive, also recorded angst. Beaumont and Tocqueville asked whether "an enlightened and humane society" should punish people through such isolation—a "terror more profound than chains or beatings," exerting "an incredible dominion . . . beyond the strength of man."[25] Lieber registered no hesitation about Eastern, which he characterized as "more philosophical in its principle, more radical and thorough in its operation, more practical and easier in its application, more charitable in its whole spirit."[26] A decade later, Beaumont and Tocqueville endorsed Eastern State's system. While acknowledging it had reportedly driven some people mad, they countered that "imprisonment of any kind creates susceptibility to insanity" and enforced isolation protected against schooling people in crime.[27]

"OBEDIENCE" THROUGH "THE THREAT OF CORPORAL PUNISHMENT," WHIPPING INCLUDED

"[S]ilence and order are maintained by labor and the thorough conviction of the unavoidable necessity of obedience;
. . . obedience is produced by the threat of corporal punishment; corporal punishment is rendered effectual by its certainty and instantaneousness."

—Francis Lieber, *On the Penitentiary System*, 1833[28]

Even as Lieber, Beaumont, and Tocqueville differed somewhat on how to accomplish reformation, they shared a theory that prison design (as a concept and in practice) ought to aim for profound regimentation ("one hour . . . follows with overwhelming uniformity the other"[29]).

What was the point? Why would one want to make people be silent, move in lockstep, and work incessantly? These men *reasoned* (differing somewhat) about the domination they commended. The goal, according to Lieber, was to "break" a person of his habits and return him to society—but not anywhere. Lieber called for legislation to prohibit "convicts" from living in cities, where "temptations" were "more frequent."[30] Beaumont and Tocqueville also wrote about breaking people; they chose the French word *dompté* which, as Sheldon Wolin explained, generally referenced mastery over animals.[31] Nonetheless, they worried about gaining obedience only through oppression; "absolute solitude . . . deprives the prisoner's submission of its moral character."[32]

That analysis drew an objection from Lieber, who pointed out that submission was produced "by the threat of instant corporal punishment," and thought Pennsylvania's system preferable because it led "to contemplation." Beaumont and Tocqueville concurred that Philadelphia's absolute silence (in theory) produced "more honest men," whereas Auburn's system produced "more obedient citizens." Lieber's replied that Eastern had fewer "recommittals" (today's recidivists), either because of reformation or to "avoid the severity of solitude."[33]

Nonetheless, the three converged on the desired end state: *control*, maintained through a mix of admonition, solitary confinement, starvation, and whipping. Beaumont and Tocqueville devoted a section to "Disciplinary Means" that, if successful, instilled habits (a "discipline") that became routine. Discipline also referenced punishment for rule violations. The two facets conflated in the description of the Philadelphia penitentiary; discipline was "as simple as the system itself. . . . The solitary cell of the criminal is for some days full of terrible phantoms." The only "chastisement" needed beyond that isolation was "imprisonment in a dark cell with reduction of food." Beaumont and Tocqueville reported that, within two days, darkness and food deprivation usually worked to "curb the most refractory prisoner."[34] (They were wrong; more forms of horrific oppression were used. A 1830s Pennsylvania legislative investigation revealed that Eastern's staff imposed a host of violent and lethal punishments, including putting metal chains around the necks of prisoners deemed to have breached rules.[35])

Whipping was a source of disagreement among the three men. Lieber approved; even as the whip was "not a very intellectual or moral means of discipline," the threat ("the knowledge of an inevitable and immediate punishment") exerted a "moral" force. Lieber offered a testimonial; he had "devised a means to obtain . . . personal knowledge" (to wit, he hit himself) and reported that, while the "the pain inflicted by this whip, . . . is very acute, . . . criminals have defied punishments much more severe than this." Lieber added a utilitarian argument. Given the ratio of staff to prisoners (thirty-five people to one thousand in some places), whips were needed. Nonetheless, forced labor "contribute[d] much more to maintain order than the whip." Thus, he linked his principles of "silence, labour, and immediate punishment."[36]

Beaumont and Tocqueville hesitated. "[C]ould these various penitentiaries dispense with corporal chastisement? This is a question which we dare not solve." Mixing descriptions of whipping's prevalence and utility with normative concerns, they reluctantly approved. "[S]ociety has the right to do everything necessary for its conservation," and if "it cannot arrive at the same end by milder means," it could use harsher techniques. Moreover, relying on the deaths and violence in French prisons as their *normative baseline*, the whip was painful but not "injurious to health."[37]

ADVOCATING FOR PRISONERS, OVERSIGHT OF KEEPERS, AND "ENERGETIC REPRESSION"

High-profile individuals like Beaumont and Tocqueville were not the only visitors welcomed. The relatively few penitentiaries were tourist attractions. As Lieber noted, "many curious persons" came to observe; in 1830, Auburn prison made more than $1,500 from visitors paying a quarter each to enter.[38] (In the twenty-first century, "prison tourism" remains, but mostly through the display of abandoned institutions. In a few instances, including Eastern State, the site has been turned into a platform to argue the imperative of prison reform.[39]) Bentham had called for public access so that prisons could serve as frightening deterrents; Beaumont and Tocqueville argued for systematic inspections and public reports to constrain the power of superintendents ("'the soul' of the administration").[40]

Given Tocqueville's work on democracy, commentators have tried to make sense of how, in *The Penitentiary System*, he and Beaumont endorsed totalizing control of prisoners. The term "othering" provides one explanation: Beaumont and Tocqueville put prisoners outside the political community and treated them, in Wolin's terms, as "pure objects of pure power."[41] Aspiring for reformation through repression, Beaumont and Tocqueville were committed to profound subjugation that, by virtue of uniform application, could have an aura of egalitarianism if providing the same treatment (single cells and manual labor) to people (generally lower class) convicted of ordinary crimes (as distinct from political crimes).

What may not be intuitive for contemporary readers is that Beaumont and Tocqueville were *passionate advocates for* incarcerated people. They pressed the French Parliament in 1833, 1843, and 1844 to enact reforms. Beaumont argued that society had "the right to punish, but not to corrupt those punished" and wanted authority for an "inspection commission" to enter at any time, as well as activities and exercise protocols. (A "cell without any kind of work is a tomb.") Tocqueville likewise decried "deplorable conditions" that were "repugnant to humanity."[42] Citing figures from Philadelphia, Tocqueville asserted that while single cells were expensive, they lessened recidivism, which could cut France's prison population by a fifth.[43]

Proposals to reform French law ended with the 1848 coup and, in the 1850s, France began its brutal transportation of prisoners to colonies, which continued for a century.[44] The country's subjugation does not fit with some accounts that the egalitarianism of the French Revolution paved the way for better French prisons and for Europe after World War II to require better treatment of all prisoners.[45] Even as the Revolution promoted that "dignity" was an attribute shared by all persons rather than limited to the aristocracy, prison authorities were licensed to impose "despotic" control, as described by Beaumont and Tocqueville in their discussion of discipline.

In 1833, the two explained that "citizens subject to the law are protected by it; they only cease to be free when they become wicked."[46] A decade later, in his 1844 addresses to the French Parliament, Tocqueville reiterated this position in response to a comment about prisoners and rights. Tocqueville concurred that prisoners had a "right to live," but not with their "fellow men." Society had both the right and the obligation to reform prisons (which were "sewers of crime and vice") by making them "sanctuaries where repentance and morality could penetrate."[47] Doing so did not entail recognizing prisoners' liberty and dignity. As he told Parliament, until returned to society, prisoners were outside the arena of "The Rights of Man."[48]

3

THE INVENTION OF "CORRECTIONS" IN THE "CIVILIZED WORLD"

John Howard, Cesare Beccaria, Jeremy Bentham, Gustave de Beaumont, Alexis de Tocqueville, and Francis Lieber illustrate how much *thought* can go into the political decision to impose gruesome punishments. Aware of incarceration's violent toll, they urged governments to maintain brutally controlling prisons in the name of promoting community safety. In contrast, some artists and writers recorded imprisonment's miseries. Yet, without an infrastructure, commendations and critique had limited impact.

This chapter's focus is the people who built the requisite scaffolding through generating professions named "penology" and "corrections" and launching formal associations that laid the groundwork for what today we call the carceral state, with its seemingly insatiable desire for social control. Yet even when shaping institutions disabling millions, the men and women I discuss were not comfortable (as others of their era were) leaving people in filthy jails and prisons. They argued that governments ought to separate children from adults and provide adequate food, light, and doctors. They coupled these "humanitarian" concerns to lessen misery with commitments to dominion over human movement; their enforcement techniques were horrific to experience and are (again) painful to recount.

PHILANTHROPIC SOCIETIES FOR PRISON REFORM
ON BOTH SIDES OF THE ATLANTIC

"The construction should be simple but not destitute of all elegance, solid but not massive."

—Second Resolution of the 2d International
Penitentiary Congress, Brussels, 1847[1]

Some reformers, such as John Howard, took it upon themselves to go on inspection tours. Others were drawn in by what sociologists call "agentic prisoners"—people who, refusing to cooperate, created (in authorities' terms) "disturbances" and "riots."[2] Prisoners stopped work and went on hunger strikes, used sheets to make signs, threw food, cut their Achilles tendons, started fires, and attempted escapes. They infuriated keepers (who regularly retaliated) and, at times, caught the attention of local philanthropists. By 1831, when Beaumont and Tocqueville toured US prisons, groups—such as London's Society for the Improvement of Prison Discipline and for the Reformation of Juvenile Offenders, Philadelphia's Society for Alleviating the Miseries of Public Prisoners, and Boston's Prison Discipline Society—had reform agendas. They argued that instead of warehousing, officials should organize prisons by age and sex and structure time around work and religion.[3]

Such organizations were hands on. The Philadelphia Society (later the Pennsylvania Prison Society) oversaw Eastern State Penitentiary and in 1845 began the *Journal of Prison Discipline and Philanthropy*. The Boston Society dispatched Francis Gray to study "prison discipline in America." Filing a report with the federal court in Massachusetts, Gray gave a scathing appraisal of what Philadelphians admired. "That stinted food, constant confinement, total privation of social intercourse, should form no part of any system." The Prison Association of New York supported the 1877 opening of the Elmira Reformatory aiming, per its name, to change behavior.[4] "Patronage societies" focused on assisting (and controlling) "discharged" prisoners. Then (and now), incarcerated individuals needed housing and employment when returning to their communities.

Steeped in ideologies of capitalism, Christianity, and colonialism, these reformers were unselfconscious about sustaining inequities

based on class, race, and gender. That condescension can be found
in the "duties" promulgated by the Prison Association of New York,
chartered in 1846. Its bylaws called for frequent visits to "endeavor to
improve both the physical and moral condition of the prisoners in all
suitable and practicable ways." Members were to "ascertain, previous
to discharge of each prisoner, his feelings, views and capabilities"
and help find work and "suitable boarding places . . . where they will
not be exposed to corrupting influences"—such as former prisoners.[5]

By the time Beaumont and Tocqueville renewed pleas for reform
to the French Parliament in the 1840s, the prison movement had
enough steam to hold cross-country gatherings in Europe. (The
antislavery, peace, women's rights, and labor movements also entered the transnational stage and used modes of organizing long
deployed by religions.[6]) In 1846 and 1847, two back-to-back ad hoc
"congresses," the first in Frankfurt and the second in Brussels, welcomed Europe's "best authorities in prison administration" and a
few from the United States. They issued "resolutions" on prison
construction, administration, and confinement.[7]

The impact of Beaumont, Tocqueville, and Lieber can be found
in the attendees' enthusiasm for "separate confinement" (justified
as promoting repentance and reformation) and their rejection of
"associated confinement" (presumed to school prisoners in crime).
Per Beccaria, on the Frankfurt 1846 agenda were questions about
how to "prevent" or "decrease" crimes, and per Howard, the 1847
Brussels Congress endorsed well-ventilated buildings and spacious
cells in which "moral and material" education could take place.[8] Per
Bentham, that Congress called for prison construction to include
a "central observatory" for oversight. The attendees also wanted
differentiation by age and less punitive treatment of juveniles than
adults who, if noncompliant, could be put into "punishment cells"
defined by their darkness.[9]

Efforts to change France's prisons were interrupted by Louis
Napoleon's return to power; uprisings thereafter around Europe
paused subsequent meetings until 1857, when about 170 people
(primarily from Germany) went to a Third Penitentiary Congress in
Frankfurt. Their output reflected more concern about prisoner well-
being than had the earlier convenings. Indeed, the 1857 Congress

called for treatment in some respects better than what the League of Nations' Rules endorsed in 1934 and Arkansas provided in the 1960s.

The Frankfurt 1857 Congress' prescriptions ("factors") included that "in general all corporal and infamous punishments be abolished," along with "extraordinary and supplementary punishments." Outsiders were to impose "constant and active supervision and surveillance." Prison authorities were to attend to the "physical, mental and moral well-being of prisoners," to provide health care, and to govern through "punishments and encouragements" recorded via "statistical means." Continuing the commitment to "absolute separation" of prisoners for work, religious instruction, and exercise (under a "capable, strict, benevolent and zealously devoted" staff), the 1857 mandates also called for opportunities for prisoners to "complain to the authorities" and to have social interactions through "frequent visits from relatives and other persons from without the prison."[10]

"CONVICT LEASING": FORCED LABOR ENFORCED THROUGH TORTUROUS DISCIPLINE

Institutionalization takes money. In the United States, financing came through "convict leasing" that brought funds into New York's Auburn Penitentiary, which sold prisoners' labor to the private sector at cheap prices. During the 1830s, the free "workingmen's movement" protested prisoner–laborers, billed at below-market rates that undercut efforts by "honest" workers to improve wages and hours. Mechanics organized a national campaign that made inroads toward limiting leasing. Yet by the 1850s, the loss of income for prisons, coupled with rising numbers of prisoners, resulted in overcrowded facilities and cycles of uprisings.[11]

During the Civil War, both North and South commandeered prisoner labor through contracts with private-sector producers. The Thirteenth Amendment, ratified in 1865, could have imposed a constraint, given its ban on slavery and "involuntary servitude." But that constitutional amendment included the words "except as a punishment for crime whereof the party shall have been duly convicted." This phrasing, borrowed from the 1787 Northwest Ordinance governing US

territories, might have been read narrowly to protect *statutes* authorizing judges to sentence people to "hard labor." Instead, the Thirteenth
Amendment was seen as licensing prisons to require labor without
compensation. Southern states enacted Black Codes criminalizing all
sorts of activities; standing on a corner or walking on a street became
illegal "loitering" or "vagrancy" that sent many Black people into confinement, where they were forced again to work the fields.[12]

The price prisoners paid was clear. The brutality of the plantation prisons and convict-lease camps meant that "leased Southern
convicts died at up to eight times the rate of convicts in other parts
of the country." Exploitation was not (then or now) limited to that
region. By the 1870s, "large-scale industrial interests set up shop in
the American penal system"; an 1887 report for the first US Commissioner of Labor found that 70 percent (45,000) of incarcerated men,
women, and children worked for profit-making enterprises.[13] Prison
authorities justified violent punishments as requisite to production
quotas. Thus, the phrase "forced labor" needs to be read not only to
reference *obligations to work* but also *enforcement* through the torture
of ice baths, shackling, strapping, dungeons, and starvation.

ENOCH COBB WINES, THEODORE DWIGHT, AND THEIR SURVEY OF PRISON DEGRADATION

"The science of punishment, the philosophy which investigates the
treatment of criminals, holding the just balance between coercion
and reformation, must [be of] profound interest for all lovers of the
human race."

> —Enoch Cobb Wines and Theodore William Dwight,
> 1867 Report to New York State's Legislature

"Penology was then no more than a small philanthropy; it had not
risen to the dignity of a social science."

> —1883 Report of the National Prison Association[14]

Two major critics of the prisoner-for-private-profit system were Enoch Cobb Wines and Theodore William Dwight,

nineteenth-century educators and prison evangelists who succeeded in changing the scale and scope of the prison reform movement. In addition to analyzing prison practices around the United
States, Wines and Dwight launched two professional organizations—
the National Prison Association and the International Penitentiary
Commission—to generate management principles.

Wines began his career as an educator, became a Congregation-
alist minister in 1849, taught classical languages at a state college,
served as the president of the City University of St. Louis, and found
his calling in prisons. In 1862, Wines became the Corresponding
Secretary of the Prison Association of New York, a perch from
which he was an incessant networker. Dwight, a New Yorker, attended Hamilton College and Yale University. Between 1858 and
1873, Dwight was the one and only professor in Columbia University's new department of law. In the 1860s, when the two wrote their
massive account of US prisons, Wines was employed as the Secretary (akin to an executive director) of New York's Prison Association, and Dwight chaired its Executive Committee as well as served
(along with Francis Lieber) as one of several vice presidents.[15]

After the US Civil War, struggles for social control included expansive criminal sanctions and institutionalization. The founding
documents of the 1865 American Association for the Promotion of
Social Sciences (soon folded into the longer-lasting American Social
Science Association) capture that effort. The goals included "Prevention and Repression of Crime, the Reformation of Criminals,
and the progress of Public Morality, the adoption of Sanitary Regulations," predicated on "sound principles . . . of Economy, Trade,
and Finance." To pay "attention" to "Pauperism" and to fulfill the
"responsibility of the well-endowed and successful, the wise and
educated, the honest and respectable, for the failures of others,"
social scientists needed to "collect all facts, diffuse all knowledge,
[and] stimulate all inquiry . . . bearing on social welfare" about
"prison discipline in England and America."[16]

The Prison Association of New York took up that mission. It
chartered Wines and Dwight to survey "penal and correctional institutions of the states of our Union" so as to "improve and perfect"

New York's "penal and reformatory system" and impress upon it "a character worthy of our civilization." (Translation: Local jails and prisons were abysmal, and looking outside the state could provide political leverage for reform.) Walking in the footsteps of Howard, Beaumont, and Tocqueville, the two New Yorkers sent hundreds of questions to officials around the country and embarked on their own grand tour. The resulting 1867 *Report on the Prisons and Reformatories of the United States and Canada* recorded that these men were appalled at most of what they saw. They relied on their descriptions to generate *prescriptions* ("principles grow out of facts").[17]

When submitting findings to New York State's Constitutional Convention in 1867, Wines and Dwight noted that the "Empire State" had given "the world a model system of prison discipline" (referencing Auburn) but that, due to "undue influence of party politics," New York had not achieved all it could. Echoing 1780s Amsterdam's appetite for detention, their recommendations centered on institutionalizing all sorts of people. Wines and Dwight argued for mandating public schools for young children, confinement in industrial schools for "truants," and incarceration for convicted people in penitentiaries run by educated staff. (Wines' 1880 book, *The State of Prisons and Child-Saving Institutions in the Civilized World*, expounded on salvation through confinement.)[18]

Yet these men worried about convict leasing and hyper-control. Wines and Dwight argued (per today's "political economy") that the state was a "loser" when selling prisoner labor at a discount instead of relying on prisoners to fund incarceration. Moreover, by outsourcing to profiteers focused on production (making "nails" instead of "men"), opportunities for reformation were lost. Despite a veneer of savings, the practice was "very expensive" because it did not "correct the majority of prisoners." They also objected to degrading uniforms and to "minute regulations" resulting in unnecessary, in-prison punishments. Their survey documented "disciplinary" measures of dark cells, shackles, balls and chains, the "cat, switch, or lash," freezing-cold shower baths, shaving people's heads, and the "yoke or crucifix" (hanging people on bars)—which they called "cruel and degrading" and "unworthy of the civilization of the nineteenth century."[19]

Wines and Dwight reported regularly thereafter to the New York Legislature, where they promoted (without much success) central-ization to shift power from locals to professionals and to enable oversight. In 1895, New York took a small step by chartering a Commission of Prisons to "visit and inspect" all facilities for "sane adults charged with or convicted of crimes"; prison managers were to per-mit entry and report yearly.[20]

THE 1870 DECLARATION OF PRINCIPLES OF THE NATIONAL PRISON CONGRESS

The "supreme aim of prison discipline [was] the reformation of criminals, not the infliction of vindictive suffering."

—The 1870 Cincinnati Principles[21]

". . . [T]he proposition, submitted to all . . . interested in the future of prisons, [is] to convoke an international reunion of specialists and jurisconsults, who, under the patronage of their respective governments, should be charged with the duty of giving to penitentiary science its definitive principles."

—Count W. Sollohub, Director-in-Chief, Moscow's House of Correction and Industry, 1868[22]

The aspirations of Wines and Dwight became the nation's and then the globe's. Wines published Count Sollohub's proposal for an interna-tional prison congress, got funding, and persuaded Ohio's Republican Governor Rutherford B. Hayes (who after a contested 1876 election be-came the President of the United States) to welcome some three hun-dred delegates from twenty-five states to the first-ever National Prison Congress. Assembling in 1870 in Cincinnati, they listened to Wines describe the "great principles" of punishment upon which he claimed widespread agreement existed. Wines turned the recommendations of his 1867 report into the Congress' official proclamation—"The Dec-laration of Principles Adopted and Promulgated by the 1870 Congress of the National Prison Association."[23] As the street sign (installed a hundred years later and reproduced as figure 3.1) reflects, the Cincin-nati meeting codified a "a far-sighted philosophy" that "remains today as the basic guide for modern correctional systems."

OHIO
HISTORICAL MARKER

FIRST NATIONAL CORRECTIONAL CONGRESS

On this site in October, 1870 a group of enlightened individuals dedicated to the reformation and improvement of penal systems met. This first Congress of the National Prison Association, now known as the American Correctional Association, adopted a far-sighted philosophy of corrections. This philosophy, embodied in its Declaration of Principles, remains today as the basic guide for modern correctional systems.

THE AMERICAN CORRECTIONAL ASSOCIATION
THE OHIO HISTORICAL SOCIETY
1970   THE CINCINNATI HISTORICAL SOCIETY   5-31

FIGURE 3.1 *First National Correctional Congress Marker* (Side A), Cincinnati, Ohio, Historical Marker Database, installed 1970 on the one-hundredth anniversary of the Congress, courtesy of the photographer William E. Fischer Jr.

The pillars of punishment erected by the thirty-seven Cincinnati Principles rejected as "unchristian in principle . . . [and] unwise in policy" the commitments of Howard, Beccaria, and Bentham to depersonalizing regimentation. Indeed, the great "mistake" had been an "infliction of vindictive suffering" through a "studied imposition of degradation" that "destroys every better impulse and aspiration." Punishment's new goals were to produce "upright and industrious free men, rather than orderly and obedient prisoners," as the "interest of society and the interest of the convicted criminal [were] really identical"—that prisoners be "trained to virtue." Because "reformation" was "a work of time," not a "lapse of time," both "progressive classification" and indeterminate sentences needed to be in place so that "satisfactory proof of reformation" could be determined by prison staff. A "well-devised and skillfully applied system of rewards" and religion ("of first in importance") would help prisoners regain "self-respect," their "manhood," and agency over their own "destiny."[24]

Formulated soon after the Civil War, the Cincinnati Principles tried to shore up the coffers and the authority of states by requiring forced labor by prisoners, but not for the benefit of private contractors. The "maintenance of penal institutions" (aside from county jails) was to come from "the earnings of their inmates, and without cost to the state." The Principles specifically condemned "the contract system" as "prejudicial" to "discipline, finance, and . . . reformation" and "injurious to the interest of the free laborer." Moreover, while referencing John Howard about work, the Principles rejected useless, demeaning activities in favor of "industrial training."[25] Further, by declaring that states should be in charge of prison construction, the Principles aimed to limit local power, except for pretrial detention.

Echoes of Bentham come from the proposed internalization of costs, decent provisioning, and the focus on infrastructure and oversight. The 1870 Cincinnati Principles, like the 1857 Frankfurt Resolutions, sought "substantial structures" that would be "moderate" in size, well designed, and not too "costly or highly ornate." Paralleling the European 1857 resolutions, the Principles called for sanitation, health care, decent ("wholesome") food, bedding, and clothes, as well as adequate ventilation ("sunlight, air and water . . . in the abundance with which nature has provided them"). As for staff, "special training, as well as high qualities of head and heart" would make "the administration of public punishment . . . scientific, uniform, and successful." Like Beaumont and Tocqueville, whose monographs were laden with numbers, the Principles called for more statistics (by "competent working committees in every state") to learn the "true character and working of our prison systems."[26]

Although written soon after the ratifications of the Thirteenth, Fourteenth, and Fifteenth Amendments, the 1870 Principles made no mention of race, due process, or equal protection. Wines had strategic reasons to skirt politics; he wanted support from across the barely reunited country, and many in Ohio had close ties to the South.[27] The 1870 Principles' only mention of "personal liberty" and "right" came in reference to "innocent" people; upon "unquestionable proof of its mistake," governments needed to provide "reasonable indemnification for such wrongful imprisonment."

Gender made it into the Principles' text, as white women were then active in reform societies; "the agency of women may be employed with excellent effect" in "official administration" and volunteer positions.[28]

The rightlessness of prisoners, reflected in the 1870 Principles, was assumed on both sides of the Atlantic. Convicted people could not contract, marry, or own property. Likewise, constitutional changes excluded the "duly convicted" from the ban on involuntary servitude and people participating in "rebellion and other crime" from national voting rights.

NATIONAL PRISON CONGRESSES' DEBATES ON DARK CELLS, CHAINS, BREAD AND WATER, AND WHIPS

"The Association has been organized . . . for the purpose of influencing legislation, executive control, and prison management, in the direction of a humane and intelligent effort to prevent the spread of the contagion of crime, within or without prison walls. . . ."
—Preface, 1887 Proceedings of the National Prison Association[29]

"[W]e have to put a ball and chain on a prisoner."
—Warden of a New Jersey prison, 1893 Proceedings of the National Prison Congress[30]

The National Prison Congress was not a one-off, and Rutherford B. Hayes hung in.[31] As Hayes recounted in an 1887 address to the National Prison Congress, Cincinnati's "most important action" was launching a "permanent National Prison Association" (incorporated in 1871) to improve "laws in relation to public offenses and offenders, . . . penal, correctional, and reformatory institutions," and the care and employment of "discharged prisoners." Yet the National Prison Association struggled to turn its precepts into practice. Convict leasing was one example—continuing, albeit with a few larger scale manufacturers in the 1870s replacing a "diversity of small and middle-scale business enterprises." Over decades, pressures from the labor movement and prisoner protests prompted a few constraints. For example, New York's Constitution required that "after

December 31, 1896, no person in any prison . . . shall be . . . allowed to work . . . whereby . . . work . . . shall be farmed out, contracted, given or sold to any person, firm, association or corporation."[32]

While not stopping convict leasing, Wines *succeeded* on an important metric: he generated a new organization to embed a new profession. Wines enlisted associations of Protestant chaplains and of wardens; within short order, wardens dominated the congresses. Speakers also included academics lecturing on statistics, physicians opining on mental and physical health, and Christian ministers (and once, a Jewish rabbi) giving sermons on redemption.[33] Meetings lasted for days, and proceedings appeared in thick annual volumes. As far as I can tell, all the speakers were white; very few were women.

What Wines could not get was a solid economic base. He aimed for federal legislation ($10,000 for "the collection of criminal and penitentiary statistics") that did not pass. After Wines died in 1879, the organization stalled. Revival came with support from the proponents of the American Social Science Association, New York's Prison Association, and Rutherford Hayes (whose US presidency ended in 1881). He agreed in 1883 to be the National Prison Association's head. Calling himself its "advertising agent," Hayes attended every meeting until his death in 1893. By the 1890s, "all the leading prison men of the country" were members, along with philanthropists, academics, and the future president Theodore Roosevelt. The organization claimed credit for elevating prison management "to the dignity of a profession" at a time when more than 82,000 people were incarcerated; estimates were that, by 1900, some 100,000 would be.[34]

Dipping into the thousands of pages of proceedings is one way to know what prisons were supposed to do, from *management's perspective*. Speakers regularly invoked a tripod (or trinity): "labor, education, and religion" as the "three bases of a reformatory discipline in prisons." Lecturers mixed pop psychology and armchair philosophizing with racism. Reading (plowing through) is uncomfortable, as many exchanges characterize "the negro" and make claims about heredity, biology, and race.[35] The materials are also boring. Participants had appetite for endless discussions about the virtues and vices of indeterminate sentencing, the "conditional liberation" of parole and probation, special treatment for juveniles and women, and help for discharged prisoners. Several lecturers discussed better prisons in Europe, with Ireland as an oft-cited model in which lessening restrictions and conditional release followed an initial period of isolation.

In addition to building norms and networks, the focus was on the public. Leaders sought to get statutes changed and budgets funded. On the question of "how to popularize prison reform," one answer—on the view that "prison reform is the child of Christianity"—was to persuade churches to discuss "prison topics" on "prison Sundays."[36]

Despite the 1870 Principles' rejection of suffering, chilling glimpses of the actual treatment of prisoners and of what constituted "discipline" come through. As the Association's president explained in 1896, when any "person encroaches upon the rights or privileges of others it is the right and the duty of society to deal with the offender in any way that may seem best to put an end to his encroachments." What was best? One standing committee devoted to prison discipline described taking away good time and privileges and using whips, starvation, chaining, hanging people by their nails, and dungeons. The point, as a warden from New York's Sing Sing prison explained in 1890, was that discipline "endorce[d] perfect subjection, and a willingness to obey the rules. . . . Therefore the severer the punishment, the less it will have to be resorted to, and the severity is really kindness."[37]

Whipping came up regularly. For example, in 1897, a Texas warden said that he would not know "how to manage without the strap." A New Jersey warden, who reported that he "never used the lash," noted that "a dark-cell, with a man chained to the wall, is corporal punishment, is it not? Well sometimes we are compelled to use that kind of punishment." A California warden explained he did not "resort to any harsh or severe punishment. We use only the dungeon and bread and water." When queried about what was regarded as the "most humane, to lock up a man in solitary on bread and water, or to give him half a dozen strokes with the lash?" that warden replied, "Emphatically, bread and water."[38]

Accounts of violence abounded. Elmira Reformatory recorded more than 2,500 beatings of prisoners between 1889 and 1893; the weapons were rubber hoses and paddles. Popular magazines provided illustrations, including of "shower baths" (the "water cure" and today, "water boarding"), in which a person was "stripped,

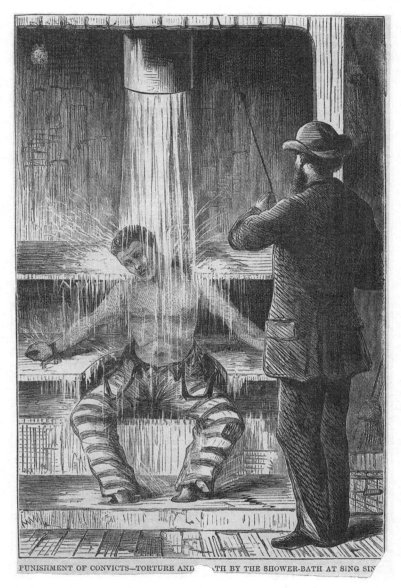

PUNISHMENT OF CONVICTS—TORTURE AND ＿＿TH BY THE SHOWER-BATH AT SING SIN

FIGURE 3.2 *Harper's Weekly*, accompanying *Punishment of Convicts*, April 17, 1869, made available by the New York Public Library

... manacled in a ... bath tub," and faced a stream of water that one author described as producing "indescribably horrible" sensations. An exposé in 1858 in *Harper's Weekly* prompted the New York Legislature to require "the advice and guidance" of a doctor. In 1860, New York's Sing Sing prison recorded using "shower baths" 161 times, while the New Jersey Legislature banned it.[39] Some depictions, as the one from 1869 in figure 3.2, show the torture of a dark-skinned man.

THE 1870 PRINCIPLES IN THE TWENTIETH CENTURY: THE DISCIPLINE/PUNISHMENT MODEL

Before following Wines across the Atlantic to the founding of the International Penitentiary Commission in 1872, a note on the endurance of the 1870 Cincinnati Declaration is in order. It was not a foregone conclusion that governments would create special entities devoted to punishment, as compared to agencies with a welfarist agenda led by experts on *care* rather than *confinement*. Indeed, the National Prison Congress faced competition from the National Conference of Charities and Corrections, begun in 1874 and becoming in 1917 the National Conference for Social Welfare. Yet racial and class hostility, coupled with political savvy, helped the National Prison Association enshrine authority by claiming to deliver community *security* through confinement. In an 1887 meeting in Toronto, Canada, a proposed name change (official in 1908) turned the entity into the American Prison Association, denoting its openness to non-US residents.[40] (In 1954, the organization adopted a broader appellation—the American Correctional Association—which continues as a trade organization and, as discussed later, offers "accreditation" used to buffer against prisoners' lawsuits.)

The 1870 Cincinnati Principles became, with modest modifications, the basis for the American Prison Association's set issued in 1930. Strides in professionalization were marked by referencing "prison executives and guards." Shifting attitudes toward mental health can be seen by "mental disorder" replacing "lunacy," and an emphasis on health care (a "competent and adequate medical staff is essential"). The word "individual" made its debut in reference to prisoner classification, and the word "prisoner" was substituted for "convict." Moreover, describing "recreation . . . [as] an essential part of education [and] . . . an indispensable factor of normal human life," the 1930 Principles suggested that incarcerated people ought to partake in aspects of *normal* life. Yet another innovation—ignored into the twenty-first century—was that "steady, honorable work" was the basis for all "reformatory discipline," and therefore labor ought to come with "reasonable compensation to the prisoner."[41]

A brief summary of the sixty plus years sketched here is in order. First, post–Civil War punishment theorists and practitioners abandoned degradation as a *goal*. Second, that shift came in part through the ongoing invocation of "civilization," denoting both that the treatment of incarcerated people was a reflection on society and that incarceration's purpose was to "civilize" the deviant. Third, people running prisons sought power to determine practices during confinement and indeterminate sentencing to get some control over detention's duration. Fourth, the reference to "normal life" in the 1930s—had it been embraced—suggested the metric of outside life that could have limited prisons' harms. But, and fifth, despite eschewing suffering as an aim, the trinity of "labor, education, and religion" left degradation in place as a *practice*.

Michel Foucault titled his iconic 1970s book *Discipline and Punish*; the "and" could mark a distinction between those two words. That space collapses in the micro-managing regimes that prison officials constructed.[42] Correctional staff aimed for *discipline* in the sense of an organized day. Managers saw control as essential in the violent spaces they created, where fear was pervasive and all kinds of normal activities were turned into breaches of prisons' peculiar rules. Violations become justifications for imposition of *discipline* in the sense of punishments on people's bodies, sometimes resulting in death. Discipline/punishment becomes a description of, as well as an abstraction about, prison. The professionalization of corrections thus gave stature to shocking forms of treatment. One reason to look back at what was *then* "normal" in prisons is to interrogate what is *now* taken for granted. The next step in understanding twenty-first-century practices requires following the path from Cincinnati to the capitals of Europe, where "prison men" shaped norms for the globe.

4

A GATHERING OF EXPERTS, A GEO-POLITICAL BUREAUCRACY, A "MARCH OF PROGRESS," AND WORLD WAR I

"The problem which the congress proposes to study—how to diminish crime—is one in which all civilized nations have an interest in common, and the congress of Stockholm seems likely to prove the most important convention ever held for the study of this grave question."

—President Rutherford B. Hayes, message to the US Senate and House, October 15, 1877

"Civilized nations" showed their stripes repeatedly in the decades to come as they drew lines between permissible and impermissible punishments. Winning support in Cincinnati for "an International Congress on Penitentiary and Reformatory Discipline," Enoch Wines sought the "official power to make reform effective" and, as his successor put it, "secured" it through creating the International Penitentiary Commission (IPC), which, as noted, was also known as the International Prison Commission.[1] When begun in 1872, the IPC was at the front end of dozens of new international governmental organizations aiming to "reform the world." For example, two years later, more than twenty countries formed the Universal Postal Union, making worldwide correspondence possible; to borrow from Leonard Woolf's 1916 description, it worked "a revolution in the constitution of the society of nations" while enjoying its own "placid obscurity."[2] The success of the Postal Union helped the IPC, which relied heavily on mail to coordinate its far-flung membership and, like the Postal Union, the IPC transformed government practices without garnering much attention.

Once again, *thought* poured into prisons, this time laden with "science." IPC proceedings were replete with debates about punishment's purposes, crime's pathologies, prison management, and worries about the financing, structure, and impact of national prisons and of the organization. The IPC, renamed in 1929 the International Penal and Penitentiary Commission (IPPC), pursued these topics for decades. Reconvening after World War I, the IPC/IPPC promoted policies that became a *source* of corrections' professional stature. After the IPPC's collaboration with fascist countries and its dissolution in 1951, its practices of border crossings and standard-making came under the UN's umbrella and became a *resource* for others. Many have since used the transnational platform Wines built to advocate for prisoners' human rights; others aim to garner larger market shares of private-sector prisons. Rather than a tidy skim of what could, in hindsight, be seen as an inevitable production of authority, in this and the following chapters, I explore how these men made, and then lost, some of their power to define punishment's parameters.

SEEKING GOVERNMENT AUTHORIZATION, FUNDING, AND PARTICIPATION

For the IPC to be an arm of government, Wines needed buy-in from the United States. In 1871, Wines engineered a joint resolution of Congress authorizing the President to appoint "a commissioner to attend an international congress on penitentiary and reformatory discipline." President Ulysses S. Grant asked Wines to represent the country at the 1872 London Congress. Thereafter, Wines gathered commitments from European countries to support the IPC, which he chaired. For the 1878 Congress, Sweden's monarch, Oscar II, directed his ministry to invite "all civilized governments . . . to send" official delegates. After Rutherford B. Hayes became US President, he asked Congress for $8,000 to send his designee to that "most important convention" on "how to diminish crime."[3]

The IPC structure, set forth in its "permanent constitution" adopted in 1880 and confirmed in 1886, called for jurisdictions to appoint "commissioners" and send "delegates" to congresses. Unlike other transnational geo-political bureaucracies, countries did not join directly.[4] While comprised of countries' officials, the IPC promised not to speak for or bind any governments, who were to pay modest dues keyed to populations: 25–50 Swiss francs (then about US$5–$10) per million inhabitants. The volume of IPC correspondence devoted to collection reflected that budgets were a perennial problem. Indeed, despite its centrality in launching the IPC, the United States was often in arrears. The meager finances reflected the marginality of prisons as a political problem and the IPC's dependence on country affiliation. In theory, payment was requisite to having a commissioner; in practice, nonpayment did not translate into losing a slot on the IPC.[5]

Although struggling with fundraising, IPC leaders were astute in bringing people into its fold. In advance of a congress, the IPC sent out detailed questions and enlisted rapporteurs. For example, for the 1895 Paris Congress, the IPC recruited some 240 reporters whose production amounted to 2,500 pages of materials, circulated three months in advance. Twenty-five countries sent official delegates, and more than two hundred foreign delegates joined five hundred French attendees.[6] Each congress devoted days to segments (designated "legislation," "administration," "prevention," and, in some years, "juveniles") at which one person presided along with several vice presidents.

IPC congresses produced what today is called "a product." Discussions culminated in a "general assembly" voting on "resolutions" that, through "highly skilled draftsmanship, were often loosely formulated and minimally prescriptive."[7] Along with reporters' papers, the IPC's "procès-verbaux" (edited transcripts) were published after congresses. Aside from London's 1872 meeting and the final 1950 Hague Congress, all materials were in the IPC's official language of French, with an occasional speech in English (and several in German at Berlin's 1935 meeting). In addition, some delegates filed reports in their own countries about debates, outcomes, prison tours, and elegant dinners. After its opening London 1872 meeting, the IPC met in Stockholm in 1878; Rome in 1885; St. Petersburg in 1890; Paris in 1895; Brussels in 1900; Budapest in 1905; Washington,

DC in 1910; and London in 1925. The renamed IPPC convened in Prague in 1930, Berlin in 1935, and at The Hague in 1950. That list reflects a world as leaders of the IPC/IPPC conceived it—dominated by Europeans and the United States, with a few attendees (often colonial subjects) from Asia, Africa, and Latin America.

One quick way to glimpse the IPC's initial scramble for authority comes from efforts to quantify its output. In 1891, US Commissioner Caleb Randall tabulated the number of members, topics, and "solutions" achieved at four congresses. A few years later, his replacement, Samuel Barrows, sent the US House of Representatives

STATISTICS OF INTERNATIONAL PRISON CONGRESSES.

	London (1872).	Stockholm (1878).	Rome (1885).	St. Petersburg (1890).	Paris (1895).	Brussels (1900).
Total number of members	341	297	234	740	817	395
Members from abroad	149	142	93	177	287	234
States represented	24	25	25	26	24	29
Official delegates	76	45	48	69	88	85
Questions on programme:						
First section: Penal legislation..	10	4	6	8	8	5
Second section: Penitentiary institutions	13	6	8	11	9	4
Third section: Preventive institutions........................	5	4	8	6	5	3
Fourth section: Questions relative to children and minors ...					8	4
Total.......................	28	14	22	25	30	16
Preliminary reports on questions of the programme:						
First section	9	11	25	46	61	52
Second section....................	3	21	24	57	64	49
Third section	4	17	18	36	31	19
Fourth section					78	53
Total.......................	16	49	67	139	234	175
Average number of reports per question	0.6	3.5	3.0	5.6	7.8	10.8

FIGURE 4.1 *Statistics of the International Prison Congresses*, in Samuel J. Barrows, *Report of the Proceedings and Conclusions of the Sixth International Prison Congress held at Brussels, Belgium, August 1900*, US House of Representatives, Doc. No. 57-374 (1903)

(in which he had served a term) an updated tally, shown in figure
4.1. By Barrows' calculations, in 1900, five more countries had representatives than in 1895, and the number of reports per question
had increased twofold, with more than ten reports per question.[8]

Whatever the debates, IPC congresses did not reject the vast res-
ervoir of officials' punishment power. And whatever claims were
made for progressive views, practices were oppressive, as seen
in figure 4.2, a photograph taken in an English prison in the early

FIGURE 4.2 *The Tread Wheel at Preston Prison, Lancashire,* 1902, courtesy of the
Mary Evans Picture Library/The National Archives, London, England

1900s. Prisoners were made to walk the seven steps of treadwheels that turned in endless, useless, and painful rotations.

Eurocentric imperialism was regularly on display. The 1890 St. Petersburg Congress came at the "invitation of the Emperor of Russia." At the 1895 Paris Congress, the French Society of Prisoners hosted a dinner at the Eiffel Tower (opened just a few years before) where the assembled celebrated the "march of progress." At the 1900 meeting in Brussels, "under the patronage of His Majesty the King" (Leopold II, infamous for horrific exploitation of the Congo), Belgium's Minister of Justice discussed the "upward march of civilization" and pronounced prison reform the "watchword for the century." Archduke Joseph "honored" the 1905 Budapest Congress by commending the assembled for choosing "charity, the controlling idea in modern culture" as the "weapon in the combat" against crime.[9]

PAINFUL OBLIVION, CASUAL RACISM, AND INSISTENT AUTHORITARIANISM

"Do we really know, in a scientific sense, what are the actual effects of this slavery?"

—Charles Henderson, US Commissioner, opening
the 1910 IPC Congress in Washington, DC[10]

The IPC's last congress before World War I was its first and only in which the United States was the host. Delegates arriving in Washington, DC were "charmed" by a handshake from President William Howard Taft, welcoming them at a White House reception. Attorney General George Wickersham, one of the meeting's honorary presidents, extolled civilizations' advances. He credited the US with proposing the IPC and with rejecting what law had once done: "branded [a convicted person] as an outlaw . . . with the gates of Hope and Mercy forever closed in his face." Instead, a "great change has occurred in the attitude of civilized communities toward the subject of the prevention and punishment of crime." The modern approach aimed not only to "deter by making an example of offenders, but by convincing the offender of the wisdom of obeying law." Yet, a hint of concern emerged in Wickersham's call for law to empower independent visitors as a guarantee against "abuse of power by prison officials."[11]

What could have been heard to be a head-on critique came from the other opening speaker, Charles Henderson, the US Commissioner selected by President Taft to replace Barrows, who died in 1909. Henderson was a minister and sociologist who had received his PhD in 1901 from the University of Leipzig, chaired the University of Chicago's Department of Practical Sociology from 1904 to 1915, and was the University's Chaplain. Henderson's writings on crime, deviance, and corrections, and his former presidency of the US National Prison Association, made him a leader in his field. In his address, he described incarceration, the "chief instrument and sanction of modern penal law, as *'reduction to slavery.'*"

> Capital punishment is rare. Torture is forbidden. Slow starvation is illegal. Only bondage, deprivation of free movement and choice of occupation and recreation, remain. Do we really know, in a scientific sense, what are the actual effects of this slavery?[12]

Twenty-first-century readers might assume that Henderson's invocation of "slavery" would be followed by a call for abolition. Don't. Henderson did not reject "this slavery," even as he questioned its utility as a deterrent and as building character. Henderson did call for some limits, including keeping youths out of adult prisons and sentencing certain adults (if not "vicious or criminal") to time suspended and placed under "surveillance." The point was to save a person from "a criminal reputation" and to help "the taxpayer, the man and his family." On the other hand, for professional criminals and others "dangerous to society," Henderson endorsed the "indeterminate sentence" to provide "social protection and re-education." Henderson ended by calling on the audience to be "[c]ourageous to defend our own conclusions, eager to learn new truths, courteous in presence of opposition [as] we are at the gate of our high duty. Forward!"[13]

Rather than "forward," what followed was familiar, with resolutions reflecting compromises limiting their operational impact
and coherence. For example, intense debate continued about the
"principle of indetermination," championed by US delegates as essential to reformation. Some representatives ("notably those from
the Latin countries") believed that penalties had to be keyed to the
"gravity of the crime"; "a definitely prescribed penalty" ought to be
set after a trial that respected the "rights of the accused." The grid-
lock ended with statements that left all doors open. Indeterminate
sentences could be "applied to moral and mental defectives" and
for some other "criminals," but only if doing so did not conflict with
"prevailing conceptions of guilt and punishment."[14]

What IPC delegates did agree upon was holding people for a long
time. Because "no prisoner, no matter what his age or past record,
should be assumed to be incapable of improvement," reform was
"incompatible with short sentences." Another resolution, recognizing the economic marginality of most prisoners, called for compensation for prisoners "according to their industry" and for sending
some earnings to their households.[15]

As was customary at IPC congresses, delegates made a "journey of inspection"—in this instance, to institutions in New York,
Ohio, Kentucky, Illinois, and Indiana. One of the US hosts described the logistics of taking "a hundred delegates, representing
forty foreign nations . . . on a 3,000 mile tour" via a "special train
of Pullman cars," where US racial hierarchies were on display.
"Uncle Sam's guests" never had to worry about luggage; citizens
volunteered their "motor cars" for the travel to the facilities, and
"even the colored porters had been selected for politeness and
competency."[16]

Windows into some of what the IPC visitors saw comes from two
essays—*An Excursion into Reformatory America* by Dr. Simon van der
Aa (a Dutch professor who had just become IPC's new volunteer
Secretary-General) and *Some European Comments on the American
Prison System* by Count Ugi Conti (a professor of penal law at the
University of Rome) and Adolphe Prins (a Belgian professor and
inspector of his country's prisons). Conti and Prins were prominent

members of the International Union of Penal Law, formed in 1889 by theorists insisting that crime was a "social . . . phenomenon" rather than an abstract wrong.[17]

In some respects, van der Aa shared the Americans' view that their punishments were progressive; "the vindictive character of penalty appears to have quite vanished, and that even the idea of retributive punishment seems here to be losing its hold more and more." Moreover, the United States was "certainly far ahead of old Europe" in its use of parole and probation. Yet conditions at many facilities were terrible. Van der Aa noted cells without outdoor light or air that were not "sufficient . . . at least not according to our general standard." At Philadelphia's Eastern State Penitentiary, he observed four people in cells fashioned for one. In the "Tombs" (New York City's jail) and in many other pretrial detention facilities, people were kept idle for months in spaces Conti and Prins called "defective" and "detestable."[18]

Conti and Prins saw layers of prejudice at work. They described the "many negroes" imprisoned, the news of "the lynching of two Italians in Florida," and the impact of the Eugenics Movement, with footprints on both sides of the Atlantic. While van der Aa praised an Indiana facility that had "taken the leadership in experimentation in the direction of sterilization of the defective" through a "daring attempt at solving one difficult problem of prevention," Conti and Prins were appalled. "[I]n the name of race-purity," governments had no "right to take away a person's virility"; doing so was a "moral degradation" of a society. A "civilized country . . . in modern times" ought not let doctors and prison superintendents use "the penalty of mutilation."[19] That understanding was *not* shared by the US Supreme Court, which, in 1927, upheld Virginia's compulsory sterilization law in an opinion infamous for its statement that "three generations of imbeciles are enough."[20]

What happened after the 1910 DC Congress was at first bumpy and then tragic. Even as the IPC scrambled for recognition and money, it made plans for its next congress, scheduled for London in 1915. In the fall of 1912, the IPC's English President Sir Evelyn Ruggles-Brise and van der Aa, again soliciting funds from the US

Secretary of State, argued the 1915 meeting would prove useful to "prison administration and preventive agencies in all the world." The two also reached out for permanent endowment funds to US-based philanthropists, including Andrew Carnegie, who demurred in 1912 and again in 1917.[21] (In some sense, Carnegie has, by giving me a fellowship to write this book, enabled the IPC to reach another audience.) By March of 1914, the IPC had produced a detailed agenda for its London convening. In June, Archduke Franz Ferdinand was assassinated; Europe moved toward war, and the IPC canceled the London Congress.[22]

After Henderson died in 1915, President Woodrow Wilson selected John Koren to replace him as US Commissioner. Koren, a Lutheran minister, had turned himself into a professional statistician for the federal government. Active in the Massachusetts Prison Association, the American Statistical Association (its journal's first editor and a president), and the American Prison Association, Koren gave speeches arguing that governments needed to generate uniform data on prisons and provide care for discharged prisoners.[23] In 1916, at the annual meeting of the American Prison Association, Koren chose chilling prose to capture the unfolding horrors of World War I. He reported he had

> just returned from that part of the world in which the forces and passions that we combat have been let loose. . . . This much . . . is certain: the great calamity which has befallen the world seems to have unhinged men's power of reason and to have perverted their sense of right and wrong.[24]

5

AFTER THE WAR

ENVISIONING AN INTERNATIONAL "CHARTER OF PRISONERS' RIGHTS"

"[T]he goal [was] the gradual elaboration of a sort of charter of prisoners' rights which should be internationally adopted, and should serve to fix the *minimum* below which no country aspiring to be called civilised should dare to fall."

—The Howard League, 1926[1]

Before World War I, criminal law experts and corrections officials aspired to bring social sciences to bear on crime and punishment. Experts on "penal law" hoped to harmonize prohibitions and sanctions across borders, while those running prisons shifted their goals (if not their practices) from retribution to rehabilitation. Amid the many discussions, books, pamphlets, and proposals from the 1700s through 1920, no one suggested "a sort of charter of prisoners' rights" until members of the Howard League, an English reform society, did. This chapter's subject is the story of the origins of this wholly new ambition to limit states' punishment powers.

To understand the imaginative leap putting this reconceptualization of government obligations onto the world stage requires meeting the people involved. To appreciate the political acumen surmounting formidable opposition entails dipping into the run-up to the International Penitentiary Commission's (IPC) 1925 London Congress, where speakers once again congratulated themselves on "civilization's progress." Thereafter, Margery Fry, Gertrude Eaton, and Cecily Craven (finally women come into this narrative!) at the Howard League called for "Minimum Rights for Prisoners in All Civilised Countries" and for the League of Nations to formulate "an international convention" to address conditions in all forms of "captivity." The Howard League sought recognition of what it alone called the "rights" of prisoners and the end of "torture" rampant in most prisons; its examples were beatings to extract evidence, over-crowded cells, brutal floggings, and disease.[2] Decades before the United Nations' promulgation of its Universal Declaration of Human Rights and the US Civil Rights Revolution, the Howard League persuaded the IPPC to draft and the League of Nations to adopt guidelines in 1934 aiming to change how sovereigns treated people they detained. These "ladies" (as the men called them) merit credit for saving the lives of some prisoners by putting prison reform onto the international agenda, for the idea of an international charter to protect prisoners, and for their campaigns in Great Britain to end whipping and capital punishment.

Why would the prison managers running the IPPC join in precepts that could limit their powers? The answer (one of many spoiler alerts) is that, initially, they did not. But the IPPC was vulnerable—worried about money, authority, and displacement by the Howard League and the League of Nations. Through adopting the standard-making project, the IPPC gained control over content and created a template for international discussions on punishment that endures in the twenty-first century.

Why should readers in this century know last century's disagreements about rules on prisons? Because debates about transnational prohibitions on in-prison disciplines (then whipping, dark cells, chains, and food deprivation) emerged first in the 1920s and continue to this day. Moreover, watching Fry, Eaton, and Craven at work provides lessons in morality, persuasion, and political economy—all the more impressive given men's dominance in the pantheon of punishment practices. Knowing what the three women fought for and fought about is not only for those fascinated by political–legal history but for contemporary impatient or jaded activists. The link between prisoners and rights forged by these women reemerged in

1955 when the United Nations promulgated its first Standard Minimum Rules for the Treatment of Prisoners. The UN's Nelson Mandela Rules, issued in 2015, come closer to what the Howard League envisioned in the 1920s. Yet no international convention has been adopted, and the track record on the rights that prisoners do have is uneven in content and application. The vision and the resiliency of these aspirations, despite the horror of enslavement and concentration camps, have much to teach now.

INTERNATIONAL COMPETITION AND MINIMAL FUNDING

Germany surrendered on November 11, 1918; World War I's formal end was marked on June 28, 1919, when Britain, France, Italy, Russia, and Germany signed the Treaty of Versailles. In 1920, John Koren returned to the American Prison Association to bring "greetings from abroad." IPC President Sir Evelyn Ruggles-Brise, who had "presided over the administration of the Prisons of England and Wales for a quarter of a century," hoped that "when world-rest is restored," he would greet delegates.[3] Five years later, after the IPC cajoled support from some two dozen countries, its 1925 London Congress opened.

A glimpse at the IPC membership underscores its roots in imperialism. In addition to Great Britain, the roster included "France, Belgium, Italy, Holland, Spain, Denmark, Sweden, Norway, Greece, Hungary, Switzerland, Czecho-Slovakia, Servia, Bulgaria, Luxemburg, United States of America, Japan," along with the British "dominions" of South Africa and India. When drafting the invitation for the British Home Office to send, Ruggles-Brise explained that the IPC welcomed "states who are officially represented" and "all other civilised States" (unless an exception was "advisable") as well as British "Crown Colonies" such as Palestine and Nigeria. The German states of Baden and Bavaria, but not the "Imperial government," were invited, as was Russia (which never returned after its 1917 Revolution).[4]

The IPC termed its plans a "fresh starting-point for the renewal of international activity in the domain of 'la science pénitentiaire.'"

What was "fresh" was competition. The League of Nations, formed in 1920, had advisory committees on child welfare, slavery, health, women, children, and "opium and other dangerous drugs."[5] The Howard League, reconfigured in 1921 through a merger of the How-ard Association (begun in 1866) and the Penal Reform League, had links to parallel organizations in Commonwealth countries.[6] The IPC was wobbling financially and worried about the United States, whose support was in question. After Koren died in 1923, van der Aa and Ruggles-Brise coupled condolences to the US Secretary of State with a request for a replacement. The subtext was funding.[7] Despite Koren's profile as a statistician-sociologist employed by the federal government, he had never secured payment of US dues.

Van der Aa and Ruggles-Brise were heartened when, in 1923, President Calvin Coolidge appointed Benjamin Ogden Chisolm, a banker with appealing credentials. Active in New York's Prison As-sociation, Chisolm explained in a 1919 talk ("Human Awakening") to the American Prison Association that personal encounters with individuals who had been derailed by criminal records propelled him to visit "sixty per cent of the prisons of this country." Arguing the economic incoherence of cutting off access to earning a living, Chisolm mixed concerns about unfair treatment and impoverished families with fears of class warfare. If treated "unjustly and humil-iate[d]," a man could get "anarchistic ideas" that could result in "a class more dangerous than the 'Reds.'"[8]

Chisolm had three prescriptions. First, unless a prison was "curative," it had "no more right to exist than a hospital which would . . . cripple its patients." Second, a man who committed a crime ought to be "regarded as a human being and treated as such." Third, depriving a man of liberty did not include the "right to bring suffering upon his family." Therefore, an imprisoned man should receive wages to "keep his family alive on the outside." Chisolm also objected to "the dark cell and solitary confinement" and the "occasional flogging." Chisolm's arguments that prisons did more to "corrupt rather than improve men" were reported in *New York Times* articles, along with his comment that "no self-respecting dog would go into [local jails] unless forced."[9]

Chisolm took pride in his IPC appointment—reflected in the seal, reproduced in figure 5.1, that he affixed to letters.[10] And, while he did help the IPC get some US dollars, he was high maintenance. Chisolm pressed Ruggles-Brise ("my dear Sir Evelyn") to alter the IPC custom of limiting official delegates to six. Looking at the issue "from the American stand-point," the cap would hinder efforts to gin up enthusiasm. In 1924, van der Aa demurred, but lost. The United States appointed twelve delegates. Chisolm also persuaded his country to pay some dues. Chisolm obtained a "check in the sum of $2,700" that, at $900 per year, covered 1919 through 1921. Yet, as Chisolm wrote van der Aa ("my dear Doctor"), the State Department had posed a question for which Chisolm had no answer, asking, "what does the Commission do with the money it receives?"[11]

B. OGDEN CHISOLM
66 BEAVER ST. NEW YORK

FIGURE 5.1 *US IPC Commissioner B. Ogden Chisolm's Stamp,* facsimile from letter to Secretary-General Dr. J. Simon van der Aa, January 17, 1928, courtesy of IPPC/UN Archives, S-0915, Box 5, File 4

"THE TRUMPET-CALL OF PRISON REFORM"
AND ITS OPPRESSIVE CONTENT

When the IPC convened in London, attendees (paying the one pound "fee of membership"[12]) included individuals who would be central to prison rulemaking in the decade to come—during which time minimum standards for prisoners were drafted, women twenty-one and older got to vote in England, the American economy toppled, and the Nazis seized power. In 1925, IPC leaders were confident about their mission. Britain's Home Secretary, Sir William Joynson-Hicks, welcoming attendees, was central in shaping his country's prison policies. Nicknamed "Jix" after defeating Winston Churchill for a seat in the House of Commons in 1908, Joynson-Hicks was vehemently anti-Communist, anti-alcohol, and possibly antisemitic. Yet he was pro–prison reform, reportedly because he was appalled by conditions.[13]

Joynson-Hicks supported probation and England's "borstal system"—reformatories for people under twenty-one. His speech coupled concerns about prisoners' humanity with commitments to authoritarian control over their bodies. By depriving people of liberty, Joynson-Hicks explained that a government "has undertaken a new responsibility of the very gravest kind, namely, that of the treatment and training of the offender during the period of incarceration" so as to "release him no worse off than he had been on entry." Painting a rosy picture of England's progress (the "old system of stern repression and personal degradation" replaced by "strenuous and efficient training and education"), prisons had become institutions of "hope rather than despair." England had centralized its system, adopted daytime communal spaces and single cells at night, provided music and libraries, and limited flogging. Although a "man does not lose his rights as a human being because he has broken the laws of his country," the state was "entitled in the interests of the community to experiment on the prisoner with physical, mental, and moral forces with a view to his restoration to the standard of normal citizenship."[14]

Another welcome (with its "trumpet-call" for reform) came from IPC President Ruggles-Brise, who praised probation and the indeterminate sentence (the "inventions of the last half century"), along with incarceration as "generally accepted as the only security against any infraction of law and order in things both great and small."[15] The resolutions resulting from the London Congress reflected the strength of the Eugenics Movement, a fear of motion pictures (a new source of "immorality" for which censorship was the proposed antidote), and acceptance of indeterminate sentences as one of many methods to control convicted people. Prisons needed "laboratories or clinics" for "scientific study" to understand the "biological and sociological causes of criminality" and provide "suitable treatment."[16]

The 1925 meeting intersected with changes at the IPC, which moved its operations from Groningen in the Netherlands to Berne, Switzerland and turned its volunteer position of Secretary-General into a paid job. The IPC sought to find its niche as a sender of surveys and collector of statistics; a publisher of reports, proceedings, and a freestanding journal; and an overseer of a library. In 1929, the IPC became the International Penal and Penitentiary Commission (IPPC) to denote its purview included the purposes of criminal law and of punishment as well as methods to accomplish the aims espoused.

But the leadership missed what it had made: a *network* it could not control. Indeed, as Howard League members noted, the value of the 1925 Congress came not from its resolutions but exchanges at prison visits and social gatherings, where discussions reflected that prisoners were no longer "a vague abstraction." Howard League members reported that many foreign visitors "expressed frankly their horror that flogging and hanging should still find a place in English law."[17] Joynson-Hicks, who the next year blocked England from openly supporting a movement toward international standards, was *right* to fear that challenge to unbounded sovereign control over punishment.

END TORTURE, ADD RIGHTS

"All forms of torture should be forbidden. No corporal punishment of a severity liable to result in permanent injury shall be allowed."

—Margery Fry, Howard League "Suggested Draft of Minimum Rights for Prisoners in All Civilised Countries," 1926

The Howard League described the IPC 1925 London meeting as ending without a "basis of action," but the League had its own plan. A first effort, "much easier" to obtain given "friendships linked by the Congress," was a "systematic collection of information" on prisoners. A second ("the object of future work") was a "sort of charter of prisoners' rights which should be internationally adopted."[18]

That "future work" came fast because of Fry, Eaton, and Craven. They knew a good deal about incarceration from visiting England's prisons and from firsthand accounts by Stephen Hobhouse (a World War I conscientious objector), Oscar Wilde (imprisoned for his sexuality), and from suffragettes, socialists, and Irish nationalists—subjected to solitary confinement, bread and water, and obligatory silence. Hobhouse's and Fenner Brockway's 1922 tome, *English Prisons Today: Being the Report of the Prison System Enquiry Committee* was, Fry said, "the Bible of prison reformers."[19] As one of her admirers put it, Fry's "reactions" became English agendas[20] and, given her efforts, those of the international community.

The impact of Fry, Craven, and Eaton on what became the 1934 League of Nation Rules was barely acknowledged at the time and is less in view in the annals of transnational punishment analyses than it should be.[21] When I first read the 1934 Standard Minimum Rules for the Treatment of Prisoners, I wondered where they came from. I reverse engineered the document and located a Howard League private "memorandum of the attitudes of the British Government towards the proposed schedule of minimum conditions for prisoners" in Howard League archives and in IPC correspondence stored at the UN.[22] I have thus been able to piece together the people to whom Fry, Craven, and Eaton spoke, the roadblocks they encountered, and their successes in Geneva.

Margery Fry was one of several high-profile siblings of a prominent English Quaker family. Two of her sisters were chaplains who visited imprisoned conscientious objectors. Her brother was the artist Roger Fry—the painter of her portrait (figure 5.2), a member of the Bloomsbury Circle, and the subject of a biography written by Virginia Woolf. For a time, Roger and Margery lived together in a London house with a "fine view of Holloway Jail," London's women's prison.[23]

FIGURE 5.2 *Margery Fry, Principal of Somerville College,* by Roger Eliot Fry, 1927–1931, with permission of the copyright holder, Principal and Fellows of Somerville College, Oxford University

Fry, who studied math at Oxford's women's college, Somerville, later became its "Principal," a role akin to a university dean. After England enacted its 1919 Sex Disqualification (Removal) Act, Fry was one of the first woman to be a magistrate; she was a prominent participant in its "feminist-criminal-justice reform network."[24] After World War II, Fry was a regular radio and television commentator and campaigned for crime victims' compensation. The gender stereotypes she encountered can be found in a book on English prison reform; for example, a dedication to her stated that Fry "not only saw clearly what was needed but with charm, wit, and good sense turned vision into reality."[25]

Cicely Craven and Gertrude Eaton were likewise pivotal at home and abroad and praised in gendered terms. Craven took up the position of Howard League Secretary when Fry left for Somerville and led campaigns to end flogging and birching. Craven was, as one man put it, adept "above all [at the] linking of criticism with constructive and practical proposals."[26] Eaton, an accomplished musician, a suffragette, and a "dedicated and dogged worker for penal reform," was appalled at "the disgusting conditions of women's prisons."[27] Lord Robert Cecil (Britain's Foreign Secretary, an architect of the League of Nations, and in 1937 a Nobel Peace Prize winner) noted that when Eaton called, it was "ostensibly to ask his advice, but really to tell him what to do at Geneva."[28] Indeed, between 1926 and 1934, Eaton went to Geneva each year, where she "*made* the delegates . . . listen to her appeals on behalf of prisoners the world over" (his italics).[29]

After the IPC's 1925 Congress, the three women asked the IPC to circulate their proposal that the League of Nations adopt a resolution that "political prisoners of all nations, as well as other prisoners" be given access to outsiders such as "members of authorized societies" promoting welfare.[30] The larger goal was to move beyond a group denoted "political" to generate a "practical working machinery for the protection of [all] prisoners."[31] In the fall of 1925, and joined by the Joint Committee of the Friends' Council for International Service, Fry's "Suggested Draft on Minimum Rights for Prisoners in all Civilised Countries" called on the Council of the League of Nations to produce an "International agreement" that would "underlie the treatment of prisoners of every class."[32]

Those provisions sought "a public trial within 6 months of arrest"; a state-provided lawyer when "the penalty is death or prolonged imprisonment"; and a right to call witnesses at trial. Access to the outside world was to come via a right to "a visit from a relative or friend at least twice a year" as well as from "representatives of authorised societies working solely for the welfare of prisoners."

Detention facilities were to have sanitary conditions; classify prisoners and separate women, men, and children; as well as provide all with "food sufficient for health" including ample water for "drinking and washing." In addition, the draft Minimum Rights stated that political prisoners were to be treated "no less favourably" than others. The Howard League also sought disclosure of persons sentenced to death. Further, "[a]ll forms of Torture should be forbidden" before trial, as should corporal punishment that was at the "discretion of the police or prison officials." The draft acknowledged the use of flogging after conviction, but insisted that none "of a severity liable to result in permanent injury shall be allowed."[33]

CAJOLING THE ENGLISH ESTABLISHMENT

One way to understand what these women had to overcome is to look at the difficulties in getting their own government on board. In January of 1926, when Fry met Lord Cecil for help at the League of Nations, Cecil responded that prisons were "internal government" matters. Fry countered that national disturbances in prisons had international implications. Explaining she would be "satisfied" to have laid down "certain general principles of minimum treatment," she handed over her draft. Cecil reported that he was "personally in complete sympathy" and wrote to Ruggles-Brise about whether he should urge the League to become involved, especially because the treatment in "Central and Eastern European States . . . , particularly [of] political and minority prisoners, was abominable."[34] Home Secretary Joynson-Hicks objected, and his "private" opposition made public advocacy by the British government unlikely.

The IPC leadership, annoyed that Fry had gone directly to Lord Cecil, called the Howard League document "not well drafted"—complaining contradictorily that the provisions did not "raise, on the whole, the actual standard" and yet that "such rules could never be enforced." Moreover, Scotland's Prison Commissioner Lord Polwarth thought the plan "very undesirable"; if adopted as a "minimum," the Rules could well "become a maximum." Further, the Howard League's efforts might "prejudice" whatever the IPC wanted to do.[35] (When the IPC took over drafting, it protected the autonomy of people running prisons by permitting deviations from its Rules.)

The Howard League made headway via a "strictly private and confidential" meeting with two English IPC members, Maurice Waller and Alexander Paterson, who were potential allies.[36] Fry had suggested that Waller replace Ruggles-Brise in 1921 as head of England's Prison Commission. Once in charge, Waller ended some degradation rituals, such as "the close cropping of convicts' hair." Waller enlisted Paterson who, after graduating from Oxford, had lived in "one of the worst tenements" to direct an "association for discharged prisoners" and later gained a reputation as a "liberal progressive" steward of England's Commission. Patterson was cited for saying that men "come to prison as a punishment not for punishment" and that it was "impossible to train men for freedom in a condition of captivity."[37]

At their meeting, Fry told Wallace and Paterson that the IPC could be central, given its "strengths" in drafting materials. (Eaton later wrote that government officials were "notoriously averse to treading on each other's toes." As the IPC was "composed of those engaged in penal administration," it was "likely to be very conservative in its views.") Fry explained that, "in practice," neither the League of Nations nor the IPC could "actually enforce a Charter of this kind" but could gather "the force of public opinion." The Howard League's private notes reflected that, to avoid "active opposition from England," they needed other governments to make a proposal to the League of Nations. The Howard League, with affiliates in other countries, was networked to do so; it knew of "keen interest" in Germany and in Sweden. In 1927, Eaton traveled to Berlin to lobby the Federation of League of Nations Societies, which issued a resolution calling for inquiry into framing an international convention.[38]

Given the subsequent rise of the Nazis, the idea of help from Germany requires explanation. That country's varying attitudes illustrate my point that punishment choices are always embedded in politics. During the first decades of the twentieth century, Germany was a model of "liberal" prison reforms.[39] What liberal meant then can be found in a 1924 article, published by the Howard League's journal, on "new German Prison Rules," explained by a professor as having turned prisons into "a school of education and labour." Prisoners were to be treated "'justly and earnestly,' but above all humanely." Germany had abolished "close shaving" as "unworthy and degrading" and rejected corporal punishment (meaning whipping) but had not ("at this date") prohibited solitary confinement (putting people into cells with "lessened, or totally abolished, lighting . . . for at most four weeks") or giving prisoners a "lessened quantity of food for at most a week."[40]

INTERNATIONAL LOBBYING

"[T]here is injustice and cruelty in the law courts, police cells and prison in the world."

—Convention for Prisoners, An Appeal to the
League of Nations, Flyer, Howard League, 1927

Seeing resistance, Fry, Eaton, and Craven developed a theory about why their issue was appropriate for an international body, a plan for coalition politics, and a public relations campaign. One hurdle was the fear that transnational action could encroach on national prerogatives. ("Very Important People said that prisons were a domestic affair for each State."[41]) In 1927, the three women put together their talking points in "Arguments in Favour of the Proposition That the Treatment of Prisoners Is a Matter for International Action." They explained that the shared goals of controlling crime, keeping international peace, and providing humanitarian aid meant that detention was a transnational issue. Invoking new technologies (the "motor car, telegraph, the telephone"), they discussed the externalities of crime that turned "domestic" issues into cross-border problems. Furthermore, extradition treaties, authorizing countries to refuse to send people elsewhere, recognized the interjurisdictional "moral responsibility for the treatment of prisoners." Analogizing to conventions on enslavement of women and children, the three posited that a prison convention entailed no "greater interference with the internal affairs of nations" than those already adopted. In addition, victims of "barbarous and unjust penal methods" were often members of "racial or political minorities," and mistreatment could be the basis for "international friction."[42]

By 1927, the Howard League had orchestrated support for international rules through engaging parallel organizations in Canada
and Germany, women's groups, and church-based associations.
Eaton set up in Geneva a pop-up office (figure 5.3) with an exhibit
on "the development of the prison during the past 200 years"; an
international organization of university women helped it to garner
"world-wide publicity."[43]

The Howard League enlisted the British League of Nations when
circulating a pamphlet providing examples of the "flagrant abuses
and of the use of flogging and tortures." To show that degradation knew no national boundaries, the pamphlet detailed "twelve
instances of abuses" drawn from the United States, Germany,
Hungary, Poland, Bulgaria, Romania, China, Yugoslavia, and Peru.
The horrors included prisons in which, during the day, "men wearing a heavy iron chained to their ankle . . . [had to wheel that ball]
in a wheelbarrow round and round the prison yard" and, at night,
were in dark, solitary cells. In another country, nine people were
held in a small cell with no ventilation. The antidote was a "draft
Convention" based on "efficiency, decency and humanity" toward
prisoners.[44]

The Howard League won an initial round at the League of Nations, itself fledgling and needing projects to gain traction in "the
ranks of international organizations [that] matter." In the summer
of 1927, the Assembly of the League of Nations called for inquiry
into an international convention that would, taking into account
country conditions, address treatment (including the labor) of people in detention.[45]

By then, the leadership of the IPC had come to understand
it needed to get on board. At a meeting in Bern in 1926, the IPC
charged Waller with doing an initial draft. Joined by the Scottish
Polwarth and the English Paterson, Waller produced a long set
of rules in April of 1927 and asked van der Aa for input. Polwarth
sought a prompt response so that the IPC could "keep hold" of
standard-making rather than cede it. Further, the IPC hoped that
countries would turn to it for expert advice on compliance with
whatever standards were promulgated. Within short order, van der
Aa circulated a draft with comments to all the IPC commissioners.[46]

FIGURE 5.3 *International Bureau of the Howard League for Penal Reform*, Geneva, 1927, with permission of The Howard League for Penal Reform Archive, housed at and courtesy of the Modern Records Centre, University of Warwick

"In the room where it happened" is a phrase from a song written for a 2015 play about the United States Revolution.[47] The next chapter puts today's readers back into the many rooms across the Atlantic where debates about the boundaries of in-prison punishments produced norms calling for clean and safe prisons while licensing—with medical oversight—whipping, dark cells, and food deprivation as "discipline" for prisoners.

6

NEGOTIATING WHIPPING, DARK CELLS, AND FOOD DEPRIVATION

THE 1934 LEAGUE OF NATIONS RULES FOR THE TREATMENT OF PRISONERS

Punishment should not leave "permanent marks . . . visible on ordinary occasions to the eyes of his fellow citizens so as to degrade him in their esteem."

—Maurice Waller's Draft for Standard Minimum Rules on the Treatment of Prisoners, 1927[1]

This chapter unearths decisions that produced the first Standard Minimum Rules for the Treatment of Prisoners. Propelled by the seven points in the 1925 Howard League's "Suggested Draft of Minimum Rights for Prisoners in all civilized countries," England's Maurice Waller elaborated fifty-two propositions that, after exchanges with the League of Nations, became fifty-five provisions disseminated around the world. The resulting code for prison administrators called for "food sufficient both in quality and quantity," a "maximum number of hours" for daily work, and cells kept "scrupulously clean."[2] But these Rules neither spoke in the Howard League's language of "rights" nor called for a ban on "torture." And, while drafts circulated between 1927 and 1933, the world situation darkened with the US stock market crash, economic strife, Stalinist Russia's expanding influence, and Hitler gaining control of Germany.

The archived, annotated versions of drafts ("destiné seulement à l'usage des membres") provide entrée into confidential discussions among prison leaders about how to treat prisoners. Just as federal judges would struggle in the 1960s to delineate the import of the US Constitution's ban on "cruel and unusual punishment," International Penal and Penitentiary Commission (IPPC) commissioners puzzled about which to rule out. Whipping was a constant source of disagreement. The practice had statutory status under English law, which authorized judges to sentence people to flogging and licensed the "birching" of children. Several members outside the British Commonwealth found whipping noxious, even as some thought chains and food deprivation were not. Those debates, detailed here, resulted in an IPPC proposal that the League of Nations adopted, which licensed whipping and dark cells "for exceptional cases"; the caveats were that, if used, they were to be regulated by law and overseen by medical personnel. Also permitted were food deprivation and chains, if temporary and deemed needed.[3]

To require law and medicine was to *acknowledge* the violence of these practices; their instantiation in what was styled "the minimum conditions which should be observed in the treatment of prisoners from a humanitarian and social point of view" was a defeat for that very predicate. Commitments to *control* permeated the project that generated an understanding of what was "normal"— and hence normatively permissible—in prisons. This history makes plain that the lines drawn have, like the punishments imposed, left lasting "marks"—whose *permanency* this book contests.

HUMANITY'S REQUIREMENTS

"Written under the Anglo-Saxon influence and spirit, the project forbids placing a prisoner in a dark cell but did not forbid striking him with a baton—while . . . in other countries . . . public opinion considers whipping a degrading punishment . . . [whose] prohibition" humanity requires.

—Comment from a Belgian Member, fall 1927[4]

Maurice Waller sent his draft rules to the Secretariat and, in June of 1927, Simon van der Aa provided a line edit and memo raising conceptual and practical concerns. In his view, the goal was not to set out the "rights of prisoners" ("a juridical question of great interest") but a guide for prison administrators. Van der Aa proposed what in this book's introduction I termed a "prison discount"—in this context, that the Rules might not be used in small prisons or places with economic challenges. Van der Aa's formulation that the Rules were predicated on a "humanitarian and social point of view" and on the need for variation based on "special circumstances" became part of the League of Nations' 1934 "preliminary observations."[5]

In some aspects, drafting was easy. The people running prisons did not want individuals to starve, and they did want leverage for resources. All of them were "for" sanitation, clothing, classification, and safety—again with room for local deviations. But sharp disagreements arose about in-prison punishments. Recall that the Howard League's draft had a complete ban on corporal punishment only for people pretrial; for convicted individuals, that draft sought the end of bodily inflictions "of a severity liable to result in permanent injury."[6] That formulation likely reflected a political judgment that, given statutory licensing of "flogging" in England, calling for prisoners' rights conditioned on ending whipping would have had no chance of British support.

Waller, who came from a prison system where shaved heads and tread-wells had been the norm along with whipping, offered a text reflecting his worries about unleashing (irony intended) too much pain. Waller proposed centralizing decision-making to control the duration and impact of beating. Punishments "for prison offences" were to be meted out only "by the Governor himself, or by his authorised Deputy," after a "full inquiry" with opportunity for prisoners to be "heard," through translators if needed. (In 1965, federal judges in Arkansas sought to constrain whipping with similar rules.) Waller further specified that corporal punishment

should be limited to beating. The rod or other instrument to be used should be approved by the central prison administration. The number of strokes should be limited, and should be named in the award of punishment. It should not be inflicted until after the Medical Officer has pronounced the prisoner fit to receive it.

No other forms of physical pain should be inflicted on a prisoner. No punishment, corporal or other, should be either a) unduly severe; b) such as to do lasting injury to a prisoner's health, or c) such as to result in any permanent marks which will subsequently be visible on ordinary occasions to the eyes of his fellow citizens so as to degrade him in their esteem.[7]

Whether Waller was a moralist or a utilitarian (echoing Jeremy Bentham's opposition to branding as uselessly disfiguring a *person* rather than deterring a *crime*), his non-degradation precept referenced prisoners as "fellow citizens"—a status not often acknowledged. Yet Waller's text addressed degradation *after* prison rather than *inside*, which could reflect the view that incarcerated people emerged as citizens only upon release. And his vantage point was what other people *saw*, rather than what incarcerated individuals *experienced*. In contrast, van der Aa was clear that "châtiment corporel" ought to be "absolutely forbidden." Given laws authorizing whipping, van der Aa's compromise was that, if legally provided, prison rules should fix the number of strikes and put control under a director and doctor.[8]

Waller's 1927 draft addressed other forms of bodily aggression. He proposed that a "reduction of food below the amount ordinarily needed to maintain health and strength should not be permitted for more than a strictly limited period," to be "prescribed either by law or by the central prison authority." Likewise, restraints ("such as irons or handcuffs") that were "of such a nature as to deprive a prisoner of the use of his limbs either altogether or almost entirely" were not to be used as "punishment" but for "temporary control of a violent prisoner" if necessary to prevent injury. On the other hand, Waller proposed banning dungeons. "Prisoners should not be placed in dark cells, even as a punishment."[9]

In July of 1927, when circulating a revised twenty-page draft in English and French, van der Aa described the project as of "great importance" and "delicate character"; in a "P.S.," he reminded commissioners of the need for "great discretion," which was to say they ought not make the proposed Rules public.[10] Responses would have given a headache to any person coordinating the revision. Objections were all over the map—of Europe, as well as metaphorically.

Commissioners disagreed about the desirability and scope, the substance of specific proposals, and the authority of the Commission (as distinct from its congresses) to put it forth. Some commented that the Rules were passé rather than future-looking, while others found the draft overbroad, or vague, indecisive, and unclear. Some wanted a proviso that prison administration was a matter of internal governance, and whatever the content, the Rules would not affect or bind any affiliated countries.[11] Calls to forbid whipping came from several commissioners including Ernest Delaquis from Switzerland (who in 1938 took over from van der Aa as the Secretary-General).[12] Indeed, a Belgian commissioner thought the whole project ill-conceived—at once too ambitious (if taking up the natural rights of men) and manifestly incomplete (to the extent it pretended to provide an outline of how to organize prisons). He preferred abandonment but, if it went forward, that the Rules should state that no punishment be inflicted "to undermine human dignity."[13]

Going *forward* (albeit with no discussion of "human dignity") was, from van der Aa's vantage, critical. The Howard League had publicly prompted the project, and he wanted the Commission's brand attached to prison rules. Van der Aa sent a revised draft to the League of Nations, which agreed in late 1927 to circulate materials broadly. The Commission, in turn, consented to reviewing new comments as long as nothing the League did would *bind* countries in their decision-making on prisons.[14]

". . . PROGRESS IN VIEW"

The ambition to be central to punishment practices can be seen in the formal name change in 1929 from the International Penitentiary Commission (IPC) to the International Penal and Penitentiary Commission (IPPC).[15] Van der Aa published a revised draft in the 1929 IPPC Bulletin; Lord Polwarth provided an English translation. Seeking to ward off changes, van der Aa, who directed Holland's system, recounted that Britain's Waller, Polwarth, and Paterson were the authors, and that he had joined Erwin Bumke, Minister of Justice in Germany, and a Swedish prison director in providing advice. Van der Aa explained that, while "endeavors may be made" for alternatives to prison, incarceration would "always continue to play a prepondering part." Van der Aa underscored that this set gave "the heads of the central administration of Prison Institutions . . . arguments to support their efforts to obtain the necessary funds for the realization of the progress in view."[16]

The 1929 version included the definition urged by the Howard League, that "prison" was used in the "largest sense of the word," including facilities for people held before trial. And, despite objections from its members that a "scientific body" like the IPPC should not support "corporal punishment . . . , an anachronism contrary to the rehabilitation of the culpable, the spirit of which inspires the modern penitentiary system," whipping remained in place. The concession was that, if "*in certain countries, for exceptional cases*," corporal punishment was permitted, its execution was to be "determined by law" and "never [to] be carried out unless the Medical Officer certifies that the prisoner can bear it." Continued was procedural protection; the prisoner was to have "the opportunity of expressing whatever he wishes to say in his defense."[17] (As Margery Fry explained in her autobiography, it was "largely to obtain the adherence of England . . . that the rule regarding corporal punishment" remained.[18]) Dark cells, where people then (and decades thereafter) were regularly kept without access to natural or artificial light, were likewise permissible.

Lost were Waller's limits on the number of lashes, as well as a freestanding rule that no punishment be too severe, cause permanent health harms, or leave "permanent marks." Moreover, even as the 1929 draft recognized that some forms of discipline could "by their nature or on account of the condition of the prisoner" have "consequences prejudicial to his health," the Rules explained *how* such punishments were to be administered. Food deprivation "below the ordinary ration, or the reduction . . . of open air exercise" should be for a "strictly limited period"; the "maximum period" was to be "prescribed by law," and the individual decision imposed "in accordance with the decision of the Medical Officer."[19]

The draft singled out shackles as presumptively prohibited ("handcuffs, chains and straightjackets"), but caveats muddied the waters. Restraints could be used temporarily when "necessary for preventing [people] from doing injury to themselves or to others or from continuing to destroy property." Moreover, "chains . . . not intended to deprive the prisoner of the use of his limbs, but only to prevent him from escaping, should always be light"; prison officials were to "watch to see" that the application did not "cause wounds or bruises."[20]

I have made no mention of comments about the Rules from the United States, which had not joined the League of Nations. The vocal US Commissioner Ogden Chisolm, appointed in 1923, resigned in the spring of 1929. Instead of the "competent man" van der Aa hoped for,[21] President Herbert Hoover chose Caroline Wittpenn, part of the high-profile Stevens family, whose inventive entrepreneurs endowed New Jersey's Stevens Institute of Technology. Wittpenn devoted her considerable energies to women's suffrage and women's prisons. Fluent in French and a member of the European Relief Commission administered by Hoover, Wittpenn had pressed for the creation of a Woman's Reformatory in New Jersey and became president of its Trustees. Sanford Bates, the Superintendent of Prisons of the United States (and Wittpenn's 1932 replacement on the IPPC) told van der Aa to "feel perfectly safe in reposing great confidence in her judgment," as she was a "lady of culture and experience in prison matters." Wittpenn reported that her IPPC colleagues modified their "etiquette" in light of her being the "only member of her sex" there. She explained to them that, because her country was not a member of the League, she would not address the Rules.[22]

By then, the IPPC had laid claim to the draft. Yet at the League of Nations, a Cuban representative credited the Howard League as the "first" to call for attention to the plight of prisoners and to enlist the Women's International League for Peace and Freedom, the International Federation of League of Nations Societies, and many others. In 1930, and in light of the IPPC's limited number of affiliated countries (and "only one" from Latin America and two from Asia), the League's Council called on its Assembly to send the set to many organizations "to assist in the development of prisons in accord with modern economic, social and health standards."[23]

THE IPPC'S 1930 PRAGUE CONGRESS AND RULES
FOR THE "WHOLE WORLD"

On one account, the IPPC's leadership had gone rogue by giving the League of Nations rules that were not blessed by its congress, which met in August of 1930 in Prague, where references were made to the economic crises shrouding the world. The presentation of the draft Rules records a fleeting moment when European prison leaders stood together to extol efforts to "ameliorate the situation of prisoners."

The commissioners treated the Rules as a *fait accompli* and did not seek a resolution to endorse them. Rather, the Congress' host, Professor August Miřička, explained that the IPPC's "official character" (with delegates appointed by governments) would make the Rules influential.[24] As the meeting was drawing to a close, the German Edwin Bumke (by then the Chief Justice of Germany's Supreme Court) presented this "important chapter in the history of international collaboration." Apologizing for awkwardness in French, Bumke spoke of his "sincere joy" at discussing the project, "inspired by the work of Waller." Noting that some would find the Rules "too modest" or "retrograde," Bumke deflected criticism of the "restrained" draft by arguing that the IPPC's "field of action [was] the whole world." In addition to different theories about incarceration's purposes, the draft had to take into account detainees who were difficult to manage and countries less "civilized" than those with a "homogenous population and a profound, or deep civilization." (Germany was the obvious subtext.) In addition, streams of funding varied (especially given World War I) and, therefore, the Rules were not set in stone but were a framework on which to build.[25]

Bumke highlighted key points confirming that the corrections establishment had left behind John Howard's redemptive suffering in favor of rehabilitation. The draft Standard Minimum Rules proposed to separate young from old and women from men, and to provide activities, along with adequate light, air, food and cleanliness, medical care, and separate cells for sleeping. Bumke stressed the attention paid to prisoners' well-being through physical and mental examinations on entry, doctors at facilities, and encouragement of development, "intellectually and spiritually," through religious services, libraries, and (screened) correspondence. Education and work were to enable released prisoners to earn a living; remuneration for labor was to encourage better behavior.[26]

Bumke also addressed discipline needed to safeguard prison personnel and maintain state authority. (One could not have "acts of subordination or efforts to evade" requirements.) Punishments were only to be meted out after prison authorities examined allegations and individuals could respond. The licensing of whipping and dark cells was not made "light-heartedly," as many countries had renounced such measures. Bumke added that objections were reflected in statements that whipping and dark cells were to be used only "in exceptional circumstances" and under stringent controls. Bumke noted that because rationing food could be a health risk, the draft called for officials to get doctors' advice. Given that punishments could prompt complaints, prisoners were to have access to prison officials. Bumke characterized this aspect as expansive in enabling prisoners to bring their grievances to light. He also discussed the importance of training prison personnel and of support for released prisoners.[27]

Having sketched the content, Bumke explained the hoped-for effect. He emphasized that the IPPC had neither the power nor the competence to instruct governments. Rather, the draft was the "advice of experts" to which all in the "civilized world" would listen. In closing, he told delegates that the League of Nations was interested. (He knew the IPPC was sending the Rules to the League's Eleventh Assembly, soon to start in Geneva.[28]) The published proceedings record that Bumke's comments were met with "prolonged applause." Also accorded "lively applause" was Margery Fry, chairing the Howard League and joined by Cecily Craven (Secretary) and Gertrude Eaton (Vice President). Making no mention of the credit due the Howard League, Fry expressed hope that adherence would be a "great stride forward." Indeed, aside from a few "exceptions," the

Howard League welcomed "the draft rules . . . as forming a great and courageous contribution."[29] (Two decades later, Fry dedicated her 1951 autobiography, *Arms of the Law*, to "the memory of Maurice Lyndham Waller, Chairman of the Prison Commission, 1922–28."[30])

Nonetheless, Fry registered disagreement with "the use of dark cells and of corporal punishment . . . as legitimate." (Fry was at work in England to end the "brutal and stupid penalty" of flogging, and she had accounts from her brother Roger of ritual lashings administered by a sadistic boarding school clergyman.[31]) Criticizing the draft for not outlining the treatment of individuals "*before* conviction," Fry asked the IPPC to "complete the good work it has begun" by doing so. Moreover, Fry did not assume what many IPPC members did—that their "civilized" countries complied; rather, she described the provisions as "precious to young communities engaged in building up their penal systems . . . and far from valueless even to older countries."[32]

Bumke's presentation and Fry's commentary came toward the end of the 1930 Prague Congress that, like its predecessors, forecast plans for the next convening. The Howard League of Australia (whose "platform" included the abolition of corporal punishment and more freedom for prisoners) had invited the IPPC to Sydney for 1935, and Rome was another option. Instead, the IPPC agreed to Germany, which had yet to host a meeting. The 1930 Congress thus closed with Bumke, speaking on behalf of the German government, extending hopes to greet IPPC delegates in 1935 in Berlin.[33]

SOVEREIGNTY OBJECTIONS AND SOVEREIGN INPUTS

"[T]he right to punish, and above all the execution of sentences [are] essentially linked with the exercise of the State sovereignty."

—Member of the League of Nations, objecting to an international convention[34]

The day after the Prague Congress closed, van der Aa asked the League of Nations' Secretary-General Sir Eric Drummond to circulate its draft. Within the month, the Eleventh Assembly met in

Geneva and, as reported in the October 1930 IPPC Bulletin, sent the Rules to member and nonmember governments, subcommittees on health and economic issues, the International Labour Organisation, the Commission for the Protection and Welfare of Children and Young People, and L'Union Internationale de Droit Pénal.[35]

To keep up pressure, the Howard League called for an international convention and the launch of a new "expert Committee on Penal Administration" to gather statistics and serve as a clearinghouse. That proposal put the Howard League at odds with the IPPC, which saw itself as "the expert" in the field. The Howard League, arguing that "men and women who have the complete freedom of expression" were needed, advised the IPPC to join forces (admittedly at "the price of yielding a little independence and a little exclusiveness") and seek to be a part of such a committee. At this juncture, the Howard League lost. On the advice of a League of Nations subgroup called its "Fifth Committee" and charged with advising on "penal and penitentiary questions," the League deferred action.[36] (Decades later, the United Nations created a successor institution looking much like what the Howard League had proposed.)

Responses dribbled in. In 1931, the League of Nations' Secretary-General reported that twenty-nine countries had commented. Germany, for example, described its own "progressive prison system," and asserted that the draft did not go far enough; the League of Nations ought to "recommend the complete abolition . . . of corporal punishment and confinement in dark cells, both of which are unknown in German penal practice." The United States, not a member of the League of Nations, nonetheless offered its general agreement with the draft rules, subject to variation by "local bodies" (a reference to state control over much of criminal law). Other countries provided detailed comparisons, rule by rule, of their practices. The Howard League was unwavering and again took exception to licensing of corporal punishment and dark cells as "a form of torture" to which no international set of rules ought to "acquiesce" and called for "complete abolition."[37]

All told, some forty-one countries and the Committee on Hygiene of the League of Nations sent in materials.[38] Once again, whipping was a focal point. Romania and Spain protested the licensure of corporal punishment, while the UK's representative argued that "corporal punishment in exceptional cases was an effective form of discipline, subject to all requisite legal and administrative guarantees for the avoidance of abuses." Sanford Bates, by then head of the newly chartered US Bureau of Prisons and the US' IPPC Commissioner, wrote to van der Aa that "officially, corporal punishment is almost unknown in adult prisons, although . . . reported from time to time as existing in some Southern prison camps." In juvenile institutions, however, "spanking or switching of boys [was a] salutary form of punishment when properly controlled."[39]

THE 1933 FINAL FORM AND ADOPTION IN 1934 WITH—"IN EXCEPTIONAL CASES"—DARK CELLS AND WHIPPING

When the fifty-five Standard Minimum Rules took final form in 1933, their stance was close to what the IPPC had circulated in 1929. In addition to whipping, dark cells were permitted. Repeated was that it would be "desirable to reach a stage where disciplinary punishments no longer include the placing of a prisoner in a cell without light" and that "if in certain countries, for exceptional cases," such placement was "permitted, the restrictions which govern it should be regulated by the law."[40] (In a 1933 memorandum to the Prison Association of New York, the IPPC emphasized "the prospect" of "the abolition of such special coercive measures as corporal punishment and the dark cell."[41]) The Rules continued to countenance deprivations of food and exercise, even as both could be "prejudicial to health"; the caveats were imposing "in accordance with the decision of the Medical Officer" and within a "period . . . prescribed by law." In contrast, routine shackling ("restraint, such as handcuffs, chains and strait-jackets" for punishment) was prohibited but could be used temporarily when "necessary for preventing" self-harm or harm to other people or property.[42]

Thus, the 1933 Rules incorporated law and medicine *into* prison administration. For example, the discussion of "discipline" began with a general admonition: Punishment ought "never, either by their nature or by their application, depart from the prescriptions of the law," which ought to "determine the individual or the authority to whom should belong the right of inflicting disciplinary punishment."[43] The word *right* was invoked as an *entitlement to punish*, with no mention of prisoners having rights to stop punishments violating the Rules. Moreover, the Howard League lost its effort to obtain specific protections for political prisoners. The IPPC, characterizing its rules as neither opposing nor calling for "special treatment," explained that its silence as the result of the "great divergence" on what constituted "political offenses and political offenders."[44]

The League's Assembly instructed its Secretary-General to recirculate the 1933 version, this time to learn whether member and nonmember states were "in a position to consider the approval and the practical application . . . in whole or in part." By 1934, some twenty-nine countries had replied; most favored adoption. Several (Austria, Denmark, Hungary, Monaco, Norway, Czechoslovakia, and Estonia) reported that such rules comported with their practices. Local variations and fiscal challenges were also recorded. For example, Estonia noted that providing work for prisoners was not plausible during economic depressions when few opportunities existed outside of prisons. India commented that its noncompliance with some rules reflected that "the penal system of a country ought to be related to general social conditions."[45]

During this period, the Howard League characterized the Rules as "modest," continued its lament that they did not ban corporal punishment, and called on the United Kingdom to champion a convention developed from the Rules. Fry and her colleagues did not prevail. In Geneva in 1934, the UK delegate Florence Horsbrugh made public what the Home Secretary Sir Joynson-Hicks had privately said the decade before: The British government was opposed to the idea of an international convention—in part because one country's prisons ought not to be affected by another's. Other delegates agreed, while some tempered objections with the possibility of a convention after "a great number of States, following the recommendations of the Assembly, had brought their penitentiary systems into harmony with the Standard Minimum Rules."[46]

The denouement was a proposal—formally approved on September 26, 1934, by the General Assembly—to adopt the fifty-five Standard Minimum Rules. The League of Nations described the Rules as "a minimum below which no State's penitentiary system should fall" and recommended that governments consider them for "every individual deprived of his liberty." Yet the League built in the escape clauses that van der Aa had fashioned in 1927. The Rules acknowledged that an "economic or financial situation" could constitute a temporary "obstacle" to compliance, and that efforts to do so be undertaken as soon as possible, with help from "qualified associations." As for implementation, the League called for reports from each country.[47] (Self-reporting has since become familiar; for example, the 1981 Convention on the Elimination of All Forms of Discrimination Against Women relies on ratifying countries to file periodic compliance reports.)

By 1934, when the Rules were formally adopted, Hitler controlled Germany. In 1931, a German commentator had called for the League of Nations to "recommend the complete abolition . . . of corporal punishment and confinement in dark cells, both of which are unknown in German penal practice."[48] Those propositions were smashed as the Nazi regime demonstrated a capacity for human annihilation—in the name of and beyond the imagination of "civilization."

7

KEEPING THE "SCIENTIFIC" DISTINCT FROM THE "POLITICAL"

1935 NAZI BERLIN AND THEREAFTER

"Our Commission . . . should not be afraid to declare that certain practices are directly contrary to the dictates of humanity, and should not be tolerated under any circumstances in a civilized community. . . ."

—Alexander Paterson, May 1935[1]

What ought an organization of prison leaders do if aware of "certain practices directly contrary to the dictates of humanity"? That question runs from the inception of the corrections profession to the present and throughout this book. From the 1870 Cincinnati Declaration and the 1934 Standard Minimum Rules to today's "accreditation" by the American Correctional Association (ACA), experts have advised governments about how to incarcerate people. In the 1930s, nongovernmental groups like the Howard League tried to lessen detention's harms through documenting conditions, refusing to cooperate with fascist regimes, calling for "rights," and condemning "torture" in prisons. The League of Nations, with limited means of enforcement as an international organization, pressed for reports on prisons. In contrast, the International Penal and Penitentiary Commission (IPPC) archives reflect inaction and complicity in the face of stunning violations of the 1934 Rules it had just produced.

Twenty-first-century critics insist on prison's embeddedness in slavery and plantations. Detention camps provide another horrific template. To escape legacies of enslavement and concentration camps requires *acknowledgment* of these historical links. To *break* those connections entails shouldering the burden of finding modes of punishment respectful of the individuals subjected to state power. The beginnings of such aims (at a formal level and only partially) came in 1955, when the United Nations revised the 1934 Rules to state that detained people were individuals with rights and dignity.

To understand the political forces producing that shift entails tracing interactions in the 1930s of the Howard League, the IPPC, and the League of Nations. The leaders of all three believed that promulgating rules about decent treatment, followed by inquiries into implementation, would make a difference in the lives of detained people. Their innovations were tested during an era filled with grotesque expressions of sovereign power. Yet, even as Margery Fry described the air of "unreality" in her work, she insisted it was "illogical as well as cowardly to abandon attempts to make the world better because the outlook is dark."

In this chapter, I sketch how these three organizations responded to evidence of fascist violence coming from several sources, including a short-lived organization, the Center for Rights and Liberty in Germany, which sent the IPPC haunting details of Nazi detention. The memorandum demonstrated the wisdom of Fry and the Howard League calling in the 1920s for protection of *political prisoners*. Their first proposal to the League of Nations was for a resolution on "the welfare of all prisoners, regardless of the nature of their crimes" so that "political prisoners of all nations, as well as other prisoners" could gain access to the outside world. Two years later, when calling on the "world's conscience" to announce seven minimum rights for prisoners, the Howard League reiterated that "conditions [should not] be varied in any adverse manner for any prisoner or class of prisoners whatever."[2]

The term "political" referenced prisoners at special risk for oppressive treatment because of their beliefs and identities. It should also be read to underscore the *political* judgments governments make about the treatment of *anyone* in detention, including in an unbounded (totalitarian) fashion. As I detail, IPPC leaders kept claiming that "science" and "expertise" exculpated their institutions from politics, just as some correctional leaders today use "security" to justify radical isolation and hyper-density. Neither science, expertise, or security should support the ruination of people, and politics always frames punishment practices.

EN ROUTE TO NAZI BERLIN IN 1935

"One of the questions which has received some attention by persons in America . . . and will, I expect, come before the Commission for decision, is a matter of some delicacy and concerns the degree to which persons of Jewish extraction would be welcome in Berlin in the summer of 1935."

—US Commissioner Sanford Bates to IPPC
Secretary-General Simon van der Aa, June 5, 1934[3]

On January 30, 1933, Hitler became Chancellor of Germany. In September of 1934, the League of Nations formally adopted the Standard Minimum Rules for the Treatment of Prisoners. The IPPC was to meet in Berlin in 1935. Members of the Howard League warned IPPC Commissioner Paterson and van der Aa in July of 1934 that the Congress would be "doomed to complete futility" unless relocated or if Nazis guaranteed "complete freedom of the press" and "complete freedom of all delegates . . . to express their views . . . , including criticism of . . . Germany and elsewhere." Moreover, it was "difficult to conceive" of taking part in "any gatherings" where "Jewish members" would not be welcomed.[4] In contrast, US Commissioner Bates downplayed fascist practices. In his 1934 letter, Bates explained he had "the highest regard and admiration for Dr. Bumke," and thought it "premature and unwise" to propose "changing the place of the meeting" without giving an "opportunity" for the hosts to "reassure our Jewish friends. . . ."

By then, Erwin Bumke's role as the Chief Justice of the Reich's Supreme Court was well-known. After meeting with Hitler in 1933, Bumke became a "most important convert," covering up the purge of judges and twisting law to support Nazi practices.[5] In August of 1934, van der Aa wrote Bates and the Howard League that IPPC President Bumke had "submitted the matter to the Government of the Reich," which determined that each country was to decide for itself who would be qualified to come and that "foreign members of the Congress will certainly be treated in Germany with . . . the . . . natural international courteousness." The "usual liberty" would be "granted" for discussion and facilities made available to accredited foreign and domestic press.[6]

That answer did not stop the planners. Moreover, during 1934, Paterson organized an exchange between Germany and England in which each country hosted the other's prison personnel. Paterson thought the visits exemplified how the IPPC could expand its "scope and activities" to study "new methods" and common solutions, provide staff training around the world, create a "pocket primer" in different languages for "subordinate officers of the prisons," and learn about alternatives to imprisonment. A memorandum detailing the German visit noted that the Englishmen heard of the "criticism of the treatment of political prisoners in Germany" but did not attempt "to enquire." They "visited no concentration camps," as the tour was "strictly limited to an examination of the methods of the treatment of the ordinary prisoner."[7]

In January of 1935, Harvard Law Professor Sheldon Glueck wrote to van der Aa that, although he had been a US delegate to Prague in 1930, "in view of the fact that Berlin is now the center of tyranny," he would not attend. Van der Aa also heard from Nora Adler, an English expert who had agreed to report about sanctions for juveniles. She withdrew, explaining she was a "Jewess" and "so many of my co-religionists are now no longer permitted in Germany to practice in the juvenile courts." Even as Paterson told van der Aa that Adler's "father was for many years the Chief Rabbi in this country" and had "strong views about the political situation in Germany," he recruited a substitute.[8]

Yet Paterson had qualms. In May of 1935, he told his co-commissioners that he needed to "tread on difficult ground"; while "the delicacy of the diplomat" might be appropriate, Paterson preferred "the directness of a practical friend." Paterson described firsthand accounts of "the permanent use of chains, the leasing of gangs of prisoners to outside employers under conditions akin to slavery, the extortion of confessions or information under torture, [and] the refusal of the right or the means to worship." Given the allegations of "cruelty and brutality" and the IPPC's Minimum Rules, Paterson argued the IPPC ought "with all its resources of information and experience," not "be afraid to study facts . . . and to play a part" that no others were "so qualified to play in the solution of these problems."[9] I did not find an archived response until, after the 1946 Nuremberg Trials, the organization—in a statement likely drafted by Paterson—condemned the atrocities.

In June of 1935, Cicely Craven, on behalf of the Howard League, officially withdrew from Berlin. Margery Fry wrote separately to reiterate the importance of getting "all possible support" for the Minimum Rules. Distressed at the "horrible failure of many governments to apply, not only the minimum rules but even the ordinary standards of decency accepted in most countries," Fry told van der Aa it was "almost useless to discuss minor questions of penal regime whilst we know what awful barbarities are going on in Germany itself and in some other countries." Nonetheless, even as the IPPC and Howard League might disagree, their "common interest in the prevention of injustice and cruelty" was stronger.[10]

LISTENING TO NAZIS' VILIFICATION OF THE "FALSE PRINCIPLE OF HUMANITY"

"The main object of the Berlin Congress . . . in the view of the hosts . . . was to present to a politely applauding international audience the latest innovations in German penal and criminal practice."

—British delegate Geoffrey Bing, 1935[11]

Staging the event in the Knoll Opera House, the Nazis got the photographs they wanted. Bing, a British delegate and barrister, reported in the 1935 Howard League's journal that "distinguished foreign officials, criminologists and reformers [were depicted] cheering the monstrous proposals put forth by Dr. [Franz] Gürtner and Dr. [Hans] Frank."[12]

The attendees came from countries that the Nazis would later invade, ally with, or fight in World War II, as well as a few that sought to remain neutral or were outside the theater of war. And while Bing termed the event a "Congress in Chains," the IPPC described it as though it had been a normal event with some 700 participants and delegates from forty-nine countries.[13] The published proceedings in 1936 began with IPPC Chair Bumke conveying Adolf Hitler's "best wishes" and the "hope that the foreign members" would come to understand the "new Germany." Bumke made no mention of the Standard Minimum Rules he had extolled in 1930 Prague's Congress; instead, he explained that "our Führer" had accomplished grand reforms based on "ideas fundamental to the Third Reich." Justice Minister Gürtner likewise discussed the "renaissance of the German penal law," incorporating the "national will" by giving judges the freedom to punish crimes, whether or not that power was enumerated in law.[14]

Bing described the address by Frank, "the Reich Jurist Leader"— later known as the "Butcher of Poland" for overseeing the murders of millions; Frank was convicted in the 1946 Nuremberg Trials and executed. In his Berlin address, Frank announced that, because criminals were a "menace to the health of the nation," German penal policy advanced the interests of the people, and eugenics was one way to do so. Joseph Goebbels argued the utility of concentration camps. The "imminent danger [of] . . . the chaos of anarchy" required "an act of defense that was impossible to accomplish with only humanitarian procedures." Goebbels added: "What importance does the surveillance of a few thousand individuals, all sworn enemies of society, have if it assures the existence of a populace of 66 million souls?" Nazis also discussed "procès monstres" ("monstreprozesse" in German and "group trials" in English) designed for quick convictions; Bumke explained that "everything must be kept out of the proceedings that is not indispensable for finding the truth."[15]

Another account comes from American criminology professor Negley Teeters, who produced a chronicle (subsidized by the IPPC) of congresses from 1872 to 1935. Amid details of the debates and resolutions, Teeters mentioned that the Nazis had run the proceedings, that the atmosphere was "intense," and that delegates resisted some proposals but German attendees blocked efforts to modify what the Nazi regime endorsed. Teeters also reported that IPPC delegates were given regulations governing concentration camps, an issue "so delicate at the time" that it occasioned "wide differences of opinion." Delegates learned that "anyone who makes derogatory or sarcastic remarks about an S.S. official" or who "intentionally omits to observe the prescribed salutes" was to be punished by eight days of "strict arrest and 25 strokes." The regulations also provided that, if individuals engaged in "political discussion in the camp," the penalty was hanging.[16]

Bing, the IPPC, and Teeters converged in reporting that delegates discussed detention for "security measures," sterilization for convicted criminals, and castration for sexual offenders. Even as the Nazis ran the show, a few people voiced concerns. For example, in the sessions on "prison administration" chaired by US Commissioner Bates, Nazi delegates (joined by colleagues from Italy and Hungary) argued that community interests took precedence over "the individuality of the prisoners." A French delegate, the noted lawyer Jerome Ferrucci, objected and argued that Germany's statistics proved its new regime a failure; the prison population had doubled since 1930. Ferrucci added that those figures did not include "the 49,000 prisoners of the many concentration camps registered by the Reich's office of statistics"; he urged the Berlin delegates to address the "legal and material conditions of prisoners" in camps.[17]

These exchanges troubled Bates, even as he had promoted American participation. Bates tried to prevent Nazi ideology from becoming IPPC policy. Rather than permitting a decision about punishment's purposes, Bates dispatched a subcommittee of German, Italian, English, and Greek delegates who could not reach agreement on a text; the Berlin Proceedings recorded that "fundamental differences" precluded voting on a resolution. Discord also emerged in a session devoted to "prevention" that centered on eugenics, which had appealed to some IPPC members as well as to lawmakers in England and the United States. The resolution proposed that "compulsory sterilisation for eugenic reasons is a recommendable measure of prevention, as it will reduce in the future the number of abnormal people from among whom criminals are recruited to a great extent." The caveat was that national legislatures were "to guarantee, from all points of view, that compulsory castration and sterilisation is undertaken with the greatest precaution only, and in proper proceedings which provide for a thorough investigation of the case by a committee of jurists and medical men." Bing reported that German delegates (numbering more than 420) outvoted everyone else, and that some attendees thought they had defeated the pro-sterilization resolution when it had carried.[18]

The proceedings ended with formal thanks from Paterson and from American James Bennett, who thereafter became head of the Federal Bureau of Prisons and later an expert witness for Arkansas' prisoners in the 1960s. In Berlin, Bennett was quoted as noting that Bumke had provided a tour of the Reich's Supreme Court. At the IPPC commissioners' private meeting, Paterson and Bates reportedly objected to the invitation extended by Italy's Mussolini for the 1940 Congress in Rome, but neither wished to do so "publicly."[19] Interest in staying at the perceived center of international crime and punishment outweighed evidence of the decimation of the Standard Minimum Rules that the IPPC had generated. The "Nazification" of the IPPC was underway.[20]

DISSEMINATING THE STANDARD MINIMUM RULES TO KEEP PRISONS FROM FALLING "INTO THE BACKGROUND"

One hope was that 1934 Standard Minimum Rules could provide leverage to lessen violence and improve conditions. In theory, that was their point. In practice, evidence of their ineffectiveness was apparent, as they did not pause the barbarism underway. Nonetheless, in Fry's views, were the Howard League to stop pushing, the prisoner issue would "soon . . . fall into the background." The Howard League documented violations and pressed for an international convention, while the League of Nations called for reports.[21]

The official rapporteur for the League of Nations' Fifth Committee, charged with advising on "penal and penitentiary issues," was Vespasian V. Pella, a prominent Romanian law professor and IPPC member. At the 1935 Geneva meeting, Pella counted some twenty countries responding about the impact of the 1934 Rules. The United Kingdom and Australia reported conforming before adoption, while Ecuador, Estonia, Iceland, India, Poland, Romania, South Africa, and Sweden indicated compliance at some facilities. Belgium and the Netherlands described limited or non-implementation and budget challenges. The United States, Latvia, and Turkey noted their dissemination of the Rules within their countries.[22]

Fry pushed for the League of Nations to ask its members to "state categorically whether they accept" the Standard Rules' application to all persons, convicted or not, to publish that acceptance, and extend the standards to people imprisoned without trial. Fry appended a document labeled "Violations of the Standard Minimum Rules for the Treatment of Prisoners," organized by rule and identifying countries by number. Included were radical reductions in food, the herding of "287 prisoners" into a "cold, damp, unsanitary prison," terrible overcrowding, lack of health care, and beatings.[23]

The Fifth Committee did not adopt Fry's call for categorical statements of adherence but did request a resolution that no one be subjected to "treatment inconsistent with the Standard Minimum Rules." Borrowing from the Howard League, the Committee reported allegations of "deprivation of the opportunity . . . to worship according to their religion," violence before and after trial to extract information, "employment of prisoners in gangs under conditions akin to slavery," "[p]rotracted underfeeding," and unsafe conditions for women. Another rapporteur called on the IPPC to recognize that these "reprehensible practices" could not be "considered to be in conformity" with the 1934 Rules. In 1935, the League's General Assembly requested governments to adopt the Standard Minimum Rules, disseminate them in official publications, and instructed its Secretary-General to call on countries to stop the "reprehensible practices" enumerated by the Howard League and the Fifth Committee.[24]

The 1934 Rules thus went into distribution. In the United States, Bates ordered "a sufficient number" to send to all the states. England's Home Office offered an introductory "note" to its distribution—that the "Rules have been accepted by His Majesty's Government" and were to be given "all possible publicity by means of official publications and otherwise." Printed by "His Majesty's Stationery Office," the frontispiece, reproduced in figure 7.1, included the royal lion and unicorn of His Majesty's crest.[25]

Between 1936 and 1938, League of Nations reports gave some credence to Fry's view that the Rules were part of what kept prisons

HOME OFFICE

**STANDARD MINIMUM RULES
FOR THE TREATMENT
OF PRISONERS**

drawn up and revised by the
International Penal and Penitentiary Commission
and recommended to Governments by
the Assembly of the League of Nations
at its Fifteenth Ordinary Session
September, 1934

LONDON
PRINTED AND PUBLISHED BY HIS MAJESTY'S STATIONERY OFFICE
To be purchased directly from H.M. STATIONERY OFFICE at the following addresses
Adastral House, Kingsway, London, W.C.2; 120 George Street, Edinburgh 2;
York Street, Manchester 1; 1 St. Andrew's Crescent, Cardiff;
80 Chichester Street, Belfast;
or through any Bookseller
1936
Price 2d. Net

FIGURE 7.1 Frontispiece from England's Home Office distribution of *Standard Minimum Rules for the Treatment of Prisoners*, London, 1936, courtesy of IPPC/UN Archives, S-0915, Box 48, File 4, 2

from falling into the "background." Pella discussed governments (including Afghanistan, the United States, Canada, Chile, Denmark, France, India, Iraq, Latvia, Sweden, Switzerland, the Union of Soviet Socialist Republics, and Yugoslavia) that had responded. The news included a decision of "great importance"—France had "decided to abolish" its penal colonies. (A decree ending transportation to French Guiana was entered in 1938; the penal colony was not "liquidated" until 1953.[26]) Chile, making an "improvement in the lot of prisoners," was said to pay prisoners for work and protect them as if free workers.[27]

"FOR ALL PRISONERS," DESPITE THE "NOTE OF UNREALITY"

"[I]t is illogical as well as cowardly to abandon attempts to make the world better because the outlook is dark."

—Margery Fry and Cicely Craven, August 10, 1936

The words "to make the world better" despite the darkness come from a cover letter to a memorandum, "The Prison Population of the World," which called on the League of Nations to launch an international effort to document "the immense number of human beings . . . deprived of liberty, of all that makes life worth having, and almost of hope itself." A form asked for those who "DEPLORE THE SIZE OF THE CAPTIVE POPULATIONS OF THE WORLD [TO] SIGNIFY THEIR GENERAL SUPPORT." As Fry and Craven explained, "quite apart from the treatment of prisoners, . . . a co-ordinated attempt" was needed to "reduce their actual numbers." If "scanty" information could be replaced with a fuller accounting, "[s]omething would be achieved if the world could be made aware of the actual number of those living in the shadow of prison or concentration camps." Fry and Craven hoped that the IPPC would join, but it stood back. Van der Aa replied that, while he would try to be helpful, he did "not see [his] way to do so" officially.[28] Pressing on, Fry provided a hand-drawn poster, reproduced in figure 7.2, to summarize extant information on the ratio of people in detention to a country's population.

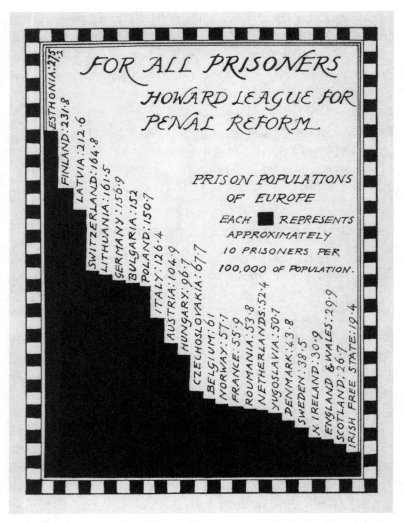

FIGURE 7.2 *For All Prisoners*, by the Howard League for Penal Reform, 1936, Howard League for Penal Reform Archive, housed at and courtesy of the Modern Records Centre, University of Warwick

The Howard League's "admirable work" prompted the Fifth Committee in 1936 to call for gathering statistics. The League's Assembly resolved that, by March of 1937, the IPPC should provide information on "the number of persons deprived of their liberty in the various countries of the world." In addition, the IPPC was

to learn whether the 1934 Rules presented "difficulties . . . of principle . . . [and/or] practice within the framework" of each jurisdiction's prison system.[29]

Getting replies was difficult. By 1937, Rapporteur John J. Hearne
of the Irish Free State recorded information from the Free City of
Danzig, Finland, British India, Mexico, Norway, Portugal, Siam,
and Sweden. Lauding this progress toward a "more scientific and
humane treatment," Hearne spoke of a "great transformation" resulting from the Rules. Reiterating the call for reports, Pella underscored what the Howard League had raised—the treatment of the
accused held without or before a trial.[30]

Attending the 1938 Nineteenth Assembly of the League of Nations, Fry said it had "a note of unreality."[31] Hitler had by then
annexed part of Czechoslovakia, and many understood that war
was imminent. The proceedings briefly mentioned the Standard
Minimum Rules, as France, British India, Norway, Portugal, and
Sweden had submitted reports. The IPPC's inquiry into the number
of prisoners worldwide had resulted in a count of almost a million
people in the fifty-three countries responding. The push to generate
new rules specifically for the "accused" produced a meeting in June
of 1939 at which the Howard League, the IPPC, and others were
among the "technical" organizations asked by the League of Nations
to make proposals. Fry, who was then the Britain's IPPC Commissioner, planned to go to Geneva to continue to press for protections
at the League of Nations' Assembly, scheduled for September 11–25,
1939—with the caveat "if it is held!"[32]

"REGIME HITLERIAN"

"I myself am always keeping strictly distinct political and scientific
considerations."

—Ernest Delaquis, IPPC Secretary-General to
Alexander Paterson, May 2, 1939[33]

Despite what IPPC commissioners had seen in Berlin and learned
thereafter, they continued working with the Mussolini government

to plan the 1940 Rome Congress. They did so throughout 1938, after
Nazis annexed Austria in March and after *Kristallnacht*—the night
of broken glass. One photograph published on November 11, 1938,
in the *New York Times* had the caption "Jewish Shop and Synagogue
Wrecked by Nazis." Reports described the "reign of terror" in Munich, where "every Jewish-owned shop in town was completely or
partially" destroyed, four hundred Jewish men rounded up and
taken into custody, and listed fourteen other German cities, including Berlin, Cologne, and Leipzig, where parallel destruction had
occurred. The following day, the paper reported that Goebbels—a
presenter in 1935 to the IPPC—voiced "no regret." All told, mobs destroyed 260 Jewish synagogues, ransacked more than 7,000 Jewish-
owned businesses, and killed hundreds in Germany, Sudetenland,
and Austria. More than 30,000 Jews were rounded up, arrested, and
shipped to concentration camps. In the United States and Canada,
mobilizations by religious organizations prompted protests, even as
those governments did not break relations with Germany.[34]

Months before, the IPPC leadership got a firsthand report of Nazi
atrocities that I found in its archives. In January of 1938, a Paris-based
group, the Centre International Pour Le Droit et La Liberté en Allemagne (the International Center for Rights and Liberty in Germany)
sent van der Aa its twenty-five-page memorandum marking the fifth
anniversary of Hitler proclaiming himself Chancellor and asking
that it be circulated to IPPC commissioners. Apparently distributed
elsewhere, the memorandum included the names and dates of the
deaths of ninety people killed between 1933 and 1938 and discussed
murders and violence in Greece and Macedonia.[35] The Center's memorandum has terrible parallels to descriptions of prisons by John
Howard, Alexis de Tocqueville, Gustave de Beaumont, Enoch Wines,
and Theodore Dwight, and to firsthand reports by many incarcerated
and enslaved individuals. Hence, I bring the Center's account, with
its cover page shown in figure 7.3, into punishment's annals.

Reflecting the Center's erudite membership, the memorandum was replete with references to speeches, laws, specific incidents, tribunals, and academic commentary amid nauseating
accounts of the torture, detention, and deaths of specific individuals as well as of hundreds of people identified as Jewish, Catholic,

FIGURE 7.3 Cover page of the *Mémorandum du Centre International Pour Le Droit et La Liberté en Allemagne*, Paris, January 3, 1938, courtesy of IPPC/UN Archives, S-0915, Box 55, File 5

Communist or otherwise deemed opponents by the Nazis. The writers poignantly invoked Germany as the "land of Goethe and Einstein" when charging Hitler with violating German traditions in pursuit of world domination. The Center aimed to mobilize humanitarian forces to stop Hitler, who planned to annex Austria, Czechoslovakia, Romania, the Netherlands, and other European countries. The *cri de coeur* was for the world not to be confused by Hitler's disclaimers of wanting peace, as he had already gone to war inside Germany, organized to invade elsewhere, and done grievous harm.

The information presented was stark, specific, graphic, and painful to read. "All the perfumes of Arabia could not dissipate the smell of cadavers" from the more than 100,000 people executed or tortured to death. The memorandum detailed violence at the Dachau concentration camp, the "orgy" of fascism that by 1938 had exterminated a half million German Jews and resulted in the arrest of seventy Catholic clergy, and funds diverted to the military while the country struggled with famine, economic instability.

Thus, Germany's interior was one of the "theatres of war"; Heinrich Himmler, the head of the Gestapo, had called for the crushing of the Reich's enemies and deployed terrorizing tactics, paralleling the Spanish inquisition. The Center provided tragic accounts of several individuals, German and not, who had been beaten, tortured, imprisoned, or murdered. The Center explained that the Nazis did their work through "legalized terror," as judges were subjugated to the will of the Führer. Nazis used law to put Jews outside the law, banished them from professions, and physically brutalized individuals in a campaign to "exterminate" them.[36]

Several pages were devoted to sadism at concentration camps. Included were texts of 1934 camp "discipline" rules—echoing what participants in the 1935 Berlin Congress had been told. A person liberated in 1936 from the Sachsenburg Camp described a whip brought out, a prisoner's arms and legs strapped, the lashing, and the blood that ran down. The Center named several prominent individuals, including Carl von Ossietzky, then still alive, who died in May of 1938, and who in 1936 had won the Nobel Peace Prize but was prevented from receiving it. Another was Ernst Thälmann, a leader of the German Communist Party, whom the Nazis imprisoned "without any juridical process." (Thälmann spent more than a decade in isolation and was shot to death in 1944.) The memorandum discussed that some people were asphyxiated and that others, imprisoned for lacking loyalty to Nazi ideals, were chained hand and foot, beaten, and starved.[37]

If IPPC members discussed the Center's 1938 documentation or other Nazi atrocities, I did not find notes in the IPPC war-year archives. Nor did the memorandum appear to have been circulated to commissioners. Instead, and to expand on Fry's comment about "unreality," the preserved IPPC letters take a business-as-usual attitude that is surreal to read. The IPPC's summer 1938 Bulletin featured a "Memorandum on the Vocational Training of Penitentiary Officials" to underscore the importance of education for prison staff. Around the same time, the IPPC offered some countries visits by commissioners to provide advice on the "practical application" of the 1934 Rules.[38] Letters discussed new publications, more questionnaires, and the agenda for the 1940 Rome Congress.

Those activities were the last under the superintendence of van der Aa, who retired in the summer of 1938. That fall, Ernest Delaquis took over. Before then, he was among the first to join the organization Kriminalbiologische Gesellschaft (KbG), formed in 1927 by German and Austrian scholars and focused on the link between biology and criminology. Delaquis also launched the Société Internationale de Criminologie, in which Giovanni Novelli, later at the helm of Italy's prisons, was central. Delaquis began the plans for the Rome Congress by soliciting papers, and Bates suggested dozens of people to write reports. Thereafter, the IPPC took up the League of Nations' request to send a questionnaire on "measures that might be proposed to protect witnesses and people awaiting trial against the use of violence and other forms of physical and mental constraint."[39]

By then, the IPPC had published the results of its inquiry into the "number of prisoners and the measures taken to reduce it"; information came from fifty-six countries including Italy, Austria, and Japan. The IPPC set forth a series of block charts, detailing country by country the number of prisoners over the age of eighteen. The IPPC concluded that, despite the "very simple and general wording" of questions, what came back was so varied that "the figures collected" and information on alternatives to incarceration were not "comparable" across jurisdictions.[40] The Howard League offered its own analysis—through another hand-drawn chart—reproduced in figure 7.4.[41] Ever polite, the Howard League explained (in French and English) that it had provided the graphic for those "studying" the IPPC report.

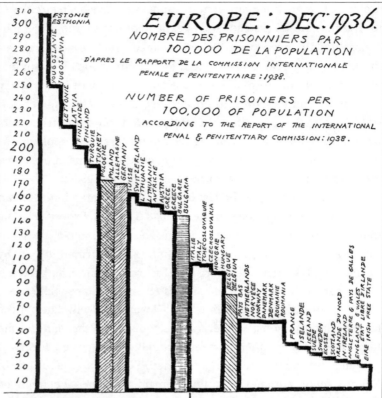

FIGURE 7.4 *Europe: Dec: 1936 . . . According to the Report of the International Penal and Penitentiary Commission,* by the Howard League, 1938, courtesy of IPPC/UN Archives, S-0915, Box 48, File 8

As if life were normal, in the winter of 1939, the IPPC called for reports due by June 30, 1939. Seeking to avoid the Berlin discord about punishment's purposes and eugenics, the 1940 printed "programme of questions" noted that some topics would be the basis for an exchange "without . . . concluding by a vote."[42] The subjects chosen included some perennials, such as the use of conditional sentences and the treatment of juveniles. Other questions were about whether remunerations for prisoners' labor should go to their families and, if so, how to justify such funds when "needy honest" families received no help from governments. Another topic was whether the importance "of exploiting and developing the colonies economically" affected incarceration. Ought colonial prisons focus on the "suppression of crime" or "the general requirements of colonization by preparing for the exploitation of the territory by means of prisoners' labour?"[43]

5

WHO "SPEAKS FOR" CORRECTIONS, AND WHAT TO SAY?

PUNISHMENT AND POLITICS IN WORLD WAR II AND IN ITS WAKE

"It would seem to be impolitic to attempt to hold the Congress in the midst of a conflict involving four or more of the major powers of Europe."

—US IPPC Commissioner Sanford Bates to
IPPC Secretary-General Delaquis, September 13, 1939[1]

"It is a matter of fact that the International Commission has always been, and intends to be, an absolutely <u>unpolitical body</u>."

—IPPC's funding request to the
US State Department, December 11, 1942[2]

"I suppose that the important thing is not, fundamentally, whether the IPPC lives or dies but whether international effort in this field improves or deteriorates."

—IPPC Secretary-General Thorsten Sellin to
IPPC President Bates, May 26, 1950[3]

Throughout World War II, the Secretary-General of the International Penal and Penitentiary Commission's (IPPC) insisted on its "absolutely <u>unpolitical</u>" character. Of course, the IPPC was far from unique in positing the autonomy of knowledge and administration from political, legal, and moral commitments or in suggesting that making change entails compromises. Indeed, the question of what stance to take is ever-present for today's critics—worrying that their work supports the longevity of oppressive institutions.

IPPC leaders missed, however, that the question was not about whether to be "in politics" but about what *kind* of political values guided its participants. By the 1940s, the IPPC was confronted with a distinctive problem: While detention had long been a part of colonialism and enslavement, fascism embraced *imprisonment* as a major *tool*. Moreover, the IPPC-drafted rules permitted—even as they sought to curb—whipping, dark cells, and food deprivation, which were among the tortures endorsed by fascist countries.

This link between "regular" and fascist prisons makes it important to understand how prison experts used their collective voice during World War II and the power struggle thereafter about what entities were to "speak for" corrections. By way of a preview, from 1939 to 1950, the IPPC tried to retain preeminence by arguing that, as a discrete intergovernmental organization devoted to punishment practices, it would generate better guidance than if the issue was "mainstreamed" (in contemporary terms) as part of a general social welfare program. The IPPC was *right* that once its hegemony ended, rules would change, and it was *right* that prisoners would have to compete for attention with other groups needing state services.

The IPPC was, however, wrong in objecting to the United Nations' form of *politicizing* punishment. After its founding in 1946 and its Universal Declaration of Human Rights in 1948, the UN revamped the standard-making process to welcome participation from people other than prison executives. By moving rulemaking beyond that exclusive professional domination, the UN opened the door to making human rights relevant to detained populations. In 1955, the UN's version of the Standard Minimum Rules for the Treatment of Prisoners recorded that impact by calling on countries to recognize that incarcerated people had "dignity" and "rights." Moreover, the 1955 Rules called for the end of whipping and dark cells. That repositioning came in tandem with more general acceptance by welfarist governments of commitments to enhancing the well-being of all, incarcerated and not.

Yet a simple narrative of a binary between social justice activists and correctional experts misses that after World War II, some prison officials joined the push for legal recognition of prisoners as rights-bearing citizens. Furthermore, even as the IPPC died as an entity, many of its practices (a leadership subgroup, congresses, and rules) did not, and professional prison officials continued to have sway.

The network spawned by the IPPC not only generated the 1934 Rules but also the 1955 UN Rules and the much-revamped 2015 version—named in honor of Nelson Mandela and calling for prisoners' rights far beyond earlier versions. These rules were developed *with* corrections officials and gained legitimacy in some quarters *because* of that involvement. Likewise, as I recount in this book's next section, when federal judges considered prisoners' claims, the correctional experts (including individuals active in the IPPC and drafting the 1955 UN Rules) testified on behalf of prisoners that whipping and unsafe conditions were abhorrent. In short, mid-twentieth-century struggles over the power to define correctional norms have shaped twenty-first-century practices in which rights, entangled with security, are center stage.

IGNORING FASCISM AND THE WAR

"Should a European War occur, you will, no doubt have formed some plan for carrying on the [IPPC's] Bureau during its continuance."

—Alexander Paterson to Ernest Delaquis, August 30, 1939[4]

During World War I, the International Penitentiary Commission (IPC) paused its operations, as soldiers from its members killed each other in trench warfare. The logistics were simple; the IPC had no paid staff. After its 1925 London Congress, the renamed IPPC turned its volunteer Secretary-General into a paid position, bought a building in Berne, Switzerland, navigated competition from the Howard League and League of Nations, and succeeded in branding itself as the source of rules to improve the treatment of prisoners. As fascism permeated Europe's streets, prisons, and detention camps in the 1930s, the IPPC declined to suspend operations or condemn the violence. Fearing for its own longevity, the IPPC continued when parallel organizations ceased to function. Moreover, until the Nazi invasions made it "impolitic" (the word proffered in 1939 by US Commissioner Bates), the IPPC planned to meet in Mussolini's Rome.

On March 15, 1939, Nazi troops marched into Czechoslovakia. In April of 1939, IPPC Secretary-General Delaquis wrote to Giovanni Novelli, who in 1935 had become the IPPC's president to host the planned 1940 Rome Congress. Novelli was Italy's General Director of Institutes for Penal and Preventative Institutions, a position he held from 1930 until his death in 1943. Mussolini's use of criminal law to control people deemed harmful to the "health and integrity of the race" was a model for the Third Reich. Novelli was a proponent—stressing that "chastising" criminals was punishment's "essential element." In the early 1930s, Italy limited defendants' rights, called prisoners by number rather than name, demanded silence, and sent "surveillance judges" to ensure prison staff enforced those mandates.[5] Nonetheless, Delaquis pressed forward on going to Rome to keep the "political" distinct from the "scientific."[6]

On September 1, 1939, the Nazi bombing of Poland began. On September 3, England and France declared war on Germany. Commissioner Bates wrote to van der Aa on September 12, 1939, about the "tremendous disaster that has befallen Europe"; without a mention of the Nazis, he added that "to many of us it seems as unnecessary as wicked."[7] In contrast, Margery Fry was unequivocal in understanding the horror and that the IPPC ought to be "entirely in abeyance."[8] Delaquis wrote to the commissioners on September 20, 1939 that the IPPC Bureau planned to "continue its work in a normal way" (albeit with a staff reduction) and asked governments for their 1939 and 1940 "contributions." (A subsequent accounting described 1939 as a "banner year" for dues, which totaled $21,000—with about $5,000 from the United States; $3,000 from Germany; $2,500 from Japan, and less than $2,000 from England and Italy each.)

Delaquis' year-end missive of December 16, 1939, said he hoped 1940 would be as "normal as possible." Two days later, Delaquis reluctantly accepted the obvious and informed Novelli that the United States had advised it was "absolutely impossible" to hold the Rome

Congress.[9] Some six weeks later, on May 10, 1940, the Nazis invaded France, Belgium, Luxembourg, and the Netherlands and, within two months, had occupied all but Luxembourg.

As if the world were not imploding, in his December 1940 year-end letter, Delaquis chatted about publications, asked for articles on new criminal legislation, and reminded member countries to make their annual contributions. Thereafter, Delaquis and IPPC President Novelli corresponded about the potential to substitute articles for the customary reports for a potential 1942 congress and about obtaining a written history to mark the IPPC's seventy years.[10] On December 7, 1941, the Japanese attacked Pearl Harbor, and on December 11, the United States entered World War II. The day before, Delaquis sent his yearly letter, describing publications and reiterating the need to pay dues.[11]

In that overview, Delaquis did not inform the commissioners that he had received a letter from Stefan Glaser, a Polish professor and criminal defense lawyer who had been a delegate to the 1935 Berlin IPPC Congress and who, after World War II, worked on drafting provisions for war crime prosecutions. Glaser, who had escaped Poland, wrote that he was part of a Polish Government in exile, described news ("always very sad") about Polish intellectuals and professors sent to concentration camps, and asked whether a representative of the "Légation de Pologne" in London might participate in the IPPC. Delaquis responded that he would send IPPC reports and that Poland had become an affiliate in 1925.[12]

SURVIVAL FOR WHAT AND FOR WHOM

"The long and terrible torment is over, leaving behind it ruins and grief."

—Ernest Delaquis to IPPC Commissioners, December 7, 1945[13]

"If the prison problems of the world are to be solved, it will be by those who have given their lives to their solution . . . the students and professors, the wardens and administrators, the physicians, psychiatrists and social workers who have met the prisoner face to face."

—Sanford Bates, *One World in Penology*, 1948[14]

At the close of 1943, Delaquis' customary December mailing began with "sad news"; the referent was not the war's violence but the death of Novelli. The following year, Delaquis described the work awaiting when the "terrible turmoil" passed. World War II ended in the West in May of 1945; Japan's surrender on September 2, 1945 closed the Eastern Front. The founding of the United Nations followed on October 24, 1945. The world was awash with refugees, displaced and stateless people, and small numbers of concentration camp survivors. The Nuremberg Trials documenting the Nazi extermination began in October of 1945. Delaquis' December 8, 1945 letter to the commissioners called for an "early revival" of activities and, "not least," "regular payment of the annual contribution of your Government."[15]

The commissioners went to Berne for a first post-war session in August of 1946, by which time Margery Fry was among them.[16] There, they finally acknowledged what had transpired. Their "resolution" began with "remembering" that the IPPC, for seventy years, had as "one of its main tasks . . . to propose adequate measures for the custody of all our fellow human beings who have offended against the law of their respective countries." Therefore, the commissioners were "constrained to express the horror with which we have read of the atrocities perpetrated in so-called concentration and internment camps during the war of 1939–1945. The facts adduced of the trial of those responsible . . . leave . . . no . . . shadow of doubt that the treatment accorded to many thousands of defenceless persons . . . has afforded an example of barbarism . . . and involves all of those concerned in shame and degradation that must be attached eternally to all who have taken part in those atrocities or favored them."[17]

In addition to suggesting "doubt" could have existed before 1946, the meeting's minutes reflected obliviousness to the emerging post-war values. Rather than address what to do with Francisco Franco's Spain, then one of the IPPC's twenty-one affiliated countries, the commissioners discussed "whether the best method of collaboration [with the UN] was fusion or merger" and set out terms for involvement. The commissioners wanted to keep the IPPC's form and function intact through congresses convened every five years and maintenance of its office, staff, and assets; they proffered "six principles" to ensure

the endurance of an entity "composed of persons with a professional, technical or scientific experience in penal and penitentiary
matters."[18] Whether governments (and specifically the United States)
might have funded both the UN and another organization dedicated
exclusively to policymaking on criminal law and punishment is a
question that was never answered, as the IPPC's track record and
toleration of Franco made its continuation untenable. Yet, the IPPC
kept on planning, and its tenacity paid off in some respects: the UN
took up its template and redeployed several IPPC leaders.

The unraveling of the IPPC was not immediately apparent to its
leadership. Needing US support, the commissioners designated
Sanford Bates president to be the IPPC's "chief negotiator" with
both the United States and the United Nations.[19] The choice of Bates
provides another window into the attitudes of US prison officials of
his era and the treatment of people in detention. After training as a
lawyer and serving briefly in the Massachusetts Legislature, Bates
became that state's Commissioner of its Department of Correction
and, in 1926, the president of the American Prison Association.
Bates moved to the federal government where he was Superintendent of the federal prisons, pushed for creation of the Federal Bureau of Prisons, was appointed its first Director in 1930, resigned in
1937 to run the Boys Club of America, and from 1940 to 1943 was the
president of the American Parole Association.[20]

Bates' golden resume looked less glittery from the vantage point
of human liberty. Illustrative was his advocacy in the 1920s for an
"honor system" for prisoners, explained not in terms of autonomy
and respect but to ensure the "protection of society" by making "better men, with less desire to prey upon the public"[21] After he became
a NY State Parole Commissioner, Bates bridled at criticism leveled
in the early 1940s by Hans von Hentig, a criminal law professor and
German refugee. Hentig explained that parolees were subjected to an
"unlimited domain of doings and omissions" that required people to
"lead a childlike and pastoral life" for years. Parolees were forbidden
to drink alcohol, go to "public dance halls," speak publicly or affiliate
with "any political party or group," borrow money, or make purchases
on an installment plan; their obligations included monthly reports

on money spent and being home by 9:00 p.m. (Twenty-first-century parole obligations do not look much different.) Hentig argued for an end to the "rigidity of the present system" and of the overuse of violations (varying "widely in graveness and scope") to reincarcerate. Bates retorted that parole was a "matter of grace" and that "control and surveillance" was demanded by "good law enforcement."[22]

As I noted, by the 1920s, Bates was ensconced in the international corrections network; in 1932, he replaced Caroline Wittpenn as the US Commissioner. After World War II, Bates sang the IPPC's praises (and hence, his own) in a 1948 essay, *One World in Penology*. Bates mentioned that Erwin Bumke joined the London 1925 Congress (the "most distinguished gathering of . . . practitioners of penal law") but did not discuss Bumke's work for the Nazis. Bates lauded the IPPC's promotion of indeterminate sentences, "crimino-biological studies of prisoners," and the Standard Minimum Rules, made available to "any government that desires to be informed" about them.[23]

In 1946, pushing at the UN for "professional domination" over crime and punishment policies, Bates presented to US officials the IPPC's "conditions" for merger with the UN's Social Commission, whose domain included crime and punishment. Handwritten notes from the 1946 commissioners' Berne meeting and dozens of memoranda, confidential exchanges, transcripts, and resolutions penned thereafter detail the IPPC's struggles to stay afloat.[24] Time and again, most of the IPPC leadership sought an autonomous role as an apolitical expert body, while many at the UN opposed working with the IPPC because of its World War II involvement with fascist countries and the membership of Franco's Spain.

"NEW SOLUTIONS" FROM THE UNITED NATIONS

"[T]he International Penal and Penitentiary Commission has but one main objective, that is to contribute to the progress throughout the world in accomplishing a humane, efficient and protective penal system."

—IPPC President Sanford Bates' speech to the
UN Social Commission, April 9, 1948[25]

In the future, "people will be . . . astonished" at the backwardness of
the "penal system and administration."

—Adolphe Delierneux, UN Assistant Director,
Division of Social Activities, 1949[26]

Between 1947 and 1949, interactions among the IPPC, United States,
and UN officials generated the template for the decades to follow. In
a forty-page, "confidential" memorandum on a "plan for the negotiations with UNO" (UN Organization), the IPPC reiterated many of its
prewar topics, such as expanding the use of probation and revamping
punishment for juveniles to shift to "medical and educational methods." In addition, the IPPC called for a study of the "increase in crime
due to the war" and more rules "to secure" that prisoners were afforded "fair and human treatment and to prevent abuse of authority."

The IPPC also raised the prospect of a *convention* (presumably
more powerful than its Standard Minimum Rules) on the treatment
of prisoners, to which countries would be "free to adhere." Further,
the IPPC proposed what it had declined in the past: draft "measures . . . to protect witnesses and persons awaiting trial against
the use of violence and any other forms of physical and mental
constraint." Moreover, joined by Delaquis in "observations" about
"international action" in "the prevention of crime and the treatment of offenders," Bates suggested studies of the "treatment of
political prisoners," of the "death penalty and its abolition," and
of "[c]orporal punishment and its abolition." In addition, the IPPC
put money on the table. Styling itself an "intergovernmental consultative agency composed of experts in penal and penitentiary
science and practice," the IPPC proposed a cooperative agreement
and explained its 1947 budget was then 79,640 Swiss francs, about
US$18,500 (more than $265,000 in 2024).[27]

The IPPC also printed the 1934 Rules with a revised set of "preliminary observations" modifying the introductory materials. First,
the IPPC recast its rules as recommended *regardless* of the legal,
social, and economic conditions in a country. Second, the IPPC
advised that, because large prisons made individualized treatment
more difficult, governments should avoid big facilities. Third, still

not repudiating whipping and dungeons, the IPPC added a bolded sentence stating that it *was* "desirable" that neither corporal punishment nor dark cells "be understood as among the disciplinary punishments."[28]

The UN was, however, more than a few steps ahead. The *New York Times* reported it had launched a "world-wide survey of crime and punishment" under the leadership of Adolphe Delierneux, then the Assistant Director of the Division of Social Activities. Delierneux had been a World War I prisoner held by the Germans ("I felt prison life in my bones") and wrote that "ignorance" drove the reliance on "high walls, bars, [and] repression," that reformers were "just beginning to understand and to perceive new solutions," and that (as quoted), in the future, "people will be . . . astonished" at how retrograde the contemporary "penal system and administration" was.[29]

OUT OF MONEY AND POWER

Lacking funds, the IPPC would have to "live on [its] income, or ask the UNO to take over, or just fade out."

—Lionel Fox to Sanford Bates, April 23, 1949[30]

"The IPPC would disappear as a legal entity subsequent to this Conference."

—Confidential US memorandum, May 10, 1949[31]

In 1949, the IPPC was on the skids. England's Lionel Fox wrote Bates that the finances were the "crucial question"; having consulted with Paul Cornil, who had run Belgium's prisons and was the IPPC's treasurer, Fox reported that funds would not last much more than a year. Thereafter, the IPPC would be at its end. Bates tried to avoid the "fade" but did not succeed. He pursued negotiations with the UN, but a confidential, unsigned US memorandum detailed plans for the IPPC's dissolution. While the United States would not announce it was stopping its contributions, its 1950 payments would be the last. In the interim, the United States would not object if Thorsten Sellin (a US-based professor of criminology at the University of Pennsylvania and UN consultant) became the IPPC's chief of staff. Given that "of all the members of the IPPC, the United States has pushed most vigorously for dissolution," the IPPC had no alternative.[32]

The IPPC convened its final congress in 1950. Invitations reflected facets of a new world order. The IPPC reached out to the International Labour Organisation; the World Health Organization; the UN's Educational, Scientific and Cultural Organization; the International Bureau for the Unification of Penal Law; the International Criminal Police Commission; the International Statistical Institute; the International Law Association; the International Union for Child Welfare; and the Howard League. When planning, IPPC commissioners debated whether its congress should continue to be open to individuals regardless of the status of their country, and whether to bar people from Germany and Japan. But the real decision-maker was the Allied High Commission occupying Germany, which sent in names of proposed German invitees. As to topics, the themes were largely familiar—prison administration, sanctions for juveniles, and probation and parole ("méthodes de libération conditionnelle") to afford a modicum of freedom.[33]

REPLACEMENT, ABSORPTION, AND RESUMPTION

The UN would convene "an international congress similar to those previously organized by the IPPC" every five years.

—Report of the UN Secretary-General, 1950[34]

Delaquis, citing health reasons, tendered his resignation as Secretary-General in 1949, and Thorsten Sellin took up the post. Keeping the custom that the IPPC Secretary-General represented his country, President Harry Truman appointed Sellin an alternative US Commissioner.[35] A multilingual sociologist, Sellin had emigrated from Sweden via Canada to the United States. In the 1940s, he wrote a book lauding the sixteenth-century Dutch for "pioneering in penology," even as what he described (as I discussed) was gruesomely rigid, albeit clean. In the 1960s, Sellin celebrated the IPPC's apolitical professionalism; he wrote that IPPC delegates, "appointed by their respective governments," worked "completely unhampered by politics"; the group was comprised of "professors of law or high correctional administrators . . . dealing with professional questions" and "free to follow their own judgments."

Most of the IPPC's August meeting was devoted to its ending. Sir Raphael Cilento, the Director of Social Affairs at the UN, joined to explain why the IPPC should agree to lose its "autonomy." Being folded in enabled the IPPC's expertise to have "a wider range and greater force"; the UN had fifty-nine members as compared to the IPPC's twenty-six, and the UN had funding "for actual action." Cilento also counseled that IPPC congresses had been "frankly a European matter" and the UN would, through convening regional conferences, broaden participation.[36]

Before folding, Fox suggested that, because the IPPC's "most essential" document was the 1934 Standard Minimum Rules, the IPPC should "raise the minimum." Within the month, Delaquis circulated a questionnaire; in "pursuance of a Resolution," he had "the honour to request that your government" furnish replies to questions that would "serve as the basis for a revision of the Standard Minimum Rules for the Treatment of Prisoners."[37]

The Berne meeting drew to a close on August 6, 1949. On the same day, the *New York Times* reported that the UN had convened a meeting of "leading criminologists," including Bates and Sellin, as part of an "international committee of experts" to advise on crime and punishment; its program was underway, dispatching experts to provide technical assistance and providing fellowships for prison studies. Within the week, the UN's Economic and Social Council reiterated its belief that the "purposes" of the IPPC could be "carried out within the United Nations while fully safeguarding the expert and professional character of the work undertaken," and the United States publicly called for the IPPC's end. On October 14, 1949, that UN's Council made official the IPPC's impending demise.[38] Delaquis closed the year with what was the last of his ritual letters, dated December 24, 1949. He assured the commissioners that "whatever the solution to be given to the problem of the [IPPC's] future status," he was confident The Hague Congress would be a success.[39]

In June of 1950, the UN set out the steps for the IPPC's replacement, absorption, and dissolution. The UN invited its members and IPPC members to designate "representatives of expert qualifications or experience, professional or scientific, in the field of the prevention of crime and the treatment of offenders" to meet together as the "United Nations Consultative Groups." The IPPC was the "first group set up" to provide recommendations. In addition, an ad hoc "Advisory Committee of Experts" was to meet annually. Further, the UN committed that, every five years it would convene "an international congress similar to those previously organized by the IPPC."[40]

THE ABSENCE OF A LANGUAGE OF RIGHTS

". . . I had a feeling that they should have gone further and enumerated some of the specific rights of prisoners."

—Sanford Bates' account of the August 1949 UN meeting of the International Group of Experts on the Prevention of Crime and the Treatment of Prisoners[41]

Amid thousands of pages of IPPC materials over seventy years, I found no use of the term "rights" in relationship to prisoners until 1949, when that word was mentioned a few times. Likewise, aside from the eventual acknowledgment of the Nazi exterminations, participants did not discuss the role of race, ethnicity, and nationality in the subordination and violence endemic to prisons. Moreover, the few references in 1949 to rights evidenced a limited appreciation of what that concept could mean for prisoners and its impact on people who, like the IPPC commissioners, ran carceral institutions.

In the summer of 1949, Bates recorded regret that the UN meeting had not "enumerated some of the specific rights of prisoners." Bates' illustrations—the "Segregation of Sexes, Freedom of Religion, Freedom of Restraints, etc."—were, he claimed, all "amply covered in the IPPC Minimum Standards" that, however, made *no* mention of rights. That fall, Bates again argued that the IPPC's 1934 Rules could be the basis for "a statement of principles or declaration of rights on behalf of prisoners throughout the world." Bates urged US Secretary of State Dean Acheson to convey to the UN Social Commission that the IPPC would have a revised version to submit.[42]

The first document I found with the phrase *human rights* in IPPC files came from the UN's Human Rights Division, explaining in the winter of 1950 that the Commission on the Status of Women had asked for materials "on the penitentiary aspect of the problem of the status of women." Attached was a five-part questionnaire focused on "equal opportunity" for women after arrest. The survey sought information on women's eligibility for bail; availability of legal counsel; "adequacy of lodging facilities"; segregation by sex to ensure that women supervised female detainees; eligibility for probation and parole; "maternity services and the care of infants"; and the "extent and suitability of institutional occupations" for training and education.[43] No mention was made of the diversity of women detainees in terms of race, ethnicity, religion, or age.

The IPPC responded by collating materials received from fifteen countries and dozens of NGOs. The resulting preliminary report by the UN Commission on the Status of Women did not focus on the treatment of incarcerated women; it described the "most important instance of discrimination against women in criminal law" to be "in the field of adultery." In many countries, if men found women "at the conjugal home" in an adulterous relationship, those who killed wives were not punished, although women murdering their husbands under similar circumstances were. In addition, women were punished more severely than men for prostitution and for "offences in the general realm of sexual immorality."[44]

The IPPC's lack of engagement with the concept of prisoners as rights-holders fit snugly within the paradigm of the corrections establishment at that time. In 1946, the American Correctional Association had published its *Manual for Correctional Standards*, a discursive account of practices in the United States. In 1952, the committee chartered to do revisions included IPPC regulars Sanford Bates, James Bennett, Edward Cass, Austin MacCormick, and Thorsten Sellin. They endorsed rehabilitation, discussed the challenges of discipline, and rejected corporal punishment. Yet they described permissible restrictions to include bread and water and a "monotonous diet" of combined foodstuffs into a tasteless loaf.[45] That 1954 publication did not discuss obligations to protect the human rights of prisoners.

Thus, over the course of seventy years, when arguing (as they did repeatedly) about punishment practices, IPPC delegates invoked morality, charity, humanitarianism, Christian love, medical and social sciences, punishment's goals, community safety, and the expense of running prisons. No part of the discussion (aside from Margery Fry and the Howard League) focused on prisoners whose rights required respect. Moreover, whatever the variation in viewpoints, a majority of prisons' officialdom (who understood themselves to be passionately committed to the betterment of prisoners' lot) explained and condoned the pervasive, persistent total (and hence in twentieth-century terms, totalitarian) subordination of incarcerated people.

These decades of international gatherings revealed what they tried to suppress: punishment decisions are nested in the political values of the social orders imposing them. The IPC/IPPC was one of colonialism's "technologies," shaping definitions of crime and punishment, collecting statistics, and spreading visions of proper prison practices around the world.[46] When political movements battling fascism, imperialism, and racism gained traction and wars erupted, the grip on power of these prison men loosened. I turn in the next chapter to the denouement, the IPPC's last 1950 Congress and its return to rule drafting. In 1955, after many alterations, the UN promulgated Standard Minimum Rules that included calls for protection of prisoners' "dignity" and "rights," albeit with a discount if security demanded it.

9

FUNDAMENTAL RIGHTS "EVEN IN PRISON"

THE UN'S 1955 RULES ON PRISONERS' DIGNITY AND PUNISHMENT'S PARAMETERS

"Imprisonment and other measures which result in cutting off an offender from the outside world are afflictive by the very fact of taking from the person the right of self-determination by depriving him of his liberty. Therefore the prison system shall not, except as incidental to justifiable segregation or the maintenance of discipline, aggravate the suffering inherent in such a situation."

—Rule 57, 1955 UN Standard Minimum Rules
for the Treatment of Prisoners[1]

The final gathering of the International Penal and Penitentiary Commission (IPPC) at its 1950 Hague Congress was the first occasion when people who ran prisons addressed what post-war incarceration should look like. Even as fascism had erased the line on which the corrections establishment depended—distinguishing an "offender" breaking a country's laws from everyone else—aspirations survived for revival of that distinction and for rules to constrain detention's violence. The 1950 Congress reflected that effort as did the IPPC's work in 1951, when it resumed its role as a drafter of blueprints for prison management.

As unfair as it was (and is) to enslaved people whose oppression has been ignored or tolerated, after Nazi concentration camps made vivid that everyone was at risk of imprisonment in devastating environments, officials in democratic countries committed to changing detention practices. Reverberations of images of people jammed into closed train cars and sent to death in concentration camps, of yellow Stars of David, branding, and of the few emaciated survivors shaped the IPPC's 1951 draft, which included provisions to prevent airless cattle-car transportation, degrading clothes, and whipping. More revisions produced the UN 1955 Rules, which announced that "respect due to [prisoners'] dignity as human beings" required governments to change their practices. Yet World War II's examples of horrific confinement did not stop rules from recognizing solitary confinement and food deprivation as licit modes of punishment.

Crafting those provisions exemplified the through-line of this book—the *redrawing of lines between permissible and impermissible punishments*. This chapter, which chronicles discussions between 1950 and 1955, marks the entrance of equality precepts in rulemaking about imprisonment. The results were recognition of prisoners' "rights" and "dignity," of the "suffering inherent" in incarceration, of calls not to "aggravate" those impositions, coupled with licensure to do so when "incidental to justifiable segregation or the maintenance of discipline." Then, as now, arguments turned on when, in the name of discipline, *suffering* could be intensified. Then, as now, many people hoped a regulatory regime that respected prisoners could lessen confinement's harms. Then, as now, balancing tests permitted prison officials' assertions of security's demands to trump prisoners' rights. Then, and more now, proposals for incarceration's abolition were put forth.

THE "HISTORIC SIGNIFICANCE"

"The exhibition has no other purpose than to present an average picture of what has been attained . . . and to arouse in the public a better comprehension of this great social work. . . . The prison régime . . . finds itself in . . . reform and renewal . . . to serve the interests of the community as well as those of the individual."

—Ernest Lamers, Director-General of
Prisons of the Netherlands, 1950

"[E]ven in prison a man has certain fundamental rights and dignities which we must preserve."

—James Bennett, Director, US Bureau of Prisons, The IPPC's 1950 Hague Congress

The "most depressing aspects of imprisonment" were being "reduced to implicit obedience, to be subject to the imperatives of the regulations and the caprices of the personnel touching on the minutest details of life."

—Paul Cornil, Secretary-General of the Belgian Ministry of Justice, The IPPC's 1950 Hague Congress[2]

The Hague proceedings reflected the centrality of the United States; the materials were printed in English as well as French, and both sets had the same frontispiece. The photograph (figure 9.1, which had a tissue overlay identifying each person) offered a view of the world as it looked from the IPPC's perspective.[3] Of the twenty-eight depicted, two were white women staffers, two were Asian men, and the rest European and American white men. At the center was the US' Sanford Bates, chairing, with Belgium's Paul Cornil and the Dutch J. P. Hooykaas at his right to denote that their countries were hosting. After the meetings at The Hague, two hundred delegates toured Belgian prisons.[4]

The IPPC had sent out 450 invitations, and about that number of people assembled. Government delegates came from twenty-seven countries as well as "learned institutions and professional organizations." As had been customary, the largest number at The Hague—more than 140—were from the host country. Formal withdrawals from the IPPC had come from several Eastern European countries (Bulgaria, Czechoslovakia, Yugoslavia, and Romania) aligned with the Soviet Union. Russia, too, was not represented—a poignant bookend given that in 1868, Moscow's Count Sollohub had proposed an international conference and in 1872 was a delegate in London. The United States sent twenty-two delegates and eight attendees; Japan had two delegates and Italy seven, while the twenty-two attending from the Federal Republic of Germany did not have the status of

FIGURE 9.1 Frontispiece, *Proceedings of Twelfth International Penal and Penitentiary Congress*, The Hague, August 14–19, 1950, with permission of the International Penal Penitentiary Foundation

delegate–voters. Observers hailed from the United Nations, the World Health Organization, the International Criminal Police Commission, and the Holy See. The contingent from the United Kingdom included Cicely Craven from the Howard League. One of the plenary session reporters was Sheldon Glueck, a Jewish professor from the United States who, as discussed, had in 1935 refused to travel to Berlin.[5]

I quoted the Dutch prison director Lamers on "reform and renewal" to capture the self-congratulatory tone, as many clung to the view of corrections as a repository of apolitical expertise. Others, however, recognized that World War II had upended that conception. Bennett, the head of the US prison system, referenced prisoners' "rights and dignities," and Cornil, who had briefly been interned by the Nazis, discussed imprisonment's assault on autonomy.

Oppressiveness was not news to delegates; it had been a perennial topic for seventy years. Moreover, degradation was likewise a familiar theme; recall that Charles Henderson, the Chicago sociologist and US Commissioner, had at the 1910 Washington Congress described prisons as *enslaving*. He suggested a few ways to curb, but not to end, that "slavery."

In contrast, lectures and resolutions at The Hague rejected treating prisoners as slaves of the state, and Cornil raised the prospect that imprisonment, like corporal punishment, needed to be abandoned. Thorsten Sellin, the IPPC's Secretary-General, noted in his preface that the "historical significance" of the ending of the "distinguished series" of congresses escaped no one. Reading the published proceedings from this vantage point, its significance stemmed from direct questioning of incarceration's legitimacy and from the credit line given to prisoners for working on the printing.[6]

Following IPPC traditions, socializing was important. A reception was held at the palace of the Dutch monarch, Queen Juliana, photographed amid a sea of white and mostly male faces. One innovation was the screening of films. In the 1920s, IPPC members, railing against the corrupting influence of motion pictures, had called for censorship. In 1950, the IPPC showed documentaries about prison systems in Argentina, Chile, the Netherlands, the United States, and Switzerland, and one "made entirely by prisoners." An International Penitentiary Exhibition of photographs and artifacts, referenced by Lamers, was viewed by 1,160 people.[7]

Attendees were inundated with information. Experts from sixteen countries provided 134 reports to complement twelve general reports distributed in advance. Familiar themes returned. In his opening address, Bates reiterated that "individualization of treatment" was imperative. Hence, discussions focused on classification and on input from psychiatry in diagnosing and treating people referred to as "offenders."[8]

Yet the idea that prisons needed to alter their practices peeked through in a few resolutions. The Hague Congress supported the proposition that "all prisoners should have the right, and prisoners under sentence have the obligation to work." Such labor was not to be punitive but part of a treatment plan; "adequate and suit-able employment" was to be available, and prisoners ought—the Congress resolved—to receive wages. The Congress also called on prisons to restore prisoners "to full civil status" through education and training; another resolution called on countries to address the "restoration of . . . civil rights" for "habitual offenders."[9]

FACING FORWARD

"[I]n a not too distant future, this penalty [of imprisonment] will be considered as no less primitive than the corporal punishments of the past centuries."

—Paul Cornil, The Hague, 1950[10]

World War II's impact was evident in the three "general" lectures discussing punishment's purposes, prison practices, and individu-als' dignity, rights, and autonomy. Yet despite fascist efforts at elim-ination of people by race, ethnicity, nationality, and religion, the lecturers did not address those categories or the class hierarchies that abounded.

In "Security Measures Appropriate to a Humane System of Social Defence," Marc Ancel, a French justice, rejected harsh punishments such as exile to colonies, a practice his country was in the midst of abandoning. As elaborated in his book, *Social Defence: A Modern Approach to Criminal Problems*, punishments needed to intervene in the situations of people who might turn to crime. Further, to "save the offender from a punishment that deprives him of freedom" and out of "the respect for human dignity," Ancel promoted probation.[11] Yet, his condescending aspirations to control people he deemed under-socialized echoed the past.

Bennett, who had become the head of federal prisons after Bates retired, called his lecture "The Organization and Problems of the Federal Prison System of the United States of America." After a som-ber reminder of the "anxious moments" occasioned by the ongoing Korean War, Bennett gave an upbeat account of programs for pris-oners. As for discipline, "we in America" believed that "flogging, mutilation, branding, striped clothing, [and] the silent system" had "resulted only in the degradation of the human personality and are inconsistent with our present concept of human values and the dignity of the human being." The federal system did not "permit the use of corporal punishment under any circumstances." Those comments forecast what he would say in 1967 when testifying *for* prisoners that whipping was cruel, wrong, and unnecessary. Likewise, Bennett's general premise that, "even in prison a man has certain fundamental rights and dignities which we must preserve" was a position he took when working on the 1951 draft IPPC Rule and as Chair of the UN 1955 Rules' session.[12]

A challenge to incarceration itself came from Paul Cornil, the Secretary-General of Belgium's Ministry of Justice, a criminal law professor at the University of Brussels, and the IPPC's treasurer. Before leveling his critique, Cornil proffered his credentials: "twenty years . . . in the prison administration of my country," visits to prisons in many countries, and, due to "the circumstances of war . . . a view of the penitentiary problems as seen from the inside of institutions." Cornil had been the Inspector General of Belgian Prisons, which meant that he was a senior prison official during the Nazi occupation; in 1943, the Nazis briefly held him in detention.[13] Cornil appears to be the *only* speaker over the IPPC's seventy years who had been in prison. (In today's conferences, people who have experienced incarceration are often presenters.)

Like Margery Fry, Cornil merits attention as an outlier in his generation; unlike Fry, he had run prisons he came to condemn. Cornil argued the incoherence of pursuing both retribution and rehabilitation. The first required a sentence be proportionate to the offense; the second sought to reeducate. Even if by some "miracle . . . these two periods . . . were to coincide exactly," coexistence between "intimidation and treatment" was not possible. Out of "respect for human dignity" (on which "obvious progress" had been made), education was key in "modern" penology, borne from "reaction against abuses and cruelties committed in concentration camps" and cognizant that prisoners had "certain rights." Cornil noted that "cases of corporal and capital punishments" were "increasingly rare." Yet, while the "physical individual" was safer, governments had deliberately let "material comfort" lag far behind "the living standards of free men."[14]

Pause to take in Cornil's referent: people outside prison were the *baseline*. Moreover, he sought to undo the "principle . . . that a prisoner had no rights, except those granted to him by the regulations." Cornil explained that one "must have undergone this régime to understand its harsh nature"—the micro-control over "the minutest details of life." Instead of losing choices, access to family, a trade, free movement, and civil rights, Cornil proposed that prisoners be able to participate in "a system of self-government." His formulation was that prisoners should have "all the rights of free men except those of which he has to be deprived for the protection of society." (The European Prison Rules of the twenty-first century echo that proposition.) Thus, punishment should "be guided by the desire to limit repression to what is indispensable for the protection of society, and to safeguard as much as possible the human dignity of the offender."[15]

Yet more radical (given his audience and era) was Cornil's conclusion—which seemed to him "certain"—that imprisonment would soon "be considered as no less primitive than the corporal punishments of the past centuries." Atop moral revulsion, Cornil argued ineffectiveness: "How can one prepare a person for social life when one separates him from his fellowmen by isolating him from his environment?"[16] In 1950, Cornil was a lonely voice in the correctional establishment. He did not elaborate how to move toward prison abolition, nor did he explain how he came to be incarcerated.

Given IPPC correspondence raising concerns about Cornil's whereabouts, I had assumed Cornil had been interned by the Nazis. A 2007 government study, *La Belgique docile*, about Belgium's occupation, included a few details. In the winter of 1943, Cornil became a Nazi prisoner, held for some weeks. That report criticized Cornil's involvement with the Nazis; while having made "innovative efforts before 1940 in the accommodation of foreign Jews and Germans in Belgium," it quoted individuals accusing Cornil of participating in the creation of "concentration camps for . . . Jews . . . [and] for his own compatriots [who had been] condemned by the occupier."[17] A form of defense comes from memoranda (perhaps preserved through Cornil) recording his protests to the Nazis about the "intolerable situation," with overcrowded facilities that had insufficient food, bedding, and heat. After the war, the government appointed Cornil to a group charged with making recommendations on the treatment of collaborators.[18] Cornil may be an example of a person who buffered some of what the Nazis sought to do and hence to occupy what Martin Conway has called the "grey world between collaboration and resistance."[19] That juxtaposition has contemporary resonance, as twenty-first-century critics worry about whether they are ameliorating conditions or legitimating grievous harms.

REVISITING THE 1934 RULES: DEBATING DEFINITIONS OF DEGRADATION

"Corporal punishment, punishment by placing in a dark cell, and all cruel, inhuman or degrading punishments shall be completely prohibited as punishment for prison offences."

—Rule 24, 1951 IPPC Draft[20]

The post-war question of changing the 1934 Rules—and hence of new line drawing on what is impermissible in punishment—was initially taken up by the IPPC, which had convened a subcommittee before its Hague Congress. The task was reoriented somewhat when the United Nation's Social Commission asked for a draft that addressed conditions for people held before trial as well as post-conviction. (Margery Fry had argued that need two decades earlier.) Moreover, again echoing Fry, the United Nations told the IPPC subcommittee chaired by the UK's Lionel Fox that it was considering "an international agreement," a "convention" to have more force. Fox used that prospect to call for rules to be "as simple as possible and in terms likely to command general agreement."[21]

The subcommittee understood its legitimacy required input from others. Yet its survey and resulting draft demonstrated that the IPPC remained focused on prison systems' *needs* rather than the *harms* to prisoners. For example, one question was whether the 1934 Rules presented "difficulties (a) of principle (b) of practice, within the framework of your present penal system?"[22] Through the United Nation's outreach, the subcommittee received some suggestions. From France came a call for a statement of the rights of persons (*droit des gens*) applicable worldwide. Austin MacCormick, then Executive Director of the Osborne Society (a US prison reform organization), urged a thorough rewrite. Israel proposed rules to require outdoor exercise and a "[m]inimum time for intellectual instruction."[23]

Transcripts of subcommittee deliberations in August 1951 record a rule-by-rule review that resulted in the seventy-eight provisions published in the IPPC's 1951 Bulletin, *Select Papers on Penal and Penitentiary Affairs*. Rule 1 offered a new precept, at Bennett's suggestion—a "basic principle" that the Rules were to be applied "impartially . . . with no discrimination on grounds of race, colour, religion, or political belief, social standing or otherwise." Those words were close to but did not include all the categories protected in Article 2 of the UN 1948 Universal Declaration of Human Rights. World War II's impact could also be found in the 1951 draft's insistence on access to outsiders; prisoners were to be able to "make a complaint, through the approved channel and without censorship, to the central prison administration, the judicial authority, or such other authorities as may be approved."[24]

The drafting group converged on another principle: a prohibition on *degradation*. Debate ensued about what fell within that category. All agreed that clothing ought not (in Bates' formulation) "be of a humiliating or degrading nature nor adorned with degrading insignia."[25] (In its final 1955 form, the Rule stated that "such clothing shall in no manner be degrading or humiliating" and when outside an institution, prisoners be allowed to wear their own clothing or "other inconspicuous clothing."[26]) Most commissioners were also clear, while Bates was not, on the importance of exercise. Bates argued that sports were a "privilege to be won by prisoners." In 1951 and again in 1955, the other commissioners prevailed. Under the heading "Exercise and sport," the UN 1955 text (close to the 1951 draft) called for "suitable exercise in the open air" and that prisoners of "suitable age and physique" be provided with "physical and recreational training."[27]

As to food, IPPC commissioners from Italy and Argentina reported their countries banned diets of bread and water, and they opposed using food as punishment. In contrast, Bates asserted that "there is nothing essentially degrading about a reduced diet." He argued that, while corporal punishment was "wrong and inhuman" and a dark cell "a dangerous and degrading experience . . . , bread and water in your own cell, without a dark cell or corporal punishment is not degrading." Bates proffered a (bizarre) analogy to what "a good many mothers in American" had done, which was to send "their children to bed without dessert." For prisoners, as long as a doctor was "watching the cases," he saw no "harm or any wrong in a reduced diet."[28]

Drawing on the United States for a different lesson, Bates called for an end to physical restraints. He argued that without such a prohibition, it would be hard to criticize the "chain-gangs used in our Southern States," commonplace in the treatment of slaves, which was, he said, the "blackest chapter" (yes, he used that metaphor) in US history. That rare invocation of enslavement was the sole mention of race I found in IPPC materials on the 1951 draft. That version did (finally) call for whipping's end. "Corporal punishment, punishment by placing in a dark cell, and all cruel, inhuman or degrading punishments shall be considered prohibited as punishment for prison offences." The IPPC did not, however, propose to prohibit solitary confinement or food deprivation, even while acknowledging the potential debilitating effects. "[C]lose confinement, reduction of diet, or any other method that may be prejudicial to physical or mental health," "shall never be inflicted," yet could be imposed. The caveats were familiar: that a "medical official" was to provide a written certification that the person was "fit to sustain" a particular punishment and visit daily to advise on whether "termination" was "desirable on grounds of physical or mental health."[29]

A disheartening summary came from Cornil, who described the proposed rules as permitting each country to decide what was "degrading, inhuman and so on"; some countries might ban what others did not. Moreover, with continuing unselfconscious racialized imperialism, the draft noted that, even as the goal was conformity, "colonial prison systems" could not be "expected" to apply all the Rules, "particularly as regards physical conditions."[30]

At a last meeting in July of 1951 when the IPPC counted twenty-one countries as members, the leadership issued three resolutions reflecting its understanding of what speaking "for" corrections entailed. A first called for shifting from sentencing based on the "nature and seriousness of the offence" to "a new differentiation" to individualize punishment. A related second recommendation was that judges be accorded discretion to fashion sentences that, given the "personality of the offender," took into account "either social defence measures or measures of protection, education, and treatment." Third, the IPPC called for study of the "treatment of habitual offenders" to understand their "abnormalities."[31] No mention was made of the Standard Minimum Rules or the dignity of prisoners.

PRESERVATION THROUGH TRANSFORMATION, AND SOME TRANSFORMATION: PRISONERS' DIGNITY AND PRISON DISCIPLINE ENSCONCED IN 1955

"The regime of the institution should seek to minimize any differences between prison life and life at liberty which tend to lessen the responsibility of the prisoners or the respect due to their dignity as human beings."

—UN 1955 Standard Minimum Prisoner Rules, 60(1)

The IPPC's assets were to have gone to the UN and devoted to crime and punishment. However, the UN had no mechanism to segregate funds. Instead, the IPPC created a Swiss-based trust, the International Penal and Penitentiary Foundation (IPPF), charged with spending the funds "to promote studies in the field of the prevention of crime and the treatment of offenders, especially by scientific research, publications and teaching."[32] Initially, only people from IPPC countries could participate; in 1964, "corresponding members" of "eminent experts" from anywhere were welcome. Unlike the IPPC, the IPPF has no official relationship to governments. By 2021, its website recorded that over seven decades, the IPPF produced about fifty documents, including a 2021 volume, *Mental Health and Criminal Justice* that, in French and English, offered "international and domestic perspectives on defendants and detainees with mental illness."[33]

What the UN could do, as promised to the IPPC, was convene an ad hoc committee of "specialists on crime prevention and control" that, in the 1950s, was within the "Social Defence Section" of the Division of Social Affairs. The charge was to develop an "international criminal policy with a social purpose and a work programme" for the "readaptation of the offenders" to aid in "recovering human capital."[34] In 1954, the UN held regional meetings in the Middle East, Latin America, Asia, and Europe to vet the IPPC Rule draft and feed comments into its Secretariat, also receiving input from the UN's Division on Human Rights.[35] These efforts fit what Margery Fry had long sought—policymaking by a group not dominated by prison officials. As different people spoke "for" corrections, they proposed revisions reflecting that *professionalism* was not all that crime and punishment needed.

Yet corrections retained a sturdy force, with former IPPC members in key UN positions. Sellin and then Fox chaired the Ad Hoc Experts' Advisory Committee, and Cornil was rapporteur. At the UN's first "Congress on the Prevention of Crime and the Treatment of Offenders," held in 1955 at its European base in Geneva, those men were central, along with Bates as an honorary vice president and Bennett chairing the session devoted to reviewing the drafted rules. Participating were 475 "specialists" from sixty-six countries; familiar activities included screening films about prisons and visiting prisons. Unlike the IPPC, the 1955 UN account made no mention of entertainment at royal palaces. Moreover, while the audience at the IPPC 1950 Hague Congress heard lectures by two Europeans and one American man, speakers in Geneva included not only the French Ancel and the American Bates but also men from Asia, the Middle East, North America, and Latin America. Bates' discussion of the United States was again smug but shadowed by acknowledgment of what he called a "recent epidemic of prison riots," which he attributed to "a small group of psychopathic prisoners." Bates' reference was to national news of more than twenty uprisings around the country revealing terrible conditions, underpaid staff, and violence.[36]

Using the IPPC's format, the UN organized segmented sessions, devoted to the Standard Minimum Rules as well as to "Open Institutions and Prison Labour" and the "Prevention of Juvenile Delinquency." The Congress focused on the UN Secretariat's revised Rules, which began with general admonitions followed by different prescriptions directed at "prisoners under sentence," "insane and mentally abnormal prisoners" ("not to be detained in prisons"), "prisoners under arrest or awaiting trial," and "civil prisoners." Just as the IPPC and the League of Nations had styled their rules aspirational, the UN acknowledged that "not all" of its ninety-three rules could be applied "in all places and at all times."[37]

A question had arisen about whether to delete the word "minimum" from the title. The 1955 Report explained that the word made clear "the provisions of the Standard Rules were not purely optional but were the essential minimum requirements on the basis of which the various countries could perfect and further improve their penitentiary administration." The UN Secretariat went a step further by saying that, while not a "complete set of prison regulations," the "Rules always imply an obligation." Moreover, unlike the IPPC's 1951 draft, which had suggested that "colonies" (called by the Secretariat "trust and non-self-governing territories") were not to be held to the Rules, the Geneva Congress rejected that exception. Thus, all countries were to consider adoption of the provisions that, "on the basis of the general consensus of contemporary thought and the essential elements of the most adequate systems of today," were "generally accepted as being good principle and practice in the treatment of prisoners and the management of institutions."[38]

As I quoted, a basic principle of the 1955 Rules was acknowledgment of "suffering" and obligations to minimize oppression. Further, drawing verbatim from the Universal Declaration of Human Rights, the precepts were to be applied "impartially . . . with no discrimination on grounds of race, colour, sex, language, religion, political or other opinion, national or social origin, property, birth or other status." The caveat was to "respect the religious beliefs and moral precepts of the group to which a prisoner belongs," variations were permissible. The 1955 Rules also insisted that detention facilities record information about admission of all individuals and deny entry to any person lacking a "valid commitment order." Stateless prisoners and refugees had to be able to communicate with officials in countries that had taken charge of them. Further, prison managers were to provide prisoners with information about their "rights" and "obligations," including the "right" to let family members know of their imprisonment and, if transferred, where they were. When transferred, prisoners were not to be displayed or transported in vehicles without adequate ventilation and light. Prisoners were also to be able to get news, and prisons had to admit inspectors.[39]

The 1955 UN Rules stressed "decent living conditions."[40] "[E]ach prisoner shall occupy by night a cell or room by himself"; if "temporary overcrowding" existed, it was "not desirable to have two prisoners in a cell or room." Rooms were to have "fresh air" and "windows . . . to enable the prisoners to read or work by natural light." Showers were to be at least once a week, and facilities kept "scrupulously clean at all times." Prisons were to provide exercise, adequate food, water, and health care including "psychiatric service" for diagnosis and treatment.[41] (When Cornil later discussed these provisions, he noted that governments might well have to provide for prisoners a "higher standard of living than law-abiding citizens"; he cited Jeremy Bentham, who 150 years earlier had made that point, to which I return in the conclusion.[42])

Although not adopting Cornil's view that prisoners were to have "all the rights of free men except those of which he has to be deprived," the 1955 Rules instructed that institutions "minimize any differences between prison life and life at liberty." Yet, the Rules explained that proposition not only in terms of "dignity" but also as part of prisoners' "responsibility" in detention—which could support divesture if violations of prison requirements occurred. The

1955 version also did not follow Cornil's proposals to end micro-control, delineate work hours, and pay wages and social security. The UN did recognize that prison took away the "right of self-determination" and, when possible, should safeguard prisoners' "rights" relating to social security and other civil interests. Yet the Rules affirmed the power of corrections to use "all the remedial, educational, moral, spiritual and other forces and forms of assistance which are appropriate and available" to organize prisoners' lives. A modicum of supervised "self-government" was possible for certain "social, educational or sports activities."[43]

As for "discipline and order," the 1955 Rules called for "no more restriction than . . . necessary for safe custody and well-ordered community life." What was "necessary" was to be answered by prison officials and through statutes or regulations specifying the offenses and the "types and duration" of punishment "inflicted." A "thorough examination" of allegations was required, along with opportunities to defend, if need be, through interpreters. Prisoners were to have no role in imposing discipline on each other. Further, "[c]orporal punishment, punishment by placing in a dark cell, and all cruel, inhuman or degrading punishment shall be completely prohibited as punishments for disciplinary offenses." The 1955 Rules reiterated bans on chains, with caveats that specified circumstances could license temporary use.[44]

The 1955 UN Rules kept the IPPC's 1951 licenses of food deprivation and solitary confinement. The UN Rules repeated the need for certification by a "medical officer" that a person was "fit to sustain it." Indeed, underlying the authority to aggravate "suffering" was a commitment to letting prison authorities use isolation. Bates had been insistent that in a "modern penitentiary system, it was often necessary to maintain isolation, a measure which undoubtably aggravated the suffering of the prisoner." The 1955 Rules added that a "medical official shall visit daily . . . and advise the director if he considers the termination or alteration of the punishment necessary on grounds of physical and mental health."[45] While aiming to increase medical oversight, rule drafters again refused to see (as some governments do now) that, if conditioning a punishment on permission from the medical profession, that incursion ought *ipse dixit* be prohibited.

Upon adopting the Rules and sending them to the General Assembly, the 1955 Congress requested that the Secretary-General ask for reports "every three years of the progress made with regard to their application."[46] Thus, on paper and thirty years after Margery Fry, Gertrude Eaton, and Cicely Craven had laid out aspirations for international protections for prisoners, transnational commitments did so. Many accounts credited only the IPPC, but the Howard League's journal took "pride in the success of the long efforts to gain adoption" of its "original proposal" for rules to "protect prisoners from degradation, unsanitary conditions, inadequate food and inhuman punishment." While regretting that the word "minimum" remained, the Howard League celebrated the UN's "new and complete code of standard minimum rules" that insisted on dignity, rights, and included a prohibition on corporal punishment of which, the League hoped, England's Home Secretary would "take notice."[47] Formal approval came in 1957 by the UN's Social and Economic Council; thereafter, the UN convened congresses every five years. Just as the IPPC had, the UN cast itself as an apolitical, expert body, even as it also tried during the Cold War to use its crime program as a "lever by democratic countries against those regarded as undemocratic."[48]

Yet a dreary paper trail has documented that, in addition to a lack of specificity, the 1955 Rules were not implemented in many parts of the world, including the United States. More than a decade later, a UN overview made that point. "The fundamental question remaining . . . is . . . how [the Rules] are to become less a statement of ideals than a description of practice." Implementation was one problem, the stature of the Rules as a human rights document another, and the impact on other UN work a third. The Rules never achieved the status of a stand-alone convention.[49]

Balancing of rights against correctional needs made its way into two other UN documents addressing detention. In 1966, in its International Covenant on Civil and Political Rights (ICCPR), the UN included protections for detained individuals and stated that no one be subjected to "torture or to cruel, inhuman or degrading treatment or punishment." When considering a separate convention on torture, the UN's 1975 Congress on Crime Prevention and the Treatment of Offenders proposed to prohibit public officials from "intentionally" inflicting "severe pain or suffering, whether physical or mental," either to extract evidence or to punish a person. Muddying the prohibitions, that draft exempted the pain and suffering "inherent in or incidental to, lawful sanctions to the extent consistent with the Standard Minimum Rules on the Treatment of Prisoners." The resulting 1984 Convention Against Torture and Other Cruel, Inhuman or Degrading Treatment or Punishment (UNCAT, or CAT) repeated that formulation.[50] The result was that governments could argue that food deprivation and solitary confinement did not violate CAT. (In the twenty-first century, the UN Rapporteur on CAT labeled prolonged solitary confinement torture, as did the 2015 revised Standard Minimum Rules).

What was gained and lost, and what changed when the UN replaced the IPPC as the voice of corrections? IPPC stalwarts had been concerned that the world's many needs would dilute the focus on crime and punishment. Indeed, UN work on crime and punishment did struggle for status. In the 1950s, the Division of Social Affairs was preoccupied with resettlement and refugee relief; that Division's influence waned when economic concerns came to dominate the UN's agenda. The Ad Hoc Experts Advisory Group, hamstrung by funding and bureaucratic demands, convened once every two years and could do little without approval from other parts of UN.[51] On the other hand, benefits were argued by Manuel López-Rey y Arrojo, the first Chief of the Social Defense Section. He rejected the "oversimplification of equating the UN's work with the IPPC." Under the UN's guidance, crime was reconceptualized as a "world-wide socio-political problem." Further, in lieu of the IPPC's Eurocentric pattern, the meetings had a "more universal character."[52]

All the while, several IPPC leaders never saw the limits of their vision. An example was the 1954 publication, "Prisons in Transformation," by *The Annals of the American Academy of Political and Social Science*. Edited by Sellin, the volume included seventeen essays about reform in the United States and "abroad." Sellin gave Bates the opening words. Despite a title—*The Prison: Asset or Liability?*—suggesting a critical stance, Bates harkened back to prisons as teaching "lessons in self-control through discipline, educating men for life in a democratic civilization, ridding diseased bodies and minds of bad inclinations, inculcating habits of work, and presenting valuable opportunities for research into the nature of crime and the causes of criminality." The "hard core of determined criminals" need institutionalization; "the public has no choice" as, while prisoners were "people," they were "bad people."[53] Another essay with a promising title—*The Legal Rights of Prisoners*, by Paul Tappen—described "vague legal specifications and areas of deep shade, where the law is wholly silent." Tappen reported that prisoners lost rights to own and convey property, marry, and vote and they had virtually no remedies if harmed; moreover, prison officials often blocked prisoners' efforts to assert rights.[54]

This compendium also underscored that facets of the UN's 1955 Rules were *far* from the mainstream in corrections. As I analyze in the book's next segment, prisoners thereafter pushed US constitutional law to align with UN positions and, echoing Bates, many correctional authorities resisted.

FROM THURGOOD MARSHALL IN STOCKHOLM TO WHIPPING IN ARKANSAS

Until 1965, the IPPC and the UN meetings on crime and punishment paid no attention to the role race played in populating prisons. That silence was modestly broken in 1965 when Thurgood Marshall gave an addresses at the UN's Third Congress on the Prevention of Crime and the Treatment of Offenders in Stockholm. Marshall, who chaired the US delegation that included other Black lawyers, was by then renowned in leading the NAACP's effort to end racial desegregation in schools and housing; such lawsuits had at times, invoked the UN Charter when attacking racist practices such as exclusionary zoning.[55] In 1961, President John F. Kennedy nominated Marshall to be a federal appellate judge. His service on that bench ended when in 1965, Marshall became the Department of Justice's Solicitor General. Soon thereafter, Marshall was confirmed as the first Black US Supreme Court Justice; as I discuss later, he was pivotal in that Court's 1968 ruling that Alabama's segregation of Black and white prisoners was unconstitutional.

In Sweden, Marshall was the first Black American to speak on behalf of the United States at such conferences and the first to make a brief comment on the intersection of racial discrimination and poverty that brought too many people into the criminal legal system. His presence reflected that after John Kennedy was assassinated, President Lyndon Johnson was pressed by Dr. Martin Luther King to respond to racial subordination; landmark civil rights legislation in 1964 and 1965 followed. Anxiety about race and street protests also prompted Johnson to create a Commission on Law Enforcement and Administration of Justice that Marshall touted when in Stockholm. (The 1967 report, *The Challenge of Crime in a Free Society*, not only tiptoed around racism in the legal system but helped to launch a national "war on crime" that resulted in the over-incarceration of millions, disproportionately of color.[56])

Marshall went to the UN meeting in the same year that Winston Talley, whose handwritten petition opened this book, filed his lawsuit to stop Arkansas from whipping him. The history provided in this section is the predicate to grasping the ambitions of the UN Rules and of prisoners like Winston Talley. From the 1800s to the 1950s, an interdisciplinary, international, philanthropic, scholarly, professional elite that was overwhelmingly white, male, and dominated by Western countries, shaped "corrections" as a profession tolerating vast amounts of in-prison violence. With few exceptions for more than two hundred years, people running prisons were oblivious to the status of prisoners as persons with rights and to subjugation by race, ethnicity, nationality, and class.

While a self-described "humanitarianism" distinguished corrections experts from many of their contemporaries, they did not recognize prisoners as peers, whose agency and autonomy had to be respected. Even as the 1955 Rules discussed prisoners' dignity and rights, corrections insisted on micro-control. Rather than adopting

Paul Cornil's stance that preservation of individuals' autonomy required a profound revamping of prisons or their demise, UN provisions (like the US constitutional law I will discuss) continued to bend rights to permit claims for security to govern. Thus, whether set forth in UN documents, national legislation, or judicial decisions, the question posed by the UN Secretariat in 1970 remains today: whether those articulations would remain a "statement of ideals" or become a "description of practice."[57]

PART II

CHALLENGING PUNITIVE VIOLENCE IN THE UNITED STATES, 1965–1970

After more than two hundred years during which theorists opined about punishment, correctional officials negotiated standards for prisons, and international bodies took up the issues, the stakes changed. Instead of *largess*, the question in the United States became the *legal obligations* owed to incarcerated individuals, who asked judges *to order* the end of whipping and horrific conditions. Judges sitting in a federal courthouse in Little Rock, Arkansas and elsewhere, along with state and federal legislators, politicians, and the public joined Cesare Beccaria, Jeremy Bentham, Alexis de Tocqueville, the Howard League, the IPPC, the League of Nations, and the UN in debating modes of incarceration. Even as correctional officials insisted on their unique ability to determine discipline, prisoners obtained legal protection against some forms of government abuse.

When I first learned that, in the 1960s, three US judges licensed whipping as long as it was rule-bound, I was shocked. My effort to understand those decisions brought me to Arkansas, the people it incarcerated, its unapologetic racism, and legislative refusals to fund minimal services in and out of prisons. In this segment, I provide details of the people whose lawsuits prompted discussions of legal constraints on punishment. I focus on the prisoners, politics, and law that shaped the 1965 hearing on whipping's constitutionality, the three-day 1967 trial and decision, the 1968 ruling banning whipping, and the 1970 opinion that the entire Arkansas prison system violated the US Constitution.

Delving into Arkansas' prison litigation illuminates the impact of what Enoch Wines had launched—correctional policymaking in national and international organizations through which people and ideas crossed the Atlantic. As forecast, James Bennett, who had been in Berlin in 1935, at The Hague in 1950, and at the UN in 1955, went to Arkansas in 1967 to testify for the prisoners, and Austin MacCormick, who had counseled the IPPC, was key to the Arkansas Legislature's 1967 blue-ribbon prison commission calling for rehabilitation in prison. Robert Sarver, selected in 1968 by Governor Winthrop Rockefeller to head the newly-created Arkansas Department of Correction, echoed views espoused in 1950 by the Belgian Paul Cornil—that prisons were sources of unacceptable harms. Arkansas is an exemplar because it was at the front end of prisoners' successful structural interventions and because conflicts there have been reiterated ever since.

FIGURE P2.1 *Cummins Prison Farm, Grady, Arkansas*, photograph by Bruce Jackson, from the series *Inside the Wire*, Collection Albright-Knox Art Gallery, Buffalo, New York, 1975, courtesy of the photographer

10

"AND THE WHIPP DESTROYED"
PRISONERS LAYING CLAIM TO PERSONHOOD

Arkansas' prison staff had "threaten[ed] the lives, safety and physical and mental well-being of inmates" and thereby violated the "public trust . . . ; the dignity of human rights, as well as civil [rights]; and the laws of the state and federal government, of ethics and the moral codes of society."

—Vernon Sloan's 1965 federal court petition[1]

This book began with Winston Talley's 1965 petition that, along with handwritten filings by two other white prisoners—Vernon Sloan and William Hash—landed in the federal court in Pine Bluff, Arkansas. Newspapers and genealogical records of these men give us glimpses of the outsized role that incarceration played as a penalty for low-level crime. Yet, unlike the state officials who opposed them, the whip that tortured them, the prison that confined them, the judges who heard the cases, the lawyers appointed to represent them, and the politicians who often ignored their pleas, these three pioneering prisoners left a thin paper trail.

Talley first made the news in September of 1959 when the North Little Rock Police arrested this "white youth" for writing a $10 bad check to buy $4 pants he wore running out of the store. Bail was set at $500. Talley pled guilty, acknowledged other checks (worth $36, $60, and $79), and in 1960 received a three-year sentence. Talley's rap sheet grew thereafter. Like many others, he escaped from the state prison farm at Cummins, which had no perimeter fencing. Sent back after pleading guilty to escape, assault, and participating in a prison-based burglary ring, Talley escaped again. In 1963, after pleading guilty to breaking into a local store, he received a seven-year sentence, plus a concurrent year for that escape.[2]

Vernon Sloan, born in 1936, made the local news for his many burglaries. In the 1950s, along with his younger brother, Sloan committed more than a dozen that netted the two $1,200. After claiming he could not control his compulsion to steal, Sloan pled guilty, received a five-year sentence, and made parole after two years. Rearrested for taking $8.80 and three packs of chewing gum, Sloan was back in Cummins by 1960.[3]

William Hash was born in Kentucky in 1931, enlisted in the army in 1948, served in the Korean War, and returned with shoulder injuries. In 1956, Arkansas charged Hash with forging a government check worth $271.12. In 1959, Hash received a five-year suspended sentence for presenting a $50 check from a bank at which he had no account. In 1962, the state alleged Hash stole a letter from a mailbox, revoked his suspended sentence, and sent him to Cummins. Hash arrived to serve five years, concurrent with a three-year federal sentence for theft of the letter.[4]

Talley, Sloan, and Hash reemerged in the news in 1965 through accounts of their federal lawsuits. We cannot know what prompted their challenges, nor can we be sure who penned their documents, or who got their materials to Chief Judge J. Smith Henley. We do know that obstacles abounded. Talley's mother told reporters that she had "arranged for a lawyer to draw up the petition . . . [she] slipped . . . into the Penitentiary for Talley to sign"—likely after receiving Talley's letter to "Mother" that became part of the federal court's file. At the October 13, 1965, hearing, Sloan stated his papers were "smuggled out by mail,"[5] and Talley testified that another prisoner lost his job for giving assistance. Confirmation came from Bob Scanlon, a lawyer imprisoned for embezzlement, who told the judge he was fired from his post for drafting petitions and the "pauper's oath" needed for waivers of filing fees.[6] Given that Arkansas segregated prisoners by race, white prisoners had access to people like Scanlon that Black prisoners would have lacked.

Talley's one-page "Writ of Prohibition" stated that James Pike, a prisoner–trusty who was a "field rider" and "a convicted murderer," had "beaten and stomped" on him, and that "state warden Mose Harmon" had whipped him. Hash's two-page "Writ of Prohibition" reported he was forced to work "in the fields as a slave" and had been flogged "by a state warden." Hash described allergies to plants and that he was a "war veteran and classed a 50 percent disability for right shoulder loss." Like Talley, he called for the court to stop "ALL use of said Whipp."[7]

Vernon Sloan's neatly lettered five-page "Petitioner's Complaint," accompanied by a "Petition for a Grand Jury Investigation," detailed that "men [were struck] with clubs made from hoe handles, broken fan belts, rubber hoses and fists." A section he called "Contentions and Allegations" asked for a federal grand jury and provided a list of ten prisoners (Hash and Talley included) to call as witnesses. As quoted, Sloan argued Superintendent Stephens and his agents had violated civil and human rights laws and society's "moral codes."[8]

On August 23, 1965, the state's lawyers admitted that Talley had been "punished," that Sloan had worked in the fields, and that his mail had been censored "for security purposes." (Hash's filing came in later.) The state denied liability and asked the court to dismiss the claims and award the "costs" of responding.[9]

MAKING "PROFITS" WITH THIRTY-ONE FREE-WORLD EMPLOYEES AND ARMED TRUSTYS

Talley, Sloan, and Hash were among about two thousand men and fifty women at Cummins, an expansive site on about 15,500 acres. Although the state's population was 80 percent white, Black prisoners outnumbered whites two to one. Prisoners lived in dorm-style barracks segregated by race under a 1903 statute mandating that, "in the State penitentiary . . . and in all county jails, stockades, convict camps, and all other places where State or county prisoners may at any time be kept confined, separate apartments shall be provided and maintained for white and negro prisoners." Another 340 white men, mostly first offenders, were at Tucker Farm, a 4,500-acre spread about thirty-five miles away, which was also where Arkansas' death row held eight Black men.[10]

"Free world" was the term for the thirty-one paid staff, all white. Arkansas' 1960s budget did not have a line for prisons. The cost was about $1.3 million a year, and prisons were "self-supporting" as well as providing "profits" for the state. Cummins prisoners farmed about 8,200 acres; Cummins devoted about 1,448 to cotton, 250 to cucumbers, and 120 to okra. Tucker had another 462 acres for cotton and sixty for cucumbers. Thus, decades after most states had abandoned "convict labor" as a revenue stream and before contemporary concerns about private prisons, the "public" prisons of Arkansas were funded by sales of crops produced through the forced labor of prisoners—whipped when they did not pick enough cotton, okra, and cucumbers to sell.

Some of those who cracked the whip were prisoner–trustys ("the system's elite"), overseeing fields and housing units. (The spelling of "trustys," common in Arkansas, serves as a reminder not to confuse these positions with "trustees," legally required to safeguard the interests of beneficiaries. Prison-as-plantation also existed in Alabama, Louisiana, Mississippi, and Texas, which had prisoner-guard-trustys and employed few "free-world" individuals.[11]) Below Arkansas' trustys were "do-pops"—"allowed to work without supervision but not eligible to supervise other inmates or to carry a gun." In the mid-1960s, Talley was among the trustys, numbering between 350 and 430 and many carrying guns. The group running Arkansas' prisons with guns, clubs, and whips had vast power and few rules. A committee of five people appointed by the governor constituted a Penitentiary Board, to which Arkansas delegated the authority to prescribe punishment for prisoners.[12]

"RULED BY THE WHIP"

"[T]he leather strap in the Arkansas prison is a story going back . . . [for] as long as anyone can remember."

—George Douthit, *Prison Whipping Aired by Prisoner at Court Hearing*, Arkansas Democrat, October 13, 1965[13]

Like Talley, Sloan, Hash, and Cummins Farm, the whip (or "bull hide") had a public presence before the 1965 lawsuits challenged its legality.[14] Indeed, brutal accounts surfaced repeatedly. In 1921, Arkansas' governor appointed a teacher, Laura Conner, as the "humanitarian" member to the Penitentiary Board. Connor recounted that Black prisoners sent an "SOS call" to bring doctors to examine "how rough their flesh" was from whipping. Based on her investigation, Conner wrote a report about the brutality at Cummins and Tucker and the sexual exploitation of women prisoners, including "colored girls and women" put into houses as servants. Despite a press headline that "17 convicts are whipped for answering questions asked by member of the board," a grand jury provided "vindication of Tucker Farm officials." Conner resigned thereafter.[15]

Headlines in 1958 again brought the violence into focus. The *Arkansas Democrat*'s story, "Ex-Convict's Book to 'Expose' Pen," explained that a New York publishing house had acquired *Ruled by the Whip: Hell Behind Bars in America's Devil Island, The Arkansas State Penitentiary*. The author, Dale Woodcock, was a white, college-educated man who had been incarcerated at Cummins from 1953 to 1955 for "theft of a microscope," a crime he said he had not committed. Reading Woodcock's 131-page account of Cummins is nauseating. On arrival, after a prisoner–trusty gave him dirty clothing but no "socks, towel, soap or toothbrush," Woodcock was sent to sleep in a dilapidated building with filthy mattresses shared by other prisoners. He detailed inedible beans and drinking cups encrusted with dirt, endless hours of fieldwork in burning sun, and intense, random cruelty.[16]

Woodcock witnessed scores of whippings, whose rituals included sadistic wardens pushing for people to plead "O Captain" for the blows to end. When first whipped, Woodcock had been determined not to "cry out or beg the warden to stop," but when whipped twice in one day, he did so. He described that after "twenty-seven lashes," he was left "on the concrete floor" with blood pouring from his rectum. During one six-month period, Woodcock counted six whippings of his own and 480 among the ninety men in his unit.[17]

Arkansas' whip had by then become politically controversial. Even as brutalities were common in prisons, whipping was not. In November of 1955, Governor Orval Faubus was reported to have "abolished whipping" but, as Woodlock recounted, when the news reached the prison, the warden "whipped twenty-seven men" to show he could. In 1958, amid publicity around Woodlock's book, Cummins' Warden Lee Henslee admitted he used "straps" for discipline, disavowed the brutality described, and sought the Penitentiary Board's imprimatur to continue. In 1962, the Board adopted a resolution authorizing the Prison Superintendent's power to use corporal punishment on "prisoners when, in his judgment, it is necessary to maintain discipline and proper respect for the policies of the Penitentiary."[18]

That authorization did not quell objections, which became a headache for Faubus. After Joe Hubbard tried to dislodge Faubus as the 1964 Democratic nominee by making whipping "a hot political issue," the Penitentiary Board suggested it had ordered whippings to stop. Faubus won the nomination and reelection. The new Superintendent, Dan O. Stephens, stated that, while "few and far between," whippings had their "place in a prison disciplinary system that did not have such punishments as solitary confinement."[19]

Talley's August 1965 filing, alleging that Stephens relied on the whip "to discipline unruly prisoners," prompted Faubus to comment he had been "unaware" the whip was back in use; he had "discontinued the leather strap . . . three times since I came into office, and apparently the superintendents have found it helpful and necessary to reinstate it." After Talley's October 1965 hearing, the Penitentiary Board's Chair told a reporter that he was "vaguely familiar with an Arkansas law which places responsibility on the prison board for prescribing the punishment of convicts." He remembered that "an endorsement of corporal punishment" was put into the minutes "at the request of Superintendent Lee Henslee, afraid something was going to come out "about the prison's method of punishment."[20] That "something" could have been criminal charges, as Arkansas statutes made it a felony for prison staff to impose punishment in excess of what the Board authorized.

"CAP'N DAN": "HOPE TO THE BOYS" AND PROFITS FOR ARKANSAS

The salience to the twenty-first century of the named defendant, Superintendent Dan Stephens, comes from his repeated endorsements of Arkansas' sweat labor, trustys, and "the whip." When first reading 1950s press clippings about Stephens, I thought I had the wrong person as he did not fit the profile of other Arkansas wardens. Unlike his predecessor, Henslee, who had been a sheriff before running Arkansas' prisons for almost three decades, Stephens was a former teacher and state legislator.

Active in Democratic politics, Stephens was a local prosecutor and in 1959 the Governor's Executive Assistant for parole and prisons. Stephens headed the Democratic Party's Arkansas office for John F. Kennedy and, after the presidential election, hoped to be appointed to a federal post. In Washington, however, Stephens' identification with Faubus, infamous for his defiance of federal authority, was toxic. Faubus' consolation for Stephens was appointment as General Counsel to the Arkansas Public Service Commission and, within six months, General Counsel for the State Highway Commission. After Henslee, citing ill health, resigned at age fifty-nine, Stephens ended up with the prison post and took up residence at Cummins Farm in 1962.[21]

Legislators pressured Stephens to "perpetuate" Henslee's "praiseworthy record," which had "put the system on its feet." Newspaper readers learned that Arkansas was the "only state in the nation with a consistently self-supporting, profit-making penal program." The sale of crops more than covered costs; income was $1,908,729.15 and expenditures, $1,637,924.24. The press credited Henslee with keeping "peace" through putting "shotguns, rifles and pistols" in the "hands of convicts"—the trustys.[22] Within the year, however, the story darkened. Henslee killed himself with a shotgun.[23] The violence and corruption of Henslee's era, documented thereafter by the state's police, made headlines, and many of his successors "perpetuated" practices endangering the safety of prisoners.

Stephens was troubled by aspects of the system. He reported that, with an average age of twenty-six, education levels averaged 6.5 years; fifty-nine of the prisoners were "illiterates," while nineteen had attended college. (Stephen made no mention of race or of the fifty women housed in a converted chicken coop.) Worried that buildings could ignite from rotten wood and bad wiring, Stephens asked the Arkansas Legislature for money. He estimated repairs would cost $150,000 for the "hospital," a structure that merited no such name. Assuring his former legislative colleagues that prisoners' labor would make up the difference, Stephens got a special appropriation of $50,000. A 1963 Sunday magazine spread in the *Arkansas Democrat* showed rows of cots in the "spotless" dormitories and a "shining stainless steel kitchen" where "nourishing meals" were prepared. In addition, instead of released prisoners being "turned loose at the gate to fend for themselves," Stephens arranged for each to be given $15, some "decent" clothes, and dropped off at the closest town, Pine Bluff.[24]

That "gate fund" reflected that prisoners had no means to earn money. Instead of paying for farm work, Stephens devised a scheme for them to sell blood. In the fall of 1963, Stephens entered into an agreement, approved by the Arkansas Board of Pardons and Parole, with the Stough-Wisdom Research Company so that "volunteers" could receive $5 a week for having their blood drawn. Neither the words "volunteer" nor "blood donors" were apt; "every man" signed up. The prison skimmed fifty cents off until the prisoner had accumulated $10 (toward his "gate fund") and another $1 to go to the "welfare fund." The remaining $3.50 went to the prisoner. Within five weeks, the press reported prisoners had "earned $13,000" through blood sales. Stephens made another splash in the spring of 1965 by bringing prisoners to high schools to talk about their crimes and regrets. Photographs of "Operation Teen Age" showed four white men telling students to "avoid alcohol" and obey the law. (One was the lawyer–prisoner Scanlon.) Such activities garnered Stephens praise: This "short, heavy-set fellow with cowboy boots and a big hat and a burning, longtime concern about what will happen to 'the boys' in the prison when they get out" was bringing "hope."[25]

Stephens did not, however, touch the underlying organization, dependent on unmechanized farms to turn profits and on trustys and wardens driving people to meet production quotas of 100 pounds of cotton a day. Indeed, Stephens bragged that, with thirty-one free-world employees and a ratio of about seventy prisoners to one employee, Cummins was a less-troubled prison "than any other prison our size in the nation."[26]

Incarcerated people, however, were in fact troubled. The press chronicled the backbreaking labor, shown in figure P2.1. Prisoners called "rankers" were "marched to the fields" six days a week to work ten hours a day in what was called the "long line." In "squads of 20 each," men handpicked cotton, cucumbers, okra, and straw-berries under the authority of the trusty "line riders" and the few free-world "wardens," with a superintendent at the top of the peck-ing order. One journalist noted it took "600 men working six days a week for three months to pick the cotton that machines could pick in a few days."[27] The prisoners were not fed the food they produced, which was either sold, given to free-world staff and trustys, or used as bribes for local businesses and inside the prison.

In Stephens' first year, the prison reported a profit of $138,951, an $80,000 increase from 1962. In 1964, 200 acres of cucumbers yielded a record 4,188,777 pounds, sold to Atkins Pickle Company for $128,487.47. Cotton brought in another $456,000, contributing to in-come of more than $1.5 million. In January of 1965, Stephens bragged that during the past decade, "this institution hasn't cost the state a penny." That February, an editorial in the *Arkansas Gazette* credited Stephens with "doing good work," even as the press recorded a steady stream of prisoners (including Winston Talley) as they escaped, orga-nized burglaries from within, brutalized and, on occasion, murdered one another.[28] Moreover, as Chief Judge Henley stated in his 1965

Talley v. Stephens ruling, if a prisoner's "performance [was] not satisfactory to his Assistant Warden, he may be whipped."[29] The imposition of this "discipline" was summary, unregulated, and unlimited.

Talley's lawsuit pushed Stephens out. Ten days before the October 13, 1965, hearing, the *Pine Bluff Commercial* printed a cartoon mocking Stephens. Within a couple days, two prisoners wrote to credit Stephens (referred to as "Cap'n Dan") for improving their lives by building "a new slaughter-house, . . . [an] up-to-date, fire-proof hospital, a combined auditorium, theatre and church," starting "a school to teach illiterate adults," and cracking down "on homosexual activities." A day later, complaining about "harassment," Stephens tendered his resignation, effective January 1, 1966. Soon thereafter, the press reported that some 321 prisoners had written letters (evidently copied from each other, as most misspelled the word "appreciate") calling on Governor Faubus to "halt" Stephens' resignation. The governor praised Stephens ("your service as prison superintendent has been outstanding") and, joined by all five Penitentiary Board members, asked him to reconsider. Stephens declined. While defending strapping in the press, Stephens did not testify at the October hearing.[30]

In short, the violence of Arkansas' prisons was well-known and its predicate, forced labor, extolled by state leaders.

11

WHIPPING PERMITTED, WHEN NEITHER EXCESSIVE NOR ARBITRARY

"I do hope . . . that if I am remembered at all it won't be only for that [prison] case, I'm afraid it will, that group of cases, but that's all right too. [There's] a saying . . . that 'A person is not dead so long as his name is remembered,' so maybe they'll keep me alive, the prison cases will keep me alive awhile."

—J. Smith Henley's 1987 Oral History[1]

JUDGING WHIPPING AND PRISONS

Chief Judge Henley correctly anticipated that his legacy would be the prison cases; at his death in 1997, the *Arkansas Democrat-Gazette* announced, "Judge Who Reformed Prison System Dies."[2] One might assume that ending whipping would *not* have been hard the decade after the UN's Standard Minimum Rules for the Treatment of Prisoners called for its abolition. Indeed, by 1965, a chorus of penologists, criminologists, psychologists, psychiatrists, pediatricians, religious leaders, and philosophers had identified the harms.

But it was not easy. In this and the chapters that follow, I delve into why federal judges struggled with whipping's legality. As I forecast, they worried that banning this in-prison punishment could (as it did) open the door to challenging other prison practices. Moreover, in 1965, Arkansas was not alone in using that "discipline." In the UK, prison officials had license to do so until 1967. Canada permitted judges to impose sentences of flogging until 1972. Back in the United States, the Supreme Court refused in 1977 to forbid teachers from "paddling" students deemed "recalcitrant." In the twenty-first century, the Canadian Supreme Court rejected arguments that hitting children violated its Charter of Rights and Freedoms protecting "security of the person" or the UN Convention on the Rights of the Child. Instead, that court left standing a statute permitting parents and guardians to use "corrective force" on children if by hand (no belts, rulers, or whips), "reasonable," "transitory, and trifling" in nature. In 2015, Singapore's highest court ruled statutory authorization of caning violated neither its constitution nor international human rights norms. In the United States, capital punishment remains constitutional.[3]

Winston Talley, William Warren Hash, and Vernon Sloan aimed to dislodge this embeddedness of violent punishments. Chief Judge Henley distinguished himself from many of his colleagues by not rejecting their petitions but linking them together, enlisting outstanding Arkansas lawyers to represent them, and ordering a state response. Then Henley disappoints. After taking testimony on October 13, 1965, and concluding that prisoners had the constitutional right to be *in* court, he did not agree that they had a right to be free *from* whipping. Reasoning that discipline was up to prison authorities, Henley concluded that officials merited "wide latitude and discretion," albeit with guardrails he fashioned that echoed the International Penal and Penitentiary Commission (IPPC) and UN Rules, even as he likely did not know them. Henley ruled that whippings could only be imposed based on "standards" and with specified "safeguards" to buffer against angry, arbitrary decision-making, coupled with a limit on the lashes imposed.[4]

By way of a preview, Arkansas did not appeal. In 1967, three more white prisoners, William King Jackson, Lyle Edward Ernst Jr., and Grady W. Mask, argued that the state had not complied and (again) that its whippings were unconstitutional. Two of Henley's colleagues on the Arkansas federal bench—Judges Oren Harris and Gordon Young—followed his approach. They called on prominent lawyers to represent the prisoners and held a trial—producing the only transcript of a challenge to whipping's legality in US history. Like Henley, these two judges condoned whipping as long as it was regulated. In 1968, the appellate court disagreed and outlawed whipping.

The following year, Henley clumped together several prisoners' petitions protesting abysmal conditions in "solitary cells"—where four to eight men were crammed into a small space with filthy mattresses and toilets they could not flush. Henley enlisted more lawyers, found the conditions unconstitutional, and ordered a report on progress from the new Commissioner of the recently created Arkansas Department of Correction. Six months later, with more than twenty additional prisoners before him, Henley called on other lawyers to bring a class action, required the prison open its doors, and in 1970, ruled Arkansas' prisons "a dark and evil world" that was unconstitutional. Yet, within three years, Henley concluded that sufficient progress had been made to end the case, only to be reversed by the appellate court, chastising him for retreating too soon. Thereafter, Henley oversaw implementation until after he was appointed to sit on the circuit and turned the case over to another federal judge, Thomas Eisele.[5]

When I went to Little Rock in 2019 to research this book, I had questions about Henley. He does not have the visibility in legal circles of several other Republican-appointed judges, described as "unlikely heroes" of the 1960s Civil Rights Movement when they insisted—at personal peril—that schools be desegregated.[6] Henley did not press for desegregation. Yet he was pathbreaking in providing lawyers for prisoners and, although initially deferential to the state on whipping, he became the first judge in the United States to hold a state's "entire System" in violation of the US Constitution and then spent years dealing with the implications.[7]

I pieced together some insights about Henley through an amalgam of sources. The state's press—including the Pulitzer Prize–winning *Arkansas Gazette*, along with the *Arkansas Democrat*, the *Pine Bluff Commercial*, and the *El Dorado Times*—devoted hundreds of stories to the exploitation, brutality, escapes, and violence at the state's prisons, as well as the "profits" generated by prison farms.[8] More about life in the prisons came when prisoners published their own newspaper, *The Pea*

Pickers Picayune, later renamed the *Cummins Journal*. These prisoners understood that pleas for changes needed to be directed not only to judges but also to other prisoners, staff, lawyers, the media, members of the public, the governor, and legislators.

To augment accounts from these outlets (through which, over the years, information unfolds like a bad serial novel), I visited the town of Pine Bluff, the prison at Cummins Farm, and the state's libraries and historical society. More of the horrors of Arkansas' prisons spilled out, including in archivally correct boxes preserving the whips and torture devices admitted into evidence in criminal trials against prison staff. I met the two lawyers (Philip Kaplan and Jack Holt, then in their eighties) who had represented the prisoners in the class action. I spoke with a reporter, Ernie Dumas, whose beat included Henley's court, and to relatives of Edward Wright, the lawyer who represented William King Jackson in the 1967 whipping trial and appeal. The incarcerated individuals bringing the lawsuits were not, to my knowledge, alive, but I found routes to some family members. Below, I chart the interplay among these individuals, constitutional law, racism, criminal law enforcement, and state politics that explains why Henley—along with Talley and many others—should be kept "alive" for limiting some of incarceration's horrors.

EMBEDDED IN RACIALIZED POLITICS: HENLEY'S HISTORY, ARKANSAS' HISTORY, US HISTORY

One of many judges appointed by President Dwight Eisenhower, Henley started his judicial service in 1958, served sixteen years as the Chief Judge of Arkansas' federal trial court, and more than two decades on the Eighth Circuit. That appellate court stretched from Arkansas to the Canadian border because, after the Civil War, Congress grouped Arkansas, a former Confederate state, with Iowa, Missouri, Minnesota, Nebraska, and North and South Dakota, all overseen by federally appointed judges drawn from across those states.[9]

Practices of segregation framed Henley's career both when en route to and during his time on the bench. Born in 1917, Henley grew up in St. Joe in one of Arkansas' poorest areas, Searcy County.

People who knew Henley thought his birthplace explained his appreciation for economically strapped litigants, prisoners included. As one federal court judge recalled, he was the judge on an appellate panel who wanted to reverse a conviction of a defendant who "had only stolen 'a few slices of ham.'"[10]

Searcy was impoverished, and it was racist. Between 1877 and 1950, 492 lynchings took place in Arkansas—the fourth-highest tally in Southern states.[11] Known as a "sundown county," Searcy imposed curfews on Black people. Searcy was also the site of interfamily "blood" feuds, including between the white Henleys and Barnetts. In one encounter, Henley's cousin, Leland, was accused of murdering a bystander. Arrested in 1932, Leland was apprehended, convicted, sentenced to life imprisonment, and released after a few years. Thus, as one of the prisoners' lawyers told me, long before Chief Judge Henley assessed Arkansas' prisons, a family member had served time at Tucker Farm.[12]

In his oral history, Henley did not talk about racism, poverty, and violence, but recounted that his great-grandfather had moved to Missouri to be out of the Confederate Army's reach. On return, his family prospered. Early in life, Henley distinguished himself as smart; he entered the University of Arkansas at age fourteen. Henley was also undisciplined—kicked out before returning and graduating in 1941 from the state's law school in Fayetteville. Henley, whose medical deferment kept him out of World War II, practiced law in Harrison, a few hours north of Little Rock. (In 2000, an Act of Congress named a Harrison facility the J. Smith Henley Federal Building and United States Courthouse.[13]) Harrison shared Searcy County's history of racism. White mobs, erupting in 1905 and 1909, pushed Black residents to flee. A century later, Harrison remained more than 95 percent white.[14]

In the 1940s, Henley had a general law practice ("whatever came in the front door") before becoming the city's attorney. In 1954, the Eisenhower Administration recruited him to be the Associate General Counsel of the Federal Communications Commission and then to run the Department of Justice's Office of Administrative Procedure. In 1958, Eisenhower nominated Henley for the Eastern

District of Arkansas—"perhaps the roughest judicial post in the United States" because of school desegregation conflicts.[15] Henley had appeal in part because he was a member of a then-unusual family in Arkansas; his brother chaired the state's Republican Party. Henley ran into opposition from Arkansas' Democratic Senator John McClellan who, in 1956, had joined eighteen other senators and eighty-two members of the House of Representatives in signing the Southern Manifesto; read into the Congressional Record, it called for "massive resistance" to the 1954 Supreme Court desegregation decision, *Brown v. Board of Education.*

Senator McClellan hoped to put segregationists on the federal courts, and he did not think Henley was one. The Senator accused Henley (falsely) of working on a Justice Department's legal opinion in support of sending federal troops to desegregate Little Rock's Central High School. Blocked from obtaining Senate confirmation, Eisenhower appointed Henley during the Senate's 1958 recess. In 1959, as part of a package with the Democrat Gordon Young, Henley won Senate confirmation to sit in both the Western and Eastern Districts of Arkansas; Young was confirmed for the Eastern District.[16] In 1965, these two were joined by Oren Harris, a powerful member of the US House of Representatives whom Lyndon Johnson nominated for the federal bench. Henley decided the first whipping case—*Talley v. Stephens*—in 1965, and Young and Harris presided together in 1967 at the second whipping case, *Jackson v. Bishop.*

Once on the bench, Henley's decisions documented the breadth of racist practices in Arkansas' lunchrooms, schools, parks, and prisons. A few related to what are called "public accommodations" where, as Henley and many others put it, the "mixing of the races" might take place. In the early 1960s, "twenty-two Negro residents" asked Judge Henley to order desegregation of Little Rock's parks and golf courses; Henley ruled that municipal facilities and the state capital's cafeteria could no longer be open only to whites. The following year, Congress enacted the landmark Civil Rights Act of 1964, banning discrimination in public accommodations, and the Supreme Court affirmed that Congress had the constitutional authority to do so based on its power over interstate commerce.

The Arkansas Capitol lunchroom returned to Henley's docket because the governing board incorporated it as "Capitol Club, Inc.," nominally "private" and open only to white people. After sit-ins, violence, state troopers, and a trial, Henley ordered the cafeteria desegregated in 1965. Yet Henley rejected an effort by Black residents to apply that nondiscrimination mandate to desegregate a 232-acre amusement park ("Lake Nixon") near Little Rock. After a trial in 1967, Henley found that while it fit the statutory definition of a public accommodation, it had too little to do with interstate commerce to be covered by federal law. The US Supreme Court reversed.[17]

Henley's responses to high-visibility school desegregation lawsuits were replete with deference to state authorities. School cases, termed "structural reform litigation" to denote that reorienting practices take years to implement, became models for prisoners' rights lawyers who likewise struggled with defendants' lack of compliance with court orders. Moreover, as Henley exemplifies, many judges, toggling between school and prison cases, were asked not only to issue but also to enforce orders.

Illustrative was a case involving the Dollarway School District, near Pine Bluff, the town closest to the Cummins prison. The railroads made Pine Bluff a major lumber market and, in the 1940s, it was thriving and the site of Arkansas' only institution of higher learning in which Black residents could enroll—the Agricultural, Mechanical, and Normal College (Arkansas AM&N), founded in 1875. Pine Bluff thus became the home of Black teachers and other middle-class professionals. By the 1960s, some 2,000 children— about half white and half Black—were in segregated schools. After the parents of three Black high school students succeeded in objecting to the School Board's refusal to admit their children to an all-white school, Henley was slow to press for remedies. The Eighth Circuit reversed and insisted on affirmative desegregation efforts.[18] By 1975, Henley had shifted somewhat; in an opinion issued that year, he used "black" (lower case) instead of "Negro" and ruled in favor of a Black coach suing the Dollarway Board of Education for racial discrimination in hiring, compensation, and promotion.[19]

When I visited in 2019 en route to Cummins, Pine Bluff was eerily empty, with many deserted and boarded up buildings. It remained the site of Arkansas' second largest state university campus; the only local downtown eatery we could find open for lunch that day was Miss Margaret's Cupcakes, a two-person operation offering sandwiches and specialties like a bacon cupcake. The town's decay had begun decades earlier. In the 1960s, the federal government had tried to infuse resources—in part by siting a three-story post office and courthouse building near the town's substandard housing—that, like other urban renewal efforts, did not stop the decline.[20] In 2020, Arkansas' Education Board merged the Dollarway schools, disproportionately of color, into the Pine Bluff School District. By that time, a 1966 federal building had been named after George Howard Jr., one of Pine Bluff's few Black lawyers who had helped both the state's children and its prisoners. Howard became the first Black man appointed to serve on Arkansas' Supreme Court, the state's court of appeals, and the federal bench in Arkansas where he, like Henley, sat in both the Eastern and Western Districts.[21]

HEARING ABOUT WHIPPING, ENLISTING LAWYERS, AND BUILDING ON PRECEDENTS

Long before Henley took evidence in October of 1965, he had known about Cummins and Tucker Farms, and not only because his cousin Leland had been incarcerated. The press had detailed that the whip became an issue in the 1964 Democratic primary for the governorship, that commitments were made to stop its use, and that Dan Stephens, the Superintendent in 1965, continued to permit it.

Henley would also have known that, by the time Talley, Hash, and Sloan smuggled out their petitions, the US Supreme Court had issued four key decisions about prisoners' rights. In 1958, Chief Justice Earl Warren wrote for a plurality of justices in *Trop v. Dulles*, interpreting the Eighth Amendment's Cruel and Unusual Punishment Clause to mean that "evolving standards of decency" limited the federal government. In 1962, the Court concluded that the Clause also constrained what *states* could do. And, through the interaction of two other decisions, *Monroe v. Pape* in 1961 and *Cooper v. Pate* in 1964, the rule emerged that people—prisoners included—could use federal civil rights statutes (enacted after the Civil War) to bring lawsuits challenging state officials for violating constitutional rights.[22]

Unlike his restrictive reading of Supreme Court precedents in desegregation cases, Henley saw that remedies could be available for Talley, Hash, and Sloan. The judge innovated by recruiting two of Arkansas' most admired lawyers—Bruce T. Bullion Jr., who was President of the Arkansas Bar Association in 1964, and Louis Ramsay Jr., the 1965 President—to represent the prisoners and lend gravitas to their claims.[23] Neither were civil rights lawyers, but both had a visibility in the state beyond the bar. Their backgrounds open windows into the politics of the era and illustrate how entangled lawyers were with the judges before whom they appeared.

Bullion, the son of Arkansas' first insurance commissioner, had championed court reform when he was president of the state's bar. Bullion endorsed Henley in 1959 when, in addition to Senator McClellan, opposition came from Thomas Dale Alford, a "hard-line segregationist" who won a seat in the US House of Representative through his 1950s write-in campaign that ousted Brook Hays, a moderate voice. Bullion wrote James Eastland, chairing the Senate Judiciary Committee, that as a "life-long Democrat," he who would have preferred "a Federal Judge in this District with the same political philosophy" but that Henley, having demonstrated fairness and integrity when sitting temporarily in 1958, should be confirmed.[24] (In 1969, Henley turned to Hays' son to represent the prisoners; two years earlier, Judges Harris and Young asked Alford, also an eye doctor, to examine one of the prisoner–plaintiffs who said he could not see the okra he had been whipped for not picking.)

Henley may also have sought out Bullion because he was not quite the conventional Arkansas lawyer. In July of 1963, Bullion admitted he was getting "into deep water" when he called on the bar to "come out of hiding" and take a "greater role in commenting on current events." He suggested surveys to learn what his "fellow lawyers" thought about the "legislation on Civil Rights" proposed by President Kennedy. Bullion later championed free speech and won in the US Supreme Court, which ruled that Arkansas' prohibition on teaching evolution violated a tenth-grade biology teacher's constitutional rights.[25]

Chief Judge Henley's appointment of Ramsay as co-counsel put on the team a person known not only because he was a bar president and vocal proponent of judicial reform but also because he had been a quarterback for the University of Arkansas' Razorbacks. A World War II combat pilot, Ramsay mixed his law practice with being a bank's president. Ramsay also served on Arkansas' University's Board of Trustees, chaired the state's Sesquicentennial Commission in 1985 at the behest of Governor Bill Clinton, and in 1989, his hometown of Pine Bluff voted him the "City's Most Influential Citizen." At his death in 2004, members of the Arkansas House of Representatives entered his many accomplishments into the Congressional Record—without mention of his pro bono representation of prisoners.[26]

Even as judges are better off with lawyers, rather than people representing themselves, Henley's decision has to be appreciated for equipping the three pioneering prisoners with the means to exercise what the Supreme Court had said was their right of access to courts. Henley also hoped doing so would avert the need for other prisoners to seek federal judicial help. While "based on an individual's complaint" and not a class action, Henley noted the decision would likely result in "some type of precedent." On September 30, 1965, Henley entered a "pre-trial conference order" outlining the issues: (1) whether prison officials had "unconstitutionally circumscribed" the prisoners' access to courts; (2) whether the US Constitution forbade all corporal punishment or, if not; (3) whether the whippings were "excessive or unjustified or out of proportion to the offenses . . . as to amount to 'cruel and unusual punishment.'"[27]

Thus, about sixty days after the whipping petition had been filed, two corporate lawyers and a straight-laced judge were in a courtroom, along with Winston Talley (described as a "tall, well-built, blond-haired man") and several other white prisoners. Evidence from Sloan and Hash was deferred because their lawyers wanted a doctor to examine them. The named defendant, Superintendent

Dan Stephens (who, as noted, tendered his resignation while the suit was pending) was present with two members of the Arkansas Attorney General's Office, R. E. Wallin and Fletcher Jackson. While their careers did not mirror the prominence of opposing counsel, their boss was high profile. Elected Attorney General first in 1956 and 1958 and seeking unsuccessfully to be governor in the 1960s, Bruce Bennett was, according to the *New York Times*, a "segregationist firebrand" who opposed teaching evolution and had called the NAACP and other organizations "enemies" tied to Communism.[28]

HAVING "THEIR SAY": HOW, WHEN, AND WHY THEY WERE WHIPPED

One news report (captioned "prisoners have their say") included the photograph reproduced in figure 11.1 of six white men garbed in white jumpsuits (with ASP for Arkansas State Prison printed on the back) and sitting "outside the courtroom waiting to testify." An Arkansas reporter noted that no "Negroes were involved in any of

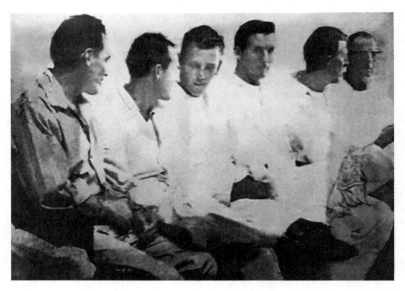

FIGURE 11.1 *Prisoners Have Their Say*, October 14, 1965, accompanying a Commercial Appeal (Memphis, Tennessee) article, University of Arkansas at Little Rock (UALR), Winthrop Rockefeller Collection, Record Group IV, courtesy of UALR Center for Arkansas History and Culture

the hearing," which took place in a "small courtroom . . . crowded with spectators, including several women."[29]

No transcript of the October 13th hearing appeared in the court's archived files; the notes from a subsequent session on November 1, 1965, were in a form of stenography that no person I contacted (including a stenographer at work in that era) could decipher. However, the extensive press coverage of "convicts" trying to end the "strapping," along Henley's decision, provide a good deal of depressing detail.

Winston Talley described repeated whippings. "Captain" Mose Harmon had told him to get down on the ground, and the twelve to fifteen strikes felt like "somebody pouring hot grease on you . . . I turned black and the tissue turned hard." Talley reported that he had been denied medical treatment. Other prisoners, including Frank C. Van Cleve, Joe Ferguson, Bob Fowler, Jack Ruark, and Bob Scanlon (the lawyer mentioned earlier), corroborated the violence against Talley, retaliation for going to court, and lack of medical attention. Superintendent Stephens, who did not take the stand, told the press he "won't apologize" for whipping. "Every one of those that were whipped know they needed it. We keep a record of the whippings and no prisoner is allowed to whip another prisoner." One reporter summarized the evidence as establishing that "most whippings [were] administered because the convict being whipped hadn't picked enough cotton to satisfy the wardens."[30] Attorney General Bennett complained the coverage failed to reflect Arkansas' "good, efficient and humane penal institution." An *Arkansas Gazette* editorial described the hearing as having lifted "the lid off Hell for the day."[31]

Within two weeks, that lid opened wider. On November 1, 1965, Chief Judge Henley ordered the state's response to Talley's accusation that after the October hearing, Captain Harmon had whipped him for "lying on the stand and making fun of him." Previewing the opinion he would file two weeks later, Henley explained he was "not prepared at the moment to enjoin corporal punishment at the prison" but believed "prisoners should know what was expected of them so that they could avoid floggings." A few days later, Superintendent Stephens filed the required "statements of parties and witnesses" about the "punishment of Winston Talley." Those materials confirmed that Harmon had hit Talley nine times with the strap; Harmon said he had done so not because Talley had testified but because he was "insolent" and had advocated a work slowdown.[32]

THE *TALLEY* RULES

In his November 15, 1965, opinion, Chief Judge Henley repeated what he said at the hearing—that while not "a class action," the decision would "have a collateral effect on the future treatment of other inmates." The judge addressed four issues: his power to hear the merits, the permissibility of forced labor, the constitutionality of whipping, and whether officials tried to block access to courts and retaliated thereafter. Citing a string of recent precedents, Henley explained his authority.

> Although persons convicted of crimes lose many of the rights and privileges of law-abiding citizens, it is established by now that they do not lose all of their civil rights, and that the Due Process and Equal Protection Clauses of the Fourteenth Amendment follow them into the prison and protect them there from unconstitutional administrative action on the part of prison authorities carried out under color of State law, custom, or usage.

Henley gave some solace to both sides. He specified that prisoners had legal protection from "cruel and unusual punishments for violations of prison rules" and from "invidious" discrimination, as well as affirmative rights to go to court to challenge sentences and protect other constitutional guarantees. Yet, Henley explained, "convicts must be disciplined," and prison officials had "wide latitude and discretion in the management and operation of their institutions, including the disciplining of inmates."[33]

Turning from the governing law to the facts, Henley noted disagreements about how many *times* Talley had been whipped since his 1961 arrival at Cummins. Talley testified it was more than seventy times; Assistant Warden Mose Harmon said whippings had happened "only six or seven times." Concluding that Talley was not "particularly worthy of belief" nor was Harmon (who had "patent interest" and whose conduct was called "into serious question"), Henley said the differences were not "material" to the legal questions. Everyone agreed that, at times, prisoners were whipped by a "leather strap five feet in length, four inches wide, and about one-fourth inch thick, attached to a wooden handle . . . about six inches long."[34]

The legal questions of access to courts and retaliation appeared easy for Henley, who devoted little of his decision to explaining *why* prison officials could not lawfully screen prisoners' filings. Chief Judge Henley held unconstitutional regulations authorizing prison officials to ensure filings had "no derogatory, insulting or slanderous remarks concerning the Judiciary or law enforcement officials," and rejected officials' explanation that they usefully screened for "obscene, abusive, or otherwise objectionable allegations or statements." Henley recorded that, on August 6, 1965, when the prison was notified of lawsuits filed, officials separated Talley and others into "special squads," treated worse than others. After the October hearing, Henley held that even if Talley was "agitating to some extent," Harmon ought not to have whipped him. Those factual findings translated into Henley's ruling that prisoners had rights to "unrestricted access to the Courts, whether State or federal, for the purpose of seeking judicial determinations or relief with respect to their confinement or with respect to alleged deprivations of civil rights within the Penitentiary."[35]

What did the Constitution have to say about forced labor, violence, and whipping? Henley did not have to decide the labor question because the skilled lawyers he picked peeled off that issue by negotiating a settlement on behalf of Hash and Sloan, who had been scheduled to testify November 1, 1965. After hearing several prisoners on October 13 recount so much violence, Henley had called off that plan for more testimony and, in late October, Attorney General Bennett consented to a judgment that neither Hash nor Sloan would be assigned work they were "not physically able to perform." The press reported that Sloan, who had broken an ankle when attempting to escape from a Georgia prison, had a misshapen foot, been denied access to doctors and courts, and was subjected to physical abuse. The press quoted Bennett that he wanted to avoid more publicity from two "partially crippled" prisoners, one a Korean War veteran: "Even if he had the whipping coming because of his conduct, it still wouldn't seem right to the public."[36]

Henley recorded that agreement in his published opinion and issued a warning: Compelling people to work "beyond their strength" would breach the Cruel and Unusual Punishment Clause and violate the substantive liberty protected by the Fourteenth Amendment. In the order that followed, the judge mandated that Sloan and Hash not be required to "perform labor . . . inconsistent with their respective physical conditions" and directed Stephens to ensure "reasonable medical attention for injuries, disabilities, and illness at all reasonable times."[37]

Remaining was the constitutionality of whipping, which Henley equated with corporal punishment. Henley's conclusion was that the Constitution tolerated whipping if done according to "safeguards." His explanation was, as law professors say, under-theorized (i.e., analytically wobbly). Henley wrote that to determine whether whipping was cruel and unusual punishment, he had to decide whether it had become "abhorrent to the modern mind."[38] Before getting to his answer (which was "no, but"), more needs to be said about where that formulation came from, and how the judge—or we—could know what is "abhorrent to the modern mind."

Henley's test reflected a decision he did not cite but would have been on his "modern mind"—the 1958 *Trop v. Dulles* plurality opinion I discussed. The Court held unconstitutional a federal statute imposing denationalization of a "native-born American," Albert Trop, who had walked off a stockade in Casablanca during World War II. On behalf of himself and Justices Black, Douglas, and Whittaker, Chief Justice Warren wrote that the Eighth Amendment "must draw its meaning from evolving standards of decency that mark the progress of a maturing society." Reasoning that the Eighth Amendment's "basic concept" was "nothing less than the dignity of man," denationalization was impermissible because it destroyed an "individual's status in organized society . . . [T]he expatriate has lost the right to have rights."[39] Warren's phrasing evoked (without citation) Hannah Arendt's 1951 book, *The Origins of Totalitarianism*, which famously used the "rights to have rights" formulation. *Trop* was one of several decisions reacting to the searing experiences of World War II by reading the US Constitution to require some insulation against state aggression for individuals held by the government.

Warren also drew on *Weems v. United States*, one of a few Supreme Court decisions addressing the constitutional limits of punishment. Paul Weems had been convicted of falsifying a "public document"; he was sentenced in the Philippines, then a US territory, to twelve years of "hard and painful labor," with a "chain at the ankle, hanging from the wrists" and a permanent loss of all civil rights. In 1910, the Court responded that "a precept of justice [is] that punishment for crime should be graduated and proportioned to [the] offense." Describing the need to reformulate punishments as "public opinion becomes enlightened by a humane justice," the *Weems* Court termed Weems' punishment excessive and "unusual in its character"[40]

Weems and *Trop* thus took the words "cruel and unusual" as directions for what has come to be called "proportionality," a precept championed by Cesare Beccaria and Jeremy Bentham in the nineteenth century; the Court called for judges to assess the suffering imposed in relationship to the wrongfulness of the conduct. Furthermore, neither decision assumed that the Court was locked into what was understood to have been "cruel and unusual" in 1791, when the Eighth Amendment was added as part of the Bill of Rights. *Trop* and *Weems* were about punishments imposed by the *federal* government; in 1962, the Supreme Court issued *Robinson v. California*—its first decision holding that the Cruel and Unusual Clause constrained *states* as well. Henley's 1965 *Talley* opinion cited *Robinson* for that proposition, and the standard Henley put forth— "abhorrent to the modern mind"—embodied a dynamic approach and proportionality.

The *Weems–Trop* evolving analysis has since become a target for some Supreme Court justices. Proponents of "originalism," a variegated concept sometimes described as relying on a "common understanding" or an "original public meaning" at the country's founding, argue that grounding constitutional interpretations in eighteenth-century meanings is loyal to the text and cabins judges' power.[41] Yet choices abound. Interpretations could focus on "Framers' intent," referencing the individuals who selected words (in this case, from the 1689 English Bill of Rights) for the US Constitution. Others might argue that the relevant inquiry should be about what the people ratifying these amendments understood their meaning to be. Methods of probing what would (or could) have been the common understanding include scouring dictionaries from the 1790s, reading commentators of that era, using computer analyses of words in various documents, and learning what punishments were in use prior to ratification (and in England), and which continued or were abandoned.

A version of this foray was undertaken in 1963 by Delaware's Supreme Court, which upheld statutes authorizing judges to sentence people to whipping. That court described the "barbarous" practices that England prohibited in 1689 included "breaking on the wheel, public dissection, and the like." Delaware's eighteenth-century constitution banned "cruel or unusual punishments." (Note the use of "or" in this and some state constitutions, as contrasted to the "and" in the federal constitution.) Delaware's justices recounted that, after enactment, "a list of horrors" continued under statutes providing for "death by hanging, drawing and quartering for . . . treason, . . . standing in the pillory, cropping of ears, branding, wearing a convict's badge, and selling into servitude." Commenting that Delaware's legislature did not end "the pillory" until 1905, the Supreme Court ruled that the decision about ending whipping belonged to the political branches. A decade later, the state's legislature abolished the practice in its 1973 criminal code revision.[42]

This inquiry into history continues to have purchase. In 2019, a five-person majority of the US Supreme Court undertook a similar analysis when permitting a method of execution that would entail severe pain. Justice Neil Gorsuch's opinion for the Court described in disquieting detail the punishments at the time of the founding of the country, as he concluded that "the Eighth Amendment does not guarantee a prisoner a painless death" but forbids "long disused (unusual) forms of punishment that intensified the sentence of death with a (cruel) 'superadd[ition]'" of "terror, pain, or disgrace."[43] Justice Gorsuch reiterated that view in 2024 by describing the Eighth Amendment as aiming "to ensure that the new Nation would never resort to" punishments like "disembowelment, quartering, public dissention, and burning alive," "others like them," or those that had "fallen into disuse."[44] The references to comparisons and disuse require judges applying that frame to pick locales—England and places in the United States—as relevant and to assess records from eras when documentation and retention were erratic.[45] Thus, as critics of originalism point out, whatever method of constitutional interpretation is used, judges have to make choices. If claiming to be yoked to history, decisions include which materials to valorize. Once amassing sources deemed reliable, originalists need to select a "they" to count and assume a shared understanding, an identifiable purpose, and an intent to have the meaning of words fixed forever.[46]

Another approach rejects a frozen document in favor of a "living tree"—a metaphor common in several constitutional democracies[47] and exemplified by Warren's discussion of "evolving standards of decency." This school of thought argues that profound changes in social ordering may require revisiting earlier interpretations. Even as the words of the 1791 Bill of Rights resonate today, they were written when most Black people were enslaved, and married women (of all races, to the extent Black people were permitted to marry) had, in accordance with English common law, no legally recognized capacity to enter into contracts or own property independent of their husbands. Black people and white women could not vote. Alterations to the Constitution through the Thirteenth, Fourteenth, Fifteenth, and Nineteenth Amendments could therefore be read to require reconsideration of interpretations stemming from when so many people were not counted as full members of the country.

Henley's reference in *Talley* to the "modern mind" suggested he was supposed to think beyond history. Moreover, Henley had measures of the "modern mind"; the local press had raised objections to whipping; during the 1963 Democratic primary, the state's Penitentiary Board seemed to have called for its end; and after election, Governor Faubus recorded concern. What held Henley back from ruling whipping "abhorrent"? Henley's brief explanation was that "corporal punishment has not been viewed historically as a constitutionally forbidden cruel and unusual punishment."[48] His reference to modernity rested largely on Delaware's statutory authorization for judges to sentence people to whipping. As lawyers know, Henley could have distinguished that approach because, unlike Delaware, Arkansas had no statute on whipping. On the other hand, as this book's readers know, Henley could also have also gotten support for his view from England and other Commonwealth countries where flogging remained. But none of the lawyers in the case appear to have supplied those citations or the 1955 UN rules calling for whipping's end.

Yet, the plot thickens. Rather than give state officials the blank check they sought, Henley implicitly determined that the "modern mind" abhorred *something* Arkansas did, and that revulsion may have been entangled with his thoughts on constitutional protections of liberty. Henley incorporated ideas about proportionality as well as a modicum of the dynamic approach by ruling that constitutionality *rested* on imposition in accordance with procedural constraints he embroidered into the Eighth Amendment. Whipping's legality

> presupposes that its infliction is surrounded by appropriate safeguards. It must not be excessive; it must be inflicted as dispassionately as possible and by responsible people; and it must be applied in reference to recognizable standards whereby a convict may know what conduct on his part will cause him to be whipped and how much punishment given conduct may produce.

Chief Judge Henley continued that it was not his "function" to translate those parameters into rules. He noted disapprovingly that "no established schedule of punishments" existed and whippings were inflicted "summarily" by people who "may or may not be men of judgment and temperate nature." Thus, Henley ordered whipping on hold

> until such time as the Arkansas State Penitentiary Board or the Superintendent of the Penitentiary, by and with the approval of the Board, shall establish by appropriate rules and regulations safeguards surrounding the infliction of corporal punishment on inmates so that the infliction of such punishment will not constitute cruel and unusual punishment prohibited by the eighth and fourteenth Amendments to the Constitution of the United States, respondent be, and be hereby is, enjoined and restrained from inflicting such punishment on petitioners for violation of disciplinary rules, for insufficient or unsatisfactory work, or for any other reason.[49]

Translating Henley's locution, the Arkansas press reported that, in the name of judicial restraint, the judge had failed to "rid Arkansas prisons of such a primitive and repugnant instrument of punishment."[50] Instead, what the prison called the *Talley* Rules" were born.

12

THE VIOLENCE CONTINUED
THEREAFTER

On paper, something had changed. Chief Judge Henley's November 1965 decision forbade whipping unless and until Arkansas had written rules that organized the process, prohibited summary imposition, and provided notice to prisoners of offenses that could prompt it. The judge also required that whipping, "inflicted as dispassionately as possible," was not to be "excessive." As creepy as those obligations sound, Henley likely assumed his "appropriate safeguards," coupled with political pressure that two years earlier had caused the Penitentiary Board to gesture toward ending whipping, would prompt the Board to stop the practice.[1]

Instead, in January of 1966, the Board wrote regulations (kept secret initially) to govern whipping. What became known as the *"Talley* Rules" moved from the court's ruling to a printed manual, whose cover is shown in figure 12.1, that set forth an internal criminal code authorizing the whip "in black and white."[2]

In 1966, Arkansas' Attorney General filed in court "a copy . . . drawn in order to comply with the decree rendered in this cause." Prison staff later testified that they distributed the "12-page mimeographed booklet" to prisoners. The Rules licensed corporal punishment for "major offenses," defined to include "homosexuality," "agitation," "insubordination," "refusal to work," "making or concealing weapons," and "inciting a riot." A "Board of Inquiry," comprised of the Superintendent or his assistant and a warden or associate warden,

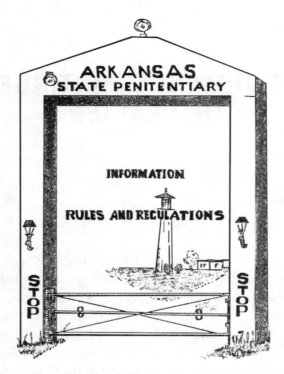

FIGURE 12.1 Cover of the Arkansas State Penitentiary Rules and Regulations, an exhibit in the 1967 *Jackson v. Bishop* trial, National Archives and Records Administration, facsimile by Jeanne Criscola

made decisions; no infraction was to result in more than "ten lashes with the strap." Prisoner–trustys were no longer allowed to whip other prisoners; whippings were not supposed to take place in "the field"; and each prisoner was to be given his own "work quota" dependent on "age, experience, health and other factors." Those 1966 Rules echoed what Laura Conner, the sole woman briefly on the Penitentiary Board in 1921, had proposed. In her unsuccessful efforts to stop brutality, she drafted "suggestions for better humanitarian measures" that, in addition to providing decent food and a "negro preacher," prohibited corporal punishment for minor infractions; when deployed, whipping were not to "exceed ten strokes."[3]

The violence did not stop in the 1920s or the 1960s. Within months of his *Talley* decision, Henley had to know his ruling had little impact. What sounded like a partial victory in 1965 for prisoners was a nightmare on the ground. News of the failure came through new lawsuits, protests, and scandals revealing that whipping was but one of the horrors in Arkansas' prisons.

"THE FIRST TEST" OF THE WHIPPING RULES

On August 19, 1966, William King Jackson filed his "neatly written" petition in the Arkansas federal court. Jackson said he had been whipped for not picking okra that, because of damaged vision, he had not seen. The state, agreeing that Jackson had been hit eight times, explained his failure to pick the required amount was a rebellion to be squelched; after being disciplined, Jackson was sent back to the fields, where he "picked all that was supposed to be picked."[4] Lyle Edward Ernst and Grady W. Mask brought similar claims soon thereafter. These three white men, each in their twenties and held at Cummins Farm, alleged that prison officials were not complying with the *Talley* Rules and that corporal punishment ought to be banned. Noting the "constitutional questions" raised, the local press called Jackson's petition the "first test of prison rules for whipping."[5] They were right. The state had not appealed the 1965 *Talley* decision, and Jackson filed a new case in 1966. As forecast, after losing the 1967 whipping trial, the prisoners appealed and won. Thereafter, the *Talley* and *Jackson* lawsuits snowballed into a comprehensive legal attack on conditions in disciplinary segregation and throughout the prisons.

Jackson began that sequence when he sued O. E. Bishop, who took over as Cummins Superintendent on January 1, 1966. News reports described Bishop as an able "investigative officer, a convivial politician, an energetic deer hunter, and a cheerful civic worker." Born in 1908, Bishop ran a gas station and the Bishop Brothers Motor Company; he said his service in the Navy during World War II reminded him he wanted to be a policeman. On return, Bishop won his first election in 1946 for a six-year term; despite a subsequent loss, Bishop won. By the end of seventeen years as Sheriff of Union County, Bishop was in charge of a fourteen-person office and credited with improving the local jail.[6]

Bishop's political skills were evident in his gaining presidencies of the Arkansas Peace Officers Association and of the Arkansas

Sheriffs Association. When Dan Stephens resigned "in the wake of controversy over the use of a strap to discipline convicts," Bishop joined other sheriffs in a resolution praising Stephens for his "great work" and criticizing "bleeding hearts" for protecting criminals who resisted "authority in our prison system." Within short order, Governor Orval Faubus offered Bishop the prison post. In addition to $12,600, the Penitentiary Board supplied Bishop with a house at Cummins. Once there, Bishop told the press that "if force is necessary, it will come, but only as a last resort."[7] In fact, Bishop often resorted to force.

The *Arkansas Gazette*, bemoaning Bishop's lack of "professional training," concluded that the state's prisons would remain "as removed from modern penology" as they had been. That proposition proved more than true with reports of a "chilling scandal" at Tucker; stories streamed out of lurid tortures, beatings, extortion, and fired staff.[8] Because judges always know more than what they learn in court, understanding *Jackson v. Bishop*, tried in January of 1967 and decided on June 3, 1967, requires knowing what people in Arkansas (and beyond) read about the state's prisons. Bizarre as it is, whipping was but a facet of the violence at Arkansas' prisons.

STRIKES, STRAPS, RATS, ROACHES, AND TORTURE

"All because we ask to be treated like human being and men and not like animals, which here we are treated much worse . . ."

—Forty-Four Cummins Prisoners' September 1966 letter[9]

Lawsuits were one route to try to get help and work stoppages another. In April of 1966, four months before Jackson filed his petition, "144 prisoners—102 Negroes and 42 whites—refused to go to the fields." Their "demands" included "better food, free toothbrushes, a five-day week and eight-hour workdays and more visits from relatives and friends." Bishop responded by shutting the prison. He later told the press that after guards released tear gas, fired "shots over [the prisoners'] heads," and whipped "nine Negroes and one white prisoner" in front of others, he had gotten "the prison back to normal."[10]

"Normal" was awful, as prisoners made plain in September of 1966, when more than 140 went on strike again. Faubus blamed "recent court decisions" for encouraging a "trouble-making group" who had a "'mistaken assumption' that the use of the strap . . . had been abolished." Bishop again responded with violence. The *Arkansas Gazette* headline, "Strap Ends Strike by 146 Prisoners; Tear Gas Is Used," captioned its report that gas was fired at the "barracks housing the 104 Negro prisoners," ten men each received ten lashes, and that the "same procedure" was used "at the white barracks," where one man was lashed.[11] That September, newspapers ran a photo (figure 12.2) captioned "The Strap for Punishing Prisoners."

Both Faubus and Bishop sought to distance themselves from that image. They said they were personally opposed to strapping, but it was necessary for "discipline" in light of a lack of enough solitary confinement cells and a maximum-security building.[12]

FIGURE 12.2 *Controversial Strap*, photograph by Larry Obsitnik, accompanying George Douthit, *Bishop Says Prison Situation in Hand*, Arkansas Democrat, September 7, 1966, courtesy of the publisher

Much more than the whip needed to end. On September 17, 1966, the *Arkansas Gazette* reported its receipt of a letter from forty-four prisoners who also contacted Pine Bluff civil rights lawyer George Howard, "a Negro" who chaired the "State Legal Redress Committee of the National Association for the Advancement of Colored People" and, as mentioned, later became a judge. The Cummins prisoners pleaded for protection against "brutal" treatment—food not "fit for hogs," work twelve hours a day, six days a week, and no medical attention. They described overcrowded barracks with "rats, roaches" and humiliation through beatings with sticks and forced "homosexual acts." Bishop responded with blanket denials.[13]

Bishop could not, however, deny what unfolded in public about Tucker Farm, which Assistant Superintendent Jim Bruton had run for twelve years. A report labeled "VERY CONFIDENTIAL" from a state police investigation led by H. H. Atkinson went to Governor Faubus on August 27, 1966. By then, Bruton and a few others had been fired. On August 30, 1966, Governor Faubus ordered the state police (with thirty-eight-year-old Atkinson at the helm) to take control of Tucker. Faubus instructed that all wardens be "relieved from their positions" and many trustys replaced. The press said that a "chilling scandal" had been the reason for the "shake up" at Tucker, and that the State Police's Criminal Investigation Division had given local prosecutors materials for the "possible filing of charges." On September 3, 1966, Governor Faubus, accompanied by reporters, visited Tucker, then holding about three hundred white prisoners. Faubus told reporters that prisoners "expressed appreciation" for the investigation, and a governor's aide credited prisoners with "courage" in bringing to light "misconduct at Tucker."[14]

GOVERNOR WINTHROP ROCKEFELLER'S "BURDEN": FILTH, BRIBES, AND THE "TUCKER TELEPHONE"

A few months later, Winthrop Rockefeller became the first Republican Governor of Arkansas in almost a hundred years. On January 10, 1967, about two weeks before the trial of *Jackson v. Bishop*, Rockefeller's inaugural address promised a new "Era of Excellence."

Proposed reforms included creating a Department of Administration to coordinate the state's 187 independent boards, of which the Penitentiary Board was one.

Unlike his predecessors who had heaped praise on the prisons, Rockefeller ended his speech by saying that "no burden rests more heavily on the conscience of the people of Arkansas, hour by hour, than a prison system regarded by professional penologists as being generally the worst in the United States." Committed to "clearing up deplorable conditions," Rockefeller asked the legislature to make it "the very highest priority." Rockefeller knew more. Within days of taking office, an aide to Faubus had leaked part of the sixty-seven-page state police report; Rockefeller then ordered release of the full report, which one reporter said read like "an account of German atrocities to the Jews in World War II." Some papers printed excerpts and photographs of instruments of torture, whips included. A local prosecutor postponed his felony docket because he "couldn't get up and ask a jury to send a man down there if conditions are as bad as they say."[15]

The report, chronicling events through September 7, 1966, detailed bribery, extortion, corruption, and daily violence inflicted by whippings, clubbing, and specially designed torture devices. The sadism, some of which Bruton had recorded on tapes, is painful to recount. Doing so is the only way to enable contemporary readers to understand that anyone looking at newspapers in Arkansas (and nationally) knew about the rampant degradation.

Arkansas' Criminal Investigation Division explained that on August 18, 1966, a group of prisoners left the prison and returned drunk. The state police credited Bishop, whose authority included Cummins and Tucker, with calling them in to find out how prisoners had gotten so much alcohol. Within a week, the inquiry moved beyond drunk prisoners. The state police's memorandum's "Subjects" were "robbery, larceny, maiming, extortion, liquors into prison, excessive punishment, personal use of provisions, [and] gifts to officers or personnel." Under the header of "Victims," the list included the "State of Arkansas" and dozens of individuals who had feared being "killed" if they talked.[16]

What Atkinson described in his "very confidential" report matched what Dale Woodcock, incarcerated in the 1950s, had detailed in his "very" public book, *Ruled by the Whip*, that I discussed. In 1966, the barracks were filled with "filthy and rotten" discolored mattresses, leaking showers, and commodes that did not flush. Weapons were everywhere; state police found knives, clubs, and a hatchet. Tucker's kitchen was also "filthy"—food uncovered; windows without screens; "flies . . . very thick," and utensils in total "disrepair." Despite the farm's produce, men were given meat once a month and an egg at Christmas. The result was malnutrition; prisoners, wearing ill-fitting shoes in "terrible" shape, appeared to be "forty to sixty pounds under their normal weight."[17]

Bribes allocated work, and prisoners ran much of the system. Winston Talley, "in charge of loans," had $12.50 owed to Vernon Sloan (with whom Talley's 1965 case had been joined). One prisoner recounted being beaten by Talley, and another identified him as the person selling laundry jobs. Talley admitted he was part of the racket headed by Bruton. Prisoners told Atkinson that goats, hogs, other produce, equipment, and labor were siphoned off to "free-world" staff and their relatives. "'Free-world' horses" were housed at Tucker and shod by prisoners.[18]

Atkinson reported that on arrival, police found Bruton taking goods out of the house. Bruton threatened Atkinson ("keep your mouth shut") and offered to make him Assistant Superintendent. Bruton bragged about his $8,000 a year salary, unlimited accounts, and the twelve-room furnished house. Bruton assured Atkinson that he could have the run of the place; to keep control, he should "hit" prisoners "with anything you can get your hands on."[19]

Bruton had much to want to suppress, including "field straps" for whipping prisoners on the farmlands—a direct violation of the *Talley* Rules. Hidden in Bruton's house was a contraption known as the "Tucker Telephone," with wires to be hooked up to naked men's genitals and toes. When the electric generator with dry-cell batteries was hand-cranked, electric shocks ran to those body parts. One prisoner gave Atkinson a list of people who had been "rung up."

Another torture method, the "teeter board," consisted of two planks nailed together. A few nails protruded, and prisoners were for hours to balance the nails on the floor. Atkinson found tapes of Bruton whipping prisoners, "on the bare buttocks and without benefit of a Board hearing, as prescribed in the Prison Regulations." Atkinson stated that "Mr. Bruton's voice and demeanor during the course of said whippings seemed to be that of a very excited person bordering insanity." Prisoners knew well Bruton's terrifying wrath, which Atkinson documented in pages of gruesome descriptions and photographs.[20]

CHARGING CRIMES AND BRINGING IN PROFESSIONALS

Within weeks, a local prosecutor brought felony charges against Bruton and three others for "excessive punishment," a crime that could result in five years imprisonment. In the winter of 1967, national coverage linked those "torture" indictments with the "hearing under way" in *Jackson v. Bishop*; the *Washington Post* described, a "16-year-old convict" testified he had been "beaten three times with the strap . . . for not picking enough cotton."[21]

The *Jackson v. Bishop* trial also coincided with reform efforts by Rockefeller and the legislature. Because "prisoners [were] living in fear of their lives," Rockefeller fired Tucker's Assistant Superintendent Pink Booher and hired Arkansas' first "professional penologist," Tom Murton, who had a degree in criminology from the University of California at Berkeley. Rockefeller put Murton in charge of Tucker, where he ended whipping. Rockefeller also appointed John Haley, then thirty-five years old, to the Penitentiary Board. Haley had been a lawyer for the Little Rock School Board, supported desegregation at Central High School, worked on the Rockefeller campaign, and was at the Rose Law Firm (which Hillary Rodham Clinton later joined). Rockefeller's brother Nelson, Governor of New York, sent examples of manuals and policies developed by that state's correctional leadership. Arkansas' legislature chartered a "blue-ribbon commission" to which the governor, the legislature, the bar association, organizations of prosecutors and sheriffs, and the judiciary each appointed two people. Winthrop Rockefeller's choices included Louis Ramsay, who had represented Talley, Hash, and Sloan in 1965.[22]

MORE JUDGES TO JUDGE WHIPPING

The accounts of sadism were front-page news in August of 1966, when Jackson, followed by Lyle Ernst and Grady W. Mask, sought federal court help. Jackson's "petition for a writ of habeas corpus" was assigned to Judge Oren Harris. Ernst's filing, docketed September 7, 1966, and called a "petition for a writ of mandamus," went to Judge Gordon Young. The words "Motion and Petition" were at the top of Mask's November 29, 1966, filing, also sent to Judge Young.[23] In lieu of the typical solo work of trial judges, Harris and Young presided jointly over the whipping trial.

Like Chief Judge Henley, both jurists were steeped in Arkansas politics and culture. Their backgrounds and opinions on other civil rights claims provide windows to the state's legal establishment. Harris had joined the bench less than a year before after serving in the US House of Representatives for twenty-five years, where he chaired the Committee on Interstate and Foreign Commerce and co-sponsored landmark 1962 legislation authorizing the Food and Drug Administration to improve regulation of medications. During the prior decade, he had joined dozens in the House of Representatives and signed the 1956 Southern Manifesto denouncing the Supreme Court's 1954 ruling in *Brown v. Board of Education*.[24] In addition to complaining in 1957 to President Eisenhower about federal troops (a "dangerous encroachment upon the prerogatives and responsibility of state and local affairs"), Harris voted against the Civil Rights Act of 1964. President Lyndon Johnson nominated Harris, who was sixty-two when he took office in February of 1966. The *Arkansas Gazette* called Harris' installation an "emotional" event at which Senator John Mc-Clellan joined other Washington luminaries at the packed Little Rock Courthouse proceedings. During the decades that followed, echoes of Harris' views in Congress carried over into his judging;

he was reversed by the Eighth Circuit in several cases related to race discrimination.[25]

Eisenhower had nominated Young, a Democrat, in 1959 to mollify Senator McClellan, who had stalled Henley's appointment. Young did not have Harris' national profile, even as both were central to Arkansas' political and legal community. Young had been a deputy prosecutor for one county and served as Malvern's city attorney before opening a law practice in Pine Bluff, where he was president of its school district; in 1954, Young advised compliance with *Brown v. Board of Education*. When sworn in on September 25, 1959, Young called himself a "country lawyer." Edward Wright, the state's delegate to the American Bar Association (ABA), described Young as a "lawyer's lawyer," with wide-ranging practical experience.[26]

Once on the bench, Judge Young appeared somewhat open to the emerging rights of criminal defendants. For example, Young ruled that that the 1963 Supreme Court *Gideon v. Wainwright* decision, requiring states to provide appointed counsel to indigent felony defendants, meant Arkansas had to do so for misdemeanor cases that entailed imprisonment. Yet Judge Young also shared with Judge Harris a record of Eighth Circuit reversals of decisions displaying limited understanding of the importance of racial equality.[27]

CALLING IN PREEMINENT LAWYERS

While new to judging, Oren Harris was an astute politician who understood Jackson's case raised significant constitutional questions. On September 1, 1966, he followed Henley's model by asking for help from two experienced lawyers, Edward Wright and William Arnold, whom he described as "leaders in the legal profession in Arkansas and in the nation."[28] The lawyers responded that, while "busy," in the "finest traditions of the bar," they would help. Two days later, after Ernst's petition landed on Judge Young's desk, the judge turned to Wright and Arnold. The two lawyers proposed consolidation and, thereafter, Mask's November filing was added.[29]

The appointed lawyers were, as Harris described, legal luminaries. Wright, a senior partner in a successful Little Rock
commercial law firm (one of its "big three") was the lead lawyer.
Wright had been the President of the American College of Trial
Lawyers in 1965; in 1970, he became the President of the ABA.
William Arnold, about twenty years younger, was a partner in the
small-town law firm of Crossett and Hamburg. Arnold was then
the Vice President of the Arkansas State Bar and became its president the following year.

Wright's and Arnold's credentials gave the prisoners' claims legitimacy, and their advocacy skills helped both prisoners and judges.
Yet they were improbable attorneys to establish—for the first time
in US history—that the Eighth Amendment prohibited correctional
officials from using an in-prison punishment of their choice. Both
were commercial lawyers who helped to craft Arkansas' Probate
Code, and both spent time as the state's representatives to the
Uniform Law Commission, a national organization that generates
model laws. Neither was involved with criminal law, nor were they
known for representing activists in the civil rights upheavals that
produced so much federal litigation in Arkansas. Indeed, none of
the published discussion by or about the two that I have found mentioned their work on the whipping case.

Arnold, the younger lawyer, took second seat. A eulogy when
he died at age seventy-four in 1996 described him as committed
to his town, Crossett, where his father had been the general manager for the local lumber company. Arnold went to law school
in Arkansas, served in World War II, and received a masters in
law from Columbia University. Returning to Arkansas, Arnold
was known for helping elderly neighbors with legal issues. Decades later, Crossett's 5,500 residents needed help of a different
kind. The 2016 documentary, *Company Town*, mapped the toxic
pollutants that the local paper mills had spewed into the air, soil,
and water.[30]

Much more has been written about and by Wright. Born in
1903, Wright spent his childhood in Little Rock, attended its local

college, and received a law degree from Georgetown University in 1928. Forty years later, Georgetown bestowed on him an honorary Doctorate of Law. In the interim, Wright became a member of the Catholic Knights of Malta and represented the Diocese of Little Rock in its successful rebuff of state efforts to tax income-producing property of churches. In 1957, Wright became president of the state's bar association. From 1962 to 1964, he chaired the ABA's House of Delegates. Wright's prominence grew after the 1963 assassination of President Kennedy and the issue emerged of presidents unable to complete their terms. Senator Birch Bayh of Indiana, at the helm of the drive to put what became the Twenty-Fifth Amendment into place, credited Wright as the "invaluable" force gaining the ABA's endorsement.[31] (The Twenty-Fifth Amendment has since been widely criticized for vagueness about what constitutes an inability "to discharge the powers and duties of the office.")

Wright's other major initiative was reforming rules governing lawyers. In 1964, he chaired an ABA committee that replaced the 1908 Canons of Ethics with a new Code of Professional Responsibility, adopted by the ABA in 1969 and thereafter in many states. In 1970, Wright became the ABA's ninety-fourth president and hence wrote monthly columns in the *ABA Journal* and gave many talks. Reading his speeches to bar associations, law students, and lawyers, one meets a man focused on the legal profession and anxious about the upheavals of the 1960s. Acknowledging protests, Wright commended change through "law and reason" and warned against "hero-worshipping that too often glorified lawless and unreasonable men." Wright wrote little about civil rights and race relations. He mentioned criminal justice reform on a few occasions; he was critical of criminal defendants' rights while calling for prison reform to stop the 200,000 people then incarcerated from becoming "permanent residents" through the "revolving door" of recidivism.

Wright's memorabilia, stored in his granddaughter's attic, attested to Wright's pride in the whipping case. Included was a photo

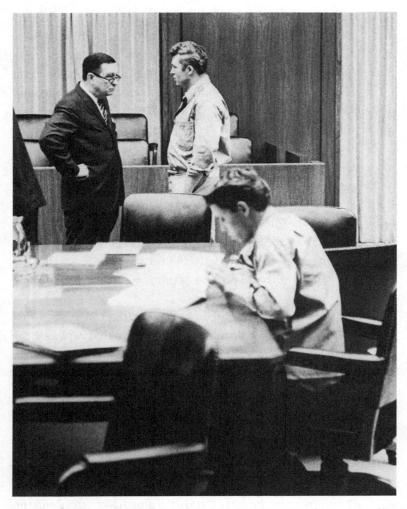

FIGURE 12.3 Edward Wright with his clients in federal court, 1967, courtesy of his granddaughter, Kate Askew

(figure 12.3) with his clients in court and correspondence with Judge Harry Blackmun after he issued the Eighth Circuit opinion vindicating Wright's approach. By 2019, while court filings and the trial transcript remained in the National Archives, neither Wright's nor Arnold's notes on the case could be found.[32]

13

WHIPPING'S TRIAL

In "pursuit of life, happiness, and attempting to live as a human being."
—William Jackson, Petition for a Writ of
Habeas Corpus, August 1966

William Jackson, Lyle Ernst Jr., and Grady Mask put into motion the only trial in US history about whipping's constitutionality. On January 26, 1967, the three men, depicted in figure 13.1, were brought to Little Rock's federal courthouse where their lawyers, Edward Wright and William Arnold, presented evidence to Judges Harris and Young, as did defending Superintendent O. E. Bishop, represented by Don Langston and Robert Smith from Arkansas' Attorney General's Office. Because the judges' decision on that trial was appealed, the 641-page transcript of the three days of testimony and a trove of related documents are part of the US National Archives. Along with news reports and my interviews, we know a fair amount about Jackson, a bit about Ernst and Mask, and what was recorded in court.

Echoing 1930s debates among members of the International Penal and Penitentiary Commission (IPPC), the white men in federal court in Arkansas disagreed about whipping's legitimacy. But unlike IPPC discussions, the trial was replete with graphic descriptions. More than twenty witnesses explained why, how, and where Arkansas whipped, and one prisoner lowered his pants to show his scars to the judges. A few experts testified—including former Bureau of Prisons (BOP) Director James Bennett who, as discussed, had been in the 1955 UN meetings resulting in Standard Minimum Rules calling for whipping's end. At issue in Little Rock was whether US law would do so as well.

Paralleling the 1965 *Talley* plaintiffs, Jackson, Ernst, and Mask had little education and few economic resources. In many respects, these men were stand-ins for hundreds who could also have attested to the violence in which they lived; these three offer a window into white people's encounters with criminal law. Glimpses of the aggression suffered by Black prisoners come from transcript references to screams from "the colored end" of Cummins' segregated barracks.

WILLIAM JACKSON, LYLE EDWARD ERNST JR., AND GRADY MASK

Born in 1939 in South Carolina, William Jackson was one of more than ten children. His older brother Linwood Jackson told me the family moved to North Carolina and lived on a "poor farm" from

FIGURE 13.1 *Principals in Latest Lawsuit Over Prison Whippings*, Arkansas Gazette, photograph by Larry Obsitnik, January 27, 1967, courtesy of the publisher

which William was eager to escape. William quit high school in the ninth grade, entered the Navy at fifteen, left, worked a variety of jobs, married, had children, and walked out. On January 23, 1967, when questioned by the state's lawyers days before the trial began, William reported he could not "remember when" he had first been arrested. By twenty-one, Jackson had been convicted in North Carolina of assaulting his wife and "abandonment and non-support." Managing "to escape several times," Jackson served twenty-three months before being paroled, arrested in Arkansas, and charged with "burglary and grand larceny" (taking $35 or more) at a grocery store.[1]

The interconnectedness of Arkansas' legal and political establishment is marked by Jackson's encounters with its courts. Joe Holmes was Jackson's appointed defense lawyer in 1964; later elected Jefferson County prosecutor, Holmes received the state police report on sadism at Tucker and filed criminal charges against Jim Bruton and others. In February of 1967, Holmes was picked by the Arkansas Prosecutors Attorney's Association to serve on the legislature's commission investigating the state prisons. That year, Holmes prosecuted Winston Talley, rearrested in October of 1967 on burglary and grand larceny charges.[2] When Jackson challenged his conviction in Arkansas' Supreme Court, he was represented by the law firm of Louis Ramsay, whom Chief Judge Henley had appointed in the 1965 *Talley* case.

For reasons that neither the court records nor my interviews illuminate, Jackson invoked his constitutional rights repeatedly in state and federal courts. When imprisoned in North Carolina, Jackson filed three state habeas writs, all denied. After an Arkansas jury found him guilty of stealing $35 and a pistol, and he was sentenced to five years "at hard labor," Jackson argued that Arkansas police violated his federal constitutional rights by holding him ten days without an arraignment, failing to advise him of his right to silence, interrogating him without a lawyer, and entering into evidence the fruits of that questioning and of a search. On January 30, 1967, three days after the federal whipping trial had begun, the Arkansas Supreme Court disagreed.[3]

Jackson said at his January 23, 1967, deposition that he did his "own writing"; his six pages, docketed on August 29, 1966, do not read like what most people leaving school before completing ninth grade might produce. In neat block letters, Jackson alleged that Superintendent Bishop, joined by "Clay Smith, Mose Harmon, and Jim Bruton have and are now violating petitioner's constitutional rights set forth in Amendment Eight." Jackson added that, forced to sleep in barracks with a person who had tuberculosis, the state violated due process and equal protection guarantees of the Fourteenth Amendment. Jackson listed six witnesses to support his claims and began his "prayer for relief" with the statement I quoted about "attempting to live as a human being." Jackson asked for a "restraining order" to stop Bishop and others from destroying legal mail, pushing him to work unreasonable hours in unreasonable conditions, and permitting trustys to pull teeth and to whip other prisoners. Jackson also requested medical attention and eyeglasses.[4]

The second petitioner, Lyle Edward Ernst Jr., a twenty-four-year-old "man of slight stature," weighed 145 pounds. Ernst grew up in Little Rock and left school in the tenth grade. The armed robbery to which he pled guilty was his first conviction. By 1967, Ernst had spent four years of his fifteen-year sentence at Tucker. Grady Mask, age twenty, reported he quit school in the seventh grade, had been in and out of reformatories thereafter, and had been arrested for "[b]urglary, grand larceny, drinking under age, [and] reckless driving." Having pled guilty to grand larceny when he was nineteen, Mask was at Tucker on an eight-year sentence.[5]

Ernst's and Mask's handwritten petitions were shorter, harder to follow, and less eloquent than Jackson's. Ernst alleged that "field Warden Capt. Mayes . . . acting upon the authority of Asst. Superintendent Jim Bruton," took Ernst from the fields and, because he had not picked enough cucumbers, lashed him ten times on his "bare buttocks," and within an hour, whipped him again. Mask's November 1966 filing said that he had been lashed six times and that doing so was unconstitutional, as was denial of medical treatment.[6]

THE LAWYERS' REWRITE

The prisoners' counsel clarified the claims and reframed the remedies to help all of Arkansas' prisoners. Instead of calling the cases "habeas petitions" (usually referencing individual arguments about unconstitutional convictions), Wright and Arnold filed amended "complaints" that relied on the Civil Rights Act of 1871 ("Section 1983"). They alleged that the state was depriving prisoners of their "constitutional rights to due process of law and equal protection of law under the Fourteenth Amendment" and that whipping "constitutes cruel and unusual punishment in violation of the Eighth Amendment."[7]

The lawyers invoked the Fourteenth Amendment for two reasons. First, the Fourteenth Amendment specifically addressed state action and was a route to "incorporating" (applying) the Eighth Amendment's ban on cruel and unusual punishment to states. Second, understanding that Judges Harris and Young would likely defer to Chief Judge Henley's *Talley* decision that whipping (with safeguards) did *not* violate the Eighth Amendment, Wright and Arnold added that whipping's unconstitutionality also stemmed from Fourteenth Amendment mandates that no state deprive individuals of "equal protection of the laws" or take away "life, liberty, or property without due process of law."

The reference to "equal protection" was not—as it might have been—based on reports that Black prisoners were whipped more than whites or that segregated prison barracks were unconstitutional. The argument was that inequality stemmed from retaliatory whippings. The due process arguments, predicated on the idea of prisoners' "liberty" not to be whipped, had two prongs—one based on what during the twentieth century came to be called "substantive due process" and the other "procedural due process." Wright and Arnold argued that whipping's incursion on liberty was beyond the pale of what states could do to anyone; moreover, if whippings were to occur, more procedural protections were needed to prevent arbitrariness.

The lawyers added facts specific to each plaintiff. For Jackson, they alleged he had been placed in solitary confinement and fed bread and water in violation of the Eighth Amendment, and that denial of access to mail violated his Sixth Amendment right to counsel. The allegations for Ernst included that after having been whipped, he was made to stand for four hours "on a board . . . two by four, three feet long, with another small strip or board on top of it." For Mask, the lawyers detailed that, despite a doctor's recommendation that Mask be taken out of the fields because of a knee injury, Mask was whipped for "allegedly failing to 'chop' enough cotton."[8]

Documents starting a civil lawsuit end with what lawyers call a "wherefore" clause to request relief, which can include options. Wright and Arnold asked for a total ban on "corporal punishment of any kind as a disciplinary or penal measure or in the alternative," for prohibitions on "the use of the strap or any other device used to whip or flog prisoners," or to stop "the use of the strap on the bare skin of prisoners." They also requested that no prisoners be made to do work that person was "physically unable" to do, and they sought money damages for the individual injuries suffered by Jackson, Ernst, and Mask.[9]

What the lawyers apparently did not do, as civil rights lawyers might have, was go out to Cummins, identify Black plaintiffs, and help them file cases that could have been consolidated with those pending. The inclusion of Black prisoners would have inscribed whipping's link to slavery and the oppressive exploitation of Black and white prisoners. Having none of the lawyers' notes, I do not know whether the lawyers consulted their clients about broadening the scope, made a strategic decision to avoid delay and capitalize on white victims to whom judges steeped in segregationist culture would likely be sympathetic, or took the assignment as it came to them.

What the records do reveal is that shortly before trial, the state's lawyers deposed Jackson, Ernst, and Mask, which meant that each previewed what they could say in court. The defense lawyers grilled the prisoners on who had hit them and how. Those accounts prompted the prisoners' lawyers on the eve of trial to agree that no evidence would show that Bishop "personally mistreated or harmed" the three and, therefore, to strike, as the state had requested, the damage requests.

EXPOSING HIS BUTTOCKS

"The petitioner, Lyle Edward Ernst, was in Chambers in the presence of the two Judges . . . and, at the request of counsel, was permitted to drop his trousers to expose his buttocks and to exhibit to the Court certain darkened areas on his left cheek of the buttocks which he identified as being scars or marks remaining from the strapping in July of 1966."

—Whipping Trial Transcript, January 26, 1967

The local press included photographs of the prisoners and their lawyers who—along with the defending prison officials and their counsel, the witnesses, the experts, and the judges—were white. Yet the lawyers and judges treated the lawsuit as if it were a "class action relating not only to the petitioner personally but to all inmates similarly situated."[10] What was on trial was Arkansas' practice of whipping any prisoner—Black or white.

Before delving into the transcript, a pause is in order to reflect on how unnecessary it ought to have been to need to "prove" whipping was impermissible. Shortly before the trial began, a reporter had likened Arkansas' prisons to concentration camps, the newspapers brimmed with details of sadistic violence, and state police took control of Tucker.[11] Yet the state continued to want to be allowed to whip, and Chief Judge Henley had ruled that whipping was *constitutional*, when regulated.

To win, Jackson, Ernst, and Mask had to prove either that Henley's ruling was wrong as a matter of law, that the *Talley* Rules were not actually followed, or that constitutional law required stricter procedural regulation. Their witnesses needed to attest to the uncontrollable brutality of whipping, beating, clubbing, and kicking at Cummins and Tucker. Therefore, the prisoners' lawyers repeatedly posed the same questions—about the ostensible reasons for whippings, who made decisions to whip, who hit whom where with what emotions, and how it *felt* to be whipped. In contrast, the defense's position was that the whippings were licit before the *Talley* decision and thereafter complied with its rules that whippings were "inflicted as dispassionately as possible" by staff acting under "reference to recognizable standards."[12] Like the prisoners' witnesses, defense witnesses discussed who decided to whip, who hit whom, with what emotive affect, and why.

Lawyers use trials to tell stories by shaping a narrative structure. The transcript and news stories permit readers to learn what the judges and public heard about daily life in Arkansas' prisons. Each side was unselfconscious when describing miserable living conditions, racial segregation, racialized violence, and forced labor. Despite allegations by Jackson, Ernst, and Mask that pushing prisoners to work unendingly constituted a distinct illegality, their lawyers made whipping *the* focal point. The judges' rulings *accepted* the brutal working regime in which white men lorded over Black and white prisoners who were made to work ungodly hours to produce revenue—an exploitation termed racialized "carceral capitalism" by twenty-first-century critics. Thus, as bizarre as it was to put whipping on trial, it was even more bizarre that the underlying system of slave-like labor was *not* at the center of the trial. And, in the 1970s, when prisoners and their lawyers tried to persuade federal judges that sweat labor violated the Thirteenth Amendment's prohibition on involuntary servitude, they lost, as other prisoners have since.

One other preview—a "trigger warning" in today's terms—is in order. The impressive stone facade of Little Rock's federal courthouse offered a veneer of respectability to proceedings detailing grotesque behavior. Having sketched that violence in the introduction and detailed brutality, racism, and filth in these last chapters, why do so again? My purposes are threefold: first, to record, out of respect, the suffering to which Jackson, Ernst, Mask and many others experienced; second, to document what people in Arkansas heard (again and again) about that violence, and third, to underscore that notwithstanding the baring of buttocks with a residue of blood, federal judges refused to use constitutional law to stop the whip, even as they issued an order they might have (like Henley had) assumed would cause others to end its use.

"OH, CAPTAIN, PLEASE DON'T HIT ME NO MORE"

Jackson was the first of fifteen prisoners to take the stand. He described how, in June of 1965, while "hoeing a row of beans," he was beaten and whipped by James Pike, the same prisoner–trusty who had whipped Talley. Jackson also recounted being called out for picking insufficient cotton (thirty-five pounds). Captain Mose Harmon (another repeat player from *Talley*) made Jackson lie down in the fields and, in front of others, hit him with the whip "as hard as he could." Just as Dale Woodcock's 1950s account, *Ruled by the Whip*, described, Harmon wanted Jackson to cry out "Oh, Captain, please don't hit me no more." Jackson refused and "went back to the field and picked cotton." Jackson reported that being whipped "put a lot of hate in me."[13]

A third whipping, late in July of 1966, took place inside. Jackson said "Captain Harmon . . . charged me with overlooking okra." Saying he picked what he saw, Jackson was told to lie down on the concrete floor, where he was whipped until "shaking" from pain. ("Captain Dean generally whips a man worse, to the extent he cuts the prisoners where Captain Harmon don't cut them with the strap.") On September 3, 1966, soon after filing suit, Jackson was held for about two months in solitary confinement at Tucker, where he was crammed into cells with other prisoners and, at times, fed only bread and water. Jackson also recounted an awful episode in which a captain told Clifford Dobbs to sing and, when Dobbs could not complete a verse, the captain hit him "three or four times" and then put a rope around his neck. (Lynching haunts this description; testimony did not mention his race, and genealogical records suggest Dobbs was white.)[14]

Ernst described seven whippings as "very painful" ("it leaves you real bad bruised and you can't hardly walk for two or three days"). The "reasons" ranged from "not working hard enough," "talking back to the yard man," and "scuffling" with another "boy." Ernst recounted that, after his clothes were soaked with blood, Bruton made him balance for hours on the teeter board—a wood and nail block entered into evidence as Exhibit No. 3. Ernst briefly went into the judges' chambers where he showed his scars to the judges.[15]

The state's cross-examination of Ernst and other witnesses reads oddly for experienced lawyers. Bishop's lawyers asked a sequence of inept questions prompting witnesses to repeat gory details and the many violations of the *Talley* Rules. For example, the state had Ernst explain that he was whipped for "juveniling" (with its sexual connotations), for throwing his hat on the ground, and for not picking enough pickles. The one answer that might have helped the defense was Ernst's report that, "if it wasn't for the Rule Book," another prisoner would have whipped him rather than turning him over to a captain.[16]

Mask, the next witness, reported that as a teenager, he had been "shoved into the tractor," injured his knee, had surgery, and continued to have pain. Because Mask was imprisoned after *Talley* was decided, his six whippings were supposed to be under that new regime. Instead, he testified that no procedural protections were provided. Mask's first whipping was for being "behind" on picking cotton; Captain Fletcher hit Mask "with ten 'oil burners.'" A week later, for allegedly leaving cucumbers in the field, Mask was whipped on his "bare buttocks." Two months thereafter, "putting rotten tomatoes" in a box was the basis for another whipping. The next two times, the rationales were the same: "not picking enough cotton." Mask said that after he filed his writ in November of 1966, Captain Goodwin punched him "on the chin," hit him several more times, and left him for eight days in isolation for "insubordination"—ostensibly for taking a fifteen-minute smoking break.[17]

"DOWN IN THE COLORED END"

Three more prisoners testified that day. Billy Utah Scott corroborated Jackson's description that, in July of 1966, several prisoners were lashed and, like Jackson, whipped for "not picking enough cotton." Scott reported that it made him "feel kind of like a dog."

The prisoners' lawyers used Scott, who had served time in other federal and state prisons, to establish that whipping was not used in those systems. Robert Styles, who had filed his own writ "for injunction," said that because of "not picking enough cotton," two captains had whipped him; Styles said whipping "builds up a lot of hate in me, makes me want to kill the man that whips me."[18]

The day ended with William Dale Tash, a sixteen-year-old at Tucker serving a five-year sentence for burglary and grand larceny. His first whipping (for "not picking enough cotton") was in October of 1966, where he was made to lie face down on the floor for "all eight licks," which got "harder" as they went and left him sore for days. Two weeks later, for "insubordination" due to the "low weight on the cotton," he was whipped, and then again in December. These three prisoners also described the cracks of the whip and cries of other prisoners subjected to the violence. It was in this context, during the late afternoon of the trial's first day, that *race* made its first appearance in the record. Styles said that he could not provide the names of the people whipped at night because it was "down in the colored end," where prison staff or trustys were "whipping the colored boys."[19]

THE STATE POLICE'S 155 INTERVIEWS

On the second trial day, January 27, 1967, eighteen people testified— nine for the prisoners and nine for the defense. The first was Duke Atkinson, who had written the state police's 1966 Tucker report. By being subpoenaed, he avoided seeming to have volunteered to help the prisoner–plaintiffs. Atkinson testified that the criminal investigation was based on interviews with 155 prisoners, and he authenticated the police's graphic photographs introduced into evidence. Atkinson explained that one was of "the buttocks of William Ponderley Casey who received ten licks on the bare buttocks by Captain Hayes in my presence." Another depicted bruises of James Edward Stephens, and a third, taken a month after a whipping, showed bruised hips and buttocks of Jerry Ivens. Three pictures were of a "field strap" (around three and a half feet by four inches,

FIGURE 13.2 *Straps Found by Police at Prison Farm*, photograph by the Arkansas State Police, circa 1967, University of Arkansas Little Rock (UALR), G. Thomas Eisele Papers, courtesy of UALR Center for Arkansas History and Culture

"carried by the wardens in their trucks to the fields"), and another of the "building strap" ("five and a half feet long by four inches"), all about a quarter inch thick with wood handles.[20] Figure 13.2 provides one example.

Because Atkinson was also listed as a witness for the defense, Bishop's lawyers guided him through questions aiming to show that whipping occurred according to the *Talley* Rules and that whipping was useful. Atkinson, who had served briefly in 1966 as Tucker's Assistant Superintendent, explained that "we had 35 prisoners who had picked less than 50 pounds of cotton. We had 12 that had picked less than 40 pounds of cotton." After a "board hearing," twelve men were whipped, four by Atkinson, who reported that he and the others had done so "dispassionately." The next day, Atkinson recounted, the "shortest count [of cotton] . . . was 125 pounds." Atkinson also stated that whipping was "preferable" to other forms of punishment.[21]

But there were glitches. Through Wright's cross-examination, Atkinson conceded that Captain Mayes (subsequently discharged) had not whipped people "dispassionately." Moreover, Atkinson acknowledged that prisoners might have preferred whipping to the awful possibilities of the teeter board or the Tucker Telephones that Atkinson had confiscated. Wright also understood that the judges wanted him to acknowledge Atkinson's contributions in uncovering the sadism. Wright therefore asked a question to which he knew the answer: whether the "telephone crank and the teeter board and perhaps some other instruments used on prisoners . . . [had] been discontinued" because of Atkinson's work. Atkinson replied they had, which gave Wright the opportunity to say that, "as a citizen," he thanked him for what he had "done down there."[22]

Before Atkinson could leave the stand, Judge Harris wanted to know whether it was "common knowledge" that the teeter board had been "used as a form of punishment." Atkinson responded with a spirited defense of Bishop whom, although officially in charge of both Cummins and Tucker, "had no way to get into the penitentiary and find out exactly what was transpiring." Atkinson dated the teeter board from when Superintendent Lee Henslee was in charge, and that it ended at Cummins after Dan Stephens took over. At Tucker, the teeter board had been "used on a continuing basis . . . for twelve years." Judge Harris also asked about the "straps." Atkinson explained that the police had confiscated "the long strap because our examination . . . indicated to us that it was cruel and unusual, that the reinforcement was too thick and extended too far down the shaft of the lash." When he had whipped prisoners, Atkinson used a four-foot strap with a "single thickness reinforcement." Judge Young closed the questioning of Atkinson by asking if "those who were responsible for that brutality" had been "terminated," and Atkinson responded "Yes, sir."[23]

THE WHIPPINGS AT THE "WHITE END" AND THE "COLORED END"

Whipping "makes me feel like an animal to lay on the floor and get cut all up with a piece of leather."

—Jerry Neal Curtis, Cummins prisoner, January 27, 1966

Trial judges do not like repetition any more than readers do. But without putting more people on the stand, Wright and Arnold could not establish that widespread brutality persisted throughout 1965 and 1966 at both Cummins and Tucker. Anticipating an appeal, they needed evidence in the record of rampant violence. Even as they cut back to present "non-cumulative matters" and "shorter and shorter"[24] exchanges in light of the judges' impatience, Wright and Arnold called eight prisoners, each of whom recounted their feelings of abuse when whipped.

Gerald Lawson testified he had been whipped twice, once for leaving weeds in the strawberry patch and the other during the "Jackson whipping," when Harmon lashed several men. Lawson said the whipping caused him "the most pain that I ever had without really being put in the hospital or something like that." He added that he had "never seen an animal beat like that and I hate the man that did it and I hate the system that would permit any man to whip another human being like that." Lawson also described being hit with a four-iron golf club that left his shoulder scarred.[25]

Charles Eugene Kelly spoke about three whippings in 1965 (before, as Bishop's lawyers insisted, the *Talley* Rules were distributed to prisoners) and reported seeing Lyle Ernst forced onto the teeter board. Kelly talked about how awful it felt to be whipped ("every time they hit you, you burn more and more . . ."). Kelly described hearing other people whipped, and spoke about the sounds—the popping of the whip and the cries of a prisoner "hollering 'Oh, Captain.'" When prompted by another inept cross-examination, Kelly described that after January 10, 1966, the captains continued whipping people, and "they didn't hold no hearing."[26]

Jerry Neal Curtis' imprisonment included an interval when his conviction had been reversed by Arkansas' Supreme Court; because he could not post bond, Curtis remained until convicted again. Curtis reported that, since May of 1965, he had been "beaten with a whip" six times. He said whippings "produced a lot of hate" in him and recounted how a "yard man," who was a "convict that runs the penitentiary" and in charge of all in "the white end," had kicked and beaten another prisoner.

That reference was that day's first mention of race, and it prompted Judge Young to ask what he meant. Curtis explained that the "white end" was where "white prisoners" slept and ate. Thereafter and again, Bishop's defense lawyers helped the prisoners' case by eliciting more about the degradation; asking if what Curtis disliked was having to "lie on the floor, . . . and . . . receive punishment," Curtis replied: "No sir . . . It's the idea of getting down on the ground and being whipped like a dog and you get cut up pretty bad." Questioned about a refusal to work, Curtis replied that the captains "grabbed" people, "choked" them, and "just forced them out into the fields."[27]

Recall that Jackson had alleged he had unconstitutionally been exposed to infectious disease because he was forced to sleep near Howard Warrington, who had tuberculosis. Warrington took the stand to explain that he was first diagnosed in 1947, currently felt "pretty sick," and was assigned to prepare food at Cummins. The prisoners' lawyers followed with four more witnesses, some of whom had been in other prison systems. They were asked about discipline elsewhere so as to substantiate that Arkansas was "unusual" as well as "cruel." Illustrative was testimony by Carl Raymond Osborne, who had been imprisoned in Iowa, in Kansas, and in the federal facility at Leavenworth; he said none used the whip. Osborne also described ongoing whippings at Cummins and made a reference to violence against Black prisoners; "very few nights there isn't some [whippings] on the colored end." Two prisoners, Elmer Fred Welling and Jesse Spigner, both held at Tucker, had seen the whippings of Ernst and the teeter board ordeal. Jerry White reported eleven whippings for "not working fast enough or not working to suit them."[28]

By the end of the morning of January 27, the judges were unwilling to hear more from prisoners. Before everyone paused for lunch, Wright described what a few other prisoners would have said.

"ENTIRELY SATISFIED WITH THE TESTIMONY . . . PRESENTED"

As the proceedings resumed, Wright made a statement for the record that rings oddly for those used to reading trial transcripts. Wright explained he had talked to "Mr. William King Jackson, Mr. Lyle Edward Ernst Jr., and Mr. Grady W. Mask" and asked if they knew of other testimony their lawyers should have presented. Wright stated on the record that "each expressed himself as being entirely satisfied with the testimony that has been presented." Wright then asked each man individually, and each concurred.[29]

Why would an experienced lawyer, enlisted to represent people who had no constitutional right to counsel, ask clients in open court to affirm the adequacy of his work? An explanation of this recitation (repeated at the trial's close on February 16) comes from an exchange in mid-November of 1966. Held in solitary confinement, Jackson complained to the judges that his lawyers were not pressing his case quickly enough. Judge Harris reassured Jackson that his lawyers were "capable and reputable attorneys" and that the judge would schedule the case when he could "get to it and they, of course, will be ready for trial."[30]

Wright and Arnold asked to be "relieved" of the assignment, but Judge Harris told them that he had learned that Jackson wanted them to continue "without further unnecessary delay." Judge Harris told the state to bring Jackson to court for a hearing on November 30, 1966, and on December 1, the lawyers filed an amended complaint on his behalf.[31] Given the timing of the amended complaints, it appears that Wright and Arnold interviewed the plaintiff–prisoners in December; they filed amended pleadings for Ernst on December 22, 1966, and for Mask on January 14, 1967. In short, Jackson's *pursuit* of his own lawyers produced the January 26 trial.

THE DEFENSE: "RAISED BY THE STRAP"

"I was raised by the strap, . . . and my boys is raised like I was."
—Guthrie Goodwin, Assistant Tucker Superintendent[32]

The afternoon of January 27, 1966, belonged to the defense, who put on staff to disagree with the prisoners. None had training in corrections, and several described decision-making procedures (which they often called "court") that did not comport with the *Talley* Rules. Many argued the reasonableness of whipping, evidenced by how they disciplined their own children. The defense could not, however, escape the Tucker torture. Three of the state's witnesses learned of their pending criminal indictments for "excessive punishment" the day they appeared in court.

The first person called was O. E. Bishop, who aimed to impress upon the judges that he had nothing to do with Tucker's atrocities, understood the *Talley* Rules, and did all he could to ensure compliance. In January of 1966 after the Penitentiary Board's rules arrived, Bishop "went to the colored section first, and read every page in the rules" before going to the "the white fellows" and reading the rules again. Thereafter, as new people entered the prison, they were given "a copy of these Rules and Regulations." Bishop reported telling wardens that, if they did not follow the rules, they would be fired, and that wardens told trustys not to do "any roughing" or they would be demoted. Bishop said that he "advised Captain Bruton to do the same as I did, and he did." Bishop reported he did "some of the court [him]self," with two wardens present; he charged prisoners with offenses and gave them opportunities to respond. The result (which happened "often") was that some people were not punished.[33] Focused on the 1,600 people at Cummins, Bishop went only a few times a month to Tucker ("50 miles away"), which was "hard" to oversee. Taking credit for launching the Tucker investigation, Bishop testified that "any man that would commit what I've learned was done" would be fired and that he had discharged Captain Mayes for whipping "someone with their pants down."[34]

Bishop said that since September of 1966, when the state police report came out, he had not heard of violations at Tucker until listening to the prisoners' testimony. When questioned about forms of "corporal punishment other than the strap," Bishop brought up the use of "solitary over at Tucker now" and hoped for a similar unit at Cummins. Asked to explain what "solitary" meant, Bishop described days on "bread and water," followed by a respite with more food. Bishop reported he had "promised the boys"—the term he and others used for prisoners—that he had ordered that they be regularly given portions of milk, eggs, and vegetables.[35]

William Arnold's cross-examination established that Bishop had no professional training. Bishop admitted he had never heard of James Bennett, the just-retired Director of the Federal Bureau of Prisons who was to testify for the prisoners. Bishop had not read the 1958 book, *Ruled by the Whip*, marked as Plaintiffs' Exhibit No. 9 for "identification." Bishop acknowledged that before he visited Tucker, alerts were sent that he was en route. Moreover, Bishop had no direct knowledge of whether Tucker staff held hearings as set forth by the Penitentiary Board's rules. More damning were the inconsistencies between what Bishop described and what the Rules required. Bishop conceded that at Cummins, the boards of inquiry often took place without either the superintendent or an assistant superintendent, which is to say that Bishop admitted violating the Board's rules.[36]

The second defense witness was Guthrie Goodwin, a forty-five-year-old man who testified he had never read any books on penology nor been part of prison administration until, from September to December of 1966, he became Tucker's Assistant Superintendent. Like Bishop, Goodwin had been a sheriff; he then spent a decade in the state's parole department, where he "put a lot of time and effort to trying to help these boys when they came out." As for whipping, Goodwin stated that, while necessary, no one "enjoys using it." He said that he whipped his children, which was the "discipline" he had experienced growing up. He "honestly believe[d]" that whipping was a substitute for what young offenders did not get at home. And, while it "stings," it was not more than that.[37]

Asked about incidents involving Mask, Goodwin reported he had sent Mask to the prison doctor (a "free-world" doctor), who found nothing wrong. Goodwin said he then "sentenced" Mask to "six licks" for picking only ninety pounds of cotton, while others had done more. When Goodwin was asked if he had "whipped him . . . passionately" (explained to mean "emotionally upset, real mad"), he replied no. Goodwin recounted another sentence of "eight licks" because Mask had taken a break. A third incident was when Mask had "made light" of a work order; Goodwin grabbed him by the shirt and told him to do "an honest day's work" or Goodwin would "have court."[38]

Arnold's cross-examination underscored that "court" did not comply with the Penitentiary Board rules. Goodwin admitted that in some instances, one of the "judges" was also the "accuser," and at times Goodwin was the sole decision-maker. When asked why he left, Goodwin said his employment was terminated "for the betterment" of the prison system. Some news reports said he was too lenient with prisoners[39]—a perception plausible only if the baseline was brutality.

Arkansas' next witness was Maurice Heston, who had been a deputy sheriff before becoming a "long line warden," overseeing fieldwork at Tucker. Heston testified that he often held "court" at night. The state's lawyer elicited that prisoners were given a chance to talk, and that no whippings took place in the fields. Heston said he had not enjoyed whipping, that he and other wardens took turns whipping, and that doing so "was part of my job." Upon cross-examination, Heston admitted that he and Captain Goodwin would alternate on the board of inquiry, which meant that some of the hearings at Tucker had neither a deputy superintendent nor a second prison official.[40]

The state's decision to call the three fired staff members (E. G. Mayes, Ernest Fletcher, and Jess Wilson) is mystifying, not only because they provided further proof of the violence but also because they had, on that day, received news that a Jefferson County Grand Jury had returned an "information," which meant they were about to be indicted. (Jim Bruton, also indicted, was in the hospital and not on the witness list.) Mayes, then fifty-three, had ended his schooling in ninth grade and been a barber and a policeman before being a "long line" warden at Tucker. Mayes stated he had not been given rules but knew he was not supposed to "hit anybody over ten licks." Mayes explained that because Ernst had not picked enough cucumbers and was "destroying the vines," he took him to Captain Bruton, who found Ernst "guilty," at which point Mayes whipped Ernst. The two others, Fletcher and Wilson, had ended their schooling after eighth grade. Fletcher worked for four years in the highway department and went to Tucker for thirteen years where he was in charge of the "rice operation," involving about 1,100 acres. Fletcher did not recall whipping Mask.[41] Wilson, in charge of the "tractor squad," gave prisoners "a spanking" after proceedings, and had likely done so "a hundred times."[42]

The state ended its day with three staff witnesses. Ray David Deam had been at Cummins since 1959; he testified he whipped only after hearings and was not "mad" when whipping. Warden Mose Harmon noted he had been "here once before." The reference was to the *Talley* case, in which Chief Judge Henley had described Harmon as aggressively assaultive. Harmon, then forty, had been at Cummins since 1955 as a field warden in charge of about a hundred men. He agreed that he had whipped Jackson, but reportedly only after he had taken him to "court" where two other people made the decision. Harmon said he did not like to whip but it was his "job." He noted that, having been "wondering" what it felt like to be whipped, he and another warden whipped each other, and that it did indeed "hurt."[43]

The state's closing witness was Clay Smith, who in March of 1966 became Cummin's head warden. (A photograph of him holding the whip became Plaintiffs' Exhibit 1.) Smith, who had been a prison employee since 1960, stated that, when holding "court," he gave the "boy" a chance to explain and not all were punished. Discussing one whipping, Smith said that an "average man can pick 250 pounds without trouble," and a prisoner had only picked seventy.[44]

On cross-examination, Arnold established that no system existed to protect against mistakes in the weighing of crops. Arnold elicited a description of a whipping on January 25, 1967, when Smith strapped two "colored boys" because they "were fighting." Smith was the first state witness to acknowledge hearing prisoners say "Oh, Captain," in "hopes" of the whipping letting "up a little," which he did when hearing those words. Arnold read to Smith excerpts from the 1966 American Correctional Association's (ACA) Manual for Correctional Standards (the domestic counterpart to the 1955 UN Rules) that called for the end of whipping as part of a long list of prohibited corporal punishments. Arnold asked if Smith knew of the ACA's manual. Smith replied he did not.

The state lawyers asked Smith about the people who had not been whipped; Smith concurred with the suggestion that "at least 1,400" of the prisoners were not subjected to whipping. Judge Young followed up: "Is it a relatively small group that we are talking about?" Smith responded, "extra small."[45]

14

THE EXPERTS OPINE
WHIPPING'S PARTICULAR HARMS

"[W]e are not trying the prison itself in Arkansas."
—The defendant's lawyer,
Jackson v. Bishop Trial, February 16, 1967[1]

The last day of trial was February 16, 1967, scheduled to accommodate the "experts"—two prison directors, James Bennett and Fred Wilkinson for the prisoners, and Thomas Dale Alford, an eye doctor for the defense.[2] Their educations and income aligned these white men with the lawyers and judges and set them apart from the prisoners and their keepers. Bennett and Edward Wright shared professional networks—the American Bar Association (ABA) and the American Law Institute (ALI). Bennett also knew Judge Harris; as head of the Federal Bureau of Prisons (BOP), Bennett had interacted with Harris as a powerful member of Congress. When the state's lawyers raised objections to Bennett's comments, Judges Harris and Young responded they would "give wide latitude" to his opinions as a "penologist," while of course deciding the legal questions.[3]

Stepping into the federal courthouse on *behalf* of prisoners, Bennett and Wilkinson were another set of "firsts." Almost one hundred years after the 1870 Cincinnati Declaration of Principles on prison conditions, these correctional professionals invoked the UN's 1955 Standard Minimum Rules on the Treatment of Prisoners and the 1966 Manual of the American Correctional Association

(ACA), calling for bans on corporal punishment. Their careers and testimony documented that, despite those standards, degradation was standard fare in federal and state prisons during much of the twentieth century. Both men saw themselves as changing that paradigm. Insistent on rehabilitation as incarceration's *raison d'être*, Bennett became a critic in the 1960s of the national turn to a retributive "law-and-order" ideology. Wilkinson, who had worked in the federal system before becoming the Director of Missouri's prisons, joined Bennett in an unequivocal condemnation of whipping. And, while neither their views nor the profession's standards persuaded Judges Harris and Young to rule whipping unconstitutional, their testimony supported the appellate judges' ban.

WAS THE UNITED STATES "REALLY A CIVILIZED COUNTRY IN THE SECOND DECADE OF THE TWENTIETH CENTURY"?

"To oversimplify, society wants men to be taught to use liberty wisely while deprived of it."

—James Bennett, *I Chose Prison*, 1970

In his autobiography, Bennett described turning to prison work out of horror at conditions he saw in the 1920s. His "motive was never . . . that of a visionary or a radical changer of lives or laws, but solely of a man who hates intolerance, injustice, and defeatism." The son of an Episcopal minister, Bennett graduated in 1918 from Brown University in Rhode Island and married a social worker. After serving in the Army Air Corps, Bennett joined the federal civil service while getting a law degree at George Washington University. The government assigned Bennett to the US Bureau of Efficiency, a predecessor to the Office of Management and Budget. Bennett recounted that Department of Justice officials asked him to evaluate the economics and logistics of requiring labor from federal prisoners. His tour took him to the Ohio State Penitentiary, which was the "decisive experience" of his life. The "enormous cellblocks depressed" him "beyond measure," as did the deplorable conditions of "the hole" where prisoners were left for days in tiny cages. Seeing such "atrocities," Bennett wrote, made him question whether the United States was "really a civilized country." In lieu of working at the Veterans Administration, Bennett "chose" prisons.[4]

Federal prisons in the mid-1920s confined about seven thousand people in five facilities—three penitentiaries at Leavenworth, Kansas; Atlanta, Georgia; and McNeil Island, Washington; along with two reformatories. When Bennett left in the early 1960s, about 20,000 people were federal prisoners; at that decade's end, the system held close to 25,000 people, which (as Bennett noted) was a small subset of the 400,000 people that was, by then, the "largest prison population of any nation in the world." (By 2024, the United States detained close to two million people, of which the BOP housed about 160,000 in 122 facilities across the country.[5])

Bennett's lengthy report, *The Federal Penal and Correctional Problem*, published in the 1929 Congressional Record with his testimony before the House Special Committee on Federal Penal and Reformatory Institutions, documented crowded, deteriorating, underfunded, and poorly staffed facilities too disconnected to be a "system." Men, "sleeping in dark, poorly ventilated basements, with inadequate toilet facilities," were double celled; that "vicious system of doubling up" was "universally condemned by prison authorities."[6]

Bennett proposed Congress create a centralized federal agency and build smaller prisons around the country. He wanted a focus on rehabilitation through education and vocational training and a few facilities for narcotics addicts. Although ill-timed given the 1929 Depression, Bennett's views fit snugly into progressive agendas of his era, during which several federal agencies were founded and professional expertise lauded. Bennett's report also reflected the influence of the burgeoning correctional establishment that he would soon join. As discussed, decades earlier, the new fields of penology, criminology, and psychology conceived of crime as a disease to be treated. Embracing that view, Bennett advocated for individualized assessments and indeterminate sentencing, which he thought could result in some shorter terms of confinement but, in practice, were interminable.[7]

Sanford Bates, at the helm of the federal prison conglomerate in 1929, asked Bennett to become his deputy, and the two contributed to drafting the statute President Herbert Hoover signed on May 14, 1930, to launch the BOP. That year, Hoover chose Bates as the BOP's Director. Bates, naming Bennett one of his three Assistant Directors, charged him with creating a prison industries program. (Another was Austin MacCormack, heading up "academic and vocational training and the formulation of prison discipline training"; in the late 1960s, he advised Arkansas on reforms.)

Persuading organized labor not to object, Bennett launched a federal prison industry system. He helped draft legislation to expand probation, a parole system, and permit the US Public Health Service to provide medical and psychiatric services in federal prisons. In 1937, after Bates became the Executive Director of the Boys Clubs of America, President Franklin Roosevelt selected Bennett to run the BOP. As discussed, Bates had been pivotal at the International Penal and Penitentiary Commission (IPPC) and brought Bennett in. Both were at the 1935 Berlin Congress, the IPPC 1950 Hague Congress, and the UN's first Congress in 1955.[8]

After becoming BOP Director in 1937, Bennett addressed the "'gut issue' of prison reform—brutality." What he *banned* tells us what was *in use*: he ordered guards to stop carrying nightsticks, clubs, "lashing, . . . the strap, . . . handcuffing men to the bars, [or] improper solitary confinement," and required his office's approval to take prisoners' good-time credits away. In addition to lessening violence, Bennett reported that, in some facilities, prisoners could "walk to their meals at any time the mess hall was open" and sit where they chose. ("In the first of several moves to desegregate the federal prisons, we urged Negro and white prisoners to sit at meals together, work together, and share cells and dormitories.") Bennett helped create a health care system, supported programs for youthful offenders, halfway houses, work release, probation, and education ("What makes a criminal is in large part lack of education, . . . [that] sets up the magnetism of crime.") In 1965, a year after Bennett retired, Congress enacted the Prisoner Rehabilitation Act putting some of those measures into law.[9] Bennett also joined Bates and Thorsten Sellin in advising the ALI, which in 1962 adopted a "model penal code" calling for corrections to "promote the . . . rehabilitation of offenders; to safeguard offenders against excessive, disproportionate or arbitrary punishment; . . . [and] to differentiate among offenders with a view to a just individualization in their treatment."[10]

Bennett was unwavering when the "war on crime" became a drumbeat that, infused with racial hostility, pushed for more policing and prosecutions. Bennett opened his 1970 memoir by discussing crime statistics, the 1967 Newark "tragic riot," and the "spread of crime, the talk about crime, and the fear of crime" in the 1967 report from Lyndon Johnson's Presidential Commission on Law Enforcement and Administration of Justice. Bennett reminded readers of his bipartisan credentials (appointed as BOP's Director by Presidents Roosevelt, Truman, Eisenhower, Kennedy, and Johnson) and warned that "equal justice under law" was "in danger of submersion . . . [to] the simpler, more savage shout of law and order." Rather than putting a "policeman on every corner" (a proposal of the Commission), Bennett called for education, jobs, and humane prisons. His book-long argument was that the "true way to fight crime" was to find the "treasure in the heart of every man."[11]

Unlike Paul Cornil, who at the 1950 IPPC's Hague Congress had suggested that prisons would one day be viewed to be as reprehensible as flogging and branding, Bennett called for prison's revitalization for the "space age"—a referent to US astronauts' 1969 moon landing. Bennett sought reliance on the "unalloyed professionalism" of correctional officials to build "new, modern, open prisons" (holding no more than six hundred) bearing "no resemblance to the penitentiaries" then in use. Before leaving the BOP, Bennett ordered the closure of Alcatraz, which was "too costly" and "too typical of the retributive justice that has no place in our philosophy." Further, incarcerating "sick people" was "cruel and unusual punishment" and likely unconstitutional. Bennett argued that "drug addicts, alcoholics, sex deviants, and mental defectives" should be moved out of prisons and into "clinics for cure."[12]

THE "GRISLY REVELATIONS OF THE ARKANSAS PRISON SYSTEM," THE "REPULSIVE" SUFFOLK COUNTY JAIL

After retiring, Bennett testified for Arkansas' prisoners and elsewhere. His participation was pathbreaking (as were the lawsuits in which he appeared) and also *consistent* with his commitments to his profession. He viewed Arkansas' officials as undermining obligations he held dear. Discussing his 1967 appearance in *Jackson v. Bishop* and other cases, Bennett wrote: "The grisly revelations of the Arkansas prison system hardly came as a surprise to me, nor to anyone even vaguely acquainted with the history of penology in the southern states. Beatings, lashings, bludgeonings, and murders of prisoners in the midst of unspeakable living conditions are commonplaces of penal history in the Delta region of the Mississippi River." Yet—seared by the federal facility he saw in Ohio in the 1920s—Bennett knew he was not telling a Southern story. "Governors and budget directors of many northern states" had let "poor facilities and programs cramp the rehabilitation of many offenders."[13]

Bennett's appearances elsewhere on behalf of prisoners reflected that Arkansas was awful but not uniquely so. In upstate New York, Bennett took the stand on behalf of a prisoner challenging "punitive segregation," where, without a bed, he was left "in a state of complete nudity"—conditions a federal judge held "constituted cruel and unusual infliction of punishment." That judge explained that Bennett had testified that discipline in prisons was a "very difficult, perplexing problem"; nonetheless, a prisoner should never be made to "sleep on a bare floor."[14]

Bennett also weighed in on the Suffolk County Jail in Boston, Massachusetts,[15] which he called a "dehumanizing museum piece." The federal judge in that case visited the jail and, citing Bennett's description of the "positively repulsive" plumbing, added that sinks and toilets were "corroded, filth-encrusted and often a serious health hazard. . . . A fecal smell emanates from many toilets."[16] In one reported decision, Bennett testified for the defense. In 1968, prisoners had challenged conditions in Missouri, which had been terrible and, as Bennett noted in his memoir, had improved under the guidance

of his former deputy, Fred Wilkinson,[17] who had joined him the year
before as the other expert in *Jackson v. Bishop*.

"BRUTAL, MEDIEVAL AND BRUTALIZED THOSE WHO ADMINISTERED IT"

"I am appearing here because of my interest in this matter . . . in the
hope that I may be helpful to the Court."

—James Bennett, testifying February 18,
1967 in the Whipping Trial

"Corporal punishment in any form should never be permitted."

—ACA 1966 Manual for Correctional Standards,
read into the transcript of the Whipping Trial[18]

Once Bennett took the stand in Arkansas, Edward Wright's questions established that Bennett was not paid for his testimony or
expenses and that he had an impressive career. Judges Harris and
Young heard about Bennett's role in shaping the BOP, his recruitment as Assistant Director, appointment as Director and retirement
in 1964. Bennett testified he helped the population drop from 24,000
prisoners in 1963 to 19,500 in 1966, had been involved with the ABA,
been president of the ACA, and chaired the US delegation to UN
congresses on criminal law enforcement.[19]

Wright asked Bennett his opinion on whipping, as it was described in the Arkansas Penitentiary Board's rules. Bennett responded the federal system did not whip because "we felt it was
brutal, medieval, and brutalized those who administered it and did
not do any real good, was not effective." Bennett stated that "certain
methods of treatment create hostilities in the prisoner"—making it
"extremely difficult, if not impossible, for him to adjust normally
to society to which he must return." Wright then asked about what
had been read at the trial's second day to Captain Clay Smith and
marked for "identification"—the 1966 ACA Manual for Correctional
Standards, in its third edition running more than six hundred
pages. Wright pointed to the statement "Corporal punishment in

any form should never be permitted" and "verbatim" put into the record what, under the header "Physical Punishment," the Manual termed "inhumane":

> flogging, strapping, beating with fists or clubs, spraying with a stream of water, stringing up by the wrists, exposure to extremes of heat or cold or to electric shock, confinement in the stocks or in camped sweat boxes, handcuffing to cell doors or posts, shackling so as to enforce cramped position or cut off circulation, standing for excessive periods on the line or barrel-heads, painted circles, etc., deprivation of sufficient light, food or exercise to maintain physical or mental health, forcing a prisoner to remain awake until exhausted, etc.

(This list of prohibitions was based on what prisons did to people, as Arkansas exemplified.)

Bennett stated he had contributed to the manual's drafting and affirmed that those punishments "should never be practiced in any circumstance." Wright also asked about the statement in the 1955 UN Standard Minimum Rules for the Treatment of Prisoners that "[c]orporal punishment by placing in a dark cell and all cruel, inhuman or degrading punishments shall be completely prohibited as punishment for disciplinary offenses." Bennett explained he chaired the drafting committee; the aim was to protect "American prisoners in foreign countries and vice versa."[20]

As to individuals who were whipped, Bennett opined doing so was "cruel" as he understood its meaning, as well as "degrading and certainly . . . unusual in this day and age." Bennett said he knew of no place he had visited in the United States and Europe, aside from Arkansas and perhaps "one other state" (later identified as Mississippi), that permitted whipping. Further, Bennett thought that "the great overwhelming majority of Americans will look upon the strapping of prisoners on this day under any circumstances for any cause [as] cruel and unusual." Wright linked that "discipline" to Arkansas' revenues by telling Bennett of the parties' stipulation (an agreed-upon fact)—that "for the fiscal year 1964–1965 . . . the profit of operation of the Arkansas Prison Farms, excluding the value of the services of the prisoners, was $677,488.75."[21]

The cross-examination was not helpful to the defense. The state's attorney elicited another critique of Arkansas' rules from Bennett; they were "quite indefinite and . . . any person who wanted to circumvent them could very easily do so." Walked through the procedures for whipping, Bennett found each aspect insufficient, including the lack of a "cooling off period" before making decisions and the absence of a "civilian person." When asked about how to discipline, Bennett explained providing prisoners with incentives and, if necessary, taking such privileges away. Bennett noted two other measures: solitary confinement and "administrative segregation" (with "full meals" inside cells) as responses if people were threatening. Bennett stated that punitive "solitary confinement" was rare, such as when a prisoner hit an officer or attempted an escape.[22]

Before Bennett could leave the stand, Judge Harris asked him what he thought about "repeaters"—people re-incarcerated after release and "hardened criminals." Bennett responded that institutions needed to provide "training" to equip people with "some skill" and "after-care." He added that some repeat offenders were easier to manage because they were "prison-wise." As for difficult people, Bennett said a small number ("four or five percent of the population") needed separate housing.[23]

". . . WHIPPING AND TORTURING ARE AS OUT OF DATE AS WOOD STOVES AND KEROSENE LAMPS"

—Fred Wilkinson, *The Realities of Crime and Punishment: A Prison Administrator's Testament*, 1972[24]

To buffer against arguments that Bennett, expert in *federal* prisons, would have little understanding of *state* prisons, Wright and Arnold called Missouri Director Wilkinson, running prisons in a state that, like Arkansas, sat within the Eighth Circuit. Unlike Bennett, Wilkinson had worked from the bottom up—starting in

1938 as a "substitute guard" at the federal penitentiary in Atlanta, Georgia.

Wilkinson marched through the ranks, becoming a full-time "correctional officer" and then "lieutenant, captain, associate warden and . . . warden of four institutions"—a camp at Mill Point, West Virginia and penitentiaries in McNeil Island, Washington; Lewisburg, Pennsylvania; and Atlanta, Georgia. Aside from Marine service (when he was wounded at Iwo Jima), Wilkinson spent his working life in prisons, ending up Deputy Director of the federal BOP before moving to Missouri, where 3,513 people were confined and eight hundred people employed. Wilkinson presided over the closing of the federal prison at Alcatraz, consulted with states around the country, and authored chapters of ACA manuals. One mark of Wilkinson's stature came from his role in the exchange of Rudolf Abel, a federal prisoner and "an important international spy," who was handed over in East Germany to enable US pilot Francis Gary Powers, shot down in 1960 and held by the Soviet Union, to return home. Wilkinson "escorted Abel out"[25]—as dramatized in Steven Spielberg's 2015 movie *Bridge of Spies*.

Wilkinson wrote an autobiography, *The Realities of Crime and Punishment: A Prison Administrator's Testament*, published in 1972 by a short-lived Missouri press and introduced as a "must read" by the state's governor. Wilkinson called for indeterminate sentences, more rehabilitative prisons, and better funding, yet decried the rise of criminal defendants' rights (the Warren Court had "upset the whole course of justice," and "tipped the scales"), opposed prisoner "self-government" ("mis-government"), and use of courts. Wilkinson criticized the 1969 US Supreme Court decision, *Johnson v. Avery*, which held that, unless Tennessee provided alternative assistance for prisoners, the state could not bar one prisoner from helping another draft documents for courts. Wilkinson described that right as "[o]ne of the influences most disruptive and demoralizing to administration," because it forced prison administrators to permit individuals (such as "sex partners and escape-minded prisoners") to be together in "conferences on . . . 'legal matters.'"[26]

Nonetheless, Wilkinson joined his former boss testifying against whipping. The prisoners' lawyer asked Wilkinson about an article in which he wrote "All forms of corporal punishment should be strictly prohibited." He affirmed that was his "policy" when in charge. Wilkinson described how different prisons were from days when he routinely "carried a . . . wooden club." Shown the straps that had been admitted into evidence, Wilkinson called whipping "cruel and unusual and unnecessary" and "abhorrent to public opinion." Wilkinson used other modes of punishment—losing privileges, good-time credits, and separation, and distinguished disciplinary solitary (a maximum of ten days) from "administrative segregation," where people having "difficulty in the prison population" could remain longer. He noted that administrative segregation was necessary for "trouble makers or agitators." ("We have a great deal of trouble today with Muslims, for example, and must control them about holding meetings"). In both the federal prison system and Missouri, "we rarely use solitary." Wilkinson added that putting someone into what prisoners called the "hole" was inefficient, as it required checks "every 15 or 30 minutes" to be sure the person was all right.[27]

Again, the state's lawyers used cross-examination to make matters worse for their client. They broke the rule good lawyers follow—not to ask open-ended questions whose answers they do not know. The state's lawyer asked Wilkinson if Arkansas' rules were "good workable rules to follow." Wilkinson listed their faults, including that not enough people did the investigating and judging. Moreover, Wilkinson declined to use the word "reasonable" in reference to ten lashes. Questioned about discipline, facilities, staffing, and problems, Wilkinson provided a lecture on how to deal with difficult people without whipping. The key, Wilkinson explained, was not to "give up on them." Asked about farming, Wilkinson explained that Missouri prisoners ate what they harvested and surpluses were given to "a training school or an orphanage or sometimes county jails." If someone missed picking tomatoes, Wilkinson commended counseling or another job.[28]

SEEING OKRA DESPITE IMPAIRED VISION, "SATISFIED" PLAINTIFFS, AND A 641-PAGE RECORD CLOSED

The day belonged to the prisoners' experts with one brief exception. The state called Dr. Thomas Alford, who, in the 1950s, won a term in Congress for his segregationist credentials. Returning to his medical practice thereafter, Alford had been asked by Judge Harris to examine Jackson. Alford concluded that chronic infections in both Jackson's eyes could obscure vision, and yet not prevent seeing "an object as large as a piece of okra." The caveat was that if Jackson had an allergy to okra, his vision could be more limited near that crop.[29]

This last trial day ended with the recitation paralleling the conclusion of the prisoners' case on January 27. Wright asked Jackson, Ernst, and Mask if additional evidence should have been presented. After each agreed with Wright's statement of being "satisfied with the trial as it has been conducted," the record in *Jackson v. Bishop* closed.[30]

To recap, these 641 pages documented that distinguished and able lawyers provided evidence of terrifying violence and that two penologists of impeccable credentials decried whipping. Three of the defense witnesses were told they faced criminal charges the day they joined other prison staff in providing incredulous accounts. Clumsy cross-examinations of the prisoners and their witnesses underscored the horrors and bizarre practices in Arkansas' prisons. Yet Judges Harris and Young refused to ban the whip even as they called for more procedure as a predicate to its use. To understand their June 3, 1967, decision and its impact requires knowing both what they said and what they knew was going on in Arkansas' prisons and politics.

15

SLOWING THE WHIP THROUGH LAW AND POLITICS

The question haunting this book is why judges—and everyone else—have not done more to end the abysmal treatment of incarcerated people. Learning about why Judges Oren Harris and Gordon Young stopped short of banning the whip and how Winthrop Rockefeller's reform efforts were thwarted is part of piecing together answers.

Below, I analyze the trial judges' ruling that whipping was not "cruel and unusual punishment." By contrasting their decision with opinions of federal judges elsewhere and the Supreme Court's toleration a decade later of "paddling" students, I clarify what Jackson, Ernst, and Mask *won* as well as what they *lost*. Further, through describing more revelations of scandals in Arkansas' prisons, as well as Rockefeller's new appointments to the Penitentiary Board and legislative proposals for the state's first Department of Corrections, I explain why Judges Harris and Young may have assumed that they did not *need* to spend federal "judicial capital" banning the whip. The high-profile lawyers the judges enlisted succeeded in shifting the punishment question to the executive and legislative branches; the publicity produced by the trial prompted state officials to call whipping to a halt. But the state's commitment to profiting from prisons by extracting endless labor while leaving prisoners in violent conditions with abysmal food and shelter meant that much more than whipping needed to end.

"OVERLOOKING OKRA," "LEAVING CUCUMBERS," AND "CRUELTY" UNDER THE EIGHTH AMENDMENT

On June 3, 1967, Judges Harris and Young issued their *Jackson v. Bishop* decision. In about a dozen pages, they condensed the 641-page transcript, exhibits, and underlying documents into a short summary of the facts and law undergirding their ruling. Readers learned that William Jackson had been whipped "for not picking enough cotton" and "overlooking okra," that Lyle Ernst had been whipped "on the bare buttocks" after being charged with "leaving cucumbers on the vines," and that Grady Mask had been whipped for "working too slow." The judges explained that these men had been made to lie "face down on the concrete floor." Further, "twelve other inmates" corroborated what Jackson, Ernst, or Mask had said and provided more instances of whippings that, the judges noted, made that testimony "cumulative."[1]

The judges recounted the state police investigation and the discovery of "torturous devices," including a machine delivering electric shocks and the teeter board. They explained that some whippings were "administered without a formal hearing" and others had only one warden present. The judges described Bishop's defense that he tried to enforce the Penitentiary Board's whipping rules and knew nothing of Tucker's horrors. Harris and Young summarized the testimony of five witness–wardens ("discharged or permitted to resign") that they viewed whipping "as just another part of their jobs" and "had no personal feelings" about individuals they whipped. Before turning to the "applicable law," the judges acknowledged the input of the two penologists, James Bennett and Fred Wilkinson. They described Bennett's opinion that the whip was "brutal and medieval and did no real good," and Wilkinson's position that "all forms of corporal punishment should be abolished."[2]

Yet Harris and Young concluded that whipping *was* constitutional, as long as an "unguarded use of the strap" was avoided. (Perhaps they chose the word "unguarded" as a reminder that prison guards were in need *of* guarding.) Their brief discussion of law offered little illumination. Noting that it was "well settled that the administration of state prison discipline" was the "primary responsibility of state officials," the judges described the "extremely limited area in which" federal courts could act. Yet, it was "equally well settled" that "exceptions" existed when "constitutional rights" were involved. Making no mention of the prisoners' claims under the Equal Protection or Due Process Clauses, Harris and Young focused on a lack of a "satisfactory definition" of the Eighth Amendment's prohibition on cruel and unusual punishments.[3]

For guidance, they looked to the Eighth Circuit law they were obliged to follow. The judges cited two 1965 appellate decisions holding that prisoners had constitutional protection when the "character or consequence" of treatment in prisons could "shock general conscience" or was "intolerable in fundamental fairness." Harris and Young did not, however, discuss whipping's relationship to the "general conscience" and "fundamental fairness." Instead, they quoted Chief Judge Henley's unwillingness to say that the "use of the strap in and of itself is contrary to the Eighth Amendment's prohibitions."[4] In addition, Harris and Young drew on *Wright v. McMann*, issued in 1966 by another federal judge, Stephen Brennan, sitting in upstate New York; he opined that

[e]very punishment in a sense involves cruelty since it imposes by force conditions at odds with the concept of the freedom of the person from all forms of trespass and freedom of action. More than this is required to violate the Eighth Amendment.

Relying on Judge Brennan was surprising. Unlike Harris and Young who had enlisted distinguished lawyers to help the prisoners, Brennan dismissed the claims of the unrepresented Lawrence William Wright, as he complained about a "continuous flood of applications by state prisoners . . . occasioned by the expanded concept of an individual's constitutional rights. . . . That the vast majority of such applications are without merit does not relieve the court from the burden imposed."[5]

Not only was Judge Brennan nasty, he was governed by law from another appellate circuit, and he was wrong. Soon after Harris and Young quoted Brennan, the Court of Appeals for the Second Circuit reversed his decision that tossed the prisoner out of court. That court quoted the prisoner's description of his treatment at New York's Clinton State Prison.

[T]he said solitary confinement cell wherein plaintiff was placed [for 54 days] was dirty, filthy and unsanitary, without adequate heat and virtually barren; the toilet and sink were encrusted with slime, dirt and human excremental residue superimposed thereon; plaintiff was without clothing and entirely nude for several days . . . until he was given a thin pair of underwear to put on; . . . denied the use of soap, towel, toilet paper, tooth brush, comb, and other hygienic implements and utensils; . . . compelled under threat of violence, assault or other increased punishments to remain standing at military attention in front of his cell door each time an officer appeared from 7:30 A.M. to 10:00 P.M. every day . . . therefore; . . . [in] subfreezing temperatures causing plaintiff to be exposed to the cold air and winter weather without clothing or other means of protecting himself.

The appellate court sent the case back to a different judge. Two years later, represented by lawyers who turned for expert help to James Bennett, that prisoner, along with another, won after a seven-day trial, recorded in a 1566-page transcript. The judge, noting that the "eminence of Director Bennett was recognized in *Jackson v. Bishop*," held that putting a person nude for days in an unfurnished cell "constituted cruel and inhuman punishment in violation of the Eighth and Fourteenth Amendments."[6]

My description of the degradation in New York's prisons serves as another reminder that, while Arkansas was unusual in licensing whipping, it was not unusual in treating prisoners horribly. Indeed, the practice in upstate New York had a shorthand—"strip cell"—and was used East to West.[7] And, just as Winston Talley and William King Jackson were beaten for insisting that the Constitution protected them, Lawrence Wright and scores of other prisoner–pioneers encountered vicious retribution after reaching out to judges, the press, and each other.

WHAT JACKSON, MUSK, AND GRADY WON

My discussion of upstate New York has another purpose. Learning that a federal judge there accused a prisoner of a mistakenly "expanded concept of an individual's constitutional rights" and refused to consider that being left, naked, in a freezing cell was unconstitutional makes it possible to appreciate the victories in *Talley* and *Jackson*. Getting federal judges to appoint lawyers and protect their access to court was a feat in 1965 and in 1967. Moreover, obtaining a court order telling prison officials to change *anything* was also a win. To be sure, what Harris and Young permanently enjoined ("the crank telephone or teeter board" and whipping "the bare skin of prisoners") had been the bases for criminal indictments.

Yet the judges also ordered a pause on whipping people whose clothes were on: Arkansas' officials were "restrained from the 'use of the strap' on any prisoner until additional rules and regulations are promulgated with appropriate safeguards." The prisoners' lawyers succeeded in establishing that the 1966 Penitentiary Board rules did "not provide the adequate safeguards required" by *Talley*. Invoking "Dr. Bennett," who called the rules too "indefinite," Judges Harris and Young required revisions. While couching their directives as "observations" (it was "neither this court's duty nor its inclination to tell" prison administrators what to do), the judges added to Chief Judge Henley's parameters. To be compliant, "more than one person's judgment" was necessary before administering corporal punishment. The accuser was not to be "counted among those who sit in judgment." One prisoner's "report on another" was not acceptable without "further investigation."[8]

Judges Harris and Young labeled one facet of whipping "intolerable"—action by "an official in a time of anger." For Harris and Young, the *timing and emotions* of the people doing the punishment mattered, just as these factors had been salient for Henley, insistent that whipping be "inflicted as dispassionately as possible." (One hundred and fifty years earlier, Jeremy Bentham had, as discussed, proposed a "whipping machine" to ensure evenhanded and nonarbitrary lashings.) For Harris and Young, whipping required an "objectively reasoned, dispassionate decision." This focus on the attitudes and feelings of the people *imposing* punishment forecast interpretations of the Eighth Amendment in decades thereafter. Instead of centering an assessment of "cruel and unusual" on the experiences of people *subjected* to punishment, Supreme Court opinions often look to the *intentions* of those meting out punishments to assess whether they sought to be "unnecessarily" cruel or to layer on a "superaddition" of pain.[9]

Even as the Associated Press ran the headline: "Prison Ordered to Bar Strap," the prisoners *lost* their labor claims. While reiterating Henley's 1965 statement that prison officials were not to "compel convicts to perform physical labor which is beyond their strength, or which constitutes a danger to their lives or health," the two judges relied on medical reports to find that the three were not pushed beyond their abilities.[10] The judges discounted the prisoners' testimony of painful, forced labor and left *intact* the economic drivers of the whipping system.

Thus, it was the prisoners and not the state that appealed. Eighteen months later, in December of 1968, the prisoners won a ban on corporal punishment. Before analyzing what moved the Eighth Circuit, I sketch why Harris and Young could have believed that whipping *was* constitutional and how their decision *did* push the political branches to halt whipping.

"PADDLING" CHILDREN AND CIVIL RIGHTS RETRENCHMENT

More than once, prison staff stated at trial that they had been "raised by the strap" and whipped their children. It is possible— although hard to fathom given whipping's nexus to slavery—that the judges thought "strapping" people, if regulated to comport with "fundamental fairness," was not a "shock to general conscience."

That testimony was not all the judges had for declining to outlaw whipping. As discussed, whipping had a long pedigree in countries regarding themselves as the epitome of "civilization." The "Anglo-Saxon influence and spirit" had sustained toleration of "striking . . . with a baton" in the 1930s, when the International Penal and Penitentiary Commission (IPPC) formulated, and the League of Nations adopted, the Standard Minimum Rules for the Treatment of Prisoners.[11] Until James Bennett became BOP Director in 1937, federal prison staff carried clubs. Thirty years later, when *Jackson v. Bishop* was tried, the English Parliament ended flogging in prison. Other Commonwealth countries, including Canada and Australia, then permitted whipping; as noted, the Supreme Court of Singapore ruled in 2015 that caning did not violate its constitution or international law.[12]

One does not need to go abroad to find examples of body blows *condoned* in US constitutional law. A decade after *Jackson*, the US Supreme Court refused to outlaw "paddling" in schools. In *Ingraham v. Wright*, a majority of five described the Dade County, Florida school district's policy; the "authorized punishment consisted of paddling the recalcitrant student on the buttocks with a flat wooden paddle measuring less than two feet long, three to four inches wide, and about one-half inch thick. The normal punishment was limited to one to five 'licks' or blows. . . ." Akin to arguments made by Arkansas wardens, Florida officials asserted that physical punishment was less harsh than suspension and expulsion. Moreover, paddling was commonplace. As the *Ingraham* Court explained in 1977, twenty-one states had legislation regulating it. "Only two states (Massachusetts and New Jersey) prohibited all corporal punishment in their public schools."[13]

As in Arkansas, evidence of paddling's injuries was plentiful. The record in *Ingraham* was replete with testimony about the harms suffered by sixteen students hit for trivial, alleged infractions. The lead plaintiff, James Ingraham, was in junior high school when he was accused of being "slow to respond to his teacher's instructions" and sent to the principal's office. Ingraham insisted he was innocent and "refused to assume the paddling position." As the Court described, a school official then gave him "more than 20 licks with a paddle while being held over a table in the principal's office." Doctors concluded that the paddling caused a hematoma from which fluids oozed. Other students provided parallel accounts, including one paddled "four times within a twenty-day period."[14]

Many commentators thought that the aggressive paddling in Ingraham's school, where children were predominantly Black, would move the Supreme Court to ban the practice.[15] Instead, the Court ruled the Constitution did not prohibit it. The decision was written by Justice Lewis Powell, who thereafter was central to cutting back on prisoners' rights. He had chaired the Richmond, Virginia School Board throughout much of the 1950s and was appointed to the Presidential Commission on Law Enforcement and Administration of Justice. Powell joined three other commissioners in making a separate statement when the Commission's Report, *The Challenge of Crime in a Free Society*, was issued in 1967. They wrote about the need to study the "difficult and perplexing problems arising from certain of the constitutional limitations upon our system of criminal justice." Translation: They objected to the Warren Court's interpretations of the Fifth and Sixth Amendments, which they thought gave criminal defendants too many rights at the expense of law enforcement. Their complaints centered on the 1966 decision in *Miranda v. Arizona*, which they believed unduly hampered police interrogations; their call for "the people of this country" to "strike" the right balance was directed at legislators to try to limit the impact.[16] (In 1971, ABA President Edward Wright, who had been Jackson's lawyer, likewise registered objections to *Miranda*.)

Once on the Court, Justice Powell repeatedly deferred to local decision-makers. Justice Powell's insistence in *Ingraham* on keeping federal judges' "hands off" (the term in the 1960s when judges declined to hear prisoners) meant that school administrators could literally use their hands to paddle students. Justice Powell's justification was that the Eighth Amendment's "cruel and unusual punishment" provision applied only to "punishment" after conviction and not to school discipline. Moreover, said Justice Powell, unlike prisons, a public school was "an open institution" subject to "supervision" by its community. Rejecting the dissenters' view that the Due Process Clause required more procedural protections, Justice Powell wrote that state tort law was the only source of remedies.[17]

The impact of the Court's licensure can be seen in data on paddling. According to the National Education Association, as of 2024, twenty-three states permitted or had not banned paddling. In 2015, data from the US Department of Education's Office of Civil Rights identified about 93,000 students paddled; the highest numbers were in Mississippi, Texas, Alabama, and Arkansas, and children of color disproportionately bore the brunt. By 2020, estimates were that COVID school closures had resulted in numbers falling to about 20,000, with "Black students and students with disabilities . . . twice as likely to" be hit "as white students without disabilities."[18]

REMEDIES FROM POLITICS: WINTHROP ROCKEFELLER, DRUGS "DISPENSED LIKE WATER," AND ADMINISTRATIVE REFORM

In addition to little law ruling out whipping and paddling, Arkansas politics gave Judges Harris and Young reasons to pause. As their opinion explained, the state police had investigated, the legislature had launched a special commission, the Penitentiary Board had made inquiries, and "many desirable changes" had resulted.[19] What the judges did not mention was that sixteen days before the trial began, Winthrop Rockefeller took over the governorship. As discussed, he pledged in his inaugural January 10, 1967, speech to reform "a prison system regarded by professional penologists as being generally the worst in the United States."[20] By June, when the judges issued their opinion, Rockefeller had picked Tom Murton, the first trained penologist employed by Arkansas, to run Tucker.

Thus, Harris and Young may have thought that they did not need do more than an interim ban, as the governor or legislature would act. More than that: Judges Harris and Young could have believed that they were *pivotal* in bringing about whipping's end. These judges had appointed two of Arkansas' premier lawyers to make a stunning record aimed not only at the court but at public opinion and, if needed, an appeal. And the judges were *right*. The Arkansas Legislature's Study Commission called for whipping's end; the Penitentiary Board prohibited it, and the trial transcript enabled the prisoners' lawyers to get the judges reversed on appeal.

However, whipping was not the only problem. As the press chronicled, the violence, filth, corruption, racism, and endless labor in

Arkansas' prisons did not abate. About two months after the judges' ruling, the Penitentiary Board selected a thirty-four-year-old, Dr. Edwin Barron Jr., to be the prisons' part-time physician. By then, the newspapers had reported that Cummins had hired its "first Negro warden," T. J. Jasper who, like others, had served as a deputy sheriff. Before Barron's October 1, 1967 start date, he reported to the Board about his inspection; what he said reiterated much of what Dale Woodcock wrote more than a decade before.[21]

Dr. Barron described food served in fly-infested areas and utensils uncleaned for hours; the lack of sanitation put prisoners at risk of "infections and food poisoning." Moreover, the only fresh fruit was to be bought at "inflated" commissary prices; many prisoners suffered from "infected gums, colon problems and constipation." Barron saw a prisoner who was in shock and, but for his intervention, would have died; he identified at least eleven cases of "endemic hepatitis" and suspected twenty more. The medical equipment was abysmal, and prisoner–trustys handed out old medicines "long since taken off the market." The Penitentiary Board responded with a call for rules, statistics, and quality controls.[22]

After Dr. Barron began and tried to establish a "permanent tuberculous control center" at Cummins, he learned that trustys gave, without recordkeeping, about one hundred doses of penicillin a day. After a prisoner asked him to sign off on an order for ten stethoscopes, Barron became suspicious. Looking at accounts (such as they were), Barron found that the prison had spent "an incredible amount of money" ($8,000 during three months) on drugs that prisoners "dispensed like water." Cummins had a stock of 50,000 aspirin tablets, hundreds of antibiotic pills, and injectable penicillin vials worth about $9,000. Barron also learned that the solitary cell for women had a can for a toilet and that the institution's X-ray machine gave off dangerous emissions. The local press described this prison-based "drug and narcotics ring" ("One More Scandal") as a new source of "shame." An editorial concluded that Dr. Barron's report "should sicken all right thinking citizens who take pride in their state, their church and their civilization." Instead, a Lincoln County grand jury complained that Dr. Barron had wrongly made public the information and declined to indict anyone. All it called for was a "'free-world' pharmacist" to dispense drugs.[23]

Yet pressures were mounting. Bishop had survived the Tucker scandal but had no way to distance himself from Barron's report and was losing the power struggle with Murton, who wanted his job. Murton's high-profile efforts included an unsuccessful attempt to have prisoners put on a play ("Of Prisons and Men") at the local arts center and providing the legislature's Study Commission with a 103-page set of "observations on the correctional needs of the State of Arkansas" running from the "ancient philosophy" of punishment to the twentieth century. Murton called for reforms including incentive pay for prisoner labor. Rockefeller, "greatly impressed," commented that the "unbelievable medieval, concentration-camp conditions which existed just one year ago at Tucker have been corrected." Further, whipping had ended there, although "[u]nfortunately," it was still in use at Cummins, even though Bishop did not "personally like this form of punishment." On November 1, Bishop submitted his resignation, effective at year's end. "Many circumstances and a number of people have rendered it impossible for me to do my job in the manner in which I think it should be done."[24]

That fall, Penitentiary Board member John Haley made the "case for reform." His six-page memo proclaimed that "dramatic changes" were underway. Legislative commitments "to expenditures in excess of profits that can be generated from the farms" would let the state move away from the "prisoner-run penal system"; funds would support the Board's plan to increase "personnel from 36 to 113"—the "most significant step . . . in penitentiary reform in fifty-four years." Yet so much was needed. At the end of 1967, Cummins housed "492 whites and 727 Negroes, including 18 white and 20 Negro women." Tucker confined "265 whites and 9 Negroes" on death row. The state had no records of their ages, crimes, lengths of sentences, education, or families. Prompted by Arkansas' Legislative Commission, staff from the Federal Bureau of Prisons (BOP) interviewed 175 prisoners and estimated that more than half could have been put on probation or parole, and about 60 percent were "suitable for minimum custody."[25]

After the 1968 resignations of Faubus' appointees to the Penitentiary Board, Rockefeller got control and promised, given that 60 percent of the prisoners were Black men, that "at least one of the new members will be a Negro." The governor chose W. L. Currie, a teacher, a farmer, and the "first of his race" to serve. The whiteness of Rockefeller's other appointees (a psychiatrist, a minister, and another farmer) went unnoted in the press. Rockefeller elevated Haley to the Chair. Within short order, the Penitentiary Board made Murton, then thirty-nine, Superintendent and called for an audit of the prison system.[26]

REHABILITATION AND RACIAL SEGREGATION

"That the form of corporal punishment commonly called whipping . . . be abolished at Cummins Farm, as it was at Tucker Farm early in 1967."

—Arkansas State Penitentiary Commission
recommendation, January 1, 1968[27]

The Legislature's Study Commission met its statutory January 1, 1968, deadline and disbanded. A central influence was its expert volunteer, the New York–based consultant Austin MacCormick who, like James Bennett, was at the corrections profession's highest echelon. MacCormick had worked at the BOP, been president in 1938 of the American Prison Association (later the American Correctional Association), proposed a rewrite in 1951 of the IPPC's Rules, and by the 1960s headed the Osborne Association that, like the Howard League, had grave reservations about incarceration. Arkansas' newspapers, noting MacCormick served without charge, explained he had "surveyed every prison system in the country at least once."

MacCormick's monograph, *Adult Correctional Institutions in the United States*, was submitted to the President's Commission on Law Enforcement and Administration of Justice. MacCormick also reported to the UN that instead of self-congratulation, "we Americans will do well to think of our country, in terms of correctional progress, 'as a developing nation.'" In many jurisdictions, he wrote, institutions were "mediocre or less." Without naming Arkansas, MacCormick ranked it at the bottom, as a state where prisoners guarded other prisoners, pressures were intense to produce money through farming, and whips were used.[28] MacCormick was the source of Governor Rockefeller's reference that Arkansas' prisons were seen as "generally the worst in the United States."

Under MacCormick's tutelage, the Study Commission cited the 1966 ACA Manual and quoted the paragraph read into the trial record at *Jackson v. Bishop* that "corporal punishment should never be used under any circumstances," with its list of horrific practices. The Commission described alternatives, such as losing privileges and good time and, if necessary, solitary confinement (preferably in single-person cells) where a person was to be fed a "restricted diet" such as "bread and water three times a day, with a full meal or all three meals every third day."

In addition, the Commission added the "r" word— rehabilitation—into the state's lexicon. "Citizens of Arkansas, and its governmental officials and legislators, accept the concept almost universally endorsed in America by correctional administrators that prisons have a legal and moral obligation to rehabilitate prisoners, and not merely to confine them." That shift supported restructuring prison administration and obtaining appropriations for construction and programs. The Commission called for a "Department of Correction," headed by a commissioner (of "high character") to be in charge of Cummins, Tucker, and the Women's Reformatory, as well as field officers responsible for probation and parole. The Penitentiary Board was to be replaced by a Board of Correction, comprised of five citizens to make policy, oversee the commissioner, and be "responsible for seeing that its policies are carried out."[29]

Another "r" word—race—was part of the report. The Commission recommended a reorganization so that Tucker, all white, would include young adults who were "white and Negro." Cummins would continue to hold older men of both races. (Not discussed was whether barracks were to be mixed.) In addition, the Commission recommended construction of a "relatively small maximum-security facility," single-occupancy cells, and to put a prison for women on a separate campus.[30]

The Commission did not, however, call for revamping the labor structure and ending the trusty system. Making money from farming drove the "discipline," and field work limited time for education or other programs. The Commission did suggest replacing *armed* trusty guards with paid professional and custodial staff. Further, it proposed "mechanization wherever it is practical and profitable" to improve "working conditions" for prisoners.[31]

MORE VIOLENCE, CALLS FOR WHIPPING, AND LEGISLATIVE REFORM

Rockefeller needed money from the legislature, but it was controlled by Democrats. Armed with the legislature's own commission's recommendations, Rockefeller asked for an appropriation of $1,750,000 for construction, staff, and a new corrections department.[32] To Rockefeller's chagrin, however, Murton put Arkansas' prisons back in national news. Acting on information from a prisoner, Murton found three unmarked graves on the prison grounds; two had detached skulls, and the Penitentiary Board approved a search for bodies. As the press explained, since 1917, at least 200 prisoners had been listed as escapees, and one theory was that "prison officials and guards killed inmates and secretly buried them over the years." The *New York Times* noted that evidence was already plentiful "that prisoners had been flagrantly beaten and tortured."[33]

On January 30, 1968, the state police were at Cummins, joined by a television camera crew. That digging was aborted when Arkansas' Attorney General said a court order was required. According to a quickly filed investigation that the state police gave to the US Attorney General, the three skeletons were relics of old paupers' graves. On February 13, 1968, a grand jury began and, in early March, declined to indict. Its report called the search a "publicity stunt," recommended Murton's firing, and proposed returning to whipping as discipline. In contrast, a national magazine linked the story ("Bodiesburg") to the *Jackson* trial's account of the teeter board, the Tucker Telephone, whippings, and beatings. A local story described parolees' accounts of having to scream "Oh Cap'n, . . . between each lick or they'd hit you harder and longer." Castigating the state for its cover-up, one reporter commented that in Germany "they still try to forget Dachau. In Arkansas they'd like to forget Cummins."[34]

Atop questions of murder came more violence. One story described prisoners trying to get into isolation cells to protect themselves from rape. A reporter quoted Murton that crowding made safety impossible and the "homosexual rate [was] about 85 percent." Rockefeller and his allies (including a key staffer, Tom Eisele who became a federal judge and presided over later phases of the prison litigation) were appalled. In February, the Penitentiary Board invited MacCormick, along with the dean of Berkeley School of Criminology from which Murton had graduated, to a meeting; I found its transcript in Judge Eisele's archived papers. Murton was described as an inept administrator who could not tell his "friends from his enemies," and MacCormick advised finding a way to end his tenure.[35] (In 1980, Murton's account became the basis for the Robert Redford movie, *Brubaker*.)

Arkansas' legislature convened a special session on February 6, 1968, to consider its Study Commission's proposals. Rockefeller's staff put in draft legislation, but the bills soon "ran into heavy weather." On February 14, the Arkansas House of Representatives voted 60–27 to "strike a prohibition against corporal punishment" from the packet. The proponents explained they spanked their kids, told children's teachers to do the same when children "get out of line," and that Chief Judge Henley has said whipping was not cruel and unusual punishment. Further, the request for special appropriations ($1.75 million requisite to continuing employment for 114 "free-world" staff) stalled. After ninety-seven Democrats supported putting off prison reform until the May session, a revised bill was proposed with fewer reforms and no ban on corporal punishment.[36]

Yet in Arkansas, even that stripped-down bill was a landmark. The legislature adopted the Study Commission's call that Arkansas align itself with rehabilitation; the new correction statute no longer required prisoners to do "hard labor"; instead, incarceration should be for "treatment, rehabilitation and restoration of adult offenders as useful, law-abiding citizens within the community." That bill, enacted February 21, 1968, also created a Board of Correction, a Department of Correction, and a Commissioner of Correction. The local press celebrated the end of "Days of Brutal Punishment."[37]

In March of 1968, before the Arkansas Penitentiary Board became the Board of Correction, the group made three key decisions. First, spending less than two minutes ("with no debate and little comment"), the Board voted "unanimously to prohibit any form of corporal punishment"—by which it meant whipping. Second, with the assent of Rockefeller, the Board refused to promote Murton to head the department. The third decision left intact the brutal labor system that undercut prospects for reform. Worried about harvesting cucumbers and sweet potatoes and the lack of mechanization, the Board authorized a *ten-hour* workday that could grow longer or shorter depending on demands.[38]

A week later, Haley joined in firing Murton for "insubordination, lack of cooperation with other state agencies and fiscal irresponsibility," on top of his "intractability." Writing to Victor Urban, head of pardons and parole, to persuade him to become the temporary new Superintendent, Rockefeller said that "[a]ll of us regret that a change has become necessary . . . However, personalities are not as important as the prison reform program." Rockefeller pledged his "full personal support . . . We have just begun."[39]

HARVESTING VERSUS SCHOOLS AND RACIAL SEGREGATION IN THE BARRACKS

"[T]o have a progressive program we must have funds above what can be earned on the prison."

—Victor Urban, Acting Commissioner of Correction[40]

The need for sweat labor intensified, as farm income declined, machinery broke down, and the legislature appropriated only $700,000, less than half of what had been requested. In June of

1968, a school started at Tucker where teenagers as young as fifteen were confined. Yet when 183 of the 298 prisoners were in classes, one headline complained "Manpower shortage delays harvesting of crops at prison."[41]

By then, forty-year-old Victor Urban had signed on to be the Acting Commissioner of Correction. Urban was Arkansas' second correctional professional, brought to Tucker in 1967; he had a criminology graduate degree from the University of Arizona and had been employed by the federal prison system. Asking the Board to get farming machinery and stop trusty authority over other prisoners' punishment, Urban explained "to have a progressive program we must have funds above what can be earned on the prison."[42]

The Study Commission had called for racial segregation to end but steps toward implementation did not come until after March of 1968, when Norman Chachkin wrote Arkansas officials to explain the March 11, 1968, Supreme Court decision of *Lee v. Washington*, upholding a desegregation order for Alabama's prisons. (I discuss that litigation and its glacial impact on Arkansas in later chapters.) Arkansas' Attorney General's Office advised the Board of Correction that, while it was "illegal" to segregate in prisons, race could be "a factor" in "particular circumstances," such as "maintaining security and discipline" when an "imminent danger" stemmed from "purely racial tensions." Those words echoed what Justice Black, joined by Justices Harlan and Stewart, wrote in the Alabama case—that prison officials, "acting in good faith and in particularized circumstances" could, when security concerns existed, "take into account racial tensions." Arkansas' Board directed Urban to develop a desegregation plan, and a month later, Urban tried to rebuff an angry state senator, insistent that Black Muslims advocated the "overthrow of the United States government by force." Urban explained that "Black Muslims' Meetings" were not a source of "trouble" in that the "followers of Elijah Muhammad of Chicago" numbered about three to ten.[43]

In September of 1968, the new Arkansas Department of Correction (ADC) filed a "progress report." The ADC stated that "by administrative action corporal punishment in all forms has been abolished." Further, instead of prisoners running financial matters, paid staff was in charge of the books. The first stage of Tucker's desegregation had begun; "twenty-one Negro inmates," aged fifteen to twenty-seven, were transferred from Cummins. When new prisoners arrived, they received physical and psychological evaluations. Mail was no longer censored, prisoners were permitted to publish their own newsletter, and food was better.[44]

But within the month, bleaker aspects were in the news. Dr. Barron left because of an unsustainable workload, and prison officials complained that the decline in the prison population made harvesting crops difficult. Moreover, the fledgling prison administration was under siege. According to Murton's 1969 memoir, the prisoner "power structure" remained, complete with a currency ("brozene") by which prisoners bought and sold jobs and food. Moreover, without funds from the legislature, Urban came to believe the farms had to make profits; he also pushed for a new maximum-security facility at Cummins to hold about forty people. Inside, the awful food, health care, and work prompted 120 men to refuse to work in October of 1968. Associate Superintendent Gary Haydis persuaded about twenty (all "Negroes," the press said) to go to the fields and fired "birdshot" on those who refused. Twenty-four prisoners were wounded, and one lost an eye. Haydis argued that his response was standard practice when orders were defied. Urban agreed: "No inmate is going to tell Mr. Haydis or I or the prison board that we should run the prison this way or that."[45]

Rockefeller condemned the gunfire, as did the Board of Correction. Haydis left, and Urban made the news again. In early November (days before the election for the next governor), the press reported that another warden had "chained" prisoners overnight to a fence in an "open-air stockade." Urban went on record that he did not object. ADC proffered a budget with funding for an "isolation unit" that, with prisoner labor, could be in place by December of 1968. As the press reported, until a maximum-security facility was built, the outdoor stockade—a "Dog Pen"—would be used.[46]

MORE FIRSTS: A COMMISSIONER OF CORRECTION, ROCKEFELLER'S SECOND TERM, AND TWO LAWSUITS CHALLENGING CONDITIONS OF CONFINEMENT

On November 8, 1968 (three days after Rockefeller won his second term), the Board of Correction appointed Robert Sarver from West Virginia to be Arkansas' first Commissioner of Correction, a post (the press noted) for which no one from Arkansas had applied. A graduate of West Virginia's law school, Sarver had been a prosecutor, a law firm partner, and the head of that state's correction department, but had lost that position in a political conflict in which he was fired for "insubordination."[47]

Rockefeller hoped he had found his next reformer. The press called Sarver a "blunt-spoken advocate of rehabilitation." Sarver said he was in for the long haul: "I want my staff to believe in what they're doing. . . . It will take 10 years of slow, steady work." Sarver went to the state legislature on November 26, 1968, where he was "well received." At a budget meeting, Sarver asked for $2,689,236 for 1969–1970 and approximately $2,725,000 for 1970–1971, which included $180,000 to "replace farm equipment," $350,000 for a "maximum-security unit," $470,000 for "farm mechanization," and $200,000 for "income producing rehabilitated industries at the prison."[48]

Spoiler alert: Within two years, the legislature had pushed Sarver out. Before leaving, Sarver wrote the first ADC report, issued in 1970. In his preface, Sarver borrowed from MacCormick in calling the prisons the "worst in the world."[49] By the time of the report's publication, Sarver had not only joined Murton as another penologist tossed out but, like Dan Stephens and O. E. Bishop, was a defendant in cases brought by Arkansas' prisoners. Unlike his predecessors, however, Sarver welcomed the lawsuits, which he understood could be routes to funding. The prisoners' lawyers told me in 2019 that Sarver helped them get the evidence to win *Holt v. Sarver* (*Holt I*) and *Holt v. Sarver* (*Holt II*), decided in 1969 and 1970. In those cases, as analyzed in later chapters, Chief Judge Henley held conditions in Arkansas' disciplinary cells, and thereafter its entire system, unconstitutional.

The filing of those lawsuits in 1969 made plain (as did the daily news in Arkansas) that not much had changed since 1965. The legislature had added the "r" of rehabilitation to statutes, and the Board of Correction had acknowledged the other "r" of race by moving a few white and Black people between Tucker and Cummins. Yet Arkansas' prisons remained racist, violent institutions imposing outrageous work demands, and the legislature refused to fund any real improvements. Even as Rockefeller appointees hoped that farm mechanization would make time for rehabilitative programs possible, that Board followed in its predecessors' footsteps in pushing for profits.[50]

The new conditions lawsuits went to Chief Judge Henley. Before he addressed those prisoners, led by Lawrence Holt, the Eighth Circuit issued its *Jackson v. Bishop* decision. On December 9, 1968, just a few weeks after Sarver became the Commissioner of Correction, William Jackson, Lyle Ernst, and Grady Mask prevailed. The next chapter explores the reasons provided by the appellate judges who outlawed the whip.

16

STOPPING THE WHIP
BUT NOT THE DEGRADATION

The *Talley* and *Jackson* decisions "go amazingly far for Arkansas justice. They grant a substantial amount of the relief requested."

—Judge Harry Blackmun's confidential memo to his
Eighth Circuit colleagues, March 1968

THE MEN WHO HELD WHIPPING UNCONSTITUTIONAL

The Eighth Circuit supervises, as discussed, the lower federal courts in Arkansas as well as Iowa, Missouri, Minnesota, Nebraska, and North and South Dakota. In 1968, eight white men—sitting in those different states—were on that court.[1] On occasion, including in *Jackson v. Bishop*, district court judges sit "by designation" to augment the ranks. The three who heard the whipping trial's appeal were circuit judges Martin Van Oosterhout from Iowa and Harry Blackmun from Minnesota, along with Robert Van Pelt, a district judge from Nebraska.

Van Oosterhout, who that year became the circuit's Chief Judge, presided. Born in 1900, he grew up in a prosperous household in a small Iowa community. After graduating in 1934 from the state's law school, Van Oosterhout joined his father's law practice and became active in the Republican Party. In 1938, Van Oosterhout won a seat in Iowa's House of Representatives, served four years, was elected to the state trial bench and, after twelve years, was nominated by President Dwight Eisenhower to the Eighth Circuit and confirmed unanimously on August 20, 1954. Gerald Heaney, a liberal Democrat nominated by Lyndon Johnson and appointed in 1966, described Van Oosterhout as regularly deferring to trial judges and with a "judicial philosophy neither liberal nor conservative." Yet Van Oosterhout had narrow views on race discrimination remedies and, while at times concerned about liberty (ruling in 1955 that "the United States has no jurisdiction over permanently insane persons for an indefinite period"), Van Oosterhout had the "reputation of a law-and-order judge." Heaney speculated that Van Oosterhout's experiences in an "all-white community in which strong parochial and well-supported public schools had operated amicably" shaped his colleague's views.[2]

Robert Van Pelt, born in 1897, grew up in Stockville, Nebraska. His single mother, an immigrant, ran a boardinghouse. To make his way through college and the state's law school, Van Pelt worked as a schoolteacher, deputy county treasurer, bail insurance underwriter, waiter, and salesman. After graduation in 1922, Van Pelt practiced law in Lincoln and served part-time in the 1930s as an Assistant US Attorney. In a career path once familiar for federal judges, Van Pelt was involved in his local community and connected to state legislators. He was President of the Rotary Club and the Lancaster County Bar Association. Like Van Oosterhout, Van Pelt was a Mason and a Republican loyalist; he was a Nebraska delegate to the 1940, 1944, and 1948 Republican National Conventions. President Eisenhower selected Van Pelt for the district court in May of 1957; the Senate confirmed him in less than a month. Van Pelt's colleagues described him as modest, unassuming, exacting in his expectations, and at times inspirational. Two years after the *Jackson* decision, Van Pelt took senior status, which meant he had a reduced workload level. The Supreme Court appointed Van Pelt four times as its Special Master, finding facts and making recommendations in conflicts between states disputing their boundaries.[3]

The most famous member of the *Jackson* panel was Harry Blackmun, who wrote the opinion and soon thereafter became a

Supreme Court justice. In 1959, Blackmun was the last man selected by Eisenhower for the Eighth Circuit. Born in 1908 in Illinois, Blackmun grew up in Minnesota, attended Harvard University and its law school, and returned to his home state. Blackmun's practice centered on tax law; from 1950 to 1959, Blackmun was general counsel for the Mayo Clinic, an experience seen as relevant to his 1972 *Roe v. Wade* opinion identifying the constitutional right to abortion. President Richard Nixon chose Blackmun in 1970 for the Supreme Court after the Senate declined to confirm G. Harrold Carswell and Clement Haynsworth.[4]

DISCUSSING THE CASE BEFORE THE ORAL ARGUMENT

It was "obvious from the record that any so-called safeguard is entirely unworkable."

—Judge Blackmun's March 1968 Memorandum to
Judges Van Oosterhout and Van Pelt[5]

Blackmun's papers at the Library of Congress include files on hundreds of cases from his Eighth Circuit tenure. Thus, we can read exchanges among the judges before they heard argument on April 5, 1968, at the Circuit's headquarters in St. Louis, Missouri.[6] On March 13, 1968, Judge Blackmun volunteered to write the opinion; *Jackson* "would be an interesting case to work on from the historical point of view. I would not mind having it." His typed memo was, in some respects, a first draft of the opinion that was issued on December 9, 1968. Blackmun explained that, as the prisoner–appellants did not seek release (the signature remedy of habeas corpus petitions), Judges Harris and Young had properly treated the case as a civil rights action. The legal question was the constitutionality of whipping, which Blackmun described as "the predominant disciplinary measure" in Arkansas.[7]

Blackmun started (as judges are supposed to) with the facts. Discussing the unworkability of "any so-called safeguard," he pointed to the "uncontroverted" testimony by Ernst and Mask of "instances of six whippings administered without a hearing."

Moreover, the "record clearly shows that such punishment does not have a beneficial effect upon the recipient. Whipping is not a sound practice," as "[p]assions and excesses of Arkansas wardens cannot be curbed and controlled by mere paper rules." Turning to the law, Blackmun criticized the lower court judges in *Talley* and *Bishop* for using "[t]he historical approach to corporal punishment," when "[c]onstitutional standards are evolving and are not static." On the other hand, the decisions were "amazingly far for Arkansas justice" even if stopping "short of holding that corporal punishment per se is an Eighth Amendment violation."[8]

Yet not "far" enough. "My sympathies . . . are in favor of going all the way to hold . . . the administration of corporal punishment . . . unconstitutional." Doing so, he predicted, would not "much outrage" the public. But, and "fortified . . . by the flat testimony" of the correctional experts, Blackmun wrote, "I am not willing to say that other disciplinary provisions, such as solitary or withdrawal of benefits and the like, are unconstitutional." Blackmun wrote a checklist of issues, including thanking counsel and considering reimbursing out-of-pocket expenses. Blackmun also noted the need for more research—to learn whether other state statutes permitted corporal punishment and the rules issued since the *Jackson* decision. Blackmun flagged two other items: whether the fact that Jackson had been paroled affected the case, and whether any "question of race" was involved, to which he answered with a handwritten "No."[9]

"RACE, AS SUCH"

"Although we are advised that a substantial percentage of the Arkansas prison population is black, the three plaintiffs, the prison officials concerned, and the witnesses are all white. No issue of race, as such, is present."

—*Jackson v. Bishop*, 1968

Eighth Circuit judges had seen dozens of cases involving racism in Arkansas' schools, parks, and workplaces. During the years between 1965 when *Talley v. Stephens* was decided and December of 1968 when *Jackson* was issued, protestors had marched in Selma and been beaten, uprisings in cities around the country recorded the scope of racism, and two national leaders—Robert F. Kennedy and Martin Luther King Jr.—had been assassinated. Moreover, race is indelibly linked to prisons, as whipping is to slavery. Thus, when Blackmun wrote "<u>No</u>" in his pre-argument memo and again in the opinion that race was not "as such . . . present," he may have referenced his own surprise that the prisoners challenging whipping were white.[10]

But why weren't Black prisoners in these cases? By then, and with help from George Howard and other NAACP Legal Defense and Education Fund affiliated lawyers, a few of Arkansas' Black prisoners had argued—at times successfully—that racial discrimination in jury selection and instructions rendered convictions and sentences unconstitutional.[11] And, as discussed, the utility of attacking corporal punishment with prisoners of both races would have been to use the privilege of whiteness and the subordination of Blackness to underscore whipping's violence.

What we know is that the cases were started by white prisoners who had "writ-writer" assistance, including from a white imprisoned lawyer. Arkansas' segregated barracks would have meant that Black prisoners had less in-prison help, and the appointed lawyers did not add more named plaintiffs. In 1969, another white prisoner, Lawrence Holt, challenged conditions in Arkansas' disciplinary cells, and Chief Judge Henley enlisted more white lawyers including Philip Kaplan, a civil rights lawyer in Little Rock's only integrated firm. In January 1970, Kaplan and his co-counsel filed an amended complaint; when they included that the prisons' *segregation* violated the Equal Protection Clause, they named "race, as such." As I discuss in later chapters, Chief Judge Henley held that segregation was unconstitutional, but officials were slow to comply with that and many other of his orders.

ORDERING THE "STRAP'S" END

"[The] use of the strap, irrespective of safeguards, is to be enjoined."

—*Jackson v. Bishop*[12]

Given that Arkansas' Penitentiary Board ordered whipping's end, the Eighth Circuit had an out, if it wanted to avoid making a decision. As Blackmun's opinion noted, at oral argument the state told the judges that prison officials had adopted "new rules and regulations" for punishments and the Penitentiary Board ended corporal punishment as "a means of discipline." Arkansas' lawyers suggested the court dismiss the appeal as moot; the prisoners' lawyers countered that no information existed on the impact of whatever rule changes were in place. Choosing to reach the merits, the court cited three cases for the proposition that "voluntary cessation of allegedly illegal conduct" did not necessarily end a court's authority. As the prisoners' lawyers had argued, a party could restart whatever behavior it had decided to stop.[13]

Writing for his colleagues, Judge Blackmun reiterated a few facts (not in "real dispute") leading to the 1965 *Talley* Rules, the lashings on "bare buttocks," the state's justification of the need for discipline, and reports by prisoners of the "hate" engendered. Judge Blackmun directly quoted two of the twenty-six witnesses—the penologists. The court cited James Bennett for the proposition that whippings were "cruel, degrading and certainly they were unusual in this day and age," and invoked Fred Wilkinson's testimony that the strap was "cruel and unusual and unnecessary."[14]

As is customary for appellate judges, the bulk of the opinion was devoted to the law. Blackmun's 1968 opinion conceptualized the task as requiring consideration of "evolving standards of decency." As we know from exchanges before oral argument, Blackmun aimed to explain whipping's unconstitutionality *without* rendering other degradations (such as solitary confinement) unlawful. To do so, he laced together decades of case law and listed nine reasons why whipping fit his analysis of prohibited punishments. Blackmun mixed repugnance with arguments about disutility. Blackmun thus followed in the footsteps of Bentham's utilitarianism, coupled with Beccaria's mix of moral ("consult the human heart") concerns. Yet, analytically, if whipping was ethically wrong, its utilities would be irrelevant; if whipping had no utility, its immorality would not matter. By writing about both, Blackmun's *utilities* as an intermediate appellate judge were on display. His job was to offer all available reasons so that the Supreme Court would either not take the case or affirm it. What he did not in 1968 anticipate were twenty-first-century efforts to abandon "decency" and "dignity" in analyses of cruel and unusual punishment.

THE METRICS: "MAN'S BASIC DIGNITY, . . . CIVILIZED PRECEPTS, AND . . . IMPROVEMENT IN STANDARDS OF DECENCY AS SOCIETY PROGRESSES AND MATURES"

Judge Blackmun aimed to maximize the decision's staying power and minimize upsetting Arkansas. His carefully crafted opinion reassured state officials of the many modes of punishment available. Blackmun chose disenfranchisement as one example about which "no real controversy" existed; "lawful incarceration may properly operate to deprive the convict of certain rights which would otherwise be his to enjoy." For twenty-first-century readers, that reference is jarring. Arguments against depriving convicted people of voting have mobilized a national movement in the United States and persuaded courts elsewhere to end that sanction. Yet discussing that penalty enabled Blackmun to signal the decision's limited scope by approving an Arkansas punishment that aligned with three other Eighth Circuit states—North Dakota, Missouri, and Minnesota.[15]

Another subtle element was Blackmun's framing the case to lessen the confrontation between federal judges and state officials. Whether addressing *state* or *federal* prisons, he explained, courts were naturally reluctant "to interfere with a prison's internal discipline," but—offering four cases involving federal institutions—judges did so when constitutionally required. As Blackmun explained, "the due process and equal protection clauses . . . follow [a prisoner] through the prison doors." Blackmun made that point in part by citing *Wright v. McMann*, the 1967 Second Circuit decision that, as discussed, had overturned the ruling on which Judges Harris and Young relied for the proposition that "every punishment in a sense involves cruelty."[16]

To develop a metric of "cruel and unusual" punishments, Judge Blackmun extracted phrases and examples (critics would say

"cherry-picked") from a hundred years of Supreme Court majorities, dissents, and concurrences. He intertwined commitments
to the "humanity of modern Anglo-American law" with concerns
about "excessive" and "disproportioned" punishments, "unnecessary pain," revulsion at "man's inhumanity to his fellow man," and
"standards of decency." As Judges Harris and Young had, Blackmun cited Eighth Circuit precedents that a "general conscience
and sense of fundamental fairness" had "some relationship to the
human concepts and reactions of present-day social climate." From
these "guidelines," Judge Blackmun turned to Chief Justice Earl
Warren's 1958 *Trop v. Dulles* plurality opinion rejecting denationalization as a punishment for a "native-born citizen" deserting a
military base. Blackmun quoted Warren that the "Eighth Amendment's basic concept 'is nothing less than the dignity of man,'" and
that the amendment served to ensure that punishment powers were
"exercised within the limits of civilized standards." Because the
"scope of the Amendment" was not "static," its meaning came from
"evolving standards of decency." Judge Blackmun's synthesis of this
progressive narrative put the "emphasis" on "man's basic dignity,
on civilized precepts, and on flexibility and improvement in standards of decency as society progresses and matures." From these
"applicable standards," courts were to assess whether a particular
punishment evidenced "disproportion, both among punishments
and between punishments and crime." When doing so, "broad and
idealistic concepts of dignity, civilized standards, humanity, and
decency are useful and usable."

"[T]hese principles and guidelines" meant that there was "no
difficulty in reaching the conclusion that the use of the strap in the
penitentiaries of Arkansas is punishment which, in this last third
of the 20th century, runs afoul of the Eighth Amendment." Whipping, "irrespective of any precautionary conditions which may be
imposed, offend[ed] contemporary concepts of decency and human
dignity and precepts of civilization which we profess to possess."
Blackmun added that whipping "also violate[d] those standards of
good conscience and fundamental fairness," the test used in prior
Eighth Circuit cases.[17]

THE NINE REASONS

By referencing earlier Eighth Circuit precedent, Judge Blackmun discreetly told the district judges they had been wrong under the law as it *was*, as well as wrong in light of his discussion.[18] But how did moving invocations of "human dignity," "decency," and "civilized standards"—or the Circuit's 1965 formulation of "general conscience and sense of fundamental fairness"—turn into a ban on whipping? And if whipping fell outside these parameters, what other in-prison (and very *corporal*) practices did as well?

Blackmun answered by listing nine "reasons" that could have been rolled into one: the uncontrollability of the violent, interpersonal assaults called strapping. By delineating separate rationales, Blackmun leaves us puzzled about the weight accorded to each, at times converging with others. Yet while the list lacked clarity, his purpose was not. He wanted to convince readers that whipping was noxious in ways that could allow state officials and judges to distinguish other punishments to avoid what lawyers call a "slippery slope"—for example, that a prohibition on whipping could be the basis for a ban on solitary confinement.

Number "1" was that the Court was "not convinced that any rule or regulation," no matter how "sincerely conceived," could "successfully prevent abuse." Second, testimony demonstrated that extant procedures went "often . . . unobserved." Third, the regulations had been "easily circumvented," as exemplified by "whipping upon bare buttocks, and with consequent injury." Reasons four and five shifted the focus from procedure to the substantive horror of whipping. Number "4" was that whipping was "easily subject to abuse in the hands of the sadistic and the unscrupulous," and "5" objected to delegation of legal authority to diverse individuals; when the power to punish was given "to persons in lower levels," limits were difficult to enforce.[19]

The sixth concern addressed directly what lawyers call "line drawing." As quoted at this book's beginning, Judge Blackmun stated the core problem all state punishments face: "[I]f whipping were to be authorized, how does one, or any court, ascertain the point which would distinguish the permissible from that which is cruel and unusual?" Blackmun prefaced that question with a description of forms of whipping ("excessive . . . or studded or overlong straps") that he termed clearly unconstitutional and then declined to delineate lawful versions. Responding to his own question, Blackmun mixed morality and disutility—that ("7") corporal punishment was "degrading to the punisher and the punished alike," generated "hate toward the keepers who punish and toward the system which permits it," and "frustrate[d] correctional and rehabilitation goals." The related point, numbered "8," was that whipping created "other penological problems and [made] adjustment to society more difficult." The ninth reason was that whippings had been abolished elsewhere; its rarity demonstrated that "public opinion is obviously adverse."[20]

Judge Blackmun made three more (unnumbered) points in closing about the costs and the breadth of the standards elaborated. Relying on notes of Edward Wright's oral argument that the Constitution ought not to "depend on [the] thickness of denim pants," Blackmun rejected Arkansas' claim that it was "too poor to provide other accepted means of prisoner regulation. Humane considerations and constitutional requirements are not, in this day, to be measured or limited by dollar considerations or by the thickness of the prisoner's' clothing." (That proposition, built on a dozen cases—mostly prisoners' wins—from around the federal circuits, was later invoked in other prison cases, as judges rejected resource constraints as justifications.) Judge Blackmun then erased the "and" in the federal constitutional phrase of "cruel and unusual punishments" and also declined to draw a distinction between legislative and executive decisions. Although Arkansas was unusual in whipping, Blackmun wrote the court would not condone a punishment if shown to be only "cruel" *or* "unusual." Further, whether prescribed by statute or by administrative practice, corporal punishment (by which he meant whipping) was unconstitutional.[21]

SLAVERY AND PROFESSIONAL STANDARDS IN THE SHADOWS

The opinion made no mention of whipping's association with slavery. The trial and appellate briefs did not draw the links between enslavement and prisons-as-plantations. Perhaps Blackmun's comment that "race, as such" was not at issue was his way of explaining why he did not address whipping's history in slavery.

Also not discussed were the professional standards to which experts James Bennett, Fred Wilkinson, and the prisoners' lawyers adverted repeatedly. The trial record included the 1966 ACA (American Correctional Association) Standard that stated that "[c]orporal punishment should never be used under any circumstances," and listed examples, including

> flogging, strapping, beating with fists or clubs, spraying with a stream of water, stringing up by the wrists, exposure to extremes of heat or cold or to electric shocks, confinement in the stocks or in cramped sweatboxes, handcuffing to cell doors or posts, shackling so as to enforce cramped position or to cut off circulation, standing for excessive periods 'on the line' or barrel-heads, painted circles, etc., deprivation of sufficient light, ventilation, food or exercise to maintain physical and mental health, forcing a prisoner to remain awake until he is mentally exhausted, etc.[22]

I repeat this paragraph, quoted earlier, because the ACA's 1966 list includes punishments thereafter challenged—such as Alabama's chaining a person charged with not working enough to a hitching post and leaving him for hours without water or access to a toilet that, in 2002, the Supreme Court found clearly unconstitutional.[23] Other punishments on the ACA's catalogue of impermissibility included forms of solitary confinement entailing "deprivation of . . . food or exercise to maintain physical and mental health;" twenty-first century examples included the treatment of detainees at Guantánamo.

Writing the *first* decision in the country ordering a state to stop a punishment it defended, Judge Blackmun went no further than needed, in part to avoid inviting the Supreme Court to step in and to discourage more lawsuits. In addition, we know from his exchanges with other justices once on the Supreme Court that Blackmun was hesitant to constrain prison officials. Yet by making no mention of the UN and ACA Standards, Blackmun lost the opportunity to educate judges and lawyers about the boundaries corrections itself sought to impose.

Also unaddressed was the structure prompting "discipline." The lawyers had not appealed the other issues their clients raised—the excessive labor, risk of infectious disease, and lack of health care.[24] In sum, both the lawyers' appeal and Blackmun's opinion were carefully constructed and deliberately circumscribed to produce an insulated victory. That success was coupled with principles that paved the way for judicial review of other practices, including conditions of confinement.

PRAISE FOR A "MILESTONE" AND PUZZLEMENT ABOUT SOLITARY CONFINEMENT

"In the next similar case you may be called on to give a definition of 'corporal' punishment. Now pending is a prisoner's petition claiming that solitary confinement is 'cruel and unusual' punishment."
—Letter from Gordon Harris to Harry Blackmun, December 12, 1968

Judge Blackmun's files preserved letters sent to him before and after the December 1968 opinion. Two came from his appellate colleagues to whom he had sent his proposed decision on November 22, 1968. Blackmun wrote that, while "not very well satisfied with the opinion," he had "already spent too much time on it." He explained that, even as Arkansas said it had "abandoned the whipping process," the "proposed holding" was a "step forward." Blackmun added he thought the state was not likely to appeal and, if it did, that the Supreme Court would not likely reverse.[25]

Both of his colleagues agreed on November 25, 1968 to join the draft. Judge Van Pelt mentioned that he had considered proposing discussion of evidence that "there were rivets in these straps, which could cause some damage to the skin," but thought adding that point might spur efforts to distinguish "riveted and unriveted straps." Concluding that the decision "constitutes a milestone in Eighth Amendment decisions and is an opinion of which you will always be proud," Van Pelt hoped it would change the "internal management of these prison farms." Officials would need to "grant some privileges" to have something to take away as discipline, and prisoners' lives would be better for it. Chief Judge Van Oosterhout likewise endorsed the "proposed opinion," which he thought "handled the difficult problem presented in a very satisfactory manner." Given that "the federal prisons and all but two of the states are able to handle prison discipline without the use of the strap, it would seem that Arkansas should be able to conform." Van Oosterhout noted that the lawyers "took pleasure in assuming responsibility for representing the prisoners" and were "well able to absorb the expenses"; he advised not to raise the compensation question unless asked.[26]

The day after the decision was published, Pat Mehaffy, the only Eighth Circuit judge from Arkansas, told Judge Blackmun that he had "made the front page of the *Arkansas Gazette*." Blackmun's files included a few other press clippings, including from his hometown of Rochester, Minnesota. His picture was next to the headline "Blackmun Decision—Use of Whips on Prisoners Banned in Precedent Case."[27]

Judge Blackmun also heard from Judges Harris and Young, whom he had reversed. Both told him that he was right. Judge Harris was "constrained to conclude" that he had "reached the correct decision," while Judge Young was more exuberant—writing to "congratulate" Blackmun on the "excellent opinion in the prisoner cases. While the law may have taken half a step forward, it is a step that I think should have been taken, and I thoroughly agree with it." (Perhaps Young had tried to persuade Harris that they should have ruled whipping out.) Both judges raised the question of defining corporal punishment. Judge Harris correctly forecast, "sooner or later, the courts will be called upon for clarification." Judge Young noted that, in a similar case, "you may be called on to give a definition of 'corporal' punishment." Blackmun responded to Young that he hoped neither he nor Harris was "too disturbed about by what was done in these cases. I cherish my friendship with the Arkansas judges." Blackmun told Harris he shared the "concern about the meaning of the phrase 'corporal punishment,'" and wrote to Young that he was not "so sure about" whether solitary fit it.[28]

What Jackson, Ernst, and Mask thought about their victory has not been preserved; had their lawyers' papers been saved, we might have heard from them. Justice Blackmun's files did include correspondence with Edward Wright who sent a letter dated March 4, 1969—after he was sure Arkansas was not going to seek Supreme Court review. Thanking Judge Blackmun for extending well-wishes on Wright's selection to be the President-Elect of the American Bar Association, Wright noted that, for "the first time," he was writing to a judge in a case in which he had been the lawyer. Wright said that putting aside "my naturally strong partisan interest," the opinion was a "landmark of the law. It is simply a classic," whose effect will be "vital for generations."[29]

Judge Blackmun also received letters from corrections officials, including Bennett, who described the decision as a "significant contribution to civilized prison treatment not only in Arkansas but elsewhere in the United States." Blackmun responded that the decision was not the "easiest one to prepare," in part because "one necessarily becomes somewhat emotionally involved in the record."[30] Another letter came from Hans Mattick, describing himself as a "stranger," yet interested as the Associate Director of the University of Chicago's Center for Studies in Criminal Justice. Mattick had been a sociologist in Illinois' notorious Stateville Penitentiary and an Assistant Warden at Chicago's Cook County Jail. As I discuss later, he was the rare voice in the 1960s arguing that prisons were useless in lessening crime or reforming individuals and should be abandoned. Mattick told Blackmun that men did not often "have the opportunity to contribute to the relatively small store of rationality and decency in an overburdened criminal justice system," but Blackmun had done so by giving prisoners "a gift of justice" that would shape the "humanity" of the administrators "whether they know it or not." Blackmun, noting that it was "good to receive an approving letter once in a while," replied he was "overwhelmed by the kind remarks."[31]

The accolades continued as Judge Blackmun became Justice Blackmun. His April 29, 1970, confirmation hearing took four hours and, within a few weeks, the Senate approved his nomination by a unanimous vote.[32] Blackmun's *Jackson v. Bishop* opinion was among those referenced by the Justice Department in its memorandum of notable rulings submitted to the Senate. In the May 12, 1970, discussion on the Senate floor, Senator Edward Brooke of Massachusetts, then the lone Black member of the Senate, praised Blackmun for holding that "any use of a strap on convicts in the Arkansas State Penitentiary was a cruel and unusual punishment under the Constitution." Arkansas' Senator John McClellan submitted a profile of Blackmun from the *Arkansas Democrat* quoting the *Jackson* opinion's explanation that "corporal punishment generates hate towards the keepers who punish and towards the system which permits it. It is degrading to the punisher and to the punished alike. It frustrates correctional and rehabilitative goals."[33]

Once on the Supreme Court, Justice Blackmun described himself as "privileged" to have written "the whipping case," which he called the most important of his appellate career. For many years, the ruling was regularly invoked by the Supreme Court and lower federal courts.[34] Furthermore, Blackmun made his papers public after his death and, in the Library of Congress' compilation, *Jackson v. Bishop* got pride of place. "Blackmun wrote over two hundred signed opinions. . . . His opinion in *Jackson v. Bishop* was one of the first decisions to declare unconstitutional the use of corporal punishment in prison under the cruel and unusual punishment clause of the Eighth Amendment."[35] His decision forecast that, as Linda Greenhouse captured in her book's title, *Becoming Justice Blackmun*, on that bench, the Justice deepened his appreciation for equality and liberty, even as on prisoners' rights, he hewed more closely to the mix of protection for prisoners and deference to state authorities evident in *Jackson*. Yet, even as *Jackson v. Bishop* has been appropriately praised as being both right and just, the decision only began to limit Arkansas' prison horrors.

17

"SECURITY, DISCIPLINE, AND GOOD ORDER"

RACIAL DESEGREGATION, MUSLIMS' RELIGIOUS FREEDOM, AND REMEDIES

Justice Blackmun was right in naming *Jackson v. Bishop*'s importance; it was a watershed in banning a "discipline" that prison officials championed. Yet Blackmun's comment that "race, as such" was not in issue requires discussion: US criminal law enforcement is drenched in racial subordination, and race cannot be bracketed.

Indeed, white Arkansas prisoners were able to get *into* federal court because, in 1964, Thomas X Cooper—persecuted as a Black Muslim—opened that door by prompting the Supreme Court's ruling in *Cooper v. Pate* that prisoners *could* bring civil rights claims against state prison officials. Four years later, race was at the core of the Court's first prisoner class action. *Lee v. Washington* held Alabama's segregation of its prisons and jails unconstitutional. In both, the Court rejected unabashedly racist defenses—from Illinois, arguing it could prohibit members of Islam from their observances, and from Alabama, asserting that "convicts" such as Caliph Washington had no right to object to segregation. These decisions imposed the Supreme Court's *first* structural boundaries on state authority to control prison life.

Yet these landmarks were brief (per curiam, "by the Court") decisions with no account of the injustices inflicted. *Cooper v. Pate* never mentioned that the prisoner knocking on the courthouse door was a Muslim man slammed into solitary by prison officials. And while *Lee v. Washington* named the illegality of in-prison "segregation of the races," the concurring justices imposed a caveat that has shrouded prisoners' rights ever since. In the name of "security, discipline, and good order," prison officials *could* take race into account. And, despite help from talented civil rights litigators, both Cooper and Washington remained for years in prison *because* of race discrimination.

Here, I detail how race discrimination operated in the name of prison security and under the guise of discipline. I sketch similarities across the state and the federal system, as all-white prison officials tried to stop Black Muslim observances, punished adherents, and segregated facilities, including the Federal Bureau of Prisons (BOP).[1] Using race as a proxy for danger continued into the twenty-first century, as evidenced by a 2005 Supreme Court decision objecting to California's racial and ethnic classifications, justified as buffers against "gang" violence.

The cases discussed in this chapter differ from the Arkansas litigation in that several of the prisoner-plaintiffs aligned themselves with transnational human rights challenges to capitalist, colonial practices.[2] These cause-based activists, assisted by a nascent prisoners' rights bar, reshaped US law. Once justices agreed in the 1960s that prisoners—like everyone else—*had* federal constitutional rights and could pursue relief through class actions, the skein of power of prison officials unraveled a bit. Yet, as this chapter documents, *prisoners' rights* were and are regularly cabined by officials' views of *security needs*, in which "race, as such" is omnipresent and results in more punishment imposed on dark-skinned people.

ILLINOIS' PANOPTICON AND THOMAS X COOPER

"The Question Presented . . . was [whether] the plaintiff was denied his day in court and the right to a fair and impartial trial . . . [and] whether . . . [Illinois] . . . properly exercised its authority [when preventing] the free choice of religion, ideas, faith and worship."

—Thomas X Cooper, "Notice of Appeal" January 9, 1963[3]

From John Howard in eighteenth-century England onward, religion—that is, Christianity—has been central for prison reformers. But people affiliated with Islam faced oppression, which was the basis for *Cooper v. Pate*, the Court's first recognition that civil rights laws crafted after the Civil War gave *prisoners* access to the federal courts.

Key to that conclusion was the innovative litigator, Thomas X Cooper. In 1953, Cooper began his long confinement in Illinois' Stateville. Like Amsterdam's proud portrayal of its detention centers, a 1920s postcard (figure 17.1) advertised the new penitentiary, sitting on 2,220 acres; sixty-four were "enclosed in a concrete wall, 30 ft. high, 1 ¼ miles long." Stateville's "roundhouse" drew on Jeremy Bentham's Panopticon, designed to facilitate surveillance.[4] The roundhouse endured (as seen in an eerily gleaming 2002 depiction in figure 17.2) until Illinois' governor announced in 2016 that, "[i]n the name of justice, I'm closing Statesville's F. House" because the "loud, chaotic environment" was dangerous and costly.[5] (In 2020, it reopened to isolate individuals with COVID.)

However photogenic, Stateville was terrifyingly violent. In the late 1940s, Harry Siegel, Robert Harp, and Maurice Meyer sued its

FIGURE 17.1 *Interior View of Cell House, Stateville, near Joliet, Illinois,* circa 1925, postcard collection and courtesy of Alex Wellerstein

FIGURE 17.2 *F House, Stateville Correctional Center, Illinois*, 2002, photograph by and courtesy of Jim Goldberg and Doug DuBois

warden Joseph Ragen. They alleged that, in retaliation for going to court, guards had beaten and put the three prisoners into solitary confinement, where they were forced for months to endure filth, darkness, and sleeping on "the cold, damp, concrete floor." Both trial and appellate judges dismissed the lawsuits as raising matters of "internal discipline" that belonged to prison officials' unfettered discretion.[6]

In the 1960s, when Cooper was there, not much had changed. In July of 1962, Cooper filed his handwritten "Petition for Relief Under Civil Rights Act" and sued Warden Frank J. Pate and Ragen, by then Illinois' "Director of Public Safety." Unlike Winston Talley's 1965 petition, whose author had high hopes and skimpy knowledge of legal rules, Cooper had a remarkable command of US law.[7] Penned in a dense cursive style, Cooper invoked the post–Civil War statute ("Section 1983") and explained that defendants, acting under "color of state law, had deprived him of his First, Eighth, and Fourteenth Amendments rights." While other prisoners could "obtain the King

James and Revised version of the Bible," he was in isolation for trying to get a Quran. Cooper alleged that Pate objected to the potential "900 inclined to Islam and about 800 sympathizers," and feared Cooper and his "associates would be able to control" the prison. About half of the 4,400 people held were Black prisoners.[8]

Cooper lost at the trial and appellate levels. Instead of sending the case back to get evidence, the Seventh Circuit relied on an appendix to the state's brief—"Muslim Cult of Islam-Nation of Islam . . ." written by the "Security Section, Intelligence Division, Bureau of Inspectional Services, Chicago Police Department." The appellate judges described Islam as the "pretext of a religious façade" for a violent agenda, reiterated that federal judges were not to "superintend the treatment and discipline of prisoners," and ruled that Cooper had "no basis for coming into a federal court" to prove that discrimination landed him in long-term solitary confinement.[9]

VICTORIOUS WITHOUT A MENTION OF MUSLIMS

In the Supreme Court, Cooper had lawyers and a receptive audience. Appearing on his behalf were Bernard Weisberg and Alex Elson, both graduates of the University of Chicago Law School, ACLU-affiliated, and knowledgeable. They edited a 1959 ACLU report, *Secret Detention by the Chicago Police*, documenting thousands held for "extended periods of time without being charged with any crime, without bail and without communications with the world outside."[10]

When describing the racism, Weisberg and Elson were not bringing news to the Court. In 1961, its *Monroe v. Pape* opinion described that James Monroe, his spouse, and six children had alleged that "13 Chicago police officers broke into petitioners' home, routed them from bed, made them stand naked, and ransacked rooms, emptying drawers and ripping mattress covers." Not mentioned but detailed in the briefing were the racial slurs ("black boy" and more). At issue was whether police, lacking a search warrant, were "acting under color of state law," as Section 1983 requires. The Court announced that, whether or not authorized by statutes or courts, the police were state actors subject to Section 1983 liability. On remand, an all-white jury awarded Monroe $13,000 in damages, later reduced by a judge to $8,000.[11]

Cooper's lawyers asked the Court to apply that precedent when addressing "whether a prisoner in a state penitentiary has a right to obtain the Koran . . . under the free exercise clause of the First Amendment and the due process Clause of the Fourteenth," and whether state officials had violated those and the Equal Protection Clause "by isolating Muslim prisoners and prohibiting them" from practicing their religion as other prisoners could. After receiving the state's opposition, the Court's clerk telegrammed the Seventh Circuit: "CERTIORARI GRANTED JUNE 22 COOPER AGAINST PATE. JUDGMENT BELOW REVERSED." The Court used Cooper's lawsuit to make one point: that its 1961 *Monroe v. Pape* ruling applied to incarcerated people.[12]

The Court's paragraph-length opinion requires decoding. As the Court recounted, Cooper had alleged that, "because of his religious beliefs," Illinois prison officials had denied him permission to purchase "certain religious publications" and "privileges" of observance that other prisoners had. "Taking as true the allegations of the complaint," Cooper had to be given a chance to prove he was right. Yet the Court did not use the words "Islam" or "Muslim," just as its *Monroe v. Pape* decision did not mention the race of the Monroe family.[13]

To know what "religious beliefs" were at issue required reading the Seventh Circuit opinion, as well as lower court decisions the Court cited approvingly without mentioning their content. In all, federal judges *had* recognized incarcerated Muslims' religious rights.[14] On remand, the same trial judge who had thrown Cooper out ordered the state to let him purchase the Quran and communicate with religious advisers. But while the judge detailed the enormous personal costs to Cooper of almost a decade of isolation ("a record length"), the judge rejected Cooper's retaliation claims, and an appellate court affirmed the conclusion that solitary confinement was for "normal disciplinary reasons" rather than "religious beliefs."[15]

MORE SOLITARY CONFINEMENT FOR BEING A "BLACK MUSLIM": WILLIAM FULWOOD, THOMAS X A SEWELL, AND MARTIN SOSTRE

"[That] cell . . . is approximately eight feet by twelve feet, with a stone floor and stone walls on three sides. There is no window, so that no natural light enters the cell, and the single artificial light is controlled from outside the cell. There is no bed; a mattress is placed on the floor at ten o'clock at night and taken out at six o'clock in the morning. The toilet has no top and in most cases is not flushable from inside the cell. There is no wash basin."

> —Federal District Court Judge Burnita Matthews'
> description of William Fulwood's Virginia cell, 1962 [16]

[Martin Sostre] "secured for Black Muslim prisoners their rights to certain unrestricted religious liberties."

> —Federal District Court Judge Constance Baker Motley, 1970[17]

"For a federal court . . . to place a punishment beyond the power of a state to impose on an inmate is a drastic interference with the state's free political and administrative processes . . . [even if] to us the choice may seem unsound or *personally* repugnant."

> —Federal Appellate Judge Irving Kaufman for the
> Second Circuit, *Sostre v. McGinnis*, 1971[18]

Around the country, people asserting their religious rights were regularly punished—ostensibly for "normal disciplinary reasons." Two examples came from the mid-Atlantic. William Fulwood, held at Virginia's Lorton Reformatory, alleged he had been held in solitary confinement because he was a Black Muslim leader. When Judge Matthews (the first white woman to sit on the federal district courts) received his materials, she enlisted a high-profile lawyer, E. Barrett Prettyman Jr., who had clerked on the Supreme Court. Holding the discriminatory retaliation unconstitutional, Judge Matthews described the cell, lacking natural light, a sink, and a place to sit.[19] That decision dovetailed with *Sewell v. Pegelow*, from the Fourth Circuit and cited by the Supreme Court in *Cooper*. Thomas X A Sewell and others also at Lorton alleged that "solely because of their religious beliefs," prison officials had put them for ninety days into solitary confinement, where they were fed "one teaspoon of food for eating [and] a slice of bread" three times a day. The Fourth Circuit insisted these men had a right to a hearing because the law protected religious observance, including when incarcerated.[20]

The other appellate case cited by the *Cooper* Court was *Pierce v. LaVallee*, a 1961 Second Circuit decision responding to three prisoners held in long-term isolation in New York's Clinton Prison: James Pierce, William SaMarion, and Martin Sostre. The state had not permitted them to purchase the Quran or contact spiritual advisers and punished their "agitating." The three received help from Edward Jacko and Jawn Sandifer, NAACP-affiliated lawyers and graduates of Howard Law School, where they were mentored by the renowned civil rights litigator Charles Hamilton Houston. A *New York Times* story, "Muslim Negroes Suing the State," tallied about one hundred such filings aiming to stop New York's vindictive discrimination.[21]

Pierce, SaMarion, and Sostre went before Stephen W. Brennan, the same jurist who (as discussed) had refused to hear Lawrence Wright's challenge to being locked up naked in a filthy, cold strip cell. In dismissing their claims, Brennan complained that, rather than being "uneducated, inexperienced, and helpless plaintiffs," their filings evidenced they had help from "outside sources" as part of a "movement." Because New York changed its policy and permitted access to the Quran, Brennan addressed only solitary confinement; he ruled it was a discipline issue for prison officials and, perhaps, state courts.[22] On appeal, the Second Circuit recognized the three men were entitled to a hearing on whether they had faced "religious persecution." But they lost after testimony was taken on remand. Judge Brennan shared prison officials' views that *being* Muslim *was* grounds for discipline because the Muslim Brotherhood was "not a religion" and the men were punished for "fomenting . . . unrest." This time, the Second Circuit, finding no "clear error," affirmed as it likewise described the plaintiffs as "leaders of the 'Muslim Brotherhood'—a self-organized and self-styled group, which pursued the study and furtherance of Islam, but had overtones of secrecy and intrigue."[23]

Had judges wanted to fortify their negative rulings with professional standards, they could have found support from a 1962 resolution of the American Correctional Association (ACA) that characterized the Nation of Islam as a "pseudo-religious sect . . . [that] lacks the generally recognized characteristics of religion" and encouraged prison administrators not to permit members of the faith to attend services. James Bennett, director of the BOP, was in sync; he chafed against what he called the disruptive force of "the Black Muslim group . . . [and] their rebellious and violent activities."[24]

A chronicle of the aggression prisoners experienced comes from Martin Sostre, whose published letters and lawsuits won him the appellation as the man "who reformed America's Prisons from his cell." Sostre, arrested on drug charges in 1952, spent several years in solitary confinement at Attica, where he joined the *Pierce v. LaVallee* litigation. After release in 1964, Sostre opened an Afro-Asian Bookshop in Buffalo. In the summer of 1967, in the wake of uprisings there and elsewhere, the police charged Sostre with an illegal $15.00 drug sale; after conviction by an all-white jury, a judge sentenced him to decades more in prison.[25]

New York officials again put Sostre in solitary, where he stayed until his new lawsuit was assigned to the Honorable Constance Baker Motley, who required his transfer to general population while she considered the merits. (Like the white woman jurist in Fulwood's case, Judge Motley was another first as a Black woman on the federal bench; in 2024, the US Postal Service issued a stamp with her portrait.[26]) Sostre's case was high profile; during the five-day hearing in October of 1969, courthouse picketers wore "Free Martin Sostre" buttons. Represented by civil rights attorneys Victor Rabinowitz and Kristen Glen, Sostre provided searing details of his time in the "hole," with lights on 24/7. Expert witnesses analyzed the physical and emotional harms; the state defended that Sostre had contraband ("racist" materials from the Black Panthers) and practiced law without a license. (In 1969, the Supreme Court concluded that prisoners could help each other prepare legal materials.)[27]

As Judge Motley recounted in her May 1970 decision, the parties agreed on key facts—that Sostre had spent more than a year in solitary and lost 124 days of "good time," that he had limited food, a once-a-week shower, no law library access, and no recreation unless submitting to a "strip frisk" entailing "a rectal examination." Motley concluded that the state had retaliated against Sostre "because of his legal and Black Muslim activities during his 1952–1964 incarceration" and his current lawsuit. Motley found the lengthy punitive segregation to be "physically harsh, destructive of morale, . . . needlessly degrading, and dangerous to the maintenance of sanity"; "the totality of conditions" violated the Eighth Amendment. The judge concluded that, if New York wanted to put Sostre in solitary, it had to hold a hearing, provide a lawyer, and find he had committed serious offenses. Further, she put a fifteen-day cap on the time that could be spent under solitary's grueling conditions. (In 2015, the UN's Nelson Mandela Rules on the treatment of prisoners used fifteen days as its benchmark and deemed longer stays akin to torture.) Motley also awarded $13,000 in compensatory and punitive damages to be paid by the prison officials, whom she found had acted in "bad faith and [with] malice."[28]

The Second Circuit, sitting as a full bench of active judges, issued its decision in February of 1971, some seven months before the uprising at Attica Prison. Although disquieted by what it termed Sostre's "black militancy," the judges did not set aside Judge Motley's findings that prison officials had punished him for successful religious rights advocacy. The appellate judges were, however, unwilling to uphold the remedies ordered. While noting solitary was "harsher" than general population, Chief Judge Irving Kaufman called it neither "unendurable or subhuman or cruel and inhuman in a constitutional sense." Even if a punishment was "unsound or personally repugnant," federal judges were not to interfere "with the state's free political and administrative processes."[29] Although Sostre had, as Judge Motley concluded, "secured for Black Muslim prisoners their rights to certain unrestricted religious liberties," and he later became "the symbol of the prisoners' rights movement," he remained under the thumb of New York state prison officials until, in 1975, New York's Governor Hugh Carey granted him clemency.[30]

THE EMBRACE OF RELIGIOUS LIBERTY

Discrimination against Muslim religious practices continued. When I represented prisoners in the late 1970s in Connecticut, I helped them file lawsuits against both federal and state officials refusing to provide pork-free diets or modify serving meals to enable observance of Ramadan, a month-long period when eating is to occur only before sunrise and after sunset. At the federal facility at Danbury Connecticut, the BOP's chaplain told me he did not see a problem. "A non-denominational Bible service was available every Sunday." That attitude was replayed elsewhere. In 1987, the Supreme Court upheld a New Jersey regulation preventing prisoners who worked outside a facility from returning to join a weekly afternoon Jumu'ah service. Even as the five-person majority noted the observance was "commanded by the Koran," the Court acceded to limiting prisoners' free exercise rights because of the prison's "legitimate penological objections" about logistics and safety.[31]

Yet a rising commitment *to* religion—in states, Congress, and on the Supreme Court—has since given more protection to prisoners. After the Supreme Court declined to protect religious rights in a case unrelated to prisons, Congress enacted a statute in 2000 protecting places of worship by calling on state governments not to burden free exercise rights when making land use decisions. Further, if limiting religion for "institutionalized persons," a policy had to be the "least restrictive means of furthering [a] compelling governmental interest."[32]

Application of that approach benefited a prisoner in Arkansas in 2011. Abdul Maalik Muhammad ("Gregory Holt" in court records) challenged the state's ban on wearing beards and sought a "compromise" of permitting a short half-inch beard. In response, prison officials threatened discipline. When defending, state officials argued that beards could hide contraband, a claim that, in 2015, Justice Samuel Alito, writing for the Court, found "almost preposterous" and "hard to take seriously."[33] Yet, even as religion gained statutory protection in prisons and the Court ruled out segregation by race, "normal disciplinary reasons" have continued to sustain discrimination.

CALIPH WASHINGTON'S RACIST PROSECUTION AND
ALABAMA'S *DE JURE* PRISON SEGREGATION

"[W]hite and colored convicts [cannot] be chained together or . . . allowed to sleep together."

—Alabama Code, title 45, § 52 (1958) (repealed 1972)

The 1966 lawsuit to end segregation in Alabama's prisons was aptly (and deliberately) named *Washington v. Lee*, even as the parties' first names were neither George nor Robert E. The case pitted the national norm of desegregation against Alabama's statutory segregation of its prisons that prohibited white and Black prisoners from being "allowed to sleep" together. Unlike Thomas X Cooper, who wrote his own court papers, institutional litigators—the ACLU and the NAACP's Legal Defense Fund (LDF)—represented Caliph Washington, Hosea L. Williams, Julia Allen (for her minor, incarcerated son, Willie), Agnes Beavers (for her minor son, Cecil McCargo), Johnnie Coleman, and Thomas E. Houck. This group of "one white and five Negro citizens" filed on behalf of everyone held in Alabama's jails and prisons. They named the head of the state's prisons (Frank Lee) along with the sheriff in charge of the Jefferson County Jail, the warden of the city jail of Birmingham, Alabama, and two others to serve as "representatives of all . . . wardens and jailers of the city and town jails of Alabama." (*Washington* was one of the first class actions under the 1966 revision of the federal class action rule, and defendant class actions were, and remain, unusual). The Alabama prisoners sought a declaration that, under the Eighth and Fourteenth Amendments, "Negro citizens, male and female" had the right "not to be segregated . . . or otherwise subjected to racial distinctions" when confined in Alabama's prisons or jails.[34]

Racism is what landed Washington in prison. Caliph Washington was accused of having shot a white police officer in Bessemer, a small city a few miles from Birmingham. A federal appellate court recounted that "a police officer . . . received a fatal wound from a bullet fired from his own pistol. Two days later . . . a 17-year-old Negro boy, able to 'read and write a little,' was arrested in Mississippi" and had a gun. As Washington's biographer later commented, this

remarkable man "read up on criminal procedure," escaped execution, and eventually succeeded in gaining release.[35]

Washington's defense lawyer was David Hood, then the only
Black attorney in Bessemer; he regularly faced violence, including dynamite thrown at his house. Hood sought dismissal on the
grounds that the state had systematically excluded Black people
from jury service. After losing, an all-white jury convicted Washington, and a judge called for "death by having a current of electricity"
run through his body. After ups and downs in the Alabama Supreme Court, help from more lawyers, and a second trial ending in
a conviction, Washington again faced execution. Governor George
Wallace granted a reprieve in 1963 and thereafter federal judge
Frank M. Johnson Jr. stayed the execution in 1964; he later decided
that Alabama had violated Washington's right to a fair trial.[36]

While confined awaiting a new trial, another of Washington's
lawyers, Orzell Billingsley, asked for help from Charles Morgan Jr.,
an Alabama lawyer who had in 1964 opened the ACLU's Southern
Regional office in Atlanta. Aiming to end Alabama's segregation of
jails and prisons, Morgan enlisted Washington as the lead plaintiff
and filed the lawsuit on February 18, 1966, in Montgomery, where
Judge Johnson, already famous for civil rights rulings, sat.[37] Given
that the suit sought to enjoin a state statute, federal law required
three judges to hear the case. Appointed were an appellate judge,
Richard Taylor Rives, from the Fifth Circuit, overseeing the lower
courts in that area of the country, and another federal district court
judge, Seybourn H. Lynne, to join Johnson.[38]

The prisoners argued that segregation was unconstitutional punishment under the Eighth Amendment and a violation of equal protection under the Fourteenth. At the hearing, John O. Boone, who
had worked at the BOP's Atlanta Penitentiary, testified that desegregation had been rapid and easy. ("Overnight," he reported, followed
by a decrease in racial tension and violence.) Likewise, one of the
local sheriffs, "up for reelection in 1966 and courting black voters,"
admitted that segregation was not the lynchpin to his jail's safety.[39]

Writing for the three-judge court, Judge Johnson explained that
state-wide statutes mandating racial segregation met the rule's

criteria of "questions of law and fact common" for both plaintiff and defendant classes. The judges rejected the Eighth Amendment claim (racial segregation was not, in itself, "inhuman, barbarous or torturous punishment") but agreed that organizing prisons by race violated the Fourteenth Amendment. The judges could "conceive of no consideration of prison security or discipline which will sustain the constitutionality of state statutes that on their face require complete and permanent segregation of the races in all Alabama penal facilities."

In crafting a remedy, the opinion underscored state officials' authority. The "operation of penal institutions . . . is a highly specialized endeavor" requiring the "sober judgment of experienced correctional personnel." The judges laid out a sequence beginning with immediate desegregation in the "honor farms," educational programs, youth centers, and prison hospitals. Minimum-level and medium-level facilities and jails had six months, and maximum-security prisons a year to desegregate. The court added that "some isolated instances" could exist when prison security and discipline required "segregation of the races for a limited period." Saying that it issued no "formal injunction," the three-judge court declared unconstitutional the statutory mandate of segregation "solely by reason of race," ordered compliance with its timetables, and required Commissioner Lee to report every three months on implementation.[40]

WHO DECIDES WHERE TO JAIL MARTIN LUTHER KING?

Do people convicted of crimes have "the constitutional right to question the validity of state statutes requiring the separation of prisoners by race?"

—Alabama's Jurisdictional Statement, *Lee v. Washington*, 1967

"You're not talking about school children now. You're talking about the most violent, the most vicious element of our society, the most dangerous."

—Alabama's attorney defending segregation, oral argument, November 1967[41]

When bringing the case in March of 1967 to the Supreme Court, Alabama held "1546 white and 2510 Negro" prisoners. At the time, Black people were about 30 percent of the state's 3.3 million population and 60 percent of the state's prisoners. Under the Court's rules, Alabama had to list "substantial" and unsettled questions in need of the Court's attention. Alabama questioned whether *convicted* people could even bring a challenge. Further, the state argued that even if its statutes were unlawful, administrators ought to be able keep prisoners with others "of [their] own race." The state also asked the Court to address whether federal judges could instruct prison officials to take specific "steps" to desegregate and whether the Fourteenth Amendment "contemplate[d] the substitution of judicial opinion for the opinion of competent prison administrators . . . for the maintenance of prison discipline and security." The state achieved an initial win when, before oral argument, the Supreme Court stayed the desegregation order pending decision.[42]

By November of 1967, when the Supreme Court heard oral argument, the Court itself was no longer all white. Thurgood Marshall, nominated by President Lyndon Johnson, took his seat that fall, more than a decade after Marshall had represented children in *Brown v. Board of Education*. As the transcript of oral argument and archived exchanges among the justices make plain, even as the Court was clear that *Brown* applied, Marshall tried but could not stop his colleagues from outlining means to circumscribe the lower court's ruling.

Alabama's lawyer got the picture when he stood up to argue. The first question came from Justice Hugo Black, who had been one of Alabama's senators before joining the Court in 1937. Black asked whether the state would concede its segregation statutes were unconstitutional. Asking for that retreat made clear the Court was not going to accept blanket segregation. The attorney for Alabama responded he was "not in a position to concede," but spent little time defending *de jure* segregation. Instead, he argued against the authority of a federal court to treat as a *class* all the various people housed in jails and prisons and the remedy ordered.[43]

Hoping to convince the justices that "public parks, schools, and similar public facilities" had nothing in common with prisons,

Alabama's lawyer called detained people (convicted or not) "the most vicious element of our society." Alabama insisted that jail and prison officials needed to fashion their own rules: "even if you hold those statutes as unconstitutional, . . . the decree should be modified. It's too rigid. It destroys unnecessarily reasonable administrative discretion" to separate prisoners when security required it.[44]

Pushback came from some justices. Marshall elicited at oral argument that state officials had planned to end prison segregation by 1969. Chief Justice Warren got the concession that, if problems arose, the state could ask the lower court to alter the desegregation schedule. Moreover, the prisoners' lawyer, Charles Morgan, was clear that officials retained some discretion. When asked by Justice Black about separating two drunks, one a Black man and the other white, Morgan replied dryly to his fellow Alabamian that in their state, the two races did not drink together. Yet Morgan added that there was "no question in my mind there are certain kinds of prisoners that you wouldn't want Dr. King to be confined with and there's not a thing in this decree . . . that prevents the exercise of responsible discretion . . . in a nondiscriminatory manner."[45]

Reading the oral argument transcript now, one might think that Morgan's image of Martin Luther King in jail was a clever rhetorical move to underscore that the lower court order was not rigid. Anyone in the courtroom knew it was a reference to current events. Dr. King had been in Alabama's jails—on October 30 of 1967, in Jefferson County Jail (where Caliph Washington was detained) and then in Birmingham's Jail, where King served less than his five-day sentence. After the November argument, Alabama's lawyer submitted clippings headlining racial conflicts in prison. In response, the prisoners' counsel wrote that the "recent confinement" of Dr. King was an "excellent example" that "security of any prisoner is a paramount consideration." The lawyers noted that "problems" could emerge if "Dr. King and his associates" were to be placed with "certain Negro prisoners" and with certain whites "dangerously antagonistic to him." The ACLU brief concluded that the focus ought not to be "related to the race of the prisoner but, instead, to the prisoners themselves."[46]

Discussing Dr. King's detention was gutsy, given that he had been put into jail *because* of the Court's 1967 opinion in *Walker v. City of Birmingham*. That ruling addressed the legality of the protest by King and fellow ministers when they marched in April of 1963 on Good Friday and Easter Sunday. Birmingham, citing its local regulation, refused to issue a permit, and state courts ordered the demonstrations to stop. When arrested and detained for contempt, the marchers argued they did not have to comply with the court order that left to the "unfettered discretion of local officials" the authority to violate the constitutional rights of "free speech and peaceful assembly." (Dr. King's famous "Letter from Birmingham Jail" elaborating ideas on nonviolent civil disobedience was written during that detention.) Thereafter, the question went to the Supreme Court; five justices upheld the contempt ruling as predicated on a lack of "respect for [the] judicial process." Justice Brennan, filing one of three vehement dissents, called Birmingham "a world symbol of implacable official hostility to Negro efforts to gain civil rights, however peacefully sought." A few years later, in another famed case, *Shuttlesworth v. Birmingham*, the Court agreed that the city's regulations violated the First Amendment.[47]

WINNING WITH CAVEATS

As the argument forecast, the Supreme Court's affirmation of the three-judge court was a foregone conclusion. The Supreme Court's per curiam decision found no problems with the innovative class action. On the other hand, the justices split six to three when addressing federal judges' powers. Understanding the Court's March 1968 decision in *Lee v. Washington* entails knowing its backstory—that proved to be a forecast of prisoners' rights litigation thereafter.

Memoranda preserved in the archived papers of Chief Justice Warren and of Justices Abe Fortas, Potter Stewart, and Byron White reflect that the justices spent a fair amount of time *disagreeing* about what (if anything) to say. On November 13, 1967, Justice Black, objecting to White's "Per Curiam" circulated two days earlier, argued that "We should not hesitate to let . . . [prison officials] know that they do have a discretion as long as the Warden's actions are not based on race." Justice White responded with a "longer version" including excerpts from the lower court and a sentence that the Court read Judge Johnson's order as not "intended to prevent Alabama officials from separating prisoners according to their race temporarily, or from segregating particularly troublesome individuals, when required by considerations of security and discipline," and therefore, the decision was "unexceptionable."[48]

Justice Marshall said he could not "settle" for anything other than the originally circulated affirmation. Marshall argued that the "only thing struck down was [the] statute," that all other rules "with respect to prison discipline" remained in effect, and Judge Johnson's decision had noted modifications were possible. Marshall sent around excerpts from the record; Alabama had not asked, as it was supposed to, for clarification from the lower court. Justice John Marshall Harlan responded that the point of holding oral argument was for the Court to say more. Fortas (a Johnson appointee) suggested noting that the district court had "established a schedule for desegregation . . . and retained jurisdiction for all purposes." Warren told his colleagues the first draft by White was best and saw "no reason for enlarging upon it." In February of 1968, Brennan endorsed that recirculated draft ("I still agree").[49]

Black persisted, writing that the Court's opinion needed to indicate that "there are circumstances under which Wardens may consider racial matters in connection with racial strife in prisons." Stewart offered that the lower court opinion had not "prevent[ed] those in charge . . . from separating prisoners of different races in particular instances to meet the legitimate needs of security, order, and discipline." The denouement was a paragraph decision for the Court, rejecting Alabama's argument that "the specific orders directing desegregation of prisons and jails make no allowance for the necessities of prison security and discipline." The Court did not, "so read the 'Order, Judgment and Decree' of the District Court, which when read as a whole we find unexceptionable."[50]

Justice Black, joined by Justices Harlan and Stewart, concurred to "make explicit . . . that prison authorities have the right, acting in good faith and in particularized circumstances, to take into account racial tensions in maintaining security, discipline, and good order in prisons and jails." They added that they were "unwilling to assume that state or local prison authorities might mistakenly regard such an explicit pronouncement as evincing any dilution of this Court's firm commitment to the Fourteenth Amendment's prohibition of racial discrimination."[51]

Pause to sort the shift in emphasis. The Court's order recognized federal judges' power to permit variation (an "*allowance*") under specific circumstances, while the concurring justices spoke about the "*right*" of prison officials to take racial tensions into account. Then and thereafter, justices disagreed about when deference to prison officials' views on institutional safety should trump prisoners' constitutional rights and the evidence needed when analyzing the scope of those rights. As detailed in later chapters, the concurrence's approach triumphed.

STRUGGLES OVER COMPLIANCE AND CALIPH WASHINGTON'S FREEDOM

In June of 1969, Commissioner Lee reported that "good progress had been made" toward "a more equitable assignment of prisoners in all institutions"; he aimed for movement "toward further equalization of the number of colored and white assigned to the camps." Yet, as the prisoners' lawyers noted in private correspondence, the state had only provided information on "the relative percentages of black and whites in the state institutions" and not on the "degree of integration." Judge Johnson responded by asking for more "effective" efforts "toward compliance."[52]

As metrics for desegregation were contested, prisoners brought new lawsuits detailing the terrible conditions in which they lived; in 1975, Judge Johnson held that Alabama had violated the Eighth Amendment by leaving people in squalor and violence. Windows were

> broken and unscreened, creating a serious problem with mosquitoes and flies. Old and filthy cotton mattresses lead to the

spread of contagious diseases and body lice. Nearly all inmates' living quarters are inadequately heated and ventilated. The electrical systems are totally inadequate, exposed wiring poses a constant danger to the inmates, and insufficient lighting results in eye strain and fatigue.[53]

The judge's exposure to that havoc framed his response to a motion by the *Washington* plaintiffs alleging that one prison remained segregated. Without prejudice to its renewal, Judge Johnson denied their request. Given "grossly inadequate funding, . . . totally inadequate physical facilities, and dangerously insufficient custodial personnel" and the need to "meet the emergency situation, . . . [the] exceptional circumstances" could be the basis for "separation of the prisoners by race" if done as a "temporary measure" and security could not "otherwise be achieved or maintained through the use of acceptable penological procedures."[54] (In short, Justice Marshall was right that no concurrence was needed.)

Succeeding on the law did not liberate Caliph Washington. Just as Thomas X Cooper and Martin Sostre lived in solitary confinement long after they "won," Caliph Washington remained detained for years. In April of 1970, two years after the Supreme Court affirmed the obligation to desegregate, these lawyers convinced a state judge to release Washington, who had been confined since 1957.[55]

Washington's third trial began a few days later; this time, the jury was eight white women, three Black men, and one Black woman. That group convicted him of second-degree murder and sentenced him to forty years. With the help of the steadfast lawyers depicted in figure 17.3, Washington succeeded in 1971 in reversing his conviction and continuing to live in his community. The state appellate court held he had a right to prove the "systematic exclusion" of Black people in the 1957 grand jury, which had been the basis for the two subsequent trials and convictions. In 1972, Alabama indicted Washington again. He remained on bond; prosecutors did not dismiss the charges until after Washington died in 2001.[56]

FIGURE 17.3 *Attorneys David Hood (left) and Orzell Billingsley (center) consult with Caliph Washington before his 1970 trial,* courtesy of the Birmingham Public Library, Department of Archives and Manuscripts

RACE, POLITICS, GANGS, AND RACIALIZED CLASSIFICATIONS, STATE AND FEDERAL

"[Y]ou don't have to go to Alabama to be segregated."

—Thomas X Cooper, 1965

Illinois' penitentiary in 1965 was "segregated into black and white sectors."[57] Throughout the federal system, segregation was commonplace—a practice made visible by World War II conscientious objectors. In August of 1943, several went on an extended strike to end the segregated dining hall at the federal facility in Danbury, Connecticut. Around that time, BOP Director Bennett wrote a memorandum criticizing "extremist conscientious objectors" for aiming to "force us to permit indiscriminate intermingling of the white and colored groups." Yet even as Bennett was leery of racial mixing, he recorded concern about racially discriminatory assignments; "'dirty' jobs or poor paying jobs should be equally divided."[58]

In his oral history, Bennett reported that desegregation of BOP facilities began around 1946; the federal system was "the first among all the prisons of the United States to desegregate, but . . . began with one institution after another. . . . It took . . . five years, I guess, once the policy was adopted." Bennett also described the BOP's "active goal of improving the ratios of black guards in federal prisons," made difficult by civil service requirements and because most BOP facilities were in "small all-white towns" to which Black staff would not want to move.[59]

Other, less upbeat, sources record the snail's pace of desegregation. In 1948, Myrl Alexander (who became BOP Director after Bennett's 1964 retirement) reported that "Black personnel were employed in only ten [federal] institutions and constituted about one percent of the total institutional personnel." In 1951, at the federal penitentiary at Terre Haute, Indiana, 250 of the 1,200 were "Negro prisoners"—"segregated from the white prisoners in the dormitories, in the mess-hall and at entertainments." Discrimination came in other ways, as various privileges, such as good time, were denied "to negro prisoners with equally good behavior." One writer described a BOP facility as a "jimcrow institution" in which Black prisoners "must go into one of two specified dormitories no matter how crowded it may be, or how empty one of the others" was.[60] Again, prisons reflected the segregation across the country. Desegregation of the military did not begin until July of 1948 when President Harry Truman issued an executive order.

In 1954, when *Brown v. Board of Education* was decided, Director Bennett ordered a survey of racial integration in housing, recreation activities, and work details. He learned that three facilities—Englewood, Colorado; La Tuna, Texas; and Tucson, Arizona—were "fully integrated"; spaces were shared for sleeping, eating, and work. Those facilities had few Black prisoners—8 percent in Englewood and 4 percent in La Tuna and Tucson. In contrast, segregation remained in the federal prison in Atlanta, Georgia, where 30 percent were Black prisoners, and in Lewisburg, Pennsylvania and Milan, Michigan, where 54 percent were Black people. A decade after *Brown*, the BOP issued a formal policy that "no inmate" in any of its facilities "shall be discriminated against on the grounds of race, color, creed or national origin, in any phase of institutional activities," and that no activity be segregated.[61] (Those words echo what Bennett had proposed in 1951 for the International Penal and Penitentiary Commission's Standard Minimum Rules.)

In the 1960s, after Congress had enacted major civil rights legislation, the federal government made funding for vocational state prison programs conditional on desegregation. In 1966, a prison administrator in Tennessee—the "first . . . in the state to integrate"—explained that the funds were the reason he did so. He reported "everything" was integrated "except the individual cells" and that the results were fewer incidents and a better atmosphere among the 1,500 prisoners. In addition, the Justice Department did not permit federal detainees to be in segregated local jails.[62] Yet the federal government's "war on crime" resulted in disproportionately policing and prosecuting Black people, which landed more Black people in prison and began a steep upward spike in prison populations.[63]

COLOR-BLIND OR RACE-BASED CLASSIFICATIONS IN PRISONS: THEN AND NOW

"[T]he very nature of prisons may require the use of race-based criteria in official decision-making under limited circumstances."
—Ninth Circuit judges, *Johnson v. California*, 2003[64]

Whatever the aspirations of desegregation mandates, they did not translate into ending racial segregation in prisons. Correctional officials from the East to the West Coast repeatedly described explosive conditions within prisons, identified race as a driver, and responded by using race and ethnicity—explicitly or embedded through classifications by "security threat groups," otherwise known as "gangs."

Of course, the people running prisons were and are *right* that violence has been endemic in the institutions created by the correctional establishment. And they were and are *right* that "racial tensions" produced throughout the entire social order replay on the streets and in prisons. But race is not the only variable in a world of metal and concrete facilities, double celling, hyper-density, noise, terrible food, a lack of health care, poor training of underpaid staff, inadequate programs, and micromanagement draining autonomy—on top of a population of large numbers of people with physical and mental health issues and histories of trauma and violence. Instead of structuring facilities and interactions to generate what social scientists call "race group contact," prison officials—along with many judges and legislators—assumed that "race, as such" was a *given*, rather than an artifact of structures to be revamped.

Here I provide two examples, fifty years apart, on the East and West Coasts. I start in Virginia in 1966, when DC prisoners held in Lorton, Virginia challenged segregated housing. The proportion of Black prisoners was stunning; an assistant superintendent told a federal judge that the facility held "1104 Negroes . . . and 109 whites." He noted that some two hundred Black prisoners attended "Black Muslim religious services" as required under a court order (that I have discussed). Adding that some "radical" white prisoners were "anti-Negro," he testified that race needed to be a factor in housing; given the small number of white prisoners, integration in six of twenty-two housing units ought to be constitutionally sufficient.[65]

Federal district court judge Luther Youngdahl agreed. Recounting that some prisoners were members of the Ku Klux Klan and others were Muslims, the judge commented that a "basic feature of Muslim religious activity is the kindling of intense racial hatred of the white man." As a result, contact between the two groups "could clearly prove explosive."[66] Not only did he appear to equate the two affiliations, he offered no reflection on the disproportionate numbers of Black people brought into prison. Instead, acknowledging the end of all-white units, he ruled that the prison could cluster the few whites and leave sixteen of its housing units populated by Black men.

A half century later, anxiety about an "explosive" mixing was how California justified its use of race and ethnicity when classifying prisoners. In 2005 in *Johnson v. California*, the state argued that institutional safety required reliance on race and national origin when making initial cell assignments. People entering California's prisons or transferring within were evaluated during sixty days, when housed in double cells. Factors included health, background, gang affiliation, and race. Yet, the state reported race was "a dominant factor," as "very important to inmates and . . . a significant role in antisocial behavior." California delineated "four general ethnic categories, black, white, Asian, and other" and subcategorized to ensure that "Japanese and Chinese" prisoners and Northern and Southern California Hispanics were not together. The result was that "the chances of an inmate being assigned a cell mate of another race is '[p]retty close' to zero percent." Prisoners were not segregated when eating, working, and in whatever recreation existed. Yet staff explained, people spent "much of their day" in the double cells. If placed in dorms, race remained relevant to keep some "balance."[67]

By 2003, when the federal appellate court heard arguments, competing lines of Supreme Court doctrine offered different answers about its constitutionality. The Supreme Court had applied a "strict scrutiny" test to racial classifications; several justices, suspicious of using race as remedies for prior discrimination in schools and employment, called for a "color-blind" approach to end affirmative action. On the other hand, the Court was also insistent on deference to prison officials' decisions. As exemplified by the Court's upholding of New Jersey regulations in 1987 that prevented Muslims from observance, as long as prison administrators could show a rational relationship between their approach and what courts viewed as a "legitimate penological purpose," their policies trumped prisoners' rights. Another 1987 decision, *Turner v. Safley*, became a shorthand within prison-law circles for courts' deference to correctional authorities.[68]

Where did California's race-based classification fit? The answer from a panel of three Ninth Circuit judges was that fear of "racial tensions" justified deference to prison authorities' racial classifications.

The judges opined that if race were not used in double celling, the level of violence would increase. (California's Corrections Department "simply does not have to wait until inmates or guards are murdered specifically because race is not considering in assigning an inmate's initial cell mate.") The decision quoted the 1968 *Lee v. Washington* concurrence that prison authorities could on occasion "take into account racial tensions in maintaining security, discipline, and good order." In response to the prisoners' request for rehearing, four other judges vehemently recorded their opposition. Giving "*carte blanche* to prison officials to impose their own notions of racial hatred and conflict upon prisoners" violated equal protection.[69]

Before the Supreme Court, that disagreement was reiterated. Several states—Utah, Alabama, Alaska, Delaware, Idaho, Nevada, New Hampshire, and North Dakota—joined California in insisting on the need to use race.[70] In addition, the National Association of Black Law Enforcement Officers argued that race-based analyses for "compelling . . . public aims" were permissible.[71] Objections came from the US Justice Department, explaining the federal prison system did not do so, from the ACLU, and from a group of former correctional officials who had not used race for classification.[72]

The Court's answer, written by Justice Sandra Day O'Connor, was that strict scrutiny applied to all racial classifications, including prisons. O'Connor underscored that prisons were a site of the *production* of race's meaning as well as a repository; "racial classifications 'threaten to stigmatize individuals by reason of their membership in a racial group and to incite racial hostility.'" Justice O'Connor cited "The Caged Melting Pot," a study reporting that prisoner-to-prisoner assaults in integrated double cells were no more than when cells were segregated. Interpreting *Lee v. Washington* as implicitly deciding that the "integrity of the criminal justice system" required race be used only if "narrowly tailored" to address a compelling state interest, the Court remanded to give California an opportunity to show its policy was.[73]

Justice Ruth Bader Ginsburg, joined by Justices David Souter and Stephen Breyer, concurred in an effort to protect race consciousness elsewhere as a remedy for past discrimination. Writing separately, Justice John Paul Stevens argued that strict scrutiny governed but argued no remand was needed as California's policy was clearly unconstitutional. Stevens noted that the BOP, running more than one hundred facilities, eschewed that criterion, while only two states (Texas and Oklahoma) relied on race when people entered their systems.[74] Justice Clarence Thomas, then the sole Black jurist on the Court, dissented. Joined by Justice Antonin Scalia, he explained that *Lee v. Washington* had recognized that prison officials could look to race under certain circumstances and, given that the "dangers California seeks to prevent are real," *Turner v. Safley's* deference standard governed.[75]

Not discussed in any of the opinions was that California relied on its practice of *double celling* to justify the need to use race. Density was linked to violence, as federal government studies had documented in 1980 and as ACA standards calling for single cells reflected. Yet in 1981, the Court had rejected an Eighth Amendment challenge to double celling in Ohio prisons and thus was itself part of the infrastructure that licensed putting two people into cells built for one.[76]

Soon after the 2005 Supreme Court's decision, the parties settled. California agreed to house prisoners in reception centers "without using race as the determinative housing criterion, while minimizing any potential impact upon inmates' safety and that of the institutions," their personnel, and the public. Those carefully crafted words forecast that, when implemented in 2008, California's policy did not let go of race even as it appeared to lower its salience by indicating that race "will not be used as a primary determining factor in housing."

What "primary" meant was one question and another was race's relationship to the other factors—a person's "history of racial violence," the offense of conviction and length of sentence, a "classification score," custody level, education, and a person's "disciplinary history." Just as in evaluations of individuals for bail and sentencing, these metrics are interwoven with racialized policing and prosecution. Several prisoners returned to complain that not all facilities had implemented the Court's ruling in *Johnson*. Other lawsuits challenged California's practice of responding to violent incidents by putting prisoners who shared the same demographics into lockdowns for extended periods of time. Thereafter, for lockdowns, California relied on membership in "security threat groups" that, again, interlocked with race and ethnicity.[77]

DISCRIMINATION, FEAR, CONTROL, AND NO SAFETY

As this chapter documents, the legal ruling that prisoners cannot be segregated or punished because they are Black people does not mean that prisoners are not segregated by race or that dark-skinned people are not punished more than white prisoners. In 2020, the Prison Policy Initiative identified Black prisoners to be 43 percent of the population in the men's prisons it evaluated, and 46 percent of the solitary confinement population in the prisons studied. Black prisoners comprised 23 percent of the population in women's prisons, and 40 percent of women's prisons' solitary confinement population.[78] In another report, *Time-In-Cell*, based on data reported by prison officials in 2019, Black prisoners constituted 40.5 percent of the total male custodial population, 43.4 percent of the men in solitary confinement, 21.5 percent of the total female custodial population, and 42.1 percent of the women in isolation.[79]

Furthermore, prisons are not safe. Pursuant to a congressional statute, the federal government collects data on "death in custody." Reporting on sexualized aggression comes because of another statute, the Prison Rape Elimination Act. Even as the information is incomplete and projects are underway to increase "transparency" about death in custody, the statistics document a volume of assaults and deaths that means that people in prison have significantly higher risk of being murdered while in confinement than others in the US population.[80]

Everybody is therefore *right* that prisons are scary. Yet instead of questioning why and how governments put people at risk of violence, many justices defer to the very profession that has structured volatile institutions that make vulnerable people living and working in them. On occasion, evidence of the violence overwhelms deference. Arkansas is a case in point to which I return in the next chapter, for it was the utter lack of "security, discipline, and good order" that moved Chief Judge Henley in 1970 to pronounce the entire prison system a violation of the constitutional ban on cruel and unusual punishments.

1S

TOLERATING DEATHS AND ACQUITTING SADISTS OF TORTURING PRISONERS

The blatant racism in Alabama and the violent whipping in Arkansas were part of prison life that federal judges held impermissible in 1968. Those decisions were building blocks for challenges to the lack of safety, too little food, arbitrary discipline, and no health care. In 1969 and 1970, Chief Judge Henley was the first jurist to find that a totality of conditions likewise imposed unconstitutional punishment.

To understand the genesis of *rights* to minimally decent conditions requires returning to the miseries of Arkansas where Henley, who in 1965 had *deferred* to state prison officials when not banning whipping, changed his mind. In 1969, as evidence of beatings, extortion, and filth piled up, Henley consolidated three petitions about Cummins' disciplinary confinement cells, appointed another eminent Arkansas lawyer, heard witnesses, and in June of 1969 concluded in *Holt v. Sarver* (*Holt I*) that jamming several people for days into a dirty, small cell was unconstitutional.[1] Meanwhile, Henley— and anyone reading the newspapers—learned about people dying and injured in Arkansas' jails and prisons. Henley saw firsthand the state's willingness to put and to leave prisoners *in* harm's way— despite revelations of sadistic torture at Tucker and the creation of the Arkansas Department of Correction (ADC).

After Arkansas' prosecution of the Tucker sadists fizzled in 1969, the US Department of Justice (DOJ) asked Henley to convene a federal grand jury to bring criminal civil rights charges against Jim Bruton and fourteen others. Federal criminal cases followed, as did more prisoner filings about squalor and violence at Cummins, while legislators balked at allocating funds for improvements. In the fall of 1969, Henley presided at criminal trials where prisoners detailed terrorizing violence. Nonetheless, juries acquitted an array of predators, including two men directing an assault ending the life of Curtis Ingram, an eighteen-year-old Black man held at Pulaski Penal Farm for failure to pay a $110 fine.[2]

Through this unremittent exposure to what was well-known and ignored, Henley came to understand that, whatever Supreme Court justices might assume in *Lee v. Washington* about prison officials' interest in maintaining "security, discipline, and good order," Arkansas' prisons were terrifyingly unsafe. Moreover, Judge Blackmun's 1968 *Jackson v. Bishop* ruling clarified that the Eighth Amendment protected "evolving standards of dignity." In December of 1969, Henley put together a new team of lawyers, called on them to shape a class action addressing an array of conditions, ordered the prison doors open for evidence gathering, had a hearing in January, and, in February of 1970 in *Holt v. Sarver* (*Holt II*), found an entire prison system unconstitutional.[3]

This chapter follows Henley's path getting there. I sketch Winthrop Rockefeller's unsuccessful efforts to secure sufficient funds for prisons, press accounts of deaths at county prison farms, and the failed prosecutions. Chapter 19 unpacks the *Holt* decisions.

THE FIRST TAXPAYER MONEY FOR PRISONS: WHY JOHNNY CASH HAD IT RIGHT

"When I get out of Cummins,
I'm going up to Little Rock.
I'm gonna walk right up those Capital steps. . . .
If the legislature's in session,
There's some things I'm gonna say, . . .
You say you're trying to rehabilitate us,
Then show us you are."

—Johnny Cash, April 10, 1969, Cummins Farm Concert[4]

In 1968, Governor Rockefeller wanted to get reelected and to reduce the horrors of the state's prisons. Rockefeller enlisted a local hero, Johnny Cash, whom he paid $20,000 to perform at several rallies, and Cash helped the "ineloquent Rockefeller to get the political message across."[5]

Cash wrote *Folsom Prison Blues* in the 1950s when in the US Air Force Security Service and, on return to the states, he began performing in prisons. Albums recorded in the late 1960s—"At Folsom Prison" and "At San Quentin"—sold 6.5 million copies. Cash sang at Cummins the week after Martin Luther King's assassination and in the wake of street protests that, in Dr. King's words, relied on "the language of the unheard." As the lyrics Cash wrote about Cummins reflected, he understood that his home state's legislature did not want to provide funds *for* prisons while making money *from* prisoners' forced labor.[6]

As glimpsed in figure 18.1, Cash appeared before "all of the farm's 900 prisoners," about twenty women prisoners, and a few from Tucker; ABC broadcast the concert on its Arkansas affiliated station. Robert Sarver, the first Commissioner of Correction, joined the governor, and noted that the eight state legislators in attendance were a sign that "the prison did have some friends in the legislature."

Cash received an "honorary life sentence," got a ride from Rockefeller in the prison's "wobbly mule-drawn prison wagon" (shown in figure 18.2) and announced he would add $5,000 to the $10,000 Rockefeller had donated towards building a chapel. Thereafter, the legislature appropriated "the first tax money that had ever been allocated" to prisons.[7]

That "first" was not enough to hire employees or improve sanitation, and pressures mounted for prisoners to generate more money. The prison farm manager, complaining that "good men" were being paroled or "just standing around," claimed that the infirmary's forty-two beds were full because doctors were afraid "prisoners will write a petition against them to a federal judge." He warned that the "manpower shortage" would result in a deficit of $194,000—instead of a $1.6 million profit—on July 1, 1969.[8]

FIGURE 18.1 *A Last Handshake with the Star before Going Back to the Barracks*, photograph by Larry Obsitnik, accompanying *Hello, Cummins Prison Farm, I'm Johnny Cash*, Arkansas Gazette, April 13, 1969, courtesy of the publisher

PROSECUTING TORTURE: UNCONSTITUTIONAL DELEGATIONS OF STATE POWER AND FEDERAL CRIMINAL CIVIL RIGHTS INDICTMENTS

"Charges Filed in Arkansas Prison Terror"

—*Los Angeles Times*, January 28, 1967[9]

Rockefeller had made public the state police report's grim details of a litany of crimes—"robbery, larceny, maiming, extortion, liquors into prison, excessive punishment, personal use of provisions, [and] gifts to officers or personnel." Calling the "67-page report . . . 'shocking,' . . . he hoped it would 'shock the Legislature and the people of this state into action.'" Rockefeller's reference was literal; the state police had tapes recording the apparent pleasure Superintendent Bruton took in the use of electric wires to inflict pain.[10]

FIGURE 18.2 *Governor Rockefeller Squeezes in Beside Cash in Prison Doby Wagon*, photograph by Larry Obsitnik, accompanying *Hello Cummins Prison Farm, I'm Johnny Cash*, Arkansas Gazette, April 13, 1969, courtesy of the publisher

On January 27, 1967 (as the *Jackson* whipping trial was underway), Arkansas prosecutor Joe Holmes indicted Bruton and three former Tucker wardens: E. T. Fletcher, E. G. Mayes, and Jess Wilson. The charges against Bruton included that he "ordered an inmate doctor to attach wires to the big toe and the private parts of an inmate," that those wires were hooked into an "old-fashioned telephone" and that, when cranked, the machine sent "electrical charges through the inmate." Rather than indict on other state crimes, the prosecution based the crimes on an 1893 Arkansas statute giving the Penitentiary Board authority to "prescribe the mode and extent of punishments to be inflicted on convicts for the violation of the prison rules." Imposition of "any greater or more severe punishment" constituted a felony punishable by one to five years; if a person died, penalties for murder or manslaughter applied.[11]

The prosecutions collapsed thereafter. Bruton persuaded a judge to postpone his October 1967 trial on the grounds he was hospitalized in a "state of depression." Bruton and his co-defendants then moved to dismiss; they argued that the legislature's delegation to the Penitentiary Board to decide what behavior constituted a crime violated the state's constitution. Winning in a lower court, they won again in March of 1969 in the Arkansas Supreme Court, which concluded that the legislature could not lawfully authorize an administrative agency to choose actions subject to felony prosecutions. Two other defendants, facing felony charges for transporting liquor into the prison, pled guilty to misdemeanors and were fined $100.[12]

A pause is in order to reflect on the concept of an "unconstitutional delegation"—in this instance, that the legislature had exclusive authority to define crimes. In the twenty-first century, critics of the Food and Drug Administration, the Environmental Protection Agency, and other agencies have filed lawsuits making parallel arguments—that Congress cannot give power to agencies to decide "major questions" and that courts ought not defer to agency interpretations of the statutes that created them. While several justices have championed these approaches and, in 2024, enshrined them in majority opinions,[13] they have not done so for corrections agencies. Just as the Arkansas Supreme Court in 1969 faulted the state's statute for providing "no guidelines," laws on correctional departments are sparse on how prison officials should exercise their powers and, as discussed, aside from racial segregation and religious liberty, the Court has insisted on deference to their decisions.[14]

Return to the 1960s in Arkansas, where new federal indictments followed after the state charges were dismissed. Federal power to do so comes from a statute drafted after the Civil War to prosecute lynchings of Black citizens. In 1939, the DOJ created a special Civil Rights Unit (renamed the Section on Civil Rights) within its Criminal Division. In 1957, amid school desegregation battles exemplified by Little Rock's Central High School, Congress elevated that section into a Division, headed by an Assistant Attorney General nominated by the President and confirmed by the Senate. The use of federal criminal law expanded in the 1960s, when civil rights workers were murdered in Mississippi, children killed in a church bombing in Birmingham, and scores killed or injured elsewhere. After Richard Nixon succeeded Lyndon Johnson as President, the

Justice Department retreated on many issues—exemplified in 1969 by its failure to prosecute Chicago police for the murders of Fred Hampton and Mark Clark.[15]

Washington, DC is not, however, the only site of federal litigating power. Another set of presidential appointees—US attorneys selected for each of the ninety-four federal district courts—can initiate lawsuits. In March of 1968, President Johnson appointed W. H. (Sonny) Dillahunty the US Attorney for the Eastern District of Arkansas. Dillahunty, who served for more than a decade, became "relentless [in] prosecution of white collar criminals and errant public officials."[16] Arkansas had come under scrutiny from the Federal Bureau of Investigations when Tom Murton, then Cummins Superintendent, went to the national media with his finding of unmarked graves. More press—and scrutiny—came after Murton was replaced with Victor Urban, who ordered birdshot fired at prisoners refusing to work. The county penal farms came into federal focus after Curtis Ingram died at the Pulaski County facility and beatings at Mississippi County Penal Farm made news. Responding to Dillahunty's request, Chief Judge Henley empaneled a special grand jury on July 8, 1969.[17] Henley's charge to the grand jurors tracked the 1866 federal criminal rights statute; they were to decide whether individuals "acting under color of state law" had "willfully" violated the civil rights of people held in state prisons or the county penal farms.[18]

Thus, in the same courthouse where Winston Talley and other prisoners had testified about whippings, Dillahunty put on some seventy witnesses. One was Talley, held under a thirty-year sentence for burglary and grand theft. He was joined by five other prisoners, twelve former Arkansas prisoners serving time elsewhere, and ten not then in custody. After listening to nauseating accounts of Tucker, Cummins, and the county penal farms, the grand jury "returned" (in law's parlance) indictments on July 11, 1969. Fifteen people were charged; Bruton headed the list with nineteen felonies. Three Cummins employees firing birdshots were among the indicted, along with defendants at the two penal farms.[19]

MURDERING BLACK MEN AND EXCLUDING BLACK
CITIZENS FROM GRAND JURIES

In this century, murders by white police officers of Black men and women have galvanized movements pressing for change. Reading about the death in 1968 of Curtis Ingram is painfully familiar; he lost his life as a result of government actions that were unconstitutional at the time or soon thereafter—an unlawful stop, search, and interrogation; a trial without a lawyer; and evidence that should have been suppressed.

Ingram's nightmare began on July 22, 1958; when driving his mother's car, two white police officers stopped him, took him to a police station, searched him, and recorded a waiver of a right to a lawyer and that he said the seven barbiturates in his pocket came from someone else. Ingram went to trial without a lawyer on what the judge later insisted was a misdemeanor—thereby trying to avoid the 1963 *Gideon v. Wainwright* requirement of appointed counsel for indigent defendants facing felony prosecutions. The police testified that they had advised Ingram of his rights and that he gave different accounts about the pills. Another white witness, a state chemist, identified the pills as anti-depressants for which a prescription was necessary. Ingram—likely the only Black person in the courtroom—testified that he had neck pain from a wound (that had left a visible scar) and a doctor gave him the medicine. After his conviction on July 31, the trial judge sentenced Ingram to a suspended prison term and sent him to Pulaski County Prison Farm to work the $110.50 fine off at $1.00 a day—the rate set by an 1875 Arkansas statute.[20]

Ingram spent his first—and only—night there on August 1, 1968; he was killed the next day. The press provided details—that Ingram had an "allergic-asthmatic condition," that nonetheless he was sent to the fields, and after vegetation made him sicker, he said he was too ill to continue. According to the 1969 federal grand jury indictment, a thirty-four-year-old white prisoner–trusty, Bruce Mc-Corley, acting at the behest of white warden Herman Belk, beat Ingram with a three-foot long wooden stick. The federal government charged another white warden, Gene Emmerling, with choking Ingram and pouring hot water on him when on the ground. Soon thereafter, Ingram was dead.[21]

Five months after Ingram died, the Eighth Circuit held whippings impermissible. Two years later, the Supreme Court found unconstitutional a sentence to "work off" a fine unless a judge found a person had the ability to pay and willfully refused to do so.[22] And federal judges concluded the following year that conditions at the county farms were unconstitutional; both Pulaski and Mississippi Counties agreed to conform to "constitutional standards."[23]

Protests in Little Rock after Ingram died "at the hands of white men" were met with the largest deployment of the National Guard since the 1957 school desegregation battles. During three days of fires, gunshots, and curfews, marchers clashed with National Guardsmen and property was destroyed. The police arrested more than 160 people; charges included assault, weapons possession, curfew violations, and disturbing the peace.[24] Pushed by this public outcry, a state prosecutor investigated Ingram's death and charged only the prisoner–trusty McCorley with manslaughter. At McCorley's guilty plea in 1968, the trial judge reduced the charges from voluntary to involuntary manslaughter and sentenced McCorley to serve at least one year of a three-year term before parole eligibility. A Pulaski County grand jury listened to sixteen people and concluded it was "unable to find sufficient evidence to bring any indictments" against Belk and Emmerling. On August 12, 1968, Dr. Jerry D. Jewell, president of the Arkansas State Conference of NAACP branches, joined by twelve other "black leaders," asked the federal courts to halt that grand jury—whose term was to expire on September 23, 1968—because its members left out all Black men but one.[25]

That lawsuit went to Chief Judge Henley, who held a hearing on September 4; he ruled on September 10, 1968 that the county used a racially-biased selection process. The judge recounted that US constitutional law was clear. States were not to discriminate on the basis of race in choosing people for either grand or petit juries; "token inclusion"—of one or more "Negros"—did not suffice.[26] Between

1953 and 1967, more than 20 percent of the Pulaski County's population were "Negroes" and, if a "truly proportional representation"
existed, one would expect to find three or four on a panel. Yet, for
twenty-eight terms, not more than "one Negro" had served as a regular grand juror and in five terms "no Negroes [served] on either the
regular or alternative panel." Moreover, no woman, no "person under 50 years of age, nor a day laborer, nor a mechanic, nor a farmer"
had been a grand juror. Instead, grand jurors were "prominent and
successful citizens . . . closely identified with its large business and
financial interests."

What was the remedy? Loath to enjoin state criminal prosecution
practices (a view endorsed by the Supreme Court in 1971[27]), Henley
concluded that he did not "anticipate that the Grand Jury would return
any new indictment" before its term expired. In practice, his ruling
meant that, if the grand jury had, any defendant could have moved
to quash an indictment as resulting from unlawful discrimination.[28]

VIOLENCE AS A "FRONT-LINE DEFENSE FOR LAW-ABIDING CITIZENS"

"'[T]he most vicious, sadistic, and inhumane treatment' of human
beings since Hitler."

—A federal prosecutor quoted as heralding
the July 1969 federal indictments[29]

The "rug in the courtroom took a beating" as three people
"demonstrated to the jury their version of how a leather strap was
used to punish inmates."

—Press account of October 9, 1969, trial[30]

The defending prison wardens "were your front-line defense for law-
abiding citizens" [against] 78 outlaws sent to the penal farm."

—Defense closing arguments, November 7, 1969[31]

Attorney General John Mitchell, President Richard Nixon's appointee, announced the federal indictments against fifteen defendants.
The charges of torture by electric shocks, blackjacks, pliers, hypodermic needles, and whips made headlines in and beyond the

United States. Although a federal prosecutor made an analogy to Hitler's techniques, federal statutes limited the penalties. Absent a victim's death, a year in prison and a $1,000 fine were the maximums then authorized.[32] Nonetheless, Governor Rockefeller told the press he was "pleased that at the end of 30 months of my administration and after some persistent efforts on our part to get some action taken, federal authorities have seen fit to issue some indictments."[33]

Within a week, Bruton's lawyers tried to stop the coverage, move the trial, and get the charges dismissed as too vague. Bruton's lawyer counted some seventy articles in local newspapers and national outlets such as *Time*, *Life*, and *Newsweek* magazines, chronicling the "hell" of Arkansas prisons. Chief Judge Henley refused Bruton's requests; he commented that, despite "sensational news stories, . . . the purported revelations about the institution have not seemed to have made much lasting impression upon the people of Arkansas." Henley's appraisal was repeatedly borne out.[34]

In early October, the government dropped charges against one Cummins employee involved in the birdshot shooting after learning he had shot into the air, not at prisoners. That week, the first civil rights criminal prosecution began against Tucker Warden Ernest Fletcher, accused of aggressively lashing a prisoner with a leather strap. Henley empaneled a jury of seven men and five women—likely all white, as the newspapers did not mention their race. A first witness during the two-day trial was twenty-three-year-old Jerry Ivens, returning from California, and recounting that he had put a letter into the Tucker prisoner mailbox to tell his mother that he was "starving and . . . needed help." That "knock" at the prison system did not get mailed but prompted Bruton to direct Fletcher to "hit him at least 11 times" in view of many prisoners. Until a trusty told him that "the procedure" was to "moan 'Oh, Captain' after each lick," Ivens, with only underclothes, did not; once he did, the whipping stopped, and he was left bleeding and bruised. Corroboration came from another witness who saw Fletcher whip Ivens "14 or 15 times."[35]

The whip was admitted as an exhibit, which is why, decades later, I found it and the Tucker Telephone archived in boxes at the Arkansas Historical Museum. The state police investigator, Duke

Atkinson, described it as "four feet long and five inches wide, attached to a one-foot wooden handle." Reenactments—by a former warden and a prisoner—simulated the violence by whipping the courtroom's rug in front of the jurors. Taking the stand to defend himself, Fletcher testified he had never lashed more than ten times and only people fully clothed. Fletcher's lawyer had subpoenaed Bruton; citing the Fifth Amendment, Bruton declined. Fletcher's lawyer argued that Fletcher always conformed to the rules and pointed to Fletcher's sons, both state policemen, in the courtroom.[36]

The jurors had to decide whether to believe the prisoners' account of a bloody beating or find credible Fletcher's defense that he had whipped in compliance with the "*Talley* Rules." That distinction was important, as reflected in Henley's jury instruction to "consider the history of the strap," which was "not legally considered cruel and unusual punishment until 1965." On October 8, 1969, the jury acquitted Fletcher. About a week later, the US prosecutors dismissed eight of the nineteen charges against Bruton.[37]

Later in October, Herman Belk and Gene Emmerling went on trial for Ingram's death. Judge Gordon Young died a few months earlier and a visiting federal judge, Edward J. McManus, based in Iowa, presided. The press reported that the federal prosecutor told the "all-white jury that Belk, a former assistant warden, had ordered the whipping of Ingram, and that Emerling, also a former assistant warden," did the "choking," "whipping," "kneeling him in the back and pouring hot water on him." Bruce McCorley—the prisoner incarcerated for a year after pleading to involuntary manslaughter—testified that, at Warden Belk's direction, he had "hit Ingram 28 times" on the afternoon Ingram died, and that Emmerling poured "hot water" on him thereafter. McCorley explained that his prior inconsistent statements (that Ingram had attacked him with a hoe) were based on reassurances from the two wardens that doing so would keep him from going to prison. Corroboration—of the beating and the blood—came from a medical technician who was in on a twenty-day vagrancy charge. In addition, Arkansas' medical examiner testified that the cause of death was "blows to [Ingram's] head with a blunt instrument." An editorial in the *Arkansas Gazette* described witnesses testifying that "beating of prisoners" at the County Farm was "standard operating procedures."[38]

One line of defense was that Ingram had epilepsy (of which the state medical examiner found no evidence) and had a seizure; the other was that the defendants' response to Ingram was not abusive. The defendants won again; the all-white federal jury acquitted within a day of the trial's beginning.[39]

On November 5, the trial of defendants Edwin Lucas and Howard McCain began, with Chief Judge Henley presiding. At issue was why Oscar Lee Phelps had died in July of 1965, five days after arriving at the Mississippi County Penal Farm. Phelps had been sentenced to eleven months and twenty-nine days and fined $136.10 for swindling a local merchant "out of $9.70." Unlike the Ingram prosecution, no mention was made of race; genealogical records indicate that Phelps was white. The federal prosecutor argued Phelps had been beaten "unmercifully" to death. As the judge explained to the jury of nine men and three women, the federal charges were that the wardens had violated Phelps' constitutionally protected civil rights. The defense lawyer countered that the wardens had not "dished out cruel and inhuman punishment" but were the "frontline defense of law-abiding citizens."[40]

The first witness was Phelps' mother, who testified her son had epilepsy. Evidence came from former prisoners who described that Phelps appeared confused, and wardens attacked him. A carpenter serving time saw Lucas and McCain use a rubber hose and an axe handle to beat Phelps, described as having had a seizure when "chopping soybeans." Three others (two brothers serving "a six-month term for the theft of a typewriter" and another in for "six months on a burglary conviction") provided graphic accounts of the blows and the victim's efforts fighting them off. The defense argued that Phelps, pretending to be sick to escape, was the aggressor and "lunged" at the wardens. Prosecutors also put on a pathologist who found "three lacerations" and blood stains; she reported the cause of death was "swelling of the brain" that could have been caused "by a severe blow to the head or by a sustained epileptic seizure." In closing arguments, the defense lawyer insisted that "rough and tough" wardens were the "buffer between prisoners and society."

The case went to the jury on the 6th of November. Within a few hours, the jury requested "more instruction on the term 'willfully,'" and the judge explained that the prosecutors had to prove that the defendants had "acted intentionally and deliberately and with the purpose of violating the law or disregarding the law." About an hour later, the jury acquitted Lucas and McCain.[41]

Bruton's trial began some ten days later.

NO "LASTING IMPRESSION"

"It is very hard indeed for the court to see how a person of ordinary intelligence would or could believe that such punishments were proper."

—Chief Judge Henley's comment to the
Bruton jurors, November 21, 1969[42]

On the first day of Bruton's trial, one prisoner recounted having been "stripped of pants, strapped to a table, and wired to the telephone" that delivered shocks to his genitals and toes. A former prisoner, who had "rung up" that prisoner at Bruton's direction, provided more details. Another witness—Bruton's prisoner– "secretary"—testified that Bruton had struck him with a cane and ordered Warden Fletcher to "whip him on the buttocks with a leather strap" while Bruton looked on. Three more people recounted their torture with the Tucker Telephone that sent "jolts of electricity through them."[43]

Bruton did not testify but his son, along with two doctors and "nine character witnesses," did. After being "crippled" in a car accident and overwhelmed by his wife's death, Burton's witnesses claimed he knew little about what occurred at Tucker and did not have the physical strength to whip people with the "large leather strap used in those days." Arguing that the prisoners were not to be believed, Bruton's lawyers succeeded. Despite the week's gruesome details, on November 21, 1969, the seven women and five men deliberated for eight hours and acquitted Bruton.[44]

Unpacking the interactions between Henley and the jury reveals how revolted he was by what he had heard. After he sent the jury to deliberate, their questions brought them to the courtroom three times for the public to hear the exchanges. Henley told the jurors that using the strap was not "necessarily" cruel and unusual punishment, as it was permitted at the time (indeed by virtue of his court's 1965 and 1967 decisions), but that whipping *could be* cruel and unusual, depending on the circumstances. As to other bodily incursions, Henley told the jury that "such devices as the 'Tucker Telephone,' pliers and hypodermic needles never had been authorized for punishment," that a state lawyer had two years earlier conceded their use would be unconstitutional, and that such inflictions were "the very kind of punishment that the Eighth Amendment was designed to prohibit." Thus, if the devices were "in fact used, as charged in the indictments," and done "willfully and knowingly," a violation of prisoners' civil rights had occurred. Moreover, in "the court's personal opinion," it "is very hard indeed for the court to see how a person of ordinary intelligence would or could believe that such punishments were proper."[45]

Such a statement is extraordinary; judges are not supposed to tell jurors how to interpret the evidence. (Had Bruton been convicted, the instructions would have been grounds for an appeal.) And Henley said more, apparently prompted by Bruton's defense that the prison system's problems were being pinned "on the shoulders of one man." Henley told the jury that the penitentiary system was "not on trial" and that cruel and unusual punishment was not justified "merely because [a person] may be employed as a head of a penal institution that is characterized by brutality, or is inadequate, out of date, understaffed or underfunded." Therefore, "[y]ou should not on the one hand, convict the defendant merely because he was working for a bad or deficient system, if he was. On the other hand, you are told that the mere fact that he was working for such a system, if he was, is not in and of itself a defense in this case."[46]

Henley's comments explain why—when the jurors returned after seven hours—he said they "have had the case about long enough," and "if they did not complete their deliberations shortly, he would suggest that they give him any decisions they had made on any charges, and he would discharge them on the remaining charges." For lawyers, that pressure to reach a verdict (sometimes called an "*Allen*" or a "dynamite" charge) is thought to push holdout jurors to capitulate and *convict*. Henley likely assumed that a holdout was for acquittal and his pressure would result in a conviction. Instead, within an hour, the jury acquitted. Recall that in August of 1969, when rejecting Bruton's efforts to gag the press and move the trial, Henley had commented that "the purported revelations about [Tucker] have not seemed to have made much lasting impression upon the people of Arkansas."[47] Nonetheless, Henley had held out hope that Bruton's trial would end with a conviction.

After the verdict, Henley remained appalled and said so repeatedly. About a month later, the federal prosecution of Gary Haydis began—predicated on his order to fire birdshot that hurt twenty-four people. Government witnesses described the peaceful sit-down protest for minimally decent medical attention. Haydis' lawyer told the jury that Cummins held "1,000 of the most hardened criminals that the State of Arkansas . . . has ever produced," and Haydis testified he had negotiated, fired one shot in the air and the other at the ground, and admitted he knew some prisoners could be hit but, with birdshot, "no one would be killed."[48]

Chief Judge Henley ended Haydis' trial without letting the jury deliberate. He told the jurors it was "wrong to fire into a group of prisoners with a gun" and, in general, he was "reluctant to take the case away from the jury." But, Henley said, just as he "had not been reluctant to tell the jury in similar prison trials that it should return a verdict of guilty," he would not let them convict Haydis. The judge explained that, despite injuries, the evidence could not sustain finding that Haydis had the "evil intent" requisite for a conviction.[49]

What was left of the federal prosecutions? While the government had dropped several counts against Bruton before and during trial, one charge remained, based on Bruton's subjecting two prisoners in 1964 to the electric shock telephone. That trial was to have begun on January 22, 1970, but on January 16, 1970, Bruton entered a plea of "no contest," neither admitting nor disputing the charges of torture.

Henley told Bruton he did not ordinarily accept such a plea and considered Bruton "convicted." Regretting that more severe penalties were not available, Henley imposed the statutory maximum of a $1,000 fine and a year in prison, suspended. The judge told Bruton he did not "believe you would live 60 days in prison because one of the prisoners or a friend of prisoners with whom you have dealt would kill you, and I don't want to give you the death sentence."[50]

That statement reflects Henley's understanding of the inability of Arkansas prisons to provide safety. Henley knew so because he had by then held in *Holt I* that Cummins' disciplinary cells were unconstitutional and he was on his way to ruling Arkansas' entire prison system ("a dark and evil world") unconstitutional, which also meant he would have had little interest in spending political capital putting Bruton into prison. Yet Henley was insistent that Bruton had tortured; in the *Holt II* decision, issued February 18, 1970, Henley repeated his evaluation that the "evidence in all of the cases was ample to convict."[51]

REJECTING ACCOUNTABILITY

A summary is in order of the forty-six federal counts against fifteen people. No one went to federal prison, and most people were acquitted or the cases dismissed. Late in January of 1970, the federal government dropped charges against the "last five" defendants (including three of five prisoner–trustys) as well as Tucker Warden E. G. Mayes and Cummins Prison Farm Supervisor G. W. Thompson, who had been with Haydis when birdshot was fired.[52] Thus, aside from Bruton's nolo contendere plea, the only people subjected to any federal criminal liability were prisoner–trustys. William James Morgan, entering a nolo plea on using the Tucker Telephone, was fined $500 and given one year of probation.[53] Ray Vern Varner received a three-year suspended sentence, which he served in his home state, Oregon.[54] And, as described, Bruce McCorley, charged in state court for Ingram's death, pled guilty in 1968 to involuntary manslaughter and served one year before being paroled. Despite McCorley's testimony in the federal prosecution,

Belk and Emmerling were acquitted in October of 1969. Bruton's no-contest plea meant that he continued to draw his monthly pension of $333.33, which he had received since August of 1966 until his death in 1975 at age sixty-five. At that time, the Conway County sheriff announced mourning the loss of this "good man and a good law enforcement officer."[55]

The refusal to hold accountable white men who had caused grievous injury and death to Black and white people in Arkansas is part of a long sequence that has not ended. Some people, like Curtis Ingram, died after having been taken into state custody, and scores more have lost their lives in encounters on the streets or by lynchings. Some became the subject of extensive press coverage, including four young Black girls, Addie Mae Collins, Denise McNair, Carole Robertson, and Cynthia Wesley, all dying in the 1963 bombing of the Sixteenth Street Baptist Church in Birmingham; and one Black man and two white men, James Chaney, Andrew Goodman, and Michael Schwerner, killed in 1964 in Mississippi where they worked to protect the rights of Black voters. In some of these deaths, investigative reporters and prosecutors convinced juries (often decades later) to hold some members in the networks of murderers (at times linked to the Ku Klux Klan) responsible.[56] However, in Arkansas in 1969 and many times before and since, government officials and juries declined to condemn violence perpetrated by people "acting under color of state law." Moreover, in the opening decades of the twenty-first century, the US Supreme Court developed new doctrines of immunity that shielded many such actors from civil liability.[57]

19

A "TOTALITY OF PRISON CONDITIONS" AS UNCONSTITUTIONAL PUNISHMENT

> "[E]ach of us bears responsibility for the hell holes that are
> our penal institutions . . . [which operate] the way most of
> us want them."
>
> —Editorial, *Arkansas Gazette*, December 21, 1969[1]

In 1969, the phrase "totality of conditions" did not come trippingly off the tongues of prisoners, lawyers, and judges, although it does today. Arkansas litigants pioneered this new application of the constitutional prohibition on "cruel and unusual punishment." While prison reformers had since the eighteenth century called for decent facilities, in the 1960s in the United States, few prisons operationalized that precept. Rather, "cruel" conditions and vicious modes of discipline were commonplace, not "unusual."

To make *structural* changes required political will and money. For a brief period in Arkansas after the police reports of torture and the whipping decision, improvements seemed likely. The Arkansas Legislature had made "rehabilitation" a stated *purpose* of incarceration and charged its new Arkansas Department of Correction (ADC) to provide it. Governor Rockefeller chose a reformer, Robert Sarver, as the Commissioner to implement that mandate. Yet, as Chief Judge Henley said when refusing Jim Bruton's request to move his criminal torture trial away from Little Rock, gory headlines and photographs had not made a "lasting impression." To accomplish

Sarver's goals of trained staff replacing gun-carrying prisoner–trustys (who sold food, jobs and, at times, protection against violent assaults), legislators had to put taxpayer dollars *into* prisons instead of using prisons to generate money *for* the state.

The question was how to get them to do so. That task was complicated because Rockefeller, a Republican, faced a legislature run by Democrats. Moreover, prisons were but one of the many miserable state services that gave Rockefeller headaches. Throughout 1969, Rockefeller made direct appeals to the citizenry to drum up popular support for all kinds of funding. Johnny Cash concerts were one route; another was a regional tour Rockefeller took. At one hearing in December of 1969, the chair of the state's Labor Standards Committee reported that Arkansas ranked *last* in salaries paid to its employees. Arkansas was also at the bottom of the fifty states in municipal revenues. One official reported $12 million needed for "a minimum level of municipal services," and the State Police Director called for another $11 million to improve salaries, hire more officers, and make "some basic improvements in the state prison system." Presidents of the University of Arkansas, Arkansas State University, and Pine Bluff's AM&N College (formerly the all-Black Arkansas Agricultural, Mechanical, and Normal College) added teachers' salaries and buildings to the list. Democrats responded by lambasting Rockefeller for overspending and for pushing for a tax hike that would be unfair to working-class citizens.[2]

Lawsuits were another path to funding. In this and the next chapter, I map the hopes prisoners pinned on federal court intervention. Henley rendered two decisions that gave Sarver and Rockefeller some leverage—*Holt v. Sarver* (*Holt I*), decided in June of 1969 and addressing conditions in disciplinary cells, and *Holt v. Sarver* (*Holt II*), issued in February of 1970 and taking on the whole system. As I unfold in the book's next segment, more prisoners' victories produced a new regime of minimal constitutional protection. Yet those rights did not dim the punitive appetite of many sectors of the electorate, repeatedly endorsing aggressive imprisonment. When pushed, Arkansas' legislature—like those of many states—was willing to appropriate dollars for more security beds but not fund services to alter conditions substantially. Constitutional rights raised the floor in important respects but left it far below what an egalitarian social order owes to the people it subjects to 24/7 control.

SARVER'S REFORMS ON A SHOESTRING

The prison system Sarver took over in the winter of 1969 was segregated and impoverished. At the 1967 *Jackson v. Bishop* trial, witnesses had described the sounds of whippings at the "colored end." Two years later, "Negro prisoners—who comprise[d] half of Cummins 985 inmates" were in three barracks at one end, white prisoners slept in three barracks at another, and everyone ate in a divided dining room. In the women's unit, "15 Negro women slept in one wing and the 18 white women in another." Sarver convinced the state's Board of Correction that the US Supreme Court's 1968 *Lee v. Washington* holding unlawful Alabama's segregation meant Arkansas had to alter its status quo, which, at a glacial pace, he began to do.[3]

Other Sarver initiatives included authorizing a prisoner newspaper; the editors of the *Pea Pickers Picayune* called it the "only uncensored paper in penal presswork." (Rockefeller paid personally for the equipment). The name echoed a famed New Orleans' paper, the *Times-Picayune*, begun in 1837 and referencing the French "picaillon," a Spanish coin of trivial value. "Pea Pickers" came into parlance a century later as a shorthand for impoverished farm workers, epitomized in the 1930s photograph by Dorothea Lange of an emaciated woman and her children. In contrast, *The Pea Pickers Picayune* was a robust resource for Arkansas' other newspapers, which cited its stories and reprinted editorials.[4] Sarver facilitated other collective actions, including a letter, describing "food unfit for human consumption," which 250 prisoners sent to Rockefeller, who promised milk and meat would soon be served. In addition, Sarver licensed an Inmate Council that, in the fall of 1969, provided a "form letter" for prisoners to write legislators to support prison reform through increasing taxes.[5]

Sarver also looked for donations. Through what is now called a "GoFundMe" campaign, Sarver made a brief appearance in a telecast by Reverend Rex Humbard, who had left Arkansas to become the leader of an interdenominational church in Akron, Ohio and whose show attracted more than eleven million viewers. On the air, the men pitched a chapel at Tucker; budgeted at $30,000; within a week, individual donations tallied more than $4,000.[6]

But Sarver could not surmount the lack of public funds. In the spring of 1969, Sarver fired his "two chief fiscal officers" because neither had the education nor experience requisite for the job. Meanwhile, a legislative committee "trimmed" back Sarver's $171,000 request for new farm machinery to replace "worn-out equipment" for planting. The Joint Budget Committee reduced the amount to $100,000 and deferred action on Sarver's proposal for $2.3 million for the coming two years.[7] As his budget gap grew, he laid off several employees and put himself in the role of Superintendent of Cummins where, on some nights, he was one of only two free-world employees in that facility. "Picayune" was an apt description of legislators' view of prisoners—whose lives, aside from extracting labor, were treated as if of trivial value.

ENTER THE COURT VIA A "62-INCH" TOILET PAPER ROLL

"A mockery is being made of providing even the barest necessities needed to sustain a person's health."

—May 1969 filing from a person in a Cummins disciplinary cell[8]

In April of 1969, Harvey Cecil Poe filed a handwritten petition on a "62-inch roll of toilet paper." The press reported that "[c]ourt clerks cut the petition into five pieces and stapled it to conventional legal-size paper." Poe's filing was one of many arriving "over a period of several days," including from Lawrence J. Holt, who claimed that his twenty-five days in solitary confinement violated the Eighth Amendment. George W. Overton, who had filed lawsuits before and wrote "for and by the request of the inmate population of the Arkansas state penitentiary," alleged terrible healthcare and that the prison charged prisoners $0.10 for $0.06 stamps.[9]

As Chief Judge Henley recounted in his June 20, 1969, *Holt I* opinion, he chose three petitioners—Holt, Overton, and Travis Eugene
Fields—held in the "cells in the isolation unit" at Cummins. Henley
told us no more about them, but the impressive Arkansas press
enables glimpses of these white men. Holt was in his thirties and
serving three years for burglary; Fields and Overton were in their
twenties. Each had escaped Cummins (sometimes more than once)
and been recaptured.[10] Their back-and-forth did not distinguish
them. The prisons were chaotic, and trustys had access to trucks,
mules, and guns. Between January of 1967 and April of 1970, when
about a thousand people were at Cummins, the press counted 180
people escaped, and 160 recaptured.[11]

Just as Henley had in 1965, he recruited lawyers and treated the
petitions as a "class action on behalf of all Penitentiary inmates."
Henley created that structure for two reasons: whatever rules he
ordered had to apply prison-wide and, as chief judge of a court
with a growing docket, aggregation permitted economies of scale
for judges and lawyers. Like other federal judges, Henley sought
to manage an influx of cases from an array of claimants relying on
new federal statutory and constitutional rights.

In *Holt I*, Henley described the "experienced and capable trial
attorney," Steele Hays, and his associate Jerry D. Jackson, who had
served without "expectation of compensation or reimbursement"
and had traveled to Cummins, photographed cells (for which they
needed Sarver's assent or a court order), and "vigorously represented" the prisoners during a "rather extended hearing which con-
sumed two full trial days and part of one night." Henley's opinion
did not mention what locals knew well: Steele Hays was not only
a hardworking lawyer in a powerful firm but also part of a high-
profile family. His grandfather was a judge and his father, Brooke
Hays, had spent fourteen years in the US House of Representatives
until defeated in 1958 in a write-in contest by segregationist Thomas
Dale Alford (a doctor who, as I discussed, testified in the 1967 whipping trial). Soon after *Holt I*, Rockefeller appointed Hays to a circuit
court judgeship; in 1979, after the legislature created an intermediate appellate court, Governor Bill Clinton elevated him to that

bench. Within a year, Hays was elected to the Arkansas Supreme Court, where he sat for fourteen years and consistently argued the unlawfulness of the death penalty.[12]

In short, Henley picked a lawyer with a general practice and a commitment to civil rights. The lawyers asked for injunctive relief, a decision that had to be made by a judge, not a jury. Because Eighth Circuit law had already rejected direct challenges to solitary confinement, the lawyers did not request abolition but that prisoners be able to defend themselves against disciplinary charges and safeguards be put into cells to "prevent assaults, spread of disease, and other dangerous and unsanitary conditions."[13]

TOXIC DENSITY IN ISOLATION, FED "GRUE," AND FEARING STABBINGS

"'Only good' can come out of [the] federal court hearing."
—Defendant Commissioner of Correction Robert Sarver,
May 26, 1969, before testifying in *Holt I*[14]

Local newspapers provided detailed coverage of the *Holt I* hearings that began on May 26, 1969. The press counted eighteen named plaintiffs representing all prisoners held in Cummins' isolation cells. The testimony, which was grim, was also redundant, varying "only slightly from one witness to another." A "universal" example was revulsion at "grue"—a baked patty of meat and vegetables pressed into a four-by-four square. Lawrence Holt testified that grue was placed on a floor that was never mopped. Holt catalogued more filth (dirty mattresses at night and nothing to sit on during the day); the lack of showers (five in twenty-five days); and intense proximity (seven men crowded into a cell with space for four or five mattresses).

Violence abounded. Among the "principal complaints" was prisoners' fear of being "stabbed while they slept" by "creepers." Daytime violence was also common. Fields, another lead plaintiff, reported being beaten by a staff member. Twenty-year-old William E. Eaton said that he had been "knocked down by an officer" the morning of his testimony. James Standridge had requested protective custody, been denied, and then stabbed.[15]

Sarver, as Commissioner, was the state's chief defense witness. Sarver attributed the lack of running water to prisoners who "tore the pipes out and have destroyed everything they can get their hands on." Yet, counter-culturally, Sarver agreed with prisoners about the violence and inadequate medical care. Sarver explained that the Department employed a total of "17 free-world guards" for 940 prisoners; when he was West Virginia's Commissioner, 170 staff were assigned to 900 men in one maximum-security unit. At Henley's request, Sarver explained what "creepers" were: if "one man . . . happens to have a personal vendetta with another . . . and one of them goes to sleep before the other," that person could be stabbed. Sarver said that without staff, he could not prevent it. (Cummins' chief security officer later testified that "four free-world guards were on duty at night . . . but . . . none" were in the barracks.)[16]

Sarver also told the judge (and the larger audience reached through the daily press) that the "prison system went broke about three weeks" before the hearing and was "operating on borrowed funds" from state coffers. Sarver's defense was to be patient (and hopeful). Medical care would be improved because a full-time doctor (to be paid $20,000 plus housing) was to be hired, and a new maximum-security unit would relieve the crowded disciplinary cells. Sarver said the legislature had appropriated $250,000 with another $200,000 to come the following year. That comment prompted Henley to ask: "What benefit is it going to be for a man who gets killed next month to have a maximum-security unit a year from now?" The judge later reiterated his concern: "A man who dies in the next six or 12 months as a result of a violation of his rights will be just as dead as if the state did eventually correct the conditions." The prisoners' lawyers entered into the record the "death reports of nine Cummins inmates who had been killed or died of violent deaths in the last 18 months and 17 reports of stabbings," and the hearing ended.[17]

FORCED PRISONER LABOR INSTEAD OF TAXPAYER FUNDS

"Correction Agency Says It Is Broke"

> —*Arkansas Gazette* headline, June 12, 1969[18]

"The money is in the ground."

> —Robert Sarver, June 18, 1969[19]

The *Holt I* hearing produced a sorry record of fear, filth, and illness. The ADC was out of money. Sarver tried to rally public support by going to civic clubs and explaining that the prison system, known as "one of the country's worst," had fostered "torture, beating, starvation, extortion" and more.[20]

But the public also heard another refrain. Cummins' farm manager said "a shortage of manpower" was worse than "the shortage of finances" because it was delaying harvesting. Critics argued that the "labor shortage" stemmed from "the new philosophy . . . of rehabilitation and paroles," which meant "hundreds fewer convicts" were available to do farm work. They were right that the number of incarcerated people had declined. In 1965, the state's penitentiaries had housed more than 1,600 people; by 1969, about 950 were held. Sarver asserted that only 100 were available for harvesting; 300 were trustys doing security, and the remainder were in the kitchen, laundry, as clerks and mechanics, or unable to work.[21]

Thus, two weeks after the *Holt I* hearing and a week before the judge issued his opinion, the *Arkansas Gazette* reported the "correction agency says it is broke." Sarver cited decrepit equipment, no staff, fewer prisoners, and a recalcitrant legislature, resulting in a "critical" financial situation. He told reporters prisoners needed "new clothing and shoes" and without funds, that ADC could not meet its payroll. In the short term, Sarver asked for $100,000 from the Governor's Emergency Fund. The Board of Correction, to which Sarver reported, had another proposal: that Sarver, living in Little Rock and dealing (mostly unsuccessfully) with the legislature, should move to Cummins and stop being an "armchair director."[22]

Holt I was decided on June 20; a legislative committee paid a visit to Cummins a few days later. That site tour was not prompted by concerns about the grotesque conditions Henley described but by harvesting shortfalls. The legislators, traveling in air-conditioned cars, encountered one prisoner on a "lie-down strike" and others making "obscene gestures." After complaining about the allocation of prisoner–workers and when about "ready to leave," the legislators "inspected the isolation-cell building" where they found "five Negro prisoners" in one of the eight-by-ten "cubicles."

Neither the judge's condemnation of conditions, Sarver's requests for shoes and equipment, nor the inspection resulted in funding. Instead, Sarver was told to extract more work from prisoners. Rearranging assignments to send another 100 people to the fields, Sarver told the prisoners: "The money is in the ground." The local press, citing the prisoners' *Pea Pickers Picayune*, reported that Sarver had tried to cushion sending people to the fields with promises of help in parole for people with "good work records."[23]

CREEPERS CUTTING THROATS AS UNCONSTITUTIONAL CONDITIONS

"[I]nmates in barracks . . . ought at least to be able to fall asleep at night without fear of having their throats cut before morning."

—Chief Judge Henley's June 1969 *Holt I* ruling[24]

The conflicts over funds and farming illuminate why Henley's *Holt I* opinion provided a gruesome account of filth and violence but did not order specific changes. Henley began by citing his 1965 *Talley* opinion that the "Court may and should intervene . . . to put an end to unconstitutional practices," and he quoted from *Jackson v. Bishop* that the Eighth Amendment embodied a "flexible and expanding" understanding. Practices that offend "concepts of decency and human dignity and precepts of civilization which Americans profess to possess, is disproportionate to the offense, or violates fundamental standards of good conscience and fairness" were unconstitutional.[25]

Those words do *not* necessarily result in finding isolation cells unlawful. As Henley explained, other courts had declined to hold solitary confinement *per se* unconstitutional; two months earlier, the

Eighth Circuit affirmed Judge Harris' dismissal of Robert Courtney's 1967 habeas petition contesting placement in Cummins' solitary confinement.[26] Yet, Henley explained that specific "circumstances" could render solitary confinement unlawful. As an exemplar, Henley drew from a 1966 decision—*Jordan v. Fitzharris*, written by Chief Judge George Harris of the federal court for the Northern District of California.[27] Henley's discussion reminded his immediate audience (and serves to do so for today's readers) that the degradation *in* Arkansas was not sui generis *to* Arkansas.

In 1966, Robert Jordan was at the California Correctional Training Facility in Soledad, a prison that became infamous with the 1970 publication of *Soledad Brother: The Prison Letters of George Jackson*.[28] California authorities put Jordan into a "strip cell"—the prisoner and the cell were bare. Jordan alleged that he had spent twelve days in the dark, naked and cold, in a space that measured six by eight feet. He had no light and no furnishings, and the toilet could only be flushed from the outside. In chapter 15, I quoted Lawrence Wright who described similar grotesque conditions in a strip cell in upstate New York. Jordan's handwritten complaint did so as well.

> The floors and walls of the cell were . . . encrusted and filthy with the body and urinary wastes of the previous occupants. . . . Plaintiff hand and body (being naked) were continually coming into contact with filthy wastes and again no possible chance of washing or cleansing his hands, face or body was given plaintiff and he was forced to eat and handle his food with his hands contaminated with other human beings' filth and urinary wastes.

California argued that Jordan's "general allegations [were] insufficient to state a claim for relief under the Civil Rights Act." The state insisted that "placing unruly or dangerous prisoners" in such cells comported with the "penological practice in the prison systems of both the federal government and the state's." Chief Judge Harris appointed a lawyer for Jordan and convened a hearing "for the first time in federal history" at the prison. Finding that California had not given Jordan the "essentials for survival" such as "water and food and . . . basic sanitation," the judge concluded that neither a "beast" nor a human should have to endure such treatment.[29]

Chief Judge Henley quoted both Harris' description of the filth and his constitutional analysis. Because prison authorities had "abandoned elemental concepts of decency by permitting conditions to prevail of a shocking and debased nature," Henley (using Harris' words) said that he, too, had to "intervene promptly—to restore the primal rules of a civilized community in accord with the mandate of the Constitution of the United States." Henley described Arkansas' eleven cells as "close" confinement; each cell held, on average, four men, and sometimes as many as eleven. The cells, ten feet long and eight feet wide, were "bare of furniture," save a "drinking fountain" and a "concrete toilet" that could be flushed only from outside. Foul toilet odors "pervaded" the area; the mattresses were "uncovered and dirty." Violence was pervasive, evidenced by the stabbings of seventeen people and the deaths of four.[30]

Henley wrote of the prisoners' terrible circumstances, pressed to labor for unending hours in fields and "paid nothing, either actually or constructively." (That phrasing hinted at the idea of a quid pro quo; a "constructive" payment could have been decent food and lodging.) With "few privileges . . . and incentives," Henley opined, developing a "rule-observing" community was improbable. Yet Henley also called "many of the inmates . . . psychopathic and sociopathic"; some were "aggressive homosexuals" and "hardened criminals . . . prone to destroy State property, even items designed for their welfare and comfort." Crediting thus the state's need to discipline, Henley sought to delineate the "uncomfortable" and the "unpleasant" from the "unconstitutional." Even as disciplinary confinement "must be rigorous, uncomfortable, and unpleasant," it was not supposed to be "degrading and debasing."[31]

What practices fell under each category? What triggered Henley was not the lack of medical and dental care nor the noxious blob of grue "pushed through the gratings" and sometimes tainted by "dogs or birds," but the filth, density, and danger. "Prolonged confinement of numbers of men" in "dirty and unsanitary cells" was "hazardous to health, . . . degrading and debasing," "offend[ed] modern sensibilities," and hence was "cruel and unusual punishment." Prisoners "ought at least to be able to fall asleep at night without fear of having their throats cut before morning, and . . . the State has failed to discharge a constitutional duty in failing to take steps to enable them to do so" and failed its "constitutional duty to use ordinary care to protect [prisoners'] lives and safety while in prison."[32]

REPORTING AS A REMEDY

Although Henley invoked Chief Judge Harris, he did not follow his model in specifying remedies. Harris instructed California that, in addition to "regular change of bedding, clothing, bathing and feeding," the "punitive segregation section and all the cells in it should be evenly heated and adequately lighted and ventilated. Artificial ventilation is usually necessary. . . . Toilets which the occupant of the cell cannot flush need constant supervision by the officer. Wholly dark cells should not be used and if there is a solid door on the cell, it should be so designed that it does not exclude all light." Because the case had not been formulated as a class action, the plaintiff with the power to enforce that remedy was Jordan. California sent him away from Soledad and continued to use strip cells. One official described the cells as "humane": "We don't use the dark dungeons or handcuff them and hang them to the wall as they once did in Folsom."[33]

Unlike Judge Harris, Henley declined to "prescribe" steps for compliance. Instead, he pointed a finger at the legislature, which had left Sarver "severely hampered" by the lack of money. Henley noted that legislators continued to look at Cummins as a "profit-making institution" that ought not require taxpayer dollars in light of "under-funded" other services "for law abiding people." Henley wrote about the need for free-world guards and also suggested transferring some prisoners to Tucker, lowering the number in disciplinary cells, and doing "something about the sanitary conditions." Henley told Sarver "to make a prompt and reasonable start toward eliminating the unconstitutionalities" and return within thirty days to explain in writing what "he has been able to do and what he is

willing to do to provide additional protection for inmates and allevi-
ate such things as overcrowded conditions in the cells." By flagging
that officials were assuming their "prisoner trusty system" would
"survive" a constitutional challenge, Henley forecast they were likely
wrong. (A few months later, Henley held in *Holt II* that Arkansas
could not arm trustys or let them control privileges and discipline.[34])

READING AND SPINNING THE RULING

Commissioner Sarver tried to use Henley's June ruling, which he
said "slapped . . . rather hard," to make headway with the legislature; figure 19.1 showed him "reading" the decision alongside two
key legislators. Sarver said the court's decision could mean that

FIGURE 19.1 *Director of Correction's Robert Sarver, and State Senators Knox Nelson and
Richard Earl Griffin "Reading the Judge's Order on Prisons,"* photograph by George
Clinton Douthit, accompanying Tucker Steinmetz, *State Told to Better Prison
Conditions*, Arkansas Democrat, 2, June 21, 1969, courtesy of the publisher

the state needed to end its prisoner–trusty system ("replete with evil") and that doing so would require hiring at least 200 employees. Sarver also reported that he had taken many people out of the disciplinary cells, but left six, for "their own safety."[35]

The prisoners, their lawyers, and the judge knew that the key audience was the legislature. Without new funds, closing facilities, or releasing people, not much could change. If remedies were to come, they would depend on buy-in from legislators. When no money was forthcoming, Sarver laid off free-world employees.

On September 19, 1969, under a headline "Prison Abuses Again Charged," the papers explained that Lawrence Holt, Robert Courtney, and Thomas M. Hildebrandt had filed new petitions about abuse and beatings in isolation cells. Within days, another prisoner, Jerry Denham, alleged that, because he and other prisoners had not "picked okra fast enough," they had been made to sit in an open field "for 24 hours without food or water." Jack A. Barber, also at Cummins, told the court that he had no shoes. In early October, another "toilet paper petition" ("a four-foot roll of yellow perfumed toilet paper") made its way into court from six people in isolation at Tucker; they said the prison gave them no paper on which to write. The same week, a prisoner complained of a lack of food and that, so hungry, he "ate a rat." Henley's response, recorded by the press, was that while he knew many prisoners' claims were "frivolous," experience had shown him that conditions "give the court serious constitutional concerns." Therefore he would allow the petitions to be treated as a class action, and other prisoners did not need to file more complaints.[36]

BROKE AND GOING BACKWARD

"We're right back to where we were four years ago, only we don't have the strap."

—Robert Sarver, December 2, 1969[37]

By December, the federal prosecutions had ended with a string of acquittals, and the penal system had no money. ADC gave Rockefeller a private report detailing the "tragedy of wasted lives" of people in custody. "We have an Arkansas Department of Correction in name only, not in fact. We <u>do not</u> have a correctional program."[38]

ADC's materials made the case in a prescient (albeit unsuccessful) mix of stories and statistics; the point was to "sell to the people that it will be a good business policy and a sound investment to provide additional funds now" by investing in human capital rather than destroying "savage lives." That approach, today called "justice reinvestment" and championed by self-described conservatives who are "right on crime," sought funds for more productive uses.[39] The December 1969 memorandum told Rockefeller that the Department was operating on a "totally inadequate" budget of $1,800,000," of which more than $1,100,000 came from farm production and $300,000 was borrowed from the state. Funds went to "bare necessities and sometimes not even these"; the state spent "$3.90" per day per incarcerated individual—with 1,345 people, about $5,245.00 per day and $1,888,380 per year.[40] Included in the analysis was that people in prisons had families, often supported by state welfare assistance that ran into the millions.

Sarver was not allowed to run a deficit of more than $300,000, which meant he had to take "one gigantic step backward." Sarver announced that he told "23 to 25 Corrections Department employees" they were losing their jobs (to be filled with trustys) and the governor that any "hopes for the immediate future . . . went up in smoke."[41] Sarver repeated to the press that prisoners' deaths were the responsibility of the legislators refusing money for employees.

A prominent Democratic legislator responded that Sarver was "politically motivated." And of course, he was *right*. Sarver knew full well that the treatment of prisoners was a political question. So did the local press. One editorial opined Arkansans needed "to face the bitter truth that each of us bears responsibility for the hell holes that are our penal institutions . . . [which operate] the way most of us wanted."[42] Johnny Cash was also *right*: Sarver needed the legislature, and *Holt I* had not sufficed to get that body's ear.

20

CORPORAL OPPRESSION IN PRISON

"However constitutionally tolerable the Arkansas system may have been in former years, it simply will not do today as the Twentieth Century goes into his eighth decade."

—Chief Judge Henley, *Holt II*, February 18, 1970[1]

TRYING TO KEEP PRISONERS ALIVE

That prisons were horrid was not news. Yet, with the exception of the English Howard League in the 1920s, prison reformers did not suggest that governments should be legally compelled to make profound changes. In the two *Holt* decisions, Henley moved the dial by setting forth that living 24/7 in filth and violence without a potential for rehabilitation turned incarceration, otherwise licit, into a form of punishment forbidden by the US Constitution.

Before unpacking *Holt II*, a word is needed about the legal and political environment that framed it. While Henley's decision (and many thereafter) pivoted on the Eighth Amendment, it was not the only constitutional predicate available. Prisoners then (and now) can invoke edicts in the Fifth and Fourteenth Amendments that neither the federal government nor states may deprive people of "life, liberty, or property without due process of law." During the latter part of the twentieth century, courts recognized that punishments such as the loss of good-time credits to shorten sentences could violate "procedural" and "substantive due process." The first kind acknowledges that the state *can* take away liberty and property, but only through a fair process. The phrase "substantive due process" encapsulates the proposition that states cannot impose certain harms on people, no matter how much process is provided.

Because, as discussed, the Supreme Court has interpreted the word "punishment" to apply only when states aim to punish, the ban on cruel and unusual punishment has not been applied *before* conviction.[2] Therefore, when people in pretrial detention allege the Constitution protects their right to safety, they rely on substantive due process. Likewise, children challenging "paddling" in schools, parents arguing protection of their relationship with children, and people asserting reproductive and gender-identity freedom argue about infringement on their substantive liberties, often intertwined with autonomy, privacy, and equality. Yet the Court's reliance on freedom and liberty in the early part of the twentieth century to invalidate state laws regulating wages and hours prompted criticisms that made some jurists leery of substantive due process. The Court's refusal in the twenty-first century to protect abortion has prompted a resurgence of attention to rights, "enumerated" and not, that the Constitution protects. The nuances and complexity were part of why, in the *Holt* cases, Eighth Amendment constraints on punishment took center stage.

Turning to what prompted Henley to pioneer such constraints, his comments from the bench about "creepers" stabbing sleeping prisoners and his 1987 oral history provide answers. While reporting ambivalence that he would be known for (kept "alive" by) the "prisons cases," Henley wanted to keep prisoners *alive*.[3] Torture prosecutions had not worked. A ban on specific practices—whipping in *Jackson v. Bishop* and segregation in *Lee v. Washington*—had not unraveled the web of violence, racism, and disabling conditions. Nor had Chief Judge Henley's initial foray into what became known as "structural reform litigation" been a success. After his detailed discussion in *Holt v. Sarver* (*Holt I*), Arkansas neither complied nor appealed, and it paid no attention to the signals that Henley sent (and Sarver saw) about disarming trustys. Instead, funding for the Arkansas Department of Correction's (ADC) collapsed. Twenty-three employees were laid off, with only thirty-five remaining.[4]

Henley then took on the entire prison system. On December 12, 1969, Henley pulled eight filings together, linked them to *Holt I* to incorporate its findings, and again designated Lawrence Holt as the lead in the "three cases . . . never actually terminated, . . . presently before the Court along with five additional cases which the Court permitted to be commenced." Naming them the "Penitentiary Cases" to be litigated for the benefit of all prisoners, Henley did not return to Arkansas' commercial bar for help but instead selected criminal defense lawyer Jack Holt Jr. and civil rights lawyer Philip Kaplan. Henley told them to challenge the trusty system, forced labor, omnipresent violence, unfair discipline, inadequate sanitation, lack of health care, programs, and inedible food and commented that:

> The court expects that its inquiry will take a wide range that will include not only complaints about specific alleged practices and abuses but also the constitutional validity of the Penitentiary System itself characterized as it is by trusty guards with few paid employees and by the working of convicts on the Penitentiary Farms without compensation.[5]

From the vantage point of people living in fear of their lives, this order was *long* in coming. From the perspective of people on the outside, Henley moved with stunning *speed*. He selected the lawyers in December, held a hearing in late January, and issued a decision in February that he positioned as a grand finale. He told the press on Christmas Eve of 1969 that "after the consolidated cases were decided, it would not be necessary . . . to hear any more such prisoner suits."[6] He was wrong. Chief Judge Henley and his successors lived with this and related lawsuits for years thereafter. Indeed, the *Holt* docket previews the arch of prison reform litigation in the decades thereafter. The first entry, dated April 17 of 1969, marked Henley's decision to consolidate filings into *Holt I*. Thirty-four pages later, the docket noted a formal end on April 20, 1982, followed by requests to open sealed documents and, on March 15, 1989, to transfer materials to the University of Arkansas Little Rock Library.

This voluminous record included nauseating accounts of mistreatment, occasions when defendants hoped court orders would enter *against* them so they could get funds for improvements, and repeated instances of recalcitrance. Along the way, Chief Judge Henley issued dozens of orders and several opinions. The case was heard three times by the Eighth Circuit (calling it in 1977 a "seemingly endless litigation") and once by the US Supreme Court. The names changed from *Holt v. Sarver* to *Hutto v. Finney* after Commissioner Sarver was forced out and a new Governor, Dale Bumpers—a Democrat to whom Rockefeller lost—took office in January of 1971. Bumpers made the disastrous decision to replace Sarver with a former Texas corrections official, T. Don Hutto, who repeatedly pushed back against court orders.[7]

Judges and governors moved on too. President Gerald Ford nominated Chief Judge Henley to the Eighth Circuit, which he joined in 1975. In 1978, after the Supreme Court upheld Henley's rulings, the parties agreed to a consent decree, signed by the prisoners' lawyers (who had stayed the course) and by Bill Clinton, then Arkansas' Attorney General. As in many such cases, the settlement did not end the disputes. The focus shifted to disciplinary hearings, as detailed in *Finney v. Mabry*, named for James Mabry who replaced Hutto in 1976 when David Pryor became governor. By then, G. Thomas Eisele, a key Rockefeller staffer and a federal judge in 1970, inherited the litigation.[8]

Below, I unpack the facts, law, and political conflicts embedded in *Holt II*, a saga about what lawyers and witnesses told Judge Henley, about what the governor and legislators said about raising and spending taxpayer money, and about how prisoners persisted in claiming the impermissibility of their confinement. Winning Henley's pronouncement that they were confined in "a dark and evil world," the prisoners could not persuade him to condemn the forced labor at its center. Perhaps Henley assumed that, given legislative hostility, the potential for improvements required *income* flowing from the prisons. If that was Henley's compromise, it did not work. Henley spent several years trying to get pitiful levels of compliance; in 1976 he held officials in "bad faith" and ordered fees paid to the prisoners' lawyers.

HENLEY'S MATCHMAKING: JACK HOLT, PHIL KAPLAN, AND THE NASCENT PRISONERS' RIGHTS BAR

In December 1969, Chief Judge Henley reached out to lawyers whose profiles were markedly different from those appointed before. Henley coupled an outsider (Kaplan moved to Little Rock for civil rights work) with a consummate insider (Jack W. Holt Jr., no relation to plaintiff Lawrence Holt, was a member of a family central to Arkansas' law and politics).

I met Kaplan and Holt in 2019 and learned of the friendship that developed and endured between these two white men.[9] Kaplan grew up in Massachusetts, went to Harvard College and the University of Michigan Law School and then to the National Labor Relations Board in St. Louis, Missouri. He moved in 1967 to Little Rock, became an "ACLU cooperating attorney," and joined "civil rights icon" John Walker in the city's "only racially integrated law firm." Walker, who was from Hope, Arkansas, went to Yale Law School where he was one of few Black students. After working at the Legal Defense and Education Fund (LDF) of the National Association for the Advancement of Colored People (NAACP), he returned to Little Rock to be LDF's "go to" counsel, representing school desegregation and other civil rights claimants for decades.[10]

Henley's choice of Kaplan meant that the prisoners had a pipeline to a small network of lawyers focused on racial discrimination in criminal law enforcement and prisons. In 1970, Kaplan corresponded with Chuck Morgan, the ACLU lawyer who had represented Caliph Washington in the Alabama desegregation litigation, as well as with LDF's William Bennett Turner. At Kaplan's behest, Arkansas' branch of the ACLU "committed" to the *Holt* case. Kaplan, with a shoestring budget, asked for funds for fact-finding and securing expert witnesses from outside the state."[11] Thereafter and responding in part to the 1971 Attica uprising, foundation support enabled the ACLU to found its National Prison Project (NPP) in 1972 and to print a first edition in 1973 of "The Rights of Prisoners" (one of a series of ACLU user-friendly "rights handbooks") in which the *Holt* litigation was featured. The longevity of the NPP, at work decades into the twenty-first century, is one marker of the difficulties in altering prison conditions; Kaplan's career was another. He spent a good deal of the 1970s on Arkansas prisons, argued *Hutto v. Finney* in the Supreme Court in 1978, and represented detainees suing county farms and jails.[12]

Holt Jr.—who in 1984 became the Chief Justice of the Arkansas Supreme Court—was Henley's choice for other reasons. Holt, who defined himself as a "conservative," had not been "active" in civil rights organizations. Holt's folksy manner ("I like to refer to myself as a street lawyer. I interviewed everybody who came in off the streets.") belied his sophistication and his family's position. Between 1936 and 1984, three Holts were justices on the Arkansas Supreme Court; two were elected and one appointed to be the state's Attorney General, and two had sought (and lost) elections for the governorship and the US Senate. The Holts were longtime Democrats; Holt Sr., a "Dixiecrat," had joined other Southerners in opposing their own President, Harry Truman, because of his commitment to equality.[13]

The Henley and Holt families had interacted for decades. Holt Jr. explained the relationships in an oral history, taken in 2012 by Ernest Dumas, a storied Arkansas reporter and historian. When the senior Holt was the prosecutor in Boone County in the 1930s, he brought a case against Henley's cousin Leland, accused (as discussed) of killing a man as part of a family feud. Holt Jr. recounted that Leland's trial was halted after the Henley clan walked, with guns drawn, into the courtroom. Thereafter, Holt Sr., promising to "restore law and order in Searcy County," won the race for circuit judge, convinced the governor to send troops to Harrison to "round up the Henleys, Leland in particular." Leland, convicted, was sent to Tucker Farm and later walked away. Chief Judge Henley knew the senior and junior Jack Holts, who lived in Harrison where Henley had practiced law and where Holt Jr., born in 1929, grew up. (Holt told Dumas the judge's wife "babysat me.")[14]

Holt Jr. graduated in 1952 from law school in Arkansas, spent three years as a lawyer in the Air Force, worked as Chief Assistant to his uncle Frank when Attorney General and, in private practice, did criminal defense. Henley, who had seen Holt Jr. in court, knew him to be a talented lawyer, willing to take cases for people who could not pay. Holt Jr. described what transpired in December of 1969 (which he repeated to me when I met him). The judge called him into chambers and said:

> Jack, I've got a Christmas present for you. I don't know if you want to accept it or not. . . . Do you know Philip Kaplan? . . . a young lawyer who's got a pretty full beard and does civil rights work. . . . I would like to perfect a marriage of you two. He's a civil rights lawyer but he's not had much experience with the criminal element. Having served as a prosecutor and attorney general and defense counsel, you pretty well know the language and know the people. . . . [T]he federal court had been getting all these habeas corpus writs about the food, about the abuse by the trusty system and the like. . . . We've had three or four cases where I have made appointments involving the use of the strap. . . . We keep getting all these individual writs, and . . . I'm thinking that probably—I've got twenty-one writs here on my desk—it might be better for you and Mr. Kaplan to look at it and see about consolidating them into a class action.[15]

SARVER PAVED THE PRISONERS' WAY

"If it hadn't been for Bob Sarver our problem resolving this case would have gone on for much longer."

—Jack Holt Jr., 2012 Oral History[16]

Getting appointed is not the same as winning, which these two lawyers largely did within two months. I asked them how they found the evidence they needed. In litigation today, prisoners' lawyers seek "discovery" by making requests for documents, interviews, and site inspections; defending officials often oppose, delay, and then limit the information turned over. In 1969, Kaplan and Holt encountered no such problems. Sarver helped them obtain an injunction *against* him. "Sarver . . . opened up everything. He did not obstruct, and, in fact, he was a lot of help—very cooperative and very insistent on the reform."[17]

Proving that conditions were despicable was straightforward. The lawyers saw segregated barracks, few state-employed guards, and fearsome prisoner–trustys, whom Holt Jr. described as "someone who was willing to carry a gun, [and] shoot and kill another inmate, if necessary." Prisoners "were abused, they were punished, and they were raped. If you did not have the means and wanted to go see the dentist you had to go to a [trusty] . . . and give him some money or sex or something else to get on sick call. The whole thing was abusive." Holt Jr.'s knowledge of Arkansas politics meant he wanted public support for a sweeping order. Interviewed before the *Holt II* hearing began, Holt Jr. invoked the specter of a shutdown. "It would be a possibility that the [Arkansas] prisons would be closed by Henley . . . until certain conditions are corrected."[18]

MORE HOSTAGE TAKING, DEATHS, AND HOPES BEFORE THE *HOLT II* HEARING

"I don't like federal courts to tell us what to do any better than anyone else does. We know what we have to do but if it takes a federal court order to make it happen, then I'm for it."

—Commissioner Robert Sarver, January 3, 1970[19]

Within two days of Henley's December 1969 outline for the new class action, the state police reported an "uprising" at Cummins, where prisoners had taken four hostages: two civilians and two trustys. Sarver and another staff member "made themselves hostage" to secure two releases and defuse the situation. A few days later, a nineteen-year-old trusty, Randy Arnold, was (according to Sarver) "fooling" with a gun when he killed another prisoner—a twenty-one-year-old man incarcerated on a "bad check charge." By then, and "for reasons of economy," Sarver was also Cummins'

Superintendent. He told the press that responsibility for the violence lay with "the public as a whole and the legislature"; as long as trustys were given shotguns, such deaths would be part of the system. Sarver reiterated that point when another prisoner at Tucker was fatally shot—the fourth in fifteen months. The *Arkansas Democrat* echoed Sarver: "the public and the legislature were responsible for violent deaths in the prisons."[20]

The Speaker of the State Assembly retorted that Sarver wanted to "blame all the ills . . . on the legislature . . . in anticipation of a special session, and the governor proposing tax increases." As Christmas approached, Sarver let some prisoners get home to a safer setting and described prisoners' generosity in contributing their $1 Christmas present from their "welfare fund" for holiday decorations and fruit. Tucker prisoners "voted to contribute their $1 to two poor families—one white and one black—living near the prison."[21]

The press kept the spotlight on the miseries, including a story about the few women (about thirty) at Cummins; many were held for alcoholism or prostitution charges and living with mice, mildew, and no privacy. Sarver said that, nationwide, women were the "most neglected" of prisoners. In fact, competition for being the "most neglected" was intense. In a "very peaceful protest" before the court hearing, more than 235 prisoners ("both Negroes and whites") highlighted terrible food, facilities, clothing, medical care, and the lack of security. After "talking with prison authorities," more than 170 people ended that action, while some forty men, described as chanting, continued the sit-in. A banner news headline on January 13, 1970, cited Sarver's account that trustys were working twelve-hour shifts, seven days a week, and that "$1 million a year" was needed to replace them with paid staff. Yet, the Board of Correction could not "visualize operating the two prison farms . . . without the use of armed trusty guards." Instead, John Haley, the Board's Chair, laid out a six-year construction plan seeking a million dollars for a maximum-security unit and another million to mechanize farming, build a diagnostic center, and construct a pre-release facility.[22]

Robert Sarver's critique continued. In early January, Sarver told the Arkansas Association of Women Lawyers that the state's prison system was in a "desperate situation." While not wanting "federal courts to tell us what to do," if that would make a change, he was "for it." Answering press questions one night at Cummins by phone, Sarver told a reporter he was one of two "free-world personnel on duty . . . to supervise about 1,300 inmates" and prisoners lacked "basics," like "socks."[23]

LEGAL THEORIES AND DEPRESSING FACTS

In their January 14, 1970 amended complaint, Holt Jr. and Kaplan named twenty-four individuals at Cummins or Tucker as plaintiffs and requested class-wide relief on behalf of current Arkansas' prisoners and "persons who will in the future be committed to the custody of defendants." The defendants were Commissioner Robert Sarver, along with the five members of the Arkansas Board of Correction, sued as individuals and in their official capacity. While Holt Jr. and Kaplan did not use the phrase "a totality of conditions," the harms they outlined in seven pages spanned all aspects of life.

The newspapers reproduced much of that filing that, by contemporary standards, was short. The prisoners alleged that they were "insufficiently fed, clothed and housed" in barracks that left them "subject to frequent assaults, murder, rape and homosexual conduct." The trustys (mostly people "convicted of serious and aggravated crimes of violence such as murder and rape") subjected prisoners to "acts of brutality or the constant fear of brutality." The barracks were "segregated by race." The prisoners alleged they were disciplined unfairly because they were not "informed or appraised of standards of conduct" that could result in punishment, "denied minimal procedural safeguards" before punishment, and isolation cells were "in and of themselves . . . cruel and unusual punishment." Another claim focused on censorship of mail to attorneys. The claim of forced labor picked up Henley's *Holt I* suggestion of a lack of a "quid pro quo"—that rather than money or compensation

in the form of "safe and adequate lodging, food, and clothing," prisoners got nothing. The prisoners also objected to the failure to provide them with materials for shaving, writing, and smoking (then
common in prisons and elsewhere).[24]

For the *sources* of rights not to be subjected to those conditions,
the lawyers invoked state and federal law. The 1968 legislative charge
to the ADC was to provide "rehabilitation and restoration of adult
offenders as useful, law abiding citizens within the community."
The complaint quoted that provision (authorizing the Department
to "establish programs of classification and diagnosis, education,
case work, counseling and psychiatric therapy, vocational training
and guidance, work, and library and religious services," and "other
rehabilitation programs or services" as needed) and alleged it required an "affirmative program" that had not been put into place.
The other basis for the requested injunction was the federal civil
rights statute ("Section 1983") authorizing remedies when people,
"acting under color of state law," deprive individuals of rights protected by federal law. As discussed, Thomas X Cooper's 1964 win in
the Supreme Court had paved the way for Winston Talley, William
Jackson, Caliph Washington, the *Holt* plaintiffs, and many others
to bring Section 1983 claims. The *Holt II* complaint stated that the
Arkansas defendants ("charged with overall policy making and
administration for all correctional institutions in the State") had
violated prisoners' constitutional rights to "due process and equal
protection" guaranteed by the Fourteenth Amendment. In addition,
requiring prisoners to perform "forced labor without compensation" violated the Thirteenth Amendment's guarantee against involuntary servitude.[25]

The lawyers tied the facts to *rights* "not to be imprisoned without meaningful rehabilitative opportunities"; "to be free from cruel
and unusual punishment, . . . from arbitrary and capricious denial of rehabilitative opportunities, . . . from the abuses of fellow
prisoners in all aspects of daily life, . . . from racial segregation,
. . . forced labor, . . . and from the brutality of being guarded by
fellow inmates." Those prohibitions were coupled with obligations:

to be provided with "minimal due process safeguards in decisions determining fundamental liberties," "to be fed, housed, and clothed so as not to be subjected to loss of health or life," to have "unhampered access to counsel and the courts." The requested remedies included adequate clothing, food, medical and dental care, trained personnel, fair decision-making, and the end of forced labor and the "trusty guard system."[26] On reading that filing, the *Arkansas Democrat* circled back to points made by Sarver, Johnny Cash, and Rockefeller—that money was the core. The editorial noted that the Arkansas Legislature had approved $4.5 million for prisons in 1969 but *never* appropriated those funds.[27]

Given the centrality of dollars, I need explain why the prisoners' lawyers did not ask directly for them. Efforts in all kinds of lawsuits to require payments from state treasuries are generally met with the defense that states are "sovereigns" and thus "immune" from such orders by virtue of the US Constitution, common law, and history. The prisoners' lawyers knew these precepts and neither mentioned money nor named the state as a defendant. Nonetheless, the defendants' lawyers asked Henley to dismiss the case because he lacked authority to "coerce" the legislature to provide funding. Not surprisingly, Henley disagreed and let the lawsuit proceed.[28]

Before the *Holt II* hearing began on January 26, 1970, a route to funding was clear, even if success was unlikely. As discussed, Governor Rockefeller had put on his own version of a trial through convening public hearings addressing the dire straits of the state's health care, educational institutions, and law enforcement apparatus. After he called for "$35 million in new taxes" to relieve these "hard-pressed agencies, cities, and counties," the legislature agreed to a special session in March. The lawyers for the prisoners, the state, and the judge understood that while the prisoners' presentations were addressed to the court, the audience to be persuaded were state legislators and their constituents. Inside the courtroom, the prisoners' lawyers put into the record photographs and a film; local readers saw pictures like figure 20.1 of a trusty "herding" prisoners to the fields.[29]

FIGURE 20.1 *Trusty Guard on Mule Herds Cummins Prisoners Across Road*, accompanying the story by John Bennett, *Inmate Tells of Cummins Extortion, Assaults*, Commercial Appeal (East Arkansas Edition), January 27, 1970 © The Commercial Appeal–USA Today Network

WITNESSES FOR THE PRISONERS

"Sarver, testifying before Judge J. Smith Henley, tended to agree frequently with the complaining inmates."

—A newspaper's overview, February 5, 1970[30]

Over the course of five days, Chief Judge Henley heard testimony from thirty-seven people, of whom thirty were prisoners (this time, not all white), and received thirty-five exhibits. During a pause, Henley signed orders dismissing—at the prosecutors' behest—the last of the 1969 federal criminal charges against five Tucker employees and trustys for torturing prisoners.[31]

Chief Judge Henley got the record he needed to put federal court power in service of protecting prisoners' lives. This painful account is unnerving ("triggering," again) and repetitive, as witnesses provided yet more examples of violence, filth, and inedible food. Chief Judge Henley's opinion said so too; the "large volume of testimony . . . was really a repetition of what the Court heard when it tried *Holt I*." Moreover, as Holt Jr. told the press, many similar incidents had been "exposed before." What he said in 1970 remains true today. The public knew and nonetheless: "What's disturbing is that they continue to exist."[32]

The prisoners' lawyers began with James Bennett, the former Director of the US Bureau of Prisons, who had testified in that courtroom in 1967 that whipping was "medieval."[33] The prisoners' closing witness was Robert Sarver. While a defendant is not often called by plaintiffs suing him, Holt and Kaplan were wise to do so. Sarver reiterated what he had told the press: he had no funds to hire staff to keep prisoners safer. In addition to these two professionals as bookends, Holt and Kaplan called other witnesses, including twenty-one "convicts," as one newspaper described them.[34]

Beginning with Bennett meant that Kaplan and Holt sought condemnation of the system. Bennett was unequivocal: "I don't think [the trusty system] has any correctional value," he opined and, moreover, it led to corruption as well as "various types of homosexuality and to other types of anti-social behavior." Designed, Bennett explained, to make prisons profitable, all states had abandoned trustys except Arkansas and two others (Mississippi and Louisiana). Bennett also objected to another feature—Arkansas' use of large, dense barracks (holding 100 to 190 people) in which a jumble of people, housed together, had no ability to "get away" from others.[35]

Thereafter, four prisoners testified that they had "purchased jobs . . . from trustys" and about the violence in the barracks, where homosexual acts were a "regular occurrence," mostly "forced." The newspapers quoted eighteen-year-old, Garner S. Autry, who said "about six inmates ganged up on him in the barracks" to rape him, while the "walkers"—charged with keeping safety—did "nothing." After Autry was transferred for "safety" to Tucker, he was attacked again at knifepoint and then placed for protection in an isolation cell, where he lived with rats. Corroboration on the rats came from nineteen-year-old Otis Taylor, who said Tucker was "overrun" with them. Thomas Mitchell Hildebrandt described his attempted suicide after a rape. James Dunn spoke of "dirty" isolation cells where he was kept because "he feared for his life." The judge threatened Dunn with contempt when Dunn refused to name the prisoner that

Jack Holt Jr. questions one of the prisoners

Judge J. Smith Henley listens to testimony and makes notes

Sarver heard his name mentioned frequently

Lawrence Holt denies he tried to kill inmate

James Dunn is a told that he is in contempt

Hilderbrandt describes pressure from trusty

FIGURE 20.2 Drawings by Jon Kennedy, accompanying *I Would Rather Eat a Rat*, Arkansas Democrat, January 28, 1970, courtesy of the publisher, facsimile by Jeanne Criscola

had caused him to seek protective custody. "With all respect to the court, I've got to go back down there and live and I'm not going to name any names." Disgusting food was another fact of life. The *Arkansas Democrat* headline was "I'd rather eat a rat: Inmate says its preferable to 'grue,'" accompanying drawings (figure 20.2) by a courtroom artist of some participants.[36]

The quote about eating a rat came from Taylor, one of a few Black prisoners who testified. Taylor described being put naked in a cell for forty days for allegedly burning a mattress. The awfulness of grue was discussed by Garland Joseph Prudhomme Jr., an eighteen-year-old in isolation for refusing to "pick pickles"; he reported the mixture of dough, vegetables, and meat sometimes included paper and cigarette butts. Rats (along with roaches and spiders) were, as others testified, omnipresent in the "hole" (the disciplinary cells), where people were sometimes forced to sleep on the floor.[37]

The hearing paused when two prisoners were to testify but said they had been told by a trusty that if they did, their lives would be in danger. ("*Res ipsa loquitur*"—the thing speaks for itself—is a phrase lawyers know well.) Kaplan and Holt Jr. responded by briefly putting on Sarver, who agreed he could not "assure protection of inmates" even if in "protective custody." Instead, Sarver asked the state police to keep the two. Danger, a pervasive lack of sanitation, and no health care were the leitmotifs. Upon entry, each person was given a "toothbrush and a tube of toothpaste . . . but got no replacements." That point was repeated on the second day of the hearing (January 27, 1970), when twelve prisoners from Tucker and five from Cummins testified; several recounted having no towel, toothpaste, mattresses, or sheets. A lack of medical care became clear from a few, including Lawrence Holt. Held at Cummins, he said that, despite internal bleeding, he was not permitted to see a doctor.[38]

Race and gender organize prisons, yet appeared only briefly in the accounts of *Holt II*. The state did not defend its segregation, and the prisoners' lawyers did not distinguish among groups of prisoners when arguing that omnipresent filth and violence perverted everyone's lives. I tried to track down information about all the named plaintiffs in *Holt I* and *Holt II*. As detailed in the endnotes, a few were Black men, and some had challenged their convictions on grounds of racial bias and, on occasion, succeeded.[39] At the *Holt II* hearing, one witness discussed that, as a Black prisoner, he could not get access to a "political book" like Eldridge Cleaver's *Soul on Ice* until Sarver gave him a copy.⁴⁰

The problems faced by women were not much discussed, even as they were part of the class action. The only woman (one of thirty-two then at Cummins) to testify was Valda Marlene Mize, a thirty-five-year-old serving a "seven-year sentence for voluntary manslaughter." Mize was a trusty in the sewing room where women made clothes for incarcerated men. Mize described that all the women slept in a large room except if in isolation. One woman, "fenced in as 'mentally imbalanced,'" had a bucket as a toilet. The press noted that state law permitted detention, without treatment, of women charged as alcoholics; this woman had been sent twelve times to prison. (In 1971, the legislature repealed that facially discriminatory treatment.)⁴¹

By the third day, the thirty-second witness was on the stand, Billy Ray Steed, Cummins prison farm manager and Associate Superintendent who had briefly been a hostage with Sarver during a prisoner protest. Steed testified to a "lack of funds"; he reported no money for jackets when the weather was cold, for adequate sewage disposal, cleaning supplies, or guards. At best, two "free-world supervisors" were on duty during the twelve-hour work shift, which meant trustys went unsupervised. Steed described having to scrounge for procurements—including gas to heat the guard towers—to keep the place going. The prisoners' lawyers also submitted a list of 286 trustys at Cummins of whom "33 [had been] convicted of first-degree murder, 39 for second-degree murder, four for manslaughter, 12 for assault with intent to kill, 26 for rape and 14 for assault with intent to rape."⁴²

Holt Jr. and Kaplan opened a window into the prison through film footage, "narrated from the witness stand by state Correction Commissioner Robert Sarver." Included were the barracks, isolation cells (with toilets "sunk in concrete to prevent them from being torn out"), the cafeteria, and work areas. "Close-up shots" were of "rust-stained commodes, ceilings with paint flaking off over dining room tables and water standing in pools on the farm grounds because of water-line ruptures." Thereafter, when asked what was wrong with the prisons, Sarver responded: "It would be easier—and wouldn't take half as long—to say what's right."

Explaining that "99 percent" of Cummins operations were under the control of trustys with guns, Sarver stated that no check system for other weapons was in place. ("It seems a little ludicrous to take a knife away and then turn around and give him a gun.") Henley asked: "Do you have the means to protect the life of any inmate from intimidation, rape or assault?" Sarver responded "No, sir." Sarver was likewise blunt about the lack of health care and no capacity to respond to psychiatric problems endemic in the population.[43] On the fifth and final day, the judge heard from several professionals. Dr. Jack Eardley, the "staff physician and psychiatrist," testified that, at times, the food served to prisoners was not "edible." Moreover, the drainage system for garbage was "pretty lousy" and could seep into the fresh water. The barracks were "run on fear."[44]

The defense was that conditions were not as bad as the prisoners had said and were going to get better. Tucker's Superintendent John R. Price, joined by defendant Board Chair Haley, spoke about improvements. Haley explained that during the past seventy years, Arkansas' General Assembly had only twice made appropriations for the state's prisons. But the tide had turned, and the legislature was "firmly committed to the abolition of prisons for profit." Evidence of an ironic step forward came from Larry E. Hudson, a former Pine Bluff police officer, who explained that in August of 1969, he had, for the first time, begun classes to train trustys on using guns.[45]

The *Holt II* hearing ended as Governor Rockefeller asked the legislature for $828,447 for prison operating expenses, $144,500 for construction before June, and $1,086,701 for operations, with $450,000 to follow thereafter. But on February 6, when some legislators toured Cummins and Tucker, one member concluded that "[c]onditions here certainly aren't as bad as the press has said they are. Everything seems all right to me."[46]

"ARKANSAS PRISONS, AS PRESENTLY RUN, ARE DECLARED ILLEGAL"

"The lives, safety and health of human beings, to say nothing of their dignity, are at stake. The state must be prompt. . . . The handwriting is on the wall, and it ought not require a Daniel to read it."

—Chief Judge Henley, *Holt II*, February 18, 1970[47]

That the prisoners were going to *win* had been clear from the outset. That "handwriting" had been "on the wall" (to continue Chief Judge Henley's biblical reference[48]) since the judge gave the lawyers their charter in December of 1969. What the judge would *say* and what he would *order* were the questions, and Henley's opinion was his own sermon. "Respondents are not limited to those formally before the Court but include the Governor of Arkansas, the Arkansas Legislature, and ultimately the people of the state as a whole."[49]

The *Arkansas Gazette*, headlining its story "Ruling Terms Arkansas Prisons 'Dark and Evil World,'" ran long excerpts. The *Arkansas Democrat* reprinted Henley's findings that trusty guards had the "power of life and death over other inmates," that they could "murder another guard with practical impunity," and that the prisons had "some of the worst features commonly attributed to Mafia techniques in organized crime."[50]

Readers of the full opinion learned more. The judge prefaced his findings by describing that, upon receiving "eight class actions," he determined that "substantial" constitutional questions existed and appointed Holt Jr. and Kaplan, who provided "yeoman service." Unlike prior actions involving "specific practices and abuses," the lawsuit was "an attack on the System itself" (Henley's capitalization) and, to his knowledge, the "first time" that "an entire penitentiary system" was at issue. The judge recounted that he had received testimony from many prisoners and a few staff, a "motion picture film," numerous photographs and documents, and had "the benefit of the expert testimony" of James Bennett. In addition and "indirectly," Henley credited Austin MacCormick, who had not been in court but was cited in the 1968 Legislative Commission's Penitentiary Report to the state legislature.[51]

Henley sketched a history in which, after the state was "admitted to the Union in 1836," a first "jail type structure" went up in Little Rock. Land purchased in 1902 turned hundreds of acres into Cummins Farm, where "hardened white convicts" were kept along with "Negro convicts" in separate barracks. Another area became Tucker Farm, "designed primarily for . . . young white convicts" and "both white and Negroes awaiting execution." After 1913, when the state formally abolished convict leasing, prisoners had to work "for the State," for which "they are paid nothing either actually or constructively."[52]

Henley characterized incarcerated individuals as a mixed "lot," some not "particularly vicious," while others could "properly [be] classified as either sociopathic or psychopathic, if not psychotic." As for the system, the state had "very few paid employees," which meant that "armed trustys" ran the prisons; it kept large numbers of men in overcrowded barracks; and it provided "no meaningful program of rehabilitation" at Cummins and only a "minimal" program at Tucker. Moreover, the periodic "exposés" had made "little, if any, lasting impression" on the "Arkansas public." Describing accounts of the prison as a "country club," Henley blamed people who provided "glowing reports of . . . conducted tours" where they are "shown in daylight hours what their conductors want them to see." In contrast, Henley credited "Arkansas convicts" for becoming "more articulate about the conditions under which they lived" and having had "more success in bringing their complaints to the attention of free-world authorities," including his court.[53]

LOSING THE LABOR CLAIM

Three legal claims were before Henley. Racial segregation was straightforward; in 1968, the US Supreme Court had ruled it unconstitutional. The two other issues raised novel questions: Did the Constitution limit forced labor, and did it require different conditions of confinement? Citing the Thirteenth Amendment, Henley did not find his way to holding involuntary servitude illegal, but he did rule that the prison conditions violated the Eighth Amendment.

History was one problem for the labor claim; menial work ran from seventeenth-century Amsterdam and England to US statutes authorizing "hard labor." Moreover, internalizing the costs of incarceration had moralistic and political dimensions, that taxpayers *ought not* have to foot bills for people who violate the law. Many jurisdictions today impose per diem rates that incarcerated individuals rarely have the resources to pay. "Carceral liens" is a shorthand for taking money from prisoners' commissary accounts or, upon release, from other sources of income.

Moreover, state power to force labor survived slavery through statutes, such as Florida's authorizing county commissioners to summon "[e]very able-bodied male person," twenty-one to forty-five, to spend "six days of not less than ten hours each year" on "road duty." People could buy out by paying three dollars for each day. Upholding a thirty-day jail sentence for a man who did not comply, the US Supreme Court in 1916, cited English mandates for state-conscripted labor for road construction and approved the practice under the rubric of "civic duty." That concept has since been invoked to justify jury duty, military service, labor for failure to pay child support, and obligations of pretrial detainees to maintain facilities.[54]

Another problem was the text of the Thirteenth Amendment, which promised the end of involuntary servitude, except as "punishment for crimes." As noted, that phrase was in the governing document, the Northwest Ordinance of 1787, which prohibited slavery and involuntary servitude "otherwise than in punishment for crimes." While some historians have argued that this "Punishment Clause" was limited to judge-imposed sentences of "hard labor,"[55] Henley did not see his way to that outcome. Instead, he gave readers a graphic picture of debilitating conditions: "stooped labor," six days a week, hot or cold, with or without adequate shoes, under the authority of gun-carrying trustys who might randomly shoot and, occasionally, kill. Further, Henley reported that the only avenue to earn money came from "bleeding at the blood bank," for which prisoners could get $5 and from which the state took money it used for the $25 provided to people at release.

FIGURE 20.3 *Cummins Prison Farm, Grady, Arkansas*, photograph by Bruce Jackson, from the series *Inside the Wire*, 1975, courtesy of the photographer

Henley concluded that, as a matter of law, this labor was both servitude and involuntary, and moreover, it was not "humane." Yet the judge ruled that Arkansas could require such work because of the Thirteenth Amendment. Citing a 1944 Fifth Circuit decision rejecting a challenge by a World War II conscientious objector arguing he should not have to work for "nominal" pay, Henley ruled that the Constitution licensed forced labor for the imprisoned.[56] Henley thus preserved a stream of income for Arkansas while, perhaps, thinking documentation of inhumane labor conditions could move legislators to fund equipment for efficient production instead of the stoop labor that figure 20.3, also on the book cover, shows. Yet by keeping the structure of subordination intact, the opinion kept prison officials in power and left prisoners no time for any form of rehabilitation that the Arkansas statute had promised and that Henley thought relevant, albeit not dispositive.

"CONSTITUTIONAL SIGNIFICANCE" AND
"CRUEL AND UNUSUAL PUNISHMENT"

"For the ordinary convict a sentence to the Arkansas Penitentiary today amounts to a banishment from civilized society to a dark and evil world completely alien to the free world, a world that is administered by criminals under unwritten rules and customs completely foreign to the free world culture."

—Chief Judge Henley, *Holt II*[57]

For the analysis under the Eighth Amendment, Henley had to answer two questions. First, could structural features of a prison, not aimed personally at individuals, ground a violation? Second, what kinds of deficits were cruel and unusual? Henley explained that the Eighth Amendment was not "limited" to a specific punishment directed at an incarcerated individual, who might "personally . . . [be] subject to any disciplinary action." Rather, "confinement itself within a given institution may amount to a cruel and unusual punishment" where the "conditions and practices [are] so bad as to be shocking to the conscience of reasonably civilized people." Echoing Judge Blackmun, Henley opined that what was cruel and unusual "tends to broaden as society tends to pay more regard to human decency and dignity and becomes, or likes to think that it becomes, more humane." His examples included torture, "grossly excessive" punishment, or practices that were "inherently unfair," "unnecessarily degrading," or "shocking or disgusting to people of reasonable sensitivity."[58]

As applied, Henley (again like Blackmun) did not rely on correctional standards as the touchstone. He noted that Director Bennett had described Arkansas as "substandard and outmoded when measured by accepted penological standards" and that Sarver had said "radical improvements" were needed. Like the two correctional experts, Henley focused on three idiosyncratic facets—the trustys (who "take bribes, . . . engage in extortion, . . . smuggle . . . , steal food," and "form a living barrier" to what other prisoners need), the barracks (where assaults from "crawlers" and "creepers" were commonplace), and the lack of any program of rehabilitation (while so many prisoners were "ignorant and unskilled . . . [and] illiterate"). Using testimony from both *Holt I* and *Holt II*, Henley concluded that, working "in combination," the "cumulative impact" was unconstitutional.[59]

Linking trustys and violence to the Eighth Amendment was easier than drawing legal import from the dearth of programs to make rehabilitation plausible. In *Holt II*, Henley reiterated what he said the June before, that a "convict, however cooperative and inoffensive he may be, has no assurance whatever that he will not be killed, seriously injured, or sexually abused." Arkansas' inability to "protect him" violated the Constitution. "It is one thing for the State not to pay a convict for his labor; it is something else to subject him to a situation in which he has to sell his blood to obtain money to pay for his own safety, or for adequate food, or for access to needed medical attention."[60]

Yet Henley struggled to articulate what was *constitutionally wrong* with Arkansas providing no activities other than grueling work. Henley had a legal hook he did not use; the state's statute creating a right to rehabilitation could have been characterized as a kind of property/liberty right (a statutory entitlement) that could not be deprived under the Fourteenth Amendment without procedural protections.[61] Moreover, after Henley ruled, other judges explained that a lack of recreation and education produced "debilitation" and "deterioration" that violated the Eighth Amendment, and, in 1976, the US Supreme Court identified an affirmative obligation in *Estelle v. Gamble* when ruling that deliberate indifference to known medical needs was unconstitutional.[62]

In contrast, Henley did not conclude that states were required *to provide activities* to improve the lives of prisoners. He explained that, in an "otherwise unexceptional penal institution," a lack of educational and vocational programs would not be unconstitutional. However, given other conditions that "militate against reform," the absence of rehabilitation could "have constitutional significance." Henley coupled that rehabilitative deficit with "other aspects of prison life" that did not, individually, "rise to constitutional dignity." On his list were the lack of medical and dental care, inadequate clothing and food, and "deplorable" sanitary conditions; people slept on "filthy bedding" and had no toothbrushes or toothpaste. *In combination*, the factors totaled cruel and unusual punishment. While some improvements (limited by "financial difficulties" causing a "retrogression") had been made since *Holt I*, Arkansas had failed to "discharge" its duty to use "ordinary care" to protect prisoners' safety.[63]

SAVING LIVES THROUGH A "PROMPT AND REASONABLE START"

"The lives, safety, and health of human beings, to say nothing of their dignity, are at stake."

—Chief Judge Henley, *Holt II*[64]

Lawsuits are about remedies, and even though "lives [were] . . . at stake," Henley did not demand immediate changes. He began with what was easy—declaring that "confinement in the Arkansas Penitentiary System under existing conditions amounts to a cruel and unusual punishment constitutionally prohibited." Likewise, "racial segregation," a "violation of the Equal Protection Clause," had to be "eliminated."[65]

Before issuing orders, Henley underscored that his decree would not "disrupt" Arkansas, a "sovereign state," which had the power to enforce law and "maintain order and discipline in its prisons." Quoting himself from *Holt I*, he understood the "financial handicaps" under which Sarver and the Board of Correction labored; they could not "make bricks without straw." Henley's remedies, *out of sync* with the violence prisoners faced, were *in sync* with his hopes that the dozens of pages of facts and law would prompt the legislature going into session March 2 to provide funds requisite to change. His "order" (whose crafting was both "difficult and delicate") called for a "prompt and reasonable start toward eliminating" unconstitutional conditions under a threat that, "unless conditions . . . are brought to a level of constitutional tolerability, the farms can no longer be used for the confinement of convicts." One reporter credited the "prospect" that Henley would send "prisoners back to the counties" with getting the legislature's attention, as legislators were responsive to local sheriffs and county judges who did not want prisoners sent their way.[66]

What would compliance with that "start" look like? The judge laid down "guidelines" and "minimum requirements," coupled with a pep talk to legislators. Given the needs, there was "no reason to believe that, subject to the overall financial needs and requirement of the state, the Legislature will be unwilling to appropriate necessary funds." Moreover, even with "unlimited funds at their disposal tomorrow," the state needed time to hire staff. To employ "venal, corrupt, sadistic, and underpaid civilians" would just "substitute another form of tyranny for that which now exists." The touchstones Henley laid out included that the "remaining vestiges of racial segregation must be eliminated." Yet, noting that prisoners were not "school children" and prisons were not "theaters, restaurants, or hotels," Henley gave no timetable.[67]

As to trustys, Henley did not call (as Sarver had hoped) for total elimination "at this juncture"; instead, the system needed to be "overhauled." The trustys, "whether guards or not, are going to have to be stripped of their authority over the lives and living conditions of other convicts," which meant they were not to decide about jobs or access to the infirmary. Once "deprived of their authority over inmates," trustys would "lose the power of extortion." Henley noted armed trustys could be "tower guards and picket guards" but not "gate and field guards." To lessen danger in the barracks, the number of people had to be limited. For those in isolation, and even if that "plight . . . [was] largely of [their] own doing," trustys had to be cut back, and food taken off the floor, as prisoners had no "decent Christian way to eat their food." As to "subsidiary problems" (health care, food, and filth), they would "tend to take care of themselves."

While not "dogmatic about time," Henley called for a first report by April 1 and warned: "If Arkansas is going to operate a Penitentiary System, it is going to have to be a system that is countenanced by the Constitution of the United States."[68]

PART III

THE POLITICAL AND THE DEMOCRATIC IN PUNISHMENT

THE 1970S TO TODAY

In *The Problem of Slavery in the Age of Emancipation*, David Brion Davis explained that slavery had, in Western political and moral thought, long been viewed as a natural practice; during the nineteenth century, its end became an imperative.[1] Yet, even as Enlightenment thinkers came to object to slavery and began to question how sovereigns exercised their power to punish, they took prisoners' enslavement for granted. The assumption that incarceration entailed a loss of citizenship endured in prison–plantations, in amendments to the US Constitution after the Civil War, and long into the twentieth century, as reflected in the 1970s photograph of the hoe line at Cummins in figure P3.1. As discussed, the Thirteenth Amendment distinguished people "duly convicted" from others when banning involuntary servitude, and the Fourteenth Amendment could be read to exclude convicted people from expanded voting rights.

As I explained, a new proposition, coming into view after World War I and to fruition in light of World War II's concentration camps, was that facets of *liberty* survived during incarceration and that prisoners were people with rights to be respected. The Arkansas litigation opened the door wide to questions of what "rights" sat inside prison gates. What happened thereafter—in Arkansas, around the United States, and across the Atlantic—is the subject of this book's closing segment.

FIGURE P3.1 *Cummins Prison Farm, Grady, Arkansas*, photograph by Bruce Jackson, from the series *Inside the Wire*, 1975, courtesy of the photographer

In the decades following *Holt II*, what the US Constitution "countenanced" in prisons took center stage. Even as prison abolitionists may argue that the phrase "a constitutional prison" is oxymoronic or useless, incarcerated people kept asking for law to be deployed on their behalf. In the 1970s, the Supreme Court, intent on distinguishing the United States from Communist countries, instructed trial judges to take prisoners' claims seriously, required officials to accord some procedural regularity before imposing in-prison punishments, and determined that prisons had to provide a modicum of safety, freedom to observe religion, and health care. Following in Henley's footsteps, federal judges issued injunctions across the country—in Mississippi, Alabama, Louisiana, Texas, Rhode Island, Massachusetts, New Hampshire, Ohio, New Mexico, and more. Some judges built on Henley's decision to require that prisons provide opportunities for "reform and rehabilitation," and the Eighth

Circuit underscored the obligation to promote rehabilitation when it affirmed *Holt II* in 1971.[2]

This project of prison reconstruction was not court-centric, in part because, when Warren Burger became Chief Justice, the Court limited what federal judges could do. Yet Burger worried about prisons and, at his urging in 1971, the federal government convened a national meeting—held months after the Attica prison uprising—about the need to improve prisons. For some, Attica was a beacon, bringing the racist and violent degradation of incarceration into public view; for others, it was a reason to put aggressive imprisonment measures in place. At the front end of the 1970s, state and federal legislators took up statutes to mandate better conditions and considered a model code of prisoners' rights, as well as funding for community-based rehabilitation programs. Civic institutions—from the Ford Foundation to the US Chamber of Commerce—came on board, as did the American Bar Association and the American Correctional Association, in support of efforts to respect prisoners' rights and to reduce racism in criminal law enforcement. Money flowed to the ACLU's National Prison Project, the NAACP's Legal Defense and Education Fund, the Nation of Islam's lawyers, and to more than sixty law schools (including in Arkansas) for prisoner legal services. In 1976, Congress enacted the Civil Rights Attorney's Fees Awards Act, authorizing successful plaintiffs in all kinds of civil rights cases to recoup fees from losing defendants. That statute was part of why, in 1978, Arkansas paid prisoners' lawyers Kaplan and Holt about $50,000.

Through these various modes, a significant restructuring of incarceration seemed *plausible*. On the ground, life changed on some dimensions. Before *Holt II*, Arkansas' legislators left prisoners without shoes, clothes, food, and farm equipment. After *Holt II*, the state spent millions on prison—some for improved conditions, even as so much went to building maximum-security units. The contours began to take shape of what, in this book's introduction, I called an *anti-ruination principle*, reflecting the constitutional prohibition on "excessive fines" that were "ruinous." Excessiveness, a term borrowed from England and implanted in the 1791 Eighth Amendment, aimed to stop governments from economically devastating people. For a time in the 1970s the idea of anti-ruination (albeit not so named) for imprisoned people gained traction in courtrooms and legislatures.

However, as forecast, the "war on crime," begun during Lyndon Johnson's presidency, ramped up. Chief Justice Burger made arguments from *morality* for improving prisons while opposing *legal* reforms and sought to dismantle the rights revolution of the Warren Court era. Prison officials, once champions of rehabilitation, began to claim that "nothing works." Political appointments changed the composition of the federal judiciary; new sentencing laws put more people in prison for longer periods of time; and Congress funded more prison construction. In 1981, the Supreme Court pulled judges back by concluding that the Constitution permitted officials to confine two people long-term in a cell constructed for one; in 1995, the Court licensed assigning a person to thirty days of solitary confinement without buffers against arbitrariness through procedural protections. By the twenty-first century, constitutional mandates to aim for safe prisons and health care were threatened by reinterpretations of the Eighth Amendment to mean it banned only punishments deemed "barbarous" in 1791.

Yet, outside the United States, the post–World War II commitment to "rights" and "dignity" had gained traction sufficient to alter twenty-first-century versions of the transatlantic networks that had their genesis in nineteenth-century organizations generating the profession of "corrections." As discussed, in 2015, the United Nations, revisiting its 1955 Rules, set forth a more robust set. Moreover, "rights," along with "care," became bywords in the transnational commercial market to provide prisons and supervision. The difficulty of delivering both, however, came from a mix of a lack of will and insufficient staff for the large number of facilities dedicated to detention. Employee vacancy rates reflected the stress of being a prison "guard," and abolition movements gathered force as they registered objections to incarceration's incursions on people's autonomy and life course. In the third decade of the twenty-first century, prisons of the kind and scale now extant seem unsustainable in polities aiming to be democratic social orders. This closing segment unfolds and analyzes these decades in which "rights" and "prisons" have shared space.

21

"COUNTENANCED BY THE CONSTITUTION" IN THE 1970S

In this chapter, I explain why understanding responses to prisoners' claims in Arkansas requires looking outside that state. During the early 1970s, the US political and legal establishment put its weight behind three propositions: prisons were a disaster, the focus ought to be on rehabilitation, and community-based alternatives were preferable to penitentiaries.

What such views meant in practice was unclear, and what role courts were to play was contested. Here, I sketch discussions—in Williamsburg, Virginia; in Kyoto, Japan; in congressional hearings convened around the country; and in the US Supreme Court—addressing the problems prisons posed for democratic orders. For a few years, support for significant changes came from many venues, including the Supreme Court, which ruled that the Constitution limited arbitrary decision-making about punishment and required the provision of some health care. The undisciplined power of corrections was, for a time, to be bounded—but not without pushback, spearheaded by the federal government during the Nixon Administration.

CHIEF JUSTICE WARREN BURGER AND THE 1971 NATIONAL CONFERENCE ON CORRECTIONS

"[I have a] deep conviction that when society places a person behind walls we assume a collective moral responsibility to try to change and help that person. The law will define legal duties but I confess

I have more faith in what a moral commitment of the American
people can accomplish than I have in what can be done by the
compulsion of judicial decrees."

—Chief Justice Warren Burger, National Conference
on Corrections, Williamsburg, November 1971[1]

Warren Burger, well-known for objecting to the expansion of criminal
defendants' rights, said he cared about prisoners. In a 1993 foreword
to a book about privatizing prisons, Burger described that, when a
Boy Scout, he visited a prison in Stillwater, Minnesota, saw prisoners
"warehoused," and wanted "to reverse this human deterioration." In
the late 1960s, in his first speech as Chief Justice to the ABA, Burger
discussed decrepit facilities where two men lived "in a cell 6 by 8 feet"
and in which education, vocation, and mental health services were
"nonexistent." The ABA responded in 1970 by launching a Commission on Correctional Facilities and Services and installing Richard
Hughes, New Jersey's former governor, as Chair. With support from
the Ford Foundation, the ABA spawned a Resource Center for Correctional Law and Legal Services and a Joint Committee on the Legal Status of Prisoners to draft Standards Relating to the Rights of Prisoners.[2]

In 1969, Burger called for a "National Conference on Corrections"
(NCC), which fit his agenda of deflecting legal challenges to prisons
through spurring reform without "the compulsion of judicial decrees." In June of 1971, President Richard Nixon directed his Attorney
General, John Mitchell, to convene a group to address the "failure" of
prisons in "correcting and rehabilitating criminals." That December
1971 Williamsburg, Virginia meeting was reminiscent of those convened by the IPPC and the UN; it included about 350 people (mostly
white and men) who attended plenary sessions (including on "correctional problems and programs in other nations") and issued a 198-
page report.[3]

Burger and Mitchell opened the proceedings by promoting improvements in and *alternatives* to incarceration. Burger repeated
his critique of prisons. "[C]onsistent with orderly administration,"
incarcerated people had to learn to "think and walk and talk as we
will demand that they do when they are released." (The *New York
Times* described Burger as calling on "prison heads" to "give inmates

some voice.") Mitchell's talk, "New Doors, Not Old Walls," recommit-
ted to the 1870 National Prison Congress goals—reformation in lieu
of punitive incarceration, classification, and education. Mitchell
proposed performance standards for corrections, increasing "minority employment," and deferring prosecutions to divert some
defendants to community-based programs.[4] (Mitchell later went to
prison after conviction for conspiracy, obstruction of justice, and
perjury in relationship to Watergate.)

Chief Justice Burger's concerns were echoed in a US Chamber
of Commerce December 1971 booklet, *Marshaling Citizen Power to
Modernize Corrections*. Its preface quoted Richard Nixon's "Presidential Call for Action to Modernize Corrections": "To turn back the
wave of crime, we must have more effective police work, and we
must have court reform to ensure trials that are speedy and fair.
But let us also remember that the *protection of society depends largely
on the correction of the criminal*." In making what is today called the
"business case" for reform, the Chamber described the terrible
physical conditions in some 460 state and federal prisons, the "jail
mess," and the "unfulfilled promises" of parole. The Chamber complained about "patchwork programming, . . . by guess and by golly,"
personnel problems, and underrepresentation of "minority groups,
[and] females," and a "loss of self-respect and human dignity."

The Chamber's solutions included creating a "National Corrections Academy to train federal, state and local corrections personnel" and community corrections to provide a "cheaper and
more humane" response. To get there, the Chamber championed
additional federal funding for Congress' Law Enforcement Assistance Administration (LEAA) that began in 1968, more halfway
houses, and new prisons. The Chamber called for "business leadership" to ensure that "equal employment opportunities shall be
extended to all citizens."[5] Its agenda included what later became
known as "ban the box"—ending employer inquiries into appli-
cants' prior involvement with criminal law enforcement. But the
Chamber's approach, like Burger's, left prisoners dependent as
they had been in prior centuries on their keepers and on volunteers who might—as a matter of grace rather than as of right—put
such programs into place.

FROM "SLAVES OF THE STATE" TO WINNING LAWSUITS
AND NAMING "INSTITUTIONAL RACISM"

In "the making . . . [is a] fundamental . . . right to rehabilitative
treatment, . . . a measure of progress toward our goals in
corrections."

—Judge William Bryant, National Conference
on Corrections, Williamsburg, December 1971[6]

Even as the Williamsburg Conference repeated themes of meetings
past, it departed in two respects: plenary speakers described the
new field of prisoners' rights and a formerly incarcerated individual
detailed the racism he faced. An overview of "the law" came from
Eugene Barkin, the general counsel of the US Bureau of Prisons
(BOP), and from William B. Bryant, a federal trial judge in the District of Columbia. They explained that a sea change had occurred.
Barkin reported that prisoners, once seen as "slaves" of the state,
were winning lawsuits. He cited "considerable authority" (including
Lee v. Washington and Jackson v. Bishop) for the proposition that "the
only rights a prisoner loses are those which are relevant to security,
discipline or [the] program." Barkin suggested that professionalism
could "forestall many unfavorable judicial decisions" and court orders could bring needed resources.[7]

Judge Bryant struck a less begrudging tone when discussing
the "Substantive Rights of the Prisoner." He invoked Holt v. Sarver
as one of several decisions exemplifying that the Eighth Amendment meant that "inhuman cell conditions" and "assaults must be
prevented." In addition to prisoners' "civil rights" to religion, expression, and nondiscrimination, Judge Bryant saw—as quoted—a
"fundamental . . . right to rehabilitative treatment." A commitment
to more legal regulation was elaborated in a session, "New Directions in Corrections," producing recommendations "so bold as to
be breathtaking, albeit quite timely." One was that legislatures or
prisons "formulate a code of rights for prisoners." Another was that
the federal government provide "aggressive leadership" to promote
such codes and make visible "the basic standards established by the
United Nations."[8]

In addition to the theme of prisoners' rights was discussion of race. Both the international and American corrections conference proceedings had been littered with racist references and casual colonial imperialism. At Williamsburg, the over-incarceration of people of color was a subtext for a few speakers, noting the need for more "minorities" to join their workforces, and the text for others. A direct account came from Eddie M. Harrison, who described his sixteen months on death row while serving eight years for felony murder. After a reversal based on illegally admitted evidence, a re-conviction, and commutation by President Nixon, Harrison became director of a pretrial intervention project. Discussing pervasive "institutionalized racism," Harrison told the group that "Black prisoners . . . have begun to consider themselves political prisoners" and that time had come to face racism's perpetuation.[9]

Racism was also central to comments by Christopher F. Edley, head of the Ford Foundation's Government and Law Program. "No black person of my generation . . . would dare assume that inmates are harmful and undesirable citizens, and no black attorney . . . who has served as a criminal prosecutor and defense counsel as I have would dare write-off the black men and women who have gone to prison." Pressing for community-based responses, Edley argued that prisons had not proved their value in 200 years. Norval Morris, a high-profile criminologist directing the University of Chicago's Center for Studies in Criminal Justice, followed with analysis of "black and minority prisoners . . . finding new leaders and a new political activism." Because "reform and unrest" were moving together, Morris called on the corrections establishment to be "innovative" and "activist."[10]

CLASHING READINGS OF ATTICA

"Attica is every prison; and every prison is Attica."

—*Attica: The Official Report of the*
New York State Special Commission on Attica, 1972[11]

As the Williamsburg audience knew well, the "unrest" Morris referenced was the September 9, 1971 uprising at Attica. Incarcerated people took over that maximum-security prison in the sparsely populated, poor, and white upstate New York. In her book, *Blood in the Water*, Heather Thompson caught the bleakness: "massive grey walls [with] a gun tower from which guards could scan the fifty-five-acre penal complex for any trouble." In 1971, Attica held 2,243 prisoners—"overwhelmingly young, urban, under-educated, and African American or Puerto Rican." Thompson chronicled the miseries that echoed those in Arkansas; people were given few items of clothing and "one bar of soap and one roll of toilet paper" every month. Fed what $0.63 a day would buy, many went hungry.[12]

In early September of 1971, incarcerated people made "demands"; New York's Congressman Herman Badillo, who went to Attica during the protests, later described twenty-eight "proposals" that had been "accepted by the State." One was "provide adequate food, water, and shelter for all inmates"; others were "true religious freedom," ending censorship and adding education, as well as mechanisms to bring grievances. Badillo testified about those proposals at a hearing in the House of Representatives. At another hearing, Vincent R. Mancusi, Attica's Superintendent, proffered a different account. He listed the "causes" to include a "fiscally starved" corrections department, "militants" and "troublemakers" fueled by "Federal court decisions exercising authority" over state facilities without "taking responsibility for results," and "the doctrine of permissiveness in society [that meant] freedom without responsibility."[13]

Yet much of what Attica's *prisoners* sought aligned them with the *professional* views of corrections. As explained by consultants to the UN's Fourth Congress on the Prevention of Crime and the Treatment of Prisoners, the Attica "demands" were "parallel if not identical" to what the 1955 UN's Standard Minimum Rules for the Treatment of Prisoners ("accepted by all mankind") had outlined. For example, "Demand #11" sought "'modernization' of the 'inmate education system'" and a Spanish-language library; the UN Rules called for education and libraries available "for the use of all categories of prisoners." "Demand #12" asked for "adequate medical treatment" and Spanish-speaking doctors and interpreters; the UN Rules called for medical officers to examine individual prisoners and interpreters as necessary. "Demand #15" was "a healthy diet, reduce the number of pork dishes, increase fresh fruit daily"; UN Rule 20 stated that prisons were to provide "food of nutritional value . . . and wholesome quality."[14]

The scale of the uprising at Attica was unusual, but as my account of Arkansas made plain, the fact of protest was not. A year before, prisoners at Cummins went on strike and took a few hostages. With Governor Winthrop Rockefeller's approval, Commissioner Sarver negotiated the release, and people were not punished for complaints that, as Rockefeller acknowledged, were well-founded. But Rockefeller's brother, Nelson, who was New York's governor, did not seek to de-escalate at Attica. Instead, on September 13, 1971, he made the tragic decision to call in untrained, heavily armed state law enforcement who stormed the facility, killed dozens, beat scores more and, as Heather Thompson documented, tried to cover up their brutality.

Thereafter, New York State's Chief Judge Stanley Fuld appointed a nine-person commission to investigate under the leadership of a lawyer in private practice, Arthur Liman, who documented "what it was like to live—and die—at Attica." The Attica Commission's 1972 report began: "Forty-three citizens of New York State died at Attica Correctional Facility between September 9 and 13, 1971. . . . With the exception of Indian massacres in the late 19th century, the State Police assault which ended the four-day prison uprising was the bloodiest one-day encounter between Americans since the Civil War." Along with that awful fact, the report insisted on the *ordinariness* of Attica. "The Attica Correctional Facility in September 1971 was not perceptibly better or worse than the other maximum-security prisons. . . . That the explosion occurred first at Attica was probably chance . . . Attica is every prison. . . ."

The Commission proposed several reforms, centered on the premise akin to what Paul Cornil had proposed at The Hague in 1950; prisoners retained "all the rights of other citizens except those that have been specifically taken away by court order." This proposition meant that "prisoners should retain all rights except that of liberty of person." Included were "to be adequately compensated for work performed, . . . to receive and send letters freely, . . . express political views, . . . to practice a religion or to have none, . . . to be protected against summary punishment by state officials, [and when] released . . . not [to] be saddled with legal disabilities which prevent them from exercising the rights of free men." That 1972 *Attica Report* called for prisons not "shrouded from public view and closed to the communities in which they are located and whose offenders they house." It did not locate the sources of the problem in upstate New York alone; "criminal justice will never fulfill either its promises or its obligations until the entire judicial system is purged of racism and is restructured to eliminate the strained and dishonest scenes now played out daily in our courtrooms."[15]

Back at Williamsburg, Norval Morris described the "appreciable restraint" prisoners had exercised in their "revolt." In contrast, Chief Justice Burger called for classification to separate "riot-prone inmates . . . who would disrupt and destroy a penal institution" from people "trying to learn and to prepare themselves for the future." Russell Oswald, the Commissioner of New York State's Department of Correctional Services, who had styled himself a reformer before Attica, argued that prisoners' pursuit of legal remedies showed their disrespect for authority. Oswald proposed "maxi-maxi" facilities to lock down the "unreasonably militant."[16]

Aligning with Oswald was an opinion essay written by Spiro Agnew, Nixon's Vice President, and published by the *New York Times* on September 17, 1971; two years later, Agnew resigned after pleading "no contest" to a felony tax evasion charge based on kickbacks from Maryland contractors. In his 1971 commentary, Agnew extolled Nelson Rockefeller for acting "courageously" and decried giving the "'demands' of convicted felons . . . equal dignity with legitimate aspirations of law-abiding American citizens." Agnew's account was incendiary; he conflated prisoners, Black Panthers, "extremists," "revolutionary leaders," and "black power militants." Warning of the ascendency of the "forces of violence and crime," Agnew argued the uprising recalled the "era of Hitler's Storm Troopers," when a "most civilized of societies" offered a "cloak of respectability . . . [to] thugs and criminals."[17]

A REPORT TO THE 1970 UN CONGRESS AND A "MODEL ACT" TO PROTECT PRISONERS' RIGHTS

"It is now clear that the past immunity from judicial intervention has fostered situations that have shocked the conscience of courts and have stimulated intervention by reluctant courts."

—Honorable Roger Traynor, former Chief Justice of the California Supreme Court, 1970[18]

Imprisoned people "shall retain all rights of an ordinary citizen, except those expressly or by necessary implication taken by law."

—Model Act for the Protection of Rights of Prisoners, National Council on Crime and Delinquency, 1972[19]

Despite Agnew's rhetoric, proposals from the 1971 Williamsburg Conference, along with recommendations from the Attica Commission Report, gained steam. In New York, "most of the practical proposals the Attica Brothers had fought for were in fact implemented." The Department of Correction revised food and clothing requirements, rules on mail censorship and visiting, and staff training.[20]

Another sign of the times came from Roger Traynor, chosen by Chief Justice Burger to head the US delegation to the Fourth United Nations Congress on the Prevention of Crime and the Treatment of Offenders in Kyoto, Japan. As the *New York Times* reported, in his 1970 speech on the "role of the law in protecting the rights of prisoners," Traynor, former Chief Justice of California's Supreme Court, outlined "new trends in American legal thinking, notably that the judiciary should be concerned with treatment of prisoners even after sentencing." Traynor cited the "indictment of the entire system" in *Holt v. Sarver*, as he discussed rights of access to courts ("clearly and unmistakably guaranteed"), due process, and religious accommodation, including for the Nation of Islam. Identifying the judiciary's involvement in "areas that have long been regarded as solely within the discretion of the administrator," Traynor was confident that, when the UN Congress met five years later, the US delegation would be reporting that "the United States will have advanced at least 25 years in the protection of prisoners' rights."[21]

One way to operationalize Traynor's forecast was through leg-islation. Congress had convened many "oversight" hearings on the BOP but had not imposed directions.[22] In 1971, Representative Charles Rangel, recently elected from New York and a founder of the Congressional Black Caucus, introduced the Prisoner Treatment Act of 1971. That proposal (made again in 1972, 1973, and 1975 but not enacted) set forth fifty provisions that were modeled on and, at times, taken verbatim from the 1955 UN Rules on the Treatment of Prisoners.[23] New York representative Herman Badillo—who, as noted, had been at Attica during the uprising—proposed a "Prisoner Rights Act" to ban "inhuman treatment of prisoners" and create "minimum rules" of treatment.[24] Representative Robert Kasten-meier from Wisconsin made the link to the UN repeatedly in his "Resolution Expressing the Sense of the House of Representatives that the United States Government Should Formally Record Its En-dorsement of the United Nations Standard Minimum Rules for the Treatment of Prisoners." Had it been approved, the House would have called on the Attorney General to "secure incorporation" of the UN provisions in the regulations of the Federal Bureau of Pris-ons unless the UN Rules were in conflict with the Constitution or "higher or more exacting standards" were in place.[25]

Another route to codifying prisoners' rights came from the Na-tional Council on Crime and Delinquency (NCCD), founded in 1907. Having generated "model acts" for states to adopt on juvenile courts and sentencing, it formed a committee of ten white men, several of whom ran prisons, including BOP Director Norman Carlson. The resulting 1972 Model Act for the Protection of Rights of Prisoners aimed to "establish law" where there had been "little," and offered to describe a set of rights that courts were recognizing.[26]

NCCD's Counsel Sol Rubin had done the drafting before Attica, which "demonstrated its need." A decade earlier, Rubin had been a principal author of *The Law of Criminal Correction*—a "hodge-podge" that mostly chronicled prisoners' rightlessness. The 1971 Model Act, like the 1955 UN Rules and the Attica Commission, called for impris-oned people to "retain all rights of an ordinary citizen, except those expressly or by necessary implication taken by law," a formulation with a large loophole. Nonetheless, the model specified adequate and nutritious food, health care, sanitation, "reasonable opportunities for physical exercise and recreational activities," a minimum of fifty square feet for cells, and a ban on solitary confinement as punishment but not for administrative reasons. Further, if judges found conditions in violation of the statute or the Constitution and "extensive and persistent" breaches continued, courts were to "prohibit further commitments" or close institutions for a six-month period.[27]

The Model Act never gained traction; lawyers may not have known to invoke it to judges, and states did not enact it, although aspects were incorporated in a few regulations. More specificity came in 1977 when the ABA set forth standards for prisons. Thus, as Judge Bryant had told the Williamsburg conferees, during the early 1970s, the *legality* of incarceration appeared as if it might turn on recognizing that prisoners had to be kept safe, free from arbitrary decisions and violence, and provided—in service of rehabilitation—with meaningful activities. Commentators predicted a robust rights regime in which, to diminish the "degradation process in our prisons," the Constitution protected prisoners' right to "privacy, autonomy, and dignity."[28]

IN CONGRESS: "AMERICAN PRISONS IN TURMOIL"

"The corrections system in the United States is a national disgrace. It corrects little. It rehabilitates few. It does nothing for most of the people who serve time in it. And it does precious little for the society which hopes that it will help prevent crime."

—Richard W. Velde, LEAA Administrator, US
Senate Hearings, May 20, 1971[29]

A new statute is needed to end the "misguided maiming
of human beings."

—Senator Jacob Javits, US Senate Hearings, June 2, 1972[30]

To understand the political energy behind a series of congressional hearings requires reading hundreds of pages of testimony from 1971 and 1972. Many witnesses expressed hope that the volatility in

prisons and on the streets, coupled with the emerging legal framework of prisoners' rights, would spark new laws and practices. More
than 100 "separate pieces of legislation directed toward improving
correctional programs and practices" were put forth. Prompts for
those bills were federal law enforcement agendas; uprisings at Attica, New Jersey's Rahway State Prison, California's San Quentin,
and elsewhere; and the "avalanche of court litigation in the field
of prison reform."[31] Proposals ranged from improving prison conditions to imposing longer prison sentences. While legislation to
ameliorate prisons was not enacted, calls for mandatory minimum
sentences and more construction funds succeeded in later years.

My point here is to catch aspirations for a different future. One
hearing, "American Prisons in Turmoil," convened in late fall of 1971
by the US House of Representative's Select Committee on Crime,
took five days. Under the guidance of John Conyers of Michigan and
Father Robert Drinan of Massachusetts, another eight hearings by a
subcommittee of the House's Committee on the Judiciary were held
around the country to focus on "Prisons, Prison Reform, and Prisoners' Rights."[32] As illustrated by Velde, the LEAA Administrator,
dozens of witnesses converged on the need for significant changes.
Many supported cutting back on incarceration. Ronald Goldfarb,
whom the Ford Foundation had funded to study corrections, explained that whether the metric was "standards of economics or
public safety or basic efficiency, administrative efficiency, or decency and humanitarianism, . . . the system fails."

Attention to life after prison came from a proposed "Commission
on Penal and Post Adjudicatory Systems Development and Reform."
Several speakers—including Richard Hughes, chairing the ABA
Commission on Correctional Facilities and Services—bemoaned
the difficulties facing formerly incarcerated individuals; he listed
dozens of occupations for which they were legally ineligible. The
Director of South Carolina's prison system told the Senate Judiciary
Committee's Subcommittee on National Penitentiaries in May of
1971 that "failures" abounded in his system and proposed a "model
corrections program" (akin to the then-popular "Model Cities Program") to develop community-based solutions. Counterclaims came

from a few prison directors and a union representing staff, insistent that progress had been made and that violent "offenders" needed to be isolated.[33]

New York Senator Jacob Javits introduced a National Correctional Standards Act to create an Advisory Commission on Correctional Standards, funded with a half million dollars and tasked with holding public hearings and developing standards for the US Attorney General to adopt. The bill's "declaration of policy" called for responses to "the dehumanizing causes of discontent within our prisons," which imposed a "variety of indignities" on prisoners that "debase and degrade our society as a whole." Javits gave a full-throttled endorsement of the "human rights" of prisoners and of rehabilitation to "eliminate the sometimes vicious, arbitrary, and unproductive punishment which can rob inmates of their self-respect and their humanity, and rob society of every glimmer of hope for the peaceful return of such individuals to the community." He underscored that "nearly all of the guards and prison officials are white," while prisoners were increasingly of color. Javits cited Judge Bryant on the need to promulgate "a statement of prisoners' rights." To end the "misguided maiming of human beings," Javits' bill outlined "thirteen general objectives" for rehabilitation including standards on health care, sanitation, "bilingual programs" for education, fair disciplinary hearings, access to religion, the right to vote, and more.[34]

Javits was joined by James Bennett, the former head of the BOP who had testified in the Arkansas prison litigation and who "enthusiastically support[ed]" the objectives of the legislation, albeit not the means. Bennett did not like the "one-shot commission" and advocated instead for a National Institute of Corrections. Norval Morris supported the "enunciation of minimum standards" and detailed the entities, such as the UN's 1955 Rules, that did so. A law professor, Richard Singer, provided dozens of pages of cases about prisoners' rights. Arguing the contours existed for a right to rehabilitation, Singer quoted *Holt II*, which had described the lack of rehabilitation as relevant to the court's conclusion of the unconstitutionality of Arkansas' prison system.[35]

An oppressive voice from the federal government can be found in debates about another statute (the Community Supervision and Services Act), which proposed diversion for some individuals. The US Attorney for the Southern District of New York supported the bill, while the US Department of Justice (DOJ) opposed diversion programs until an "exhaustive analysis of [the] implications" was completed. Moreover, BOP Director Carlson lauded a new federal facility for "mentally disturbed and violent offenders" and insisted that many needed to be "confined in institutions—some for many years—because of the serious threat they present to the community." That view fit with his work for the Nixon White House in shaping the federal government's "10-year plan" to expand the federal prison footprint. Between 1970 and 1977, the percentage of people who were Black and Latino within the federal prison system grew from about 25 percent to close to 40 percent, as Carlson joined a chorus endorsing deterrence and retribution and objecting to rehabilitation as an illusory goal for "violent offenders."[36] The federal government's position held sway. Legislation for diversion, reform, and rights did not pass; enacted was one provision "for narcotic addicts" on conditional release to be provided care.

THE COURTS AND THE COLD WAR

For a short period, the US Supreme Court seemed in sync with the many proposed statutes trying to lessen prison's harms. Soon after *Holt II*, the Supreme Court told lower court judges more than once that their job was to provide some oversight on the treatment of prisoners. Two brief 1972 decisions, responding to unrepresented prisoners held in Illinois and Texas, made that point.

Francis Haines alleged that, after a fight with younger prisoners, Illinois placed him in dark isolation. The lower courts dismissed Haines' lawsuit based on the view he had no right to redress. After accepting his case, the Court appointed Legal Defense Fund lawyers to represent him. At the 1971 oral argument, Illinois did not dispute that Haines was left for fifteen days to sleep on the floor, given a meal midday and bread and water morning and night, permitted one shower a week, and provided no soap or towel. Illinois' defense was that Haines, who admitted hitting another prisoner, deserved it; the state's lawyer told the Court that "to make isolation effective, you have to make it severe." Haines' lawyers countered that putting an "elderly, partially disabled prisoner" in a dark cell, where his false teeth became rancid and his physical condition deteriorated, violated the Eighth Amendment and that the lack of fair process to decide the rule breached the Fourteenth Amendment.[37]

By then, Harry Blackmun had joined the Supreme Court. In notes for the oral argument, Justice Blackmun indicated his reluctance "to interfere with matters of prison administration and discipline," even as not doing so "opens wide the door to abuse." He did find distasteful "the deprival of hygienic facilities . . . [and] having dark cells," yet he "would not hold solitary confinement, *per se* . . . a violation of the Eighth Amendment." Blackmun would "go so far as to say a prisoner [was] entitled to some kind of a hearing when . . . charged with an infraction of prison discipline." Given that staff members "not connected with the incident" had decided on the punishment, Blackmun was "inclined to affirm although there are some fringe matters that concern[ed]" him.[38]

Blackmun did not carry the day. On January 13, 1972, the Supreme Court issued a per curiam opinion, with "no view whatever on the merits," that the lower courts had wrongly dismissed Haines' complaint without providing "the opportunity to offer supporting evidence." Two months later, the Supreme Court reiterated that prisoners had rights to be heard; it reversed another lower court ruling that had tossed out Fred Cruz, who had filed his complaint on toilet paper and alleged that Texas prison officials discriminated against him as a Buddhist. Cruz reported that Texas would not give him access to the chapel; because he shared religious materials, the state put him in solitary confinement on a bread-and-water diet for two weeks. On March 20, 1972, in another per curiam decision (with Justice William Rehnquist as the lone dissenter), the Court insisted that judges had to give Cruz a chance to substantiate his claims.[39]

Haines v. Kerner and *Cruz v. Beto* became pillars of the growing law of prisoners' rights. Both told federal judges to read unrepresented litigants' filings liberally and to entertain civil rights claims alleging unfair process, unconstitutional in-prison punishment, and religious discrimination. The reminder, however, is not to equate a person's getting *into* court with obtaining the relief sought. Francis Haines did make it to a jury, which found that Illinois did not owe him money. On appeal, Haines lost again before a Seventh Circuit panel that included John Paul Stevens before he went to the Supreme Court. The appellate judges explained that the question of cruelty was to be assessed by legal standards when the acts took place; given that solitary confinement had "traditionally been an appropriate means of maintaining prison discipline," Illinois had not punished Haines "excessively" in response to conduct risking harm to another.[40]

On his case's remand, Fred Cruz faced an unsympathetic judge who dismissed the case as moot. Cruz forged on and, in 1971, a federal court held unconstitutional Texas' ban on prisoner-to-prisoner help with court filings. In a 1976 lawsuit, a judge found Texas had illegally barred a particular lawyer from representing prisoners and unlawfully imposed onerous conditions on the prisoners who had sought the lawyer's help. Yet in 1972, Cruz and the others lost their claim that Texas had violated the Eighth Amendment when putting them in solitary confinement ("pitch black" cells and bread-and-water diets). Five years later, Cruz gained a measure of vindication when a federal judge enjoined those practices and awarded damages and fees to their lawyers.[41]

ARBITRARINESS, PROCEDURAL DUE PROCESS, OR "CRIPPLING" CONSTITUTIONALIZATION

Given "the hundreds of Federal Court decisions concerning state prison administration, . . . prison administrators must wonder if incarceration is any longer a legal form of punishment for those convicted of crimes."

—Brief filed on behalf of Nebraska,
April 6, 1974, *Wolff v. McDonnell*[42]

If prisoners' protected interests were "no greater than the State chooses to allow, he is really little more than the slave described in the 19th century cases."

—Justice John Paul Stevens, dissenting in
Meachum v. Fano, 1976[43]

Around the country, prisoners were hyper-regulated, while prison officials could do as they pleased. In 1974, the Court addressed the procedures to be used in a case from Nebraska, which disciplined punished prisoners for "escape" and "mutiny, riot, or insurrection," possession of "any negotiable item, such as stamps" or money, referring to others "either in writing or orally, by any other than his correct name, or commonly used name in good taste," and not addressing "officers and staff" by their "titles." After Ronald McDonnell, at the helm of a group of self-represented prisoners, challenged the disciplinary process, a trial judge explained that prisoners could lose "good-time" credits for "messing up the count, cussing a guard, [and] bringing a sandwich into the shop," as well as for fighting and organizing protests. The judge ordered good time restored because of the lack of fair procedures, and the Eighth Circuit affirmed.[44]

The "primary issue" at the Supreme Court in *Wolff v. McDonnell* was how much process was due. Underlying that question was whether incarcerated people had "liberty" akin to that of people on probation or parole, for whom the Court had held that due process hearings were required before being incarcerated. The *Wolff* litigants and amici presented radically different pictures of prisons, discipline, and the procedures in place.

Drawing on materials from the Attica Commission and the ABA's Commission on Corrections, several filings discussed the utility of lawyers and witnesses at prison hearings and the hopes of incarcerated people that accuracy and fairness would replace arbitrary exercises of power. The NCCD wrote about prisoners' isolation, fear of "injustice" at the hands of "poorly trained and poorly educated" staff, and that the procedures required for disciplinary hearings could lower tensions, express respect, and foster reintegration by showing that disputes could be resolved fairly. The prisoners'

advocates referenced the ABA's Survey of Prison Disciplinary Practices and Procedures ("the collective judgment of correctional
administrators, judges, lawyers, prisoners, and others about the
appropriate balance of interests"), which found that most states
had written policies requiring notice, opportunities to present
evidence, an impartial tribunal, and written decisions with some
review. Thirty-nine states permitted some "counsel substitute" to
assist prisoners; thirty-one authorized confrontation of "accusing
witnesses," and twenty-eight licensed "cross-examination of adverse witnesses."[45]

The US government pushed back. Solicitor General Robert Bork
paid lip service to "accurate fact-finding in the context of prison
disciplinary proceedings," but Bork asserted that "the unique conditions of the prison environment and the nature of the interests
served by the disciplinary process" meant that the Court ought
not apply its procedural mandates for parole and probation revocation, even if "there may be a slightly increased risk of factual
mistakes in a few cases." The government opined that "the impact
of prison discipline on the individual, although not unimportant to
him, was almost invariably far less grave than the consequences
of a criminal conviction or of revocation of parole or probation."
Discipline altered prisoners' liberty but "only marginally—and
often only briefly." Because prisons were "tense and volatile," the
brief reported that some prison officials thought "that testimonial
confrontations between an inmate and staff members or other inmates can be dangerous and are to be avoided whenever possible."
In short, "substantial governmental interests and needs" ought to
trump risks to prisoners of a less fair and accurate process.[46]

At oral argument, the defending state, joined by Bork, shifted the
focus from *prisoners* to *prison administrators* and to *judges*. Bork told
the justices that the Eighth Circuit's constitutional mandates could
"impair the freedom of the Bureau of Prisons to continue its evolution of prison disciplinary procedures." The lawyer for Nebraska
characterized the Eighth Circuit's ruling as a "great extension" of
prisoners' rights that would cause chaos for judges; "a terrific increase in the number of cases . . . [would result because] inmates

will sue on every conceivable possible thing." Moreover, the "basic question" was whether a conviction extinguished a person's liberty, which Nebraska said it did.[47]

As was often true, the defending state was *right* in some respects. As prisoners in the 1960s and 1970s challenged prison officials, courts responded by directing administrators to make changes, and legislatures considered new statutes, it could have been the end of "prison" as it then was. Once practices like whipping and losing good-time credits were no longer at the discretion of officials, other aspects *of* prison could also have become impermissible. That prospect was part of what propelled some justices to pull back, as can be seen in the mixed message sent by Justice Byron White's *Wolff* decision. The Court both required prison officials to hold hearings before taking away prisoners' good-time credits and limited the kinds of procedural rights to be accorded.[48]

One aspect of the opinion, invoking Cold War Era terminology, affirmed prisoners' status as rights-holders. *Wolff* was issued in 1974, the year that the English edition of *Gulag Archipelago* was published. Written by Aleksandr Solzhenitsyn who had won the Nobel prize in 1970, *Gulag* chronicled life in Soviet prison camps. Justice White insisted that no "iron curtain" separated prisons from the Constitution. While "[l]awful imprisonment necessarily makes unavailable many rights and privileges of the ordinary citizen," it did so to accommodate institutional needs; prisoners retained many constitutional rights, including the guarantees of the Due Process Clause. The Court held that, given that Nebraska had statutory good-time credits and authorized officials to take away time earned for specified misconduct, due process protections were required to buffer against arbitrary retraction.[49]

Wolff was the Court's first announcement that prisoners were protected by the Fourteenth Amendment's guarantees of "due process" as a predicate to deprivations of "liberty" and "property." Justice White explained the core concern with "protection of the individual against arbitrary action." His opinion was not clear whether prisoners, as humans, had inherent liberty interests; it could be read that procedural fairness was required only if states imposed on themselves obligations to respect prisoners' interests. White wrote that prisoners had no constitutional right to "good time" but, because the state provided for it and limited the grounds for its withdrawal, process was due. Justice White's opinion distinguished the "grievous loss" (a term from other cases) of losing parole or probation from good time. Taking a future release date away was not the "same immediate disaster" for a prisoner, as it might not "work any change in the conditions of his liberty."

Furthermore, drawing on the volatile picture presented by state and federal governments and ignoring the ABA study, White deemed cross-examination and confrontation too risky because prisoners "may have little regard for the safety of others," and an "unwritten code . . . exhorts inmates not to inform on a fellow prisoner." The majority, invoking the "incorrigible," manipulative prisoner and the "personal antagonism[s]" that put "safety" at risk, rejected "encasing the disciplinary procedures in an inflexible constitutional straight-jacket" or imposing "unduly crippling constitutional impediments." Hence, the majority selected a few procedures required for probation revocation, including advance written notice (in this context, at least twenty-four hours) of charges, an opportunity to speak and present witnesses, and a written statement of reasons for a sanction. But the Court licensed prison staff to bar evidentiary presentations if they believed that doing so would "create a risk of reprisal or undermine authority" or be "unduly hazardous to institutional safety." Moreover, prisoners were not entitled to lawyers; prisoners with limited abilities were to have access to aid from staff or from other prisoners.[50]

The dissenters (who agreed that process was due) focused on prisoners, in need of protections that were demonstrably feasible. Justice Thurgood Marshall, joined by Justice William Brennan, argued that the Court had hollowed out the "essential" components of a defense: the right to have witnesses testify and to confront and cross-examine others. Citing the ABA's prison discipline survey, Marshall noted that many jurisdictions used cross-examination.[51] Justice William O. Douglas wrote separately; he invoked the 1970 Holt v. Sarver conclusion that an "entire prison system" in Arkansas was so "inhumane" as to violate the Eighth Amendment and identified the "unchecked power of prison administrators" as the "central evil" that "due process" procedures were designed to "cure." Given the "threat of any substantial deprivation of liberty . . . such as solitary confinement," a "full hearing with all the due process safeguards" was required. While Justice White noted that the decision was not "graven in stone" and the door was open to "further consideration" as changing circumstances warranted,[52] *Wolff* turned out to be the high-water mark for in-prison disciplinary protections.

The majority in another case, *Meachum v. Fano*, rejected prisoners' argument that they should be buffered from arbitrary transfers to higher-security facilities. In a dissent, Justice Stevens returned to the question of enslavement. Stevens wrote that liberty was part of being human and was independent of, rather than derivative *from*, the state. The Court's assessment that prisoners' interests were "no greater than the State chooses to allow" would return a prisoner to "the slave described in the 19th century cases." Stevens insisted that prisoners retained "an unalienable interest in liberty—at the very minimum the right to be treated with dignity—which the Constitution may never ignore." Whenever a detained person suffered a "grievous loss," such as placement in solitary confinement or transfers to "disparate conditions between one physical facility and another," protection from arbitrary decisions was required.[53] Instead, Justice Rehnquist's analysis prevailed, permitting all sorts of punishments, including long-term solitary confinement, unless doing so imposed an "atypical and significant hardship on the inmate in relation to the ordinary incidents of prison life."[54]

Even with its limits, *Wolff* is one of several decisions imposing *affirmative obligations* on prison officials that rendered hearings regular artifacts of incarceration. Before the decision, as the ABA reported, most prison systems called for some process when imposing certain punishments. After the ruling, all systems were to do so if taking away good time. The volume of hearings—in the 1970s and the twenty-first century—document the breadth of efforts at control. The government's *Wolff* brief cited BOP data that, in 1973, it housed more than 23,000 prisoners and had conducted "19,000 misconduct hearings." (The brief did not report what percentage resulted in acquittals.) California's amicus brief, objecting to cross-examination and a right to counsel, reported its prisons "averaged over 50 disciplinary hearings every day" in 1973.[55] More than fifty years later, statistics from Oregon painted a comparable picture. In 2018, Oregon incarcerated some 14,000 people and held 10,000 disciplinary hearings. In that data set, prisoners sometimes won; in approximately 13 percent, officers dismissed charges.[56]

MORE AFFIRMATIVE DUTIES: "SERIOUS, KNOWN MEDICAL NEEDS"

One more piece of the Court's approach to prisoners needs to be explained before exploring the backlash and returning to Arkansas in 1970. The issue of health care reached the US Supreme Court in 1976 through J. W. Gamble, incarcerated in Texas. In his handwritten petition, Gamble told a federal judge that, while working, he had been hit by a 600-pound bale of cotton. Although seen by prison doctors, the prison did not follow through on prescriptions and sent Gamble to solitary confinement as punishment. Reversing a lower court decision that had thrown Gamble out of court, appellate judges noted the "woefully inadequate" medical services: one facility had a single doctor for 17,000 incarcerated people.[57]

Before this decision, a few judges had concluded that the Fourteenth Amendment's protection of "liberty" meant that prison officials had to provide some health care, generally in cases when terrible injuries had occurred. The 1976 *Estelle v. Gamble* opinion, written by Justice Thurgood Marshall, focused on what the Eighth Amendment required. Marshall reiterated what Judge Blackmun had said in the whipping case—that the ban on cruel and unusual punishments embodied "broad and idealistic concepts of dignity, civilized standards, humanity, and decency"—which, as applied, required states not to be deliberately indifferent to known, "serious medical needs."[58]

Even as this constitutional pronouncement was another "first" in requiring some health care in prisons, its formulation raised questions. Did the word "punishment" in the Eighth Amendment require the Court to link the obligation to administrators' or doctors' *intent*, as contrasted with knowledge of the need? Was the question about personal motivation or an objective assessment from which to make inferences? And why should the burden to demonstrate "deliberate indifference" rest with the incarcerated person? Those points were part of the dissent in *Estelle* by Justice Stevens, criticizing the majority.

That standard insulated prison officials, who could argue they did not have the requisite intent for injunctive orders to make changes or pay monetary damages. Less than nine months after Mr. Gamble "won" in the Supreme Court, the appellate court dismissed his case because he could not meet the "rigorous guidelines" to "satisfy" the Court's standard.[59] Yet the Court's decision also supported a host of lower court rulings requiring medical and psychiatric services for prisoners. *Estelle v. Gamble* helped to spawn new organizations of prison health care professionals, committed to making improvements. In addition, several corporations saw the potential for profits. A few obtained a large market share of lucrative contracts and long lists of complaints about their failures to provide adequate services. In the decades since *Estelle v. Gamble*, it became clear that *some* level of health care did not equate with *quality* care. Long before the arrival of COVID-19, an array of reports and lawsuits documented ongoing failures to provide care as compared to that available in the community.[60]

Nonetheless, as discussed in a later chapter, the obligations established in *Estelle v. Gamble* were central to a 2011 Supreme Court decision upholding an order reducing the prison population in California because the density precluded safety and health care.[61] Moreover, concerns about the safety and health of incarcerated people were shared in Congress. While it did not enact statutes proposed in the 1970s for prisoners' rights, Congress weighed in on behalf of prisoners and other detainees in 1980 by creating the Civil Rights of Institutionalized Persons Act (CRIPA), which empowers the federal government—after notice and mediation efforts—to file lawsuits on behalf of people held in local jails, prisons, and state health facilities.[62]

CURBING "MILITANTS": RACE AS TEXT AND SUBTEXT

Spiro Agnew, Warren Burger, Norman Carlson, Robert Bork, William Rehnquist, and others did not focus on better care when considering the problem prisons posed for the social order and constitutional law. Agnew's call to clamp down on "militants" was part of the retelling of Attica to justify being "tough" on crime. Correctional officials, even while conceding that prisoners had some rights, insisted on their need to control prisons. Although Nebraska's lawyers did not convince the Court to deny procedural protections when good-time was withdrawn, the state's view that courts were becoming too involved in prisons took hold. As Nebraska's lawyer explained in *Wolff*, "[w]e are not advocating that the 'slave of the state' concept of prison inmates should be retained or returned to, but we are seriously concerned" about how to delineate constitutional rights from "policy decisions" to be made by prison officials.[63]

One of Burger's strategies to contain the rights-based approach was to improve state officials' capacity to defend against lawsuits. Burger was instrumental in the 1971 creation of the National Center for State Courts. That organization helped judiciaries on budgets, dockets, and by training state attorneys general to defend against habeas corpus petitions and federal civil rights suits.[64] In addition, Burger's and the Chamber of Commerce's calls for a national correctional academy took shape in 1974 when Congress chartered the National Institute of Corrections (NIC), nested within the DOJ. Congress tasked NIC with activities the IPPC in the 1940s had aspired to do: training, research, and technical assistance for prison systems. Under its first Chair—Allen Breed, who had attended the 1971 Williamsburg Conference—NIC aligned itself with efforts to limit incarceration. Breed saw court involvement as generative; he served as a special master for a federal judge concluding that Rhode Island's prisons were unconstitutionally debilitating. In 1980, as the Burger Court limited prisoners' rights, Breed decried the "dangerous implications"; citing a 1979 decision, *Bell v. Wolfish*, which had licensed double celling in a federal jail in New York City, Breed feared it signaled an unwise return to the "blind deference to the views of correctional administrators."[65]

Burger's leadership in undercutting a rights-based regime returns me to this chapter's opening account of Burger's concerns about prisoners. As an appellate court judge in the 1960s and occasionally on the Supreme Court, Burger sided with prisoners' claims. More often, he joined majorities rebuffing prisoners.

Nonetheless, he kept calling for prisons to be less miserable. Burger was on record in 1972 as opposing efforts to "enlarge all sentences for all persons convicted of serious and violent criminal conduct and keep them off the streets in a sort of long-term quarantine." Burger argued that, instead, prison facilities needed to be improved to avoid "deadly monotony . . . bound to be devastating" and identify people "who should not be sent to prisons, but should be released under close supervision." Burger promoted prison industries ("factories with fences"), modeled after what he had seen at prisons in Sweden and Denmark, as salutary.[66]

The reason to record the disjuncture between Burger's concern for prisoners and his approach to improving prisons through policy changes comes not only because he had power but also because it underscores why *rights* matter. Harkening back to prison reformers of the past, Burger argued that prisons should teach that "life's problems are solved by working within the system—not by riots or the destruction of property." He regularly accompanied his appeal to "common sense" (for example, to develop grievance procedures, modeled after labor-management interactions) with a reminder that he was not talking about "legal rights."[67]

Burger's fight against rights reflected that they *mattered*. Given the contemporary breadth of prison officials' authority, it can be hard to recognize that courts made a change. As this chapter's references to Illinois, Texas, Nebraska, and elsewhere reflects, Arkansas was but one of dozens of examples of grotesque deprivations. A painful illustration comes from a description by an ACLU lawyer, inspecting an Alabama prison in the early 1970s. He saw "dozens upon dozens of old, helpless men, many in wheelchairs, incontinent or bedridden, unable to care for themselves and jammed into squalid, dilapidated living quarters which could only be described as a human death trap." Another building, "the doghouse," had "no windows and a solid front door with eight cells, each about the size of a small door." The cells held five to six prisoners, put there for violating minor rules like "talking back" to a guard.[68] Windowless, the cells had no lights, ventilation, toilets, furniture, beds, running water, sinks, or showers, and no guards.

When prisoners in the 1960s had challenged such treatment, lawyers representing states around the country told federal judges that the US Constitution had *nothing* to say about the treatment of prisoners. In contrast, in the years after *Holt II*, governments acknowledged both that prisoners *could* be heard on claims that their keepers failed to abide by constitutional requirements and that prison officials *could* be constrained by law. And it was Henley's recognition of *legal rights* that finally brought taxpayer money to Arkansas' prisons.

I have sketched the potential for rights to channel spending in ways more generative than what politics put into place—massive construction projects intersecting with expansive prosecutorial practices and aggressive sentencing laws that have kept millions of people behind bars. In the chapters that follow, I turn to the struggles over compliance with *Holt II* and how, under the leadership of Bill Clinton, Dale Bumpers, and others, Arkansas was again a model—this time for spending money to lock more people up.

22

"CONSTITUTIONAL TOLERABILITY" WITH PRISONS AS A "HOT POLITICAL POTATO"

"Judge Henley's order simply gives formal recognition to a conclusion that anyone with the barest sensitivity to the human condition realized about life at Cummins and Tucker Prison Farms long ago."

—Jack Holt Jr., February 21, 1970[1]

"The state's prison system is a hot political potato."

—Commissioner Robert Sarver, May 31, 1970[2]

"All we want to do is keep somebody from getting killed."

—Cecil Boren, Cummins Associate Superintendent,
November 21, 1970[3]

The "defilement of individuals and the inhumane treatment of prisoners practiced in the name of the state" has to stop.

—The Honorable Donald Lay, May 5, 1971[4]

Chief Judge Henley's conclusion that a totality of conditions rendered a prison system unconstitutional would have made a great closing chapter, had the consequences been the *end* of such a system. Two Arkansas prisoners thought it would be. Within weeks of *Holt v. Sarver* (*Holt II*), they sought release from that "dark and evil world." One alleged his life was "threatened daily" because he did not get epilepsy medicine, and another that the danger meant his eight-year sentence was a "death penalty." Henley's premise, however, was that the state *could* hold people in outrageous conditions for a time, if moving toward amelioration. Rejecting their pleas, Henley focused on updates from the Arkansas Department of Correction (ADC) on steps toward running prisons the Constitution "countenanced."[5] Thus, he haggled—as would judges across the country—with prison officials and state legislators for years thereafter to make modest improvements.

Trials and opinions have dramatic arcs that are reader-friendly. Translating court orders into lived experiences requires attention to micro-interactions as implementation depends on cooperation from the very people—"legislators and other high officials"—who, as Holt Jr. said, knew that the state's prisons were abysmal, dangerous places. To generate "constitutionally tolerable" punishments required political will and money. Governor Rockefeller had will but lacked access to funds; the legislature had money it was loath to appropriate. Thus, to understand the snail's pace of compliance and the choices made about what form punishment would take requires delving into the back-and-forth from courthouse to legislature and the executive.

For a few years, life inside Arkansas' prisons hardly changed. Senior staff tried to "keep somebody from getting killed"; Henley kept calling for reports; the appellate court resoundingly affirmed that "confinement of human beings at the Cummins and Tucker . . . constitutes cruel and inhuman punishment"; and incarcerated people remained unsafe.[6] Yet *Holt II* gave Rockefeller leverage to break the logjam on taxpayer funding. Arkansas' legislators thus took up the debate about the punishments they would "tolerate" as they decided about how much money to allocate for what changes. Refusing Rockefeller's requested tax increases, the legislature scraped money from other agencies and federal grants. One legislator described those trade-offs as "taking funds away from schools, welfare and other agencies and giving them to the prison,"[7] which, as Commissioner Sarver put it, became a "hot political potato."

That metaphor also described him and the conflicts gaining traction about crime, posited to require a "war" (a term echoing "social defense," used by Marc Ancel and the UN in the 1950s). Rockefeller's 1970 reelection bid pitted what Sarver termed "rehabilitation-treatment" against "securitization," championed by Democrat Dale Bumpers. After winning, Bumpers replaced Sarver with T. Don Hutto, who became infamous for his "bad faith" in complying with Henley's orders and later founded a private prison company. This chapter chronicles how, between February of 1970 and the end of 1971, "securitization" won.

EXECUTIVE ASPIRATIONS TO COMPLY VERSUS APPEALING

"We take no exception to the findings of fact . . . or to the Court's judgment . . . because this is no more than has been stated time and again by legislative study groups, our board, and others conversant with our problems."

—John Haley, Chair, Arkansas Board
of Correction, March 1970[8]

I will not "abandon the operation of our state penitentiary system to the federal courts."

—Joe Purcell, Attorney General of Arkansas, March 1970[9]

The local press broadcasted Chief Judge Henley's February findings and featured a photograph (figure 22.1) of Jack Holt Jr. and Philip Kaplan, "pleased" by the forty-four-page opinion, even as Holt Jr. reminded readers the opinion offered "no information that should be news to Arkansas and certainly not to legislators and other high officials, elected and appointed, in the state government." Rockefeller agreed; in 1967 he had begun his tenure by saying that "no burden rests more heavily on the conscience of the people of Arkansas" than its prison system. Committed to "clearing up deplorable conditions," Rockefeller was "elated" that *Holt II* would be the "turning point."[10]

Sarver, the governor, and Correction Board Chair Haley did not want to contest Henley's decision. But the state's Attorney General, Joe Purcell, pushed an appeal. Despite norms that a lawyer's advice is confidential and clients make decisions, that disagreement was front-page news. As the *Arkansas Gazette* noted, the decision was about politics, not law or ethics. Echoing Arkansas' infamous opposition to school desegregation, Purcell explained he needed to stop the federal judiciary from regulating "the day-to-day operations of a state

FIGURE 22.1 *Winners: Jack Holt Jr. (left) and Philip E. Kaplan*, photograph by Larry Obsitnik, accompanying Bill Lewis, *Convicts' Lawyers Pleased by Ruling, Raise Few Points*, Arkansas Gazette, February 20, 1970, courtesy of the publisher

prison system." Agreeing, the *Arkansas Democrat* quoted Chief Justice Burger's 1969 ABA speech: "We take on a burden when we put a man behind walls, and that burden is to give him a chance to change. If we deny him that, we deny his status as a human being, and to deny that is to diminish our humanity and plant the seeds of future anguish for ourselves." Yet, the editorial continued, while Henley's opinion was a "good decision," the question was whether it was "the right one," given the "delicate boundary between state and federal powers in the Constitution." The way to find out was to get the case "all the way to the Supreme Court." The state did just that, and eight years later, Chief Justice Burger joined in affirming most of Henley's remedies.[11]

LEGISLATORS' TOLERANCE

Despite Purcell's drama, he did *not* dispute the prisons were awful and he did not ask the courts to stop the effect of Henley's decision pending appeal. The question of punishment turned, therefore, on what the legislature would fund. In February, Rockefeller requested $4.2 million; the legislature cut it to $2.3 million; it earmarked $200,000 for a maximum-security unit, $350,000 for operations, and another million for the next fiscal year, with $152,225 left for a vocational-rehabilitation unit. After the building contract was signed, the Board of Correction reported a shortfall of $104,993. By then, Sarver was hospitalized; having endured combat duty in Korea that garnered him a Purple Heart, Arkansas had exhausted him.[12]

The day before Henley's April 1 deadline, Board Chair Haley had little to report. ADC acknowledged that, with limited funds, it could not fill the 246 positions authorized by the legislature for "inmate care and custody," nor the twenty-seven farming jobs. The matter of "immediate urgency" was "free-world supervision over the barracks," ideally in place by July 1.[13] Henley, knowing he was in a dance with the legislature, was "most pleased" to see potential responsiveness to "fiscal needs" but not pleased by how unsafe the prisons were. On April 15, 1970, he said again that it was "small comfort to a barracks inmate to know that he may expect to be reasonably safe . . . if that safety depends on his being able to live that long." The *Arkansas Gazette* reported violence was "almost commonplace." Henley ordered updates on May 10 and July 10 about measures to "preserve order in the barracks and in the yard and prevent murderous assaults by inmates on inmates." Henley suggested that ADC search for weapons, enlist the state police, and increase surveillance.[14]

The state's May 10th filing, parroting Henley's language, said it aimed to remove weapons. Acknowledging that not all toilets worked, the state blamed prisoners for the "malfunction of the sewer system." Not "entirely satisfied," Henley spoke about the "'considerable distance to go' before the Penitentiary reach[ed] 'constitutional tolerability.'" In its July report, addressing thirty-five items as required, ADC told the judge that Cummins had been "completely integrated," that trustys, "stripped of their authority," no longer had "immediate direct or indirect control over other in-mates," and that routine "shakedowns" had recovered more than sixty weapons. Henley ordered periodic reporting and set mid-1971 as the deadline for full compliance. The Board of Correction pinned its hopes on a new unit with "punitive cells, quiet cells and adminis-trative cells." With the intervention of Wilber Mills, Arkansas' pow-erful Chair of the Ways and Means Committee of the US House of Representatives, more than $60,000 in federal funds came in. In August of 1970, the cost estimate was up to $610,000 and prisoners were constructing concrete walls that were to confine them.[15]

But after going to inspect Cummins, legislators pushed back and called for a prisoner to "earn his keep at the penitentiary." In August, Sarver had to tell the judge that trusty "supervision of the long lines at Cummins had not changed." Only one paid employee was in the barracks at Tucker. Henley heard from three prisoners about vodka on sale and armed trusty guards in the towers. The judge also took evidence on "women's rights"; incarcerated women testified about terrible facilities and lack of health care. Cummins staff had set up a triple-bunk layout to open up floor space but gave up because bunks obscured sight lines and "too many stabbings had occurred at the back of the room hidden from view."[16]

"MONUMENTS TO DESPAIR" AWAIT A "NEW DAWN"

The "so-called 'self-supporting prisons for profit'" had been "exposed as unsanitary, inhuman, constitutionally intolerable, degrading, disgraceful and destroying institutions which stand as incongruous monuments to despair in this enlightened age. . . ."

—Robert Sarver, First Annual Report of the
Department of Correction, September 1970[17]

Sarver wrote the ADC's Report "to the Governor and the General Assembly" to account for work since the Department's inception on March 1, 1968. Reflecting his anger, Sarver invoked expert Austin MacCormick's comment that Arkansas prisons were "the worst in the world." Sarver described his experience of working "in a fish bowl" and of "progress" that was "painfully slow" because of inadequate funds. Yet he lauded the first-ever general appropriations of $500,000; Henley's ruling prompted "$2.3 million to begin major improvements"—all "evidence of a sincere effort to accomplish prison reform in Arkansas."[18]

Sarver explained that, instead of putting a man on the "Sahara Desert to teach him how to swim," ADC was launching "a comprehensive series of programs designed to assimilate the cultures of free society and the society of the penal community." A transition was underway "from a punishment-custody orientation to a rehabilitation-treatment orientation." That "battle" was hard, yet new practices would enable "the public offender to live peaceably." The reducing numbers (about 1,000 people) and new staff (twenty-six added to make eighty-seven in 1970) made his plans feasible.[19]

Moreover, new paint was on the walls, a maximum-security unit underway, and a "free-world chef" supervised meals. Athletic programs were in place, along with a clinically trained chaplain, data processing training, and music from the "Cummins Swingers" and a "gospel singing group." Even as employees worked "12–16 hours each day, seven days a week, for low salaries," a "new dawn" was evident. Sarver assured readers that, given the speed of change, his account would be out of date when published. Sad to say, he was "out of date" by then; the copy I found in the state's archives had Sarver's name whited out. After Rockefeller lost the election, Sarver lost his job.[20]

ROCKEFELLER ("FACT SHEET: PRISON REFORM") VERSUS BUMPERS ("PRISONERS REGULARLY ESCAPE")

Rockefeller's third race demonstrated an *agreement* among candidates on the need for prison reform. They disagreed about what reform meant. Rockefeller aimed for incarceration that respected the rights-bearing status of prisoners ("citizens," he stressed), while Dale Bumpers sought control.

The prison system was "a big issue" but not the only one. As Bumpers recounted in his memoir *The Best Lawyer in a One-Lawyer Town*, an odd confluence of events had propelled Rockefeller's 1966

PRISON REFORM

"When we talk of law and order, we must talk of our prisons." — *Winthrop Rockefeller*

PRISON REFORM	BEFORE GOVERNOR ROCKEFELLER	TODAY
PUNISHMENT	▶ Legalized use of the strap. ▶ Brutality and torture commonplace.	▶ The strap outlawed — no more torture or beatings. ▶ Isolation and disciplinary barracks used instead. ▶ Revocation of good behavior time used effectively.
SECURITY	▶ Work crews and barracks controlled by armed inmates. ▶ Armed "trustys" literally in charge.	▶ Civilian guards now control all work crews, isolation units, yards and barracks. ▶ Armed "trustys" being replaced as funds permit. ▶ Maximum security unit under construction at Cummins.
HEALTH AND FOOD	▶ No milk served . . . meat once a month . . . and eggs once a year. ▶ Poor sanitation in barracks and kitchens. ▶ Medical treatment often denied or sold prisoners. ▶ Plasma program conducted for private gain.	▶ Balanced diet now provided — milk and meat every day. ▶ Kitchens, isolation cells and barracks disinfected . . . clean bedding and linens issued . . . pest control program started. ▶ Infirmary now under professional supervision at both units. ▶ Income from plasma program now used for better medical service.
AGRICULTURE	▶ Crops and livestock in a state of neglect. ▶ Antiquated equipment and farming methods.	▶ Crop controls and improvements instituted — farm mechanization underway. ▶ Cummins superintendent trained in agriculture — good crop year expected.
ADMINISTRATION	▶ Prisoners in charge of all records — extortion rackets and sale of "soft" jobs common. ▶ Prisoners loaned to private deer camps and politicians. ▶ Non-professional, untrained superintendents. ▶ Ratio of prisoners-to-staff worst in nation: 58-to-1.	▶ Inmates no longer keep records or assign jobs. ▶ No more use of prisoners or prison property for private gain — strict auditing begun. ▶ Professional penologists now in charge — management study underway. ▶ Prisoner-to-staff ratio now 8-to-1, and training programs started for prison staff.
CLASSIFICATION OF PRISONERS	None.	▶ Prisoners now classified every three months as to security risk, job assignment, medical condition and psychological condition. ▶ Young offenders now sent to Tucker Intermediate Reformatory — older offenders to Cummins Prison Farm. ▶ Integration carried out peacefully.

FIGURE 22.2 *WR70 Campaign Fact Sheet on Prison Reform*, University of Arkansas at Little Rock (UALR), Winthrop Rockefeller Collection, 1912–1973, UALR.MS.0001, Record Group IV, courtesy of UALR Center for Arkansas History and Culture

PRISON REFORM	BEFORE GOVERNOR ROCKEFELLER	TODAY
EDUCATION AND TRAINING	None.	▶ Academic classes started at Tucker in 1967 — high school education completed by more than 100 inmates. ▶ Vocational training facilities completed at Tucker and under construction at Cummins. ▶ More than $1 million received from federal government for education and rehabilitation.
OTHER TYPES OF REHABILITATION	None	▶ Inmate-run newspapers started. Professional director for athletic programs. ▶ New chapel built by private donations at Tucker — one being planned for Cummins. ▶ More than 900 inmates placed in jobs as a result of new pre-release employment program.
JUVENILE TRAINING SCHOOLS	Under Governor Rockefeller, Arkansas' four juvenile training schools were placed under one board and consolidated into two desegregated institutions. In 1969, a Diagnostic, Evaluation and Classification Center was established. Education programs were accredited by the State Department of Education. Today the training schools have a returnee rate of only 15%, while the national average is 40%.	

A LOOK AT FUTURE NEEDS:

▶ Enough professional guards to stop escapes and to prevent violence in the barracks.

▶ More education and a program of prison industries.

▶ An end to crowded barracks living.

▶ More probation and parole officers. Better parole records and more time for consideration of paroles.

▶ Community treatment centers and halfway houses.

▶ Diagnosis and classification service to assist judges.

"Let's face it. Of those who go to prison, 98.5% eventually will return to live in our cities and communities. Shouldn't we try to make them better citizens while we have the chance?" — *Winthrop Rockefeller.*

FIGURE 22.2 (*Continued*)

win against segregationist James D. Johnson. By 1968, Rockefeller's "drinking, his notorious habit of being late for every function, and his interminable absences from his office . . . were becoming legendary." Moreover, Rockefeller was a "pitiable speaker . . . , uncomfortable with a microphone in front of him." Yet that year, Rockefeller won by 60,000 votes as the Democratic candidate, Marion Crank, was felled by a corruption scandal. However, Rockefeller's second term was "as acrimonious as the first"; Democrats' control of the legislature ensured that "nothing happened."[21]

In his 1970 race, Rockefeller slogan was "Arkansas is worth paying for," and one campaign flyer—reproduced in figure 22.2— was dedicated to prisons.[22] A "fact sheet" explained that "98.5% [of people in prison] eventually will return to live in our cities and communities. Shouldn't we try to make them better citizens when we have the chance?" The flyer contrasted Arkansas' prisons "before" with "today," in which whipping and torture were gone, prisoners were classified and better fed, and rehabilitative programs—a prisoner newspaper, a chapel, and prerelease jobs—existed.

Bumpers, a self-proclaimed "fresh face," did not share Rockefeller's recognition of prisoners as part of an "us" rather than a "they." Instead, an ad to "elect Dale Bumpers Governor," figure 22.3, headlined escaping prisoners.[23] The text called for more scrutiny before people were released and "better management" to make "needed improvements."

The central question was whether Democrats could oust Rockefeller, whom they portrayed as an outsider as contrasted with Bumpers, the son of a state representative and ". . . reared right before the voters' eyes." Moreover, unlike Rockefeller's awkward public presence, Bumpers knew how to use thirty-second television spots. On November 3, 1971, Bumpers won 62 percent of the votes.[24]

Prisons remained in the news before and after the election. In September of 1970, a "tower guard" trusty holding a rifle shot a prisoner seated in the baseball field's bleachers. (An investigation reported the bullet had ricocheted from the ground.) Some 200 Cummins prisoners protested. Characterized as the "largest sit down strike in the history of the Arkansas prison system," 152 prisoners refused to work; sixty remained on strike a third day. In early November, a day before the election, another eruption occurred: Prisoners in the overcrowded isolation cells took hostages to protest a lack of clothing, eating utensils, and the shots fired to make prisoners run to and from the fields. Press reports put Sarver as bringing the armed confrontation to closure. The *Arkansas Gazette* attributed the peaceful "outcome of the 13-hour revolt [as] brilliant testimony to the sincerity and courage" of Sarver. Rockefeller said Sarver's "professionalism" was key to prisoners turning over guns. Sarver commented that the "system," sorely in need of change, was the "major cause."[25]

In late November, violence broke out between a "white group and black group." That "very tense" situation began, Sarver said, because people wanted "to go back to segregated housing quarters and segregated work details." Within two days, Cummins

❝❝ Let's Talk About The Issues ❞❞

PRISONERS REGULARLY ESCAPE FROM ARKANSAS' PRISONS

We must reform our prison system instead of just talking about it, and provide the prisoners the opportunity for rehabilitation.

Better management of farm land owned by our prisons will provide yields comparable to farms in the same area, and will help finance needed improvements.

At the same time, prison reform means proper security so prisoners can't walk off when they're ready. We need a more effective and efficient parole and probation system. A parole should be granted only after a thorough and careful weighing of all factors, including consultation with local authorities and sentencing courts.

ELECT *DALE BUMPERS* GOVERNOR

The Leader Arkansas Needs For The Seventies

POLITICAL ADVERTISING PAID FOR BY GUY FENTER, TREASURER

FIGURE 22.3 *Let's Talk about the Issues, . . . Elect Dale Bumpers*, Arkansas Gazette, October 28, 1970, courtesy of the publisher

staff reported that "fighting involved blacks and whites, blacks and blacks, and whites and whites." The "very explosive" situation prompted dispatching seventy-five armed state troopers; the goal was to avoid "somebody . . . getting killed." Some press described the "forty hours of racial disturbance" as a "riot." Within three days, however, "quiet" prevailed and people went to work. Thus, as discussed, unlike his brother Nelson Rockefeller who sent untrained, armed state law enforcement into Attica, Winthrop Rockefeller did not order the storming of Cummins. Even as "state troopers moved into Cummins . . . equipped for trouble," they did not fire. A nine-hour shakedown of 1,160 people collected 500 objects—"pills, weapons, etc." Sarver rejected requests for resegregation: the system was "under a federal court order to provide integrated facilities, and we are not about to go back to segregated working or living conditions." Instead, he put the 100 "most militant black and white inmates" together in a barracks and lambasted the legislature for imposing a salary cap of $339 per month. Without "security like the human eye," he could not stop the violence.[26]

In his waning days as governor, Rockefeller continued his quest to end the death penalty. Anthony Amsterdam, a high-profile professor who had represented several people on Arkansas' death row and "more than a hundred condemned men" elsewhere, called on Rockefeller to commute a dozen people's death sentences, and Rockefeller did so. On December 31, 1970, Sarver joined Rockefeller at Tucker to visit men taken off death row.[27]

A NEW GOVERNOR AND THE PRICE OF PRISON FUNDING

"I have a very strong obligation to do something about the prisons."

—Dale Bumpers, Governor-Elect, December 10, 1970[28]

"If we had refused to dismiss Sarver, we would have gotten minimal appropriations. . . ."

—John Haley, Chair, Board of Correction, April 7, 1971[29]

"Where from Here?" was the aptly titled first long-range plan for the Arkansas prisons that, with federal funding, the Arkansas Commission on Crime and Law Enforcement published on November 30, 1970. Addressed to the "executive and legislative branches," the Commission outlined options, priorities, and costs. One plan, based on a narrow reading of *Holt II*, was "to be within constitutional tolerance, no more," while a "second plan" aimed for "a higher degree of rehabilitation." Whichever road taken, money was needed. With calculations about staff, prisoners, and infrastructure, the Commission estimated that "advanced process" would cost $74.2 million over ten years and the "minimal" approach about $40.4 million.[30]

To get funds, Bumpers echoed Rockefeller's themes of reorganizing state administration, revising revenue streams (hinting at tax raises), and ending prison trustys. Bumpers told the Pulaski County Bar Association that making prisons "a humane institution" was a priority and invited Sarver to stay "indefinitely." Armed with the Commission's budget analysis, Haley called for $12 million—with two-thirds allocated from general revenues and the rest coming from profits from farming, special allotments, and federal grants. After Bumpers took office in January of 1971 and faced pushback, he cut the request to $4 million over two years.[31]

Arkansas' prisons were not the only debilitating detention facilities. Jails for pretrial detainees and county-run "penal farms" were likewise grotesque. One lawsuit, assigned to Henley, challenged Pulaski County's Penal Farm, where Curtis Ingram had died. An attack on Mississippi County Penal Farm was assigned to Judge G. Thomas Eisele, the former Rockefeller aide who joined the federal bench in August of 1970. One plaintiff, Black fifteen-year-old Nathan Smith Jr. serving a six-month sentence, drowned after allegedly forced into a stream to retrieve a can dropped by a guard. (A Mississippi County grand jury refused to indict.) Another plaintiff, James Arthur Howerton, an eighteen-year-old white man, alleged a vicious rape and no medical attention. A "battery of high-powered attorneys from all parts of the state" sought to have all the penal farms closed as, by then, the Supreme Court had (as discussed) held unconstitutional the system of converting fines to imprisonment for people to "work off" the dollars owed. Another case, before Judge Eisele and with Kaplan as one of the lawyers, involved the Pulaski County Jail, where unlit concrete isolation cells had no toilets. In a hearing a week after *Holt II*, Eisele reminded the defending county lawyers that pretrial detainees had more legal protections than convicted people. Thereafter, he ruled that the isolation cells could not be used for teenagers or federal prisoners.[32]

While federal judges were hearing new evidence of deaths, violence, and filth, legislators came up with $1.85 million for state prisons to add thirty-four employees and $2.2 million for thirty-two more staff the following year. After a proposed $400,000 cut, Sarver announced that, while "extremely tight," he hoped the Governor's Emergency Fund could make up the difference. But a new "price" emerged: Sarver. Legislators announced that they were "very determined" to fire him, even while some objected to making Sarver a "scapegoat." However, the "handwriting" was once again "on the wall," and Sarver did not see it. Initially, Bumpers defended Sarver, but on February 24, 1971, the House of Representatives resolved that, as long as Sarver remained, it would not support "new taxes for . . . additional funds for continued progress and improvement in the state penitentiary system."[33]

Sarver's rehabilitation-rights approach gained support when, on March 10, 1971, the Eighth Circuit heard the appeal of *Holt II*. The prisoners had the good fortune to get three judges who cared about them. Martin Van Oosterhout had been on the 1968 *Jackson v. Bishop* ruling outlawing whipping. Marion Charles Matthes, from Missouri, had been nominated by President Eisenhower and was then Chief Judge, and Donald Lay from Minnesota was a Lyndon Johnson 1966 nominee who became known as a stanch defender of "the rights of women, Native Americans and convicts."

The prisoners were also lucky that, unlike today when many federal appellate courts limit each side to less than fifteen minutes, both sides had a half hour and the court let Holt Jr. show a "23-minute film taken during January and February of 1970 that documented life" at the prisons. The questions forecast the outcome. When Arkansas' lawyer began by insisting that the case should be dismissed because the state was immune from suit, Van Oosterhout "cut him off" and told him that argument was not "worthwhile to pursue." Even as Judge Henley's orders prompted some legislative funding, the judges were not receptive to the claim that *Holt II* had "in effect, ordered an appropriation from the state legislature in the amount of $4 million." Matthes commented, "something had to be done about it. . . . The legislature hadn't seen fit to do anything about it."[34]

Yet in Arkansas, nickel, diming, and deaths continued. In late March, the press reported that a prisoner held in an isolation cell with two others had died; another was accused of murdering him. One legislator blamed Sarver, who ought to have "known better than to stick a white boy in with two black boys in a situation like that." Bumpers became "convinced that the General Assembly would not approve appropriations for prisons as long as Sarver" was there and called for his resignation. Sarver refused, made his case to the Correction Board, and was fired. Bumpers explained that no one person was "indispensable." Sarver's second-in-command, Bill Steed (who "credited Sarver with teaching him all that he knew") became the interim commissioner. Sarver stayed in Little Rock, practiced law, and lectured at Arkansas' Graduate School of Social Work, where he taught a course called "Problem-Solving in Correction."[35]

Bumpers' "appeasement" (as one editorial called it) worked. The legislature approved $2,155,285 for 1971–1972 and $2,541,893 for the following year. At Bumpers' request, the legislature also supported a special unit for youthful offenders, a work-release program, and good-time credits linked to merit. Two bills addressed women: one to end sending women convicted of misdemeanors to prison and the other to fund a new facility for women. In April of 1971, Bumpers won again when the legislature agreed to raise the income tax in Arkansas for the first time since 1929, when that tax began. That new stream of revenue would produce $16.3 million for the 1971–1972 fiscal year.[36] Rockefeller had argued that "Arkansas was worth paying for," and Bumpers persuaded legislators to do so.

"EXHAUSTIVE" EVIDENCE OF INHUMAN PUNISHMENT

"Supervision over the state prisons by a federal court should of course not be kept in force for any longer period than necessary."

—*Holt v. Sarver*, Judge Van Oosterhout, for the
Eighth Circuit, May 5, 1971

Jurisdiction was to continue until an "immediate and continued emphasis is given to an affirmative program of rehabilitation."

—Judge Lay, concurring

While reviled in the legislature, Sarver's views were shared by the Eighth Circuit, which in May of 1971 spurred Henley on. While noting the limits of federal judicial power, the court insisted on its exercise. Writing for the panel, Judge Van Oosterhout praised Henley for presiding at an "exhaustive evidentiary hearing" demonstrating that "confinement of human beings at the Cummins and Tucker prisons . . . constitutes cruel and inhuman punishment." The judges opined that the structural injunction did not intrude on state sovereignty (while in some ways it did). Citing *Jackson v. Bishop* and noting it came from "the two identical prisons here involved," the court rejected the state's quarrels with Henley's reliance on former BOP Director James Bennett's testimony. Henley had the authority to decide what weight to accord to experts; the "voluminous record" contained "overwhelming substantial evidence" of unconstitutional conditions.[37]

Van Oosterhout's account relied heavily on Sarver, who had "frankly admitted" the physical facilities were in a "state of disrepair that could only be described as deplorable." No "adequate means exist[ed] to protect the prisoners from assaults." As to the remedy, the appellate court commended Henley's understanding that "conditions at a prison cannot be corrected overnight." Acknowledging that legislative funding was essential (which is why the state had said it was immune from suit), Van Oosterhout discussed the need to recruit and train staff, the "sincere effort" underway, and that court supervision would end when no longer "necessary."[38]

Judge Lay wrote separately to "express additional judicial condemnation of the conditions and practices" that were "immoral and criminal." Lay explained that Arkansas' prisons did not "vary greatly from those condemned in England in the 1700s," for which he cited John Howard on the "deplorable conditions in London," along with a reference to Cesare Beccaria on the limits of state punishment powers. The "defilement of individuals . . . in the name of the state" meant that Henley had a lot more to do. After quoting Henley on "the absence of an affirmative program of training," Lay concluded the trial court had to retain jurisdiction to ensure a "continued emphasis" on an "affirmative program of rehabilitation."[39]

Within months, Judge Lay wrote an essay, *The Judicial Mandate*, calling on judges to address the "increasing number of prisoner petitions" seeking "relief from the intolerable conditions under which they are forced to live." Lay argued judges had special obligations to prisoners, whom they had not sentenced to "20 years of brutality, homosexual rape, improper diet, poor medical care, and unemployment." Atop constitutional authority, judges had "inherent power" to address conditions experienced by people they put into prison. By 1992, when Lay stepped down after more than a decade as the Eighth Circuit's Chief Judge, he said the "disappointment" of twenty-five years on the bench was "the failure of the law to deal with fair sentencing of those convicted of crime and to provide humane conditions."[40]

T. DON HUTTO AND NOT "CODDLING" PRISONERS

Bumpers did not push to get Supreme Court review of the Eighth Circuit loss. Yet instead of insisting on a Sarver-like "rehabilitation-treatment" leader, Bumpers endorsed as a replacement T. Don Hutto, a warden in Texas in charge of a maximum-security prison holding about 1,700 people, who was credited with generating the "lowest" recidivism rate "in the nation." (One way was keeping people locked up.) Hutto had a reputation for innovative programming, such as two years of college courses.[41] But Hutto's idea of cleaning up Arkansas' prisons rested on controlling prisoners.

Hutto's name has lived on not only in dozens of court opinions but also because it was chosen by CoreCivic, a private prison company he cofounded in 1983, to adorn its Taylor, Texas facility. The T. Don Hutto Detention Center later became the subject of searing reports and lawsuits documenting disabling treatment of immigrant children and families.[42] Arriving in Arkansas in June of 1971, Hutto was greeted by legislators calling on him "to run prisons as prisons" rather than "coddling" prisoners.

Another kind of welcome came from Chief Judge Henley, directing Hutto to answer questions within a month about whether the system had been brought "up to a level of constitutional tolerability."

Henley wanted to know if the trusty system had "in fact been dismantled" or guns and control over other prisoners' jobs remained, about medical care and mail, the numbers, qualifications, and training of free-world staff and whether "consideration, if any" had been given to dismantling "the so-called barracks." Henley ordered Hutto to provide, as Sarver had, access to the prisoners' lawyers to visit, take pictures, and make tapes. A report, "as specific and detailed as possible," was due on July 20. Responding, the ADC informed the judge the armed trusty system had not been dismantled, budget restraints were significant, and conditions at the women's facility were not "good." The judge told the lawyers to be in court for hearings on November 16 and 17.[43]

BEFORE THE NOVEMBER RECKONING

A lot happened between the summer of 1971 and that November hearing—on streets around the United States, in courts, prisons, and in Arkansas. The country was at war in Vietnam, which spurred student activism and protests. The Nixon Administration tried to stop the *New York Times* from publishing the Pentagon Papers, which documented internal acknowledgments of US policy failures in Southeast Asia. That summer, President Richard Nixon declared his "war on drugs" and also reached out for a détente with China. New political efforts on the environment and women's rights were marked by the founding of two NGOs—Greenpeace and the National Organization for Women. The shifting parameters of what we now call the culture wars were evident in Little Rock. Kaplan, who had lost in a prior effort to require a Little Rock venue to open its doors to the musical *Hair*, succeeded when Judge Eisele concluded that, even with brief nudity on stage, the play could go on.[44]

Judge Eisele also called for significant reform or closure in the Pulaski County Jail. Concluding that staff was so scarce the jail was unsafe, he ruled that "[i]f the state cannot obtain the resources . . . [for] persons awaiting trial in accordance with minimum constitutional standards, then the state simply would not be permitted to detain such persons." Moreover, pretrial detainees were entitled to conditions "equal to, but superior to, those permitted for prisoners serving sentences for the crimes they have committed against society."[45]

Attica erupted in September of 1971. Soon thereafter, Kaplan and Holt Jr. were invited to a first national "Prisoners' Rights Conference," sponsored by the ACLU Foundation, the Committee for Public Justice, and the Playboy Foundation. Spearheaded by Professor Herman Schwartz, teaching at SUNY Buffalo and pivotal in representing prisoners in the wake of "the tragedy of Attica," the November meeting at the University of Chicago discussed lawsuits, Attica's "after-math," and its "probable impact on prisoners and corrections."[46] Congress in turn launched hearings, sketched in chapter 21, on the "turmoil in American's prisons." Hutto, however, commented that if New York officials had "granted the demands those inmates had, there wouldn't have been a safe employee in a prison in the country."[47]

Making the rounds of press interviews and community talks, Hutto explained his "general philosophy of prison security" in which discipline was key to prisoners' "safety and welfare." Hutto's ADC issued a new "Inmate Handbook" (to be kept "in a safe place for reference") that listed twenty-five infractions, ranging from assaults to "creating unnecessary noise" (including using "indecent or vulgar language"); "insubordination" (a "disrespectful attitude or actions toward officers or employees"); "refusal or failure to work"; and staying "in living quarters . . . when . . . scheduled to work."

The Handbook gave a four-person committee the power to impose sanctions. If people appealed, they were at risk of a "new major infraction," if making untrue or incomplete statements. Listed punishments included a reprimand; loss of privileges and good time; requiring "additional, distasteful work assignments for a period of time"; fines; and "punitive isolation" for an unspecified time. A revision in 1972 added that, if sent to punitive isolation, a person would be given "a diet of bread, grue, and water, not to exceed 15 days of continuous confinement," and supplemented every third day with one "regular meal." The Handbook authorized a person deemed suicidal or problematic to be put in a "quiet cell" for no more than twenty-four hours.[48]

The Handbook did not mention the "Texas TV," which was a "disciplinary measure" about which Chief Judge Henley learned in the November hearings addressing "what progress had been made in bringing the state prison system up to constitutional standards." Despite the court rulings, people continued to live amid violence, racism, filth, retaliation, and discrimination, often targeted at Black Muslims. Prisoners filed new lawsuits about trusty abuse, and Henley linked them to the ongoing *Holt* litigation.[49]

BACK IN COURT ON NONCOMPLIANCE, RACISM, AND VIOLENCE

"They get you up in the morning and give you two pieces of bread with syrup and tell you to pick cotton all day and when you don't pick enough they stick you on that wall so you don't get any supper or clean clothes."

—Hubert Glen Lewis, testifying, November, 1971[50]

The November 16, 1971 hearing began with several prisoners who described (and some demonstrated) the "Texas TV"—being forced to stand some feet from a wall for as long as six hours, hands behind them, trying to balance by pressing their foreheads against that wall. After witnesses told Henley they had been made to assume that position while waiting to testify, Henley called for its halt. When Hutto took the stand, he proved he was no Sarver, who had welcomed the federal court's help in getting better conditions. Hutto claimed that untrained and "overly enthusiastic prison employees" misapplied the Texas TV, which was supposed to include fifteen-minute breaks and end at two hours. Because the Texas TV could be "construed as corporal punishment" and he did not "want to have anything to do with corporal punishment," Hutto ordered its end.[51]

The Texas TV was not the only form of discipline Hutto admitted had "gotten out of hand." Several prisoners recounted shaved heads, "quiet cells," racial slurs, bars on religious observances by Muslims, beatings, a lack of sanitation, and harassment for seeking court help. Individuals reported being "stripped naked" and left on a cold, "bare concrete floor" in a tiny room whose toilet flushed (if at all) from the outside. Daniel Montgomery Jr. said he had no toilet paper, no paper to file writs, no light inside the cell, and no shower for twenty-eight days. Having been fed "grue," he lost weight and his voice. Henley heard from Hubert Glen Lewis that he had taken wax paper from food wrappings to try to get warmer in the cold cells. A few, including fifteen-year-old Tommy Oliver, spoke about beatings by Robert Britton, Tucker's Superintendent. Another described how, because he was at the hearing, he lost his job as a gate trusty and was reassigned to the kitchen. "[E]xtensive testimony" identified A. L. Lockhart (who came with Hutto from Texas and later became the Commissioner) as directing "racial slurs" at prisoners. Charles Richard Roth described that, after giving a "peace sign" to other prisoners who had attempted to escape, he had been ordered to join them atop a truck driven at high speed from the fields; because he had not been handcuffed, he avoided falling off while others had. Thereafter, they were all stripped and held for several days in the dark quiet cells.[52]

Kaplan and Holt Jr. put on a psychologist to substantiate the debilitation from the quiet cells. Such punishment was so "destructive" and "grossly detrimental" that it could leave "damage . . . literally for the rest of one's life." The state stipulated that one person had been held in a quiet cell for "28 days for refusing to work in the field," and Hutto reported it was a "mistake" to leave prisoners longer than fifteen days. The prisoners' lawyers also called Reverend J. F. Cooley, a chaplain who had resigned. He explained it was "very difficult to salvage a person" made to work nonstop with virtually no time "left for spiritual rehabilitation." Cooley told the press that segregation had returned "in full force," racial slurs were commonplace, and physical abuse widespread, with "brutality . . . the order of the day."[53]

Testimony also came from people who said they were prevented from practicing their religion. Hutto's position was that he did not want an "all-black meeting without supervision" but that, as long as no person was excluded "on a racial basis" and meetings were supervised, he would permit them. In contrast, Sarver (to whom the prisoners' lawyers had issued a subpoena) testified that he had

permitted "Black Muslims to meet and worship . . . and to use the
'X' in their names." To buttress Hutto, Arkansas' lawyers called
George Beto, the Director of the Texas Corrections Department
who had been "Hutto's boss." Beto vouched for quiet cells limited
to fifteen days, endorsed the Texas version of the Texas TV as a
good alternative to solitary confinement, and said he refused to
let prisoners change names or use "X" ("a man comes in with a
name"). He noted that Texas had put all the Black Muslims into
one prison, where they were "exceptionally good workers." As
discussed, Beto's name became inscribed in the jurisprudence of
prisoners' rights by a Supreme Court ruling against him and for
Fred Cruz, who alleged that Texas prisons discriminated against
him as a Buddhist.[54]

Chief Judge Henley also heard from Mark S. Richmond, an Assistant Director of the Federal Bureau of Prisons. Testifying for
the state, he sounded at times like a witness for the prisoners.
Richmond said he had been at Cummins in 1968; touring in 1971,
he saw improvements. Nonetheless, an "awful lot" needed to be
fixed, including ending the trusty system, developing prison industry, and lessening crowded barracks. Richmond called "inde-
fensible" the lack of adequate clothing and towels, yet "the first
order of priority was getting control of the prisons away from the
inmates."[55]

More sadness came into the courtroom when newspapers reported that Willie Stewart, a Black seventeen-year-old, had died
of unknown causes on a one-day commitment at Cummins. The
Reverend Elton Ballentine, a Service Coordinator, testified that
Stewart had "been forced to run up and down the cotton rows,"
that shots were fired at him, and that, chased by horse-riding
trustys, he fell to the ground. Ballentine saw "prison guards
drag" Stewart, unconscious, and leave him on the floor. Another
employee—Joe Lewis, a twenty-six-year-old "civilian tower guard"
who resigned thereafter—said he had been instructed to fire at
Stewart's feet "to scare him a bit. . . . I don't question it. I just
do it." The account prompted the governor to say that there was

"absolutely no excuse in civilized society" for putting a juvenile in a penitentiary.[56]

CONSTITUTIONAL "TOLERANCE": TIRED OR STRATEGIC?

"Perhaps if the sensibilities had not been dulled by revelations of Arkansas's wrenching experiences with the state penal system over the last five or six years, the responses to the testimony in the penal farm case last week would have been more decided."

—Editorial, *Arkansas Gazette*, November 27, 1971[57]

The details emerging from all Arkansas' detention centers were grotesque, and Henley had to flip back and forth between hearings on conditions in the prisons and those in the country farms. Once it became clear that more days were needed for the compliance hearing, Henley paused to take testimony about Pulaski County Penal Farm.

Over the course of three days, with Kaplan as one of the lawyers, witnesses reported violence, decrepit facilities, and segregation. Despite the 1968 *Jackson v. Bishop* and the *Holt II* rulings, jailors continued to whip and segregate prisoners. One witness described "switching" people—using a branch to strike people made to lie face down on the floor. A jailor explained he had beaten a detainee who had called him "a lot of foul names." People were held in isolation cells that had no heat, light, or plumbing; at times, no staff were on the premises. "[B]lack and white inmates" were kept separate and Black prisoners excluded from trusty slots. Henley toured the facility with its leaking roof, broken windows, and kitchen filth that exuded "the smell of death." On December 11, 1971, Henley found conditions there unconstitutional.[58]

This time, Henley was directive, as Judge Eisele had been in the Pulaski County Jail case. Henley ordered the end of whipping, racial segregation, and forcing people to spend time beyond their sentences. He called for roof repair, organized sick call, free-world employees, fixed heat and sanitation, and he forbade putting people in isolation cells during cold weather and, otherwise, for "quite short periods of time." Given that county voters had by then approved a

$3.2 million plan for a new facility, Henley required changes within thirty days.[59]

Yet when dealing with Cummins and Tucker, Henley's response seemed like what the press had described was the public's reaction to the county farm lawsuits—"dulled sensibilities." Henley's 1970 baseline of the "dark and evil world," coupled with the whipping, segregation, and filth at Pulaski, may have made the judge appreciate small changes, and he may have wanted to learn what Governor Bumpers, who said it was "inexcusable" to leave a person for a month in a quiet cell, would require of Hutto.

Whether Henley was tired or strategic, the judge's "remarks" from the bench did not include clear prescriptions. Although "much remain[ed] to be done," Henley took solace that new filings of staff misconduct were "unlike those we heard before" about "brutality, extortion, and sexual abuse." Henley credited the "people of Arkansas, speaking through the legislature," for having made "reasonable financial provision," such that trustys no longer had "power over the daily life of other inmates." Yet staff "quality" was a problem, as it was small "comfort to an inmate to have a sadistic trusty replaced by a dishonest, sadistic guard." Moreover, facilities, especially at the women's unit and in the barracks, were problematic. As for religion and racial discrimination, Henley commented that people of all faiths had a right to observe their religion, even as prison officials had a right to know the purpose of a meeting. Likewise, the prison could insist that mail use the name of the prisoner as committed, while prisoners were "at liberty" to use other names inside the prison.[60]

Henley acknowledged the "fear on the part of the inmate population"; testimony had revealed a "mood of oppression," stemming possibly from due process problems and censorship as well as from reprisals when people sought relief in courts. Chagrined about retaliation, Henley found it "most suspicious when an inmate testifies here and within a few days . . . winds up in the hole." Addressing the death of Stewart when on a one-day sentence, Henley provided a hair-raising summary: that Stewart had been "hazed," shot at, slapped, bruised, and forced to "dance with a hoe handle" while saying that "I ain't gonna to steal no more." A person on a day sentence ought not be "beaten, or abused or mistreated," yet Henley accepted the medical examiner's explanation that Stewart had died of a rare blood condition rather than abuse.[61]

To turn his remarks into enforceable orders, Chief Judge Henley read into the record a lengthy excerpt from his 1965 *Talley v. Stephens* decision ordering an end to interference with access to court. Henley noted that "technically, Mr. Hutto, you and the members of your staff are not in actual violation," but "the Court is convinced that, as some echelons at least," prison staff were trying "to convince prisoners that it is not in their best interest to file writs or to testify." Henley explained that prisoners were to have "unrestricted access to the courts." In closing, the judge noted he was considering the prisoners' lawyers request for compensation.[62]

BUMPERS: "AT THE BOTTOM"

"If the state has the right to deprive a person of his freedom, it has a legal and moral obligation to protect that inmate during his period of incarceration."

—Governor Dale Bumpers, December 10, 1971[63]

Governor Bumpers got the message: "We're at the bottom looking up." While not firing Hutto (who had legislative support), Bumpers asked the Board of Correction for action, whether Hutto concurred or not. With "safety and security of the inmates" his "top priority," Bumpers sought the end of "terrorism and brutality," gun ammunition "strictly accounted for," and no "shots . . . fired except in . . . emergency." Bumpers called for reform of discipline, limits on quiet cells, and a ban on the Texas TV along with other forms of corporal punishment. Because "racial slurs and racial discrimination shall not be tolerated," staff should be fired for such violations.[64]

On December 11, Henley set forth his bench remarks into a decree, formally retaining jurisdiction. Within days, the Board of Correction endorsed several of Bumpers' proposals, and more disquieting news surfaced. Elijah Coleman, the Executive Director of the Arkansas Council on Human Relations, sent a report to the Governor's Office about that Council's November visit to Cummins. (Since Rockefeller's first term, that Council went four times a year.) The Council recounted that more than seventy prisoners had food poisoning, apparently sourced in rotten sandwiches. Moreover, "incoming prisoners" had their heads shaved; naked and without privacy, they were sprayed for body lice. Council members saw prisoners in the cotton fields struggling to pick the amounts demanded. If they failed to "meet work quotas," prisoners were subjected to standing "for seven hours without talking, eating, [or] going to [the] bathroom." On November 11, seven prisoners were "'on the wall' for not making their quotas." Several Muslims described not getting a pork-free diet. Many prisoners told the Council that their mail was read, and some of it lost. Other common "gripes" included a "[l]ack of toilet paper and soap," and the "drastic changes with new administrators" who had brought in severe hair cutting, security, and oppressive micromanagement.[65]

When the Board of Correction visited Cummins, a prisoner was stabbed. The press noted that the population was up to 1,340; barracks were "so crowded that the beds" had to be stacked, and "as many as 30 men" had to sleep on the floor. That crowding reflected the drop in the parole grant rate. The drumbeat of dreadful life in detention continued with a settlement of the Mississippi County Penal Farm case. Judge Eisele made public the stipulated plan that included keeping all people under the age of seventeen out of the facility, new modes of classification, improved sanitation and food, clothing satisfactory for the climate, the training of staff, and an end to mail censorship.[66]

In sum, while *Holt II* had succeeded in making the prison system "a hot political potato" and state officials conceded changes were needed, incarcerated individuals continued to ask Arkansas' federal judges to bear witness to the ongoing horrors. Henley repeatedly said that promises of a better future provided "little comfort," yet he did not direct specific changes.

23

A DIFFERENT "POSTURE"

BASELINES MOVING, AND NOT

"Prison reform as a viable political issue has evolved from a totally non-topic to a matter of almost daily attention. The prison system, today, ranks as one of the top two or three issues on the governor's desk."

—Editorial, *Northwest Arkansas Times*, December, 1971[1]

The litigation was "in a posture quite different from that in which it stood in 1969 and 1970."

—Chief Judge Henley, withdrawing
Holt v. Hutto (*Holt III*), August 13, 1973[2]

By 1971's end, Henley, aware of the lack of compliance, retained jurisdiction "until . . . satisfied definitely that the institutions in question meet constitutional standards." During 1972 and 1973, he heard evidence of a myriad of failings. Yet in *Holt III* (which he called his "last long opinion"), Henley explained he did not "foresee" a need to order "closing of one or both of the prisons or enjoining the . . . reception" of people into those facilities. Moreover, even as "inmate complaints [were] going to continue to be received," it was not "necessary or desirable to retain further supervisory jurisdiction." This chapter tracks what Henley learned during that interval that kept prison *reform* a problem ("on the desk") for the various men who sat as governor in Arkansas and elsewhere, and explores why in 1973 Chief Judge Henley decided to deem the litigation done.[3]

Conceptually, something *had* changed, and Arkansas was *right* that *Holt v. Sarver* (*Holt II*) had substantially altered its "sovereignty." One example is the term "excessive force," denoting undue violence by state actors. The 1969 acquittals of Bruton and other staff who had tortured prisoners made plain that violence against prisoners went unpunished. Indeed, the words "excessive force" rarely appeared in the legal lexicon; one computer search of federal case law found a handful of mentions about prisoners before 1980.

But in the aftermath of *Holt II*, Henley and others developed the proposition that, while "force" could be licit, "excessive force" was not. In 1973, at the behest of a pretrial detainee allegedly beaten by a guard threatening to "break [him] in half" for not following orders, a federal appellate court required a hearing on whether the force aimed to "maintain or restore discipline" or was "maliciously and sadistically" imposed in violation of the Constitution.[4] More than a decade later, in *Whitley v. Albers*, the Supreme Court agreed that the Constitution protected individuals against some forms of in-custody violence but imposed a significant burden on a victim to prove that "unnecessary and wanton infliction of pain" had occurred. Hundreds of opinions debated those contours, as corrections administrators and police promulgated policies addressing limits on use of force.[5] Failures of implementation abound; audits find violence and rape; prisoners report assaults, and people in confinement often lose lawsuits. Nonetheless, force that once needed *no* justification has come to be questioned and, on some occasions—famously in 2020 after the death of George Floyd—successfully prosecuted as a crime.

Henley, at the front end of this shift, had grounds for seeing progress. Yet Henley's 1973 decision reflected that misery produced a pathetic baseline; dragging people out of utter filth and chaotic violence constituted a form of "progress" that became justification for not doing more. In addition, the prisoners' lawyers had told Henley they could not serve indefinitely without compensation, which meant the judge had two funding problems: getting the legislature to put taxpayer money into prisoners' safety and getting pay for the lawyers.

As I explain in the next chapter, prisons did not leave Henley's "desk" because, based on the "firm conviction that the Arkansas correctional system [was] still unconstitutional," the Eighth Circuit sent the case back in 1974 to him to resolve remaining, "major constitutional deficiencies."[6] In this chapter, I explain Henley's decision, which he may have written *to be reversed* and get more legal capital to push the state harder.

ENJOINING HUTTO AND "ALL" HIS SUBORDINATES

The last *Holt* docket entry of 1971 was a précis of orders flowing from the judge's discursive remarks a few weeks earlier. Responding to his own comment that current staff members were not legally bound by prior orders, Chief Judge Henley added people up and down the hierarchy. "[T]he term 'defendants'" encompassed all members of the Board of Corrections; the new Director of Correction (Terrell Don Hutto), as well as the Superintendents of Tucker (Robert Britton), of Cummins (A. L. Lockhart), the Women's Reformatory (Helen Carruthers), the Head of Security at Cummins (Cecil Boren), and "their successors; and all officers, including trusty guards, and employees of the Department of Correction and their successors." That wording aimed to make each of these many people individually liable (and subject to contempt) if "inflicting any cruel or unusual punishment" or "interfering in any way with any inmate in his right of access to the courts, whether State or Federal, or to counsel." What Henley could not do was change Arkansas Department of Correction (ADC) leadership; unlike Sarver, Hutto pushed back repeatedly. As one commentator explained, of the five people running ADC between 1968 until 1982 (the lifespan of the lawsuit), "Hutto emerged as the least cooperative."[7]

Hutto proffered an upbeat public narrative to deflect responsibility. Criticizing the press as unduly harsh *on* guards and insufficiently attentive to abuse suffered *by* guards, Hutto noted progress: "no more" armed trustys in the fields and new free-world employees would number forty-six, paid by $231,000 with money from the Federal Emergency Employment Act. Escapes were down, the physical plant improved, and fewer gunshots fired. The press lauded Hutto for launching basic and vocational education and noted he had appointed Helen Carruthers, a Black woman, to head the women's unit, housing "28 black inmates and 17 whites."[8]

Other stories were bleaker. An eighteen-year-old, on a one-day sentence at Cummins, told reporters that along with three others, "[w]e had to get down on all fours and oink like pigs, cackle like turkeys, and quack like ducks," were forced to dunk in "water and excrement" and to suck on a guard's pistol. Another reporter noted that, after Henley raised "particular concern," two staff were fired for "excessive and unnecessary force"; they had beaten prisoners after an attempted escape. Another prisoner alleged being "starved, beaten, and refused medical treatment" because he would not "play the role of an Uncle Tom." These accounts were part of why Governor Bumpers was less sanguine than Hutto. The prison farms' 1971 income tallied about $1,793,500, and Bumpers, wanting legislative funding, said the state had "not really faced up to the problems" resulting from prisons operating "very much the same way they were a hundred years ago."[9]

Instead of reducing the population as proposed by John Haley at the end of his five-year term as Chair of the Board of Correction, new construction was underway. Arkansas' Commission on Crime and Law Enforcement allocated a half million dollars in federal funds for a minimum-security, single-cell unit to hold 248 people. ADC also contracted to build a new facility for women, gained permission for a "non-geographical" school district, and planned a rodeo. Missing was money for health care, which remained abysmal; in March of 1972, when nine prisoners were treated for tuberculosis, some 1,300 had not been screened. Discrimination against Muslims was abundant, as was violence.[10]

Yet "favorable publicity" for Hutto came from former New Jersey Governor Richard Hughes who, as discussed, chaired the American Bar Association's Commission on Correctional Services. After a prison tour, Hughes, speaking to the Arkansas Bar Association, described problems that did not stem from "bad intent or nonfeasance" in the state's prisons he called "progressive." Soon thereafter, Bumpers and Hutto succeeded in getting a record $4 million for the prisons' 1972–1973 budget.[11] But those funds would not undo what prisoners were experiencing.

TERRORIZED PRISONERS, RACIST OPPRESSION, AND LAWYERS WITHOUT PAY

A "repressive psychological atmosphere designed to force the inmate into total submission and willingness to give up even his most basic rights."

—Philip Kaplan to Chief Judge Henley, December 1, 1972[12]

In the fall of 1972, after Bumpers won the Democratic primary and was en route to reelection, he commended Hutto's "masterful job"; the "reduction in escapes, improved inmate security, abolition of the trusty guard system and indiscriminate firing of weapons . . . [spoke] for themselves."[13] Were today's "fact-checking" in place, Bumpers' assertions would have been debunked. The trusty system was not fully phased out until after Bumpers left the governorship in 1975 when he defeated and replaced US Senator William Fulbright. And before then, the Eighth Circuit had directed Henley to get back to work to end "sub-human conditions" at the prisons.

The reality came through the petitions piling up on Henley's desk, and the volume was a problem. As Chief Judge, Henley told his fellow judges, Oren Harris and Thomas Eisele, that each filing should, for "statistical and case load purposes," be distributed among the three but that he would hold hearings related to prison conditions. Further, issues of discrimination against "Black Muslims" fell "into a somewhat different category" from other civil rights cases, so he would keep those, especially as "one of the reasons prompting Mr. Kaplan's willingness to remain in the overall prison litigation is his interest in the Black Muslim situation." In advance of a November, 1972 evidentiary hearing, Henley told the state that its "list of writs [was] woefully incomplete"; his staff's "Writ Writers Journal" had more. Kaplan's archived notes were full of prisoners reporting they were "fed a starvation diet," held in chains in dark "quiet cells," beaten, and "punished for not picking enough cotton."[14]

This "constant stream of complaints," Henley said, if "only partially valid," made plain that officials were not following court orders. Henley consolidated "34 individual and class action cases" with the ongoing litigation. During fourteen hearing days in 1972 and 1973, more than thirty prisoners testified. Press recounts of their testimony were depressingly familiar. One reported that prisoners were made "constantly" to run back and forth from the fields. Others testified about "verbal, physical and mental abuse," the lack of mental health care, and being beaten.[15]

Several Muslim prisoners chronicled discrimination. Alvin X Higgins, a Tucker prisoner and "acting minister for Black Muslims," testified that prison authorities had confiscated and destroyed the *Mohammed Speaks* newsletter, that Muslim meetings were relegated to a noisy kitchen, and that a list of attendees was "given to the FBI." Another described being beaten by Tucker's Superintendent Robert Britton, who said he did not like "black folks." Kaplan was back in court thereafter on behalf of Robert X White, who reported being permanently assigned to maximum security because his religious beliefs were "a threat." Another account came from Ervin X Lacy, who sent Kaplan an impressive class action complaint, citing several federal decisions and detailing violations of religious liberty.[16]

The state's defense witnesses included Cummins Superintendent A. L. Lockhart, who insisted he did not "tolerate the use of force or racial epithets"; one warden had been "terminated on the spot" for having "pushed an inmate unnecessarily." The Superintendent of Tucker denied misuse of prisoners' "welfare funds" for remodeling homes, and Hutto testified ADC's revised rulebook complied with the court's order on discipline. Dr. Thomas Wortham, a physician whom Bumpers had appointed to the Board of Correction, described convening a "seven-man advisory committee" to study health care issues. Four correctional officers also testified. One explained that "mixing [races] . . . would cause trouble." Another admitted to using racial epithets but "not in the presence of inmates."[17]

When the first phase of the hearing ended, Kaplan summarized the evidence for Henley. (Lawyers draft such documents in the hopes that judges will borrow from them when writing decisions.) Kaplan described the "continued use of physical force" as a "most troubling aspect of the testimony." The prevalence of "brutality and physical abuse" included that the Texas TV remained in use. Further, "top officials" were involved in "physical confrontations . . . to intimidate and restrain inmates from testifying." Kaplan wrote about discipline meted out and good time lost without any fair process to determine what, if anything, was merited, and he underscored targeted discrimination against Muslims. Furthermore, barracks were "severely overcrowded"; prisoners had inadequate "outerwear and undergarments"; and they suffered from a "total lack of complete dental and eye care." As to the law, Kaplan reminded Henley that prison litigation was "the fastest growing area," with new decisions coming out regularly. In addition, Kaplan told the judge he could not continue to volunteer "without some hope of compensation." Kaplan pointed out that the state was paying outside lawyers to help it defend. Henley nonetheless continued to send new complaints to Kaplan.[18]

FROM THE *PEA PICKERS PICAYUNE* TO THE *CUMMINS JOURNAL*

After *Holt II*, the legislature put some taxpayer money into prisons. In 1973, it authorized more than $7.5 million for two years.[19] And, amid continuing violence, intimidation, and discrimination, the prisoner–publishers of the *Cummins Journal* discussed improvements after the court order. The prisoners had changed the name from *Pea Pickers Picayune* because it implied "our characters and our institutions are of a mediocre, and all agrarian nature"; the new title denoted a "liberal" publication of which they could "identify . . . and be proud." For a few years, that monthly *Journal* (priced at fifty cents) mixed essays, information about activities, profiles of people, national prison news, cartoons, drawings, and an occasional glimpse abroad, such as "A Land without Prisons" about the Netherlands.[20]

A *Journal* editor commented that no one "would . . . have speculated—not even in a remote sense of the word—that the inmate council would be privileged to meet with the State's Correction Board" monthly. The informal discussions produced concessions, such as bedding and clothes, two packages per week of tobacco, a movie committee, and ending Hutto's "practice of head shaving." In addition, the kitchen, run by a former Navy man, no longer served only "cowpeas and rice" but clean and "wholesome food" protected by a new refrigeration system; some of Johnny Cash's $5,000 bought two ice machines. A tentative budget (beyond what had been "dreamed of") was pending; if funded, a million dollars were earmarked for salaries. Further, because the prisons were "under attack in the federal courts," $95,200 in federal funds went for drafting a long-range plan (as discussed). Legal aid services, federally funded at $27,655, were coming along with $37,712 more to hire a full-time lawyer. The *Journal* later noted the arrival of an Arkansas native who was a 1972 graduate of a DC law school; he was to help on civil and criminal matters, including habeas petitions, but not bring lawsuits against the prisons. The *Journal* published his monthly "law report," responding to questions such as how to get a transcript for appeal.[21]

Readers also learned about the Cummins Jaycees chapter that sponsored sports teams (the "Cummins Outlaws") and a basketball tournament; it had pulled off a "miracle" by hosting a banquet where outside speakers were given a "good meal" and awards. In addition, the *Journal* republished materials from prison newspapers such as Louisiana's *Angolite*, as well as information on lawsuits, admonitions about substance abuse, poems, profiles of the "inmate of the month," and essays about women in prison. Its national news included proposals of the National Council on Crime and Delinquency for compensation of incarcerated people's labor, the campaign for enfranchisement of "ex-convicts" in Maryland, and excerpts from New York State Special Commission on Attica's 514-page report including that "prisoners should retain all the rights of citizens, except that of liberty."[22]

The misery of Arkansas' prisons also came through. The pressure to make farm crop quotas was reflected in a photograph of the first 500-pound bale of cotton in 1972. With more acres cultivated, prison officials wanted a yield beyond the 1,669 bales the prior year. By picking 7,500 pounds in three days, five prisoners won a three-day contest that gave them time off. Incarcerated readers also learned that Bruce Jackson, described as reporting for the *New York Times*, was at Cummins to take photographs; the *Journal* encouraged people to sign a "photo release form." Although the

Cummins Journal did not explain the background, Jackson was a folklorist and ethnographer who had done a photo shoot at Texas' Ramsey Prison Farm, where Hutto had been the warden. Hutto gave Jackson open access; between 1971 and 1975, Jackson took some 5,000 photographs in Arkansas.[23] Figures 23.1 and 23.2 depict what unmechanized farming meant for prisoners.

FIGURE 23.1 *Cummins Prison Farm, Grady, Arkansas*, photograph by Bruce Jackson, from the series *Inside the Wire*, 1975, courtesy of the photographer

FIGURE 23.2 *Cummins Prison Farm, Grady, Arkansas*, photograph by Bruce Jackson, from the series *Inside the Wire*, 1975, courtesy of the photographer

"NOT THE SAME SYSTEM"

Henley's twenty-three-page opinion, *Holt v. Hutto* (*Holt III*), is a heartbreaking account of a willingness to find permissible appalling treatment of prisoners. Citing the ADC's change in written policies, which no longer officially approved unconstitutional practices, Henley concluded that inadequate staff were at the "root of most of the serious problems in the Department." Yet the judge turned the prisons back to the very people whose deficits he documented. As an incarcerated person pointed out in the *Cummins Journal*, Henley's conclusion was "confusing"; despite finding the prisons "poorly administered," he left "most of the inmate problems" to the administration.[24]

Can sense be made? Henley may well have thought that, having succeeded in getting some legislative funding and new policies, he could not fix the remaining "administrative" problems. Yet, given that Henley's decision detailed ongoing failures, he may have been worried about his "sagging authority" and wrote to pave the way for the appellate courts to be give him more leverage. Henley may also have been ambivalent, and he was clearly tired. Even as he let go, Henley called for changes, coupled with a reminder that compliance failures would subject defendants to contempt.[25]

The ruling is shadowed by what Henley had seen before. What psychologists call "framing effects" meant that Henley could describe "marked improvements." Attesting as if a witness, Henley recounted that his own "experience with the Department . . . extend[ed] over a period of at least eight years"—citing the 1965 *Talley v. Stephens* case (where this book began). Since then, the law, his work, and the prison system had changed. In 1970, the "Court was dealing with official prescribed or sanctioned conditions and practices," and the "controlling facts were essentially undisputed." By 1973, even as important facts were "sharply disputed," the ADC no longer approved and in some respects prohibited the conduct prisoners challenged. Crediting the state's legislature, Robert Sarver, Winthrop Rockefeller, and the current administration, Arkansas prisons were "simply not the same system" that had existed before.

Moreover, Henley knew prisoners *everywhere* lacked care and states provide little for *anyone*, incarcerated or not. Although the barracks remained "seriously overcrowded" and "inmate assaults on other inmates and fights between inmates still oc-cur[ed]," Henley opined that "all prisons" had such problems. Henley took comfort that Tucker, then housing 300 people, was no longer a source of many lawsuits and the Women's Reforma-tory, "capably administered by a Negro Matron . . . appears to be a constitutionally tolerable institution." Henley discounted the many complaints in the new maximum-security unit holding 10 percent of the 1,100–1,200 people at Cummins—whom Henley described as the "most dangerous and unstable inmates." Thus, while "some additional injunctive relief" was needed and "some problem areas of constitutional significance" continued, Henley largely pulled out.[26]

Henley provided a point-by-point account of facets he found constitutionally "tolerable." Henley pronounced the trusty system "essentially . . . dismantled"; he was "confident" remaining trustys did not "represent the threat" they had. Moreover, a lawyer served "full time as Legal Advisor," and the law library was adequate. Prison officials no longer opened outgoing mail to lawyers and courts; incoming privileged correspondence was opened only to check for contraband. Facilities, even as they needed "serious . . . improvement," sufficed; shortages of underwear and laundry came in part from "careless" prisoners. Yet, even as the judge aimed to "accentuate the positive," his account exposed a host of "deficien-cies," attributed to a lack of funds and the prisons' "rural locations" far from services.[27]

CONSTITUTIONAL TOLERABILITY DESPITE "DEFICIENCIES" IN HEALTH CARE

"Dental services" consisted only of "extractions and the supplying of false teeth," and "mentally ill or emotionally disturbed [people]" had no care.

—Chief Judge Henley, *Holt III*, August 13, 1973[28]

A painful example of Henley's low expectations was his unwillingness to use available legal principles to hold the state accountable
for the lack of medical services. Henley described them to be "the
best" available, given "the resources at [ADC's] command." That
"best" included no full-time physician on staff, no automatic segregation of people with active tuberculosis "from other inmates,"
no "dental services" except extractions, and no services for serious
medical and psychological needs.[29]

Henley's evaluation rested on a test he crafted—had authorities "intentionally denied medical and dental services . . . within
the power of the Department to provide"? The phrase "within the
power of the Department to provide" was deadly—literally and fig-
uratively. Henley categorized some claims as not getting treatment
"as quickly" as desired and commented that "many people in the
free world would have the same complaints." But free people could
seek doctors, while prisoners could not. Henley did not mention
testimony from prison officials about the inadequate care and by
Dr. Wortham, a Board of Correction member, about the expert
study documenting the failings.[30]

What health care could Henley have required? The issue did
not reach the Supreme Court until 1976 when, as discussed, *Estelle v. Gamble* recognized that prison officials violated the Eighth
Amendment if deliberately indifferent to serious medical needs.
Lower courts had paved the way, relying—when presented with
dire facts—on the "liberty" protected by the Due Process Clause
or the Eighth Amendment ban on "cruel" punishments.[31] Indeed,
Henley's 1970 *Holt II* decision cited the absence of medical care as
contributing to unconstitutional conditions. Moreover, governing
Eighth Circuit law included a 1970 decision by Judge Donald Lay
that Henley did not mention. After a district court reviewed a doctor's report at the federal medical facility and concluded that "reasonable medical care" had been provided, the Circuit affirmed. In
the absence of "factual allegations of obvious neglect or intentional
mistreatment," courts were to rely on prison authorities' reports,
rather than second-guess physicians. Arkansas, however, provided
no health care to "second-guess," and Henley could have found

"obvious neglect or intentional mistreatment."[32] Moreover, Henley could have drawn on a 1972 decision by Judge Frank Johnson, detailing fourteen health care failings in Alabama's prisons, issuing ten directives, and calling for reporting within six months.[33]

BRUTALITY AND RACISM

"[T]here is simply no excuse for hitting, slapping, or kicking [recaptured escapees] after they ceased to be a source of any real danger to their captors . . . The prison population was about "50 percent black" and the staff "[f]rom top to bottom . . . predominantly white."

—Chief Judge Henley, *Holt III*, August 13, 1973[34]

Henley's account of daily life provided a similarly oppressive picture. Prisoners lived with awful working conditions, verbal threats, "offensive racial and other allusions," retaliation for petitioning the court, and physical violence. Prisoners were hit with "striking weapons" ("slappers" or blackjacks) and were required to run to the fields in front of horses and cars. Henley noted that brutality (euphemistically "use of force") was common "in prisons all over the United States" and provided a litany of justifications—self-defense, "breaking up fights," "compelling obedience to lawful orders where milder measures fail in protecting State property," "preventing escapes," and recapturing individuals. Yet Henley did not find "serious" problems; the force was generally "in reasonable proportion to the violence displayed by the inmates," who "brought it on themselves." On the other hand, Henley singled out Superintendent Britton for having been "involved personally" in "unnecessary and unreasonable force" directed at individuals captured after escapes and posing no danger.[35]

Henley's account of the administration was likewise disheartening. Henley's tepid characterization of senior management (Hutto, Lockhart, Britton, and Boren) as "qualified" came with "reservations as to particular individuals." "Up to a point," they tried to do "good jobs," but "lower echelon personnel" were "unprofessional," "poorly paid," had "little training or experience," were often "uncultured" or "poorly educated," and some were "perhaps too young" for the authority they held. Moreover, staff from "top to bottom" were "predominantly white." White staff members on discipline committees could be hostile to prisoners, especially "black inmates" whom Henley described as "neither well educated nor industrious" and "highly suspicious of those in authority." The result was "friction, stress, unrest, and at times violence." Thus, although the written policies were acceptable, the practices were not; deficits, especially when "race [was] involved," were of "constitutional significance."[36]

Further, as Henley detailed, it was "thoroughly established" that Black Muslims were a "religious sect . . . entitled within reasonable limitations dictated by the conditions of prison life" to observe their religion. Yet the prison had not made accommodations. Staff imposed restrictions on meetings that did "not exist with respect to other religious groups," and "for a time at least lists of inmates who attended Muslim meetings were . . . turned over to the Federal Bureau of Investigation." Moreover, Muslims were obliged not to eat pork, but "a great deal of the food . . . [was] cooked in pork grease or fat." Henley ordered an end to "undue restrictions upon the Muslims" while concluding that officials did not "intentionally" discriminate. As a practical matter, avoiding attributing racist intent to individuals could make them less resistant to change, and at the time, a violation of the Equal Protection Clause did not require a finding of *intent*; impact sufficed. (In 1976, the Supreme Court required intentionality as a predicate to a remedy.)[37]

Henley also reported that, while Cummins had been desegregated, its maximum-security unit was not. Citing the 1968 Supreme Court's *Lee v. Washington* (discussed earlier) for the proposition that not everyone had to be assigned to "integrated cells," Henley ordered the end of the "general policy of racial segregation." Atypically, Henley was concrete: If race was used, the prison's superintendent had to provide written reasons about why the "inmate in question should not be confined in an integrated cell."[38] Turning to classification, jobs, and discipline, Henley described what today is called "implicit bias," documented through rapid association tests demonstrating the ease with which people equate doctors with white men and have negative stereotypes of men and women of color. Writing in 1973, Henley explained that discrimination, "covert, subtle, or even unconscious," was "hard to establish" and "get rid of." Moreover, the "appearance of discrimination"—even when not present—was a problem that would undermine "race relations in a prison."[39]

Henley found that, aside from maximum-security cell assignment, no "open or gross discrimination against black inmates" existed, but "some covert discrimination" did; "white prison administrators sitting in judgment on black inmates might not consciously be aware that their reactions to rule violations by blacks, as opposed to whites, may constitute a form of discrimination." Cummins' monthly reports showed that "a black inmate accused of a disciplinary violation" was not more likely to be found guilty but, if found guilty, was more likely to suffer "severe penalties." Sanctions included "reductions in classification, adverse changes in job assignments, loss of good time, and confinement in punitive isolation" that lasted longer than time served by "a white inmate."

In terms of discrimination for job assignments, Henley saw a cloudy picture, perhaps because of his *own* implicit biases. He wrote that it was "safe to say that the majority of black inmates" were qualified only for physical labor; in the "manual agricultural labor as a member of the hoe squad," white and Black laborers were roughly equal. Yet, for other job assignments, "Negroes should occupy some job slots" that they did not; the cumulative impact of disparities in punishment and jobs related to the "appearance" and to "actual existence of racial discrimination." For "black inmates . . . [to] make a better adjustment to prison life and . . . conform," they needed to "believe affirmatively that members of their race [were] being treated fairly and without discrimination on account of race."[40]

SUPPLEMENTAL ORDERS: RACISM, DISCIPLINE, AND PAYING PRISONERS' LAWYERS

Holt and Kaplan provided "valuable services not only to the inmates and to the Court but to the people of the State of Arkansas."

—Chief Judge Henley, *Holt III*, August 1973

When calling his work on Arkansas' penitentiaries to a close, Henley issued supplemental orders and retained power to "impose sanctions for violations of existing decrees." Henley reinforced prior rulings by enjoining "discrimination in any manner against prison inmates who are . . . Black Muslims," as well as discrimination in placement in maximum-security cells. The judge added three suggestions: enforce rules on "employee language" (in other words, derogatory epithets needed to stop), post rules prohibiting race discrimination, and create a recruitment plan for "black employees."[41]

Henley also addressed discipline. Henley reviewed the Inmate Handbook, counted twenty-five offenses, eleven punishments and described the decision-making process as "not ideal." The Committee, comprised usually of three staff, often met at night and provided limited opportunities to rebut accusations. Reasoning that people were entitled to be heard and to an impartial decision, Henley instructed that committees should convene during the day "within 72 hours" after an alleged infraction; tapes or transcripts had to be made and preserved.

As to the sanctions, Henley concluded that the isolation cells were no longer overcrowded, that light and ventilation were acceptable, and that grue ("nourishing but tasteless") was not unconstitutional. Further, while "administrative segregation" was "more rigorous than may be absolutely necessary," it did not violate the Constitution, nor did the "soundproof" quiet cells with no fixtures and double doors that left prisoners "in complete darkness." Because people were held for "quite brief" stays and a bit of light sometimes came in, the cells were not "inhumane." (Recall that in 1934, the League of Nations had sanctioned, "in exceptional cases," the use of "dark cells" but the 1955 UN Standard Minimum Rules on the Treatment of Prisoners called for a ban, as did the American Correctional Association's 1966 Manual.) Henley had less tolerance for the treatment of younger people. Punishing such prisoners of "comparatively tender years" by transferring them from Tucker to Cummins, with its "hardened criminals," needed to be time bound. Henley required evaluation within fourteen days and no more than an additional thirty days at Cummins.[42]

Before concluding, Henley turned to lawyers' fees. But for their work, he would not have had the facts or the law to render judgment. The judge framed his decision to compensate Holt Jr. and Kaplan not as a "punishment or sanction" but as recognition that the lawyers had provided "valuable services" to everyone in the state, to whom the prison system "belongs." For work from 1969 to the 1973 opinion, Henley required defendants to pay, "as soon as possible," $8,000 (about $49,000 in 2024 dollars), plus $502.80 for law students. Henley knew that appeals could come from both sides; he authorized prisoners to be able to appeal without paying fees ("in forma pauperis").[43]

NOT ENDING: "BE STILL"

"The Arkansas prison system encountered its most severe criticism in recent years . . . as eight former employe[e]s testified before an investigating legislative panel."

—*Arkansas Gazette*, March 22, 1974[44]

In addition to the anticipated appeal, more prison miseries made the news. "Cummins unrest" was the description of a "disturbance" erupting Christmas Eve in 1973 that involved about twenty people held in punitive isolation, where property was destroyed. The press also covered alleged misuse of public funds, unfair treatment of prison staff, and racial discrimination. In January of 1974, a former Cummins assistant superintendent claimed Hutto had forced employees out to add more Texans. Legislators called on Bumpers to investigate, who declined. The Legislative Council voted to investigate Hutto's hiring practices and the use of state vehicles. In the interim, after a three-day hearing, the Board of Correction concluded that allegations of racial discrimination (not "planned or intentional") toward both prisoners and staff members had merit, that some prison officials had used "poor judgment," and that policy changes were needed, especially in accounting for funds. About sixteen employees resigned; having talked to the Board, they said they were going to lose their jobs anyway.[45]

Hutto broadcast other news: that in 1973 the prison farms had netted a "gross profit of $3,258,020.89"—$700,000 more than the year before.[46] That accounting did not eclipse that, in March of 1974, the Legislative Council's Committee on Charitable, Penal, and Correctional Institutions heard allegations that a supervisor told a guard about a plan to "kill" a Black prisoner held in solitary, that correction officers "falsified" disciplinary reports after they had assaulted prisoners, and that Hutto "doesn't really know what's going on in the prison." Singled out for criticism was A. L. Lockhart, the Cummins Superintendent said to have used excessive force on prisoners and misused state property. Hutto again tried a counternarrative: that Arkansas was en route to having the "most modern . . . correctional facilities in the nation" by virtue of new federal funding. Almost $2.8 million was coming from the Law Enforcement Assistance Administration for a new "hospital and diagnostic center," to be in place by 1978.[47]

But press accounts of hearings before Chief Judge Henley undercut Hutto's spin. Over several summer days in 1974, prisoners testified about being "gassed and beaten," while guards described prisoners who had "curse[d]" at them and thrown whatever they could, including "excrement, urine and doorknobs." After the state described the "justified" use of mace and rested its case, the press said that Henley "begged" for people to be "still"; he would issue another opinion after the Eighth Circuit ruled on his *Holt III* decision.[48]

24

COURTS AS CATALYSTS, CONSTRAINTS, AND GREEN LIGHTS

"In thee O Lord, do I put my trust: . . . Deliver me in thy righteousness and cause me to escape . . . out of the hand of the unrighteous and cruel man."

—Robert Finney's handwritten filing, September 15, 1972[1]

"[T]here is no such thing as a 'perfect' prison system, but this does not relieve respondents of their duty to make their system a constitutional one in which the human dignity of each individual inmate is respected."

—Judge Donald Lay, *Finney v. Arkansas Board of Correction*, October 10, 1974[2]

Robert Finney was one of many prisoners seeking "deliverance" from Arkansas prisons. Chief Judge Henley had tried to step away, but the Eighth Circuit insisted—based on the record of arbitrariness, brutality, and racism Henley had compiled—that he could not. Here, I focus on what the public and Henley learned between 1974 and 1976 as Henley continued to sit in judgment of prison practices.

This chapter explains the Eighth Circuit's reversal and the responses of the litigants and Judge Henley. After being pushed to assess whether Arkansas' prisons were taking steps to improve safety and to enable rehabilitation, Henley set caps on the population and limits on the number of days spent in isolation which, he reasoned, was akin to an indeterminate sentence with no rehabilitative utility.

Yet, when shoring up directives, Henley did not insist on the level of safety the Eighth Circuit had called for, nor could Henley stop the conflicts between the state and prisoners about what was licit treatment of people in detention. Henley's 1976 opinion, which included another order for payment to prisoners' lawyers, was his swan song in the Penitentiary Cases, which thereafter continued under Judge Eisele until 1982. By then, in a case from Ohio, the Supreme Court had limited federal judges' authority to require rehabilitative efforts in their evaluations of prison conditions' constitutionality.

THE "HELL-HOLE" AT CUMMINS

When before the Eighth Circuit for a second time, the case's name had changed from *Holt v. Hutto* to *Finney v. Arkansas Board of Correction*. The first appellant, Robert Finney, made news in 1972 when describing Cummins' isolation unit as "nothing but a 'Hell-Hole,'" where guards pitted prisoners against each other. In his lawsuit's "prayer for relief" (the phrase used to request remedies), Finney added "Amen." On appeal, as part of a group represented by Jack Holt Jr. and Philip Kaplan, Finney did not get release but did get recognition of the wickedness of Arkansas prisons.

On October 10, 1974, Judge Lay, joined by Judge Gerald Heaney and District Judge Edward Devitt, issued a twenty-one-page opinion that offered a vision of a "constitutional" but not "perfect" prison far afield from what Arkansas (and many other jurisdictions) provided. Because "segregation from society and loss of one's liberty" were the sole deliberate deprivations permitted, prisons were to be "safe and sanitary," and purposeful efforts toward "rehabilitation" requisite. In some respects, that opinion is akin to a fossil preserved in amber. The decision was written *before* the Supreme Court required proof of intent for racial discrimination; *before* the Court ruled out affirmative action; *before* the Court abjured obligations to provide environments in which rehabilitation was plausible and limited the focus to a cribbed view of "life's necessities"; *before* Congress undercut the power of federal judges to require improvements in prisons; and *before* justices called into question "evolving standards of decency" as a measure of constitutional punishments. Instead, the Eighth Circuit's decision, replete with "shalls" directed at Judge Henley and the defendants, expressed its "firm conviction that the Arkansas correctional system [was] still unconstitutional" and that courts were not to be "apologetic in requiring state officials" to respond. "[A]lmost five years" after the initial ruling, "major constitutional deficiencies" remained; "inadequate resources" did not "justify the imposition of constitutionally prohibited treatment."[3]

Understanding this decision is one way to glimpse the contingency of punishment's *legal* parameters. Rather than *discounting rights* as I have discussed, these judges were "compelled to find . . . a continuing failure by the correctional authorities to provide a constitutional and, in some respects, even a humane environment . . . ." The deficits ran the gamut—in their words—from "housing, lack of medical care, infliction of physical and mental brutality and torture upon individual prisoners, racial discrimination, abuses of solitary confinement, continuing use of trusty guards, abuse of mail regulation, arbitrary work classifications, arbitrary disciplinary procedures, inadequate distribution of food and clothing, and the total lack of rehabilitative programs." Their directions were a roadmap for becoming "constitutional," by which they meant legitimately exercising sovereign power.[4]

A PROGRAM FOR REHABILITATION

"We . . . deem it necessary that the respondents submit to the court an overall program for treatment and rehabilitation of the inmates at both Cummins and Tucker."

—*Finney v. Arkansas Board of Correction,* October 10, 1974

The *Finney* opinion had a series of headings; one section was labeled "Rehabilitation," a term Judge Henley had used. Arguments for rehabilitation go back to the Enlightenment, when theorists hinged the legitimacy of punishment on *the good reasons* governments had to limit individuals' liberty. They identified reformation (rehabilitation today) as one, alongside deterrence, incapacitation, and retribution.

The question of a *right to rehabilitation* emerged in the 1960s when incarcerated people argued judges had to lessen confinement's degradation. (Prisoners had no interest in enforcing any potential "rights" to deterrence, incapacitation, or retribution.) Judges linked decent living situations and activities to utilitarian and moral arguments supporting rehabilitation in service of society's interest ("penological purposes") that individuals be law-abiding on release.

Rehabilitation has baggage from the history of efforts to "cure" people of the disease of crime, echoed in the condescending term, *corrections*, which became the name of almost all the agencies that run prisons in the United States. Yet the *Finney* judges deployed it for a different end. If rehabilitation was a *constitutional right*, it would anchor a panoply of services; that proposition scared some, worried about the burden incarceration would (and I argue should) impose. (In later chapters, I discuss the Court's abandonment of rehabilitation by using the provision of "life's necessities" as the touchstone of constitutional tolerability.)

Henley had been among the first to discuss rehabilitation. His 1970 *Holt II* ruling concluded that this "sociological theory or idea" would not alone be the basis for finding an "unexceptional penal institution" unconstitutional. Yet, as discussed, Henley wrote that the "absence of an affirmative program of training and rehabilitation" could have "constitutional significance" when conditions "actually militate against reform and rehabilitation." Likewise, at the 1971 Williamsburg Conference, Judge William Bryant told the assembled that a "fundamental right to rehabilitative treatment" was "in the making." More support came from Judge Frank Johnson who, in the context of Alabama's confinement of individuals with mental health challenges, had written about the state's obligation not to cause debilitation. A few years later, building on Henley's comments, Johnson concluded that Alabama prison conditions were "so debilitating that they necessarily deprive[d] inmates of any opportunity to rehabilitate themselves, or even to maintain skills already possessed." A prison system "cannot be operated in such a manner that it impedes an inmate's ability to attempt rehabilitation, or simply to avoid physical, mental or social deterioration."[5] (As I discuss in the conclusion, forbidding debilitation is distinct from requiring rehabilitation.)

In 1974, Judge Lay's *Finney* opinion added legal scaffolding to a rehabilitation right by invoking two Supreme Court decisions. He quoted *Jackson v. Indiana*, a 1972 ruling written by Justice Blackmun, who explained that "due process requires that the nature and duration of commitment bear some reasonable relation to the purpose for which the individual is committed." That case involved Theon Jackson, who could neither read nor write and was accused of stealing less than $10. Given the inability to understand the charges and participate in a defense, the state deemed Jackson "incompetent to stand trial" and planned to hold him indefinitely. The unanimous Court ruled the state could detain a person for a "reasonable period" to regain competency; if not, detention had no *purpose*, and the state had either to release or initiate civil commitment proceedings. Judge Lay cited another Court decision, *Procunier v. Martinez*, addressing censorship of mail. Justice Powell had written that California's licit reasons for regulations included "the preservation of internal order and discipline, the maintenance of institutional security . . . , and the rehabilitation of the prisoners."

To those two Supreme Court decisions, the Eighth Circuit added Arkansas' 1968 statute that—as recounted—put the word "rehabilitation" in the charter of its Arkansas Department of Correction (ADC). People who were "forced to labor long hours under arduous conditions, . . . [and] constant threats of physical and mental abuse . . . [were] left almost no time for self-advancing activities"; moreover, even if "time were available, rehabilitative programs" were not. The Circuit concluded that Arkansas therefore had to create a plan for rehabilitation and provide means to enable it.[6]

UNCONSTITUTIONAL VIOLENCE, CROWDING, TRUSTY POWERS, AND HEALTH CARE

A lack of funding did not excuse the failure to "provide optimum safety and sanitation for every inmate."

—*Finney*, October 10, 1974

By 1973, Arkansas held 1,500 people and, "despite Mr. Hutto's concession that the barracks cannot be successfully operated with more than 60 to 80 inmates," 125 to 135 men were in each. A minimum-security facility, to be built, would add 248 single cells, and the maximum-security unit 90, but "serious overcrowding" would not end. (Fast forward: In 2024, Arkansas held more than 21,000 convicted people in its prisons and jails.) The appellate court told Henley he "shall meet" with the parties to "devise a program to eliminate immediately the overcrowding and to ensure the safety of each inmate." Options included transfers and release.[7]

The Eighth Circuit also disagreed with Henley that the ADC had "done the best that it could" on health care. The decision quoted the expert group ("seven physicians, four pharmacologists, one hospital administrator and one psychologist") convened by Correction Board member Dr. Wortham and ignored by Henley. (Wortham's 2015 obituary described him as a family care physician and a "catalyst for major improvements in prison healthcare.") The experts cited rehabilitation as "the primary purpose of prison," linked a "basic level of medical care" to "the rehabilitation process," and concluded that prisoners had a "basic right to medical, dental and psychological diagnosis, study and treatment." In contrast, Arkansas had "a total deficiency in both manpower and equipment resources." Facilities did not meet "state licensure" requirements: no dentist, nurse, or trained staff could diagnose or treat an "emergency and acute illness." The Circuit noted that, in an eight-month period, none of 1,200 people at Cummins had seen a dentist. Indeed, that study was all that had happened. The appellate court told Henley it was "incumbent" upon him to "delineate within specific terms and time limitations" that every prisoner be seen by "a qualified physician when necessary."[8]

The appellate court identified the trusty system as a "most offensive practice." Contrary to Henley and based on 1973 information from prisoners, it had not ended. Leaving nothing for the defendants to dispute or Henley to interpret, the trusty system was to be "completely phased out within a few months." Moreover, despite formal policies, "excessive force, verbal abuse, and various forms of torture and inhuman punishment" continued. The Eighth Circuit's examples included "hoe squads" working excessive hours "under constant prodding" and prisoners made to "run to and from" the fields," at times "in front of moving vehicles or ridden horses." In sum, "profane, threatening, abusive and vulgar language, together with racial slurs, epithets, and sexual and scatological terms," and the grueling and aggressive treatment were unconstitutional "working conditions."[9]

RACE DISCRIMINATION, DISCIPLINE, AND GRUE

Discipline was another category eliciting concern. Under the Supreme Court's *Wolff v. McDonnell* ruling that prisons had to provide hearings before rescinding statutorily granted "good-time" credits, *Finney* ruled that a person making an accusation was no longer to sit in judgment of an alleged offender. Another problem was racial discrimination, recognized by Henley, but the Circuit found that his supplemental injunction stopped "short of its intended goal." The prison population was almost half Black men but "no blacks had ever sat in judgment on the disciplinary court." Moreover, whether intended or not, Black prisoners occupied "menial positions," and no progress had been made on recruitment of staff. The Circuit told Henley to "include an affirmative program directed toward the elimination of all forms of racial discrimination."[10]

As to solitary confinement, the court repeated its prior rulings, that it was not "per se unconstitutional" but specific conditions could render it so. The unconstitutionality of Arkansas' 1974 punitive isolation stemmed in part from giving prisoners "grue" instead of "the regular prison diet." This practice, "designed to break a man's spirit," crossed the "minimal line separating cruel and unusual punishment from conduct that is not." The district court was to direct that no person be deprived of "basic necessities," including "light, heat, ventilation, sanitation, clothing, and a proper diet."[11] That list implicitly ruled out Arkansas' pitch-dark "quiet cells."

The bottom line was that, while appreciating the "conscientious and responsible manner in which the district court" had dealt with the litigation and confident "a suitable end will be quickly attained," the facts and the "newly developed area of constitutional law" meant Arkansas' prisons were "still unconstitutional." Given the "inhumane treatment and brutality," Henley had more work to do, including pending individual assault claims.[12]

A "VEHICLE FOR SOCIAL CHANGE": METRICS OF IMPACT

The Eighth Circuit was not Henley's only critic. A 1976 "case study" of the *Holt* litigation chronicled his approach and its limits. That report, *After Decision: Implementation of Judicial Decrees in Correctional Settings*, sponsored by the ABA and published in 1977 by the US Department of Justice, sought to understand litigation's "effectiveness" as a "vehicle for social change" by replacing "bald assertions" with "knowledge." After reviewing more than eighty decisions, *Holt*'s stature as the "precedential base" and its "extensive litigation history" prompted its inclusion as one of four in-depth accounts.[13]

The question of methods for such studies continues to engage social scientists. The 1976 study focused on court decisions rather than analyzing legislative debates, executive actions, relationships between prisoners and their lawyers, and national developments. Yet, at the time, the work was responding to what was new—which was judicial involvement on behalf of prisoners. The research on *Holt* came from Dudley Spiller, a civil rights lawyer who had represented detained juveniles. His "narrowly focused examination" was based on dozens of meetings with prisoners and staff and on forty "separate orders" issued by Henley.[14]

I found Spiller's draft in Robert Sarver's papers; he was one of the "principal figures" asked for input. Spiller described complaints by the prisoners' lawyers about the "slow pace" of change, as well as that Commissioner Hutto, unlike Sarver, "expressed resentment toward the court's continued intervention." Hutto characterized prisoners as "frequently able to file false, outlandish, scandalous complaints that were nevertheless widely publicized." Spiller lay the lack of compliance partly at Henley's feet. The judge's orders were "broad, general and often ambiguous" (such as stop "inflicting cruel

and unusual punishment" or "interfering with . . . access to court
and counsel"), lacked "substantive definition" and standards, and
were often framed as "suggestions" and "recommendations." Rather
than appointing an external monitor, Henley relied for information
on the state's reports and prisoner filings. Spiller cushioned his criticism by adding that Henley's lack of "rigidity" (to get "compliance
by persuasion rather than force") had been useful for legislators.
Spiller noted that Henley, an "astute politician," timed court hearings in relationship to the legislature's calendar; some rulings were
a "catalyst for prison change" by prompting new funding streams,
even if what transpired was "somewhat less than ideal."[15]

LIFE IN THE "HOLE" AND IN THE FIELDS

After the Eighth Circuit's 1974 remand, Hutto told the press that
problems were under control, that errant employees had been
reprimanded or fired, and that, as to rehabilitation, more than 46
percent of the 1,900 prisoners in 1974 were "involved in academic
and vocational training programs." Yet ADC's filings document its
resistance to court orders. In January of 1975, prison officials produced a revised Inmate Handbook. The list of offenses had grown
from twenty-five to twenty-eight violations; added were breaches
of "rules of cleanliness, sanitation and appearance." The revision
required a discipline committee to convene within seventy-two
hours. Sanctions no longer included the imposition of odious work,
nor was the prison to deprive a person of "sufficient nutritional
diet or adequate rest or clothing." Yet, despite the Eighth Circuit's
specificity, punitive isolation remained with a "diet of bread, grue,
and water not to exceed" fifteen continuous days. If a person was
held for longer, he would get two days of regular meals and then
be returned to "restricted diet"; on every third day, a "regular diet"
was to be provided. Moreover, the euphemism of "quiet cells" remained, and the prison could "sentence the inmate to isolation for
[an] indefinite period of time."[16]

Henley then took new evidence. Several prisoners testified in
March of 1975 about beatings, rapes, a lack of health care, and filthy

conditions. One prisoner described life in the "hole"; the punitive wing was "very dirty," loaded with mice and roaches and without hot water. Another spoke of food, labeled as pork-free, but fried with lard. By April, Henley concluded that the volume of prison work was too much for him or "any District Court judge personally"—especially given the logistics of "bringing large numbers of inmates to Court to testify, of guarding them . . . and in returning them."[17] Henley did not mention that President Gerald Ford had nominated him to the Eighth Circuit, that he had been confirmed on March 13, 1975, and took his seat the next day. Henley ceased being the Chief Judge of the District when joining the Circuit but, specially designated, continued presiding as the trial judge in the Penitentiary Cases.

To ease that burden, Henley enlisted the Honorable Robert W. Faulkner, who had worked for Winthrop Rockefeller and, in 1973, been appointed as a magistrate for that federal district. Henley tasked Faulkner with taking "the testimony of any and all witnesses, including parties" about pending issues; the transcripts, treated as depositions, were for Henley, who ordered the (objecting) defendants to pay $2,548 for the voluminous results. In August, Henley personally toured the prisons. Furthermore, having been chastised by the Circuit for not getting updated data before issuing his 1973 withdrawal, Henley ordered the state to provide "specific information" on the prison's population by "housing, race and work assignments"—due on November 17, 1975.[18]

The press continued to report violence. A twenty-one-year-old died in the fields. "[G]iven no breakfast and transported into the field to chop grass out of ditches all day in temperature . . . as high as 90 degrees," he collapsed. A few months later, an eighteen-year-old in punitive isolation after an escape hanged himself. In February of 1976, Henley ordered the closing of the Arkansas State Reformatory for Women, a facility with capacity of sixty-nine that held ninety-five, and, in Henley's words, was "hopelessly and unconstitutionally overcrowded." Governor David Pryor (who took office in 1975) and Hutto "stated publicly" closure by June 30 of 1976 was not problematic.[19]

VIOLENCE AS "THE NATURE OF THINGS" BUT LIMITS ON CROWDING

Prisoners "no [longer lived with the] danger of death or injury at the hands of another inmate in whose hands a weapon has been placed by the Department."

—Judge Henley, *Finney v. Hutto*, March 19, 1976[20]

In March of 1976, Henley issued his last opinion, augmented by an unpublished "clarifying memorandum opinion" on April 2, 1976 and by a supplemental decree. When Henley had written *Holt I* and *Holt II*, he had aimed to persuade the legislature to fund changes. In this successor ruling, Henley also wanted to convince his appellate colleagues that *he* had complied with the Circuit's 1974 ruling. Citing another Eighth Circuit decision he had recently authored, Henley emphasized that when "constitutional deprivations" existed, judges had the "power to intervene and devise appropriate relief."[21]

Henley's format paralleled the decision that reversed him with the same sequence of topics. On his account, the people running prisons had come to understand they were subject to standards not entirely of their own making. Henley's directives included general population caps, a thirty-day-limit in isolation cells, mental health professionals on staff, revamped affirmative action, and paying attorneys' fees. But Henley's discussion of tolerable levels of violence and his formulation—that the "danger of death" from state-armed prisoners was over—reflected that he never escaped (a word used advisedly) the horrors he had witnessed when presiding at the 1960s whipping trials and torture prosecutions.

Rehearsing that sordid history and commending the ADC for no longer using "armed inmates as guards," Henley put forth a standard *below* the Eighth Circuit's 1974 "optimal safety" test. Instead, Henley described a duty "to use ordinary care for [prisoner] safety" so that institutions would not be "so dangerous that the inmates must exist in dread of imminent injury or death inflicted by other inmates." Henley described three deaths: two killings occurred "after the record" had closed and another that may well have been the result of "hazing" by other prisoners and staff, as well as other "non-fatal incidents." Henley discounted that loss of life by noting that official policies did not countenance brutality and that the "reasonable use of force by even prison authorities [was] not only permissible but positively required on occasions." Moreover, Henley condoned—as "in the very nature of things"— in-prison violence, including "homosexual violence, [which] would occur from time to time." Concluding that the barracks were "not nearly as dangerous" as they had been, Henley registered no objection to unarmed prisoners "floorwalkers" at night, along with "actual guarding . . . by civilian guards." Henley ruled that the Department had used "ordinary care for inmate safety" and that neither Cummins nor Tucker was "such a dangerous place" that raised "a constitutional problem."[22]

On the other hand, having been instructed by the Circuit to "devise a program to eliminate immediately the overcrowding of the barracks and to ensure the safety of each inmate," Henley limited the numbers to be held. He determined that unconstitutionality did not depend on square footage alone; the "quality of the living quarters and . . . the length of time" mattered as did the distribution of people throughout facilities. By 1975, more than 1,500 people were at Cummins and 501 at Tucker, while Hutto had testified barracks were not to hold more than sixty to eighty men. Hutto later "raised that figure to 100." Yet Henley pointed out, on his site-visit, the barracks had "substantially more than 100 men in them." Moreover, the ADC had put people in the commissary, gym, infirmary, in what ADC called the "dog kennel," and in "pods" (trailers). Henley refused to "accept" that the East Building—designed, as its "slick paper brochure" explained, for single-cell occupancy—could house "120 maximum-security inmates without overcrowding. . . . Three or four men" were using cells built for one, and some had "to sleep on the floor." Given "chronically overcrowded" facilities, "something must be done."[23]

Long-term solutions included new buildings; in the short term, Henley set maximum-capacity standards. Absent an emergency, the ADC could not assign more than 1,650 inmates to Cummins and 550 to Tucker. Henley drew those numbers from what ADC said it would do; Henley's mandate did not require releases at that time.[24]

ISOLATION WITHOUT ANY REHABILITATIVE UTILITY

Punitive isolation "serve[d] no rehabilitation purpose," but was "counterproductive," as it made "bad men worse" and "must be changed."

—Judge Henley, *Finney*, 1976[25]

Henley concluded that Arkansas complied with the Supreme Court's 1974 *Wolff v. McDonnell* standards; moreover, on occasion, "black employees" sat on disciplinary panels." In contrast, Henley painted a grim picture of punitive isolation where many remained "weeks or months, depending upon their attitudes as appraised by prison personnel." This "dreaded" placement put prisoners in an "extremely small cell under rigorous conditions"; three or more were in cells with two bunks. People had no exercise, and "all privileges and opportunities" were gone. Arkansas fed them grue, unless "medically contraindicated." Weight-loss checks after fourteen days made plain the harms.[26]

Henley reiterated his negative characterizations of individuals subjected to these conditions; as a "class," these were "violent men . . . filled with frustration and hostility, some of them . . . extremely dangerous . . . and others . . . psychopaths." Putting them together meant that the housing was "not infrequently a scene of violence," with noise, screams, vandalized cells, and aggression towards staff. "Hatreds" built up, and the "forcible response from prison personnel," at times "excessive" with mace and nightsticks, could have been "avoided . . . if the guards were more professional and used better judgment and common sense." Henley found it "hard" to believe that "American technology and engineering" could not equip prisons with lighting and plumbing secure against people using "bare hands" and "simple tools" to attempt destruction.[27]

Henley drew on 1974 testimony from a clinical psychologist for the propositions (which became central in 1978 at the Supreme Court) that punitive isolation "serve[d] no rehabilitation purpose"; "counterproductive," it made "bad men worse." Describing ADC's discipline as "sentencing inmates to indeterminate periods of

confinement in punitive isolation," Henley held it "unreasonable
and unconstitutional."²⁸ Henley could have offered more by way of
analysis because, not only did isolation provide no rehabilitation,
no evidence suggested that it had other "penological purposes." It
did not deter; it inadequately incapacitated, and its violence made
it an unconstitutional form of retribution. Had Henley ruled that,
as practiced by Arkansas, punitive isolation had *no rational relationship* to any legitimate governmental end, the irrationality of solitary confinement could have made its way into the jurisprudence
of punishment, where it was—and is—sorely needed.

Yet in 1976, responding to the Eighth Circuit's reversal, Henley focused on change rather than on the legal theories for it. In addition
to capping time, he addressed density and food. While not prepared
to "go so far as to say that is unconstitutional to confine as many as
two men in the punitive isolation and administrative segregation
cells," each person had to have "a bunk to sleep on at night and to
sit upon during the day." Henley prohibited having "more than two
men at any one time"—absent a "serious emergency" like a "riot."
He also outlawed "grue" and, referencing Hutto's "view that . . . the
maximum period of time" a person "should be in punitive isolation
with a restricted diet . . . [was] fourteen days," Henley allowed "a
maximum sentence of thirty days" as the "permissible" outer limit.
This time, Henley set a timetable for implementation. The "prohibition against limited diets" was effective immediately, while a
"reasonable but comparatively short period of time" to comply with
capping duration at thirty days.²⁹

Henley also imposed parallel rules on "administrative segregation" in the maximum-security unit; again citing the Eighth Circuit
ruling he wrote about assessing whether reasons for segregation
had "ceased to be valid or relevant," Henley directed Cummins
Superintendent Lockhart to identify "as soon as practicable" individuals who could be "returned without serious risk" to general
population. Henley added a comment that capping days in punitive isolation "may cause . . . consternation in the Department
and . . . outside." As solace, Henley said he "sincerely" believed
the rules were constitutionally required and "will produce both a

more humane prison system and a system that is going to be more peaceful and orderly and easier to administer efficiently in the long run."[30] (In the decades thereafter, social scientists and some prison officials agreed that solitary confinement was a *source* of violence rather than of safety.)

COURTS, HEALTH CARE, REHABILITATION OPPORTUNITIES, AND VEXING RACISM

All staff shall "refrain from verbally abusing, or cursing, inmates, and from employing racial slurs or epithets."

—Judge Henley, *Finney*, 1976[31]

After years of chastising ADC on blocking access to courts, Henley found the new policies acceptable. Legal assistance came because "fellow inmates" could help, as did an in-house legal adviser who, Henley noted, had assisted two habeas petitioners unconstitutionally convicted because of systematic exclusion of "Negroes from the jury venire."[32]

As to health care, Henley recognized that, consistent with "legitimate institutional interests," the state owed "a constitutional duty" to provide prisoners "reasonable and necessary medical and surgical care" that included "the field of mental health." Henley reported that a "full-time physician" was at Cummins, that "qualified" paramedics were on site, that the infirmaries and pharmacies were "reasonably well equipped," that an ambulance and off-site care were available along with "rudimentary dental care" for filings and extractions. Steps had been taken toward protection from contagious diseases and, except for hordes of flies, sanitation was "reasonably satisfactory." While nothing had been done for the mentally ill, a beginning group therapy plan was a "step in right direction." Henley directed the ADC to seek a study follow "reasonable suggestions" from the state's health department. Further, Henley ordered the ADC to employ one or more full-time psychiatrists or psychologists.[33]

Under the header "Rehabilitation," Henley concluded that "[u]nlike . . . 1973, the rehabilitation picture . . . is now quite bright"

and "free of constitutional deficiencies." The legislature had created
the Department of Correction School District, with programs "comparable" to public schools and access to high school and "college
level" courses. As for vocational programs, women had access to
ceramics while men learned to repair farm equipment and furniture, upholster, weld, and print. Henley noted that opportunities
for women should broaden.[34] Henley knew about ADC programs
because another prisoner, James Rutherford filed a lawsuit arguing
that, as an illiterate adult, he had a constitutional right *not* to attend
school. Henley disagreed; just as prisoners could not refuse work,
they could not reject mandated rehabilitative programs. Prisoners
without a fourth-grade education had to take ungraded classes a
few hours a week.[35]

Turning to race relations ("a major social problem all over the
United States"), Henley described it as "perhaps the most vexing
one to beset the Department." Progress had been reported about
treatment of Black Muslims, no longer "unduly restricted" and able
to hold meetings like other religious groups, and "a conscientious
effort [was underway] to supply the Muslims with a pork free diet
and to advise Muslim inmates . . . what dishes they can eat." Given
the lack of "trust," Henley reissued the injunction against serving
pork and suggested assignments of some "Muslims . . . to the kitch-
ens" and inspections "by free-world Muslims."[36]

More generally, interactions between the "Negro and the Cauca-
sian races" were "still bad." Although Black people were a minority
in the state, they were "nearly one-half" of the prison population
and lived in facilities "under the control of white people." The
Department had sought to hire more blacks, but "very few" had
"positions of any real authority." Henley noted that ADC's Affirmative Action Plan (entered into the record as Exhibit 687) had resulted in 30 percent of the new hires being Black people; of 198
staff promotions, about a third (sixty-four) went to Black staff.
That "commendable" progress had not, however, resulted in Black
people in positions of "some real authority and influence" as supervisors or on discipline committees. Furthermore, the garden
and hoe squads were about 55 percent Black men, while security

staff overseeing the fields were white. In short, Henley was "not satisfied" that Hutto and others had "really exerted themselves to the fullest extent possible," such as through outreach to the Urban League, the National Association for the Advancement of Colored People, or people connected to the nearby University of Arkansas at Pine Bluff, which was "predominantly black." Yet Henley concluded that he had "nothing really substantial to add" to the injunctions issued in 1973.[37]

"[C]ontemporaneously with the filing" of his March opinion, Henley issued a decree "defining cruel and unusual punishment." Henley recounted that, in 1973, he had enjoined "in broad terms so as to include the infliction of force in any form; the assigning of an inmate to tasks inconsistent with his medical classification; the use of any punishment amounting to torture; the practice of forcing any inmate to run to or from work, or while at work, or in front of any moving vehicle or animal, and the infliction of any punishment not authorized by the Department's rules and regulations." While Henley did not believe more relief against violence was "called for or that it would do any good," the lack of "professionalism" evidenced by employees' "foul language and racial epithets" made another directive "of some value to higher echelon employees" supervising staff. Henley thus ordered that all staff refrain from "verbally abusing, or cursing, inmates, and from employing racial slurs or epithets."[38]

FINDING "BAD FAITH" AS A LEGAL ROUTE TO REQUIRING THE STATE TO PAY THE PRISONERS' LAWYERS

The state defendants had "in a legal sense . . . acted in bad faith and oppressively."

—Judge Henley, *Finney*, 1976[39]

For most of his decision, Henley referenced the Eighth Circuit's reversal as his source of legal principles. But when writing about the fee award, Henley did more. After the Circuit had agreed that he had the power to require the state to compensate the prisoners' lawyers, the Supreme Court issued decisions that could have been read to undercut the fee award. Henley therefore detailed a mix of facts and law to substantiate two legal theories: that Philip Kaplan and Jack Holt Jr. merited money because they were "private attorney generals" rendering services to all, and that the fee award was a sanction for the state's "bad faith" failure to follow court orders.

The relevant background norm is the "American Rule," that each side pay the costs of its lawyers. This presumption got its name because in England and elsewhere, losers have to pay winners' lawyers. The idea is to screen out unworthy claims. The US rule reflects the concern that meritorious, if not always winning claimants would be deterred by a risk of fee shifts. More than that: US law has historically sought to *encourage* private parties to enforce public rights. In the late nineteenth century, Congress enacted antitrust laws offering victorious plaintiffs treble damages and attorney fees. Likewise, the 1870 Enforcement Act authorized fee awards for lawsuits aiming to protect voting rights. These examples of one-way shifts to winning plaintiffs are "litigation incentives," found in many federal statutes.[40]

The Supreme Court addressed fee-shifting in the context of the 1964 Civil Rights Act banning discrimination in public accommodations and employment and providing for winning plaintiffs to recoup lawyer fees. When affirming a fee award, the Court described such litigants in 1968 as "private attorneys general" vindicating congressional policies. But, as Judge Henley recounted, two decisions thereafter raised questions. *Edelman v. Jordan* involved a ruling that Illinois had wrongly withheld federal benefits for aged, disabled, and blind individuals. Federal judges ordered the state to pay the wrongfully withheld benefits. William Rehnquist writing for a majority of five reversed. Citing the Eleventh Amendment of the US Constitution (that does not use the word "immunity" but limits federal court jurisdiction over some kinds of cases involving states as defendants), Justice Rehnquist concluded in 1974 that courts could not order pay back benefits yet could require prospective relief—future-looking injunctions. Justice Rehnquist acknowledged that drawing a distinction between retrospective and prospective relief was not as bright as "between day and night." Henley thus had to puzzle about whether attorney fee awards were "purely ancillary to prospective equitable relief properly granted against a state or a state agency." Henley decided his fee award was part of the package of equitable relief and ordered the state to pay.[41]

Henley was too able a judge (and too eager to get money to the lawyers he had enlisted) to rest on that analysis alone and therefore discussed *Alyeska Pipeline Service Company v. Wilderness Society*, in which the federal Court of Appeals for the District of Columbia had agreed with environmental groups that the Secretary of Interior lacked power to permit a proposed pipeline. Thereafter, Congress amended the law to make construction possible, and the case returned to the DC Circuit, which ruled that, while no federal statute authorized lawyer fees, these environmental groups had vindicated "important statutory rights of all citizens" and merited fees. Recall that in 1973 when Henley ordered the state to pay Kaplan and Holt Jr. $8,000, he explained they had conferred benefits on the state and on the people of Arkansas, to whom the prisons belonged. But in 1975, the Supreme Court rejected the DC Circuit's approach and told judges that they were not to rely on a "private attorney general" theory. To order fee shifts, judges needed authorization from a statute or to make factual findings that "the losing party has 'acted in bad faith, vexatiously, wantonly, or for oppressive reasons.'"[42]

Judge Henley both distinguished and complied with *Alyeska Pipeline*. *Alyeska* had been a private lawsuit involving no constitutional questions, while the Arkansas prison litigation ("markedly different in quality") raised the "grave constitutional question of whether those in charge of the Arkansas Department of Correction and the prisons . . . deprive[d] indigent convicts of fundamental rights and immunities guaranteed them by the fourteenth amendment." Moreover, unlike lawyers volunteering "under the banner of environmental protection," Kaplan and Holt Jr. had been recruited to assist litigants who "could not . . . have intelligently" pressed their claims.

Henley also found that the state had "in a legal sense . . . acted in bad faith and oppressively," which meant that his award fell under the historical exception predicated on courts' inherent powers, as *Alyeska* had acknowledged. Although not naming Robert Sarver, Henley stated that in the "earlier stages . . . the prison administration tended to be cooperative . . . and indeed appeared to welcome the action of the court in requiring them to do what they wanted to do anyway but felt unable to do voluntarily." With the passage of time (to wit, the firing of Sarver and replacement by Hutto), the "Departmental attitudes" had "hardened" into an "unwillingness on the part of the prison administrators," with "progress . . . made to . . . date" still being "insufficient." Furthermore, prison officials had often claimed they had no knowledge of the unconstitutional practices employed. "[T]he higher echelon officials of the department" had not kept "themselves personally familiar with day to day life in the prisons including the work activities of the inmates." Even as the ADC had moved toward a "constitutional system," each step required a court mandate, and each stage revealed new deficiencies.[43]

Henley fixed an additional fee of $20,000 (about $118,000 in 2024 dollars) for the lawyers to divide; while not adequate, the amount was more than "nominal." Because he assumed an appeal would follow, Henley certified (as required by federal rules) that the case was sufficiently final to be eligible. He also noted that as much as he wanted to "relieve counsel" of their "duties," it was not "practicable" to do so, at least not until after the appeal, "if any," and decisions in the remaining individual claims. This time, Henley retained jurisdiction. Henley instructed Hutto to submit a report by July 15, 1976 to document ADC's compliance with the court orders, including providing population numbers in a format consistent with (and hence comparable to) the November 1975 data.[44]

Within days, Jim Guy Tucker, then the state's Attorney General, filed a motion arguing the lack of clarity and seeking revisions. The state objected to caps on general population and on time in isolation as well as the fee award. Henley replied on April 2, 1976 in a "Clarifying Memorandum Opinion," declining to vacate his order but slightly altering it. Henley's exasperation was plain; he was "unwilling . . . to define what constitutes 'cursing' of inmates by prison employees." The "higher echelons" of ADC knew "full well the kind of language that ought to be avoided," and it was their "duty . . . to pass that knowledge on down the line." Henley likewise reiterated rules on food in isolation; he underlined his March order that diets were not to "differ qualitatively from food served . . . in general population." While some variation was possible, Henley warned that, if prison officials were to "start making a habit of adding to the punishment . . . by deliberately serving short rations or by deliberately choosing for inmates . . . the least desirable . . . dishes, they will . . . make trouble for themselves not only with the inmates . . . but also with the court."[45]

Henley made two concessions. He had "overlooked" that some isolation cells "were designed to house four people" and permitted that number, as long as each person was "serving a sentence of punitive confinement imposed by a disciplinary committee or panel itself." Henley also modified the thirty-day time cap; if a person committed "a serious or major disciplinary infraction, and particularly one involving violence" and was found guilty, that person could be sentenced for more than thirty days. Again, Henley inferred he expected bad faith. Those in charge were to use new sentences "sparingly," not against people who were "simply loud, profane or . . . 'acting out,'" and not "as a means of evading the court's prohibitions against indeterminate sentences." Were consecutive sentences to become commonplace, it would be "constitutionally suspect."[46]

NOT OVER, AGAIN

In May of 1976, Henley directed Magistrate Faulkner to investigate and report on alleged beatings. The docket sheet reflected a series of short decisions declining requests to hold the defendants in contempt for violence toward prisoners; Henley found the evidence insufficient. Moreover, Henley had a related case to address. Another group of prisoners, consisting of "black inmates of the maximum-security facility" and spearheaded by William Graves (who later withdrew), sued Cummins Superintendent A. L. Lockhart and others. Henley had put the lawsuit on hold; the Circuit told him in 1974 to address the issues. Ruling in 1977, Henley described the plaintiffs as "dangerous and violent criminals . . . serving long terms." Henley summarized their complaints to include insufficient food, overcrowding, arbitrary discipline, and discrimination against Black Muslims—"mocked and harassed and . . . compelled to eat food . . . contaminated . . . with pork."[47]

The pretrial exchange in *Graves* substantiated a grim record of disproportionate confinement of Black prisoners and terrible conditions. According to Arkansas' documents, the charges that landed people into isolation ranged from "refusal to work," "creating unnecessary noise," "insubordination," "disrespect to officer," to destroying state property and assault. While the prison population was 52 percent Black men, Cummins' maximum-security wing was 60 percent Black men. Those cells in the East Wing were about ten by eight, with one bunk, one toilet, and one sink. The cells had no cooling system; ventilation—such as it was—came from forced air from the hall whose thermostat was set at 80 degrees. People had been fed grue plus four slices of bread, netting 962 calories a day, with a "regular meal every third day." In February of 1974, staff admitted "quelling disturbances" by spraying mace into cells. The state also acknowledged that prisoners had lost weight, had no access to the law library, and were sometimes left to sleep on mattresses on the floor. Because of his March *Finney* orders ending indeterminate confinement in crowded cells and grue, Henley concluded no more relief was needed. As to the individual claims, even as many were "legitimate" and staff had responded "unprofessionally," Henley decided the prisoners had been confrontational and no basis for money damages existed.[48]

25

SPENDING "MILLIONS OF MORE DOLLARS" TO DO WHAT?

"Terrell Don Hutto took a look into the future . . . [and] saw an increasing number of prisoners, more federal court orders, higher costs, and the need for millions of more dollars in state money."
—*Arkansas Democrat*, October 28, 1976[1]

In 1950, based on his brief internment by the Nazis and on directing Belgium's prisons, Paul Cornil observed that incarceration denuded individuals of their autonomy. After federal judges in the 1970s held conditions of confinement unconstitutional, the question was whether court interventions could limit the *autonomy* of staff by requiring opportunities for individuals to live safely in a setting that, in Judge Henley's terms, would not impede "rehabilitation" and, under the Eighth Circuit's approach, affirmatively enable their growth. To do so requires space and resources, which is why policies on sentencing, funding, and paroling are crucial. This chapter analyzes conflicts about the use of money for security versus services and for the prisoners' lawyers, and how decision-making by politicians shaped today's views about the forms of punishment permissible under US law.

While penologists had long promoted open-ended ("indeterminate") sentences to give corrections the power to decide when people should be deemed "cured" or "rehabilitated" and released, a new "science" in the mid-1970s concluded that prisons were not places for reform and that some people (read: Black men) were "incorrigible" or "superpredators" (a newer term), for whom endless incapacitation was necessary. Under the slogan "nothing works," proponents heralded "truth in sentencing," meaning people were to serve all or most of fixed terms. Criticism of indeterminacy came not only from people insistent on retributive punishment but also from those concerned that discretion often resulted in discrimination against Black people.[2]

Analytically, *fixed* terms do not have to translate into *longer* terms. Politically in the United States, they did. Racism was again a driver; people of color were prime targets of the "War on Crime." The guns were fired not only by legislatures and governors but, with Warren Burger and then William Rehnquist at the helm, by Supreme Court majorities pulling law back from protections for criminal defendants under the Fourth, Fifth, and Sixth Amendments and for prisoners under the Eighth and Fourteenth. Techniques included closing off habeas review of certain claims—such as alleged illegal searches and seizures—and, as explored later, changing criteria to make easier government defenses of crowded prisons.[3]

Yet in 1978, in *Hutto v. Finney*, the Burger Court affirmed Judge Henley's power to cap time in solitary confinement and to order the state to pay lawyers' fees. Had this book been court-centric, the 1978 decision could also have served as a closing chapter. But neither the Arkansas Penitentiary Cases nor the political debates about crime, punishment, and the miseries of prison ended there, and hence, neither does this book.

LEGALLY EASY IF "ENDLESS," CIRCA 1977

"[This is] the latest chapter in the seemingly endless litigation."
—The Eighth Circuit, *Finney v. Hutto*, January 6, 1977

As anticipated, the state appealed. Even as Arkansas grounded its arguments in state prerogatives and federal overreach, it did not question most of Judge Henley's order, including caps on general population and remedies for race discrimination. Arkansas' partial acquiescence marked what prisoners had *won*. State officials no longer contested that the Constitution governed prisons and that grotesque conditions were unconstitutional. But Arkansas did not want a thirty-day cap on isolation or to pay fees.

On January 6, 1977, the Eighth Circuit affirmed Henley in all respects by, in essence, saying "amen." The three-page ruling was written by Judge Donald Roe Ross, who had been President Eisenhower's pick in 1953 to be US Attorney for the District of Nebraska, selected as the general counsel for the state's Republican Party, and in 1970 Richard Nixon's choice to fill Harry Blackmun's seat after Blackmun went to the Supreme Court. The other circuit-level judge was Gerald Heaney from Minnesota, a Lyndon Johnson nominee who heard the first *Finney* appeal (*Finney I*). Robert Van Pelt, an Eisenhower appointee to Nebraska's district court, sat "by designation" as he had in *Jackson v. Bishop*. The three were appalled at the prison conditions and concerned more generally; in another case, Judge Ross detailed statistics on the "pervasive nature of prison assaults" that were evidence of the "failure of prisons to protect inmates from assaults" and required "judicial intervention."[4]

The 1977 Eighth Circuit ruling quoted four paragraphs Henley had written about punitive isolation—that the prisoners were violent and that isolation, serving "no rehabilitative purpose," was "counterproductive." Adding not a word of legal analysis about the cap on time, the panel affirmed on the "basis of Judge Henley's well-reasoned opinion." The Circuit spent another four paragraphs (this time of its own crafting) on the fee and cost award. In October of 1976, about six months after Henley ruled, Congress enacted the Civil Rights Attorney's Fees Award Act of 1976. The statute gave judges discretion to award the "prevailing party . . . a reasonable attorney's fee as part of costs." Relying on the legislative history, the Circuit concluded Congress had intended its statute to apply to pending cases, that state agencies could be required to pay whether named a party or not and that, because the lawyers had functioned as private attorneys general, the fee award was "justified."[5]

As support, the Circuit cited two Supreme Court decisions, one from 1927 holding that it could assess "costs" (such as filing and transcript fees) against states, and another from 1976 recognizing congressional power to authorize states to pay attorney fees if losing Title VII employment discrimination cases. In a footnote, its decision (*Finney II*) explained that, having found power in the Fee Act, it did not have to address "bad faith." Yet, the judges added that the "record fully support[ed] the finding . . . that the conduct of the state officials justified the award under the bad faith exception." As to the amount, the Eighth Circuit found the $20,000 award "reasonable" and added $2,500 for the lawyers' "services on this appeal." Arkansas paid those sums "under protest" and without waiving "its rights to challenge the authority of the Federal Courts to order such payments."[6]

MUSICAL CHAIRS IN ARKANSAS POLITICS GENERATING MORE MONEY FOR MORE PRISONS

After Henley ruled in 1976, the legislature chartered another commission on prisons that reiterated the call for *rehabilitation* and added a plea for oversight, given the dollars pouring into the state's prisons. Bill Clinton, running for Attorney General, pressed for mandatory minimums following convictions for violent crimes, while Commissioner Hutto, then forty-one years old, announced he was leaving to be the Deputy Corrections Director in Virginia. The Board of Correction named James Mabry, whom Hutto had brought from Texas, as the interim Director and later made that appointment permanent.[7]

Before departing, Hutto was in open disagreement with legislators; he labeled "disastrous" their eagerness to punish people through "stricter parole laws and good-time provisions." Hutto accurately foresaw that populations would continue to rise, costs would soar, and more court orders would come. (By Hutto's account, the price per prisoner had increased more than 60 percent over five years.) By then, Dale Bumpers had gone to the Senate and been replaced by David Pryor, a Democrat who once held Oren Harris' congressional seat after Harris became a federal judge in

1966. Pryor took on the governorship in 1975 and served until 1979 when he became a US Senator after John McClellan died.[8]

All were aligned on "tough on crime" politics, which collided on the ground with Judge Henley's caps on prison population. Building more beds was one route, and another was to get some people out. Hutto urged the state to fund work release centers and implored the legislature to protect his predecessor Robert Sarver, against whom a jury had leveled a $50,000 damage award because a prisoner was shot by a trusty during Sarver's tenure. Hutto argued that no one would serve as a commissioner "under that kind of threat" and that neither he, Sarver, nor other administrators "could have prevented" the shooting.[9] Within a year, the legislature enacted an indemnification provision.

Governor Pryor understood he was required to lock people up "constitutionally," which entailed millions of dollars "in new construction funds." Keeping abreast of prison population growth was, however, a losing proposition. While in 1970, Arkansas had about 1,200 people in its prisons, by 1976, it confined 2,300 people of whom almost half were Black men serving, on average, sentences of eight-and-a-half years.[10] Arkansas' prison population growth rate was 17 percent—significantly higher than the national rate of 11 percent. Facing that upward spiral, Governor Pryor requested a 16 percent increase for prisons for 1977 and a 25 percent increase for 1978.[11]

Flash back to Governor Bumpers' fight to get less than $3 million, for which the price was firing Sarver and that in 1965 the Arkansas Legislature had *no* budget line for prisons. The willingness in 1977 to pay the "price-tag on the new space"—an estimated $25 million on top of some $20 million for operations—was contrary to economic models in which rational actors are price-sensitive. In theory, as price goes up, demand goes down. What Arkansas did not, however, want to do was pay the small amount owed to the prisoners' lawyers under Judge Henley's 1976 ruling. Money was the through-line that drove Arkansas' efforts to profit from prisoner labor, to keep services paltry in prison, and to avoid paying the prisoners' lawyers— all the while pouring state dollars into confinement.

THE "FIRST PRIORITY": LOCKING MORE PEOPLE UP

"Crime Consensus: The Arkansas House has voted 'ninety to nothing'
to toughen state parole laws. . . . [T]he costs of building new and
upgrading old prison space are daunting enough, but we can think
about the added millions after we've tended to the first priority—
getting the repeaters off the parole list and behind bars."

—Editorial, *Arkansas Democrat*, January 23, 1977[12]

Less than three weeks after losing its *Finney II* appeal, Arkansas
endorsed more incarceration. The Senate—over a lone dissent—
approved a parole bill to "lengthen the stay" for people convicted
of felonies; instead of a sixth of a sentence, the new bill doubled
the time a person had to spend in prison before becoming eligible
for parole. Although Hutto had objected, his replacement, James
Mabry, did not. Mabry's support was (unsurprisingly) in line with
his boss, Governor Pryor, who endorsed the measure as did Attorney General Bill Clinton, sworn in on January 11, 1977.[13]

The court-ordered population caps were salient as Pryor and Clinton argued for more buildings and the increased use of probation and
of work release. As Clinton explained, without all three, "we're going
to have an unbearable financial, legal and political position, not only
for state prisons, but also for county jails around the state" that had
to take the overflow when federal population caps were breached. In
early 1977, "the limits were reached . . . and . . . prison officials were
forced to turn back prisoners" sent from local jails. A few individuals
filed lawsuits arguing that, given terrible jail conditions, they had a
"right to serve time in prison" that provided some services.

Jail crowding was also under federal court supervision, with
warnings from Judge Eisele that he would order releases if population caps were exceeded. Meanwhile Clinton argued for a "new
prison facility" and, in March of 1977, the legislature approved $3.9
million for prison construction. Within a month, the need for more
money was patent; given the new parole rules, the population was
projected to double within four years. The Board of Correction instructed Mabry to seek $17.5 million for facilities because, without
a "massive building program," the prisons would be "overflowing

and in contempt of court orders." Another estimate put $37 million as the price tag, with $30 million for building and more for operating costs.[14]

Commissioner Mabry continued to try to spin the news; the Arkansas Department of Correction's (ADC) 1977 annual report featured an organization chart of institutional, administrative, and special services. However glossy the attempt, the content revealed the racism and poverty of life in prison. Black men continued to be about half the population, and most people were "unskilled" with education levels of grade six or less. Black women were 57 percent of the women's unit. Sweat labor remained key. Arkansas directly funded $6.23 million, less than half of the $14 million budget; federal money provided almost $3 million, and income from farming and prison work programs accounted for another $5 million.[15]

GOVERNOR PRYOR'S 1977 "CITIZENS' COMMISSION" ON PRISONS: OPPRESSIVE WORK, VIOLENCE, CORRUPTION, AND NO REHABILITATION

"The history of the Arkansas prisons has not been a pleasant one, something for which the entire population of the state must share responsibility. . . . Due to the intervention of the Federal Judiciary, Arkansas has recently endeavored to raise the standards of its correctional services. . . . [P]rison facilities must be more than a dry place to warehouse criminals. They must be safe and secure, and they must entail proficient laundry, dining, recreational and treatment components. They must, in short, be humane. . . . To be frank, a person treated like rabble while in prison will respond like rabble upon his release."

—The 1977 Arkansas Prison Study Commission[16]

How was money being spent? Governor Pryor understood that Arkansas' prisons not only posed a problem of unconstitutionality but also of corruption, which could become *his* political problem. Money was going into the ADC, which had no guardrails. Pryor called for a "citizens' commission" and in 1977, the legislature created the Arkansas Prison Study Commission.[17]

Recall that in 1967, after the torture revelations, the legislature chartered a first commission whose report prompted the 1968 statute creating the state's ADC, with rehabilitation as a statutory goal. This second commission became another forum to debate the purposes of state punishment; by January 1, 1978, it was to address "all aspects of the Department of Correction"—housing, budgets, farm profits, good time, and reform of sentencing and parole laws. Pryor directly appointed most members (including Jack Holt Jr.), who joined a state senator, a member of the House, and the chairs of the Boards of Correction and of Parole. Around the same time, ADC announced it was drafting its "master plan" and offered a "Blueprint for Correction," which had neither priorities nor a timetable but called for a new four-hundred-bed prison that "could be expanded" to hold one thousand, a one-hundred-bed "intensive treatment center for mentally ill, emotionally disturbed and retarded" individuals, more pre-release centers, and better controls over inventory and accounting.[18]

In contrast, the legislature's Commission issued eighty pages to "guide in formulation of policy," albeit without "exacting and detailed recommendations." Just as court decisions, the IPPC, and the UN had proffered ideas about penological purposes, Arkansas' "citizen commission" did as well. This self-described "diverse group" sketched the history of the "treatment of offenders by Western Civilization in general, and by the State of Arkansas in particular," and credited *Talley v. Stephens* with bringing to the "free world" the terrible accounts that "beatings and torture were commonplace" and prisoners "lived under despicable conditions." Noting that as it wrote in 1977, court hearings were underway, the Commission described "dramatic changes" because of "prodding of the Federal Judiciary."[19]

Much more was needed. A "most serious" deficiency was fiscal management, which was in "shambles," implicitly because of corruption and graft. The Commission's "subcommittee on prison fiscal affairs" noted that the Department could not account for "more than $27,000 of the $29,545 in the inmate welfare fund," nor find forty-six deeds for property it "supposedly" held. In its final report, the Commission concluded that "physical inventories were incomplete or entirely lacking," as were tracking systems for safeguarding the "integrity of . . . funds" received. Another problem was that Arkansas lagged in developing alternatives to incarceration. Of the four thousand people convicted yearly, about 1,500 (35 percent) went to prison. The Commission urged fiscal management and a reduction in the numbers sent to prison, as warehousing people did not suffice.[20]

What flowed from the critique and aspirations? The Commission proposed cutbacks so that Cummins would become the only maximum-security facility and more convicted people would be sent to community-based centers. Another lower-security facility for four hundred people would be built "near a populous urban area" to enable better "rehabilitation" services, professional staff, "contact" with the community, and work release. Location was important because some employees were commuting sixty miles a day while paid terribly (first-tier staff made under $7,700 a year) and required to do "overtime to chase escaping inmates." Thus, even as Arkansas had "progressed a century" within the decade by having *state-paid* staff, the workforce had "a serious lack of professionalism," especially at the lower echelons plagued by "high turnover, high absenteeism and low morale." The Commission called for earmarked appropriations for training, managers included, and changing the pay scale ("far into the bottom half of the country").

Under the header "inmate care and treatment," the discussion matched Henley's grim descriptions. Arkansas' "hard, strict prison" might provide safety but was "made too hard for the good of both the inmate and society"; treating people "like rabble" was inhumane and unwise. Commission members observed staff "resorting to physical or verbal harassment and abuse" and "needlessly degrading inmates in front of free-world people." The recommendation was not to employ any person "who cannot maintain and demonstrate a respect for his charges."[21]

ADC did not implement these recommendations. Moreover, neither the two legislative commissions nor Judge Henley took on the *engine* of that abuse: forced labor aiming for "profits" through ruthless exploitation. Buried in the 1977 report in its discussion of agriculture was that about a third of the prisoners worked "in hoe squads," justified by ADC as teaching good work habits and creating incentives for reassignment. But the Commission found that the prison had few "non-field jobs" and the "free-world market" had little need for hoeing. Hence, the recommendation was for mechanization. As to vocational training, the Commission commended teaching electronics, welding, machine repair, furniture manufacturing and, for women, cosmetology.[22]

Violence was also in view, with "disturbing signs that inmates [were] subjected to physical abuse by Department Officers." Given that court hearings were to commence, the Commission urged "the Governor, the Legislature, and the appropriate Prosecuting Attorneys" to follow the situation "as it develops through the courts." The federal court's docket sheet provided concrete details. At the end of September, Henley turned over the Penitentiary Cases to Judge Eisele; the following April, Eisele directed Magistrate Faulkner to take evidence on allegations that two prisoners had been beaten.[23] Eisele's rulings thereafter confirmed that brutality and unfettered discretion remained central to life at Cummins.

THE "ENDLESS LITIGATION" CONTINUES: *FINNEY V. MABRY* AND "THE RULE OF LAW"

"[P]rison officials sometimes decided how to punish a prisoner before the prisoner was given a hearing."

> —A. L. Lockhart, testifying in *Finney v. Mabry*, May 26, 1978[24]

"When arrogant, unprincipled, and evil men are in control, the rule of law becomes meaningless."

> —Judge Thomas Eisele, *Finney v. Mabry*, June 30, 1978[25]

"The Arkansas prison system is already besieged with prisoner petitions and suits, averaging about one every two days filed in federal court during 1978."

> —*Arkansas Democrat*, February 18, 1979[26]

Early in the winter of 1978, a local headline, "Prison Farm Fight Continues," headed a story of prison staff who had "ambushed" potential escapees, killed one, and wounded the other. The same month, the prisoners' lawyers, Kaplan and Holt Jr., joined by Phil McMath (a year out of law school and son of former Arkansas Governor Sid McMath), filed a "Third Consolidated Amended Substituted Complaint," which, the press explained, was "actually an extension of the 1969 hearings." Entitled *Finney v. Mabry* and entered onto the ever-lengthening *Holt* docket, the prisoners' lawyers, who had received "dozens of . . . complaints of brutality," alleged "23 broad categories" of violations—including that people were held in punitive isolation without hearings, pushed to work beyond capacity, denied adequate medical care, had their mail opened, and were "beaten and intimidated if they write attorneys." Further, the prisoners asserted that the state provided inadequate clothing and personal hygiene items, no evaluation for mental illness, and failed to put "black persons in positions of meaningful authority in the prison system."[27]

The prisoners' lawyers planned to call thirty witnesses; after the first day of testimony, a reporter noted that the "hearings could drag on through the summer." Judge Eisele did not wait, however, to express his distress. After learning that new arrivals were set up to become targets of abuse by mandates that their heads be shaved, that staff continued to make prisoners run to and from the fields, and that punishment was meted out based only on information from the investigating officer in violation of ADC's rules, the judge commented that prison discipline "appears to make a farce of an honest attempt to find the facts." A few months later, Judge Eisele again recorded dismay when A. L. Lockhart, a defendant and later the Commissioner after Mabry stepped down, admitted that, at times, no investigation took place and punishment was decided before hearings were held.[28]

On June 30, 1978, a week after the US Supreme Court issued *Hutto v. Finney*, Judge Eisele issued an emotion-laden decision finding Arkansas' disciplinary practices unconstitutional. His twenty-four-page decision came eight years after Henley's indictment of Arkansas' prisons, another forty court orders, and the Supreme Court's affirmation of Henley's orders. Included was a depressing rehash of findings from 1973 about procedures "administered . . . summarily and with hostility." Eisele quoted pages of rules from the ADC's revised 1975 Inmate Handbook that were routinely violated; disciplinary findings were "frequently" based "solely on the statements of a 'charging officer.'" The judge explained: "Even more ominous," that person sometimes relied on an "unnamed informant" and "incredibly enough," the committee required no "tangible or physical evidence" of violations, nor "probe[d] a case so far as to require the questioning of witnesses in person." "[D]epressing evidence" substantiated that at times "high prison officials have ordered verdicts of guilty and have 'suggested' certain punishments"; that arrogance and evil rendered law "meaningless."

Judge Eisele moved from those facts to the governing principles and their theory. After explaining the Supreme Court's due process requirements, Judge Eisele discussed their purposes. The "utilitarian value of . . . insuring . . . accuracy" in government decisions was one; another was the "profound value in the *concept* of due process that is an expression of the very rule of law." That "intrinsic value" had special import in prisons, where "arbitrary treatment" in which "human beings are unfairly treated" was the source of "disorder and discontent" that made prisons harder to manage and undermined the potential "of attaining their correctional goals." Reminding the defendants that "prisoners are incarcerated not for punishment but as punishment," the judge ordered adherence to ADC policies to end the "type of abuse" he identified.[29]

AT THE SUPREME COURT: AFFIRMATION WITH SUBTEXTS

"[Judge Henley] has never been met with compliance. . . ."
—Philip Kaplan arguing *Hutto v. Finney*, February 21, 1978[30]

"[T]he Eighth Circuit's holding [in *Jackson v. Bishop*] . . . broke the ice in what theretofore had been a reluctance on the part of federal courts . . . to interfere with state prison administration."
—Justice Harry Blackmun to Justice John Paul Stevens, June 15, 1978, commenting on Stevens' draft *Hutto v. Finney* opinion[31]

"We felt we were on sound ground all along. But when the Supreme
Court accepts a case, it causes one to hold one's breath."

—Jack Holt Jr., June 23, 1978[32]

ADC's loss before Judge Eisele came after its loss in the Supreme
Court. The debates before the Supreme Court, in both the justices'
private memoranda and their opinions, illustrate that *Hutto v. Finney* was simultaneously a peak in prisoners' rights protection and
a harbinger of the retrenchment that followed. While confirming
the power of federal judges to provide prophylactic remedies, the
Court's decision by Justice Stevens elided the question of a constitutional "right to rehabilitation." Justice Rehnquist's dissent showed
his toleration of prison violence and his ambitions (later realized) to
limit federal judicial power in all kinds of civil rights cases. Mining
the specifics reveals the parameters of what states could then do to
and had to do for imprisoned people.

In May of 1977, Attorney General Clinton had posed three questions to the Court: whether the Civil Rights Attorney's Fees Award
Act permitted judges to order states to pay fees to victorious opponents; whether, if so, the Eleventh Amendment to the US Constitution barred payments from state treasuries; and whether the Eighth
Amendment ruled out "the use of indefinite punitive isolation for
serious infractions of prison discipline." The stakes prompted the
attorneys general of California, Iowa, Mississippi, Pennsylvania,
and Texas to join Arkansas in arguing that their sovereign immunity protected them from paying fees. Filing for the prisoners was
the US Department of Justice (steered by President Carter's Attorney General Griffin Bell), the Lawyers' Committee for Civil Rights
Under Law (formed in 1963 because of President Kennedy's "call to
the bar" to enlist law firms to represent civil rights litigants), and
the ACLU, joined by thirty other legal organizations helping "under-
represented" interests.[33]

Were this case to have been decided a few years later, Arkansas
and its supporters would have prevailed on the three issues. But anticipating a loss, Arkansas tried to convince the Court to dismiss the
petition as "improvidently granted" ("DIG"), a practice available if a

record or legal developments makes a case ill-suited for a nationwide ruling. Arkansas argued that the issues, largely governed by state law, were idiosyncratic. Clinton cited the new Arkansas law (for which Hutto had pushed) requiring the state pay fees as well as "actual . . . damages" for state officials "based on an act or omission by the officer or employee while acting without malice and in good faith within the course and scope of his employment and in performance of his official duties." Whatever federal law required, money would come from Arkansas. Moreover, Judge Henley's April 2, 1976 "Clarifying Memorandum Opinion" had solved the state's concerns; it could keep people more than thirty days for new serious offenses. The prisoners' lawyers had a different request: postpone argument and order the state to pay about $5,000 to transcribe nine days of testimony (about 1,000 pages) for the justices to read. Private exchanges among law clerks and justices noted these requests would be considered after argument; the published decision made no mention of them.[34]

As it turned out, the prisoners won, and the justices who had voted *against* granting review were part of the majority *giving* the prisoners those victories.[35] Of the four who voted to take the case— Chief Justice Burger, and Justices Powell, White, and Rehnquist— only Rehnquist was a full-on dissenter; he would have reversed the cap on isolation time and the fee order. Joining the Stevens opinion upholding the isolation remedy, Burger, Powell, and White disagreed about paying lawyer fees.

Rehnquist was not the only one pushing a different outcome. A law clerk for Justice Stevens had urged reversal. While that clerk's objections did not persuade Stevens, they aligned with Rehnquist's published views and thereafter made their way into constitutional law. This young lawyer argued that judges ought not to "substitute . . . their penological theories for those of the state's elected and appointed officials." Nonetheless, he offered his own: that because overcrowding and inedible food had ended, there was nothing "inherently barbarous about the conditions of Arkansas' punitive isolation." Further, given "the usefulness of isolation," long stays were not necessarily disproportionate. The clerk honed in on Henley's comment that punitive isolation lacked a "rehabilitative purpose" and told Justice Stevens that relying on rehabilitation as an Eighth Amendment "touchstone" was "particularly unwise," as "even the most liberal prison administrators are coming to the view that rehabilitation in prison is a delusion, and that punishing prisoners is what prison is for." Those views tracked the opinion of the head of the US Bureau of Prisons, Norman Carlson, who announced that the federal system was no longer focused on rehabilitation. "The unfortunate truth . . . is that we don't know very much about the causes or cures for crime." People could volunteer, Carlson had noted, for rehabilitative programs, but the point of incarceration was punishment. The Stevens clerk also flagged that, by describing the indeterminacy of punitive isolation as a problem of cruel and unusual punishment, Henley was "casting doubt on the sentencing policies of many states."[36]

Stevens did not adopt those positions. Rather, and with support from Justice Blackmun who pushed for clarifying that *Holt I, II*, and *III* were the "sequel" to *Jackson v. Bishop*, Stevens culled information and highlighted that Henley's conclusion was "amply supported by the evidence" that the prisons were a "dark and evil world completely alien to the free world."[37] Yet even as Holt Jr. was right that prisoners were on "solid ground," he was also right about "holding one's breadth." Digging into what Stevens and the dissenters said reveals the mixed blessings within. Stevens did not use the occasion to endorse state obligations to enable rehabilitation or to question the rationality of punitive isolation. Moreover, the arguments against the prisoners have since become the governing doctrine, which has constrained what constitutional law contributes to circumscribing incarceration's harms.

Stevens' account broadcast the horrors of Arkansas' prisons (familiar to readers of this book) to a national audience. In footnotes, Stevens fleshed out the "routine conditions that the ordinary Arkansas convict had to endure." Arkansas sent people during the day to tend "crops by hand" and at night to barracks where they were terrorized by "creepers" who might rape or slash them. Stevens recounted how prisoners were "lashed" until "bloody and bruised" and tortured with the Tucker Telephone. Stevens termed these common punishments "cruel, unusual, and unpredictable." As to indeterminate punitive isolation, Stevens relied on information from the 1969, 1970, 1973, and 1976 Henley decisions. While on average four people were held together, at times "as many as 10 or 11 . . . were crowded into windowless 8'×10' cells containing no furniture other than a source of water and a toilet that could only be flushed from outside the cell." Despite "infectious diseases," each morning the staff "jumbled together" the mattresses and returned them "at random" at night. People were also starving. Given "grue," prisoners "received fewer than 1,000 calories a day" when 2,700 were recommended for men.[38]

Stevens also recounted that, despite those conditions, Henley had declined to impose "immediately . . . a detailed remedy" and only ordered a "substantial start." After a series of hearings, findings that progress was "unsatisfactory," more hearings, and more time for ADC "to devise a plan of their own" to "cure the worst evils," Henley ended his jurisdiction. After the Eighth Circuit's 1974 reversal, Henley wrote in 1976 that either conditions had been worse than he had realized or that, with the population rising from one thousand to 1,500, "conditions had seriously deteriorated since 1973." Stevens explained that only in 1976 did Henley impose boundaries, requiring each person to have a bunk on which to sleep, food other than grue, and spend no more than thirty days in isolation.[39] In short, in the Supreme Court, Henley's years of deference to defendants was seen to be a *judicial virtue* that persuaded all but Rehnquist to affirm the cap on time in isolation.

THE CONSTITUTION, A "RIGHT TO REHABILITATION," AND THE ECONOMICS OF CIVIL RIGHTS LITIGATION

"[T]he Constitution does not require that every aspect of prison discipline serve a rehabilitative purpose."

—Justice Stevens for the Court, *Hutto v. Finney*, June 23, 1978[40]

"No person of ordinary feeling could fail to be moved by the Court's recitation of the conditions formerly prevailing in the Arkansas prison system."

—Justice Rehnquist, dissenting, *Hutto*[41]

The Supreme Court's job is to instruct the country on the legal meaning flowing from the facts it recounts. The issue—for majority and dissent—was whether federal courts had the *power* to order remedies for constitutional violations persisting since 1969 and 1970. Drawing from its 1976 *Estelle v. Gamble* health care decision that quoted Blackmun's 1968 whipping ruling, the Court had to determine whether punishments were "grossly disproportionate" or "transgress today's 'broad and idealistic concepts of dignity, civilized standards, humanity, and decency.'" Stevens concluded that Arkansas' prison conditions, "taken as a whole," did so. That formulation became talismanic for lower court judges assessing whether a "totality of conditions" rendered facilities unlawful.[42]

As discussed, some judges no longer embrace looking to "today's . . . concepts of dignity, civilized standards, humanity, and decency" and instead ask whether a particular practice violated standards in 1791 when the Eighth Amendment was adopted. Yet, in 1978, Stevens pointed out that Arkansas *agreed* with the legal principles respecting prisoners' dignity and did not contest that punitive isolation conditions violated the Eighth Amendment. The state only challenged the thirty-day remedy cap, which it argued was based on Henley's erroneous view that unending isolation constituted an indeterminate sentence serving no "rehabilitative purpose" and making "bad men worse."[43] Had the Court endorsed that interpretation of Henley's ruling, *Hutto v. Finney* would have stood for the broad, hopeful proposition that the Constitution required prisons to be useful and restorative, not do harm, and not detain indefinitely.

Whether any member of the Court would have signed onto these propositions is questionable. They did not have to because Justice Stevens avoided them by chastising the state for plucking out a few sentences from Henley's long decision and mischaracterizing their import. Considered "in its entirety," Henley had made "abundantly clear" that punitive isolation *per se* was not unconstitutional. Henley's time limit was contingent on "specific conditions": the starvation diet, overcrowding, violence, vandalism, and ill-trained staff. Therefore, as part of a "comprehensive order," the thirty-day cap was a permissible judicial response to limit the "risk of inadequate compliance" and did not rely on "a new legal test."[44]

Stevens relegated to a footnote whether a "rehabilitative purpose" was constitutionally required; his ambiguous sentence was that "the Constitution does not require that every aspect of prison discipline serve a rehabilitative purpose."[45] A cheerful interpretation was that the Constitution *did* require that *some* aspects of prisons serve rehabilitative purposes. But by then, the tide was turning, as Arkansas had pointed out by citing a 1977 Fifth Circuit decision on Alabama's dreadful prisons. The trial judge, Frank Johnson, had mandated vocational and educational programs that the Fifth Circuit reversed. That court ruled that, as long as a state furnished "reasonably adequate food, clothing, shelter, sanitation, necessary medical attention and personal safety," the Constitution did not require "any and every amenity which some person may think is needed to avoid mental, physical, and emotional deterioration."[46] The word "amenity" was hardly relevant to prisons then, nor is it now. Yet that 1977 appellate court decision presaged the law that would follow. As rehabilitation receded in politics and in law, the Supreme Court came to tolerate a host of deprivations under a revised approach to the Eighth Amendment.

Although Stevens avoided confronting, let alone delineating, a "right to rehabilitation," he could not skip over another legal question: what *nexus* had to exist between the constitutional violations found and the remedies ordered? One answer could have been that judges were to craft efficacious responses. But Chief Justice Burger had already made headway in limiting federal courts' power to shape structural remedies in his 1974 school desegregation decision, *Milliken v. Bradley*. A district court had concluded that Detroit schools unconstitutionally segregated its students. The court had ordered interdistrict busing so that inner-city Black school children and white children from suburban neighborhoods would integrate each other's classrooms. A five-person majority rejected that remedy on the grounds that the desegregation plaintiffs had neither challenged the composition of the suburban schools nor put on proof that those schools discriminated on the basis of race.

Cutting back on its prior endorsement of the "flexibility" to shape equitable relief, the Court in *Milliken* required (as Rehnquist's *Hutto*'s dissent explained) a kind of "tailoring" in which the remedy had to be related to "the condition alleged to offend the Constitution."[47]

Rehnquist was correct in identifying *Milliken* as raising questions about Henley's time cap. Rehnquist argued that, given lower court orders that had ended crowding and starvation, the limit on time in solitary was a "prophylactic" measure evidencing a "management role" he claimed belonged to the state. Further, we know from later decisions that Rehnquist found no constitutional problems with profound isolation for thirty days or longer; he termed such punishments "normal" incidents of incarceration that prisoners had to endure and that federal courts ought not address. Rehnquist previewed those views in *Hutto*: "The District Court . . . enjoins a practice which has not been found inconsistent with the Constitution."[48]

In 1978, Stevens was one of eight votes upholding Henley's remedy. Stevens explained that Henley had "given prison authorities repeated opportunities to remedy the cruel and unusual conditions in the isolation cells," that Arkansas had not "fully complied with the court's earlier orders," and therefore that Henley had the power to impose a cap. This "long and unhappy history . . . justified . . . a comprehensive order to insure against the risk of inadequate compliance," and "special deference" was owed to the "trial judge's years of experience with the problem at hand." Stevens also pointed out that Henley had extrapolated the thirty-day framework from correctional experts, including ADC Commissioner Hutto, testifying that, "ordinarily," people should not be in isolation for more than fourteen days.[49]

In contrast, the Court split five to four on the fee award order, which was the issue that had drawn state amici to support Arkansas in trying to stop state *money* from being used to finance prisoners' litigation. Requiring states to internalize some of the costs of their failings—on a rational actor model—creates incentives for different behavior. Stevens underscored that Arkansas did not "question the accuracy of the finding" about bad faith or that losing parties in bad faith could be required to pay. Rather, Arkansas insisted that the Eleventh Amendment protected the state's treasury from handing $22,000 to the prisoners' lawyers.

Justice Stevens took the same tack Henley had. Deploying Rehnquist's 1974 formulation in *Edelman v. Jordan* that state officials were "not immune from prospective injunctive relief," Stevens described the fee award as part of the "cost of compliance" and thus "'ancillary' to the prospective order enforcing federal law." Given the bad faith, Stevens concluded that federal courts did not have to be "reduced to . . . hoping for compliance"; imposing fines made more sense than having to send "high state officials to jail" for contempt. As to the fee award for time in the Eighth Circuit, Stevens concluded that Congress' fee-shifting applied to "any" action to enforce civil rights; the statute provided no "hint of an exception for States," which made sense, given it aimed to alter *state* action. Stevens also relied on the Court's long-standing practice of awarding "costs" to prevailing parties; "traditionally," states had routinely paid such costs, including when a statute made no mention of them; it would be "absurd" to require Congress make an "express reference" to states in statute on filing fees and taxable costs. Furthermore, courts had "inherent authority" to do so as part of the "orderly administration of justice."[50]

These details are relevant today not only because they provoked dissents but also because their predicates were later rejected as new majorities revised civil rights law to insulate governments. Justice Powell, joined by Chief Justice Burger, argued that fees could not be awarded against states without Congress saying so in a statute's text.[51] Powell also argued (alone) that states *qua* states could not be sued under Section 1983 because that statute referred to "persons." That issue had not been briefed; Justice Brennan had encouraged Powell not to address it and then said so publicly by filing a concurrence. Yet Powell previewed what the Court did thereafter. In 1989, the Court agreed that, although "cities" were "persons" within the meaning of Section 1983, states were not. Powell also objected to reliance on legislative history. That view likewise turned into the Court's "clear statement" rule, requiring Congress to abrogate immunity in statutes' texts and later limiting the bases of Congress' power to do so. Justice Rehnquist, who joined Powell and Burger in objecting to the fees based on the civil rights statute, wrote separately to disagree about the power to rely on bad faith; the state could not be "personally responsible for the recalcitrance." Justice White signed onto that view.[52]

CONSENTING TO COMPLY AND, AGAIN, NOT ENDING

Since 1969, "Arkansas prisons have been declared unconstitutional in every federal court up through the Supreme Court."
—*Arkansas Democrat*, September 2, 1978[53]

The agreement "binds us to do nothing more than what we are already required to do."
—Attorney General Bill Clinton, August 18, 1978[54]

The question was how to turn the legal pronouncements into practices that would change the experiences of people held in prison and of people guarding them. An obvious route by 1978 was a "consent decree," a kind of contract drafted by parties and entered into by courts to set forth binding obligations in light of judicial decisions made. Common in school and prison structural litigations, Philip Kaplan had models from Rhode Island, Pennsylvania, Mississippi, Ohio, and elsewhere.[55]

Yet Arkansas was again recalcitrant. After the Supreme Court's decision, Judge Eisele warned in September that it was "the duty of the state . . . to provide a constitutional penal system, and if it does not, it is my duty to close it down." As drafts were exchanged, the question emerged about oversight by a third party (a "special master" or "monitor"), buffering judges from day-to-day disputes. Federal rules authorized judges to appoint ad hoc "special masters," and losing defendants typically paid the costs. For Arkansas to do so, the state's legislative council had to concur. It approved the "concept" of a Compliance Coordinator and thus implicitly supported "negotiation . . . to end litigation" by agreeing "that the prison system comply with all federal court orders," and a "compliance coordinator" be hired "to report on the progress of the Department . . . in obeying those orders." Judge Eisele weighed in; he did not want to appoint a special master "who works for the judge" and hoped the litigants would give authority to a person to be responsible to them.[56]

The denouement came in nine pages, designed to remain in effect for eighteen months, signed by Philip Kaplan, Jack Holt Jr., and Phillip McMath, on behalf of "all past, present and future inmates confined in the correctional institutions of the Arkansas Department of Correction," and by Bill Clinton representing the defendants. The press ran photos, including the one in figure 25.1.[57] The state agreed to "maintaining a humane prison system consistent with the Constitution and laws of the United States and the State of Arkansas," and honoring "all prior orders and injunctions" including (but not limited to) thirty-nine provisions listed. The state also agreed to pay the prisoners' counsel fees "in full"—$29,894 ($148,000 in 2024 dollars)—and additional fees if returns to court were needed.[58]

Eisele turned that document into a court order, entered on October 5, 1978. Clinton called the accord "one of the most important

FIGURE 25.1 *Holt Offers Clinton a Pen While Lyford and Smedley Watch*, photograph by Larry Obsitnik, accompanying Dianne Woodruff, *Signings Close Suits on Prisons*, Arkansas Gazette, October 6, 1978, courtesy of the publisher

things I've done as attorney general," as it would "save state money, and state officials' time." Eisele told a judicial colleague that the order put Arkansas "far in advance of what is going on elsewhere in prison system reform by establishing the independent monitor system" through which the state was to make all information related to the decree's implementation accessible for oversight.[59]

Despite that upbeat spin, the consent decree's terms were a depressing primer in low standards of "constitutional tolerability." The ADC affirmed that employees would not "use excessive force" or "verbally abuse, curse or use racial slurs when addressing or talking with inmates" and, if an escape was attempted, a new personnel policy would specify that recaptured prisoners were not to be beaten. Further, prisoners were not to "be required to run to and from work as part of their job and training." Quiet cells were generally off limits and, if used, for no "longer than necessary." Grue was not to be served; people in punitive segregation (capped at thirty days) were to be fed "a proper diet daily," have a bunk and, in "emergency situations," be joined by only one other person in a cell. The Department agreed to new disciplinary procedures, a grievance system, access to court and lawyers, and not to retaliate for seeking help.

One innovation was a general population cap: Cummins was not to hold more than 1,650 people and Tucker 676. Arkansas also agreed to provide its prisoners with "reasonable and necessary" health care and to supply adequate food, clothing appropriate for work, towels, and soap. The consent decree also reiterated that the state could not discriminate against "Muslims on account of their religious beliefs" (entitled to the "same, but no greater, privileges . . . of religious worship" as others) and would not serve them pork "against their will." In terms of staffing, "Black employees" were to be assigned "on the same basis" as white employees and ADC would do an "immediate assessment of all Black employees" to consider promotions.[60]

As forecast, the consent decree created a new office of "Compliance Coordinator," to be occupied by a person with "suitable legal, administrative and humanistic skills." As the judge had wanted, he would not appoint a person; rather, the Arkansas Attorney General, the prisoners' lawyers, and the Commissioner of Correction were to select an individual who would be authorized to hire an assistant, have an office near Cummins, assess the "state of compliance," and file reports. Clinton assured the judge the state would pay a yearly salary of $25,000 plus expenses, and Commissioner Mabry "pledged himself 100 percent 'to make the system work properly.'"[61]

ADC was to give the Coordinator all documents requested and (absent emergencies) "unlimited access," without notice, to records and facilities and to talking confidentially with anyone. The Coordinator's recommendations did not bind the Department, which could refuse to follow them, subject to court review if prisoners requested. A final compliance report was to be filed within eighteen months and the court's jurisdiction to end thereafter. Those reports were not open to "inspection by anyone except on order of the Court," nor subject to subpoena or otherwise discoverable; if acting in "good faith," the Compliance Coordinator was to be immune from suit as if a special master.[62]

The entry of the consent decree could have been another place to end this book, except that agreement did *not* end the lawsuit, the miseries prisoners suffered, or political pressures to put more people into prison. As recorded on the court's docket during the years of litigation after 1978, prisoners continued to live amid violence borne from confinement in crowded facilities run by ill-equipped staff. Within eleven months of the June 1978 Supreme Court decision, prisoners sent in more than 800 letters alleging beatings, thefts, and terrible conditions. Court staff selected 231 to docket and thus, during that interval, prisoners' filings comprised "more than one-sixth" of the cases before that district court.[63]

Fights over lawyers' fees also continued. In October 1978, Kaplan, Holt Jr., and McMath filed another "Petition for Attorneys' Fees" for work at and after the Supreme Court argument. Arkansas, described as having spent "more than $1 million in defense costs" (more than $4.9 million in 2024 dollars), objected to a $100 per hour rate and to fee requests by lawyers at the NAACP Legal Defense and Education

Fund for assistance at the Supreme Court. Almost six months later, Judge Eisele awarded Kaplan, Holt Jr., and McMath $20,250 in fees ($91,000 in 2024) and $1,511.18 ($6,800 in 2024) in costs.[64] Thereafter, the "voices of the people"—shaped by political campaigns freighted with racist imagery—kept calling for more incarceration. Bruce Jackson's photograph (figure 25.2) captures the crowding that resulted. And as the next chapters analyze, the new majority at the Supreme Court—likewise assembled through politics—walked back what *Hutto v. Finney* portended and pulled judges away from efforts to lessen those harms.

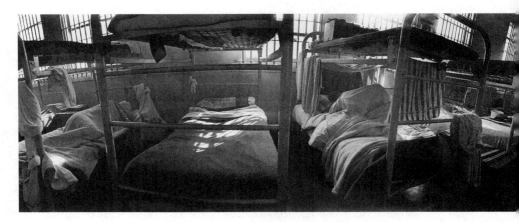

FIGURE 25.2 *Cummins Prison Farm, Grady, Arkansas*, photograph by Bruce Jackson, from the series *Inside the Wire*, 1975, courtesy of the photographer

26

"THE MINIMAL CIVILIZED MEASURE OF LIFE'S NECESSITIES" VERSUS "REHABILITATION"

"[I]t would take Jesus Christ to handle the job" of Compliance Coordinator.

—Board of Correction Chair, September 2, 1978[1]

"People shouldn't have to ask why there is violence in our prisons. All they have to do is look at the overcrowded situations and inadequate space and programs."

—Vernon Housewright, Commissioner, Arkansas Department of Corrections, December 17, 1980[2]

Arkansas had not complied with court mandates for almost a decade. The prisoners' lawyers hoped that the state's *consenting* to a court decree would make a difference. But as reflected in the call for "Jesus Christ" to connect the parties, a miracle was needed. As hundreds of pages filed by the Compliance Coordinator documented, salvation turned out to be hard to come by. Between 1979 and 1981, his office generated voluminous records detailing modest improvement amid violence, crowding, and no health care for mentally ill individuals. Yet, during that time, what sufficed for "constitutional conditions" became easier to achieve.

This chapter weaves together the power struggle in Arkansas with the national debate about what prisons had *to do* for prisoners. Had rehabilitation remained relevant to prisons' constitutionality, governments would have been required to create opportunities for more than survival. That potential was plausible not only because incarcerated people and some judges thought so but because correctional leaders did too. Rehabilitation was a central tenet of the American Correctional Association (ACA), the National Council on Crime and Delinquency, the American Bar Association, legislative commissions, state statutes, and some prisons' policies. Instead, a counternarrative—previewed in the last chapter by Justice Rehnquist's 1978 dissent in *Hutto v. Finney* and pronounced by Bureau of Prison's (BOP) Director Norman Carlson—prevailed: the point of prisons was "punishment," not rehabilitation.[3]

By August of 1981 when Judge Eisele took testimony about whether the state's compliance sufficed, the Supreme Court had undercut his power. In its decision, *Rhodes v. Chapman*, licensing Ohio to hold two people in cells designed for one, the Court ruled that what it called the "minimal civilized measure of life's necessities" were the *maximum* federal courts could require. Beneath the words "double celling" lay the question that ran from Beccaria and Bentham to the prisoner–plaintiffs about what makes punishment *legitimate*. The harms of crowding are known: it begets disease, violence, emotional distress, and noise, and it undermines whatever rules, services, and programs could do to lessen detention's harms. When users outstrip resources, pressures mount for rigid control. Thus, at stake in late twentieth-century debates about "constitutional sufficiency" were governments' roles in mitigating or fueling confinement's miseries. Below, I excavate the harms resulting from the Court's lowering the price of incarceration through a law-license to jam people in.

RACIST SLURS, NO FIRE ESCAPE, AND EIGHTY-SEVEN "TO DOS"

Prison staff exhibited "an unexplainable propensity . . . when possessing a baton or slapper to strike prisoners in the face or head area."

—Second Report of Stephen LaPlante, Compliance
Coordinator, July 1979[4]

Translating rights into material conditions framing prisoners' lived experiences requires reorganizing micro-interactions. The person selected to try in November of 1978 was Stephen C. LaPlante, a thirty-year-old whom Attorney General Clinton praised as "the best of a very good field." LaPlante had studied sociology at the University of San Francisco and the University of Chicago; he had briefly served as a "uniformed deputy" and "ombudsman" in San Francisco's Sheriff Department.[5]

Reading LaPlante's in-the-weeds accounts reminded me of when, teaching a law school clinic and representing Muslim prisoners seeking to observe Ramadan at a federal facility, we succeeded in a settlement so that, during that month-long period, individuals would be able to eat, as required, before sunrise and after sunset. Students gave me a draft agreement that, while pronouncing the constitutional right to practice religion, had no details about how incarcerated people could do so. Specifics were needed on the hours at which alarm clocks were to wake people, so that meals could be prepared, served, and eaten before the first rays of dawn. Changing times to eat and sleep in one prison was straightforward when compared to LaPlante's chronicles I found at the Arkansas State Library. While filed in court as "sealed," facets became public through the news and, later, via the library's shelves. The reasons for sealing become apparent from reading; LaPlante documented his interviews, by name, of prisoners alleging injury and of staff said to have been violent.[6]

LaPlante's uphill slog might have been avoided, given that Bill Clinton became governor in January of 1979. He inherited James Mabry as Commissioner, whose annual report sounded promising, with a "reaffirmation" of prisoners' "humanity" and a budget of $15.5 million. Yet the new governor, some funds, the parties' agreement, and LaPlante's presence did not stop the violence and racism. Failures included high-profile eruptions; 107 people from Cummins' "maximum-security unit . . . overpowered guards," and a few escaped. After gaining control and handcuffing recaptured prisoners, staff continued "striking inmates with slappers and nightsticks." The prisoners' lawyer, Philip Kaplan, said that an Arkansas Department of Correction (ADC) staffer, when clubbing a prisoner, screamed "die, you bastard, die." Among the sixteen employees accused of "excessive force" was A. L. Lockhart, later the Commissioner. Thus, LaPlante's first task was to analyze whether ADC had violated the consent decree mandates that "no ADC employee will use excessive force against any inmate" and that ADC would investigate allegations of misconduct.[7]

LaPlante's March 23, 1979 findings ("under seal") were covered by the press. The full report stated that evidence was "inconclusive" about nine named employees and violence was "definitely established" for seven. LaPlante singled out Lockhart for deciding erroneously that he had no basis to discipline staff. Within weeks, the Board of Correction fired one employee, sanctioned a couple more, and promoted Lockhart to Acting Commissioner after Mabry resigned amid questions of corruption. Kaplan protested that the Board "rewarded one official found to have engaged in violent acts."[8]

LaPlante's next report, filed in early July 1979, detailed dozens of violent incidents laced with racist epithets, quoted in the press. LaPlante described a "pattern" of beatings "behind closed doors," and Clinton called on the Board to fire a guard "for his role in the September 1978 strangulation death" of a prisoner. The next month, LaPlante devoted twenty-three pages to the lack of services for mentally ill individuals; that failure became a leitmotif of his (and then the judge's) analyses. Reflecting LaPlante's academic training, he gave a fulsome account of the many organizations that had addressed prisoners' needs—beginning with the League of Nations' 1934 Standard Minimum Rules for the Treatment of Prisoners and excerpting the 1955 United Nations' revision. LaPlante recounted that in 1976, the American Public Health Association and, in 1977, the ACA called for psychiatric consultation always to be available. Given that Arkansas had done nothing for people with mental health challenges before 1976, LaPlante noted rudimentary beginnings and the desperate need for stable, quality, organized psychiatric services, without which "the mental health program" could not be "considered constitutional."[9]

Instead, resources were going to a new $2.3 million medium-security facility, reminiscent of Jeremy Bentham's hoped for, but never built, Panopticon. Designed, as professional standards commended, so people would not share sleeping space, the building had "184 one-man cells with electronically controlled locking mechanisms" and two glassed-in control stations with a "360-degree view of two of the dayrooms and 92 of the cells."[10]

By the fall of 1979, LaPlante listed eighty-seven topics requiring attention—and thus provided the *first* document in the decade-old litigation that specified metrics of compliance. That set became a touchstone for LaPlante's June 1980, 206-page report focused on Cummins, with separate reports planned on health care, affirmative action, racial discrimination, and Tucker. LaPlante categorized findings as "compliant," "substantially compliant," "partially compliant," or "not in compliance." His approach echoed Judge Henley— cajoling to try to get cooperation from the people running the place while detailing violence and racism. Yet, unlike Henley, LaPlante invoked professional standards, such as the ACA's Correctional Law Project to craft "Model Correctional Rules and Regulations" for "good correctional management and interpretation of current case law." LaPlante found "absolutely appalling" that standard equipment of "whistles" and "handcuffs" were not provided to line staff.[11]

LaPlante identified a few areas of constitutional "compliance" and many that were not, such as the failure to integrate the maximum-security unit. LaPlante reported that the "'pattern or practice' of beating prisoners" was lessening, but mace was being used. Moreover, "quiet cells" remained, and some "mentally disordered" prisoners had been placed in soundproofed enclosures for "long periods of time." Further, racial slurs were commonplace and, at Tucker, Black prisoners were "three times more likely to be convicted of a major offense and receive time" in isolation and more likely to lose good time and jobs. As to legal services, the sole lawyer employed was "so inundated" he could not help on many legally viable claims. Yet, given that another attorney was to join, LaPlante found "partial compliance."[12]

One of many attachments to LaPlante's June 1980 "Third Report of the Prison Compliance Coordinator on the Defendants' State of Compliance" were notes of twenty-three points discussed in a three-hour "Compliance Meeting" with the Commissioner and ADC staff.

One topic that leaps out was a "fire procedure plan"; LaPlante raised the issue and learned none existed. The quantity of food to provide was another concern; after discussion, second portions were not to become available. Another question was how to tell Judge Eisele that staff wanted to keep maximum-security cells racially segregated.[13]

As LaPlante explained in a paper delivered in 1980 at a workshop of the 110th Congress of the ACA, his presence and flexibility, along with a "constant threat of a surprise visit," produced change. Having "harangued the state" for not funding mental health services, he could, for example, take the blame (as a "scapegoat") for what the Department both needed and wanted. LaPlante did offer a "word of caution" about the risk of being co-opted.[14] The risk he did not forecast was being fired. Within the year, the Board of Correction declined to renew his contract.

POLITICAL AND ECONOMIC SUPPORT FOR—AND AGAINST—COMPLIANCE: NEEDING MONEY OR MAGIC

People "are sent to prison as a punishment, not for punishment."
—Vernon Housewright, Illinois Warden, April 1971[15]

"[T]here is no way they can be in compliance by August."
—Philip Kaplan, March 31, 1981[16]

"You either have to have the money or a bag of magic tricks. We didn't have either."
—Vernon Housewright, former ADC Commissioner, Compliance Hearing, August 26, 1981[17]

Governor Clinton recruited Vernon Housewright, reputed to be a "very experienced, yet very progressive" corrections leader. Housewright made his mark running the Vienna Correctional Center in Illinois, a "model" minimum-security facility and the first accredited under the ACA standards Housewright had helped draft. On arrival in Arkansas, Housewright found few resources and little political support for funds to meet the obligations of the consent decree.[18]

But Housewright tried. Like Robert Sarver and Arkansas' Legislative Prison Commissions of 1967 and 1977, Housewright endorsed rehabilitation. His ADC 1980 annual report paid tribute to *Talley v. Stephens*, which "marked the beginning of free-world concern" about prisons; *Jackson v. Bishop* for outlawing the "strap," and *Holt v. Sarver* as the "first time in American history that the Federal Judiciary had held that an entire prison system was being operated unconstitutionally." ADC highlighted construction in 1971 of the first maximum-security unit; the first rodeo in 1972; new education and work release programs in 1973; the end and then the return of "court control" in 1974; more prison construction in 1975; and Judge Henley's caps on prison population in 1976 and his mandate to close the women's unit. The Department heralded its new building that cost $3.5 million, the resumption of capital punishment in 1976, more facilities opening in 1977, the 1978 settlement, and, in 1980, the completion of the medium-security unit and launch of a division of "Research, Planning and Management Services." ADC noted no housing existed for "mentally disordered inmates."[19]

One driver in broadcasting ADC's accomplishments was the 1980 release of the movie *Brubaker* starring Robert Redford. The script extrapolated from accounts by Thomas Murton, whom—as detailed in earlier chapters—Winthrop Rockefeller had appointed and then fired after Murton's repeated calls to the press to decry the state's prisons. A *Washington Post* headline, "Arkansas Lets the Light into 'Brubaker's' Dark Age Prisons," described ADC as "practically" begging "reporters to tour." While describing "very dramatic" changes due to litigation that pushed the state to spend taxpayer dollars, "overcrowded" barracks were staffed at night by "only four guards for a thousand prisoners." The reporter astutely identified that additional funds depended on pressure from two sets of players—federal judges calling for compliance and local sheriffs pushing for more prison beds to reduce crowded jails.[20]

To bolster arguments for larger budgets, ADC turned to the National Institute of Corrections (NIC)—created to professionalize corrections and help states ward off lawsuits. The NIC dispatched Anthony Travisono, who had run Rhode Island's prisons before becoming ACA's Executive Director in 1974. Travisono described crowding the "most serious problem," along with a "critical need" for more security staff in Arkansas. He proposed adding 44 new positions to the 112 staff at Tucker and another 99 at Cummins to its 154 positions. Travisono's involvement provides another reminder that Arkansas was not an outlier. By 1977, Rhode Island's prisons were under federal court orders based on findings of inadequate heating and light, unsanitary plumbing, filthy showers, fire hazards, "deplorable" food service, "deafening and maddening" noise, and "rampant violence" rendering detention an "imminent public health, fire, and safety hazard."[21]

In the spring of 1980, another potential source of help for prisoners came from a new federal statute, the Civil Rights of Institutionalized Persons Act (CRIPA). Congress authorized the US Department of Justice (DOJ) to notify states or localities about failings in prisons, mental health facilities, and juvenile detention centers and to file lawsuits to compel improvements. Instead of welcoming federal pressure to wrangle funds from the legislature, Clinton's staff objected; that anti-federal government posturing did not prevent Clinton from losing his reelection bid in November of 1980, which meant that the prisoners lost their chance to have any semblance of progressive corrections leadership.[22]

The new Governor, Frank D. White, requested $19.2 million in 1981—despite Housewright's view that "the absolute minimum" of $40 million was needed to run a "manageable, safe, humane, constitutional system," including $2 million earmarked for a mental health care unit. In January 1981, Housewright left; when testifying later at the compliance hearing, he explained he resigned because he could not get sufficient funds.[23] In Housewright's stead, Governor White returned the prison system to the very people who had run it unconstitutionally and corruptly—Arkansas insiders imported from Texas. A. L. Lockhart, then forty, became the acting head.

Lockhart had a reputation as a "bully," garnered in part from LaPlante's 1979 report, concluding that "clear and convincing evidence" identified Lockhart as one of the culprits who had "beat and kicked inmates needlessly after an attempted escape." The following year, LaPlante referred to the US Attorney's Office another prisoner complaint, that Lockhart stole meat from prison stocks and threatened to kill him for talking. The federal investigation, which resulted in no prosecution, slowed but did not stop Lockhart's permanent appointment as ADC Commissioner. LaPlante said he was the "last major casualty" of Clinton's defeat.[24] The casualty count was much higher because prisoners were left in inadequately funded, poorly staffed, graft-ridden, and unsafe facilities.

Kaplan objected to the "disastrous mistake" of firing LaPlante. Nonetheless, Judge Eisele acquiesced based on the consent decree (whose terms he had influenced) that required the Compliance Coordinator to be "mutually acceptable" to all parties. Eisele did order the state to "retain" LaPlante to write a final report, filed in June of 1981 "under seal . . . and placed in [the] Vault." When LaPlante's replacement described him as too political, LaPlante's responded that to "say the compliance process is apolitical is naïve."[25]

In March 1981, LaPlante had identified the two main problems as crowding and lack of care for the mentally ill. Despite these "last big hurdle[s]," LaPlante was "very confident" that improvements were "just a matter of time." At Kaplan's request, Eisele agreed to a fact-finding hearing to ascertain whether the state was acting in accord with "the 87 compliance points established by the consent decree." The proceedings, estimated to take four weeks, started August 11 and, with interruptions, continued through October 5, 1981—three years to the day after the entry of the consent decree.[26]

Before the hearing began, Kaplan outlined dozens of violations, including the ongoing use of and failures to investigate "excessive force," "racial slurs," inadequate health care, and crowding. Kaplan asked that defendants be found in contempt and for appointment of a special master. LaPlante's final report had significant overlap with the prisoners' filing. In almost 200 pages with hundreds more in supporting documents, LaPlante concluded that the ADC was in compliance with about fifty of the eighty-seven points. A glaring fault was that "inmate safety [was not] at a constitutional level." The reasons included crowding, inadequate programs for "mentally disordered prisoners," and the need for better security personnel, health care, sanitation, affirmative action, and procedures for grievances. A stark example of dysfunction came from the Cummins' "sick call," which ran for one hour starting at 4:30 a.m. and during which some eighty people might try to get care. Verification came from the *Arkansas Democrat*, running a series on "efforts to comply with federal court orders." The ADC's Assistant Director for Health Services told a reporter, "the funding isn't there." Another marker was staff turnover: "About 70 percent of the system's approximately 450 correction officers were replaced between February of 1980 and 1981."[27]

LaPlante was not wholly negative. He described significant improvements including that the women's facility had gone from being "one of the worst" to "one of the finest." LaPlante characterized the state's response as a "roller coaster," in which the "department moves at varying speeds and rises to near compliance, followed by all-too-rapid descents." LaPlante's ouster meant that determining the pitch and direction was for Judge Eisele. As federal oversight loomed, Governor White released $175,000 from his emergency funds—"every available penny . . . to bring the prison program into compliance with federal court orders to improve conditions." Nonetheless, the *Arkansas Gazette* reported that "Arkansas prison officials still [had] not complied with court orders relating to . . . [the] crowding of inmates." More than 360 prisoners were in barracks, and 250 were jammed into trailers, which meant each person had about forty-five square feet of space. Yet, before Eisele began to consider Arkansas' compliance, the Supreme Court issued *Rhodes v. Chapman* that, as the *Arkansas Gazette* explained, limited federal court powers over states' prisons.[28]

"LIGHT AND QUITE AIRY" OR THE "KINGDOM OF THE WILD": DOUBLE CELLING IN THE SOUTHERN OHIO CORRECTIONAL FACILITY

"In an era of increasing numbers of people being committed to correctional systems with limited resources, the area of greatest concern is the ability of the systems to adequately house the growing number of inmates."

—Brief of Ohio, defending its double celling in
Rhodes v. Chapman, 1980[29]

"The United States Supreme Court's ruling Monday allowing state prison officials in Ohio to house two men in a cell built for one is a source of some relief for the Arkansas Correction Department."

—*Arkansas Gazette*, June 16, 1981[30]

Throughout this book, I have stressed that *baselines* loom large in debates about punishment. The litigation about double celling in Ohio makes that point. The prison at issue, the Southern Ohio Correctional Facility, did not look like the dilapidated, fly-infested buildings in Arkansas to which it was compared. Known as Lucasville (the town in which it sat), that maximum-security prison opened in 1972 to replace the 140-year-old Ohio Penitentiary in Columbus. Within short order, Lucasville was crowded and, in 1976, two white cellmates, Kelly Chapman and Richard Jaworski, filed a lawsuit objecting to double celling. On April 1, 1976, after lawyers became involved, Judge Thomas Hogan in the federal court for the Southern District of Ohio certified a class action and, in December of that year, rejected Ohio's effort of dismissal.[31]

Just as Lucasville did not resemble Cummins, Judge Hogan's work did not fit Judge Henley's mold of lengthy opinions, patient admonitions, and reluctant remedies. Instead, in a brief, unclear decision issued on June 29, 1977, Judge Hogan ruled double celling unconstitutional, gave defendants a few months to submit plans, rejected them all, and in March of 1978, ordered the end of that practice. Confusingly, Hogan's opinion praised the Lucasville complex for its gyms, "modern" library, chapels, vocational activities, dining and visiting rooms, health care units, and tomato garden. Based on his own visit, Hogan described the facility as "quite light and quite airy." Further, Judge Hogan noted that none of the prisoners' five "main factual witnesses," along with one guard, linked violence and other harms to double celling. Moreover, the judge cited Ohio records that comparable levels of stabbings, fights, and self-inflicted harm existed in 1975 when single cells were used and in 1977 when double cells were used.[32]

The judge then offered his own causal account that had logical gaps: he found "no increase in violence or criminal activity" attributable to double celling but which could have been due "to increased population." Yet because Lucasville was designed with single cells, population increases *depended* on double celling. In the Supreme Court, the prisoners' lawyers pointed to a record thicker than what the judge's opinion had referenced. They told the Court that "five days of testimony by numerous prison officials, a prison psychologist and psychiatrist, prisoners, and correctional experts," supplemented by depositions, forty exhibits, and the judge's tour, demonstrated the prison's failings.[33]

Their account dovetailed with press coverage providing a frightening picture of warehousing, extortion, and interracial violence. Indeed, reading news accounts of Lucasville, the disjuncture between Judge Hogan's opinion and the reporting is startling. The judge did not mention that the prison was controversial when it opened, as Ohio had picked a remote area. Employment depended on the all-white town residents, while the prisoners were disproportionately Black men. Nor did the judge address legislative investigations into "the troubled Lucasville penitentiary," beset by corruption, understaffing, and violence. The prison complex had "grown too fast"—producing by 1976 a "state of crisis"; guards were "without confidence in their ability to maintain order." In June of 1976, one story ran with the headline "'Kingdom of the Wild' Exists at Lucasville," and described the "trouble almost from the day it opened," which included the risk of being stabbed "simply for sitting in the wrong chair."[34]

The *Columbus Dispatch* had detailed the "idleness" in a story headed "Unemployment Tops 40% Inside Lucasville." Lucasville had 1,200 jobs and more than 2,000 prisoners. Getting work yielded $12 a month—providing the proverbial "coin of the realm"; prisoners needed money for commissary purchases, including food stuffs. A reporter quoted Kelly Chapman, a "41-year-old jailhouse lawyer" and one of the plaintiffs, that the lack of jobs set up a system of extortion by "stronger prisoners." Further, news accounts of the trial testimony included details of physical abuse and failures of medical care, and a prisoner being raped in the "crowded day rooms." One of the prisoners' experts concluded that the mix of violence, overcrowding, and poor health care violated the Constitution. A social worker said that Lucasville "makes more problems for prisoners than they had when they came in," and a correctional officer said doubling up prisoners rendered his job "impossible."[35]

Ohio countered by calling James Estelle, Director of Texas' prisons, as its witness. Estelle was by then a name familiar in prisoners' rights circles; he was the unsuccessful defendant in the Supreme Court's 1976 *Estelle v. Gamble* ruling, concluding that the Eighth Amendment protected incarcerated people from "deliberate indifference to serious medical needs." Estelle was also a defendant in another massive prison conditions litigation, *Ruiz v. Estelle*, in which the US Justice Department joined the prisoners and Judge William Wayne Justice made hundreds of findings of horrific conditions. In Ohio, Estelle told Judge Hogan that "of the 50 prisons he had visited around the country, there were few superior to the one at Lucasville."[36]

What counts on appeal are facts found by the trial court and the legal conclusions drawn. Judge Hogan's findings and his muddled analysis set the prisoners up for a fall. Hogan had detailed temperature control, reasonable food for guards and prisoners alike, and "plumbing, lighting, [and a] law library" adequate "to meet the needs of the increased population." Even as health services were over-taxed, the administration had not been "indifferent to the needs" of prisoners. On the other hand, Hogan noted that 140 people were waiting for dental care, which did fall below what the Constitution required. Moreover, given "not enough jobs to go around," the population density "reduced an inmate's opportunity to rehabilitate himself by lessening his chances of receiving educational or vocational training or a meaningful job."[37]

In terms of double celling's harms, Hogan invoked the consensus that single celling was "desirable." Experts testified that double celling entailed a "loss of privacy" and "close contact . . . increase[d] . . . tensions and frustrations." The situation was exacerbated because "a substantial number of the inmates [were] victims of some form of emotional or mental disorder," and increased tensions exaggerated "aggressive and anti-social characteristics." Hogan concluded that the Constitution did not permit Ohio to house 2,300 people in a long-term facility with single cells designed for 1,600. Given his brief account of the governing legal principles, one reading of his opinion was that double celling was *per se* unconstitutional, and another was that the "totality of the circumstances" rendered the housing unconstitutional.[38]

In support of either a per se or totality-of-conditions ruling, the Justice Department later argued Judge Hogan had identified five factors. First, while pretrial detainees held on average sixty days or less could, according to the 1979 *Bell v. Wolfish* decision, be double celled, Lucasville's prisoners were "long-term," which meant "close confinement and overcrowding" for years. Second, the prison was 38 percent over its "rated capacity." Third, prisoners sharing sixty-three square feet were getting about half of that space per person. The ACA Manual called for seventy-five square feet; the National Sheriffs Association's Handbook suggested seventy to eighty square feet in single-occupancy cells, and fifty-five square feet in multiple occupancy units. Fourth, "a substantial number" of prisoners were in cells all the time, except for four to six hours a week. Fifth, population growth would not likely abate, and hence no evidence suggested that double celling was a "temporary measure."[39]

SINGLE CELLING AS THE PROFESSIONAL NORM AND ITS RELATIONSHIP TO REHABILITATION

"[T]he mass incarceration of hundreds or even thousands of inmates makes almost impossible any effective work of rehabilitation."

—Judge Joseph N. Ulman, *A National Program to Develop Probation and Parole*, 1938[40]

"[A]ll cells should be designed for the use of one prisoner."

—1966 Manual of the American Correctional Association[41]

Even as Judge Hogan adverted to professional standards, he did not provide a fulsome account of the depth or duration of the professional commitment to single cells. Also missing were the reasons why people running and designing prisons thought "cellular" confinement preferable to large dorms or multi-person cells. In his 1929 report, *The Federal Penal and Correctional Problem*, James Bennett termed crowding "a disaster from the health standpoint"; the "vicious system of doubling up" was "universally condemned by prison authorities" because it facilitated sexual aggression, and "generally degrades the standards of the better men to those of the lowest."

That view was reiterated in the American Prison Association's 1946 *Manual of Suggested Standards for a State Correctional System*— that jail cells were to be "for one person only and doubling up should never be practiced." The 1954 revision (issued under the organization's new name, the ACA) stated that jail and prison cells to be "designed for the use of one prisoner." In 1955, the UN's *Standard Minimum Rules for the Treatment of Prisoners* likewise endorsed single celling. A decade later, the ACA's 1966 manual called for "all" prison cells to be "designed for the use of one prisoner." For multiple occupancy and dormitories, at least "75 square feet of floor space" per person was needed. The 1977 manual reiterated "[t]here is one inmate per cell," while space per person was reduced to "at least 60 square feet."[42] Ohio followed those protocols when it designed its facility for *single* occupancy.

Standard-setting by insiders need not be equated with constitutional floors, ceilings, or requirements. Nonetheless, Judge Hogan did not explain that his objection to double celling *was* grounded in (and hence deferring to) the views of the people running prisons. Judge Hogan also gave no details on the health hazards. Whether old or newly constructed (as Lucasville was), dense congregant housing increased the risk of disease (think COVID). And the opinion did not illuminate the import of "wet" prison cells, which have open toilets and sinks, in contrast to "dry" cells with no water sources. A federal district judge in Massachusetts explained the indignity when he ruled Suffolk County Jail's double celling unconstitutional: "an inmate may not use the toilet except in the presence of a stranger mere feet away."[43] And as Judge Ullman said in 1938, crowded prisons undercuts rehabilitative opportunities.

What Judge Hogan did discuss in June of 1977 was a possible remedy. Noting a power to compel release (he said he could not order funding), Hogan gave state officials ninety days to come up with a plan and, because the November election could have opened up new souces of funding, provided more time. Ohio's Constitution capped state debt at $750,000 without public permission for more. On the ballot was a proposal to raise that cap permanently; $80 million in a bond issue was earmarked for prison construction. Voters, however, rejected the constitutional revision "by a 72–28 percent margin." Thereafter, Ohio submitted five options to Hogan—including double celling only prisoners "with jobs, school assignments or both" and turning space into dormitories. Judge Hogan found those proposals wanting and, on March 7, 1978, held a hearing that resulted in an order on April 7, 1978, requiring a reduction by twenty-five people a month until the population was at the single-cell level. After Ohio was unsuccessful in getting the order stayed, the state reopened its old Penitentiary. By the time the case was argued in the Supreme Court on March 2 of 1981, the double celling at Lucasville had—at least temporarily—ended.[44]

COMMON SENSE, DATA, AND HOUSING DENSITY

"The basic finding, which confirms common sense, is that there is a . . . measurable increase in negative effects with an increase in housing density."

—*The Effect of Prison Crowding on Inmate Behavior*,
National Institute of Justice, December 1980[45]

Ohio's September 1980 certiorari petition was in one respect a *tribute* to Winston Talley, other prisoners, their lawyers, and judges like Henley. The state argued it could double cell because it did *not* "deprive inmates of minimum constitutional guarantees to adequate food, clothing, shelter, sanitation, medical care and personal safety."[46] The acknowledgment that the Constitution *constrained* punishment was a sea change from positions taken less than two decades earlier by states asserting that the Constitution had no role to play in prisons. On the other hand, seeking a legal license to put people into dense spaces exemplified efforts to cut back on what Talley and others had achieved.

The need for privacy, shaped through cultural expectations, is visceral, as demonstrated by data gathered in 1978 and 1979. Researchers at the Justice Department's National Institute of Justice (NIJ) received information from 1,400 prisoners held at six federal prisons and, coupled with archival records, evaluated "the psychological and physiological effects of crowding and various housing arrangements." That report, with the cover reproduced in figure 26.1, was published in December of 1980, by which time the Court had agreed to review Judge Hogan's holding. The "negative effects" of "[h]igh degrees of sustained crowding" included "illness complaint rates, higher death and suicide rates, and higher disciplinary infraction rates." The mechanisms came from a lack of privacy that produced a sense of helplessness and depression, over-stimulation from the tumult of people compressed into small spaces, and fearfulness that often prompted aggression. This research identified single cells, even if small, as key to mitigating problems in crowded prisons.[47]

Given the "common sense" about the desirability of single cells and the record before Judge Hogan, the Court's decision to take the Ohio case was in one sense perplexing. At issue was a single facility—a 1970s prison built to replace an old penitentiary. Judge Hogan had written a short opinion, based on a skimpy record, and his legal conclusions did not clarify what rendered Lucasville's density unlawful. The appellate court provided no help; rather than a reasoned decision, it affirmed without explanation.[48] Doing so was part of a shift in federal appellate courts, designating a significant percentage of their decisions "not for publication" or "not for precedent." To warrant that tag, judges are supposed to select cases that are either too routine to merit explanation or so specific they ought

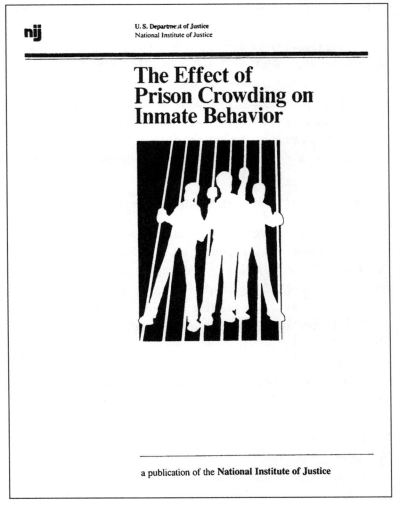

FIGURE 26.1 *The Effect of Prison Crowding on Inmate Behavior*, cover, National Institute of Justice, 1980

not be used in other lawsuits, and in theory, would not be ones the Supreme Court—focused on conflicts in the circuits about major legal issues—would take. Yet the Court has picked up other "not for publication" decisions; *Rhodes* is one example of justices shopping for cases to forward their agendas.[49]

What gave the Lucasville case appeal (so to speak) was that it was a great vehicle for members of the Court to limit prisoner litigation. Judge Hogan's messy legal analysis was catnip for justices like Warren Burger, Lewis Powell, and William Rehnquist, eager to pull lower courts out of prisons and other civil rights cases. Especially grating was the wafts of a "right to rehabilitation"; Hogan had noted double celling's negative impact on jobs and educational opportunities. Further, Hogan's discussion of lockdowns would have made some justices worried about challenges to solitary confinement.[50]

THE "PAIN THAT HURTS," AS CONTRASTED WITH "A DULL ACHE"

The stakes were reflected by the amici chiming in. Texas, which was subject to federal court oversight for unconstitutional crowding, described itself as "the largest penal system in the country" and insisted that the Eighth Amendment was "not a vehicle by which the federal courts may legislate the 'ideal' . . . in prison management and conditions." Thirty-four other states, from Alaska to the "State of Rhode Island and Providence Plantation," came together to warn that the order to reduce population by 38 percent risked the "premature releases of 1,400 convicted felons" in Ohio alone. While agreeing that federal courts had a "duty to protect fundamental constitutional rights," the "minimum standards embodied in the Eighth Amendment" ought not be transformed into an "affirmative jurisdictional base from which federal courts can impose . . . architectural and penological standards upon the states."[51]

Instead, the states pitched *pain* as the test: federal courts were to assess only whether prison conditions caused "extreme or unnecessary pain." Claiming loyalty to the text and "the commonly understood meaning" of "cruel and unusual," the states used the Court's language in death penalty decisions to argue that "cruel" meant "unnecessary cruelty" or the "wanton" inflictions of pain. The states constructed a scale on which only "pain that hurts" counted, and "not the kind of pain . . . identified as a dull ache." The states argued that whether "impermissible methods or conditions" existed depended on "the quality and quantity of pain involved," a test they claimed was less subjective than "totality of the circumstances" or "evolving standards of decency."[52]

A pause is in order to underscore the reasons for pushing individualized assessments and the complexity of inquiries into pain. A "totality-of-conditions" approach considers a prison as a whole and does not require each person to demonstrate personally debilitating circumstances. Using an individual's pain as the metric would require inquiry into experiences, prisoner by prisoner, rather than looking at the conditions as a whole. By using "pain that hurts," the states implicitly acceded to bans on whipping and chains while arguing judges should *permit* other forms of carceral constraints causing a "dull ache." Moreover, as Elaine Scarry discussed in *The Body in Pain: The Making and the Unmaking of the World*, pain's signature is its "inexpressibility." The audible moans of many sufferers exemplify what Virginia Woolf explained: when a person is in pain, "language runs dry."[53]

Nonetheless, the states' approach got traction; quoting earlier precedents, Justice Powell's *Rhodes* majority opinion included "infliction of unnecessary and wanton infliction of pain" on a list of Eighth Amendment prohibition. Those terms have become a refrain in cases challenging methods of execution. In a 2019 opinion for the Court, Justice Neil Gorsuch discussed the Court's requirement that individuals objecting to a particular method of execution had the burden to show that an alternative way of being killed would "significantly reduce a substantial risk of severe pain." And, in 2024, when writing for the Court permitting the criminalization of sleeping in public, Justice Gorsuch described the sanctions as licit in part because they were not designed to "superad[d] . . . terror, pain, or disgrace."[54]

SAFEGUARDING "PHYSICAL AND MENTAL HEALTH"

The "firm federal policy [is] that there should be no double celling in long-term correctional facilities."

—Memorandum for the United States as Amicus
Curiae, *Rhodes v. Chapman*[55]

"[L]ong term overcrowding causes and accelerates the spread of communicable disease and results in the increased occurrence of stress-induced mental disorders, tension, aggression and physical violence."

—Motion for Leave to File Brief Amicus Curiae of the
American Medical Association and the American
Public Health Association, *Rhodes v. Chapman*[56]

"There is one inmate per room or cell, which has a floor area of at least 60 square feet, provided inmates spend no more than 10 hours per day locked in . . . ; when confinement exceeds 10 hours per day, there are at least 80 square feet of floor space."

—Commission on Accreditation for Corrections of
the American Correctional Association, Manual
of Standards for Adult Correctional Institutions, 1977[57]

In January 1981, Ronald Reagan took over the White House. But in 1980, Jimmy Carter was the President, and the DOJ had already joined prisoners in challenging Texas' prisons. Yet the federal government also had a large prison system whose head, Norman Carlson, had endorsed punitive retribution, and the bipartisan "War on Crime" and the "War on Drugs" were filling federal and state institutions. In 1979, the United States won *Bell v. Wolfish*, holding that short-term pretrial detainees could be double celled in a new federal Metropolitan Detention Center in New York.

Nonetheless, in *Rhodes*, the United States filed a "memorandum," ostensibly taking "no position" but lending support to the prisoners by informing the Court of "current federal policy" governing "one of the largest correctional systems in the country." The DOJ provided copies of "new Federal Standards for Prisons and Jails." While creating no "rights," the Standards stated DOJ's firm policy" that cells "rated for single occupancy" were to "house only one inmate" so that each person in "long-term institutions" would have "at least 60 square feet of floor space." The memorandum analyzed federal jails and prisons under "five factors" of the lower court decision. Noting that some 5 percent were then double celled with less than sixty-three feet per person, the government tried to insulate itself from challenges while demonstrating a capacity to house a lot of people without double celling.[58]

The prisoners had other allies: the American Medical Association (AMA), joined by the American Public Health Association (APHA). The AMA/APHA explained that since the early 1970s, both had worked to improve health care and that "sustained overcrowding needlessly caused physical and mental harm to the prisoners," which violated "contemporary standards of decency as reflected in the standards of various professional organizations." Standards on space were not only "desirable goals" but the "minima required" for safety. They cited Arkansas data that, from 1975–1977, incarcerated people had a 6.5 times higher rate of tuberculous than those outside of prison. Other studies demonstrated crowding's association with high blood pressure, depression, and additional "psychological disturbances" and, when prolonged, increased violence. Further, given reduced opportunities for activities, crowding forced idleness, which was linked to mental and physical harms. In addition to citing the ACA Manual, the AMA/APHA quoted US Army regulations that people need "a minimum of 60 square feet" as the "lowest which may be used without unnecessary risk of abnormal disease incidence," and if an emergency, forty feet for not more than seven consecutive days.[59] California's Public Defender added its *cri de coeur*, asserting that double celling "of the most violent offenders in the most decrepit of California's prisons is all but certain to increase" violence. Its argument that rising prison populations would outstrip funds for more space was double-edged, as it added reasons not to up the price of incarceration by pinning it to single cells.[60]

TO DE-CONSTITUTIONALIZE REHABILITATION

"[I]s overcrowding a synonym for cruel and unusual punishment? . . . Well, what if a prison offered no education opportunities at all, would that be a cruel and unusual punishment?"

—Question, Justice William Rehnquist, Oral argument, *Rhodes v. Chapman*, March 2, 1981[61]

"[T]he Constitution does not mandate comfortable prisons, and prisons . . . which house persons convicted of serious crimes, cannot be free of discomfort."

—Justice Lewis Powell, for the Court, *Rhodes v. Chapman* (1981)

"[T]oday's decision should in no way be construed as a retreat from careful judicial scrutiny of prison conditions. . . ."

—Justice William Brennan, concurring, *Rhodes*, 1981[62]

The questions asked by Justice Rehnquist aimed to cut off claims of constitutionally mandated rehabilitation. Justice Powell's opinion for the Court did the same. He described the ruling as "the first time" the Court had to decide the limits imposed "upon the conditions in which a State may confine those convicted of crimes." *Hutto v. Finney* had, of course, done so just three years earlier, but Powell distinguished (and thereby diminished) *Hutto* as not involving "a disputed contention that the conditions of confinement at a particular prison constituted cruel and unusual punishment."[63] *Rhodes* was thus the "occasion to consider specifically the principles relevant" to unconstitutionality.

Powell's account of the governing principles (as distinct from their application) are more than what some contemporary justices might endorse. At the time, he made Chief Justice Burger uncomfortable. Powell described the Court as having adopted a "flexible and dynamic" interpretive "manner" that had "extended the amendment's reach beyond . . . barbarous physical punishments." Echoing Blackmun in *Jackson v. Bishop*, who had drawn on Chief Justice Earl Warren's *Trop v. Dulles* plurality, Powell explained that "[n]o static 'test' can exist" because the Eighth Amendment "must draw its meaning from the evolving standards of decency that mark the progress of a maturing society."[64]

Private exchanges reveal that, despite Burger's many speeches about the need to improve prison conditions, he wrote to Powell to "scrub" references to *Trop*. Powell declined, explaining that his law clerk had found "at least 303 federal cases" invoking *Trop*, of which 156 used the words "evolving standards of decency"; included were decisions joined by both Burger and Powell. Powell added that, if his draft opinion could garner a "6–3 majority," his decision would "help settle the law with respect to the 'prison conditions' cases." By "settle," Powell meant *end* a good many lawsuits. Burger replied that he could "live with" the *Trop* quote and hoped in the future that "pleasing but extravagant rhetoric" would be "resisted."[65] Powell did "resist" aspects of *Trop*; Chief Justice Warren used the term "dignity," which Powell did not mention but which featured in Justice Brennan's concurring effort to stave off damage from Powell's opinion.

Thus, *Rhodes* concluded that the Eighth Amendment prohibited more punishments than those considered "cruel and unusual" in 1791. The prohibition banned "the wanton and unnecessary infliction of pain," punishment that is "grossly disproportionate to the severity of the crime" or that "deprive[s] inmates of the minimal civilized measure of life's necessities." Citing the Court's 1976 *Estelle v. Gamble* health care decision, Powell explained that "unnecessary and wanton" pain was not limited to the "physically barbarous." Practices that were "totally without penological justification" such as "deliberate indifference to serious medical needs" violated the Eighth Amendment. The obligation to treat medical needs flowed from the fact that, as "recognized by the common law and state legislatures," a prisoner had no other way to obtain care. Furthermore, given Powell's list that the "goals of the penal function" included "to punish justly, to deter future crime, and to return imprisoned persons to society with an improved chance of being useful, law-abiding citizens," rehabilitation was within that rubric. Powell invoked *Hutto v. Finney* as an example of the "unquestioned and serious deprivation of basic human needs" such as clothing, sufficient food, medical care, heat, minimal physical exercise, sanitation, and some protection from violence. In contrast, "restrictive and even harsh" conditions were not unconstitutional but were "part of the penalty that criminal offenders pay for their offenses against society."[66]

By using the gross conditions in Arkansas and elsewhere as a baseline and the district court's praise of Lucasville, Powell positioned double celling as somewhat benign. To keep other justices on board, he noted courts had "a responsibility to scrutinize claims of cruel and unusual confinement and conditions . . . , especially [in] older" prisons, some of which had been described as "deplorable" and "sordid." As for the professional standards, Powell dismissed them as "an aspiration toward an ideal environment for long-term confinement." Moreover, Powell justified that "discomfort" (read: pain) by commenting that Ohio's prison housed "persons convicted of serious crimes."[67] When added to the Court's *Bell v. Wolfish* ruling by Justice Rehnquist permitting double celling of people held pre-trial, *Rhodes* provided rationales for hyper-dense facilities spanning the detention system. *Rhodes* thus lowered the dollar costs of putting people in prison. Brennan's concurrence noted that, according to the NIJ's 1980 report, "two-thirds of all Federal, state, and local prisoners" had less than sixty square feet per person and "confinement of prisoners is unquestionably an expensive proposition." In 1977, construction costs ranged from $25,000 to $50,000 per additional prisoner.

Brennan, joined by Justices Blackmun and Stevens, advised readers not to "construe" the ruling "as a retreat from careful judicial scrutiny of prison conditions." (Of course, it was.) And, as noted, Brennan quoted more from *Trop v. Dulles* than had Powell and underscored that the Eighth Amendment required assessing whether "a challenged punishment comports with human dignity." Brennan chastised the *Rhodes* district court for not having documented an *"actual effect* . . . upon the well-being of the prisoners" (Brennan's italics), and for its remedy, which resulted in reopening a nineteenth-century facility that, by 1977, had been found to be unconstitutionally segregating prisoners by race. In contrast, Brennan cited dozens of decisions declaring "individual prisons or entire prison systems" unconstitutional based on a "totality-of-the-circumstances test." He counted "at least 24 States" in which court orders properly were in place, exemplified by "gruesome detail" about Alabama conditions, as well as by facilities in Colorado, Louisiana, Arkansas, Texas, Rhode Island, and New Hampshire.[68]

Justice Blackmun filed a separate concurrence taking exception to the "perhaps technically correct observation" that *Rhodes v. Chapman* was the first time the Court was deciding a prison conditions case. The Court was not "writing upon a clean slate"; conditions were at issue in *Bell v. Wolfish* and *Hutto v. Finney*. Blackmun noted he had been "privileged to write the opinion" for the appellate court's "unanimous panel" in *Jackson v. Bishop*, "one of the first cases" to underscore that that incarceration was "not an open door for unconstitutional cruelty or neglect" and "federal courts must continue to be available to those state inmates." Like Justice Brennan, Blackmun did not want judges to take the decision as a "signal" that courts were adopting "a policy of general deference" to administrators on what constituted "contemporary standards of decency."[69]

The lone voice in support of Judge Hogan was Justice Thurgood Marshall. Lucasville was "overcrowded, unhealthful, and dangerous." The reason was a breach of the state's own "policy judgment" to build a maximum-security facility for 1,600 people housed in single cells with sixty-three square feet. Deference was due to that decision and not to its response to crowding, which was the "*only* reason" (Marshall's italics) for double celling. To make legible the dimensions, Marshall noted that most of the Supreme Court's windows were larger than the space allotted per person in double cells.[70]

All the many warnings about crowding proved tragically correct. Lucasville later exploded in violence and Ohio responded by created a "supermax prison" in which people were held potentially indefinitely with lights on 24/7 and without environmental stimuli. In 2005, Justice Anthony Kennedy wrote for a unanimous Court that before placement in solitary, a modicum of procedural due process was required.[71] In chapters to follow, I explore the permissibility of that form of punishment after I analyze the impact of *Rhodes v. Chapman*'s constraints on the Arkansas Penitentiary Cases that Judge Eisele formally called to a close in 1982. What he could not close were the resulting harms and the conflicts about whether the "minimal civilized measure of life's necessities" should be the measure of punishment's legitimacy.

27

SEQUELA

HYPER-DENSITY, SPIRALING BUDGETS, AND "WAREHOUSING"

> While "light years ahead of where it was in the 1960s," Arkansas was not likely compliant with "minimum constitutional standards established by the federal courts. Why? The reason, in a word, is overcrowding."
>
> —US Senator Dale Bumpers, *Keeping in Touch*, February 26, 1981

Writing to his constituents before Judge Eisele had ended federal oversight of Arkansas' prisons, Senator Bumpers discussed the problem of 1,650 people held in a "facility designed for 900." His comment on "overcrowding" forecast the future, in part because Bumpers and others did not support sending fewer people to prison and thinning the ranks of those there. Instead, Bumpers proposed a Criminal Justice Construction Reform Act, co-sponsored by Republican Senator Robert Dole, to provide federal incentive grants ($1 federal dollar for every $3 states invested) for the "construction and modernization of criminal justice facilities." Sounding the bell of freedom in support of massive deprivations of liberty, Bumpers wrote that the "freest nation on earth [ought not let] decent law-abiding citizens . . . [be] held captive to fears of being victims of criminal acts."[1]

While the Dole-Bumpers proposal did not become law, it previewed legislation that Bill Clinton successfully championed when he became President in 1992. In that decade, both federal and state legislatures imposed longer sentences, permitted fewer releases, and generated new financing schemes to construct prisons ("super-max") designed for density as well as for isolation. Despite federal studies documenting crowding's link to violence, Congress did not create national guidelines on adequate space and services for imprisoned individuals.[2]

This chapter maps the frantic scramble for beds and funds to accommodate all the people pushed into jails and prisons through aggressive prosecution and sentencing laws. The ending of the *Holt/Finney* litigation intersected with new Arkansas lawsuits, some about intolerable conditions in local jails and others filed by cities suing counties and counties suing the state to get paid for housing detained people. The charts and tables toward the chapter's end document the dollars poured into detention. Harder to track are the costs to the individuals packed in, to the communities from which they were taken, and to the people staffing overstuffed facilities, as well as the economic losses due to missed education and employment opportunities and the deepening divides along race and class lines. Instead of trying to make meaningful the recognition of detained individuals as political equals and fashioning social services for people in and out of prison, "warehousing" gained renewed acceptability as a permissible form of sovereign punishment.[3]

REGRESSING: CHAINING TO TREES AND STUFFING PEOPLE IN

"Without the pressure for change and responsible action brought by the court, I believe that it is only a matter of time before we begin to regress. . . . The running of our nation's prisons . . . is . . . too important to be left to the uncontrolled discretion of those of us in corrections."

—Allen F. Breed, Director of the National Institute of Corrections, 1980[4]

"We're getting an inmate a day."

—Arkansas Commissioner A. L. Lockhart, February 18, 1982[5]

Arkansas provides a lesson in law's potential to affect incentives. State officials repeatedly tried to comply with court-imposed population caps. In July of 1981, after the Arkansas Department of

FIGURE 27.1 *Five Left in Chains*, photograph by Gene Prescott accompanying George Bentley, *5 Inmates Left Chained at Wrightsville United*, Arkansas Gazette, July 18, 1981, courtesy of the publisher

Correction (ADC) refused new entrants, the Pulaski County Sheriff, dealing with his own crowded jail, "rid the county of 18 prisoners" by "literally" dumping them outside a state prison, as photographed in figure 27.1. Commissioner Lockhart, Governor White, and the Board of Correction sued and won a state court order that, instead of chaining people to fences, the sheriff had to transfer people "in a reasonable, orderly and lawful manner."[6]

Yet, as one reporter noted, "those actions . . . did more to dramatize the crowded conditions in the state's jails and prisons than months of talk." Pulaski County, the source of about a third of the state's prisoners, got access to a third of the available beds as ADC "shuffled inmates" elsewhere to "make room for about 70 state prisoners backed up in county jails."[7]

Another lawsuit resulted in federal Judge George Howard telling the Pulaski County sheriff to reject entrants until that jail was down to its designated capacity of 200 and had adequate staff, access to health care, a law library, visitors, and a grievance system. Thus, in August of 1981, the Pulaski County Jail "refused . . . three prisoners from the Little Rock City Jail." In response, that sheriff won agreement from that city's Board of Directors that municipal judges "suspend the imposition of jail sentences for minor offences until the space situation . . . improved." The *Arkansas Democrat* reported that "Little Rock's jail population [had not] been a big problem since last August when the city allowed policemen to issue a "misdemeanor criminal citation" keeping people out of pretrial detention while awaiting court appearances.[8]

But prosecutors and judges kept priming the pump. When state prisons held 3,307 people with construction for 432 beds underway, Lockhart sought funding for new prisons to hold 1,000 more. By June, Lockhart wanted money "for more room in the prisons." Thereafter, the Board of Correction contemplated sending forty state prisoners to the Pulaski County Jail and tried to persuade federal prosecutors to charge people for federal crimes so, if convicted, they would end up in federal, rather than state, prisons.[9]

THE WEIGHT OF APPLYING WORN-DOWN
CONSTITUTIONAL ASPIRATIONS

"If the State requires that certain persons be institutionalized, as it
may, it has the corresponding obligation to meet their basic human
needs, which includes some degree of protection, where necessary,
from other persons that the State also requires to live in the
institution. . . . The respondents must understand that they may not
revert to the old practices, regardless of lack of funds, or any other
circumstances that might prompt a desire to do so."

—Judge Thomas Eisele, *Finney v. Mabry*, February 19, 1982[10]

I have used the phrase "eerily familiar" before; it remains apt. Everyone stayed in role as the *Holt/Finney* litigation drew to a close:
the prisoners put on evidence of failures, defending state officials
argued they were doing the best they could, and the judge tried to
impose some boundaries. Racism and violence continued, even as
the decade of litigation had made material differences in the lives
of people forced inside prisons.

Judge Eisele's compliance hearing, begun August 11, 1981, centered (as had hearings in the prior years) on insufficient security,
staffing, and health care. Philip Kaplan put on former Compliance
Coordinator Stephen LaPlante and former Commissioner Vernon
Housewright. Housewright was damning; while a "lot of progress" had been made, the prison had not been "in compliance"
when he left in January 1981. Prisoners were doing jobs "clearly
related to security" including control over some gates ("inmate
turnkeys"), and staff turned over was at times 100 percent. A
prisoner explained to Eisele that turnkeys "commonly accept[ed]
bribes from others" to open doors. Others testified about dirt in
the kitchen ("worse" than before), kitchen-assignments despite
hospitalization for hepatitis, and violence, including being struck
while handcuffed.[11]

The state countered that grievance procedures had improved;
the Disciplinary Board was "comprised of three permanently established members, two of whom [were] black." The Chair of the Board
of Correction defended inmate turnkeys "as long as they were under

the direct supervision of a free-world guard." T. Don Hutto, then
directing Virginia's Corrections Department, opined that Arkansas
was on its way to becoming "the top five or six prison systems in
the country." Hutto did admit staffing was inadequate at night, when
only "four guards were" at Cummins. In short, versions of what had
been unconstitutional in the past remained: not enough "free-world
people" on staff, racial slurs, and a prison administration with "no
blacks . . . in responsible positions."[12]

The hearings concluded October 5, 1981, and Eisele said he
aimed to end supervision within a year if officials performed as
planned. In the interim, Eisele filed a few decisions on items not
"resolved during the five-week trial" on compliance. Included
was a December 1981 ruling holding unconstitutional procedures
for administrative segregation of individuals perceived to have a
"chronic inability to adjust," pose a "serious threat" to security, or
need protection.[13] On February 19, 1982, Eisele issued a twenty-
page opinion, supplemented on March 2 with an outline of the
coming months.

Eisele used LaPlante's voluminous reports as substantiation
that the prison system had been put on notice about areas of
noncompliance and accepted LaPlante's "uncontested findings"
of compliance on thirty-six issues. Eisele wanted to review several
not-yet-in place policies but was clear on health care for mental illness: Arkansas was "required to keep and maintain at all
times a separate facility on a permanent basis for the housing
and treatment of severely mentally disturbed inmates." In addition to and aside from Arkansas' "highly acclaimed" institution for
women, Eisele detailed continued racial segregation in Cummins'
maximum-security unit and that prisoners in barracks remained
unsafe because (akin to what Henley said in the 1970s), the "100-
man . . . open barracks" with double bunks "makes it virtually impossible for a security guard to have an unobstructed view through
the barracks from any angle." Some prisoners "drape[d] blankets
over the bunks to create some sense of privacy in the large and
crowded room." (The press reported "that sheets were hung . . .
to hide activities such as homosexual rape.") While prisoners no

longer carried guns, they were at guard posts, held keys to internal gates, and patrolled the barracks ("floor walkers") at night.[14]

Judge Eisele ruled that it was "imperative to state specifically that the practice of using inmates as security personnel, with power over other inmates, is unconstitutional." Yet, even as Eisele enjoined "placing inmates in positions of authority or discretion and control over other inmates," he made an exception for "the most serious emergencies when absolutely no alternative for control is available," and for the "minimum period necessary." Because a constant "deficiency in staffing . . . contributed to most of the problems of the system," the judge condoned reliance on "turnkeys on the riot gates" to "mechanically open and close the gate under the direct supervision of a free-world guard."[15] (Pause to imagine interactions at "riot gates" or in "serious emergencies" when some prisoners, in conjunction with guards or not, had official authority to make others more or less safe.)

In terms of desegregation, Eisele's ruling countenanced limited exceptions, as had the 1968 concurrence in *Lee v. Washington*, where three justices agreed that Alabama's *de jure* racial segregation was unconstitutional unless needed to "maintain security, discipline, and good order." Those words echoed in 1982, when 300 of the 1,650 people at Cummins were "racially segregated." Eisele wrote that integration in the maximum-security unit was not required if it would cause a "bona fide established likelihood of danger or harm to any inmate." Eisele later called for "as precise a method as possible for identifying those individual inmates the integration of whom may create a hazard for their safety or the safety of others." Those directions stemmed from his distress at ADC, which had circulated a questionnaire asking prisoners if they "objected" to integrated cells. One prisoner wrote to Eisele that a "bloodbath" and a "full scale race riot" would occur if the two-person cells in the maximum-security unit were integrated. Eisele informed the ADC that while white prisoners may object, he expected "few cases" in which a "real threat" of violence existed by putting a person in a cell with someone of another race.[16]

Aiming to wrap up, Eisele called for a final report on "factual developments concerning compliance," with time for the prisoners to "file any objections or exceptions." The state sent "a package of 17 reports" on May 8, 1982, followed by an account of its integration efforts at Cummins. Kaplan registered many objections, including that prisoners had more responsibility for security at night than permitted, integration fell short, and the barracks were too crowded. Governor White weighed in by sending some people to work release centers, where the dollar estimate cost per person was $1,800 in contrast to the $7,000 per incarcerated person.[17]

SIGNING OFF: BASELINES AND ANXIETY ABOUT "SLIPPING BACK"

"The conclusion . . . is . . . that the respondents are in compliance with the requirements of the Constitution, the Consent Decree, and all prior orders of the Court on all issues concerning the conditions of confinement at the various units of the Arkansas Department of Correction. . . . The progress made cannot be overstated."

—Judge Eisele, *Finney v. Mabry*, August 20, 1982[18]

On August 20, 1982, after a "short hearing" ten days earlier, Judge Eisele rejected the prisoners' requests for continued monitoring and more injunctive relief. Instead, he ended his tenure as an overseer of Arkansas' prisons and dismissed *Finney v. Mabry* "with prejudice." Once again, the lengthy opinion was a mix of praise, worry, and a good deal of contingency, summed up by the admonition that the "respondents are well aware of their obligation to maintain conditions . . . at a constitutional and lawful level. This obligation will not end with the dismissal of this suit." Moreover, noting the population explosion, Eisele wrote that "a similar suit could be filed tomorrow if the conditions" were not "maintained or if there is a reversion to prior unacceptable policies and practices."[19]

Eisele's ambivalence permeated the pages; he was both cheerleader and supplicant, describing "changes . . . actually made by the duly constituted state officials who have come to recognize and accept their duty and responsibility to administer the system according to lawful and constitutional standards. *Their* duty, not the Court's." As justification for handing over the reins, the judge reminded his audience of the horrific baseline he knew well. In contrast to the 1970 "dark and evil world" staffed by "a handful of paid free-world people," some 1,000 "free-world employees" were in charge. In 1970, no "mental health services were provided," while in 1982, a facility had opened for "the most severely mentally ill inmates." Eisele described improved physical safety in dense barracks due to better lighting and officers who "actually walk[ed] through" at random times. Moreover, the "inmate turnkey" system had ended; no prisoner remained "employed in positions allowing them to exercise the prohibited discretion," even as some were unarmed tower guards. Further, even as changes in "administrative segregation, integration, and racial slurs" had not been "as great as might be hoped," the effort was "great," and the result "sufficient." Eisele tolerated racial segregation in parts of Cummins; "some episodes of actual violence" could occur in "forcibly integrated" cells.[20] Not discussed was that, had the Supreme Court rejected widespread use of double celling, the question of *which* two people could be housed together would not have arisen.

Of course, Eisele was *right* that Arkansas' prisons were significantly different than they had been in 1970. The whip, teeter board, and Tucker Telephone were gone; paid staff rather than prisoners served as guards; protocols existed for discipline; the filth had been reduced; and some mental and physical health care added. As Malcolm Feeley and Edward Rubin later wrote, Arkansas had moved from a "feudal-like Plantation Model," in which "prisoners were slaves of the state . . . forced at the end of a shotgun to work in the fields," into a system functioning as a "public agency; . . . the proximate cause for the transformation was intervention by the federal courts," requiring "principles of bureaucratic accountability . . . guided by the rehabilitative philosophy."[21]

In contrast, in 1982, Eisele did not describe the federal courts as the source of change. Reflecting his understanding of *judicial dependence* on executive and legislative branch action and his knowledge of Arkansas' politics, Eisele rolled out a long list of credits. He thanked governors, heads of ADC, attorneys on both sides, the Compliance Coordinator, legislators, and the state's burdened taxpayers. He singled out "the lowest echelons of the staff" and praised "the dignity and professional status that comes from the fair and even-handed performance of their most difficult duties." Sadly missing were the prisoners who braved retaliation to insist on their humanity. Yet Eisele's accolades were, of course, *a plea* to those he named to stay the course ("how easy it is to slip back"). Given the state's representations and the law that governed, Eisele had run out of facts to support his authority to do more.[22]

Before turning to the decades thereafter, when Arkansas and other systems incarcerated high numbers of people in conditions deemed *permissible*, a word is in order about the individuals who were central to the twelve years of the "Penitentiary Cases." I discussed the firing of Commissioner Sarver, the departures of Hutto and Mabry, the resignation of Housewright, Lockhart's longevity, and Governors Rockefeller, Bumpers, Clinton, and White. Because public records provide little about the named plaintiffs, all I know is that Lawrence Holt was gone from Arkansas' prisons by 1970 and died in 1987 and that, by the 1981 compliance hearings, Lockhart reported Robert Finney "got out of prison years ago."[23]

In contrast, the professionals' paper trail is ample. Chief Judge Henley had understood that the Penitentiary Cases would be his legacy (kept "alive" by them). Thomas Eisele, who died in 2017, was known for his commitment to adjudication (reflected in his horror at prison disciplinary decision-making). He was a regular defender of public courts, jury trials, judicial responsibility, and due process. In 1980, *The American Lawyer* called him the "Best District Judge in the 8th . . . who combine[s] intellectual brilliance and a sense of humor with what may be his most prominent feature: courage." As to the prison litigation, in his 1987 oral history, Eisele did not discuss his six years presiding in *Finney v. Hutto* but did reflect that, as a Rockefeller staffer, he knew the legislature "didn't really want to spend any money on prisons."[24]

Philip Kaplan and Jack Holt Jr., who had been paired by Henley in 1969, remained prominent figures in Arkansas' legal establishment and good friends until their deaths in 2023. (They were generous resources for me in writing this book.) Kaplan became a pillar of the Little Rock bar while, in 1984, Holt Jr. ran unopposed in the Democratic primary for Chief Justice and won in the general election. Serving until 1995, Holt Jr. was credited with changing the administrative structure, decision-making in juveniles' cases, and championing a state constitutional amendment to discipline judges.[25]

(MIS)HANDLING AND FUNDING THE (OVER)CROWDING

"We must keep longer sentences for repeat offenders."

—Governor Bill Clinton, Second Inaugural
Address, January 11, 1983[26]

"Arkansas cannot realistically expect to build its way out of the current prison population."

—Woodson Walker, Chair, Arkansas Board of
Correction, the Kiwanis Club, March 1987[27]

"They cannot handle the people that they get."

—Judge Henley, visiting Cummins, 1991[28]

Neither the prisoner–plaintiffs, their lawyers, nor the judges could stop the political engine pumping lock-them-up policies. New policies, statutes, budgets, press reports, and occasional lawsuits laid bare the parameters of punishment in Arkansas. Hearing less from judges, politicians were freer to decide whether and how to invest in punishment. They demonstrated a high toleration for confining people in miserable conditions.

Prison crowding was an issue during the 1982 race for Arkansas' governorship, when Bill Clinton vied for the Democratic nomination. Clinton called for double celling prisoners and lowering new housing construction costs. Once in office, Clinton—who had not mentioned

prisons in his 1979 inauguration—spoke in his January 1983 address
about making prisons more "self-supporting." (Eerily familiar again.)

> We have to do something about the prison system. Its budget is
> increasing dramatically because of a rapidly increasing popu-
> lation and longer sentences for repeat offenders. . . . [W]e can
> reverse the trend of diverting more and more tax dollars from
> education and other needed services to prisons, but only if we
> make a determined effort to see that the thirty-eight hundred
> incarcerated men and women work more productively and pay
> more of their own way.[29]

That approach was evident in Clinton's decision not to replace Lockhart, who despite allegations of misconduct, remained the Commissioner for another decade.

These choices generated a morass. Arkansas officials understood
that the number to be housed often exceeded population caps. They
pursued funding, building, alternative placements (moving prisoners
out of state, to local facilities, and courthouse basements), and a series of back-end releases to make room for new entrants. Constantly
adding and filling beds, the governing powers occasionally tweaked
but never recoiled at the system they had shaped nor confronted the
underlying problems of overuse of criminal law and incarceration.

Specifics, as always, ground my analyses. In 1984, when the
Correction Board reported its prisons were "full to overflowing,"
Clinton called for a new infusion of taxpayer funds—$51 million
for 1986 and $58 million for 1987. In 1986, when the prisons were
again "full" and 200 prisoners were "'backed up' in local jails," Clinton sought more buildings and regional jails, as well as expanded
release programs. County sheriffs objected that reimbursements
would be "piddling"—if paid.[30] After the Correction Board sent state
prisoners to Pulaski County Jail, a lawsuit charged the county with
an "unauthorized tax usage" on the theory that local county taxes
were not to be spent to "support the state prison system." By 1991,
one headline announced, "Bill for Prisoners Mounting" and that the
ADC was "still in red." Budget cuts prompted staff layoffs.[31]

Back-end release had been disparaged in the 1970s when Arkansas' legislature cut parole eligibility. But in 1987, the legislature enacted a Prison Emergency Powers Act, triggered when the prisons were at 98 percent capacity and permitting the Board to "release parole-worthy inmates 90 days ahead of their regular parole date." In April, as its "only option," the Board for "the first time" permitted "early release of up to 447 inmates" when 451 state prisoners were "backed up" in county jails. The number of individuals identified as "eligible" for getting *out* generally dovetailed with the people in line to get *in*; in November, with 7,067 people in state prisons, the Board ordered early release of 158 prisoners as 157 men and three women in jails awaited prison beds.[32]

Meanwhile, the state went further into debt to county jails for housing state prisoners. "No pay, no jail" was what Arkansas' Sheriffs' Association threatened, warning that its members would start refusing to accept or keep prisoners. Around the same time, Little Rock's City Jail was dunning Pulaski County for more than $80,000 owed for "inmate-housing." Having gotten attention before by chaining prisoners outside a prison, the sheriff linked fifty people to trees, which produced an ACLU lawsuit resulting in a settlement of $22,500 for detainees and lawyer fees.[33]

But not much changed. "Bursting at its bars" was how one writer put it, as the state legislature added $7.5 million to the ADC's coffers to open an empty 700-bed facility, vacant for want of operating funds. Under other federal court consent decree caps, the county and city jails were "full." Officials tried to deal with the "overflow" by shipping prisoners around the state, out of state, and exploring home confinement with monitoring via "ankle bracelets." In the fall of 1987, Lockhart bragged that while other prison systems spent about $40–$50 a day, the $23 a day per inmate . . . [in Arkansas was] the lowest figure in the country."[34]

1988 sounded a lot like 1987, with "backlogged inmates" and early release on the horizon by the end of March. The news in 1989 was more of the same. The prisons were growing by "1.6 inmates a day" (an odd calculation). Everyone was clear that crowding was "the heart of the problem," and its sources were a mix of "a growing

drug problem" and "get-tough sentencing policies." Five hundred
people with life sentences had only one way out: commutation by
the governor, a practice Clinton ended "after being criticized for
a handful of commutations in his first term." Meanwhile, people
in jails and prisons kept asking federal judges for help; 677 claims
were filed between 1988 and September of 1989. Another headline,
"No Room for Justice," topped a story complaining the "public . . .
[was] caught up in the flood" as cells were full "at every level . . .
from state prisons down to city lockups."[35]

Prisons were of course competing with other government services in the "constant scrabbling by government agencies for a fi-
nite pool of cash amid stiffening public resistance to new taxes."
According to the state's Finance and Administration Department,
the public—"every man, woman and child in Arkansas"—paid
"about a nickel a day to run the state prison system." In that budget,
86 percent went to "education and human services" and 3 percent
to prisons; the *Arkansas Gazette* complained prisons "gobble[d] up"
money that ought to have gone to more deserving users. Meanwhile, Arkansas was winning a pathetic race to the bottom: the
state ranked forty-eighth in "budget dollars per inmate" and garnered praise as "among the leanest, most efficiently run systems
in the country."[36]

Inefficiencies, however, abounded. The state owed counties
money, counties owed cities, and all levels of government tried to
collect, at times via lawsuits. In 1990, after what the press called
"riots" at some jails, the Arkansas Sheriffs' Association authorized
a lawsuit against the state, and in November, Pulaski County sought
$600,000 for its "housing [of] convicted felons." Lockhart asked the
legislature for $9.7 million in supplemental funds, of which $5.4
million was to reimburse counties. After obtaining $8.7 million,
some people called for a "surtax to finance Gov. Bill Clinton's drug
war, prisons and other measures."[37]

A proposal for a sales tax to boost funds won in 1990 Pulaski
County. That February, more voters turned out than in the "last
20 years for a special election" and approved two to one (23,505
to 13,855) a 1-percent sales tax to finance a new 800-bed regional

jail. (In the words of one prosecutor, "people are willing to pay for more jail space.") Yet the state's 5,000 outstanding felony warrants outstripped beds.[38]

Taxpayer money was one route and another was trying to extract funds from prisoners. Arkansas had in 1981 enacted a Prison Inmate Care and Custody Reimbursement Act, which authorized taking money from a prisoner's "estate," including inheritances as well as social security, disability, veterans, and other federal benefits. For example, the state used that authority to seize $6,800 inherited by a twenty-six-year-old prisoner from his father; Arkansas said it had spent $55,000 for its eight years of "care." On the other hand, Arkansas lost its bid to take prisoners' federal disability benefits when, in 1988, the US Supreme Court ruled the state had no power over national programs.[39]

Arkansas did not invent that "pay-to-stay" approach, which remains widespread. Many states have statutes to recoup "room and board" and impose fees for soap, food, medical visits, and phone calls. Such measures have come under sustained criticism as a bizarre form of consumerism undermining individuals with limited economic stability and disproportionately affecting communities of color. Nonetheless, in 2023, Connecticut sought to up its recoupment from a daily rate of $249 to $323, and the federal government proposed taking 75 percent from prisoners' commissary funds, whether or not family members had sent money for food and phone calls.[40]

After Clinton became president of the United States, his successor Jimmy Guy Tucker "pitched" alternatives to lessen reliance on incarceration. "Arkansas . . . cannot build its way out of a correctional crisis," said Roger Endell, the new Commissioner of ADC and of community supervision. He estimated that a day in prison cost $30 and supervision outside $6.50. Tucker asked for more than $109 million, far outstripping Clinton's requests the decade before. Endell's brief tenure ended with reports of using state funds when moving his belongings to Arkansas; the department reverted to Larry Norris, who had been at ADC since 1971.[41]

Thereafter, the state enacted its first Community Punishment Act, permitting "options" for "nonviolent offenders" that included

"economic sanctions" (fines), home confinement, community service, boot camps, substance abuse and mental health treatment,
and parole and post-prison supervision. A related statute created a
Department of Community Punishment, tasked with "supervision,
treatment, rehabilitation, and restoration of adult offenders as
useful law-abiding citizens within the community." In 2001, the renamed Department of Community Correction sat under the Board
of Corrections; the "s" denoted oversight over more than one mo-
dality of punishment. In 2019, as part of a Transformation and Efficiencies Act, the legislature turned the ADC into the "Division of
Correction" run by a "Director" as one of several subparts within
a "Department of Corrections" (catch the "s" again), headed by a
"Secretary" who, upon confirmation by Arkansas' Senate, joined
fourteen other heads of "cabinet-level . . . agencies."[42]

That expansion reflected in part the impact of federal incentives
to build prisons and keep people locked in them. In 1994, Congress
offered federal grants for prison building—contingent on "truth-in-
sentencing" laws requiring individuals to serve at least 85 percent
of their sentences. In addition, Clinton endorsed and Congress enacted legislation in 1996 that limited prisoners' access to federal
courts. One statute "reformed" habeas corpus by cutting back on individuals' ability to challenge convictions. Another, while called the
Prison Litigation Reform Act (PLRA), imposed hurdles for people
pursuing lawsuits like *Holt v. Sarver* and for federal judges issuing
injunctions as Judge Henley had.[43]

Given Clinton's experiences with the Arkansas legislature that
had, before the late 1960s, been unwilling to spend *any* taxpayer
money for prisons, I could have understood Clinton's openness to
federal funding—if it had been conditioned on standards to improve
services, lessen prison terms, and support alternatives. The federal
legislation not only lacked those features but also provided no funds
for operating costs, which left staffing, services, and maintenance
to the states. Just as Clinton had helped in 1977 to draft Arkansas'
"first really tough repeat-offender law," Clinton-era federal enact-
ments left more people confined for longer periods of time in miserable circumstances.[44]

CORRUPT AS WELL AS BRUTAL PRISONS

"You are now an inmate within the Arkansas Department of Correction. We did not catch you, convict you, nor sentence you; but we are charged with the responsibility of confining you."

—Preface by A. L. Lockhart, ADC Inmate
Handbook, September, 1986[45]

"[A] high level of sexual harassment and fear" affected "nearly every prisoner."

—Board of Correction's investigation, 1986[46]

A decade after the Arkansas Legislative Commission had bemoaned a lack of fiscal accountability, and despite soaring budgets, not much had changed. Along with prisoner escapes, deaths, beatings, rapes, and health care failures, accusations of corruption made the news. Lockhart allegedly knew about bribery attempts of staff, thefts from the "Inmate Welfare Fund," the use of state equipment and prisoner labor for private purposes, and payments without proper bidding to businesses with whom Lockhart had relationships. Lockhart was also defending several lawsuits, including a 1984 class action brought by women alleging discrimination in vocational programs, health care, and release programs. Following the pattern of *Holt/ Finney*, this amalgamation of individual petitions specified a myriad of failures, including that women lacked psychiatric services, were heavily sedated, lived in unsanitary conditions, and had limited access to lawyers. In 1986, a federal judge approved a settlement adding vocational programs, work release, the building of a classroom, and improved health care.[47]

Another class action, filed in 1985 by the ACLU on behalf of twenty-seven prisoners seeking to represent five hundred more at Tucker's Maximum-Security Unit, alleged that conditions were "more inhumane and barbaric than ever" and sought $5 million in compensatory and $5 million in punitive damages in light of the "brutality." Sadly familiar, the lawsuit claimed that staff were making people "run to and from the fields," keeping them in isolation long beyond the "legal maximum of 30 days," and that people were held in crowded, unsafe conditions, with insufficient access to lawyers and health care. The Board of Correction commissioned its own study, which found that "nearly every prisoner" lived in "fear." In light of the evident "management problem," the consultants called for better educated staff and an end of dorms with more than fifty beds—estimated to cost more than $5 million.[48]

Until 1992, Lockhart survived what he characterized as "bad press." Key to his longevity was support from Clinton, the state's Association of Chiefs of Police, and Knox Nelson, Pine Bluff's state senator later implicated in some of Lockhart's alleged wrongdoing. In 1992, after Clinton became President and Nelson lost reelection, the Board of Correction held a "closed, two-day investigation of . . . dubious purchasing practices," and Lockhart resigned. Atop acquisition of allegedly bad equipment at high prices, Lockhart was said to have profited from marketing tainted plasma from prisoners; as discussed, since the 1960s, selling blood was prisoners' only source of income. A state grand jury convened in 1993, but it was the federal government that indicted Lockhart on fraud charges. That prosecution ended in a deal in which Lockhart received probation. (One lesson of this book is that people who run prisons rarely end up sentenced to them.) In 1998, prisoners' blood sold from Arkansas prompted a Canadian-based inquiry, identifying more than 42,000 at risk of hepatitis C. Lawsuits followed against ADC as well as two companies staffed by Clinton allies and cited by the FDA for safety deficiencies.[49]

After Lockhart's departure, the tone of the "Inmate Handbooks" shifted. In 1994, the ADC's "mission statement" was "to provide for the protection of free society by carrying out the mandate of the courts; provide a safe, humane environment for staff and inmates; strengthen the work ethic through teaching of good habits; and provide opportunities for inmates to improve spiritually, mentally, and physically." The Handbook repeated that the department was "not responsible" for the fact of incarceration ("the price you pay") but did plan "to hold you in a safe and humane manner." Yet, accounts of beatings and rapes continued under Commissioner Norris, who was also implicated in 1995 in widespread "corruption, contraband and bribery." A few employees were fired or transferred, and within the year, the press reported that the Department "bought more than

$100,000 in fuel products" of "poor quality" from a company owned by Norris' brother.[50]

EVER-SPIRALING DOLLARS: DENSITY AND THE DECADE OF COVID

"Federal judges don't like it when inmates sleep on the floor, and it creates problems for our jail staff . . . putting that many extra folks in such a small area."

—John Montgomery, Sheriff of Baxter County
Detention Facility, May 2017[51]

One accounting of ADC's operating expenses comes from a 2006 ADC report, figure 27.2, showing "operating expenses" from 1981 (as *Finney v. Mabry* was ending) through 2006.

The dollars pouring in did not "ease prison overcrowding." In 1996, ADC's 9,000 prison beds were full; 792 people were "backed up in county jails," and some "lower-security inmates" were sent out of state as a $39 million bond was floated to build "Arkansas' first two private prisons." In 1997, the Correction Board used its early release powers to permit 500 prisoners to leave. In 1998, "prisons [were] filling up at rapid rate."[52]

The ever-enlarging budgets and the numbers of people "caught" (to borrow Marie Gottschalk's title of her book about politics and punishment) continued into the twenty-first century. In 2000, for example, when 1,111 prisoners were held in local jails and the prisons were "bulging," the Board authorized 487 "parole eligible prisoners" to leave, the transfer of 150 to Texas, new construction of a medium-security facility for two hundred more, and fifty more beds in another facility. Fast construction was possible because architects had developed "prototypes"—pre-fab, cement slab, cookie-cutter cell blocks that other architects thought poorly designed.[53]

Quick construction could not, however, keep pace with prosecutors and sentencing judges. In the spring of 2001, the prisons were again 98 percent above capacity for ninety consecutive days, and more than 500 prisoners were—as the press put it—"turned loose early." Inside facilities, the experience was awful. One reporter described the noise produced by the hard metal surfaces that followed prisoners into the "hole," where people were "out of sight but not sound" as a racket drowned out everything. All the while, the counties, cities, and state continued their cycles of "squabbling over the debt" owed each other. Governor Mike Huckabee sought $189 million for fiscal year 2004 while promoting a "vision" of slowing prison construction by (again) calling for alternative sentencing and drug court diversion programs. The legislature tweaked its sentencing laws to shift decisions from juries to judges and authorize alternative sentencing, including drug rehabilitation and electronic monitoring.[54]

By 2006, when the chart (figure 27.2) ends, the ADC had a revised mission ("public safety . . . a safe humane environment for staff and inmates, . . . opportunities for spiritual, mental and physical growth," and equal employment opportunities) and another fundraising effort (a $40 million special revenue bond to build 860 beds

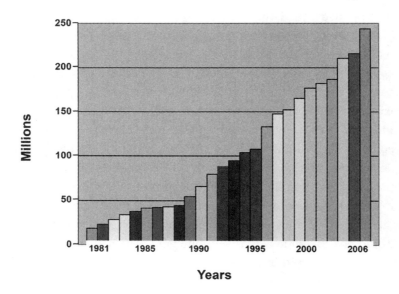

Inmate Care & Custody Operating Expenditures

FIGURE 27.2 *Inmate Care and Custody Operating Expenditures*, Arkansas Department of Correction, July 1, 2005–June 30, 2006 Annual Report, Arkansas State Library

for "geriatric, mental health, and chronically ill" prisoners). ADC then housed more than 12,600 people, categorized as Black, white, Asian, and Hispanic. A majority of the men (52 percent) and a third of the women were not white. In 2007, with almost 14,000 prisoners, ADC asked for $284 million to add another 1,400 beds; the request was winnowed down to $268 million plus another $68 million for Community Corrections. In 2008, on "any given day . . . as many as 1,000" people were held in county jails awaiting transfers to state prisons. In 2010, Governor Mike Beebe urged sheriffs to lobby to get paid for holding nearly 1,400 state prisoners. Describing prison population growth as "unsustainable," Beebe called for alternatives and appointed Ray Hobbs, an ADC member for thirty-five years and the "first African-American to head" the department.[55]

Evidence of unsustainability came from the ongoing reliance on jails; as of 2017, ADC, still paying $30 a day, owed $14 million to county jails. An effort in 2017 to slow intake came when Governor Asa Hutchinson promoted the Criminal Justice Efficiency and Safety Act to permit "nonviolent" parole offenders" to have six minor violations before being re-incarcerated and, hopefully, open up 1,650 beds. Yet demand for detention again outstripped supply. When arguing the need to expand the 100-bed jail in Baxter County, its sheriff pointed out that people were sleeping on the floor, and county's voters approved a "short-term," 1-percent sales tax to expand by fifty beds the 100-bed facility. Pressures to keep numbers within caps had become part of state statutes, providing that sheriffs could only "refuse to accept prisoners" when complying "with constitutional requirements." Violence accompanied density, and density was used to justify solitary confinement. In 2017, the state proposed four hundred more "lockdown" cells to the two thousand it had to keep people "at least 22 hours a day" in isolation. That addition meant that 16 percent or more of the "prison systems beds" would be devoted to solitary confinement. About a year later, five prisoners died within a week at a supermax unit; officials linked that "unacceptable" loss to drug overdoses.[56]

The state continued to see prisoners as a source of revenue; in addition to their forced labor, it charged exorbitantly for basics.

In 2007, Arkansas received $2.5 million in "commissions . . . on the cost of collect calls" and, after criticism, reduced the price of a fifteen-minute call from $6.60 to $4.80 and its commission from 51 to 45 percent. Fees for visits was another route; in 2018, the Benton County Jail ended in-person visits and charged $0.50 per minute for video, which required access to computers.[57]

The interjurisdictional, interpersonal search for money continued unabated, as did litigation about it. In 2018, the Arkansas Supreme Court interpreted "prisoners of municipalities" to include individuals "arrested by city police." That decision required cities to foot the bill for housing people held pretrial through misdemeanor convictions but not people held under felony charges. That fall, one county leveled a $40 fee per day, per person, for cities to use its jail space. In 2019, voters in a county approved a "permanent quarter-percent sales tax to fund" its jail operations.[58] As of 2024, ADC reported about 500 more people monthly than it released. Its prison population added more than 100 prisoners a month, with about 1,900 people held in "country jail backup" each day. In May of 2024, Arkansas launched a "Justice Reinvestment Initiative" to address why 46 percent of people released in 2017 had returned within three years.[59]

Violence and illness remained. Headlines in January of 2020 flagged prisoners' deaths, one allegedly at the hands of another, and the other deemed a suicide. COVID arrived soon after. The density proved to be the disaster public health officials had forecast. By April of 2020, "860 prisoners at Cummins, . . . almost half the population, had tested positive for COVID-19," and "at least 10 had died." That April, the "lion's share" of the state's COVID patients were prisoners, which gave Arkansas the distinction on a *New York Times* website as a "hotspot." A *New Yorker* profile captured the terror of incarcerated individuals unprotected from COVID exposure. Arkansas' prisoners turned—as Winston Talley had in 1965—to the federal courts. After getting a hearing, they lost their request for emergency relief for soap, disinfectant, social distance, and doctors.

Again, Arkansas was not an outlier. As several trial court judges required prisons to "de-densify," provide soap, and health care, some of their orders were reversed or stayed, including by the US

FIGURE 27.3 Budgeting for prisoners, Arkansas, 1965–2021

Year	State budget allocations	Percent of state budget (NASBO data available as of 1982)	Percentage change	Number of prisoners in state
1965				1,970
1966				1,864
1967				1,651
1968	$700,000.00			1,538
1969	$500,000.00		−28.57	950–1,250
1970	$500,000.00		.00	1,360
1971	$2,310,400.00		362.08	1,658
1972	$2,749,081.00		18.99	1,619
1973	$3,571,351.00		29.91	1,679
1974	$3,874,617.00		8.49	1,938
1975	$5,775,970.00		49.07	1,938
1976	$6,102,723.00		5.66	2,162
1977	$9,615,306.00		57.56	2,542
1978	$11,868,371.00		23.43	2,654
1979	$11,731,548.00		−1.15	2,963
1980	$13,329,219.00		13.62	2,925
1981	$20,732,074.00		55.54	3,328
1982	$22,972,050.00		10.80	3,925
1983	$31,455,730.00	2.83	36.93	4,246
1984	$35,000,000.00	2.25	11.27	4,472
1985	$37,000,000.00	2.53	5.71	4,611
1986	$38,000,000.00	2.67	2.70	4,701
1987	$43,000,000.00	2.76	13.16	5,441
1988	$50,000,000.00	3.00	16.28	5,519
1989	$55,000,000.00	3.09	10.00	6,649
1990	$62,000,000.00	3.33	12.73	7,322
1991	$72,000,000.00	3.74	16.13	7,681
1992	$82,000,000.00	4.02	13.89	8,373
1993	$93,000,000.00	4.23	13.41	8,911
1994	$94,689,983.00	4.00	1.82	8,808
1995	$110,000,000.00	4.42	16.17	9,378
1996	$120,678,540.00	4.60	9.71	9,760
1997	$146,000,000.00	5.14	20.98	10,455
1998	$149,905,233.00	5.03	2.67	10,890

(*Continued*)

FIGURE 27.3   *(Continued)*

Year	State budget allocations	Percent of state budget (NASBO data available as of 1982)	Percentage change	Number of prisoners in state
1999	$162,000,000.00	5.10	8.07	11,827
2000	$165,106,231.00	5.06	1.92	11,856
2001	$190,287,036.00	5.61	15.25	12,496
2002	$178,819,219.00	5.52	−6.03	12,999
2003	$209,636,947.00	5.98	17.23	13,244
2004	$209,061,947.00	5.79	−.27	13,668
2005	$248,678,484.00	6.50	18.95	13,383
2006	$257,013,387.00	6.33	3.35	13,713
2007	$278,814,017.00	6.41	8.48	14,310
2008	$275,802,921.00	6.26	−1.08	14,660
2009	$271,923,566.00	6.38	−1.41	15,144
2010	$290,303,309.00	6.48	6.76	16,147
2011	$296,737,360.00	6.48	2.22	16,037
2012	$298,842,000.00	6.32	.71	14,615
2013	$312,998,229.00	6.35	4.74	17,159
2014	$322,311,296.00	6.40	2.98	17,819
2015	$336,663,255.00	6.49	4.45	17,656
2016	$338,502,919.00	6.38	.55	17,476
2017	$349,646,130.00	6.53	3.29	18,028
2018	$353,186,149.00	6.49	1.01	17,795
2019	$343,344,977.00	6.33	−2.79	17,759
2020	$360,991,738.00	6.42	5.14	16,094
2021	$359,032,680.00	6.19	−.54	17,023

Sources: National Association of State Budget Officers; Arkansas Department of Finance and Administration; Acts of the General Assembly of the State of Arkansas; Bureau of Justice Statistics; Arkansas Sentencing Commission; Sentencing Project; and the Vera Institute.

Supreme Court. The data on COVID's impact reflected the reason to call for intervention. As discussed, prisoners were 3.5 times more likely to die and 5.5 times more likely to become infected than non-incarcerated people; staff likewise had higher rates of infection and death than people outside prisons.[60]

TAXPAYER DOLLARS FROM THE 1960S TO 2020S:
TOO LITTLE AND TOO MUCH

I have detailed sixty years of Arkansas' budgets in figure 27.3. During that time, prisoners sought better treatment, the state legislature began its input of taxpayer dollars, and then accelerated commitments to fund detention. I begin in 1965, which is when Winston Talley filed his petition and Arkansas had *no* budget line for its prisons. Figure 27.3 reflects that, once prisoners had "rights," court orders did help push dollars out of the state's treasury.[61] That funding did not stop the forced manual labor at Cummins. When I visited in 2019, I was startled to see prisoners stooped over, cutting grass with hand shears. Staff explained that task was assigned during the first months of incarceration and made no mention of its being as degrading as it was inefficient.

Figure 27.3 depicts that Arkansas' legislature first allocated for prisons in 1968, in the wake of the state police torture investigation, the legislature's creation of the ADC with a mandate for "rehabilitation," and the Eighth Circuit ruling that whipping was unconstitutional. Because that table details the number of individuals incarcerated each year, it provides a reminder that, in the 1960s, efforts to reduce prosecutions and incarceration translated into a population decline.

The years 1969 and 1970, when the first "totality of conditions" cases—*Holt v. Sarver I* and *II*—resulted in a judgment that Arkansas' entire prison system was unconstitutional, dovetailed with larger legislative allocations. That initial 1968 allotment came by way of an off-cycle special legislative session that authorized $700,000 ($5,480,889 in 2021 dollars) for prisons. The willingness to do so soared in the decades thereafter, as politicians beat the drums of crime, race, and violence and chose to incarcerate tens of thousands in impoverished conditions with few services. By 2021, Arkansas budgeted more than $359 million—a 6,550 percent increase from 1968. Given that the state housed about 1,538 prisoners in 1968, the cost per prisoner was $455 ($3,564 in 2021 dollars). By 2021, with more than 17,000 prisoners, the per-prisoner cost was about $21,091. The growth in the prison population between 1968 and 2021 was 1,005 percent, and funding per prisoner increased 492 percent.[62]

Caveats and contexts are needed. Since the mid-1980s, the National Association of State Budget Officers (NASBO), a font of information about tax revenues, special bonds, and federal grants, reported that 90 percent of state expenditures come from general tax revenues. (Before NASBO published its reports, identifying allotted dollars entailed reading state session laws). NASBO delineates expenditures by categories including corrections (prisons, jails, detention centers) as a percentage of total state expenditures. Other services tracked include elementary/secondary education, higher education, Medicaid, public assistance, transportation, and all others. Given my focus on tax revenue allocations, figure 27.3 does not include dollars from federal funds, state ad hoc appropriations, or cuts in funding, which also occurred. Moreover, after sums are appropriated, correction departments may (and did) spend them in other ways. Further, this accounting does not reflect expenditures at the local level or how the money was spent; analyses by the Vera Institute for Justice and the Prison Policy Institute do so through distinguishing new construction from facilities' maintenance, staff salaries and benefits, incarcerated people's health care, and other services.[63]

This accounting is also incomplete in that it does not include the value of prisoners' labor or the money correctional systems extract from incarcerated persons and their families. As of 2020, more than 60 percent of individuals in federal and state prisons were forced, as Robert Chase documented, into "coerced labor." While some states such as Arkansas send many people to pick crops, all jurisdictions rely on prisoners for building maintenance and food services; some systems have "prison industries" doing manufacturing or support for governmental programs and private-sector entities. One estimate is that prisoners' labor defrayed about $9 billion yearly in operational costs.[64]

Although the influence of the International Labour Organisation prompted leaders of the IPPC in the 1920s to call for real wages, as of 2024 in the United States, prisoners were generally paid less than a few dollars per hour. Moreover, neither federal nor state statutes requiring minimum wages, overtime, and safety have been read to apply to prisoners. Arkansas was one of three states (Georgia and Texas were the others) that obliged incarcerated people to work while paying nothing; in a few other states (Alabama, Florida, Mississippi, and South Carolina), most work without pay. One justification is that the state provides housing and food. (Recall that the *Holt* lawyers argued unsuccessfully in 1970 that conditions were too awful to be a quid pro quo.) As discussed, many jurisdictions also charge for some "minimal necessities of civilized life" such as soap and toothpaste and "copays" for health care; in Arkansas, that fee in 2021 was $3 for each medical appointment. Some prisons impose dollar sanctions for misconduct; $250 and more can be the result of prison disciplinary hearings. Further, "pay-to-stay" laws authorize post-release collection at per diem rates, as if a prison were a hotel and the imprisoned, volunteers.[65]

A glimpse at a few other states provides more context. I looked at budget allocations in New York, the site of the 1971 Attica uprising, and in Ohio, the system at issue in the double-celling decision, *Rhodes v. Chapman*. California is included because the harms to health and safety of density prompted a 2011 decision, discussed in the next chapter. Moving back to the South, I chose Louisiana, Texas, and Mississippi that relied in the 1960s—as did Arkansas—on prisoner labor for income. Again, the numbers do not include non-tax revenue sources; moreover, significant variations exist in the aegis of corrections departments and their budgeting methods. Hence, the numbers are rough estimates of funding to prisons and spending per prisoner. The trends in terms of state taxpayer dollars are similar to that of Arkansas, in that steep increases began in the 1970s along with expansion of prosecution, longer sentences, and prisoners' rights. In contrast to Arkansas, before prisoner litigation, many states had budget lines—often small—for prisons. Rather than narrate the details, figure 27.4 provides snapshots.

Another way to look at dollars spent comes from NASBO reports on total state corrections spending (including federal and other sources) as a percentage of state budgets—baselines that vary widely. The percentage ranged in the 1980s from a low of 0.7 percent in North Dakota to 5.3 percent in Maryland, with the median at 1.9 percent. By the 2021 fiscal year, estimates of spending were 1.2 percent in Hawaii to 4.3 percent in Utah, with the median at 2.2

FIGURE 27.4 Budgeting for prisoners: California, Louisiana, Mississippi, New York, Ohio, and Texas, 1967/1968 to 2021

		Non-Southern states			
Year	State budget allocations	Percent of state budget	Percentage change*	Number of prisoners in state	Expenditure per prisoner
California					
1967	$81,705,107	2.40		27,794	$2,940
2021	$11,984,000,000	3.00	14,748	96,472	$124,233
New York					
1968	$86,633,000	1.60		15,000	$5,775
2021	$1,277,000,000	1.70	1,374	31,262	$40,848
Ohio					
1967	$44,753,000	.89		10,393	$4,306
2021	$1,810,072,312	5.12	3,945	42,963	$42,130
		Southern states			
Year	State budget allocations	Percent of state budget	Percentage change*	Number of prisoners in state	Expenditure per prisoner
Louisiana					
1967	$3,560,088			3,700	$962
2021	$540,000,000	5.40	15,068	26,714	$20,214
Texas					
1968	$18,016,723	4.00		12,215	$1,474
2021	$2,435,000,000	4.00	13,415	117,491	$20,725
Mississippi					
1968	$4,000,000			1,544	$2,591
2021	$311,000,000	1.50	7,675	16,945	$18,353

FIGURE 27.5 Comparing state expenditures for corrections and higher education (including from federal and other funding sources), 1985 to 2021

	1985 corrections	Est. 2021 corrections	1985 higher education	Est. 2021 higher education
Min	.7	1.2	4.8	2.0
Median	1.9	2.2	9.4	8.9
Max	5.3	4.3	22.6	23.6

percent. States spent about 2.5 percent of "total state expenditures" on prisons for an aggregate of more than $62 billion.[66]

Given the large numbers of incarcerated people during years when some people are in college, prison budgets are sometimes compared with higher education funding. In the late 1980s, higher education expenditures as a percentage of total state expenditures ranged from 4.8 percent in Maine to 22.6 percent in Arizona; the median was 9.4 percent. By the 2021 fiscal year, this estimated figure was 2.0 percent in New Hampshire and Pennsylvania to 23.6 percent in Iowa, with the median at 8.9 percent. NASBO's analysis calculated that states spent a total of $225.3 billion, including federal funds, and thus about 8.5 percent of the total state expenditures.[67] Figure 27.5 is the summary.

Two more numbers and a bit of theory bring this chapter to its close. In 2019, the United States held about forty men as part of the 9/11 detention at Guantánamo Bay, and the cost for a year per person was estimated to be about $13 million. In 2021, the cost to hold a person for a year at New York City's Rikers Island, infamous for the many lives lost of people held before trial, was more than $550,000 per person; on an average day, just under 5,000 people were there. As for some theory, David Garland wrote decades ago to criticize the ways in which, in the name of "welfare," England expanded its use of detention.[68] The dollars poured into the construction and operation of prisons ought not to be conflated with generative investments in human beings and the social order.

28

"DOUBLE BUNKING," SOLITARY CONFINEMENT, MASS INCARCERATION, AND ABOLITION

"[L]inking the costs of confinement to the decision to incarcerate, more rational incarceration policies might emerge . . . [about] the . . . prison conditions that are tolerable . . . and the amount of resources the state is willing to divert from other public purposes to maintain an incarcerated population."

—*American Prisons and Jails: Summary and Policy Implications of a National Survey*, National Institute of Justice, 1980[1]

The Federal Bureau of Prisons "has recently changed its policy on using single cells to permit some double-bunking. . . ."

—*Prison Costs: Opportunities Exist to Lower the Cost of Building Federal Prisons*, US General Accounting Office, 1991[2]

"Inmates must remain in their cells, which measure 7 by 14 feet, for 23 hours per day. A light remains on . . . at all times, . . . [I]nmates are deprived of almost any environmental or sensory stimuli and of almost all human contact. . . . for an indefinite period of time, limited only by an inmate's sentence."

—Justice Anthony Kennedy, *Wilkinson v. Austin*, 2005[3]

This chapter brings this several-century analysis into the present as the cages of carceral punishment's legitimacy are being rattled. Paralleling this book's first section devoted to the scaling-up of the enterprise of corrections before the mid-twentieth century, this chapter tracks the recent decades of infrastructure expansion. Aggressive prosecution and sentencing laws generated record numbers of incarcerated and state-supervised people. I use the term massive incarceration as a reminder of its discriminatory impact; the phenomenon is often denoted by the shorthand "mass incarceration."[4] Prison construction turned corrections into a major source of employment with budgets larger than many other state agencies. In 2018, for example, the head of the Ohio system told me that one out of four employed by the state worked for him. Thus, a mix of hyper-density and expanded use of solitary confinement raised questions for judges and legislators about delineating permissible and impermissible punishments.

For a few months in 2020, as COVID provided a vivid exemplar of the harms of crowded congregate housing, some commentators thought it would prompt acceptance of a de-incarceration agenda. COVID, however, provided unnerving evidence of a political willingness to *tolerate* leaving incarcerated people at heightened risk of disease and death.[5] Even as prison populations declined between 2010 and 2022, the appetite for punishment, coupled with political polarization and backlash against affirmative action, brought "crime control" into focus again. Many candidates for elected office backed away from reforms of police and bail, "progressive prosecution," and alternative sentencing. By 2024, prison populations—in Arkansas and elsewhere—were rising.

On the other hand, social mobilizations had generated new counter-movements. "Stop Solitary," renamed "Unlock the Box," called for ending isolating individuals in tiny spaces, and "abolition" became the byword for revisiting assumptions that policing, state prosecution, and incarceration were fixtures; the goals were to move beyond "reformist reforms" to "non-reformist" transformations. Proposals to limit corrections' use of solitary confinement took shape in dozens of statutes, regulations, and professional standards; a few became judicial mandates. Prison abolition gained currency as a method for analyzing criminal law systems, even as it also engendered concerns that its ambitions would cutoff support for less sweeping goals.[6] Because sorting out events during the most recent fifty years is requisite to concluding, this chapter maps the impact of crowded prisons on standards for safe confinement promulgated by corrections, the federal government, and the courts, on density's relationship to discipline and isolation, and on social movements.

GENERATE AND FOLLOW THE (FEDERAL) MONEY

Given the girth of today's "prison-industrial complex," the reminder is that "corrections" only got rich in the last half of the twentieth century. Before the 1960s, crime was categorized as a "local" matter, the boom in state prison funding had not begun, and the federal government had a small criminal justice footprint when compared to states and localities. The tumult of the 1960s, with street protests opposing race discrimination and the Vietnam War, were fuel for a conservative agenda, which gained political sway. In 1968, Congress enacted an Omnibus Crime Control and Safe Streets Act that was the source of the Law Enforcement Assistance Administration (LEAA) which, as discussed, gave grants to states and localities. Such "broad scale" federal assistance for "Criminal Justice Planning Agencies" aimed to "advance the state of the art of law enforcement" and "reduce crime and delinquency." By 1972, Congress had appropriated $699 million to add to $860 million dedicated to LEAA, whose decade of grant-making provides another window into debates about what forms of punishment were tolerable.[7]

A bit of LEAA money was spent to *limit* detention's use. I participated in one such effort when working on an LEAA-supported New York City project to provide services for mentally ill criminal defendants. The challenge was locating needy individuals dispersed across the five boroughs; some were sent to hospitals and others to detention centers. Another LEAA grant of the mid-1970s, a "cost analysis of halfway houses," concluded that running a "model halfway house" was less expensive per person than an "average jail even though a halfway house offer[ed] a wide range of services not available in most jails."

More de-incarceration suggestions emerged from a 1976 congressional mandate that the National Institute for Justice (NIJ) survey the "existing and future needs in correctional facilities . . . and the adequacy of Federal, State and local programs to meet such needs." Five bulky volumes, published in 1980, argued for decriminalization. Researchers explained that the "largest share of growth," producing "unprecedented levels" of incarceration, came from people "sentenced for property and public order crime—precisely those groups repeatedly recommended for alternative treatment." Hence, the report "seriously" questioned building more prison beds and recommended legislatures adopt "standards defining the minimum living space and associated conditions to be provided each prisoner—a measure that would define the costs of confinement and establish implicit capacity limits for state and local institutions." Federal funding ought to depend on meeting "minimum living space requirements."[8]

In addition, the NIJ research team suggested making "accelerated release" (akin to the "operating back door" that Arkansas opened) available when facilities reached capacity. The researchers thought that focusing on the human costs and dollar prices of incarceration would sharpen public awareness of the disutility of building prisons and the need to spend state dollars elsewhere. A related publication (as discussed) concluded that "sustained crowding" had a "wide variety of negative psychological and physiological effects," including higher death and suicide rates and more disciplinary infractions. The NIJ was not alone; "overcrowded time" (as one foundation's 1982 monograph put it) needed to end through decriminalization and alternative sentences.[9]

Trying to prove its own utility, the LEAA positioned itself as the font of "reliable and comparable information about the success or failure of innovative crime prevention efforts." Yet despite its research, most of its money went to expanding criminal law's reach; "three out of every four dollars . . . during its fifteen-year span" went to police for the protection of "law-abiding Americans." Funds for prisons, in theory to enable "[t]he criminal . . . [to] be rehabilitated and given the opportunity for a truly constructive life," instead enabled warehousing; Arkansas received $61,096 for its maximum-security unit at Cummins. LEAA also funded (at $400,000 a year) the American Correctional Association's (ACA) new "Commission on Accreditation in Corrections," and LEAA gave states money to pay for the accreditation process.[10]

That accreditation was, however, ridden with problems. Instead of requiring adherence, discounts abounded: a corrections agency needed to meet 90 percent of "essential," 80 percent of "important," and 70 percent of "desirable" standards. Even when in the 1980s the ACA had its single-cell policy, the Commission deemed that standard "nonmandatory" and accredited more than fifty facilities that double celled. Moreover, unlike the IPPC and the UN's Crime Control Commission, which welcomed an eclectic group to meetings, the ACA's Commission met in private and refused to disclose prices or findings. In 1982, one of the Commission's esteemed members, David Bazelon, a federal appellate judge, made national headlines in a scathing twenty-one-page "memorandum of resignation." He explained that the public was "excluded from every stage" and the ACA exerted "too much control"; it appointed fifteen of twenty-one commissioners and oversaw the "most basic policy decisions." He wrote that panels typically spent "one hour evaluating and deliberating the accreditability of each applicant"; even when court decisions documented unconstitutional practices, they relied solely on information from an applicant. These "shoddy procedures" and "pervasive conflicts of interest" meant that instead of using accreditation to improve the "human wasteland that is our prison system," the Commission had created a "propaganda vehicle for corrections authorities."[11]

Judge Bazelon left, but the Commission continued. More evidence of failings came in 2003, when a reporter recorded the horror of noise, razor wire, and solitary confinement in an Arkansas prison accredited in the late 1990s. Twenty years thereafter, US Senator Elizabeth Warren of Massachusetts issued "The Accreditation Con," recounting investigation of the relationship between the ACA and private prisons. Like Judge Bazelon, she detailed a system that had "zero accountability," lacked "transparency," was "riddled with conflicts of interest," and produced self-serving, self-protective information.[12]

A similar set of criticisms were leveled against the LEAA. In 1979, the Justice System Improvement Act spelled its demise, with funding ended in 1980 and doors closed in 1982. Atop its "wrongheaded" assumptions about crime, the LEAA "came to be viewed as a giant pork-barrel operation that allowed state and local law enforcement agencies to go on huge shopping sprees as they purchased all kinds of policing and military hardware and established special units, most notably SWAT teams." Yet, like the IPPC, which died but whose template lived on through the UN, the LEAA anchored a federal role in criminal law enforcement policy taken up by other entities, nested in the Justice Department along with the BOP and often adopting pro-prosecution and pro-incarceration approaches. The Bureau of Justice Statistics (BJS), launched in 1979, gathered data; the Bureau of Justice Assistance (BJA), begun in 1984, gave grants. They joined the National Institute of Corrections (NIC), providing training since the early 1970s. In 1985, Congress added the Edward Byrne Memorial State and Local Law Enforcement Assistance Program, named after a police officer shot when responding to a drug crime, to expand grant-making.[13]

The federal infusion of funds to build prisons and train jail and prison officials, coupled with state investments, invigorated the market sufficiently that the American Institute of Architecture (AIA) generated a subspecialty, the "Academy of Architecture for Justice," denoting designing courthouses and detention facilities. At the prompting of Jonas Salk, the AIA helped to form the Academy of Neuroscience for Architecture, focused on the physiological impact of facilities. One NIC-funded workshop on "neuroscience and correctional facility design" explored how environments affected "inmate behavior management," even as mounds of materials had already documented that enclosures with noise and density were destructive as well as unmanageable.[14]

FEDERAL ADVICE FOR "CREATIVE FINANCING" TO SKIRT STATE SPENDING LIMITS

"There has never been a greater need for financing construction of correctional facilities. . . . We . . . know that prisons do work: while in prison an offender cannot commit additional crimes against innocent victims."

—National Institute of Justice, July 1986[15]

"Public opinion is absolutely unanimous in calling for additional
prison facilities to house violent offenders."

—Texas Governor William P. Clements Jr., July 2, 1987[16]

In addition to its own spending, the federal government's "Construction Bulletins" advised states about ways to fund prison construction. In 1986, with Ronald Reagan's Attorney General Edwin
Meese in charge, the Justice Department focused on the "crisis" of
prison and jail crowding. Sounding a good deal like Dale Bumpers
and Bill Clinton, they sought to "find less costly ways to increase
corrections capacity so convicted serious criminals [would be]
prevented from preying on people, communities, and our economy." As the NIC director explained, the "price of not expanding
capacity . . . [was] increased victims of crime and its attendant
fear."[17]

Dozens of state constitutions limited the amount of debt that
could be incurred.[18] Moreover, jails were run by counties and cities
with little (or no) taxing authority, and a "taxpayers' revolt" had undercut resources for a host of services. Special ballot measures were
unpopular, even if some voters (such as in Arkansas' counties) had
increased sales taxes to expand their jails. The NIJ had an answer—
"lease-rental" or "lease-purchase" financing agreements—touted in
a 1986 Construction Bulletin as avoiding debt limits by outsourcing
to a "leasing entity." NIJ offered the example of the "Ohio Building
Authority," nominally owning prisons until its "tenant," Ohio's Department of Rehabilitation and Corrections, completed installment
payments. A follow-up 1987 NIJ "brochure," listing several states
using lease-purchase financing, explained the need in light of "increases in incarcerated populations" and court mandates "to improve . . . prison systems."

NIJ was not clear on the downsides, but Ruth Wilson Gilmore's
Golden Gulag was. Her book charted prison expansion in California;
from 1852 through the 1960s, the state ran twelve institutions. After
1984, California built twenty-three "major new" facilities through
lease revenue bonds that, by not putting taxing powers behind repayment, avoided the need for voter approval. That mechanism

propelled California's debt from $763 million in the 1970s to $4.9 billion by 1993.[19]

Another NIJ example was Texas, where William Wayne Justice, a federal judge, concluded that the violence, arbitrary decision-making in discipline, lack of health care, and filth in overcrowded prisons rendered that state's prisons unconstitutional. In 1985, the parties' consent decree required "depopulation" of several facilities. A year later, under Governor William Clements, Texas faced more than $800,000 a day in civil contempt fines for compliance failures. Unlike his predecessor, Clements aimed to abide and, in July of 1986, talked to his legislature about financing with the "maximum flexibility and least cost." Entries to prisons had risen 112.8 percent in six years, but the capacity only 50 percent. He hoped in four years to have 20,000 more beds, double celled, except for "psychiatric inmates."[20]

As illustrated by the Texas prison litigation, the Supreme Court's *Rhodes v. Chapman*, which permitted double celling, had not extinguished all conditions claims; judges found some forms of density unlawful. By 1995, the American Civil Liberties Union tallied more than thirty jurisdictions subject to court orders or consent decrees. Those mandates were, as NIJ referenced and Heather Schoenfeld chronicled, part of the push to expand "carceral capacity."[21] Yet prison populations might not have ramped up if politicians had supported work release, shorter sentences, decriminalization and much else. Instead of crafting safe environments to which consent decrees aspired, federal and state dollars went—with few constraints—to more double cells and designs for profound isolation.

In chapter 27, I documented that Arkansas' prison construction never kept pace with its prosecution and sentencing decisions. Again, Arkansas was not alone; prisons regularly held more people than the number for which they were designed as well as their "rated" and "operational" capacities, terms loosely taking into account services, staff, and space as well as beds. The grim bars of Ohio's 1992 Department of Correction's chart, "Prison Design Capacity and Population," in figure 28.1, make plain that individuals far outstripped space.

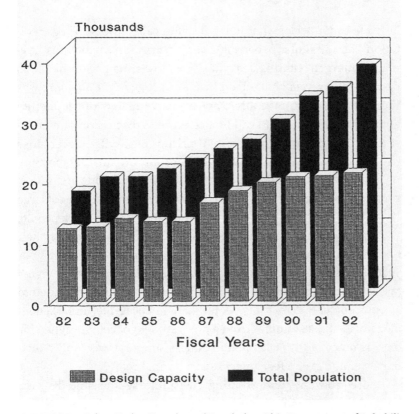

PRISON DESIGN CAPACITY AND POPULATION (as of June 30)

FIGURE 28.1 *Prison Design Capacity and Population*, Ohio Department of Rehabilitation and Corrections Annual Report, 44 (1992)

HABITABILITY, VIOLENCE, AND DOUBLE CELLING: BACK TO AN "ACCREDITED" LUCASVILLE

"Lucasville . . . is widely described as an extraordinarily violent place where people can die for something as insignificant as a pack of cigarettes."

—Dayton Daily News, May 2, 1993[22]

"[W]e have to rethink what we do and how we use our prison space" to find "other ways to punish criminal offenders, particularly the nonviolent ones."

—Lieutenant Governor Michael DeWine, May 1, 1993[23]

Terrible examples of what Judge Bazelon called the ACA's Accreditation Commission's "paper[ing] over [of] crises in corrections" regularly emerged. Ohio's Lucasville, which was the prison in which double celling was challenged in 1981 in *Rhodes v. Chapman*, was then accredited in 1992 after "an extensive review of the facility and its management." Recall Justice Powell's discussion of no constitutional right to a "comfortable" prison. Lucasville, never close to "comfortable," erupted in the "Easter Riot" on April 11, 1993.[24]

In selecting Lucasville in the late 1960s, Ohio built "one of the most remote prisons in the state"—about 100 miles from "the nearest large city in Ohio." Lucasville's 1,554 inhabitants included no Black people, while 57 percent of the prisoners were Black men, held far from their homes and cut off under a rule permitting "one five-minute call per year." Lucasville's crowding mirrored other Ohio facilities; the state's prison population had, in the prior ten years, gone from 18,000 to 39,000 people. In 1993, 2,133 people were in Lucasville, and 994 doubled up. Figure 28.2 comes from a press account of cells designed for one; as noted, a 1993 Oldsmobile Cutlass Supreme was "only 1 inch narrower and over 6 feet longer than a normal cell."[25]

Dense crowding, understaffing, racist interactions, and distrust, both within staff and among prisoners, produced violent exchanges and lockdowns. The press reported that Ohio had provided a "recipe for a prison riot" by putting "heavies" in Lucasville, where gangs ("the Aryan Brotherhood," the "Black Gangster Disciples," and a "Muslim gang," according to an Ohio Supreme Court decision) were in control. Some attributed the April uprising to a warden's order for tuberculosis testing that Muslim prisoners argued violated their religious beliefs. More than 400 prisoners took over L Block, comprised of eight units, each with eighty cells. The "demands" (echoing 1971 Attica) were for more access to the outside world, better health care, less arbitrary decisions, safety, and work. This "micro-revolution" lasted for several days, and nine prisoners and one staff member died. Staughton Lynd,

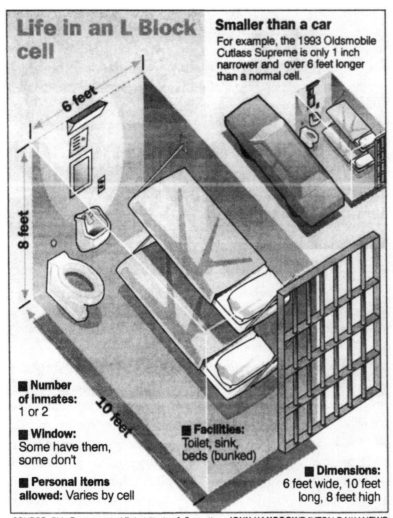

Life in an L Block cell

Smaller than a car
For example, the 1993 Oldsmobile Cutlass Supreme is only 1 inch narrower and over 6 feet longer than a normal cell.

6 feet

8 feet

10 feet

■ **Number of inmates:** 1 or 2

■ **Window:** Some have them, some don't

■ **Personal items allowed:** Varies by cell

■ **Facilities:** Toilet, sink, beds (bunked)

■ **Dimensions:** 6 feet wide, 10 feet long, 8 feet high

SOURCE: Ohio Department of Rehabilitation & Correction   JOHN HANCOCK/DAYTON DAILY NEWS

FIGURE 28.2 *Life in an L Block Cell*, drawing accompanying Sandy Theis and Tim Miller, *Racial Issues May Be Behind Lucasville Riot*, Dayton Daily News, April 15, 1993

a lawyer for some prisoners, described men from different racialized groups trying to limit the violence. Thereafter, five were charged and convicted of murdering a staff member; held in solitary confinement, they coordinated challenges to their death sentences.[26]

When reporting about the uprising, the press retold the story of *Rhodes v. Chapman* and detailed Ohio's awful record on various metrics.

The state had the "second worst ratio of guards per inmate"; "the third worst" on crowding; "fourth worst" on prison homicide rates; "ninth worst" on spending per prisoner; fifth worst on people held twenty years or more, and eighth worst on salaries for staff. The state's Lieutenant Governor Michael DeWine (in 2024, the state's governor) commented that the Lucasville violence required rethinking prison space and underscored the need for alternatives to incarceration.[27]

TOO "GENEROUS" SPACE FOR IMPRISONED PEOPLE

"[F]ederal prisons were more generous [than states] with space."

—*Prison Costs: Opportunities Exist to Lower the Cost of Building Federal Prisons*, US General Accounting Office (GAO), 1991[28]

The obvious punchline—lessen the crowding!—was not the one given by the corrections establishment or the federal government. It bears reiterating that the ACA 1981 Manual had been clear on "single occupancy" cells, explained as lowering the costs of supervision, improving safety "for both inmates and staff," and providing more flexibility "to accommodate different types of inmates." A California Corrections Department's task force concurred; "double-celling violates basic standards of decent housing, health, and institutional security." (Yet that task force also opined that this "totally undesirable" practice was necessary given population growth.) In 1985, the US Department of Justice (DOJ) reported on "data collected from 19 Federal prisons over a 33-month period"; defining crowding as more people held than an institution's capacity, the report identified it as an "important determinant in the level of assault rates for the federal prison system from October 1975 to June 1978."[29]

As my account makes plain, prisoners do *not* need constitutional rights for governing officials to create habitable prisons, but law can help, and it can hurt. In the decade after the 1981 *Rhodes* decision permitted double celling, both the ACA and the Federal Bureau of Prisons (BOP) revisited their one-person-one-cell position, substituted the words double "bunking" for double celling, and endorsed that density. Those revisions were, of course, responsive to the continuing surge of people sent to prison and to the quest for cheaper prisons, as well as to the absence of legal pressure to single cell. Between 1925 and 1974, prison populations in the United States had grown from 91,669 to 218,466 people, or an average growth rate per year of about 2.8 percent. By 1989, the growth rate was 16 percent a year, and more than 700,000 individuals were incarcerated. That year, the Justice Department concluded state and federal governments would generate "a demand for 1,600 new prison beds per week." The BOP thought it would need $3 billion to double the federal prison system's "capacity by 1995" through an "unprecedented expansion program" entailing "15 to 20 times" more in operating than in construction costs.[30]

The following year, the ACA began to narrow its mandate for single cells, still to be used "for all security levels" *except* people held in minimum custody. In its 2003 Manual, the ACA cut back further; single cells were "required" only for people "assigned to maximum custody" as well as "when indicated" for individuals with "severe medical disabilities," serious mental illness, or a risk of victimization. The 2021 ACA's Manual lowered housing "performance based standards" by reducing the size of "unencumbered space" per person from thirty-five to twenty-five square feet and further reducing single celling ("when indicated") to apply only to individuals with severe health issues, those "likely to be exploited by or victimized by others" or with "special needs." Everyone else could be housed in dormitories or in "multiple occupancy" cells or rooms—which could include retrofitting cells designed for one.[31]

In the late 1980s, when federal studies priced prison construction costs at $70,000 per bed (as compared to $55,000 in states), BOP planned to locate prisons to "facilitat[e] family visits"; proximity to urban areas was important because "60 percent of inmates . . . [were] more than 250 miles from home and 35 percent . . . more than 500 miles from home." Members of Congress asked the General Accounting Office (GAO) about how to save money. Answers came in two 1991 reports, *Prison Costs: Opportunities Exist to Lower the Cost of Building Federal Prisons*, followed by *Federal Prisons: Revised Design Standards Could Save Expansion Funds*, and the 1992 *Federal Jail Bedspace: Cost Savings and Greater Accuracy Possible in the Capacity Expansion Plan*. The GAO concluded that the "major

difference" between federal and state construction costs came because federal design standards called for single cells ("643 square
feet per inmate versus 415 square feet for state prisons"), spaces for
activities, and locating facilities closer to "inmates' homes."[32]

Describing the BOP as "more generous with space" than needed,
the GAO coupled prescriptions for "double bunking" to cut the
number of cells, toilets, and space with recommendations for "siting prisons in lower cost geographic areas," meaning rural settings.
Without apologizing, the GAO said its conclusions did not entail
analysis of "inmate quality of life issues that may be associated with
cell size or type . . . [or] enhancing prisoner rehabilitation and the
incidence of violence." One way to explain that admission is through
Ruth Gilmore's analysis of prison construction as using "surplus
land" and "surplus labor" for building.[33] The GAO treated prisoners
as "surplus people" (my words) whose well-being could be ignored.

By January of 1991, the BOP had already "increased the rated capacity" of some facilities through "substantially expanding" double
celling. Nonetheless, eighty of its eighty-four facilities were over
capacity, and seventeen "more than 100 percent" beyond. The GAO
also reported that the BOP had cut spaces for activities, used prisoners as laborers, and was looking for remote locations. Yet even as
the BOP was capitulating, the Justice Department told Congress it
had concerns about the GAO proposals. BOP was obliged to provide
"a safe, secure, and constitutional prison environment"; cost mini-
mization needed to be balanced "with the requirements of federal
law and good security" so as not to incur "disturbances which would
result in considerable human suffering, very high costs, disruption
to federal law enforcement efforts, and harm to the public interest."
The Justice Department also criticized the GAO for including in its
analyses a Florida facility that was hardly an exemplar of success
as it was under a court order because of "overcrowding, medical,
food services, and mental health issues."[34]

That pushback did not last. By 1993, the BOP cut down on measures of space each person needed. In 1997, the BOP issued a
"program statement" on "Rated Capacities for Bureau Facilities"
that noted the use of "cots in hallways and TV rooms" with no

instructions on who ought to be put where. In another directive on solitary confinement ("special housing units," whose acronym—"SHU"—described the cramped space), the BOP specified that, while "living quarters will ordinarily house only the amount of occupants for which it is designed," wardens could "authorize more occupants as long as adequate standards can be maintained."[35]

In 2012, the GAO reported the dismal results. Increased lengths of sentences had swelled the BOP's population more than 400 percent from the 1980s. From 2006 to 2011, in the 117 institutions where 38,000 staff dealt with 178,000 federal prisoners, crowding was "most severe (55 percent) in highest security facilities." The BOP was using "double and triple bunking" and reported wait lists for education and drug programs as well as increased "inmate misconduct which negatively affect[ed] the safety and security of inmates and staff."[36] The GAO's potential remedies, again eerily familiar, were combinations of reform sentencing laws, alternatives to incarceration, more prisons, and adding staff. All the while, corrections officials were responding to "management" problems by ramping up use of solitary confinement.

SOLITARY CONFINEMENT AS AN "ORDINARY INCIDENT OF PRISON LIFE"

Thirty days of solitary confinement was not an "atypical and substantial hardship" but an "ordinary incident of prison life."
—Chief Justice William Rehnquist, *Sandin v. Conner*, 1995[37]

Studies describe what everyone knows: density begets violence. The mechanisms, as Craig Haney and other social scientists have explained, are a debilitating lack of opportunities for work, education, and activities amid hours of unstructured time. The physical closeness, noise, high staff turnover, and instability generate "social complexity"; in dangerous spaces, "interpersonal mistakes or errors in social judgments can be fatal."[38] As a result, both incarcerated people and staff are right to be fearful. Yet rather than refusing (as prison officials in Arkansas occasionally did) to accept people when prisons were "full," officials pressed people together and struggled for control through expanding use of solitary confinement.

Different names have been used for profound isolation. One, categorized as "disciplinary segregations," denotes (in theory) a time-framed punishment for violation of prison rules. Another, "administrative segregation," explained by officials as for people they deem to be at risk of misbehavior; individuals can be held for years in isolation. A third rationale, "protective," confines individuals seen as vulnerable to assaults by other prisoners. Corrections officials have come to use a sanitized umbrella term, "restrictive housing,"—which well describes prison itself. For plain speakers, solitary is "the hole," "the box," or "hellhole." California and the BOP pioneered purpose-built "supermax prisons"; as of the 1990s, more than twenty-five existed. Data from Kansas substantiates that, with or without a separate prison, reliance on isolation grew alongside density. Before that state's population spurt of the 1970s, 13 percent of its prisoners spent thirty days or more in solitary. Between 1987 and 1992, more than 40 percent had; the percentages of people of color held in isolation for longer periods of time were higher than their numbers in the prisons' general population.[39]

Solitary confinement is an intense, physically violative, *interpersonal* form of degradation that makes a person utterly dependent on correction staff on the other side of the door—for food, light, exercise, toilets that flush, and more. Indeed, in the 1890s, the Supreme Court, drawing on materials from the International Penitentiary Commission, commented that people "fell, after even a short [solitary] confinement, into a semi-fatuous condition . . . and others became violently insane; others, still, committed suicide."[40] By the 1970s, federal judges regularly commented that isolation was not *per se* unconstitutional, yet at times ruled that specific conditions—filth, freezing temperatures, total darkness, no sanitation—rendered it unlawful.

People who have experienced isolation attest to its dislocation and violence. Dwayne Betts wrote of being "tossed" at age sixteen into a "cell with a door so thick no sound escaped," and how "in a fit of panic," he slammed his fist against a wall, "thought about suicide, [and] almost disappeared." A psychologist held in a federal prison testified in 2021 that he continued to gulp down his food because in solitary, plates were shoved through a floor slot and often removed before he had time to eat. Albert Woodfox found himself doing eye exercises to try to counteract the loss of depth perception from decades of isolation in Angola, Louisiana. And a federal judge, ordering release of a person after three decades, commented that the man deserved "the opportunity to shake hands with someone other than his attorneys."[41]

Different legal theories could support solitary's end. One basis is that "evolving standards of decency" mean it is "cruel and unusual punishment." Relatedly and building on Henley's *Holt* opinions, isolation has no justifications (no legitimate "penological purpose"). Given violence within such units, it insufficiently incapacitates; its retributive ends are not proportionate to its harms; and it has no rehabilitative utility. That lack of rationality could support finding isolation unconstitutional under the Fourteenth Amendment's "substantive due process" protections and, absent careful decision-making, a violation of procedural due process. Isolation could also be ruled out as failing to provide "the minimal civilized measure of life's necessities."

Judges had to address those arguments when, in the 1990s, isolated prisoners at California's Pelican Bay supermax sought a general ban under the Eighth Amendment. After a detailed trial of brutal harms, Thelton Henderson, a federal district court judge, rejected a blanket prohibition but held that seriously mentally ill people could not be placed in profound isolation. Evoking *Rhodes'* test of "life's necessities," Henderson ruled that leaving deeply mentally ill people in solitary was akin to putting "an asthmatic in a place with little air to breathe"; no decent social order would sanction such "shocking and indecent" treatment.[42] Yet Judge Henderson declined to acknowledge that solitary confinement diminishes the health of people not visibly ill on entry. His decision, followed within a year by the Prison Litigation Reform Act cutting back federal judges' powers over conditions litigation, made difficult comprehensive attacks on the legality of solitary confinement.

Focus shifted to the Due Process Clause that, as discussed, required some "process" before deprivations of life, liberty, or property. Building on the 1974 *Wolff v. McDonnell* ruling that statutory good-time credits created a "liberty interest,"[43] prisoners argued that other in-prison punishments triggered due process rights and, as discussed, the Court rejected obligations to provide hearings for various sanctions such as transfers to higher-security facilities. At issue in 1995 in *Sandin v. Conner* was whether a Hawai'i prisoner, challenging a thirty-day term in "disciplinary" segregation, had a right to a hearing about whether his alleged misbehavior fit the criteria for punishment.[44] The question was not the duration or conditions of isolation (at issue in the 1970s in *Holt/Finney*) but whether the decision to impose thirty days of isolation required procedural protections.

Chief Justice Rehnquist for the Court said no; he ruled that prisoners had no "liberty interest" because such confinement was not an "atypical and significant hardship" but part of the "ordinary incidents of prison life." Justice Ginsburg, joined by Stevens, faulted Rehnquist's "test" for leaving lower courts "at sea," as it provided "no examples" of its "key words." Additional objections came from Justice Breyer, joined by Justice Souter, who detailed the differences between disciplinary segregation and life at the same prison. Regular prisoners were presumptively out of their cells "for eight *hours* each day," while people in solitary spent their "entire time alone . . . [except for] 50 *minutes* . . . on average for brief exercise and shower[s]," during which they were "constrained by leg irons and waist chains."[45]

Ten years later, in 2005, the Court took up the question of *indefinite* isolation in a case borne from chronic overcrowding and racialized in-prison discipline. By then, reports of violent isolation of detainees held at Guantánamo Bay after 9/11, graphic images from California's Pelican Bay, and hunger strikes at both facilities, had been broadcast by the media. The Court accepted a case from Ohio that grew out of its authorizing double celling in *Rhodes v. Chapman*. Reginald Wilkinson, directing Ohio's Department of Rehabilitation and Correction, explained that Ohio Supermax Prison (OSP) was constructed "in reaction to the April 1993 riot at . . . Lucasville" to "handle prisoners who were hellbent on disrupting the orderly operation of our correctional institutions." Federal district court judge District Court Judge James Gwin found that, as a matter of fact, OSP's deprivations were "atypical" and imposed a "significant hardship," and Justice Kennedy's description in *Wilkinson v. Austin* explained why: Ohio put a person, potentially forever, in a tiny, always-lit cell and deprived him of "almost any environmental or sensory stimuli."

In the Supreme Court, Ohio conceded those conditions meant prisoners had a liberty interest in avoiding them. (Nonetheless, the US government, which ran its own gruesome isolation units, argued to the Court that "no liberty" interest was "implicated.") Justice Kennedy used Ohio's concession to craft a unanimous Court decision that a modicum of procedural protection was due. However, his opinion seemed to put its imprimatur on isolation. Not naming Lucasville, Kennedy wrote that the prison was "imperiled by the brutal reality of prison gangs" that were "[c]landestine, organized, fueled by race-based hostility, and committed to fear and violence. . . . Prolonged confinement in Supermax may be the State's only option for the control of some inmates."[46]

Yet Justice Kennedy also registered qualms. Although not citing the health care professionals' amicus brief, he underscored their concerns—that OSP provided no human contact, no parole, and no time when lights were off. Under those circumstances, the Fourteenth Amendment required opportunities to contest placements. That decision left unclear whether prisoners' liberty interests hinged on having all of Ohio's practices, whether other factors generated liberty interests, and how to weigh the factors. Moreover, noting "the difficulty of locating the appropriate baseline," Justice Kennedy concluded that OSP imposed "an atypical and significant hardship under any plausible baseline."[47] *Wilkinson* thus appeared to recognize a federal liberty interest (which could predate the Constitution, be sourced in it, derive from state law, or come from facts conceded by Ohio) in being free from almost total sensory deprivation for an indefinite period that could affect parole.

BACK TO BASELINES: FIFTEEN DAYS TO FORTY YEARS

Wilkinson v. Austin was a victory for its era—requiring some process rather than *Sandin*'s conclusion of no constitutional obligation to protect against arbitrary isolation placements if under thirty days. *Wilkinson* offered the possibility that, if states had to prove specific wrongdoing to justify isolation, they would either not be able to or not want to spend those resources, and fewer people would be isolated. But to go to court to enforce *Wilkinson*, incarcerated people (generally without lawyers) had to prove their specific confinement was an "atypical and a significant hardship." And hundreds tried to do so, which meant that *Wilkinson* provided windows into conditions in solitary confinement, as campaigns ramped up to "unlock the box." Moreover, a few correctional officials joined in the critique with amici briefs arguing that profound isolation was not necessary, even when running prisons was challenging. More press attention followed tragic losses of life including the suicide of teenage Kalief Browder, held in isolation for years at New York City's Rikers Island—but never tried—for stealing a backpack.[48]

The body of legal rulings that resulted documented the widespread use of solitary confinement, as well as that federal judges used underspecified criteria to assess the impact of time and conditions and had a high tolerance for letting corrections staff leave people in deep isolation for months, years, and decades. For example, the Court of Appeals for the Second Circuit concluded in 1999 that placement for 101 days in New York's Auburn Correctional Facility "SHU" did not itself constitute an atypical and significant hardship. Thereafter, that circuit developed a rule that "restrictive confinements of less than 101 days do not generally raise a liberty interest warranting due process protection." On the other hand, 305 days or more days in "normal SHU conditions" (twenty-three hours a day in cell, two showers a week, no work) was "a sufficient departure from the ordinary incidents of prison life," and procedural protections were required.[49]

For those of us made anxious by contemplating one, four, eight, ten, or twenty-three *hours* locked inside a cell, it is not intuitive that the 305-*day* rule was protective but, as compared to standards elsewhere, it was. Many courts condoned isolation counted by years. The Tenth Circuit (with jurisdiction over the federal ADX Florence supermax in Colorado) did not require procedural due process in cases when individuals were held thirteen, seventeen, and twenty *years* in solitary confinement.[50] The Sixth Circuit held it was "not 'atypical' for a prisoner to be in segregation" for two and a half years while an investigation (in that case, about the Lucasville uprising) was underway.[51] A tragic example of winning an "atypicality" claim came in a 2014 ruling when the Fifth Circuit concluded that the thirty-nine years Albert Woodfox spent in solitary confinement at the Louisiana State Penitentiary met that test.[52]

As the body of decisions grew, so did examples of the seat-of-the-pants approach on which Chief Justice Rehnquist had relied when deeming isolation "ordinary." Judges could have drawn on empirical research and standards promulgated. The UN's 2015 Standard Minimum Rules for the Treatment of Prisoners called for a prohibition on "indefinite" and "prolonged solitary confinement," defined as lasting more than fifteen days and termed degrading and torturous treatment.[53] In 2016, the ACA revised its standards to term thirty days or more as "extended restrictive housing." Those standards stated that no one be placed in restrictive housing solely based on gender identity, pregnant people not be in extended restrictive housing, seriously mentally ill people presumptively not be there, and prisoners in extended restrictive housing be given access to certain services and programs.[54]

One way to understand the many decisions by Supreme Court justices and lower federal courts is as a continual ceding of decision-making to prison officials.[55] Yet to focus on the power of corrections misses that the Court has been pivotal in sustaining both hyper-density and profound isolation as "ordinary incidents" of prison life. The Court has drawn the lines by inscribing its own view of prison life and permitted authorities to transfer people to higher-security institutions and to isolate people for thirty days without according them procedures to buffer against arbitrary exercises of authority.

DRIVING PEOPLE "MAD": DELIBERATE INDIFFERENCE TO HUMAN HEALTH AND NO PENOLOGICAL JUSTIFICATIONS

"[D]uring the many years you will serve in prison before your execution, the penal system has a solitary confinement regime that will bring you to the edge of madness, perhaps to madness itself."

—Justice Anthony Kennedy, concurring in
Davis v. Ayala, 2015[56]

In 2015, Justice Kennedy signaled he was ready to revisit the permissibility of profound isolation. In *Davis v. Ayala*, he joined the Court's ruling against Hector Ayala, who argued his conviction and death sentence were predicated on an unconstitutional jury selection. Nonetheless, Kennedy wrote separately to object to Ayala's *conditions* of confinement—held for decades "in a windowless cell no larger than a typical parking spot for 23 hours a day . . . [and] allowed little or no opportunity for conversation or interaction with anyone." Citing social science studies, Kennedy wrote that the "solitary confinement regime" could "bring you to the edge of madness," as he noted the "judiciary may be required . . . to determine whether workable alternative systems for long-term confinement exist, and, if so, whether a correctional system should be required to adopt them."[57]

Justice Kennedy did not explain why, as a matter of law, solitary confinement failed. Again, the options included that it was "deliberate indifference to known, serious medical needs"; a violation of "evolving standards of decency" and "dignity"; did not provide the minimum of "life's necessities" for lack of social contact; had no legitimate "penological purpose," and that its degradation was beyond what "civilized" countries could impose.[58] Whichever the reasoning, Kennedy appeared willing to join Justices Breyer, Ginsburg, Kagan, and Sotomayor in ruling out some forms of solitary confinement that, as Justice Breyer wrote, caused "anxiety, panic, rage, loss of control, paranoia, hallucinations, and self-mutilations,"[59] and Justice Sotomayor later described as a "penal tomb."[60]

But Justice Kennedy retired in 2018, and new members of the Court distanced themselves from the analyses I have discussed. Indeed, responding in 2015 to Justice Kennedy, Justice Thomas wrote that the focus should be on the individuals murdered; "the accommodations in which Ayala is housed are a far sight more spacious than those in which his victims . . . now rest." Moreover, Justice Thomas disavowed the Eighth Amendment's application to prisons in general and objected to class-wide relief.[61] Several of his colleagues, as noted, have looked to historical understandings of cruel and unusual punishments, as they have also turned to historical analogues when assessing constitutionality in decisions on gun control, abortion, and homelessness.[62]

Yet solitary confinement's legitimacy has, as Kennedy's comments reflected, been rattled. Pelican Bay was the source of another challenge that resulted in prisoners in solitary joining their lawyers to shape a class-wide settlement, approved by a federal judge in 2015. California was no longer to use membership in "security threat groups" (gangs) as the basis for placement in solitary and therefore was to move about 2,000 individuals to general population. Furthermore, the state agreed that placements were not to be indefinite; transitioning ("step-down programs") was required.[63] Systemwide settlements in New York, Arizona, and Pennsylvania likewise imposed substantive limits on when the state could place people into solitary confinement and required lessening isolating conditions. In other cases, states agreed that subpopulations, such as individuals with distinct health challenges, juveniles, or people with capital sentences, were to have less isolation.[64] And akin to the compliance struggles in Arkansas, implementation has been contested. For example, the Pelican Bay prisoners returned repeatedly to court and argued that many individuals were held in the functional equivalent of solitary confinement.[65]

Moreover, decades of research made untenable the 1995 conclusion that solitary confinement could be imposed on people who were not demonstrably seriously mentally ill. The Fourth Circuit's 2019 *Porter v. Clarke* decision is one example. On Virginia's death row, individuals spent years "alone, in a small . . . cell" with "no access to congregate religious, educational, or social programming." Citing evidence that long-term solitary confinement posed "an objective risk of serious psychological and emotional harm to inmates," judges concluded that the state was "deliberately indifferent," and required prison officials to design methods of confinement other than twenty-three hours in cell.[66] Other dents in solitary came through judicial rulings that isolation of certain individuals violated the obligations to accommodate people under the Americans with Disabilities Act (ADA) and provide access to religious practices under the Religious Land Use and Institutionalized Persons Act (RLU-IPA) and the First Amendment's Free Exercise Clause.[67]

AGGREGATING NUMBERS AND SHAPING A PROFESSIONAL AND POLITICAL CONSENSUS TO END SOLITARY

The litigation discussed is embedded in social movements pushing to reframe punishment practices. Among the critics were people running prisons, and some of them forged a relationship with researchers (myself included) to document the use of isolation and revise correctional policies. As one state's corrections director explained in his *New York Times* op-ed, he had staff put him inside and, after less than twenty-four hours, saw that the practice should end.[68] Beginning in 2013, the Association of State Correctional Administrators (ASCA), renamed the Correctional Leaders Association (CLA), joined with the Arthur Liman Center for Public Interest Law at Yale Law School (which I founded) and, over a decade, mapped policies and uses of "restrictive housing."

We began with prisons' written rules, which are artifacts of lawsuits like *Talley v. Stephens*, requiring statements of expected behavior. By the twenty-first century, every correction system had "inmate manuals" and regulations. Thus, some years ago, I spent dispiriting days reading state policies on how to isolate people. *Administrative Segregation, Degrees of Isolation, and Incarceration*, published in 2013, was the result—a meta-analysis drawn from forty-seven jurisdictions. Thousands of pages produced three conclusions. First, the criteria for placement in isolation were broad; prison officers at many levels had discretion to identify individuals as a "threat" to the "orderly operation of the institution." Second, few policies focused on how individuals were to be released. Third, when in isolation, people lived stunningly constrained lives with little space to move.[69]

To move beyond formal policies, five surveys at two-year intervals between 2014 and 2022 asked prison systems in the fifty states, the District of Columbia, and the BOP about the numbers and demographics of people held for an average of twenty-two hours or more per day for more than fifteen continuous days. That definition, related to the UN's 2015 Rules, aimed to provide an aggregate picture built from different prison systems about people "under their control." (Some states ship large numbers out of state or to county jails.) The goal was to sum what correctional systems reported, while other researchers asked detainees or did jurisdiction-specific studies. A first monograph, *Time-In-Cell*, gathered such information from thirty-four jurisdictions that, in 2014, housed about three-quarters of the national prison population. The estimate was that 80,000 to 100,000 prisoners of 1.5 million imprisoned people were held in solitary confinement.[70] About a decade later, in 2022, thirty-five jurisdictions (holding about 61 percent of the prison population) reported that, in total, 25,083 people were in restrictive housing out of 731,202 people under these jurisdictions' "direct control." Across those jurisdictions, the percentage of people reported to be in isolation ranged from none to 15 percent; the median was 3.2 percent of the total population. Extrapolating from the responding jurisdictions, the 2022 CLA-Liman Report estimated that, as of July 2021, between 41,000 to 48,000 people were in fifteen days or more of restrictive housing in prisons across the United States.[71]

Those numbers were undercounts, as other sources identified more people or questioned the accounting. For example, drawing on data released from 2019 and focused on anyone held "22 hours or more on a given day in 2019" in federal and state prisons, *Calculating Torture*, estimated some 81,000 individuals, or about 6.3 percent of the total state and federal prison population, in isolation. Using additional information from jails, the number went up to about 122,000 individuals in isolation on any one day. (Not included were detainees in immigration or under eighteen.)[72] In terms of duration, the *Time-In-Cell* series documented months and years. Thirty-four jurisdictions reported in 2021 that 6,000 people spent more than a year; about 1,000 had been isolated for a decade or more. Looking at subpopulations, this thin slice of data identified more than 1,000 isolated people categorized by their own prison systems as having "serious mental illness." In prisons for women, the percentage of Black people in restrictive housing was significantly higher than the percentage in total custodial population.

Just as comparison of prison practices in the nineteenth century generated the Cincinnati 1870 Declaration of Principles, some systems did not want to be at the high end of the comparison in terms of numbers and percentages of people in isolation. During the decade of data collection, several departments changed policies to restrict their own use of "restrictive housing." As of 2021, four states reported that they had stopped putting people into isolation for twenty-two hours or more, fifteen days or more. Ten reported that no women were held under those conditions.

Many elected officials agreed. Pressed by people held inside and other social activists, legislators who had paid little attention to isolation drafted statutes to limit or stop solitary. Colorado put in place a fifteen-day cap on holding a person in a cell for twenty-two hours or more per day. Massachusetts' 2018 requirement was that "prisoners held in restrictive housing for a period of more than 60 days" were to be provided with "access to vocational, educational and rehabilitative programs to the maximum extent possible." A 2019 statute in New Jersey prohibited "isolated confinement for more than 20 consecutive days, or for more than 30 days during any 60-day period." More generally, between 2018 and 2020, legislation was introduced in more than twenty-five states, and some fifteen statutes enacted provisions.

By 2022, dozens more had been proposed and a few became law.[73] New York's 2021 statute, HALT, and Connecticut's PROTECT ACT aimed to undo twenty-two hours a day in a cell. Several jurisdictions required data; as part of the First Step Act, the federal government reported that in 2021, more than 10,400 of its 156,542 prisoners had been placed in "segregated housing." In 2023, US Representative Cori Bush introduced the End Solitary Confinement Act, describing solitary confinement as "inhumane and degrading treatment" that had "no place in a civilized society." The proposed statute aimed (absent time-limited emergencies) to end solitary confinement in federal prisons through requiring "congregate interaction" for at least fourteen hours a day for all federal prisoners and require procedural protections before punishments. Parallel bills were introduced in the Senate, including in 2024, the Solitary Confinement Reform Act.[74]

Those legislative initiatives were supported by individuals subjected to solitary, by studies from the Vera Institute for Justice providing alternatives, by religious coalitions campaigning against the "torture" of solitary confinement, and by professionals rebelling against its use. In 2010, the ABA called for limits; in 2012, the American Psychiatric Association objected to the use for people with serious mental illness; in 2013 the American Public Health Association's policy statement called "solitary confinement" a public health problem creating "barriers" to health care, and in 2014, the Society of Correctional Physicians condemned "prolonged segregation" for individuals with serious mental illness. Architects/Designers/ Planners for Social Responsibility pressed the American Institute of Architects (AIA) to pull out of designing prisons as well as solitary cells. In 2020, the AIA, committed to "promoting the design of a more equitable and just built world that dismantles racial injustice and upholds human rights," prohibited members from designing for "execution, torture and prolonged solitary confinement"—defined in light of UN rules as more than fifteen consecutive days "for 22 hours or more per day without meaningful human contact."[75]

Thus, the project of delegitimating solitary confinement became robust, even as federal judges made their own rules about the parameters of "normal" isolation and rarely flinched at years in "the hole." When I first began working on the issue, people running prisons were insistent that isolation was essential. By 2024, directors in several systems had shifted formal policies away from reliance on restrictive housing and were looking to take the numbers down. While solitary confinement had been touted as the solution to the problem of prison discipline, solitary had itself become a problem and for many, an anathema.

DENSITY AND DEATH: THE LETHAL AND LEGAL IMPLICATIONS OF CROWDING

"For years the medical and mental health care provided by California's prisons has . . . failed to meet prisoners' basic health needs. . . . Short-term gains . . . have been eroded by the long-term effects of severe and pervasive overcrowding. . . . The State's prisons had operated at around 200% of design capacity for at least 11 years."

—Justice Anthony Kennedy, *Brown v. Plata*, 2011[76]

"Decisions regarding state prisons have profound public safety and financial implications, and the States are generally free to make these decisions as they choose."

—Justice Samuel Alito, dissenting, *Brown*[77]

Above, I excavated the relationship between density and profound isolation. Here I turn to the nexus between density and death. In decades past, what Jonathan Simon called the "old overcrowding" came from decrepit, oversized prisons (the "Big House"); back-end parole provided a safety valve to get the numbers down. After *Rhodes v. Chapman*, the "new overcrowding" is driven by the rise in prosecutions, of determinate sentences, and the decline in parole. Ruth Gilmore and Michelle Alexander underscore the results—legions of Black and Brown people dislocated from their communities and put into prisons. Gilmore linked California's rising incarceration rates to global economic crises in which rich and poor sectors divided; the state embarked on the largest prison building program as to demonstrate its prowess through containment of crime. Alexander centered incarceration's expansion as the "New Jim Crow" in which race was the central driver. The analyses converge on the result: "hyper-chronic" crowding of people, disproportionately of color, made density definitional of life in many prisons.[78]

Failures of safekeeping conclude this chapter's account of twenty-first-century conflicts over mass incarceration, solitary confinement, and incarceration's (il)legitimacy. Throughout this book, I have advised readers not to treat Arkansas' prisons and their whips as *outliers*. Here, I show that they are also not *antiques*. Litigation over hyper-density as well as profound isolation documents the *corporality* imprisonment imposes and thus continues to raise a version of questions posed by Judge Blackmun in *Jackson v. Bishop*: Can polities that claim to acknowledge the rights-bearing status of prisoners impinge on people in the way that US prisons do, and what institutions police the boundaries?

In 2011, in *Brown v. Plata*, the Court split five to four on answers. Faced with evidence of deaths and illnesses of people held in California, Justice Kennedy's majority insisted that "decency" and "dignity" authorized judges to require a population reduction. The four dissenters accused him of harming the country. Moreover, unlike Justice Rehnquist, who commented in 1978 in *Hutto v. Finney* that everyone had to be "moved" by the facts of Arkansas prisons even if he disagreed about federal courts' remedial authority, the 2011 dissenters, intent on circumscribing prisoners' access to courts, said little to acknowledge prisoners' experiences.

Writing for the majority upholding a lower court order requiring California to stop running at double its design capacity and bring its population down to no more than 37.5 percent *above* capacity, Justice Kennedy appended pictures to his opinion. I reproduce two here. Figure 28.3 shows the crammed dormitory photo but not that fifty-four people sometimes shared one toilet.[79] The metal

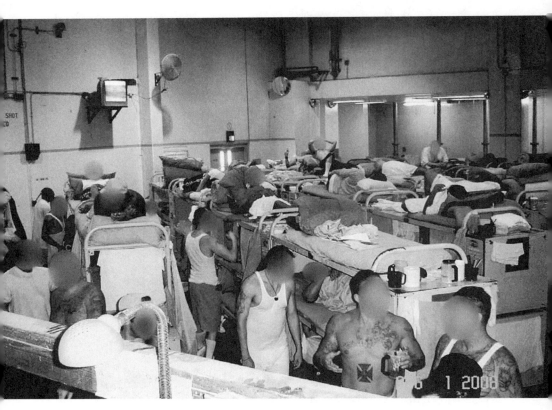

FIGURE 28.3 "California Institution for Men," August 7, 2006, Appendix B to *Brown v. Plata*, United States Supreme Court, 2011

enclosures depicted in figure 28.4 were used because "of a shortage of treatment beds"; "suicidal inmates [were] held for prolonged periods in telephone-booth sized cages without toilets."[80]

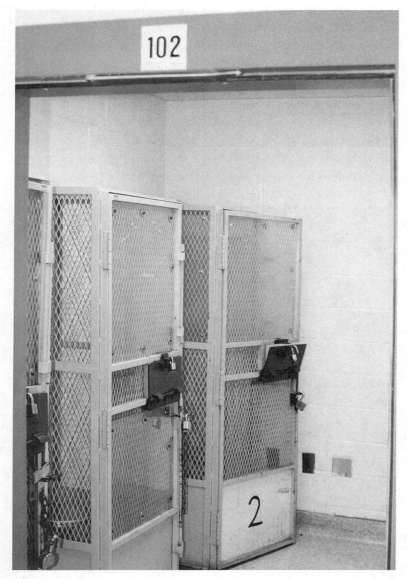

FIGURE 28.4 "Salinas Valley State Prison, Correctional Treatment Center (dry cages/holding cells for people waiting for mental health crisis beds)," July 29, 2008, Appendix C to *Brown v. Plata*, United States Supreme Court, 2011

The backdrop, as Gilmore explained in *Golden Gulag*, was that between 1982 and 2000, the population in California's prisons had grown almost 500 percent, even as reported crime rates dropped. The photos were part of an extensive record of two class actions, whose history and outcome were closer to *Hutto v. Finney* than to *Rhodes v. Chapman*. Begun when Pete Wilson was California's governor, the lawsuits continued during the administrations of Arnold Schwarzenegger, Jerry Brown, and Gavin Newson. One case focused on people with "serious mental disorders" and the other on prisoners with "serious medical conditions." The result was a nauseating record prompting judges to make specific findings about hyper-chronic, overcrowded prisons that put everyone at risk.[81]

Death haunted the Court's account. Two men "committed suicide by hanging after being placed in cells that had been identified as requiring a simple fix to remove attachment points that could support a noose. The repair was not made because doing so would involve removing prisoners from the cells, and there was no place to put them." Another person died after an assault in a crowded gym, and "prison staff did not even learn of the injury until the prisoner had been dead for several hours." California had not contested that, "on average, an inmate in one of California's prisons needlessly dies every six to seven days due to constitutional deficiencies in the medical delivery system." Thus, "in 1995, after a 39-day trial," a lower court "found 'overwhelming evidence of the systemic failure to deliver necessary care to mentally ill inmates' in California prisons." Indeed, California had conceded in 2001 that "deficiencies in prison medical care violated prisoners' Eighth Amendment rights," and the state had "stipulated to a remedial injunction" and then "failed to comply."[82]

But was that unconstitutional? And if so, could federal judges respond, given the 1996 Prison Litigation Reform Act (PLRA) that Bill Clinton had championed? Congress aimed to curtail judicial relief by telling judges that prospective relief could "extend no further than necessary to correct the violation of the Federal right of a particular plaintiff or plaintiffs," had to be "narrowly drawn," and "the least intrusive means necessary to correct the violation of the Federal right." If contemplating release, Congress required three judges to sit together and make findings. Thus, the Supreme Court reviewed not only the two class actions' records but additional materials from a three-judge court that had taken evidence for fourteen days and issued a 184-page opinion explaining why, in compliance with the PLRA, California had two years to reduce its prison population to 37.5 percent over capacity.[83]

One question was the metric of "cruel and unusual punishment." Justice Kennedy embraced Chief Justice Earl Warren's 1958 plurality in *Trop v. Dulles* that the "basic concept underlying the Eighth Amendment is nothing less than the dignity of man." Invoking the 1976 *Estelle v. Gamble* decision that correction officials not be "deliberate[ly] indifference to serious known medical needs," Justice Kennedy reasoned that "[j]ust as a prisoner may starve if not fed, he or she may suffer or die if not provided adequate medical care. A prison that deprives prisoners of basic sustenance, including adequate medical care, is incompatible with the concept of human dignity and has no place in civilized society."[84]

Another issue was the remedy. The Court concluded that the population-reduction order was justified because of the lack of sufficient improvements. In 2005, the trial judge found "the California prison medical care system broken beyond repair," resulting in an "unconscionable degree of suffering and death" as well as leaving everyone in "unsanitary and unsafe conditions." Vacancy rates across the health professions ranged from twenty to more than 50 percent.[85]

The miseries of Arkansas' 1970s prisons were invoked to explain the 2011 *Plata* orders. Citing *Hutto v. Finney*, Kennedy wrote that "constitutional violations in conditions of confinement are rarely susceptible of simple or straightforward solutions." Moreover, "chronic and worsening budget shortfalls, a lack of political will in favor of reform, inadequate facilities, and systemic administrative failures" laced California's system, as it had in Arkansas. "Only a multifaceted approach aimed at many causes, including overcrowding, will yield a solution." Thus, "[i]f government fails to fulfill this obligation, the courts have a responsibility to remedy the resulting Eighth Amendment violation." Per *Hutto v. Finney*, "the scope of a

district court's equitable powers . . . is broad, for breadth and flexibility are inherent in equitable remedies."[86]

But unlike *Hutto*, when all justices but Rehnquist approved the
thirty-day cap on time in jammed disciplinary cells, four members
launched an aggressive attack. The first sentence of Justice Scalia's
dissent, joined by Justice Thomas, offered a sound bite, condemning affirmation of "perhaps the most radical injunction issued by
a court in our Nation's history: an order requiring California to
release the staggering number of 46,000 convicted criminals."
Moreover, the "proceedings that led to this result were a judicial
travesty" and the outcome "preposterous." Justice Scalia aimed to
disable civil rights cases beyond those governed by the PLRA. He
argued the decree ignored "bedrock limitations" on judicial power
and took "federal courts wildly beyond their institutional capacity."
Disagreeing with what he termed "our judge-empowering 'evolving
standards of decency' jurisprudence," Justice Scalia argued that the
Eighth Amendment prohibited only "'indecent' treatment of individuals." Moreover, the "notion that the plaintiff class can allege an
Eighth Amendment violation based on 'systemwide deficiencies' is
assuredly wrong," as "the only viable constitutional claims consist
of individual instances of mistreatment," for which a systemic remedy was not permitted under the PLRA. While a court could potentially order release for needed treatment, no court could release
prisoners who had "suffered no violations of their constitutional
rights" to lower a risk of harm to others.[87] (The justices' interest in
limiting class actions was not unique to incarcerated people; con-
sumers, employees, and many recipients of commercial services
lost access to joint actions in court and could only proceed, if they
had the wherewithal, single file and in private arbitration.[88])

Justice Alito (joined by Chief Justice Roberts) proffered the specter of violence on the streets. Invoking *Rhodes'* test of "the minimal
civilized measure of life's necessities," Justice Alito described the
"undesirable prison conditions" in California as constitutionally
sufficient. While not disputing that overcrowding "contributed" to
health care problems, Justice Alito argued it could not be a "spring-
board" for a remedy that did not necessarily help ill prisoners and

was "very likely to have a major and deleterious effect on public safety" through "the premature release of approximately *46,000 criminals—the equivalent of three Army divisions*" (his italics). Justice Alito discounted the level of injury; "by the date of the trial before the three-judge court, the death rate had been trending downward for 10 quarters." He also posited that many cities with populations paralleling the 156,000 in California's prisons would also have "residents" with records revealing "grossly deficient treatment . . . provided." With dramatic flourish, Justice Alito concluded that, by sustaining the lower court order, the majority was "gambling with the safety of the people of California." He feared that the "decision, like prior prisoner release orders, will lead to a grim roster of victims. I hope that I am wrong. In a few years, we will see."[89]

CAPACIOUS CONSTITUTIONAL TOLERABILITY AND POLITICAL CAPITAL

What can "we see"? Justice Alito raised the question of what people can chose to see, or not. Decades after Judge Eisele formally closed the Arkansas Penitentiary Cases, the footprint of prisons has expanded, the scale of the harms to individuals and communities is vivid, and questions about the legitimacy of incarceration have become intense. The commitment to *aggressive incarceration* and the provision of *prison discounts* through deference to corrections and the licensing of hyper-density and of isolation have now bumped up against three movements—stopping "mass incarceration," "unlocking the box," and "abolition"—all contesting carceral punishments.

What can also be seen is that constitutional law once expanded to try to help prisoners and then contracted. The touchstones of the Eighth Amendment have throughout been contested, with differing tests of impermissible punishments, such as punishment practices in 1791, a minimum "of civilized life's necessities," "evolving standards," "dignity" and "decency."

Yet, as discussed, litigation is but one platform on a larger stage in which punishment is debated. During the first decades of the twenty-first century, incarcerated people marshaled political capital that brought into view their very "uncivilized" lives in prison and produced change. Some correctional directors committed to reform echoed the values of Arkansas' Robert Sarver and Vernon Housewright. Other branches of government—legislators and (occasionally) judges—insisted on limiting some in-prison practices including profound isolation. Claims for religious rights, including those of prisoners, gained new purchase,[90] as did a deepening understanding of the breadth of the "costs" of prison with its pervasive impact on communities of color. The budgetary impacts of incarceration, coupled with economic uncertainty and concerns about racism, curbed some of the enthusiasm for more prisons.

In 1997, the US Bureau of Justice Statistics (BJS) reported that the "lifetime chances" of a Black man "going to prison" was "greater than a 1 in 4 chance," while a "Hispanic male [had] a 1 in 6 chance and a white male . . . a 1 in 23 chance of serving time." An update, published in 2003 and called *The Prevalence of Imprisonment in the US Population, 1974–2001*, was dire. For people born in 2001, "6.6 percent of US residents" were projected to go to prison, and for Black men, the numbers were one in three. Thereafter, the Pew Center issued *One in 100: Behind Bars in America 2008*, which found that "cash-strapped states with soaring costs" were confronting that, for the first time in US history, "one in every 100 adults" was confined in a jail or prison. For Black men between the ages of twenty and thirty-four, the number was "one in nine." Yet all those dollars had no "clear impact either on recidivism or overall crime."[91]

The idea of prisons as "schools for crime" dates back to Jeremy Bentham, Alexis de Tocqueville, and their colleagues. The contemporary counterpart identifies the entire criminal legal system as a sorry source of education. The "hidden curriculum," explained by Benjamin Justice and Tracey Meares, socializes swaths of the citizenry about the likelihood of being deprived of educational and work force opportunities, the racial bias and erratic exercise of state discretion, and living with long-term disabilities such as losing access to public housing and other benefits. Rather than being welcomed as citizens, people are taught they belong to "a class of problem people to be excluded, monitored, and surveilled, treated harshly, and punished arbitrarily." A parallel analysis by Reuben Miller and Amanda Alexander frames the results as generating "carceral citizenship" of millions of people in a "supervised society" marked by race and class. And, social theorist Monica Bell offered the term "legal estrangement" to capture the harms spawned when, instead of evenhanded and procedurally fair treatment, so many people experience biased and arbitrary encounters with state officials.[92]

Pew's report was published as the Great Recession of 2008 was underway. That economic downturn, which was the longest since World War II, began in 2007 and ran through 2009. Given that state and federal governments were by then spending more than $80 billion on corrections, with almost $200 billion more on policing and courts, the fiscal crisis prompted reconsideration of choices made. As mentioned, in 2007, an organization called "Right on Crime," created by the Texas Public Policy Foundation, the Prison Fellowship, and the American Conservative Union Foundation, was launched. Its name pointed to being "right" on the political spectrum, being fiscally conservative, being religiously committed, and "right" that reducing incarceration would limit the waste of dollars and harms to people's souls. (At times, libertarians joined in objecting to overcriminalization of drugs and financial offenses.)

Soon thereafter, another buzzword gained currency (pun intended)—"justice reinvestment"—supported with US DOJ's help to restructure financing to keep more people out of incarceration, stem the flow of funds to prisons, and redirect resources to community-based programs. Some of those resources came from the Edward Byrne Memorial Justice Assistance Grant Program, which, as noted, had begun in 1985 and then merged with other programs in 2005 to expand its reach through the BJA. The Second Chance Act of 2008 sought to redirect efforts to what the Brennan Center termed "success-oriented funding," aiming to "nudge" people out of prison. Yet, even as the right and left converged in questioning the use of incarceration, they differed on whether the criminal law system was overused yet fundamentally sound or was an unjust instrument of disempowerment and inequality.[93]

Meanwhile, Congress began to send bipartisan signals that acknowledged the violence, disutility, and waste of massive incarceration. In 2003, Congress rallied behind the Prison Rape Elimination Act that aimed to constrain sexualized violence by requiring state facilities to provide audits on safety in prisons. Further, the 2008 Second Chance Act authorized "federal investments . . . to reduce recidivism and increase public safety" through "reentry" programs with education and services for people leaving prisons. Within a decade, more than 840 grants totaling $600 million had been made to support local services such as mentoring and substance abuse treatment. In 2018, the First Step Act (whose name reflected its limits) offered a few possibilities for reducing the number of people held in federal prisons. If serving an "eligible offense," incarcerated individuals could earn more good-time credit toward "prerelease custody." In addition, the First Step Act amended the power of the BOP and of judges to permit "compassionate release," not only for medical or age-related reasons but also for other "extraordinary and compelling reasons." Along with some state counterparts, the federal First Step Act gave some individuals routes to exit.[94]

Another facet of an economically based critique came from communities beset by the garnering of fines, fees, and assessments. In 2016, based on news and a DOJ report about how a Missouri town used its police and courts to fine Black residents for general revenues, "Ferguson" became the shorthand for localities exploiting their power to impose monetary sanctions. Around the country, counties charged families of children held in juvenile detention, assessed indigent defendants "registration fees" for "free" public defenders, and payments for time spent in detention. Debt could result in the loss of driver's licenses or voting rights and, at times, imprisonment for noncompliance with court orders or for committing infractions such as driving without a license. Political and legal organizing—including the founding of the Fines and Fees Justice Center to track the injuries and generate statutory and policy changes in many jurisdictions—has sometimes persuaded localities to end fees and on occasion, judges to find them unconstitutional. In 2023, the DOJ, building on its 2016 initiative, issued a new "guidance" to localities that poverty was not supposed to block usage of courts nor result in detention.[95]

Evidence of incarceration's many costs and harms continued to pour out through research as well as litigation. The Vera Institute of Justice calculated an average dollar cost per prisoner in 2015 to be more than $33,000, including staff and health care costs and, as discussed, not calculating the labor of prisoners and charges to them.[96] The loss of life was the focus of the Louisiana-based "Incarceration Transparency" Project, documenting that "at least 1,168 incarcerated people" had died between 2015 and 2021 "behind bars" in that state's prisons, jails, and youth detention facilities. A research team led by Andrea Armstrong identified causes to include disease, drugs, accidents, suicides, and violence. About 58 percent were Black, and their average age was under fifty-six years.[97] At the federal level, the Office of Inspector General issued an audit condemning the maintenance of BOP facilities, as dozens of institutions in disrepair put individuals at risk and some were not safe to occupy.[98] Efforts to mitigate prisons' harms came from Freedom Reads, an organization created by Dwayne Betts to bring tens of hundreds of books onto bookshelves made of wood so as to interrupt the concrete and metal of prisons and provide a gateway to worlds that prison walls tried to cut off. Another agenda focused on how prisoners' labor supported incarceration's sprawl. In the fall of 2022, voters in four states approved amendments to their constitutions that, unlike the text of the Thirteenth Amendment, did not exclude people held in prison from the ban on involuntary servitude.[99]

29

CAN IT END?

PRISONS' PERMEABILITY, PUNISHMENTS' SHIFTING CONTOURS, AND CORRECTIONS' TRANSNATIONAL GIRTH AND VULNERABILITIES

"Some grudge him every gleam of comfort or alleviation of misery. . . . [T]o others, every little privation, every little unpleasant feeling, every unaccustomed circumstance, every necessary point of coercive discipline, presents matter for a charge of inhumanity."

—Jeremy Bentham, *Postscript to Panopticon or the Inspection House*, 1791[1]

"The association between men in correctional institutions is closer and more fraught with physical danger and psychological pressures than is almost any other kind of association between human beings."

—US District Court Judge Luther Youngdahl, 1966[2]

"[T]he Eighth Amendment does not proscribe all pain . . . [but requires] distinguish[ing] impermissible methods or conditions in terms of both the quality and quantity of pain involved."

—Amicus Brief by thirty-four States and the Virgin Islands, *Rhodes v. Chapman*, filed December 1980[3]

"I am persuaded that the institution of prison probably must end. In many respects it is as intolerable within the United States as was the institution of slavery, equally brutalizing to all involved, equally toxic to the social system, equally subversive of the brotherhood of man. . . ."

US District Court Judge James E. Doyle, 1972[4]

These four quotes preview the lessons I draw from this transatlantic, three-century chronicle, documenting why undoing incarceration's harms is difficult and, nonetheless, changes are afoot. Jeremy Bentham's 1791 *Postscript* captured the conflict between people begrudging prisoners "a gleam of comfort" and those who think humanity requires alleviating "privations." I do not know whether Justice Powell had read Bentham when writing in 1981 in *Rhodes v. Chapman* that the "*discomfort*" of double celling was constitutional. Nor do I know whether Justice Kennedy had Bentham in mind when insisting in 2011 in *Brown v. Plata* that California *had* to reduce crowding to protect prisoners' health and safety. I do know that Bentham anticipated centuries of debates about whether prisoners ought to be more or less "eligible" (his term) for state assistance than others in need of support.

The 1981 court filing from dozens of states, claiming the propriety of inflicting *pain* as punishment, exemplifies the continuing salience of retribution that, along with deterrence, incapacitation, and reformation, Enlightenment theorists embraced and jurists entrenched as licit *penological purposes*. While religious reformers of that era advocated "redemptive suffering" to purge sin, contemporary retributivists argue the morality of punishment. Some assert its "just deserts" generates symmetry between the harmed victim and the wrongdoer—a proposition H. L. A. Hart rejected as analytically incoherent (transmuting "the two evils of moral wickedness and suffering . . . into a good"). Another strand—"response retributivism" is Leora Dahan Katz's term—posits a "moral duty" arising from relationships with wrongdoers; respect requires accountability that, on her account, need not result in massive incarceration or vengeful pain. What role these theories play in practice is the concern of Didier Fassin, who linked the "why" of punishment to the "who" getting punished; selective distribution lands overwhelmingly on the poor. Neither the criticisms of retribution nor nuanced retrievals have made headway in the US Supreme Court. As the states urged, the Court sorts the "quality and quantity" of pain and, in the case of executions, puts the burden on capital defendants to prove that less painful ways exist to kill them.[5]

The two quotes from federal judges provide a synopsis of law's responses to incarceration's incursions on individual rights. When Judge Youngdahl licensed segregation of some "Negro inmates" at a Virginia facility, he called prisons "more fraught" than any other human "association." Two years later, when the Supreme Court found unconstitutional Alabama's statutory racial segregation, concurring justices reflected that view: if needed for "security, discipline, and good order," officials *could* segregate. That caveat—that prisoners' rights can be cabined by institutional needs—is the *prison discount*, explained in the introduction, that continues in international and domestic law.

Judge Doyle differed. Concluding in 1972 that the First Amendment protected a prisoner's right to correspond with a relative, Judge Doyle detailed Wisconsin's control over prisoners' "total existence"—by dictating times for rising, sleeping, eating, and the clothing worn. The state prevented people from "wearing beards, embracing their spouses, or corresponding with their lovers" and required submission to "oral and anal searches" after visits. That "elaborate network of rules and regulations," with no rehabilitative purpose, sought to protect "the guards and administrators from the inmates," prisoners from each other, and to keep costs low. Linking incarceration to enslavement, the judge concluded that, if prisons could not "survive without" such rules, the Constitution required that "the prison be modified" or come to an "end."[6]

These four comments encapsulate the disjuncture and continuities between the pre–World War II regime and contemporary analyses of incarceration's legitimacy. Enlightenment reformers recognized punishment's incursions and called for rationalizing its deployment. Yet even as transatlantic movements thereafter built norms to structure incarceration, none centered on the *authority* of convicted individuals to impose constraints until World War II, concentration camps, and the Civil Rights Movement made prison a problem for polities aiming to be egalitarian. Prisoners then succeeded in gaining formal recognition that, no longer "slaves" of the state, they were individuals whose rights had to be respected. The acceptance of that proposition required translating "rights" and "respect" into practice. Doing so became a central concern of incarcerated people, social movements, politicians, government officials, judges, corrections professionals, moral and legal theorists, and transnational organizations, some of which endorse incarceration's abolition.

Atop conflicts over the impact of rights in prisons, a new fault line has emerged with the girth of the transnational corrections enterprise that makes sustainability questionable. Working in prisons, like living in them, is awful. The literature on corrections is awash with data on high vacancy and turnover rates and on the ill health of employees as well as detainees. Given the time, energy, and money spent on prisons, how "fraught" they remain, and the harms they inflict, the questions are whether prisons will collapse, be abolished, survive "as is," or be reconstructed in ways distant from the current instantiation. Formulating answers entails abstracting themes from the centuries of resiliency of both the practice of imprisonment and of the people on whom this punishment is imposed.

REPETITIVE, NOT STATIC: NORMATIVE SHIFTS STOPPING PUNISHMENTS AND LAUNCHING OTHERS

Assessments of the permissible-in-punishment change, and deeply entrenched punishments have been upended. Cesare Beccaria sought the end of executions; John Howard hated the filth and disease of imprisonment; Jeremy Bentham argued against transportation; Gustave de Beaumont and Alexis de Tocqueville objected to the chaotic jumble of people warehoused in French prisons. These men were in pursuit of "non-reformist reforms"—a term common, as noted, in twenty-first-century prison abolitionists discussions. Rather than improve a practice ("reformist reforms"), the point was to stop it. In the twenty-first century, *none* of those once commonplace punishments is admired, and most have been abolished, in part through *legitimating* incarceration. Therein lies another lesson: to bring a punishment to its end has entailed promoting replacements.

Altering the "whys" of punishment has helped change the modes of punishment. Enlightenment theorists of the eighteenth century advocated suffering as redemptive, while subsequent reformers rejected purposeful degradation. Invoking humanitarian commitments and "civilization's" obligations, these entrepreneurs argued incarceration's ameliorative qualities. Codification of this approach linked to a new professionalism came in 1870 when the National Prison Congress issued its Cincinnati Declaration of Principles identifying *rehabilitation* as incarceration's primary goal. Thereafter, corrections officials and judges pressed for indeterminate sentences that, for much of the twentieth century, gave them control over the duration of confinement. The "prison men" who ran the International Penal and Penitentiary Commission (IPPC) and built the 1934 League of Nations' fifty-plus Standard Minimum Rules for the Treatment of Prisoners were able to consolidate corrections' authority over the conditions of confinement and modes of in-prison discipline.

After the IPPC's collaboration with fascist countries brought it to an end, the UN opened up rule drafting to human rights advocates. Punishments, licit during the first half of the twentieth century, were excoriated thereafter. Revulsion at racism and detention camps supported new commitments to prisoners as rights-bearing members of the political order. The 1955 UN Rules, recognizing prisoners' dignity and rights, rejected whipping, chaining, dark cells, and starvation. As the twenty-first century unfolds, other shifts are underway. The UN's 2015 revisions, named after Nelson Mandela, call for ending food deprivation and strict limits on solitary confinement. Thus, Winston Talley, Thomas X Cooper, and their cohort taught us that Enlightenment theories of punishment are insufficient guides to twenty-first-century decisions about the sovereign act of punishment.

The concept of "rights-bearing" prisoners generated not only the potential to change punishment practices but also claims by other people that their status likewise needed to be addressed. During the last few decades, a "victims' rights" movement gained strength, in part through technology's ability to broadcast incidents of terrible violence. In the United States, constitutional law accepted the use of victims' statements at sentencing, and dozens of state constitutions required notice to victims and opportunities for input at sentencing and parole. The international #MeToo movement, spawned by victims of sexualized violence, pushed for punitive responses to those harms.

Distinguishing recognition of harms from punitive responses has been at the center of the "restorative justice" movement that aims to engage victim and wrongdoer in a future-looking, reparative relationship. A burgeoning literature recounts successes of individual and larger-scaled efforts, such as "truth and reconciliation commissions," while some critics register concerns. Exemplary is Annalise Acorn, worried about what she calls "compulsory compassion." She questioned whether "recompense, reconciliation, forgiveness, and healing" would be sustainable, given social-emotional experiences of wanting accountability for harmful acts.[7]

In short, the literature of punishment is replete with fits and starts about alternatives. However repetitive, punishment's history is not static.[8]

PERMEABLE PRISON WALLS

As Caleb Smith put it, the prison wall stands "between the captive and the world at large . . . [as] also the medium of their contact, of their common cause."[9] I have shown that the separation between prison and its social order has been overstated. I reproduced a print of Amsterdam's 1780s Men's House of Correction to illustrate that detention facilities were part of the landscape. Reflecting Bentham's theory of example-as-deterrent, spectators were invited to see the utilities of disciplined confinement, whipping included. New York's Auburn Penitentiary sold tickets so visitors could watch prisoners forced into silent oppressive work.

In addition, paid staff and religious workers came and went, and doors were opened for inquiries pioneered by Howard, Beaumont, and Tocqueville, followed by Enoch Wines and Theodore Dwight and, in the twentieth century, by Austin MacCormick, social scientists, investigative reporters, and photographers such as Bruce Jackson. More information—from the perspective of the people in charge—poured out in meetings of the National Prison Association, the IPPC, and the UN commissions thereafter. As astute entrepreneurs, corrections professionals reached out to religious leaders, the business community, and the public to garner support for funding and to enlist volunteers to help prisoners after release.

Throughout, and despite prison authorities' efforts to silence imprisoned people, incarcerated individuals recorded the degradation, petitioned government officials, and went on strike. Winston Talley smuggled papers out, and such lawsuits produced a wealth (so to speak) of materials about the radical impositions of detention. Thus, even as today, getting inside prisons and cells requires permission, the injuries inflicted by incarceration have been public, rather than veiled from sight.

The permeability, embeddedness, and radiating impacts of prisons make questionable the use of the term "reentry." While laudatory in marking the needs of people leaving incarceration, reentry suggests a world *apart* from the social order that produces it. Other terms can mark the shift; *transitions* is one alternative. The footprint of prisons extends far beyond their walls. Many communities (disproportionately of color and with limited means) bear the impact of losing individuals to confinement, and these practices impoverish the political order while stoking divides within it. Moreover, overreach alters prison's import as a sanction; when commonplace, prison loses the stigmatizing force to which some retributivists aspire as well as its utilities as a deterrent.

AWASH WITH AGENCY ALTERING PUNISHMENT'S VOCABULARY AND NORMS

Remarkable individuals have driven changes in punishment's rationales and modalities. In the 1700s, Cesare Beccaria's genius was to insist that punishment be linked to licit sovereign goals. Jeremy Bentham brilliantly (and gruesomely) elaborated those ideas in thousands of pages categorizing and cataloguing forms of punishment and their utilities. While they insisted on the need to have *reasons* for punishment and sought to limit punishments to those necessary to achieve stated purposes, they countenanced whipping, caging, fetters, and long-term confinement. Enoch Wines and his cohort propelled the infrastructures that produced the corrections profession and today's international industry.

I singled out Margery Fry and her colleagues at the Howard League because, in the 1920s, they called for the end of "torture" and international protection of prisoners' rights. I devoted a section of this book to the years between 1965 and 1980 because several incarcerated people (Winston Talley, Thomas Cooper, Caliph Washington, William Jackson, and more) upended the convention that people who ran prisons had total control over the lives of prisoners and could, without explanation or constraint, turn ordinary human movement and association into illicit acts. Whether steeped in political theory or not, these incarcerated individuals insisted that they were part of, rather than outsiders to, the political community and participated through strikes, petitions, and litigation pushing for legislative and executive branch action. Just as Bentham, Howard, Tocqueville, and others propelled a conceptual shift by seeking a rationality for punishment, prisoners altered *the acceptable* in punishment by reframing national and transnational law to state limits on sovereign powers.[10]

Prisoners' successes pushed new words—*dignity* and *decency*—into punishment's legal vocabulary. Writing shortly after Hannah Arendt's 1949 essay on the "right to have rights," Chief Justice Earl Warren explained that, because punishment ought not leave a person rights-less, evaluations required considering "evolving standards of decency." In 1955, the UN inscribed "rights," "dignity," and "liberty" into its Standard Minimum Rules for the Treatment of Prisoners. Judge Harry Blackmun applied those ideas in 1968 to rule out whipping as a disciplinary measure, as did Chief Judge J. Smith Henley when finding Arkansas' prison system to be a "dark and evil world" and calling for "constitutionally adequate" facilities. Legislators and model rule drafters proposed statutes to make rights and dignity material, as the US Supreme Court debated the liberties that incarceration had to protect.

The issue of *liberty* in prison was central to Justice John Paul Stevens; mostly in dissent, he affirmed government obligations to protect a freedom inherent in personhood. In 2011, Justice Anthony Kennedy relied on dignity and decency when requiring reductions in overcrowding to lessen illness in California's prisons and in 2015, when objecting to the psychological destructiveness of profound isolation. During those decades, *excessive force* denoted that government control did not license acts of unfettered violence. That proposition entered police and corrections manuals, even as implementation fell far short, and beatings and murders continued.

New rights and new concepts have not, to date, generated a profound revisiting of practices of incarceration in the United States, while in Europe its norms have shifted. When US judges were confronted with people like Talley, they adopted the Beccaria/Bentham approach by assuming that punishments were not to be random or ruthlessly terrorizing but in service of what the US Supreme Court described as "legitimate" aims. As discussed, judges invoked a capacious set—deterrence, incapacitation, retribution, and reformation/ rehabilitation, administrative convenience, and safety. In tension analytically, these various purposes have been deployed to justify all sorts of sanctions, including the death penalty. Jurists describe themselves as evaluating the rationales for a given sanction and, in deference to legislatures and prison officials, understanding the punishments defended by government actors. As a result, even as judicial opinions appear to impose a layer of oversight, they often read like cost/benefit inquiries that identify permissible ends ("penological purposes") and look for a minimal rational relationship. Yet at times, when confronted with degradation—such as whipping—that could have been rationalized as useful, judges rejected specific practices.

REJECTING "CORRECTION" AND "CIVILIZATION" AS TOUCHSTONES

Nomenclature reflects values, making it time not only to add but also to attrite terms within punishment's lexicon. Were one to do a word search of this book, "civilized" would be found dozens of times *before* it became central to the Court's 1981 formulation that the Eighth Amendment protected against deprivation of the "minimum of civilized life's necessities," translated as *permitting* the density and lack of privacy of living with other people in small cells. "Civilized life" has a past steeped in race and class and deployed to license subjugation—of prisoners and many others, debilitated by self-described civilized countries.

These class and race hierarchies likewise reside in the infrastructure of incarceration, with a profession calling itself "corrections" that at times focused on "curing" and "rehabilitating" the detained. Whether prisons fell under the wing of state "charity" boards governed by "philanthropists" or by professionals, practices were justified through analogizing crime as a pathology altered through "correction." Per Foucault, officials imposed a regime of discipline (as in structured days) followed by discipline (as in punishment if noncompliant with all the many rules). Pseudoscience licensed awful "treatments" and indeterminate sentences.

Who is punished and how depends on the politics within a social order. History is replete with delegation of vast swaths of decisions to people within a "Department of Correction." That licensure is ill-suited to aspiring egalitarian orders. Another set of social services sit under agencies focused on "welfare," and their mission statements name their goals as fostering "*self-sufficiency*" to improve "*well-being*" and "*health*." In contrast, the bywords for corrections are "*safety*" and "*security*." Yet the correctional profession has, at enormous expense, produced institutions that are *unsafe* for both prisoners and staff. The concrete and metal enclosures, the spools of razor wire, and the bars do not generate the "good order" claimed to be corrections' forte. The "rate of homicide in state prison is 2.5 times greater than in the US population when adjusted for age, sex, and race/ethnicity."[11] To frame another approach, the work of punishment needs to be conceived; a better description would be an Agency of Obligation, to reflect the burdens taken on by government when detaining people.

THE RISE OF AGGRESSIVE INCARCERATION

Although Dr. Martin Luther King Jr. saw that the "arc of the moral universe . . . is long but it bends toward justice," recent decades have demonstrated that "evolving standards" in the US Constitution have not all bent toward justice, dignity, decency, and liberty. As the racialized war on crime drove prison populations up, officials embraced what I termed *aggressive incarceration*. Dozens of politicians (exemplified here by Dale Bumpers, Bill Clinton, Richard Nixon, and Ronald Reagan) argued for longer sentences, mandatory sentences, and life without parole. Once the Supreme Court lowered "constitutional tolerability" to the "minimal civilized measure of life's necessities" in 1981 and licensed double celling, density undercut the ability to provide services and heightened fears of losing control.

Hence, during an era when legislatures, the correctional establishment, and many jurists continued to call for rehabilitation, and professional and federal standards remained committed to single celling to protect privacy and safety, prospects dimmed for personal space and social services. The hyper-density of warehousing became a rationale for solitary confinement, claimed to enhance safety by isolating subsets of prisoners. Corrections ideology shifted to match these conditions, and the mantra that "nothing works" became a claim of empirical truth. Politicians pressed to get money to control "deviants" reiterating centuries-long efforts (recall Amsterdam's 1780s Houses of Correction), as if doing so benefited the polity.

Aggressive punishment gained the imprimatur of constitutional conventionality in 1995; with Chief Justice William Rehnquist in charge, the Court opined that solitary confinement was not an "atypical and significant hardship" but an "ordinary incident" of incarceration. Pronouncing that *normalcy in prison* entailed radical constraints on movement sustained its use, even as a unanimous Court later obliged prison officials to provide a modicum of procedures if imposing extraordinary, indefinite sensory deprivations. Thereafter, self-proclaimed "originalist" justices gained authority and put several decades of Eighth Amendment law at risk. If the touchstone of rights is not "evolving" but a "public" or "common understanding" at the Founding Era or at the post–Civil War Reconstruction Amendments, inquiries become refocused on the status of prisoners in centuries when courts pronounced them "slaves of the state" and civilly "dead." To be clear, the Court's return to history in US constitutional law extends beyond punishment to a host of legal rules including reproductive rights, climate, guns, and administrative agency authority. Moreover, what I have documented in the context of prisons is a general proposition. Constitutional law is thin and does not, alone, sustain change but is embedded in and gains meaning from political and social movements.

THE CONSTANTS OF TRANSNATIONALISM

Rolling back the clock to the 1790s for prisons will be hard, and not only for those whom Justice Antonin Scalia styled "faint-hearted originalists,"[12] but for the corrections establishment itself, which describes its contemporary "mission" as providing "care" and respecting "rights." The people running prisons built a transnational movement that, while dating back centuries, no longer is controlled by prison managers alone. Corrections became norm-laden in the 1840s when standard-making began in Frankfurt and continued in the 1870 Cincinnati Principles and the 1934 League of Nations' Standard Minimum Rules for the Treatment of Prisoners. Once the UN took over, it opened up access, which resulted in the 1955 Rules' formal acknowledgment that individuals' self-determination meant incarceration was to interfere as little as possible with liberty. Those rules banned corporal punishment (meaning whipping and chaining) and discrimination on the basis of race, class, gender, national origin, or religion.

The transnational human rights movement did not stop there. While the UN never generated a convention on prisoners, in 1966 it promulgated the International Convention on Civil and Political Rights (ICCPR), stating that no person be subjected to "torture or to cruel, inhuman or degrading treatment or punishment." Those words, drawn from the 1950 European Convention on Human Rights, contributed to the Council of Europe's decision to promulgate European Prison Rules, issued in 2006 and revised in 2020. Along with the UN's Convention Against Torture or Other Cruel, Inhuman, and Degrading Treatment or Punishment (CAT), these provisions became bases for human rights committees and rapporteurs to investigate and for some judicial decisions ordering improvements. More protections came from the 2007 "Istanbul Statement" on solitary confinement and the 2010 "Bangkok Rules" on improving conditions for women in detention.[13]

The UN 1955 Rules were slightly modified in 1977 to reflect enactment of the ICCPR. Thereafter, twenty-first-century activists sought a major revision. A group called Penal Reform International (PRI), promoting criminal legal systems that upheld "human rights for all and . . . do no harm," was at the helm. With political acumen matching the Howard League's lobbying the League of Nations, PRI brought together NGOs to outline options (including as Margery Fry had hoped, a "binding instrument"), shape messaging to "civil society organizations," develop background materials (the "Essex Papers") from an academic human rights center, and generate a "joint-NGO submission." This collective persuaded the UN in 2012 to request its Commission on Crime Prevention and Criminal Justice to reconsider facets of the 1955 Rules. Goals included expanding "respect for prisoners' inherent dignity," improved health care, investigation of injuries and deaths, protection of "vulnerable groups," access to legal representation and independent inspections, and staff training. One sociologist described this approach as a "compromise between boldness and feasibility" that, based on an "inclusive, robust, and empirically grounded" process, succeeded in obtaining new rules.[14]

"Feasibility" meant that the point was not to upend prisons but (and again) *to improve* them. In 2015, after the United States agreed not to "undermine" the initiative, directors from the Colorado and Washington prison systems played a politically helpful role through confirming that limiting solitary confinement would not "hamper" prison safety. Meanwhile, prisoners' rights advocates signaled that they took "operational issues seriously," which meant they appreciated *staff* concerns. These negotiations resulted in the 2015 UN Standard Minimum Rules for the Treatment of Prisoners, named (as discussed) to honor Nelson Mandela's decades of incarceration and his vision of apartheid's end. The 2015 preface underscored the dual objections of prisoners' rights and corrections' authority by quoting President Mandela's charge to South Africa's Department of Correctional Services—to help prisoners become "law-abiding citizens" while not "denying them their dignity and their rights as humans."[15]

In some respects, the 2015 Rules are familiar artifacts of political compromises made from the 1930s to the present. They continued to iterate their own limitations by describing the 122-set as the "general consensus of contemporary thought" about "good principles in the treatment of prisoners and prison management" that offer "minimum conditions," even as not all countries would be able to provide them. Yet centering on the proposition that prisons must "respect" detained people's "inherent dignity and value," the rules redefined *safety* as predicated on care and specified it entailed cleanliness, adequate nutrition, programming and activity, and access to the outside world. Further, the Rules rejected food deprivation as punishment and sought to limit body searches by making them exceptional, documented, and conducted by trained staff. As discussed, the Rules restricted isolation through defining solitary confinement as twenty-two hours a day or more "without meaningful human contact" and categorizing fifteen days or more as "prolonged solitary confinement" amounting to degrading inhuman treatment akin to torture. NGO pressures did not abate with adoption of the 2015 Rules. PRI issued "initial guidance" on implementation in 2016; in 2017, the UN Office on Drugs and Crime published *Assessing Compliance with the Nelson Mandela Rules: A Checklist for Internal Inspection Mechanisms*. In 2022, a manual followed on national-level implementation.[16]

The UN Rules and many court judgments from around the world have prompted some commentators to argue that, while no prison convention exists, a transnational law of prisoners' rights has gained enough traction to be "customary law" and hence binding obligations that national courts should recognize. Moreover, since 2005, the European Court of Human Rights, which sits in Strasbourg, has repeatedly called for prisoners to be able to vote, even as it backed down somewhat in tussles with the United Kingdom over implementation. That court has also issued rulings limiting prison overcrowding and insisting that all persons—including in isolation—have a right to family life that requires visitors. Furthermore, in many countries, a raft of rules became commonplace.[17] (When I visited a French prison in 2017, its chief waved a thick red book of regulations and bemoaned its volume and detail.)

Fault lines remain. The rights-based prison reform movement is haunted by an ever-present caveat (the *prison discount*) that rights can be bent in response to perceived security needs. In 1955, the United Nations led the way by simultaneously stating that prisoners were rights-holders and yet that prison systems could, "as incidental to justifiable segregation or the maintenance of discipline, aggravate the suffering inherent in such a situation."[18] As discussed, a parallel pronouncement came in the US Supreme Court's 1968 first prisoner class action, *Lee v. Washington*. Likewise, guidance on implementing the 2015 UN Rules explained that "prisoners retain all rights *except for those taken away from them* as a specific consequence of the deprivation of liberty" (my italics). The hope, as explained by PRI, is that such discounts will be used only when necessary, related to legitimate aims, and proportionate; the issue is who makes those judgments.[19]

Thus, while detained individuals continue to live under the arbitrariness of staff decisions and often abysmal conditions, incarceration in many countries is no longer the haphazard morass that Tocqueville and Beaumont encountered in the early nineteenth century. Moreover, the "elaborate network of rules and regulations," described in 1972 by Judge Doyle, no longer aim only at invasive control. A report issued in 2023 by "HM [Her or His Majesty's] Chief Inspector of Prisons for England and Wales" is illustrative. The "unannounced" visits sought to learn whether facilities were "healthy establishments" in terms of "safety," "respect," "purposeful activity," and "rehabilitation and release planning." Rather than the "minimum of civilized life's necessities" the questions were about efforts to mitigate incarceration's suffering. Prisoners and staff were asked how they felt, whether they were treated fairly in a community with "mutually agreed values" in which esteem and consideration extended to all of their members.[20]

That report was, however, another reminder of the gap between precepts and implementation. Just as Arkansas repeatedly failed in the 1970s to comply with court orders, British prisons in 2022 regularly fell short. Finding a general decline in the quality of living conditions and staff–prisoner relationships, the Inspector described discrimination experienced by Black prisoners and staff, people in double cells with inadequate screening of toilets, too many incidents of violence, and too little "purposeful activity" such as programs, exercise, and education. The causes were shortfalls of funding and staff, and the results were what Bill Keller described as the "alarming Americanisation of British prisons."[21] Parallels—echoing what Tocqueville and Beaumont criticized—can be found in discussions of French prisons. A 2023 European Court of Human Rights ruling condemned inhumane conditions; a 2024 research report detailed unfair discipline, and a French newspaper recounted dense crowding, deaths, and disarray in a story it captioned: *"le monde pénitentiaire au bord de la rupture."*[22]

More generally, the fragility of human rights enforcement and the documented miseries in prisons around the world means that no starry-eyed ode to rights or to transnationalism is in order. I have highlighted *normative* shifts on both sides of the Atlantic, even as they have not produced the changes they portend. Awful documentation came in 2019 and 2021 from the US Department of Justice (DOJ), which provided stomach-churning reports on violence in prisons of Alabama and Mississippi. Thousands of Alabama prisoners went on strike to protest conditions in facilities that DOJ lawyers found to be "understaffed and notoriously dangerous"; more than 180 percent over capacity, these prisons had "some of the highest rates of homicide and rapes in the country."[23]

Yet that report also reflects the impact of century-long efforts at changing the contours of rights. By then, the DOJ had dozens of attorneys devoted to protecting institutionalized people; seventy years earlier, no such division existed, and states insisted they had no constitutional obligation to provide anything to prisoners. Further, many layers of law—transnational, national, state constitutional law, legislative action, and some corrections directors' regulations—are fonts of changes. Some states and localities have limited solitary confinement, and a national movement seeks to ensure people who are or have been incarcerated have access to the ballot.[24]

In short, my account of diverse domestic and international venues in which prisoners' rights have had sway is an illustration of what Seyla Benhabib described as "democratic iterations," in which ideas and practices are shaped through repeated interactions and conflicts over norms.[25] The transnational, regional, and local developments curb the influence of the cribbed constitutional approach in the United States; they make improbable in democratic political orders a return to the chattel-slave world of the eighteenth- and nineteenth-centuries' prisons.

CORRECTIONS: GLOBALIZING, PRIVATIZING, AND WOBBLING

Atop caveats *within* rights regimes and the gaps *between* regulation and incarcerated peoples' experiences, narratives about twenty-first-century incarceration need to take into account the political and economic heft of country-level prison departments and transnational corporations invested in detention. Correctional "agencies" are large employers, with leadership and staff whose livelihood depends on surveillance and confinement that, even when aiming for "healthy establishments," imposes extraordinary control over human beings. As Dirk van Zyl Smit explained, the bureaucratization of corrections can "normalize the notion of a state prison system" as if it were just another function of government.[26]

Yet, in this age of globalization and privatization, the question of a "government function" needs addressing. My focus has been on *state* obligations to prisoners; in many legal systems, private providers that serve a "state function" are subject to the same legal mandates as public-sector providers. Reformers of centuries past turned prisons into publicly run institutions. The reemergence of private prisons came during the latter part of the twentieth century when the UK's Margaret Thatcher and the US' Ronald Reagan sought to shift a host of services—policing, courts, telecommunications, transportation, education, housing, and health services—to private-sector providers. The goal was to reverse a process I have elsewhere termed "statization" as a reminder that the contours of both public and private sectors are built and change.[27] Moreover, delineating the "public" from the "private" is made complex because private labor (prisoners') and private funds (their families') play a major role in US "public prisons," which also outsource many services, such as health care, to private industry.

In the United States, an early champion of prison privatization was T. Don Hutto who, as memorialized in *Hutto v. Finney*, failed to comply with federal law when running Arkansas' prisons. As discussed, Hutto founded the Corrections Corporation of America, later renamed CoreCivic. A competitor, the Wackenhut Corrections Corporation, became the GEO Group in 2003. A decade later, the two controlled 75 percent of the US private prison market, which houses a small share of US prisoners (under 10 percent) as well as detained immigrants. The GEO Group described itself as the "world's leading diversified provider in privatized correctional work," offering prisons, detention of juveniles and immigrants, private probation, residential treatment, psychiatric facilities, and electronic monitoring under a *"Continuum of Care* model" for its "customers worldwide." By 2023, with annual revenue exceeding $2.3 billion and approximately 18,000 employees, GEO advertised itself as the "global leader in evidence-based rehabilitation." Its materials explained "what we do"—which it said was saving "taxpayer dollars . . . without sacrificing the quality of service" under "strict government oversight and accountability."[28] What it did not "do," GEO reported, was "lobby" for incarceration or "cut corners." What it also did not, in promotional materials, "do" was discuss commitments to prisoners' *rights*.

In contrast, another new entity, the International Corrections and Prisons Association (ICPA), founded in 1998 as a "worldwide organization for networking correctional professionals and practitioners," described imprisonment as "a last resort" in its "mission, vision and values." The IPCA called for detention practices to respect "the *dignity* of all individuals" and "the duty to protect their *rights*" (my italics). The ICPA welcomed members "across all sectors," including staff and management, consultants, entrepreneurs, and academics, offered an "International Centre for Exchanging Best Correctional Practices," a journal named "Advancing Corrections" available to members and, in 2016, gained "Special Consultative Status with the Economic and Social Council of the United Nations," making it eligible to send delegates to the UN Crime Commission meetings. The ICPA's financing reflected its public-private mix; in addition to dues, some corporate sponsors (such as prison telecommunications companies and the GEO Group) provided support garnering them "platinum" or "gold" status.[29]

This sketch of twenty-first-century corrections highlights features that distinguish it on several dimensions from its nineteenth-century predecessors. Transnational human rights norms and layers of national legal prescriptions make corrections less autonomous than it once was. Further, officials now discuss the race and ethnicity of the incarcerated and their keepers. Moreover, transborder private prison companies promote their products alongside the public sector that, in some places, has unionized staff. The industry as a whole controls large swaths of capital, land, and people. (As of 2023, some 350,000 people worked in the United States for corrections.)

Yet, lurking beneath this expansive public-private enterprise is the problem that prisons are hard (terrible) places to be for employees as well as prisoners. Staff vacancies run in some places to 50 percent or more, as does turnover. A mound of research documents that prison is *bad* for its workers' health. The reasons stem from the "bizarre" (apt again) propositions that, while aiming to sever association with family and friends, incarceration imposes undue proximity to strangers, many of whom have health issues including limited abilities to control their own behavior. Once in prison, staff try to undermine connections among prisoners, at times out of fear of losing control *to* prisoners, some of whom may be part of what corrections terms "security threat groups" ("gangs") that may exploit others. Add overcrowding, double cells, noise, concrete, metal, extreme heat or insufficient warmth, long stretches of overtime, and low pay. (In 2023, the median annual wages for corrections staff in the United States were about \$53,000.) Then add the "solid evidence" of staff "morbidity and mortality rates" exceeding "almost all other occupational groups."[30]

In 2022, the advocacy group Right on Crime detailed the "crisis" of staff shortages in the federal prison system, where some 38,000 staff were "responsible" for more than 155,000 individuals. Given "shortfalls" at many facilities, poor pay, violence, and stress, the results were "burnout, lower morale, and . . . safety risks." That year, Arkansas had a 47 percent vacancy rate for security staff; elsewhere, systems lost 35 percent in a year to resignations. Further, "no-shows" were commonplace at New York City's Rikers Island, a pretrial detention facility where deaths, illness, and violence have prompted repeated efforts to close it. In Wisconsin, about a thousand prisoners in 2023 were in "lockdown," left for months without sunlight, visitors, and health care; the explanation was no safe movement was possible with half of the 284 staff positions empty. Cross the ocean to England, where the Inspector General identified a lack of staff as central to the failings described. Back in the United States, the DOJ's Inspector General issued a scathing critique of the Federal Bureau of Prisons because of its crumbling infrastructures, filled with mold, broken pipes, buckling concrete, poor ventilation, and housing many more individuals than the rated capacity.[31]

An experiential report comes from an investigative reporter, Shane Bauer, who took a job at a CoreCivic prison in Louisiana and described life as "unbearable," with shakedowns, assaults, and co-workers smuggling in marijuana and having sex with prisoners. Bauer found himself trying to get prisoners' obedience and writing charges for "defiance" and "disobedience."[32] In a calmer atmosphere in an Oregon prison, I saw smaller-scale challenges. When entering a facility, I was required to check my cellphone, as was my high-level staff escort. She explained the difficulty of being on a many-hour shift without an ability to call her young child, who had recently broken a limb. Efforts to control communications and fears of generating markets in contraband seemed to preclude an obvious fix—let her and prisoners have access to some kind of cell phone.

Transforming staff–prisoner relationships is a core concern of another new entrant to the world of corrections, an organization called "AMEND," based at the Medical School of the University of California San Francisco and enlisting prison workers in making prisons less oppressively restrictive. Building on models from Norway of a less authoritarian "dynamic security," a few prisons in the United States have shifted to have staff and prisoners (or "residents") eat and join together in activities reflecting their interwoven lives. The predicate is that when prisoners and staff find common cause, they can improve shared material conditions. One example of an appreciation of shared fate can be found in the decision in 2010 of the California Correctional Peace Officers Association, representing 35,000 officers. It told federal judges that, given the hyper-density of the state's prisons, workers could not "adequately perform their duties" and therefore sided with prisoners calling on federal courts to limit crowding.[33]

Efforts to make prison "different" (and not just "better") through reorienting the role of staff can be found in various countries. Illustrative is a facility, Grendon, in England, providing incarceration for 200 "long-sentenced" individuals convicted of violent crimes. This "democratic therapeutic community," begun in the 1960s, aimed to create a "sensitive internal environment" in which individuals were able to "act with conscious and considered agency in their own lives" and gain "problem-solving skills." The authority of the community's members was made plain to me when I asked to visit; the chief officer responded he needed to consult with residents and other staff. After they agreed, I joined a routine meeting of about ten incarcerated people and two health care providers discussing daily stresses. No security staff were in that meeting, nor present when a resident took me to his cell, where his family was permitted to visit twice a year and where he kept a pet bird.[34] In contrast, when a couple of years later, I visited Arkansas' Cummins Farm, I met with the all-white leadership and was not permitted to talk with incarcerated people. I was escorted through empty halls; the warden had locked down the facility during my brief visit.

Grendon's structure entailed interpersonally labor-intensive tasks. Furthermore, it raised the issues of whether concepts of "democratic," "therapeutic," and "community" can and should sit inside an institution labeled a "prison," whether such institutions should be under the supervision of health rather than corrections departments, whether, in light of declining commitments to social welfare services, it could survive, and whether calling practices "health care" would produce radical revision or oppressive institutionalization would persist.[35]

Anecdotes meet statistics through studies of the aggregate impact of work inside prisons. Line officers die on average fifteen years earlier than the general population; explanations include elevated rates of heart disease, suicide, depression, and workplace injuries. After COVID hit, deaths and infection rates were higher for staff and prisoners than the population at large. These problems are more than visible to the corrections industry, as conferences and publications address workplace stress, the "staffing-health crisis," and enhancing "well-being."[36] Yet those measures do not respond to the structural problems of half-empty employee lines, no-shows, long hours, non-security personnel reassignments to security, poor pay, and oppressive environments. Whether aiming for progressive reform or aggressive incarceration, corrections cannot satiate its own demands *for* and *on* staff. The corrections industry is proof that prisons of the kind and scale currently in use are not viable means of punishment.

Thus, when Judge Youngdahl described prisons as "more fraught with physical danger and psychological pressures than is almost any other kind of association between human beings," he captured the misery of staff as well as prisoners. What he did not do was reject the construction that produced those pressures. Others, including people running prison systems, have. Early in the twentieth century, speakers at prison association congresses advocated "alternative sentencing"—probation in lieu of prison and the conditional release of parole—not only as back-end safety-valves to reduce populations but also as preferable to putting men behind bars and leaving their families without economic support.

The idea that incarceration was itself illegitimate came not only from Margery Fry's condemnation of the torture of detainees and convicted individuals but also from some people running prisons. As discussed, in the aftermath of World War II, individuals such as Belgium's former head of prisons, Paul Cornil, raised the specter of prison's end as he spoke at the IPPC's 1950 Hague Congress about the devastating effects of divesting people of their autonomy. In 1967, Hans Mattick, a criminologist based in Chicago who had run a detention facility, argued that "rapidly accumulating" evidence showed "imprisonment does more harm than good." Writing in the era when Erving Goffman identified the oppressiveness of "total institutions" and David Rothman saw an end to "the asylum" in sight, Mattick described a public "imprisoned in a mass delusion which, in the long run, punished society far more severely than society could ever punish a convicted criminal." Pointing out that nowhere else did "eighteen-and-nineteenth-century methods" work well, Mattick insisted that correctional professionals had a special obligation to make plain that "[i]mprisonment does not protect society from its criminal, it does not deter them, it does not reform them, and it does not rehabilitate them."[37]

In the 1970s, Michel Foucault brought the totalizing power of the state into view and used imprisonment as his major exemplar. During the last several decades, more critics—Angela Davis, Dorothy Roberts, Allegra McLeod, Ruth Gilmore, Mariame Kaba, Bernard Harcourt, Jessica Mitford, and others—developed a full-throttled rejection of imprisonment. Identifying incarceration's expansion with racial and class conflicts that target economically marginal people disproportionately of color, these commentators push abolition. Not anticipating an "overnight erasure," they call for "abolition as method" and challenge "reformers" to probe whether their proposals sustain or undermine the longevity of incarceration as a dominant mode of punishment.[38] As in centuries past, the effort to end one punishment is often coupled with suggested alternatives; some abolitionists focus on limiting state-based punishment in favor of community-generated restorative processes.

What reformers of the Enlightenment Age did not have to grapple with, but contemporary efforts do, are the millions of correctional workers whose livelihood depends on their jobs and will need redeployment akin to other sectors when industries die. What may help dismantle that enterprise is Mattick's point about the misfit of nineteenth-century methods to contemporary problems. The challenge is not only that prison has failed as a technique and is unsustainable as an industry but also that the current version does not fit what aspiring democratic orders demand of themselves in terms of punishing their members—which is my topic for this book's closing chapter.

30

REASONING FROM RUIN

INSIDE AND OUT

"Why this strange institution, the prison?" was Michel Foucault's point of departure for his lectures in the early 1970s on the "punitive society."[1] This book has responded to that question by crisscrossing the Atlantic to trace the ideas and political economy generating institutional infrastructures and laws entrenching imprisonment over centuries and the disruption produced after World War II, when universal commitments to rights emerged. The result is an ongoing struggle about the meaning of those commitments for incarcerated people.

Today's questions are: What now, and what next? For some punishment critics, the answer is abolition to end the incursions of detention. Yet as I write, the fragilities of democratic governance are in high relief, with attacks on voting, equal treatment, the rule of law, and the concept that all persons have rights and merit respect. Rather than abandon the process of "statization" that turned governments into service providers and drove new ideas about treating people fairly and equally, revitalization is needed. When crimes are committed, government *obligations* flow to the people bearing the immediate brunt, to the wrongdoers, and to the body politic. Governments bear the burden of shaping sanctions that recognize the participatory rights and equal status of all members of its social order, detained or not. Instead of continuing to create a class of "carceral citizens," governments have to recognize the punished as peers in an (ever aspiring to be) egalitarian democratic order. These ideas are the basis for my proffer of the *anti-ruination principle* I introduced at the outset and with which I close.

Honoring the personhood of all individuals, including the incarcerated, requires rejecting their "ruin" as a purpose or as a consequence of incarceration. That negative injunction produces positive obligations not to leave people in disabling conditions injurious to individuals, families, communities, corrections staff, and the body politic. In the United States, many jurists have rejected these propositions. This disdain is a reminder that reasoning, as I do, from the rights and status of detained people must not ignore Jeremy Bentham's insights about the role emotions play in punishment practices. Buffering against *ruination* entails distinguishing separation from degradation and making incarcerated people more "eligible" for government assistance than others. And, as Bentham said, doing so is *emotively* complex because of a felt unfairness that people who have done harm get benefits that others do not.

Although Bentham sketched a dichotomy between retributive and humanitarian impulses, I believe one can *both* "begrudge" (his word) the resources flowing to people convicted of crimes and see the necessity (from legality, morality, and utility) of doing so. Because prisoners are dependent on the state that incarcerates them, they have more "eligibility" (again Bentham's term) to receive services than those who are free. The ways to mitigate the distress at having to do more for the incarcerated are to incarcerate rarely, incarcerate differently, and give to others in need.

AN UNDER-UTILIZED PENOLOGICAL PURPOSE: ANTI-RUINATION

Like everything else in this book, concern about the power of the state to ruin a person has a history. The word "ruin" has been used to explain why the English prohibited the imposition of "excessive fines"; the point was to limit the King's power to defeat potential rivals by draining their assets. The proposition appeared to have also protected the livelihood ("contenement," "wainage," or "merchandise") of people of more limited means. In 1791, that precept became part of the US Constitution. In addition to prohibiting "cruel and unusual punishment," the Eighth Amendment states that "Excessive bail shall not be required nor excessive fines imposed." Although the Supreme Court determined in the 1960s that bans on cruel and unusual punishment constrained *states* as well as the *federal* government, not until 2019 did the Court conclude that the Excessive Fines Clause likewise limited state as well as federal power. Justice Thomas' concurrence described that Clause's history, traced back to the Magna Carta and embedded in the Constitution, as an aspect of a "fundamental right of citizenship." His examples of harms caused by severe economic penalties included the Black Codes enacted to reiterate slavery's oppression when the Fourteenth Amendment was ratified.[2]

To be clear, "ruin's" buffer against excessive fines existed in eras when punishments of branding, transportation, and execution were common. Eighteenth-century commentaries proffered a utilitarian rationale for the incongruity that governments could end a person's life yet not "ruin" a person economically. Benjamin Franklin wrote that taking property necessary for a person to subsist made him dependent on others, which undermined public welfare.[3] Although as discussed, many Enlightenment ideas about state punishment—deterrence, incapacitation, retribution, and reformation/rehabilitation—became part of the US constitutional law addressing punishment, preventing ruination has not (yet) been regularly invoked other than in the context of economic injury. Nonetheless, an anti-ruination principle explains some of what Supreme Court law requires. One could read the formulation of a "life's necessities" test as recognizing a minimal version—that governments cannot aim to undermine a person's physical and mental capacities by depriving them of food, sanitation, and clothing. A more robust expression is the interpretation of the Eighth Amendment to entail an affirmative mandate for health care.

Moreover, some lower courts' judges discussed anti-ruination (not by name) in the 1970s, when addressing whether prisons were fulfilling obligations to rehabilitate, which was one of the penological purposes Supreme Court justices then cited. Recall that

Chief Judge Henley in *Holt II* discussed the absence of programs and activities as part of what made Arkansas' prisons unconstitutional. As also mentioned, a federal judge in New Hampshire said more: Leaving people idle and "warehoused" caused "physical, mental, and social degeneration." He mandated programs and activities to buffer against deterioration.[4] Parallel concerns were expressed in lawsuits about the involuntary civil confinement of individuals. Although some jurists took a minimalistic approach (states had to provide a "tolerable living environment" that included protection from assault, medical care, food, heat, and hygiene), Judge Frank Johnson posited a right to "adequate treatment from a medical standpoint." The right to habilitation aimed to preserve skills people possessed upon entering forced confinement.[5] Those decisions and media exposés were part of a national movement that succeeded in shuttering large facilities holding people with limited mental and physical capacities. That deinstitutionalization was not, however, accompanied by resources sufficient to provide support in community settings. Nor did comparable accounts of violent disabling conditions—such as in Arkansas—result in closing prisons.

Reasoning from anti-ruination is distinct from "rehabilitation," even if (as explained) rehabilitation as a constitutional obligation could have been the harbinger of a regime committed to anti-ruination. Yet the term rehabilitation implies a *rescue* rather than recognition of the capacities of people in detention. Ruination, in contrast, describes both the power of governments *to harm* and its *impact* on those punished. The underlying proposition is that people enter prison with skills and experiences to be respected; they have agency, aspirations, and knowledge. Learning how to help them thrive outside of prison entails working with, not "on," them. (This approach dovetails with altering policing through a reorientation towards harm reduction, safer environments, and lessening racial inequalities.[6]) Building anti-ruination into punishment requires understanding it as a constraint *on* other punishment purposes (such as deterrence and incapacitation) as well as a goal *of* punishment, which is to respect individuals' autonomy and maintain well-being.

One possibility is that prison *is* ruination and therefore must end. Since Jeremy Bentham, punishment theorists have worried about leaving "lasting injury" and "permanent marks" on people. Rejecting disfigurement, Bentham argued that punishment's point was to deter behavior ("the offense") and not to villainize "the offender." Prison may well be unsustainable on the metric of not imposing ruin, lasting injuries, and permanent marks. An extensive literature has demonstrated the destructiveness of incarceration. Michel Foucault is one standard-bearer, analyzing the omnipresent surveillance that undermines individuals' autonomy. Dozens of social scientists have since documented the harms to health, the fears imprisonment produces, the anxiety of its indeterminacy, the disabling lack of agency, the micro-assaults and humiliation, the isolation from ordinary life, and staff arbitrariness. To capture those intrusions, Ben Crewe and others add "depth," "weight," and "tightness" to punishment's vocabulary to reflect overbearing efforts at control, the numbers of rules that could be breached, the dynamics of uncertainty, and the miserable dependency.[7]

For those such as myself who pause at total abolition of all forms of detention, the concern is not only the challenges of the politics of obtaining endorsement of prison's end but also that putting some form of confinement in place marks the radical injuries caused by an individual. Yet today's massive incarceration depends on criminalizing too many actions; the issue of what to criminalize has produced a large literature mapping changing mores over time. Recent examples of efforts to express the wrongfulness of acts include criminalization of police and family violence and of interfering with elections, just as decriminalization of drug consumption and alcohol denotes changing views of the harms flowing from sanctions for such acts.

Generating forms of incarceration that do not ruin is the aim (albeit again not by using the term ruin) of the European Prison Rules and the 2015 UN Nelson Mandela Rules. In Europe, key principles are "normalisation" and "regularisation"; prison life should approximate community life, including for people with long sentences. The Mandela Rules speak in terms of minimizing the "difference" between prison life and "life at liberty."[8]

Again, these efforts have antecedents. As I discussed, from Paul Cornil in the 1950s onward, many have put forward the propositions that incarcerated individuals retain all rights, except for what prison "requires." As also discussed, who decides what rights to discount determines the permissible-in-punishment. However rocky in practice, the point is to measure prison life against life in the community to approximate the normalcy of free movement. In contrast, US Supreme Court justices have used their own assumptions about life *inside* prisons as the baseline. Without explanation or empiricism, they have deemed isolation to be an "ordinary" hardship, as distinct from an "atypical and significant hardship." By taking in-prison degradation for granted, they helped make it commonplace.

MORE OR LESS "ELIGIBILITY"

This practice of comparing people in and out of detention dates back at least to Jeremy Bentham who, even as he was clear that jailors had to provide food, shelter, and health care for detained people, worried about making life in prison attractive to "the poorest class," whom he thought were those likely to be incarcerated. By setting forth a series of precepts and rationales, Bentham worked through this problem in his "plan of management" for his proposed 1790s Panopticon.

Bentham's "Rule of Severity" meant that, aside from "regard due to life, health, and bodily ease, the ordinary condition of a convict doomed to a punishment which few or none but individuals of the poorest class are apt to incur, ought not to be made *more eligible* than that of the poorest class of subjects in a state of innocence and liberty" (my italics). His countervailing "Rule of Lenity" was that a person "doomed to forced labor for a length of time, ought not to be attended with bodily sufferance, or prejudicial, or dangerous to health or life." Under the "Rule of Economy," prisoners had to work so that the state would not incur costs for "the sake either of punishment or of indulgence." Moreover, prisons were to create incentives through discipline to prevent misbehavior ("prison-offenses") as well as to preserve "decency" and avoid "undue hardships . . . of design or negligence."[9]

Bentham specifically called for clean "quarters," food, clothing, heat, and medicine to preserve health and safety, privacy for incarcerated women, and means for prisoners to learn to support themselves ("future subsistence") so as not to commit crimes. Bentham understood that implementation of his rules could result in some prisoners being *better off* than individuals not incarcerated, which is where his "no less eligible" (sometimes referenced as "no more eligible") analysis came into play. As Philip Schofield explained in his guide for readers whom Bentham "perplexed," Bentham's precepts meant that prisoners would be given necessities that not all "of the poorest class" had, including as much food as desired, albeit the cheapest available. Bentham justified the differential treatment: Even if the "innocent poor" did not have as much, they had the "liberty of choosing" their food.[10] Moreover, were the government to shorten prisoners' lives through deprivations, the executive would have converted Parliament's prison sentences into death sentences that had not been imposed for a particular offense. In addition, if prison officials failed to provide basics, Bentham advised, the results would be excessively severe and disproportionate.[11]

Bentham's worse off / better off quandary has echoed ever since, as correctional professionals, judges, legislators, and others considered conditions of confinement. Recall that delegates to the IPPC in the 1930s and the UN in the 1950s addressed whether mandates for adequate food, clothing, and health care ought to apply in the colonies; the question was whether prisons would offer a higher standard of living than on the streets, where the population had been depleted economically by unapologetic imperialism. Thereafter, when prisoners had "rights," the allocation of billions of taxpayer dollars concretized (pun intended) Bentham's "less eligible / more eligible" problem. States had to provide food and shelter for the incarcerated when it did not for others. Resentment at doing so was commonplace; as I quoted, an Arkansas reporter in 1989 bemoaned that prisoners, less deserving than others, had "gobble[d] up" resources.[12]

Bentham's more/less eligible point not only explains why "giving" prisoners annoys some people, it also illuminates that practices *outside* of prisons are critical determinants of in-prison treatment. In some countries (my examples come from Europe), people are provided with support for housing, education, health care, and food. When I visited a prison in Luxembourg, prisoners were given a few Euros each month; when I entered a facility in France weeks before an election, I saw the wall poster, "En 2017, Votez!" (Vote in 2017), reproduced in figure 30.1. My hosts explained that giving people

Élections présidentielles 2017

EN 2017, VOTEZ !

Le Président de la République est élu, au suffrage universel direct, par les électeurs français lors de l'élection présidentielle. Son mandat dure 5 ans et est renouvelable une fois.

Selon l'article 5 de la Constitution, le président de la République incarne l'autorité de l'État. Il veille, par son arbitrage, au respect du texte constitutionnel, et assure le fonctionnement normal des pouvoirs publics et la continuité de l'État. Il est le chef des armées et désigne seul le premier ministre. Les autres ministres sont choisis par le chef de l'État et le premier ministre.

S'inscrire dès maintenant !

Pour pouvoir voter, vous devez :
-être de nationalité française
-avoir une pièce d'identité en cours de validité
-être inscrits sur les listes électorales
-ne pas être déchu de votre capacité électorale

Dès à présent, vous devez :
-vérifier la validité de votre carte identité
-vous inscrire sur les listes électorales (fin de inscriptions le 31/12/2016)

Inscription sur les listes électorales : L'inscription se fait auprès de la mairie de votre domicile ou de la mairie de Réau si vous êtes incarcéré au CPSF depuis au moins 6 mois. Si vous ne disposez pas d'un domicile, vous pouvez vous faire domicilier à l'établissement. Pour obtenir de l'aide dans votre démarche, écrivez en courrier interne au point d'accès au droit.

Modalités du vote : Vous pourrez voter en sollicitant une permission de sortir ou par procuration (auprès d'une personne inscrite sur la même liste électorale que vous). Un officier de police judiciaire viendra au CPSF pour établir une telle procuration. Pour faire une demande de procuration, vous devrez écrire au greffe.

Une information collective sera organisée courant 2016 par le point d'accès au droit et le SPIP. Les informations vous seront transmises ultérieurement.

FIGURE 30.1 Poster, *En 2017, Votez!*, from a French prison in 2017

Euros and encouraging them to vote were routine aspects of life for everyone and hence part of the "normalisation" and "regularization" to assimilate life in prison to life outside prison.[13] What some European systems have offered (if sustainable in light of ongoing wars and the rise of illiberalism) is that, in and out of prison, governments identify themselves as having a long-term *relationship* with their populations that entailed provisioning.

Like other Enlightenment approaches, Bentham's point about more/less eligibility needs to be refurbished in this rights-status era. Acceptance of the proposition of equal status makes decisions about punishment *harder* because the state itself must fulfill its obligation of expressing the wrongness of acts of violence, aggression, and exploitation without violating its parallel obligation to shape a fair and just social order. Efforts to forge a path forward can be found in a 2014 task force, commissioned by the US National Academy of Sciences. That group recognized that, when imposing limits on the autonomy of a subset of individuals found culpable of harming individuals and the public, the goal was to be as minimally intrusive on freedom as possible. "Parsimony as a restraint on punishment" was its precept.[14]

Yet parsimony, while necessary, does not suffice. When governments take individuals away from their homes and create an alternative place to live, they have an ominous past to escape—the legacies of slavery and of concentration camps aiming to extinguish individuals' autonomy. Moreover, they have a burden to shoulder, which is to recognize the person as a member of the social order. Doing so not only limits the "ruin" of people in prison, it aims to curb ruination of the social order.

The decision to imprison thus imposes a price tag of provisioning that in some countries would be described as *equal eligibility* and in others *equal-plus* when prisoners, dependent on the state, would get more than free people. This analysis illuminates the specific challenges in the United States, sometimes identified as its "exceptionalism," explained as mixing its history of enslavement with US individualism and entrepreneurialism to generate a uniquely punitive system. However, such an *essentialist* approach, equating a jurisdiction with a specific policy, ignores the relevance of time and political leadership that has altered attitudes towards a host of government practices, incarceration included.

As my transatlantic history illuminated, many "civilized" countries imposed grotesque punishments. The photograph of the 1902 English "treadwheel" in which caged men were forced to walk endless hours on a revolving set of steps is but one example. Moreover, IPC/IPPC congresses from 1872 to 1950 entailed discussions of comparative punishment practices. During the first decades of the twentieth century, Germany was a font of "penal welfarism" to expand social service content, which crashed with the 1933 Nazi takeover. As for the United States, assessing its liberality as compared to approaches of other countries depends on the era and which of the states' prison systems is described. When the twentieth century began, the United States joined several other common-law jurisdictions in shaping conditional release programs such as probation and parole, in building "open prisons" without perimeter barriers, and at times in reducing the length of sentences. Yet on both sides of the Atlantic, leaders of prisons embraced eugenics.

Thereafter, the United States in the 1970s offered a glimpse at what could have led to a set of practices far different from those today. The number of individuals in prison declined in the late 1960s before politics propelled a racialized rise in prosecutions, in punitive policies targeting low-income communities, and in federal courts withdrawal of oversight. Politics were vivid when Congress lent its weight to that retreat through its 1996 Prison Litigation Reform Act and its new restrictions on habeas corpus. Since the 1980s, the United States has distinguished itself in its rates of incarceration of people, who are disproportionately of color and economically marginal, in its insistence on licensing the use of the death penalty, in its impoverished social services for people not incarcerated, and in its self-exclusion from transnational human rights accords, including on the rights of children and to combat discrimination against women.[15]

Likewise, while I have used some examples from Europe, its prisons are not an idyllic paradigm for incarceration. Didier Fassin's

2016 account, *Prison Worlds: An Ethnography of the Carceral Condition*, based on four years of in-prison observations, explained prisons were an "institution for the poor" and a "poor institution" to which people were consigned to "the emptiness" of time spent there. Emma Kaufman chronicled the treatment ("punish and expel") of non-citizens in England's prison and the roles race, ethnicity, and class play in populating European prisons and detention centers. In chapter 29, I discussed deteriorating prison conditions documented in recent years in England and France. Moving to the globe, by 2023, one account tallied 11.5 million people incarcerated, many were held in "deplorable conditions" despite the overlay of international human rights.[16]

In sum, central to lessening targeted harms to subpopulations and reducing the miseries of prison conditions are political commitments to all members of their population. As Nicola Lacey explained in 2007 in *The Prisoners' Dilemma*, some European countries were then turning to incarceration ("penal populism") as a facet of social policies aiming at control. Given that criminal law enforcement is not "an autonomous area of governance," countries that used it less and less harshly were those providing more support in general. Lacey cited data that political orders with "higher levels of social solidarity and trust" (sometimes stemming from the homogeneity of their populations) focused more on "reconciliation" and less on retaliatory punishment. Institutional support for solidarity, in turn, was related to the kind of capital market a country had and its efforts at coordinated, long-term investments, made in recognition of the mutual dependency of various sectors and the value of ongoing relationships.[17] The various approaches within the United States during the eras chronicled here serve as reminders that "national character" is a slippery concept. Politics, intersecting with histories of racial and class discrimination, produce punishment practices. Anti-ruination of individuals and social orders entails turning imprisonment into a rare event and responding to people's needs *outside*, as well as *inside*, prisons.

MOVING FORWARD

I have argued that decisions about punishment should not be delegated to a group of people called prison directors, nor should authority reside with medical professionals. Indeed, as I explained, calling for a doctor's assessment of a person's ability to withstand a punishment is evidence enough to ban it. Rather than a "science" predicated on expertise of various sorts, a host of political, social and (thanks to Winston Talley, Thomas X Cooper, and others) *legal* choices have to be made about the forms of punishment democracies can impose. Moreover, in terms of safekeeping for people in or outside of prison, the record is abysmal. As discussed, homicide rates and deaths from other causes *inside* US prisons are high; the acknowledged undercount of the lives lost and of the harms inflicted mean that the hegemonic control of corrections and the ever-present *prison discount* that cabins rights in the name of "security, discipline, and good order" should come to an end.

Limiting the breadth of bureaucratic authority in the name of democratic commitments should not be equated with a call for its replacement with majoritarian rule about the quantum of punishment to inflict. Anxieties about disorder and violence on the streets and in prisons have regularly been enlisted to frame arguments in politics to garner support for harsh, repressive measures. The words "democratic" and "political" have many meanings. In this book, I have shown that punishment choices are embedded in political systems and that, in democratic orders, acknowledgment of all members' equality must be reflected in the treatment of detained people. Further, to call for limited delegations of authority to prison officials is not to ignore their contributions or reject their participation in forging new practices. The development of relational obligations in criminal law enforcement emerged with curbs on policing and corrections in the second half of the twentieth century, as did a "victim's rights" movement. The concept of involving victims, perpetrators, and their communities, while not ceding the state's role as the final arbiter, should be part of the agenda of reconceiving punishment practices.

The bottom line of this long book is that the punishment system we inhabit was built through decisions authorizing stunning
incursions on individuals. Its practices need to be upended so as
to prevent the "lasting injury" and "permanent marks" inflicted on
individuals and on the body politic. The legion of prisoners I have
centered on generated a movement that has succeeded to the extent
that governments acknowledge they are punishing people who are
rights-bearing members of their polity. Ending whipping was a first
step in limiting the corporal incursions of incarceration. Doing so
entailed a shift in perspective, moving from what the state wanted
to do to what the people punished experienced.

These pioneering prisoners began to *shackle* the sovereign to its
own democratic commitments to treat each person as an equal.
That obligation does not end the government's authority to punish but revises what constitutes a legitimate state purpose when
punishing. Given that people are equals, the state cannot set out
to undercut that status by diminishing their capacity to function.
Punishment practices must prevent ruination and, as Judge Doyle
put it decades ago, prisons, to the extent they continue to be used,
have to change.

ACKNOWLEDGMENTS AND NOTES ON SOURCES

I have many thanks to give and sources to explain. Support for research came from Carnegie Corporation which awarded me an Andrew Carnegie Fellowship; from the Oscar M. Ruebhausen Fund at Yale Law School which enabled me to obtain archival materials, images, and digital enhancements; and from Yale Law School which has provided me with a genuine home for my work. The Lillian Goldman Library, under the guidance of Teresa Miguel-Stearns and now Femi Cadmus and with advice from Fred Shapiro and Kathryn James, has given me a remarkable education.

I have benefited from discussions in workshops and conferences at Yale Law School, the University of Alabama School of Law, Columbia Law School, Georgia State University, Northwestern Pritzker School of Law, Princeton University, Sciences Po, and the Collège de France. In addition, many colleagues shared insights about punishment's parameters and read drafts of this book and of related articles. Special thanks are due to Muneer Ahmad, Andrea Armstrong, Dwayne Betts, Jenny Carroll, Marta Cartabia, Brett Dignam, Fiona Doherty, Justin Driver, Didier Fassin, William Forbath, Kellen Funk, Nancy Gertner, Miriam Gohara, Michael Graetz, Linda Greenhouse, Brenda Hale, Bernard Harcourt, Elizabeth Hinton, Vicki Jackson, Johanna Kalb, Leora Dahan Katz, Emma Kaufman, John Langbein, Courtney Long, Timothy Lytton, Allegra McLeod, David Menschel, Hope Metcalf, Jamelia Morgan, Robert Post, David Rudovsky, Freek Schmidt, Philip

Schofield, Jed Shugerman, Reva Siegel, Dirk van Zyl Smit, Caleb Smith, Jennifer Taylor, Myron Thompson, Anna VanCleave, Patrick Weil, John Witt, Gideon Yaffe, and Ekow Yankah. Extra help came from Alice Kaplan and Patrick Weil guiding me on research about the French Communist party; John Witt reviewing my account of Francis Lieber; Martin Conway clarifying decisions by Belgian officials in and after World War II; Sandy Baum and Laura Geller's helpful feedback on accessibility of my account; and Emily Bazelon sharpening the narrative. When writing about Jeremy Bentham, I am always in debt to Philip Schofield, who heads the UCL Bentham Project and provided me with a roadmap to resources and reviewed my analyses, as did UCL's Tim Causer. A visit to the Centre Bentham in Paris was likewise enriching; thanks to Anne Brunon-Ernst and Emmanuelle de Champs for commenting on draft chapters.

Denny Curtis, Dirk Hartog, and Dirk van Zyl Smit, along with the Press' anonymous reviewers, read the many chapters (often more than once); their reactions enabled me to deepen my analyses. Charles Myers, who guided this book until his retirement as an editor, was a patient interlocutor, kindly pressing me to clarify the threads that weave the chapters of this book together. Thereafter, Sara Doskow at the Press brought this book to conclusion, and Erika Barrios and Rosemary Frehe assisted in moving the manuscript through publication. Wendy Strothman, my agent, forged the link to the Press and advised me on the shape this work should take. Through her indexing, Enid Zafrin made the book's contents accessible.

Obtaining usable images was an undertaking made easier by Jeanne Criscola; her expertise in graphic arts made old newspaper print and photography legible, and she conformed each image to Press specifications. Bruce Jackson—professor, filmmaker, and photographer—generously provided prints and permission to use his pictures of Cummins Farm in the 1970s. Ernie Dumas, a veteran Arkansas journalist, put me in touch with the Arkansas newspaper editors Walter Husman Jr. and Eliza Hussman Gaines, who enabled me to reproduce materials from the *Arkansas Democrat* and *Arkansas Gazette*. Permission to use a photograph from the International Penal Penitentiary Commission (IPPC) came from the leadership of the International Penal and Penitentiary Foundation. The United Nations' New York City archives authorized reproduction of documents found in the IPPC's boxes that it houses, and I navigated that collection with help from Lucie Olejnikova, Associate Director for Foreign and International Law at Yale's Law Library. Help with digitalization came from Jason Eiseman, Associate Director for Administration of the Yale Law Library, who also directed my compilation of voluminous materials culled from the United Nations, Arkansas' libraries, the National Archives, the Library of Congress, Sterling Library at Yale, and the Modern Records Centre at the University of Warwick, which houses the Howard League for Penal Reform. I made my way to many of these materials because of efforts by Michael VanderHeijden, the Head of Reference at Yale's Law Library, and Julian Aiken, the Digital Repository and Open Scholarship Librarian. Yale's Rare Book Librarian Kathryn James, who had been at Yale's Beinecke Rare Book and Manuscript Library, enabled me to find and use several items from both collections. Somerville College, University of Oxford made possible reproduction of Margery Fry's portrait painted by her brother, Roger Fry.

When Director of Rhode Island's corrections department, A. T. Wall joined me in teaching a class on incarceration. As Chair of the Association of State Administrators (ASCA, renamed the Correctional Leaders Association, CLA), Wall and ASCA's staff, George and Camille Camp, welcomed me and my students to meetings and launched a joint, decade-long venture with the Liman Center at Yale Law School to collect data on the use of solitary confinement. Working with several directors of prison systems, including Leann Bertsch, Gary Mohr, Rick Raemisch, and Bernie Warner, I gained insights into their concerns and innovations. Decades earlier, Norman Dorsen and Sylvia Law at NYU School of Law supported my interest in protecting liberties and rights for people in detention.

Archivists in Little Rock, Arkansas were welcoming and generous with their time and resources; I was guided to them by Scott Stern. Thanks are due to staff from 2019—Director David Stricklin of the Butler Center for Arkansas Studies in the Central Arkansas Library System; Laura McClellan, Assistant Director of the Center for Arkansas History and Culture of the University of Arkansas at Little Rock (UALR); Shannon Marie Lausch, Multimedia Archivist, and Kaye M. Lundgren, Archival Assistant at UALR; Sarah Cohen, Registrar of the Old State House Museum in Little Rock; Lauren Jarvis, Archival Manager for Public Services at the Arkansas State Archives; Natalie Marlin, Senior Librarian at the Arkansas State Library; Ava Hicks, Director of the Arkansas Supreme Court Library; and Holli North, Records Supervisor at the Arkansas Supreme Court. I also met with some participants and relatives of those involved in the Arkansas prison litigation. I appreciate the input from Kate and Jesse Askew, Ernest Dumas, Jack Holt Jr., Jerry Jackson, Philip Kaplan, Linwood Jackson, and Jeanette Jackson. I was able to visit Cummins prison because Wendy Kelley, then directing Arkansas' Department of Correction (ADC), authorized my entry. There, I met Dale Reed, who was Chief Deputy Director of the ADC; William Straughn, the Superintendent of the Cummins unit; and a few staff members who provided a brief tour of the facility. This book has also been informed by my visits to many other prisons, including when representing individuals in the federal system and when visiting institutions in England, France, and Luxembourg.

Yale Law School staff were great help; thanks to Bonnie Posick, Kelly Mangs-Hernandez, and Vanesa Suarez. Current and former students joined in research, translations, and analyses; they include Hirsa Amin, Sophie Angelis, Lucía Baca, Griffin Black, Alyssa Chan, Kevin Cheng, Greg Conyers, Kayla Crowell, Jenn Dikler, Ellie Driscoll, Elle Eshleman, Avital Fried, John Giammatteo, Jonathan Gibson, Natalie Giotta, Jordan Gonzalez, Wynne Muscatine Graham, Megan Hauptman, Remington Hill, Jessica Huang, Sonya Jacobs, Amit Jain, Broderick Johnson, Laura Kokotailo, Lydia Laramore, Catherine Lee, Caroline Lefever, Adela Lilollari, Yixuan Liu, Layla Malamut, Catherine McCarthy, Brian McGrail, Aseem Mehta, Michael Morse, Emma Perez, Megha Ram, Alexandra Ricks, Laila Robbins, Katie Roop, Zoe Rubin, Upasna Saha, Hannah Schoen, Sarah Shapiro, Madeline Silva, Malina Simard-Halm, Scott Stern, Kelsey Stimson, Claire Stobb, Paige Underwood, Iva Velickovic,

Hannah Vester, Alex Wang, Annie Wang, Emily Wanger, Meredith Wheeler, David Wong, and Henry Wu; and Yale College undergraduates Kevin Bendesky, Esul Burton, Susan Chen, Melat Eskender, Joseph Gaylin, Ella Goldman, Frances Keohane, and Molly Shapiro. Special thanks are due to Tor Tarantola who joined Denny Curtis and me on a trip to Arkansas and helped database thousands of pages of documents on top of extensive research. Extra shout-outs are in order for Russell Bogue, Jessica Boutchie, Romina Lilollari, Zoë Mermelstein, Anna Selbrede, and Shunhe Wang, who brought the manuscript to its close.

In terms of the many sources cited in endnotes, I identify them in the form used by the specific collection. The IPPC's archives in New York are organized by record series, box, file number, title, and date. Materials on the Howard League, held at Warwick University Library's Special Collections (and some at Harvard University), are identified by reference number, title, and date. The federal litigation materials preserved in the National Archives and Records Administration (NARA) are located by case name, docket, box, and accession number or reference group. Some filings in lawsuits are available through the University of Michigan Law School's Civil Rights Litigation Clearinghouse. Papers from ACLU lawyer Charles Morgan are archived in the Making of Modern Law (MoML) ACLU Papers, held at the Seeley G. Mudd Manuscript Library at Princeton University. The Honorable David Bazelon's Papers are held at the Archives and Special Collections Department of Biddle Law Library at the University of Pennsylvania. The Honorable Oren Harris Supplementary Papers in the Special Collections Department of the University of Arkansas Libraries are catalogued by series, box, and folder number. The Eighth Circuit made available the oral history of the Honorable Thomas Eisele and the Honorable J. Smith Henley. Hans von Hentig's Papers can be found at the University of Colorado Boulder Library's Special Collection and Archives. Materials from Carnegie Foundation Archives were provided by Jeanne D'Onofrio, then Chief of Staff in the President's Office of Carnegie Corporation of New York. Yale's Sterling Library is the repository of the Papers of Justices Abe Fortas, William O. Douglas, and Potter Stewart. The

Library of Congress hosts the Papers of Justices Harry Blackmun, Thurgood Marshall, John Paul Stevens, Byron White, and Chief Justice Earl Warren. Justice Lewis Powell's papers are available through the Washington & Lee University School of Law Scholarly Commons.

The University of Arkansas at Little Rock (UALR) has several collections I used. The Philip E. Kaplan Papers, 1932–2007, at the UALR Center for History and Culture include litigation materials, organized by series, subseries, box, and folder number, as well as title and date; the Winthrop Paul Rockefeller Papers, 1912–1973, by record group, box, file number, title, and date; the C. Robert Sarver Papers, 1928–1989, by series, box, file number, title, and date; the G. Thomas Eisele Papers, 1962–1970, by box, folder number, title, and date. The Butler Center for Arkansas Studies at the Central Arkansas Library System hosts other collections I used. The John H. Haley papers, 1917–1974, are organized by series, box, folder number, title, and date; the Laura Cornelius Conner Papers, 1921–1924, at Butler, are by box, folder number, title, and date. In addition, the Arkansas State Prison Records, 1967–1993, are at the Arkansas State Archives, and Arkansas Department of Corrections' Reports in the State Library. I also drew heavily on newspapers, some on Newspapers.com and GenealogyBank.com. Some editions of the Arkansas prisoner publications—the *Pea Pickers Picayune* and the *Cummins Journal*—are available on JSTOR; copies of some *Pea Pickers Picayune* are also in UALR's Rockefeller Papers.

In addition, an array of authors—some incarcerated and some not—have informed this book. Citations in the endnotes are my way of saying thank you.

NOTES

INTRODUCTION

1. Jackson v. Bishop, 404 F.2d 571, 579–80 (8th Cir. 1968).
2. Those events were the backdrop to Arkansas' prison litigation. Ernest Dumas, *The Education of Ernie Dumas: Chronicles of the Arkansas Political Mind* (Butler Ctr. Books, 2019); Carlotta Walls LaNier, *A Mighty Long Way: My Journal to Justice at Little Rock Central High School* (One World Books, 2010); Karen Anderson, *Little Rock: Race and Resistance at Central High School* (Princeton U. Press, 2010).
3. *Imprisoned Intellectuals: America's Political Prisoners Write on Life, Liberation, and Rebellion* (Joy James ed., Rowman & Littlefield, 2003). A contemporary counterpart is Dwayne Betts, *A Question of Freedom: A Memoir of Learning, Survival, and Coming of Age in Prison* (Avery Publ. Grp., 2010).
4. Lee v. Washington, 390 US 333, 334 (1968) (Justice Black, joined by Justices Harlan and Stewart, concurring).
5. David M. Oshinsky, *"Worse Than Slavery": Parchman Farm and the Ordeal of Jim Crow Justice* (Free Press, 1997); Larry Yackle, *Reform and Regret: The Story of Federal Judicial Involvement in the Alabama Prison System* (Oxford U. Press, 1989); Malcolm M. Feeley & Edward L. Rubin, *Judicial Policy Making and the Modern State: How the Courts Reformed America's Prisons* (Cambridge U. Press, 2000).
6. Ruffin v. Commonwealth, 62 Va. 790, 796 (1871).
7. Michel Foucault, *Discipline and Punish: The Birth of the Prison* (Alan Sheridan trans., Vintage Books, 1977).
8. Ruth Gilmore, *Golden Gulag: Prisons, Surplus, Crisis, and Opposition in Globalizing California* (U. Cal. Press, 2007); Tony Messenger, *Profit and Prison: How America Criminalizes the Poor in the Name of Justice* (St. Martin's Press, 2021).
9. Susan Mettler, *Dividing Citizens: Gender and Federalism in New Deal Public Policy* (Cornell U. Press, 1998); Elizabeth Hinton, *From the War on Poverty to the War on Crime: The Making of Mass Incarceration in America* (Harvard U. Press, 2016); Joseph Fishkin & William E. Forbath, *The Anti-Oligarchy Constitution* (Harvard U. Press, 2022).

10. Richard Rothstein, *The Color of Law* (Liveright, 2017); Jeffrey Fagan, Valerie West & Jan Holland, *Reciprocal Effects of Crime and Incarceration in New York City Neighborhoods*, 30 Fordham Urb. L. J. 1551 (2002).

11. Albert Woodfox, *Solitary: Unbroken by Four Decades in Solitary Confinement. My Story of Transformation and Hope*, v, xiii (Grove Press, 2019).

12. *Attica: The Official Report of the New York State Special Commission on Attica*, xix (Bantam Books, 1972); Heather Thompson, *Blood in the Water: The Attica Prison Uprising and its Legacy* (Pantheon, 2016).

13. Michelle Alexander, *The New Jim Crow: Mass Incarceration in the Age of Color Blindness* (The New Press, 2010).

14. Rhodes v. Chapman, 452 US 337 (1981).

15. Correctional Leaders Association, Liman Center Public Interest. Yale Law School, *Time-In-Cell: The 2019 Snapshot* (2020); *Time-In-Cell: The 2021 Snapshot* (2022); Solitary Watch and the Unlock the Box Campaign, *Calculating Torture: Analysis of Federal, State, and Local Data Showing More than 122,000 People in Solitary Confinement in US Prisons and Jails*, 3–13 (May 2023).

16. Marie Gottschalk, *Caught: The Prison State and the Lockdown of American Politics* (Princeton U. Press, rev. ed. 2016).

17. Data sources for prison population include the Bureau of Justice Statistics, *Correctional Populations in the United States, 2022—Statistical Tables*, tbl. 1, US DOJ (2024); Wendy Sawyer & Peter Wagner, *Mass Incarceration: The Whole Pie 2024*, Prison Pol'y Initiative, Mar. 14, 2024.

18. Brendan Saloner, Kalind Parish & Julie Ward, *COVID-19 Cases and Deaths in Federal and State Prisons*, 6 JAMA 602 (2020); Julie A. Ward, Kalind Parish, Grace DiLaura, Sharon Dolovich & Brendan Saloner, *COVID-19 Cases among Employees of US Federal and State Prisons*, 60 Am. J. Preventive Med. 840, 841 (2021).

19. Bureau of Justice Statistics, *Probation and Parole in the United States, 2022*, US DOJ (2024); Leah Wang, *Punishment Beyond Prisons 2023*, Prison Pol'y Initiative, May 2023.

20. Fiona Doherty, *"Obey All Laws and Be Good": Probation and the Meaning of Recidivism*, 104 Geo. L. J. 291 (2016).

21. Williams v. Illinois, 399 US 235 (1970).

22. Angela Davis, *Are Prisons Obsolete?* (U. Cal. Press, 2003); Ruth Wilson Gilmore, *Abolition Geography: Essays Towards Liberation* (Verso Books, 2022); Tommie Shelby, *The Idea of Prison Abolition* (Princeton U. Press, 2022).

23. Timbs v. Indiana, 586 US 146, 151–54; 162–63 (2019) (Thomas, J., concurring).

24. Leora Dahan Katz, *Response Retributivism: Defending the Duty to Punish*, 40 L. & Phil. 585 (2021).

25. Mary Dudziak, *Cold War Civil Rights: Race and the Image of American Democracy* 3–6 (Princeton U. Press, 2000).

26. Wolff v. McDonnell, 418 US 539, 555–56 (1974).

27. Jeremy Bentham, Panopticon; Postscript, Part II: Principles and Plan of Management, 1787, published 1791, reprinted in *The Works of Jeremy Bentham* vol. 4, 122–25 (John Bowring ed., 1843).

PART 1

1. *The Emergence of Carceral Institutions: Prisons, Galleys and Lunatic Asylums, 1550–1900*, 2–7 (Pieter Spierenburg ed., Erasmus U., 1984); J. M. Beattie, *Crime and the Courts in England, 1660–1800*, 10–15 (Princeton U. Press, 1986).

CHAPTER 1

1. Matthew Pate & Laurie A. Gould, *Corporal Punishment around the World*, xvi (Praeger, 2012); Didier Fassin, *The Will to Punish*, 46–47 (Christopher Kutz ed., Oxford U. Press, 2018).

2. Myra C. Glenn, *Campaigns against Corporal Punishment: Prisoners, Sailors, Women, and Children in Antebellum America*, 8–9 (SUNY Press, 1984); Reva B. Siegel, *"The Rule of Love": Wife Beating as Prerogative and Privacy*, 105 Yale L. J. 2117, 2169 (1996).

3. Pierre Fouquet, *Nieuwe atlas, van de voornaamste gebouwen en gezigten der stad Amsterdam, met derzelver beknopte beschryvingen* [New atlas of the most prominent buildings and vistas of Amsterdam, with succinct descriptions] (approx. 1778). Fouquet commissioned artists, including Hendrick P. Schouten, who drew the Men's House of Correction. After engravings were made, Fouquet reached out in 1783 to booksellers to create sets of the prints. Freek Schmidt, *Passion and Control: Dutch Architectural Culture of the Eighteenth Century*, 165–66 (Routledge, 2016); Freek Schmidt, Building Discipline: Two Amsterdam Houses of Correction, *Public Buildings in Early Modern Europe*, 165–80 (Konrad Ottenheym, Monique Chatenet & Krista De Jonge eds., Brepols, 2010). London's 1550s facility is sometimes cited as Europe's first; Amsterdam was likely the first in continental Europe to authorize in 1589 a "house of correction," opened in 1596. Blake McKelvey, *American Prisons: A History of Good Intentions*, 2 (P. Smith, 1977); Thorsten Sellin, *Pioneering in Penology: The Amsterdam Houses of Corrections in the Sixteenth and Seventeenth Centuries*, 27–30 (U. Penn. Press, 1944); Max Grünhut, *Penal Reform: A Comparative Study* (Clarendon Press, 1948).

4. Schmidt, Building Discipline, 165, 170–74; Schmidt, *Passion and Control*, 167, 170–79, 189–90; Pieter Spierenburg, The Sociogenesis of Confinement and Its Development in Early Modern Europe, *The Emergence of Carceral Institutions: Prisons, Galleys and Lunatic Asylums 1550–1900*, 9–63 (Pieter Spierenburg ed., Erasmus Universiteit, 1984).

5. Schmidt, *Passion and Control*, 189–90.

6. Schmidt, Building Discipline, 165–71. Women were housed in the "Spinhuis," opened the following year.

7. Antony Duff, *Punishment, Communication and Community* (Oxford U. Press, 2001); Hugo Adam Bedau & Erin Kelly, Punishment, *Stanford Encyclopedia of Philosophy* (2015).

8. E. C. Wines, *The State of Prisons and of Child-Saving Institutions in The Civilized World*, 12 (Cambridge U. Press, 1880); Michael Ignatieff, *A Just Measure of Pain: The Penitentiary in the Industrial Revolution, 1750–1850*, 49, 57–58,

72–73 (Pantheon Books, 1978); Tessa West, *The Curious Mr. Howard*, 31 (Waterside Press, 2011).

9. John Howard, *The State of the Prisons in England and Wales: With Preliminary Observations, and an Account of Some Foreign Prisons*, 1, 78, 119, 152 (William Eyres, 1777); John Howard, *An Account of the Principal Lazarettos in Europe: With Various Papers Relative to the Plague, Together with Further Observations on Some Foreign Prisons and Hospitals, and Additional Remarks on the Present State of Those in Great Britain and Ireland*, 52–78 (J. Johnson, C. Dilly & T. Cadell, 2d ed., 1791); John Aikin, *A View of the Life, Travels, and Philanthropic Labors of the Late John Howard*, 57, 61 (W. W. Woodward, 1794).

10. J. M. Beattie, *Crime and the Courts in England, 1660–1800*, 572 (Princeton U. Press, 1986).

11. Jacob Hogg, "John Howard, Esq. Visiting and Relieving the Miseries of a Prison" (1790), gift of David Alexander, 20.2 (Yale Ctr. British Art, B1980); Courtney Long, *Captive Bodies—Exhibition Text for* George Romney's "Howard Visiting a Prison," 1780–1785 (Yale Art Gallery, 2018).

12. Beattie, 573–76; Simon Devereaux, *The Making of the Penitentiary Act, 1775–1779*, 42 Hist. J. 405 (1999). One example was the Norfolk Prison, constructed in 1784.

13. Cesare Beccaria, *On Crimes and Punishments*, 1764 (Graeme R. Newman & Pietro Marongiu trans., Transaction Publishers, 2009); Cesare Beccaria, *On Crimes and Punishments, 1764* (Henry Paolucci trans., Macmillan, 1963); Cesare Beccaria, *On Crimes and Punishment, 1764* (Aaron Thomas & Jeremy Parzen trans., Toronto Press, 2008); Philip Schofield, *The First Steps Rightly Directed to the Track of Legislation: Jeremy Bentham on Cesare Beccaria's Essay on Crimes and Punishments*, 4 Diciottesimo Secolo 65, 66 (2019); Schmidt, *Passion and Control*, 178.

14. Bentham had access to a 1767 English version using the phrasing "the greatest happiness of the greatest number." Closer to Beccaria's original was "the greatest happiness shared among the greatest number." Schofield, *Bentham on Beccaria*, 67.

15. Beccaria / Newman & Marongiu, xxvii, xvi–xxx.

16. Beccaria/Paolucci, 44, 50.

17. Beccaria/Paolucci, 10, 43, 55, 99.

18. Beccaria/Paolucci, 48.

19. Sajjad Safaei, *Foucault's Bentham: Fact or Fiction? Dissecting a Perverse Fixation*, 35 Int'l J. Pol. Culture & Soc'y 47 (2020); Schofield, *Bentham on Beccaria*, 66–71.

20. A project, begun in 1959, aims to compile "a new and authoritative edition of Bentham's works, largely based on the manuscripts" to supersede the Bowring edition and augment materials posed on the UCL Bentham website. More than twenty volumes have been published, with dozens to come. Bentham Manuscripts, University College London (UCL).

21. *UCL's Jeremy Bentham Joins Exhibition in New York*, UCL News, Feb. 14, 2018.

22. Auto-Icon: Further Uses of the Dead to the Living, A Fragment from the MSS of Jeremy Bentham (not published), forthcoming with edits by Prof. Tim Causer of the UCL Bentham Project; Philip Schofield, Introduction, *Bentham and the Arts*, 1–19 (Anthony Julius, Malcolm Quinn & Philip Schofield eds., UCL Press, 2020); Carolyn Shapiro, Bentham's Image: The Corpo-Reality Check, *Bentham and the Arts*, 270–88; Chris Haffenden, *Every Man His Own Monument: Self-Monumentalizing in Romantic Britain*, 40–91 (Uppsala Universitet, 2018).

23. Jeremy Bentham, A View of the Hard-Labour Bill, 1778, reprinted in *The Works of Jeremy Bentham* vol. 4 (John Bowring ed., 1843); Jeremy Bentham, Panopticon; Postscript, Part I: Containing Further Particulars and Alterations Relative to the Plan of Construction Originally Proposed; Principally Adapted to the Purpose of a Panopticon Penitentiary-House, 1787, published 1791, reprinted in *The Works of Jeremy Bentham* vol. 4 (John Bowring ed., 1843); Jeremy Bentham, *The Rationale of Punishment* (Robert Heward ed., 1830). In 2022, a compilation of correspondence and lengthy "letters" on transportation was published as *Panopticon Versus New South Wales and Other Writings on Australia* (Tim Causer & Philip Schofield eds., UCL Press, 2022). The unsigned contract Bentham drafted for construction of the Panopticon can be found at "Twenty-Eighth Report from the Select Committee on Finance, &c. Police, including Convict Establishments," 26 June 1798, reprinted in *House of Commons Sessional Papers of the Eighteenth Century*, cxii, 66–76 (S. Lambert ed., 145 vols., Wilmington, Delaware, 1975).

24. Bentham, *Rationale of Punishment*, 1–2, 19–20, 27–31, 37–40, 76–77.

25. Bentham, *Rationale of Punishment*, 93–98, 135.

26. Maurice Waller, Outline of Draft for Standard of Treatment of Prisoners, Rule 30, 1928, IPPC, UN Archives, NY, S-0195, Box 23, File 6.

27. Bentham, *Rationale of Punishment*, 28–30, 82, 115–19; Jeremy Bentham, Pauper Management Improved, 1797, reprinted in *The Collected Works of Jeremy Bentham: Writings on the Poor Laws* vol. 2, § V, 8 (Michael Quinn ed., 2010).

28. Bentham, *Rationale of Punishment*, 196; Jeremy Bentham, On Death Punishment: By Jeremy Bentham to His Fellow Citizens of France, *Rationale of Punishment*, App. 2 (1831); Hugo Adam Bedau, *Bentham's Utilitarian Critique of the Death Penalty*, 78 J. Crim. L. & Criminology 1033, 1035–36, 1041 (1983).

29. Bruce Kerscher, *Perish or Prosper: The Law and Convict Transportation in the British Empire, 1700–1850*, 21 L. & Hist. Rev. 527, 528 (2003).

30. Bentham, *Rationale of Punishment*, 330.

31. Jeremy Bentham, *First Letter to Lord Pelham*, 7 (Tim Causer & Philip Schofield eds., UCL Bentham Project, 2018); R. V. Jackson, *Bentham's Penal Theory in Action: The Case Against New South Wales*, 1 Utilitas 226 (1989).

32. Bentham, *First Letter to Lord Pelham*, 49–50, 53.

33. Jeremy Bentham, A Plea for the Constitution, 1803, published 1812, reprinted in *The Works of Jeremy Bentham* vol. 4, 251–84 (John Bowring ed., 1843); Jeremy Bentham, *Third Letter to Lord Pelham*, 117–259 (Tim Causer & Philip Schofield eds., UCL Bentham Project, 2018).

34. Jeremy Bentham, Panopticon; Postscript, Part II: A Plan of Management for a Panopticon Penitentiary-House 1787, published 1791, reprinted in *The Works of Jeremy Bentham* vol. 4, 121–22 (John Bowring ed., 1843).

35. Jeremy Bentham, Rights, Representation, and Reform: Nonsense upon Stilts and Other Writings on the French Revolution, 1795, published 1816, reprinted in *The Collected Works of Jeremy Bentham*, 317–401, 330 (Philip Schofield, Catherine Pease-Watkin & Cyprian Blamires eds., Oxford U. Press, 2002).

36. Bentham, Plea for Constitution, 253.

37. The criticism is vast. Hugo Adam Bedau, *Bentham's Utilitarian Critique of the Death Penalty*, 1063–65 (1983).

38. Judith Resnik, The Functions of Publicity and of Privatization in Courts and their Replacements (from Jeremy Bentham to #MeToo and Google Spain), *Open Justice: The Role of Courts in a Democratic Society*, 177–252 (Burkhard Hess and Ana Koprivica eds., Max Planck Institute, Luxembourg, Nomos, 2019).

39. Michel Foucault, *Discipline and Punish: The Birth of the Prison*, 9, 16–31, 224 (Alan Sheridan trans., 1977); Michel Foucault, *The Punitive Society: Lectures at the Collège de France 1972-1973* (Bernard E. Harcourt ed., Graham Burchell trans., 2015).

40. Bentham, Panopticon; Postscript, Part I, 71–82, 80–86.

41. Anne Brunon-Ernst, Deconstructing Panopticism into the Plural Panopticons, *Beyond Foucault: New Perspectives on Bentham's Panopticon*, 17–42 (Anne Brunon-Ernst ed., Ashgate, 2012); Anne Brunon-Ernst, *Utilitarian Biopolitics: Bentham, Foucault and Modern Power* (Pickering & Chatto, 2012).

42. Jeremy Bentham, Rationale of Judicial Evidence (1827), *The Works of Jeremy Bentham* vol. 6, 355 (John Bowring ed.,1843).

CHAPTER 2

1. Samuel Edgerton, *Pictures and Punishment: Art and Criminal Prosecution During the Florentine Renaissance* (Cornell U. Press, 1985).

2. Courtney Skipton Long, *Captive Bodies—Exhibition Text for George Romney's "Howard Visiting a Prison" 1780–1785*, Yale Ctr. British Art, Fall 2019.

3. Gustave de Beaumont, *Marie, or, Slavery in the United States*, published in two volumes in 1835, and translated into English in 1958. Tocqueville's *Democracy in America*, first published in 1835, was retranslated in 2000 by Harvey Mansfield and Delba Winthrop (U. Chi. Press, 2000). Francis Lieber's books included *Manual of Political Ethics*, 2 vols. (C. C. Little & J. Brown, 1838–1839); *Legal and Political Hermeneutics* (C. C. Little & J. Brown, 1839); *On Civil Liberty and Self Government* (Lippincott, Grambo & Co., 1853); *Instruction for the Armies of the United States in the Field* (D. Van Nostrand, 1863), discussed in John Fabian Witt, *Lincoln's Code: The Laws of War in American History*, 174–96 (Free Press, 2012). When living in South Carolina, Lieber had two slaves; in New York, he became associated with abolition.

Hartmut Keil, *Francis Lieber's Attitudes on Race, Slavery, and Abolition*, 28 J. Am. Ethnic Hist. 123 (2008).

4. Gustave de Beaumont & Alexis de Tocqueville, *On the Penitentiary System in the United States and Its Application in France: With an Appendix on Penal Colonies, and Also Statistical Notes*, with introduction by Francis Lieber, 13, dagger note (Francis Lieber trans., Carey, Lea & Blanchard, 1833); Gustave de Beaumont & Alexis de Tocqueville, *On the Penitentiary System in the United States and Its Application in France: The Complete Text*, 21 n.39 (Emily Katherine Ferkaluk trans., Palgrave Macmillan, 2018); Emily Katherine Ferkaluk, *Tocqueville's Moderate Penal Reform* (Palgrave Macmillan, 2018).

5. Andre Normandeau, *Pioneers in Criminology: Charles Lucas: Opponent of Capital Punishment*, 61 J. Crim. L. & Criminology 218, 220 (1970).

6. Oliver Zunz, *The Man Who Understood Democracy: The Life of Alexis de Tocqueville*, 33 (Princeton U. Press, 2022); Normandeau, 224.

7. Alexis de Tocqueville, On Prison Reform, Speech to Parliament, Apr. 26, 1844, *Tocqueville and Beaumont on Social Reform*, 86, 88 (Seymour Drescher ed., trans., Harper, 1968).

8. Zunz, 38–39.

9. Ferkaluk, 3, 13 nn.8–10.

10. Beaumont & Tocqueville / Lieber, 15.

11. Alexis de Tocqueville, Report on Abolition, July 23, 1839, trans. and published in Boston in 1840. Tocqueville, Speech to Parliament 1844, 98–135. Emancipation, proclaimed during the 1770s French Revolution, was undone by Napoleon, and proclaimed again in 1848. The antislavery activism of this "two-man machine" included Tocqueville's report on abolition to the French Parliament; Beaumont "simultaneously presented a petition to the Chamber on behalf of the French Abolitionist Society." Andreas Hess, *Tocqueville and Beaumont: Aristocratic Liberalism in Democratic Times*, 9–10, 75–79 (Palgrave Macmillan, 2018).

12. Tocqueville's diary entries did not center on prisons. Thorsten Sellin, Introduction, *On the Penitentiary System in the United States: And Its Application in France*, xvii (S. Ill. U. Press, 1964).

13. Hess, 9–10.

14. Ferkaluk, 3–4, 101–06.

15. Sheldon S. Wolin, *Tocqueville Between Two Worlds*, 384 (Princeton U. Press, 2009).

16. Hess, 3–10, 54–59.

17. Beaumont & Tocqueville / Ferkaluk, 21 n.39.

18. Francis Lieber, Preface, *On the Penitentiary System*, viii.

19. Beaumont & Tocqueville / Lieber, 47.

20. Lieber, Preface, vii–viii; Beaumont & Tocqueville / Lieber, 47, dagger note.

21. Michael Meranze, *Laboratories of Virtue: Punishment, Revolution, and Authority in Philadelphia, 1760–1835* (NC Press, 1996); Ashley T. Rubin, *The Deviant Prison: Philadelphia's Eastern State Penitentiary and the Origins of American's Modern Penal System, 1829–1913* (Cambridge U. Press, 2021);

Norman Johnson, *The World's Most Influential Prison: Success or Failure?*, 84 Prison J. 20S, 25S (Dec. 2004).

22. Gustave de Beaumont, Second Sketch Book, Apr. 1831–Apr. 1832, Yale Tocqueville Manuscripts, Beinecke Rare Book and Manuscript Library, Yale University, Gen MSS 982, Box 14.

23. Rubin, 110–23. The vices were detailed by Francis C. Gray, Boston's "chief inspector of prisons," in *Prison Discipline in America*, 77, 185–87 (C. C. Little & J. Brown 1847).

24. Éric Keslassy, *Tocqueville et 'l'Économie' Pénitentiaire*, 23 Revue d'Histoire des Sciences Humaines 175, 200–01 (2010); Beaumont & Tocqueville / Lieber, 5–11, 34, 74–82. Rebecca M. McLennan, *The Crisis of Imprisonment: Protest, Politics, and the Making of the American Penal State, 1776–1941*, 63 (Cambridge U. Press, 2008), reported that thirteen states used Auburn as a model. In the South, plantation prisons were the norm after the Civil War. David Oshinsky, *Worse than Slavery: Parchman Farm and the Ordeal of Jim Crow Justice* (Free Press, 1996).

25. Beaumont & Tocqueville / Lieber, 5, 91–92; Wolin, 395, 405–07; Alexis de Tocqueville, *Oeuvres complètes, Écrits sur le système pénitentiaire en France et à l'étranger*, 37 (Michelle Perrot & J. P. Mayer eds., Gallimard, 1984).

26. Lieber, Preface, xi, in note.

27. Tocqueville, Speech to Parliament 1844, 86, 89; Alexis de Tocqueville, *Rapport fait au nom de la commission chargée d'examiner le projet de loi sur les prisons*, July 5, 1843; Sara M. Benson, *Democracy and Unfreedom: Revisiting Tocqueville and Beaumont in America*, 45 Pol. Thought 466, 478 (2017). Their competitor on prison reform, Charles Lucas, objected to isolation. Normandeau, 222.

28. Lieber, Preface, x, in note.

29. Beaumont & Tocqueville / Lieber, 32.

30. Lieber, Preface, xx–xxi.

31. Wolin, 396.

32. Beaumont & Tocqueville / Lieber, 40.

33. Beaumont & Tocqueville / Lieber, 59–60.

34. Beaumont & Tocqueville / Lieber, 39–40.

35. W. Fitzhugh Brundage, *Civilizing Torture: An American Tradition*, 66–67 (Belknap Press, 2018).

36. Lieber, Preface, ix–x and note.

37. Beaumont & Tocqueville / Lieber, 41–48; Richard Avramenko & Robert Gingerich, *Democratic Dystopia: Tocqueville and the American Penitentiary System*, 46 Polity 56, 72–78 (2016).

38. Beaumont & Tocqueville / Lieber, 30, dagger note.

39. *Palgrave Handbook of Prison Tourism* (Jacqueline Z. Wilson, Sarah Hodgkinson, Justin Piché & Kevin Walby eds., 2017). The "Guide-Led Tour and Discussion" on Eastern State Penitentiary's website provides a gruesome picture of confinement to set "the stage for conversation about criminal justice reform today."

40. Beaumont & Tocqueville / Lieber, 30, dagger note.
41. Wolin, 386.
42. Gustave de Beaumont, *On Prison Reform*, Sept. 7, 10, 21, and Oct. 2, 1843, 60–69, 80 (Seymour Drescher ed., trans., 1968).
43. Tocqueville, *Rapport sur les prisons*, 1843.
44. Clare Anderson, *Convicts: A Global History* (Cambridge U. Press, 2022); Linda Colley, *Part of the Punishment*, London Rev. of Books, Jan. 2023.
45. James Q. Whitman, *The Continental Abolition of Degradation in Harsh Justice*, 97–150 (Oxford U. Press, 2003).
46. Beaumont & Tocqueville / Lieber, 44.
47. Beaumont, *On Prison Reform*, 82–83.
48. Wolin, 394; Bernard E. Harcourt, *The Invisibility of the Prison in Democratic Theory: A Problem of "Virtual Democracy,"* 23 The Good Soc'y 6 (2014).

CHAPTER 3

1. Sessions and Resolutions, *The Second International Penitentiary Congress in Brussels*, 202, Sept. 20–23, 1847; English versions provided by Negley K. Teeters, *The First International Penitentiary Congresses: 1846–47*, 26 Prison J. 190 (1946).
2. Robert Adams & Jo Campling, *Prison Riots in Britain and the USA* (Macmillan, 2d ed. 1994); Ashley T. Rubin, *Early US Prison History Beyond Rothman: Revisiting the Discovery of the Asylum*, 15 Ann. Rev. L. & Soc. Sci. 1 (2021); The *Consequence of Prisoners' Micro-Resistance*, 42 L. & Soc. Inquiry 138 (2017).
3. Blake McKelvey, *American Prisons: A History of Good Intentions*, 7–19 (P. Smith, 1977); Harry E. Barnes, *The Historical Origin of the Prison System in America*, 12 J. Am. Inst. Crim. L. & Criminology 35 (1921); Jacques M. Quen, *Historical Reflections on the Sesquicentennial of the Founding of the Boston Prison Discipline Society (1825–1854)*, 3 J. Am. Acad. Psychiatry & L. 132 (1975); H. H. Hart, Prisoners' Aid Societies, *Proceedings of the Annual Congress of the National Prison Association of the US, Nashville, Nov. 16–20, 1889*, 270 (Knight & Leonard, 1890).
4. *Pennsylvania Prison Society Records 1787–1966*, Hist. Soc'y Penn., 2006; *Journal of Prison Discipline and Philanthropy, 1945–1920*, renamed *Prison Journal, 1921–1986*; Francis C. Gray, *Prison Discipline in America*, 2 (John Murray ed., 1848); Fiona Doherty, *Indeterminate Sentencing Return: The Invention of Supervised Release*, 88 NYU L. Rev. 958, 977–82 (2013); Lawrence M. Friedman, *Crime and Punishment in American History* (Basic Books, 1993).
5. Prison Association of New York, Bylaws of the Prison Association of New York, *Twenty-Fourth Annual Report of the Executive Committee of the Prison Association of New York and Accompanying Documents for 1868*, VIII(2) at xv and ix (The Argus Co., 1869).
6. Douglas Maynard, *Reform and the Origin of the International Organization Movement*, 107 Proc. Am. Phil. Soc'y 220, 220 (1963); Steve Charnovitz, *Two Centuries of Participation: NGOS and International Governance*, 18 Mich. J.

Int'l L. 183 (1997); Judith Resnik, Sisterhood, Slavery, and Sovereignty: Transnational Antislavery Work and Women's Rights Movements in the United States During the Twentieth Century, *Women's Rights and Transatlantic Antislavery in the Era of Emancipation*, 19–54 (Kathryn K. Sklar & James Brewer Stewart eds., Yale U. Press, 2007).

7. Order of Business and Resolutions, *The First International Penitentiary Congress at Frankfurt, Sept. 28–30, 1846*; Teeters, *1847 Resolutions*, 191, 200–01; Martina Henze, Transnational Cooperation and Criminal Policy: The Prison Reform Movement, 1820s–1950s, *Shaping the Transnational Sphere: Experts, Networks and Issues from the 1840s to the 1930s*, 198–202 (Davide Rodogno, Bernhard Struck & Jakob Vogel eds., Berghahn Books, 2015).

8. Teeters, *1847 Resolutions*, Second, Third Resolution, 203–06.

9. *1846 Resolutions*, Seventh Resolution; Teeters, *1847 Resolutions*, First-Third Resolutions and Principle G, 201–05.

10. Resolutions, *The Third International Penitentiary Congress at Frankfurt, Sept. 14–18, 1857*, Factors A.1–A.2, B.4; Teeters, *1847 Resolutions*, 195, 207–09.

11. Rebecca M. McLennan, *The Crisis of Imprisonment: Protest, Politics, and the Making of the American Penal State, 1776–1941*, 10, 17, 72–85 (Cambridge U. Press, 1967).

12. James Gray Pope, *Mass Incarceration, Convict Leasing, and the Thirteenth Amendment: A Revisionist Account*, 94 NYU L. Rev. 1465 (2019); Eric Foner, *The Second Founding: How the Civil War and Reconstruction Remade the Constitution*, 29, 42, 45–46 (W. W. Norton & Co., 2019).

13. McLennan, 87–90, 105–06, 129–32.

14. Nat'l Prison Assn., *Fourth Report of Proceedings*, First Annual Report, 10 (C. G. Burgoyne's "Quick" Print, 1884).

15. Edward J. Schauer & Enoch C. Wines (1806–1879), *Encyclopedia of American Prisons*, 498–99 (Marilyn D. McShane & Frank P. Williams III eds., Garland Publ., 1996).

16. American Social Science Association, *Constitution, Address, and List of Members of the American Association for the Promotion of Social Science*, 3–4, 11–12 (Wright & Potter, 1866). The American Association for the Social Sciences ended in 1912 as different social sciences spun off their own organizations.

17. Enoch C. Wines & Theodore W. Dwight, *Report on the Prisons and Reformatories of the United States and Canada, Made to the Legislature of New York, Jan. 1867*, 53 (Van Benthuysen, 1867).

18. Wines & Dwight, *1867 Prison Report*, 4, 47; Enoch C. Wines, *The State of Prisons and of Child-Saving Institutions in the Civilized World* (J. Wilson & Son, 1880, republished by Patterson Smith, 1968).

19. Wines & Dwight, *1867 Prison Report*, 52–62, 78, 145–46, 164–66, 247–64, 294–95.

20. Wines & Dwight, *1867 Prison Report*, 19–36; An Act to provide for a State Commission of Prisons, chap. 1026, 118th Legislature, Vol. 958 (June 15, 1985), as amended 1901, chap. 12, 124th Legislature, Regular Session 15, Vol. 15; W. David Ball, *Why State Prisons?*, 33 Yale L. & Pol'y Rev. 75 (2014).

21. Declaration of Principles, *Transactions of the National Congress on Penitentiary and Reformatory Discipline held at Cincinnati, Ohio, Oct. 12–18, 1870,* 541–47 (Enoch C. Wines ed., Weed, Parsons & Co., 1871).

22. Count W. Sollohub, The Prison Question in Russia, *PANY Twenty-Fourth Annual Report 1868,* 555–76; Enoch C. Wines, *International Prison Reform,* 371 (1876).

23. Enoch C. Wines, The Present Outlook of Prison Discipline in the United States, *1870 Transactions,* 15, 17; *1870 Principles,* 541–47 (available on the American Correctional Association's website); Enoch C. Wines, *Report of the International Penitentiary Congress of London, held July 3–13, 1872* (Gov't Printing Office, 1873).

24. *1870 Principles,* XIV, 543; II, 541; XIII, 542; XIV, 542; XV, 543; III, 541; XX, 543; VIII, 548; IV, 541; IX and XIV, 542; V, 541; Michele Pifferi, *Reinventing Punishment: A Comparative History of Criminology and Penology in the Nineteenth and Twentieth Centuries,* 60–68 (Oxford U. Press, 2016).

25. *1870 Principles,* XXXII, 546; XVII, 543; XVI, 543.

26. *1870 Principles,* XXX and XXXIII, 546; VII, 541; XI, 542; XXIX,545–46.

27. Paul Finkelman, *The Strange Career of Race Discrimination in Antebellum Ohio,* 55 Case W. Res. L. Rev. 375 (2004).

28. *1870 Principles,* XXIV, XXXVII, 547. Elizabeth Fry, a middle-class English Quaker working in the first half of the nineteenth century, was an oft-cited English example; the idea of detention as protection for "fallen" women in the United States is analyzed in Estelle B. Freedman, *Their Sisters' Keepers: Women's Prison Reform in America, 1830–1930* (U. Mich. Press, 1984).

29. *Proceedings of the Annual Congress of the National Prison Association held at Toronto, Sept. 10–15, 1887,* 4 (Knight & Leonard Co., 1889).

30. *Proceedings of the Annual Congress of the National Prison Association held at Chicago, June 7–10, 1893,* 110 (Knight & Leonard Co., 1893).

31. Another president of the association attributed Hayes' interest to his service on Ohio's Board of Charities, prompted by "God and humanity." Hayes opposed the "Lombroso fad"—which pinned criminal behavior on genes—and insisted that heredity was "no excuse for crime," and instead that education and industrious activities were needed by all. Rutherford Birchard Hayes, In Memoriam, *1893 National Prison Association Proceedings Chicago,* 11, 25–28, 32–33.

32. *1884 First Annual Report,* 9; *1887 National Prison Association Proceedings Toronto,* 49, 52; McLennan, 99–100, 185–91, 201–38; NY Const. of 1894, art. 3, § 29 (affirmed by law in 1896).

33. A second meeting in 1873 in Baltimore was followed by those in St. Louis in 1874 and New York in 1876. Address Gen. Roeliff Brinkerhoff, *Proceedings of the Annual Congress of the National Prison Association held at Austin, Tex., Dec. 2–6, 1897,* 12, 14 (Shaw Brothers, 1898); W. Ralph Graham & Bryn A. Carlson, *The American Protestant Correctional Chaplains Association, Inc.,* 42 J. Pastoral Care 220 (1988); *1887 National Prison Association Proceedings Toronto,* 66; *1887 National Prison Association Chicago Proceedings,* 7–9.

Charles E. Felton, Prison Management, *Proceedings of the Annual Congress of the National Prison Association held at Milwaukee, Wis., Sept. 26–30, 1896*, 33–39, 59 (Shaw Brothers, Printers, 1897).

34. *Transactions of the Third National Prison Reform Congress held at St. Louis, Mo., May 13–16, 1874*, 43–44 (Enoch C. Wines ed., Office of the Assn., 1874); Frederick H. Wines, Memorial Address in Honor of General Rutherford B. Hayes, *1893 National Prison Association Proceedings Chicago* 60, 61; *1893 National Prison Association Proceedings Chicago*, 79, 82; *Proceedings of the Annual Congress of the National Prison Association held at Cincinnati, Sept. 25–30, 1890*, 37 (Shaw Brothers, 1891); Address Gen. Roeliff Brinkerhoff, *1897 Nat'l Prison Assn. Proceedings Austin*, 9–10, 20.

35. Frederick H. Wines, Twenty Years' Growth of the American Prison System, *1890 National Prison Association Proceedings Cincinnati*, 79, 93; *1897 National Prison Association Proceedings Austin*, 191–94, 289–93; Dr. S. H. Blitch, The Negro Criminal, *Proceedings of the Annual Congress of the National Prison Association held at Lincoln, Neb., Oct. 21–25, 1905*, 273–79 (Press of William B. Burford, 1906).

36. Hon. Geo. G. Washburn, How to Popularize Prison Reform, *Proceedings of the Annual Congress of the National Prison Association of the US held at St. Paul, Minn., June 16–20, 1894*, 227 (Shaw Brothers, 1894).

37. Address Gen. Roeliff Brinkerhoff, *1897 National Prison Association Proceedings Austin*, 15–18; Warden A. A. Brush, Report of the Standing Committee on Prison discipline, *1890 National Prison Association Proceedings Cincinnati*, 189, 195.

38. *1897 National Prison Association Proceedings Austin*, 59; *1893 National Prison Association Proceedings Chicago*, 109; *Proceedings of the Annual Congress of the National Prison Association held at Denver, Co., Sept. 14–18, 1895*, 213–15 (Shaw Brothers, 1896).

39. W. Fitzhugh Brundage, *Civilizing Torture: An American Tradition*, 82–85 (Harvard U. Press, 2018); *Torture and Homicide in an American State Prison*, Harper's Weekly, Dec. 18, 1858, 808; The Prison Reform League, *Crime and Criminals*, 45–46 (Prison Reform League Publ. Co., 1910) (quoting Charles Edward Russell, *Beating Men to Make Them Good*, Hampton's Magazine, 321–22, Sept. 1909).

40. *1887 National Prison Association Proceedings Toronto*, 322; *Proceedings of the Annual Congress of the American Prison Association (Formerly the Nat'l Prison Assn.), Richmond, Va., Nov. 14–19, 1908*, 7 (W. M. B. Burford, 1909). Wines died in 1879 and his son, Frederick Howard Wines, served as Secretary for some years thereafter.

41. *Declaration of Principles of 1870 as Revised and Reaffirmed at the Sixtieth Annual Congress of the American Prison Association held in Louisville, Kentucky, Oct. 10–16, 1930*, III, 5; XII, 6; XXV, 9; X, 6; XVI, 7; VII, 6.

42. Michel Foucault, *Discipline and Punish* (Alan Sheridan trans., Vintage Books, 1977).

CHAPTER 4

1. *Transactions of the National Congress on Penitentiary and Reformatory Discipline held at Cincinnati, Ohio, Oct. 12–18, 1870*, 253 (Enoch C. Wines ed., Weed, Parsons & Co., 1871); Address of Samuel J. Barrows, *Proceedings of the Annual Congress of the National Prison Association of the United States, held at Cleveland, Ohio, Sept. 22–26, 1900*, 224 (Shaw Brothers Printers, 1900).

2. Leonard Woolf, *International Government: Two Reports Prepared for the Fabian Research Department, with a Project by the Fabian Committee for a Supernational Authority that Will Prevent War*, 118–29 (Fabian Society, 1916); Guy Fiti Sinclair, *To Reform the World: International Organizations and the Making of the Modern State* (Oxford U. Press, 2017); Nir Shafir, *The International Congress as Scientific and Diplomatic Technology: Global Intellectual Exchange in the International Prison Congress, 1860–90*, 9 J. Glob. Hist. 72 (2014); José E. Alvarez, *International Organizations as Law-Makers* (Oxford U. Press, 2005).

3. A Resolution Authoring the Appointment of a Commissioner to an International Congress on Penitentiary and Reformatory Discipline, 42d Cong., 1st Sess., 17 Stat. 21; *Prisons and Reformatories at Home and Abroad Being: The Transactions of the International Penitentiary Congress held in London, July 3–13 1872*, xiii (Edwin Pears ed., Longmans, Green & Co., 1872); Minutes, Meeting of the Commission for the Study of Penitentiary Reform, Brussels, June 1874, *Transactions of the 1874 National Prison Reform Congress held in St. Louis, Missouri, May 13–16 1874*, 559–64 (Enoch. C. Wines ed., Office of the Assn., 1874); Rev. Fred. H. Wines, Special Commissioner from the State of Ill., to the Hon. S. M. Cullom, Gov. of Ill., *Report on the International Prison Congress held at Stockholm, Sweden, Aug. 20–26, 1878*, 4 (Weber, Magie & Co., State Printers, 1879). After Wines could not travel, Illinois' governor appointed his son, Frederick Wines, a US delegate. President Hayes then chose Caleb D. Randall, from Michigan, who served as the US Commissioner until 1895. 45 Cong. Rec. 58–59 (1877); An Act to Provide for Deficiencies in the Appropriations for the Service of the Government for the Fiscal Year Ending June 30, 1878, and for Prior Years, and for Other Purposes, Ch. 3, 20 Stat. 7, 12 (1877). (That same appropriation provided $30,000 for a federal courthouse and post office in Little Rock, Arkansas, the site of the 1960s whipping litigation.)

4. Some categorize the IPC as a "quasi- or semi-official organization." Martina Henze, *Crime on the Agenda: Transnational Organizations 1870–1955*, 109 Historisk Tidsskrift 369, 377 (2009).

5. *Actes du Congrès Pénitentiaire International de Rome, Nov. 1885*, 22 (Imprimerie, Mantellate, 1887). By 1910, the United States owed about $1,625. Letter Roeliff Brinkerhoff, President, American Delegation to Samuel Barrows, Sec. to Richard Olney. *Report of the Delegates of the United States to the Fifth International Prison Congress held at Paris, France, July 1895*, 3–9 (Gov't Printing Office, 1896).

6. Règlement pour la Commission Pénitentiaire Internationale, élaboré à Stockholm en 1877, *Actes du Congrès Pénitentiaire International (IPC)*

de Washington, Oct. 1910, Vol. I, 588, 590 (Louis C. Guillaume & Eugène Borel eds., Staempfli & Cie, 1913).

7. *The International Prison Congress, Aug. 1925*, 2 Howard J. 1, 10 (1926). Whatever the number of delegates, countries had one vote on issues. Règlement 1877, Art. 3; Règlement 1877, Art. 4–6.

8. Comparing the "Labors" of the 1872, 1887, 1885, and 1890 Congresses by C. D. Randall, Bureau of Educ. Circular of Info., *The Fourth International Prison Congress, St. Petersburg, Russia*, 186–87 (Gov't Printing Office, 1891); Bureau de la Commission d'organisation du Congrès, *Actes du Congrès Pénitentiaire International de Saint-Pétersbourg, 1890*, Vol. 1, 801–02 (Imprimerie, Staempfli & Cie, 1892); Statistics of the International Prison Congress, in Samuel J. Barrows, *Report of the Proceedings and Conclusions of the Sixth International Prison Congress held at Brussels, Belgium, August 1900*, US House of Representatives, Doc. No. 57-374 (1903).

9. Randall, *1890 IPC St. Petersburg*, 9; *Report of the Delegates of the United States to the Fifth International Prison Congress held at Paris, France, July 1895*, 69 (Gov't Printing Office, 1896); *Ve Congrès Pénitentiaire International, Paris, 1895*, Vol. 6, 303 (Melun Imprimerie Admin., 1897); Samuel J. Barrows, *Report of the Proceedings and Conclusions of The Sixth International Prison Congress, held at Brussels, Belgium, Aug. 1900*, 7, 11–12, submitted to the Speaker of the House of Representatives and the Sec. of State (Gov't Printing Office, 1903); *Actes du Congrès Pénitentiaire International de Budapest, Septembre 1905* (Jules Rickl de Bellye & Dr. Guillaume eds., Bureau de la Commission Pénitentiaire Internationale, Imprimerie, Stampfli & Cie, 1907); Samuel J. Barrows, *Report of Proceedings of the Seventh International Prison Congress, Budapest, Hungary, Sept. 1905*, 14–15 (Gov't Printing Office, 1907).

10. *1910 IPC Washington*, 23.

11. President Theodore Roosevelt, who had been a vice president of the Prison Association of New York, personally extended the offer. Barrows, *1905 IPC Budapest*, 437–39; Charles Richmond Henderson, *Report of the Proceedings of the Eighth International Prison Congress, Washington, DC, September and October, 1910*, HR Doc. No. 52, 3–10, 17 (1913). In 1911, Wickersham spoke at the American Prison Association Congress; invoking Beccaria and Bentham, he detailed a new federal parole system. George W. Wickersham, Atty. Gen. US, The Parole of United States Prisoners, *Proceedings of the Annual Congress of the American Prison Association, Omaha, Neb.*, 221–38, (1911), Ob. 14–19.

12. William N. Gemmill, *Memorials to Mr. John Lisle and to Professor Charles Richmond Henderson*, 6 J. Crim. L. & Criminology 486, 488–89 (1916); *Charles Richmond Henderson*, 55 J. Prison Discipline & Philanthropy 25, 25–26 (1916); *1910 IPC Washington*, 23.

13. *1910 IPC Washington*, 26.

14. Negley K. Teeters, *The International Penal and Penitentiary Congress (1910) and the Indeterminate Sentence*, 39 J. Crim. L. & Criminology 618, 623–24 (1949). The American Prison Association held its annual congress in conjunction with the 1910 IPC Congress and reproduced in English the IPC

Resolutions in *Proceedings of the Annual Congress, held at Washington, DC, Sept. 29–Oct 8, 1910, Including Abstracts of Papers and Resolutions of the Eighth International Prison Congress*, 255–65 (W. M. B. Burford, 1911).

15. Henderson, *1910 IPC Washington Report*, 35–41.
16. Frank Marshall White, The American Tour of the International Prison Congress, *1910 Am. Prison Assn. Proceedings Washington, DC*, 228–36.
17. Michele Pifferi, *Reinventing Punishment: A Comparative History of Criminology and Penology in the Nineteenth and Twentieth Centuries*, 45–48, 59–141 (Oxford U. Press, 2016).
18. J. Simon van der Aa, An Excursion into Reformatory American, *1910 IPC Washington Report*, 13–16; Ugo Conti & Adolphe Prins, *Some European Comments on the American Prison System*, 2 J. Crim. L. & Criminology 199, 201–02, 208–09 (John Wigmore trans., 1911).
19. Van der Aa, *1910 IPC Washington Report*, 15; Conti & Prins, 199–201, 204–05.
20. Buck v. Bell, 274 US 200, 207 (1927). In a subsequent case by prisoners protesting Oklahoma's sterilization law, the Court retreated without directly overruling *Buck*. Skinner v. State of Oklahoma *ex rel*. Williamson, 316 US 535 (1942); Victoria F. Nourse, *In Reckless Hands*: Skinner v. Oklahoma *and the Near Triumph of American Eugenics* (W. W. Norton, 2008).
21. Letter J. Simon van der Aa & Evelyn Ruggles-Brise to US Sec. State, Oct. 1912, IPPC, UN Archives, NY, S-0914, Box 3, File 1, 1; Letter van der Aa & Ruggles-Brise to Andrew Carnegie, Oct. 1912, S-0914, Box 3, File 1, 1–2. IPC also sought funds from Rockefeller, who declined. Letter van der Aa to Professor D. Henderson, Nov. 9, 1913, S-0914, Box 3, File 1, 1; Letter van der Aa to Professor D. Henderson, Mar. 9, 1914, S-0914, Box 3, File 1, 1; Letter John Koren to James Bertram, Sec. Carnegie Foundation, Apr. 26, 1917; Letter Bertram, Sec. Carnegie Foundation, to Max Farrand, Gendered Dir. of the Commonwealth Fund, June 26, 1920, confirming the rejection of 1917. Carnegie Foundation Archives provided to me by Jeanne D'Onofrio.
22. Ordre du Jour de la Réunion de la Commission Pénitentiaire Internationale, Mar. 7, 1914, S-0914, Box 3, File 1, 1–2; Letter to Monsieur le Ministre, Commission Pénitentiaire Internationale, Oct. 24, 1921, S-0915, Box 3, File 5.
23. *Boston Man for International Prison Board*, Christian Sci. Monitor, 1, Oct. 15, 1915; John Koren, *Report of the Committee on Statistics of Crime*, 1 J. Am. Inst. Crim. L. & Criminology 417 (1910); John Koren, The Ideals of Prison Reports, *Proceedings of the Annual Congress of the American Prison Association, Indianapolis, Ind., Oct. 11–16, 1913*, 374, 384 (WM. B. Burford, 1913); John Koren, The State's Obligation to the Discharged Prisoner, *Proceedings of the Annual Congress of the American Prison Association held at St. Paul, Minn., Oct 3–8, 1914*, 227–30, 10 (W. M. B. Burford, 1914); *John Koren Dies at Sea: Famed as Statistician and Sociologist*, Bost. Daily Globe, Nov. 17, 1923.
24. Address by John Koren, US Commissioner, IPC, *Proceedings of the Annual Congress of the American Prison Association held at Buffalo, NY, Oct. 7–12, 1916*, 405 (W. M. B. Burford, 1916).

634 NOTES TO CHAPTER 5

CHAPTER 5

1. *The International Prison Congress, August 1925, Annual Meeting*, 2 Howard J. 1, 11 (1926).

2. Suggested Draft of Minimum Rights for Prisoners in All Civilised Countries, undated, IPPC, UN Archives, NY, S-0914, Box 2, File 2 (unless otherwise noted, IPPC/UN archival material are from S-0914); Gertrude Eaton, *The Need for an International Charter for Prisoners*, 2 Howard J. 93–97 (1927).

3. *Proceedings of the Annual Congress of the American Prison Association, Columbus, Ohio, Oct. 14–19, 1920*, 156–58 (Wynkoop, Hallenbeck, Crawford, 1920); Letter Sir Evelyn Ruggles-Brise to B. Ogden Chisolm, Sept./Oct. 1924, Box 2, File 1, 5. Appointed in the 1890s, Ruggles-Brise was to lessen the violent practices of the aptly named Edmund du Cane. Victor Bailey, *The Rise and Fall of the Rehabilitative Ideal, 1895–1970*, 21–29 (Routledge, 2019).

4. Letter Ruggles-Brise & Dr. Simon van der Aa to British Home Office, Oct. 30, 1924, Box 3, File 4.

5. League of Nations, *Index to the Records of the Second Opium Conference, Geneva, Nov. 17, 1924–Feb. 19, 1925* (1926); Paul Knepper, *International Crime in the 20th Century: The League of Nations Era, 1919–1939* (Palgrave, 2011).

6. Jubilee Retrospect, *The Howard Association Annual Report*, Oct. 1897, 3, 4, Howard League for Penal Reform Collection, Warwick Modern Records Ctr., U. Warwick, MSS.16X/1/6/26. Fry guided the merger. Cecil Leeson, *Margery Fry*, 2 Howard J. 85, 87 (1927); *Our Case*, 1 Howard J. 1, 2 (1921); Anne Logan, *Feminism and Criminal Justice: A Historical Perspective*, 31–32 (Palgrave Macmillan, 2008).

7. Letter van der Aa & Sir Evelyn Ruggles-Brise to US Sec. of State, Nov. 26, 1923, Box 3, File 3.

8. *B. O. Chisolm Dies: Retired Banker, 78*, NY Times, 19, Mar. 21, 1944; *Says Prisons Corrupt Men*, NY Times, 30, June 21, 1920; B. Ogden Chisolm, Human Awakening, *Proceedings of the Annual Congress of the American Prison Association, New York City, Oct. 20 to 24, 1919*, 235–36 (W. M. B. Burford, 1919).

9. *Says Prisons Corrupt Men*, 30; James C. Young, *Faults in Our Prison System*, NY Times, 88, Feb. 26, 1922.

10. IPPC/UN Archives S-0915, Box 5, File 4. The seal, figure 5.1, is reproduced courtesy of the UN Archives.

11. Letter Chisolm to Ruggles-Brise, Dec. 21, 1924, Box 2, File 1; Copy to van der Aa; van der Aa to E. R. Cass, General-Sec. of Am. Prison Assn., Oct. 23, 1924, Box 3, File 4; Chisolm to van der Aa, Apr. 3, 1925, Box 2, File 1, 2. Nine US delegates attended, joined by forty from the states. Amos W. Butler, *Ninth International Prison Congress*, 16 J. Crim. L. & Criminology 602 (1926); Letter van der Aa to Chisolm, Apr. 5, 1925, Box 3, File 4, 1; Chisolm to van der Aa, Feb. 25, 1925, Box 2, File 1. Archived correspondence suggests Chisolm did not receive a written answer, and Chisolm persisted, seeking "all receipts from the different Governments and what the expenditures go for in a regular statement." Chisolm to van der Aa, Apr. 3, 1925, Box 2, File 1, 1. Van der Aa replied that the information would be provided in person at the

commissioners' London meeting before the 1925 Congress began. Van der Aa to Chisolm, June 7, 1925, Box 3, File 4, 1. Chisolm continued to ask for "some figures" to present to US delegates to try to get more funds. Chisolm to van der Aa, July 8, 1925, Box 2, File 1, 1.

12. *International Prison Congress*, 1 Howard J. 187, 194 (1925).

13. *Actes du Congrès Pénitentiaire International de Londres, Août 1925, Procès-Verbaux des Séances*, Vol. Ib, 131 (Simon van der Aa ed., Staempfli & Cie, 1927); David Cesarani, *The Anti-Jewish Career of William Joynson-Hicks, Cabinet Minister*, 24 J. Cont. Hist. 461 (1989); William D. Rubinstein, *The Myth of Jix's Antisemitism*, part I, 7 Austl. J. Jewish Stud. 41, 52–67 (1993).

14. *1925 IPC London*, Vol. Ia, 4–10.

15. *1925 IPC London*, Vol. Ia, 27–33; "Présidence de Sir Evelyn Ruggles-Brise," 413–18. In *Prison Reform at Home and Abroad: A Short History of the International Movement Since the London Congress, 1872*, 3 (Macmillan and Co., Ltd., 1924), Ruggles-Brise extolled the IPC for its "remarkable human fellowship" aiming not to "strike blindly at the offender, but . . . inspired with the spirit of mercy and indulgence." Under Ruggles-Brise, the "pace of progress in humanizing prisons was glacial." Victor Bailey, *English Prisons, Penal Culture, and the Abatement of Imprisonment, 1895–1922*, 36 J. British Stud. 285, 322 (1997).

16. An English version of the questions presented and resolutions comes from Butler, 602–09.

17. *The International Prison Congress, August 1925*, 2 Howard J. 11.

18. *The International Prison Congress, August 1925*, 2 Howard J. 10.

19. Bailey, *Rehabilitative Ideal*, 24–29, 35–36.

20. Leeson, 85–86.

21. A few writers have focused on their work. Anne Logan, *The Politics of Penal Reform: Margery Fry and the Howard League* (Routledge, 2018); Logan, *Feminism and Criminal Justice*; Sir Leon Radzinowicz, *Adventures in Criminology*, 376–78 (Taylor & Francis Grp., 1999). Radzinowicz described "that brilliant woman, Miss Margery Fry (ably helped by Gertrude Eaton) [as the] *porte-parole* for a fresh initiative in the 1920s."

22. Howard League Memorandum of the Attitude of the British Government Toward the Proposed Schedule of Minimum Conditions for Prisoners (undated), Howard League Warwick Archives, MSS.16B/3/IN/1/5. A handwritten note identified it as from 1927.

23. Enid Huws Jones, *Margery Fry: The Essential Amateur*, 6, 85 (Oxford U. Press, 1966); Logan, *Feminism and Criminal Justice*, 31; Virginia Woolf, *Roger Fry: A Biography* (The Hogarth Press, 1940). Margery Fry had "arranged" for the writing of that "memoire." Logan, *Politics of Penal Reform*, 114, and Woolf, 225, quoted Roger's description of the house.

24. Logan, *Politics of Penal Reform*, 5; Logan, *Feminism and Criminal Justice*, 31–32, 147–57; *Annual Public Meeting*, 1 Howard J. 1, 6–7 (1921). In 1927, after appointment as Somerville's Principal, Fry resigned as an Honorary Secretary of the Howard League; she continued to chair its governing committee. *Resignation of Miss Margery Fry*, 2 Howard J. 77 (1927).

25. Gordon Rose, *The Struggle for Prison Reform: the Howard League and its Predecessors*, dedication page (Quadrangle Books, Inc., 1961).

26. Sir George Benson, *Miss Cicely Craven*, Times [of London], 18, Feb. 15, 1962. Cicely M. Craven, *Corporal Punishment*, 1 British Med. J. 537 (Mar. 11, 1939); George Benson & Cicely M. Craven, *The Purpose of Imprisonment*, 7 Howard J. 162 (1948).

27. Anne Logan, *The Life of Gertrude Eaton (1864–1940): Musician, Tax Resistor and Penal Reformer*, 2 Women's Hist. 5, 9 (2019).

28. *Foreign Prison Conditions, Howard League Campaign, Tribute to Work of Miss G. Eaton*, The Guardian, 10, Jan. 15, 1936.

29. Cicely Craven, *Miss Gertrude Eaton*, 4 Howard J. 133, 133 (1935) (emphasis in original).

30. Letter S. Margery Fry to van der Aa, Sept. 1925, Howard League Warwick Archives, MSS.16B/3/IN/1/1.

31. Craven, *Miss Gertrude Eaton*, 133.

32. Eaton, 93–97. Another draft did not have the language I quoted. See Joint Committee of the Friends' Council for International Service and the Howard League for Penal Reform, Suggested Draft of Minimum Rights for Prisoners in All Civilised Countries (undated), Howard League Warwick Archives, MSS.16B/3/IN/1/2. A different version is in the IPPC Archives: Howard League, Suggested Draft of Minimum Rights for Prisoners in All Civilised Countries, Mar. 17, 1926, Box 2, File 4. The Howard League labeled its first version "in consultation with the Society of Friends . . . [and] amended in consultation with the League of Nations Union." Howard League, Arguments in Favour of the Proposition That the Treatment of Prisoners Is a Matter for International Action (undated), Howard League Warwick Archives, MSS.16B/3/IN/1/7.

33. Point I and Point II, Howard League, Suggested Draft of Minimum Rights for Prisoners in All Civilised Countries Mar. 17, 1926, Box 2, File 4; Eaton, 96.

34. Letter Polwarth to Ruggles-Brise, Mar. 24, 1926, Box 2, File 2; Letter unnamed Sec. of Foreign Office to Ruggles-Brise (1926); Howard League Memorandum of the Attitude of the British Government, 1.

35. Letter van der Aa to Ruggles-Brise, Mar. 26, 1926, Box 4, File 1; Letters dated Mar. 17, 1926, and Mar. 24, 1926; Polwarth to Ruggles-Brise, Mar. 24, 1926, Box 2, File 2, 1.

36. Howard League Memorandum of the Attitude of the British Government, 1.

37. Bailey, *Rehabilitative Ideal*, 16–17, 29, 105–09, 145–56; Alexander Paterson, *Should the Criminologist be Encouraged?*, 26 Transactions Medico-Legal Soc. 180, 181–82 (1933); Ian Brown, *A Commissioner Calls: Alexander Paterson and Colonial Burma's Prisons*, 38 J. Se. Asia Stud. 293, 294 (2007); Alyson Brown, *Inter-War Penal Policy and Crime in England: The Dartmoor Convict Prison Riot, 1932*, 48–66 (Palgrave, 2013); Bill Forsythe, *National Socialists and the English Prison Commission: The Berlin Penitentiary Congress of 1935*, 17 Int'l J. Soc. L. 131, 133–34 (1989).

38. Howard League Memorandum of the Attitude of the British Government, 2–3; Eaton, 95; *The Howard League Annual Meeting*, 2 Howard J. 249, 252–53 (1928); Logan, *Politics of Penal Reform*, 122–27; V. E. Watkin, *Prisons and the League of Nations*, 2 Howard J. 356, 357 (1929).

39. Warren Rosenblum, *Beyond the Prison Gates: Punishment & Welfare in Germany, 1850–1933* (UNC Press, 2008); Gabriel N. Finder, *"Education Not Punishment": Juvenile Justice in Germany, 1890–1930* (unpublished PhD diss., U. Chi., 1997); David Garland, *Punishment and Welfare: A History of Penal Strategies* (Gower Publ. Co., 1985); David Garland, *Punishment and Modern Society: A Study in Social Theory* (U. Chi. Press, 1990); Sandra Leukel, "Reforming Women's Prisons in Imperial Germany," in *Crime and Criminal Justice in Modern Germany*, 86–112 (Richard F. Wetzell ed., Berghahn Books, 2014).

40. Professor Liepmann, *Prison Reforms in Germany*, 1 Howard J. 169–72 (1924).

41. Craven, *Miss Gertrude Eaton*, 133.

42. Howard League Arguments in Favour, 1–3.

43. Logan, *Politics of Penal Reform*, 112–16; Memorandum by Captain L. H. Green; Howard League Warwick Archives, M85/16B/3/IN/1/6. Seeking to involve the International Labour Organisation, Eaton was counseled to include "the general question of prison conditions."

44. The Howard League, Notes on the Draft Convention for the Treatment of Prisoners, 1927, 1, MSS.16B/3/IN/1/4. The Howard League for Penal Reform, An International Convention for Prisoners: An Appeal to the League of Nations, 1928, 1–2, MSS.16B/3/IN/1/9, both in Howard League Warwick Archives.

45. Rose, 317–18; Letter van der Aa to Polwarth, July 11, 1927, Box 35, File 4 (quoting the League of Nations' resolution written in French).

46. Letter van der Aa to Waller, June 6, 1926, Box 4, File 1; Waller to van der Aa, Apr. 9, 1927; van der Aa to Waller, May 8, 1927; van der Aa to All Members of the IPC, July 25, 1927; Extract of Letter from Polwarth to van der Aa, Apr. 27, 1927, S-0915, Box 35, File 4; Aperçu des réponses reçues des membres de la Commission, IPPC/UN S-0915, Box 46, File 4, 1.

47. Lin-Manuel Miranda, "The Room Where It Happens," *Hamilton*, 2015.

CHAPTER 6

1. Maurice Waller, Outline of Draft for Standard Minimum Rules (SMR) on the Treatment of Prisoners, 1927, Rule 30, IPPC, UN Archives, NY, S-0915, Box 35, File 4 (all UN/IPPC archival material in this chapter are from S-0915).

2. Rules 8, 12, 17 of the SMR for the Treatment of Prisoners, drawn up and revised in 1933 by the International Penal and Penitentiary Commission and recommended to Governments by the Assembly of the League of Nations (LN) at its Fifteenth Ordinary Session, Sept. 1934.

3. Rule 36, 1934 Rules.

4. Belgian General Observations Concerning the Project's Aims, Box 35, File 4, 2 (my translation, as are other French materials).

5. Response of M. Simon van der Aa, to Circular July 25, 1927, Box 35, File 4, 1, 3; Preliminary Observations, 1934 Rules.

6. Point IV, Suggested Draft of Minimum Rights for Prisoners in All Civilised Countries, Joint Committee of the Howard League, the Society of Friends and the LN Union, Box 2, File 2, 2; Gertrude Eaton, *The Need for an International Charter for Prisoners*, 2 Howard J. 93, 96 (1927). The draft added that '[i]f corporal punishment is permitted by the law of the country, it should not be inflicted at the discretion of the police or prison officials, nor upon unconvicted prisoners, but only upon prisoners after conviction and sentence by a legal tribunal."

7. Rules 24, 25, 26, 27, 28, 29, 30, Waller's 1927 Draft Rules.

8. Response van der Aa, July 25, 1927, Box 35, File 4, 6.

9. Rules 31, 33, 32, Waller's 1927 Draft.

10. Memo van der Aa to Members of the Commission, July 25, 1927, Box 35, File 4, 1–2.

11. Letter Ernest Delaquis, Chief of Police of Switzerland's Fed. DOJ and Police, to van der Aa, Oct. 19, 1927, 2.

12. Letter [French] Dir. of the Ministry of Justice's Office to van der Aa, Sept. 1, 1927, Box 35, 2; Delaquis Letter of Oct. 19, 1927, 1, 3.

13. Letter Charles Didion on "General Observations Concerning the Idea the Project Attempts to Achieve," Dec. 1, 1927, Box 35, File 4, 8, 9.

14. Margery Fry, *Retirement of Sir Maurice Waller*, 2 Howard J. 192–93 (1928); Editorial, *The League of Nations and the State of Prisons*, 2 Howard J. 184–86 (1928).

15. *Actes du Congrès Pénitentiaire International de Prague, Août 1930, Procès-Verbaux des Séances*, Vol. Ia, iii–iv (van der Aa ed., Staempfli & Cie, 1931); Ernest Delaquis, *L'Œuvre de la Commission Internationale pénal et pénitentiaire, 1872–1942*, Box 3, File 3, 5.

16. Letter van der Aa to Members of the Commission on Proposed Rules, Apr. 8, 1929, Box 23, File 6; Simon van der Aa, *Preface to the International Penitentiary Commission's Draft of the Standard Minimum Rules for the Treatment of Prisoners*, 5 Bull. Int'l Penitentiary Comm'n. 3–6 (1929).

17. Van der Aa letter Apr. 8, 1929; French delegate letter, Apr. 22, 1929, Box 23, File 5; Rule 36, 25, 1929 Bulletin Draft, English, 16; Rules 25, 26, Waller 1927 Draft.

18. Margery Fry, *Arms of the Law*, 161 (Camelot Press, Ltd., 1951).

19. Rule 38, 1929 Bulletin Draft, 16–17.

20. Rule 39, 40, 1929 Bulletin Draft, 17.

21. Letter Ogden Chisolm to van der Aa, Mar. 8, 1929; van der Aa to Chisolm, Mar. 1928, Box 1, File 13.

22. *Mrs. Alexander to Wed H. O. Wittpenn*, NY Times, 1, Jan. 6, 1915; *Mrs. Wittpenn Gets Post*, NY Times, 26, Apr. 12, 1929; *H. Otto Wittpenn, Banker, Is Dead*, NY Times, 18, July 26, 1931; *Mrs. H. O. Wittpenn, Civic Leader, Dies*, NY Times, 17, Dec. 5, 1932; Letter Sanford Bates to van der Aa, June 6, 1929, Box 1, File 13; *Prison Conference Abroad Described: Jersey Woman Honored by Delegates*

in Berne, Sunday Call, Sept. 15, 1929, Box 6, File 1; Aperçus des réponses reçues des membres de la Commission, undated, Box 46, File 4, 3.

23. LN, Improvements in Penal Administration, Report by the Delegate [Agüeroy Bethancourt] of Cuba (undated), C.51.1930.IV, Box 46, File 4, 1–3; Letter League Sec.-Gen. Eric Drummond to van der Aa, Jan. 30, 1930, Box 46, File 4.

24. *1930 IPPC Prague*, Vol. Ia, 16, 18–19.

25. *1930 IPPC Prague*, Vol. Ia, 473–77.

26. *1930 IPPC Prague*, Vol. Ia, 477–79.

27. *1930 IPPC Prague*, Vol. Ia, 480–82.

28. *1930 IPPC Prague*, Vol. Ia, 484; V.E. Watkins, *Penal Reform and the League of Nations*, 3 Howard J. 80, 82 (1930).

29. *1930 IPPC Prague*, Vol. Ia, 484–86; *1930 IPPC Prague* Vol. Ib, 17.

30. Fry, *Arms of the Law*, opening page.

31. *1930 IPPC Prague*, Vol. Ia, 485; *Editorial*, 3 Howard J. 6–7 (1930); Virgina Woolf, *Roger Fry: A Biography*, 32–35 (Harcourt, Brace & Co., 1940). Woolf quoted Roger Fry's account of being forced to hold the "culprit" down for a "very precise" ritual.

32. *1930 IPPC Prague*, Vol. Ia, 486.

33. Letter Honorary Sec. Norman Sachisthal to van der Aa, July 30, 1930, Box 58, File 5. German states had been IPC members; the Reich joined after World War I. Martina Henze, *Crime on the Agenda: Transnational Organizations 1870–1955* (2010); *1930 IPPC Prague*, Vol. Ia, 517.

34. LN, *Sixth Meeting, Sept. 20, 1934*, 129, LN Official J., Special Supp. 28, 32–33 (1934).

35. Letter van der Aa to Drummond, Aug. 30, 1930, Box 46, File 4, 1–2; Memorandum for IPPC with notes by Delaquis, 1930, Box 46, File 4, 6–7, 8–9 (undated, post-Prague); *Eighth Meeting (Public, Then Private), Oct. 3, 1930*, 11, LN Official J., 1527, 1529–30 (1930).

36. *Editorial*, 3 Howard J. at 8–9; LN, Penal and Penitentiary Questions: Report of the Fifth Committee to the Assembly, Oct. 10, 1932, A.58, 1932, IV, 4.

37. LN, Improvements in Penal Administration: Report by the Secretary-General to the Twelfth Assembly, A.25, July 15, 1931, IV, 1–7.

38. LN, Penal and Penitentiary Questions: SMR: Activities of the Technical Organisations, Report by the Fifth Committee to the Assembly, A.44, Oct. 5, 1933, IV, 1; *Explanatory Memorandum Relating to the Revision of the Rules for the Treatment of Prisoners Drawn up by the International Penal and Penitentiary Commission*, 1–9 (1933), Annex 1 (A.44.1933.IV), 119 LN Official J., Special Supp. 30 (1933).

39. Activities of the Technical Organisations, 2; Letter Bates to van der Aa, March 21, 1933, Box 23, File 6, 3.

40. Rule 37, 1934 LN Special Supp. 129, Penal and Penitentiary Questions, A.3, 75.

41. 1933 IPPC Explanatory Memorandum Relating to the Rules for the Treatment of Prisoners, Report by the International Penal and Penitentiary Commission, 1933, 117–25, Prison Association of New York (pamphlet).

42. Rules 38, 39, 40, 1934 LN Special Supp. 129, Penal and Penitentiary Questions, A.3, 75.
43. Rules 33 and 34, 1934 LN Special Supp. 129, Penal and Penitentiary Questions, A.3, 74.
44. 1933 IPPC Explanatory Memorandum Relating to the Rules for the Treatment of Prisoners, 123.
45. LN, *Report of the Fifth Comm. to the Assembly, Annex 3*, 129 LN Official J., Special Supp. 63, 69 (1934); 1934 LN Observations by the Governments Regarding the Revised Rules on the Treatment of Prisoners, 1–12.
46. *Editorial*, 4 Howard J. 7, 8 (1934); Howard League for Penal Reform Resolution to HM Government, July 20, 1934, Howard League Warwick Archives, MSS.16B/3/IN/1/56; LN, *Sixth Meeting of the Fifth Committee, Penal and Penitentiary Questions: General Discussion, Sept. 20, 1934*, 129, LN Official J., Special Supp. 28, 33, 129, 63, 69 (1934).
47. LN, *Resolutions Adopted on the Reports of the Fifth Committee*, 123 LN Official J., Special Supp. 14, 16–17 (1934).
48. LN, Improvements in Penal Administration: Report by the Secretary-General to the Twelfth Assembly, A.25, July 15, 1931, IV, 6.

CHAPTER 7

1. Alexander Paterson, Memorandum on Extending the Scope and Activities of the International Penal and Prison Commission, May 1935, IPPC, UN Archives, NY, S-0915, Box 11, File 1, 6–7 (all UN/IPPC archival materials are from S-0915).
2. Letter S. Margery Fry to IPC Leaders, Sept. 1925, Howard League Warwick Archives, MSS.16B/3/IN/1/1; Suggested Schedule of Conditions Observed in all Civilised Countries in the Treatment of Persons under Arrest or in Captivity on Whatever Charge, 1927, Howard League Warwick Archives, MSS.16B/3/IN/1/3.
3. Letter Sanford Bates to Simon van der Aa, June 5, 1934, Box 61, File 1.
4. Letter Cicely Craven to Paterson, July 23, 1934; Craven to van der Aa, July 24, 1934; van der Aa to Craven, Aug. 2, 1934, Box 61, File 1; Bill Forsythe, *National Socialists and the English Prison Commission: The Berlin Penitentiary Congress of 1935*, 17 Int'l J. Soc. L. 131, 137 (1989).
5. William Frederick Meinecke Jr., *Conflicting Loyalties: The Supreme Court in Weimar and Nazi Germany, 1918–1945*, 128–38, 178–80, 272–74 (PhD diss., U. of Maryland, 1998), UMI 9920971.
6. Letter van der Aa to Bates, Aug. 14, 1934; van der Aa to Craven, Aug. 29, 1934, Box 61, File 1.
7. Paterson, Extending IPPC Scope, 2–5; Visit of English Prison Officials to Germany, Sept.–Oct. 1934, Box 35, File 5, 1–19; Rapport sur l'échange de fonctionnaires pénitentiaires pratiqué en 1934 par l'Allemagne et l'Angleterre, Box 11, File 1.

8. Letter Sheldon Glueck to van der Aa, Jan. 9, 1935, Box 59, File 7; Nora Adler to van der Aa, Apr. 22, 1934; van der Aa to Paterson, Apr. 15, 1934; Paterson to van der Aa, May 2, 1934, Box 59, File 2.

9. Paterson, Extending IPPC Scope, 6–7.

10. Letter Craven to van der Aa, June 3, 1935, Box 60, File 7; Fry to van der Aa, June 4, 1935, Box 48, File 4.

11. Geoffrey H. C. Bing, *The International Penal and Penitentiary Congress, Berlin, 1935*, 4 Howard J. 195, 195 (1935).

12. Bing, 195–96.

13. Representatives came from Afghanistan, Argentina, Austria, Belgium, Bolivia, Brazil, Bulgaria, Canada, Chile, China, Cuba, Czechoslovakia, Denmark, Dominican Republic, Egypt, Estonia, Finland, France, Germany, Great Britain, Greece, Guatemala, Holland, Hungary, Iran, Iraq, Italy, Japan, Latvia, Liberia, Lithuania, Luxembourg, Mexico, Nicaragua, Norway, Peru, Poland, Portugal, Romania, Siam, Spain, Sweden, Switzerland, Turkey, United States of America, United States of South Africa, Uruguay, Venezuela, and Yugoslavia. Letter van der Aa to Dir. of the League of Nations' International Bureau Section, Mar. 24, 1936, Box 60, File 9, 2. Martina Henze, *Crime on the Agenda: Transnational Organizations 1870–1955*, 109 Historisk Tidsskrift 369, 396 (2009).

14. *Actes du Congrès Pénal et Pénitentiaire International de Berlin Août 1935*, Vol. Ia, iv, 3, 24, 184, 196–97 (Staempfli & Cie, 1936).

15. *1935 IPPC Berlin*, Vol. Ia, 86–106, 119; "Germany from the Inside: The Constructive Project of the Nationalist-Socialist State," *1935 IPPC Berlin*, 230–31; Bing, 196; Forsythe, 137–39; Philippe Sands, *East West Street* (Weidenfeld & Nicolson, 2017).

16. Negley K. Teeters, *Deliberations of the International Penal and Penitentiary Congresses, Questions and Answers, 1872–1935*, 177–80 (Temple U. Book Store, 1949). The 605 copies, published in 1949, cost $1,495 to print; the IPPC had provided Teeters with a subsidy of $1,415. Slow sales resulted in a loss, with efforts to sell the book again at the 1950 Hague Congress. IPPC Administrative Report, August 1949 to date, May 4, 1950, VII; app. VIII, Box 27, File 5; Martina Henze, Transnational Cooperation and Criminal Policy: The Prison Reform Movement 1820s to 1950s, *Shaping the Transnational Sphere: Experts, Networks, and Issues from the 1840s to the 1930s*, 207–08 (Berghahn Books, 2015).

17. *1935 IPPC Berlin*, Vol. Ia, 316, 343, 345, 510; 530–31, 101–03; 226–27.

18. *1935 IPPC Berlin*, Vol. Ia, 164, 327–49, 529–34; Vol. Ib, 88, 149–50; Bing, 196–98.

19. *1935 IPPC Berlin*, Vol. Ib, 178; Letters van der Aa to Paterson & Bates, Sept. 16, 1935, Box 60, File 12.

20. Nazis likewise controlled the International Criminal Police Commission. Paul Knepper, *International Crime in the 20th Century*, 84–85 (Palgrave Macmillan, 2011).

21. *Geneva: A Letter from Margery Fry*, 4 Howard J. 117, 134 (1935).
22. *Eighth Meeting of the Sixteenth Ordinary Session of the League of Nations Fifth Committee, Sept. 21, 1935*, 142 LN Official J., Special Supp. 49, 50 (1935).
23. *Treatment of Prisoners: An Appeal to the League of Nations, Sept. 1934*, Warwick Archives; *The League of Nations and the Problem of the Prisoner: A Plea by the Howard League for Penal Reform for the Observation of the Standard Minimum Rules of the International Penal and Penitentiary Commission (SMR)*, Sept. 1935, 2; Attachment, Violations of the SMR, Warwick Archives; Vespasian V. Pella, *Penal and Penitentiary Questions: Report Submitted by the Fifth Committee to the Assembly*, 142 LN Official J., Special Supp. 75, 76 (1935); Editorial, *A Charter for Prisoners*, 3 Howard J. 13 (1933).
24. Pella, *1935 Report*, 76–78; *Resolutions Adopted on the Reports of the Fifth Committee*, 137 LN Official J., Special Supp. 24 (1935).
25. Home Office, SMR, London: printed and published by His Majesty's Stationery Office, 1936, Box 48, File 4, 2. Figure 7.1 is reproduced courtesy of the UN Archives.
26. Clare Anderson, *Convicts: A Global History*, 24 (Cambridge U. Press, 2022).
27. Pella, *Penal and Penitentiary Questions: Report Submitted by the Fifth Committee to the Assembly*, 160 LN Official J., Special Supp. 63, 63–64 (1936); *Eighth Meeting of the Seventeenth Ordinary Session of the League of Nations Fifth Committee, Oct. 6, 1936*, 160 LN Official J., Special Supp. 42, 44 (1936).
28. Letter Fry & Craven to unnamed recipient, and Memorandum, The Prison Population of the World, Aug. 10, 1936; van der Aa to Fry, Aug. 13, 1936, Box 48, File 7.
29. Pella, *1936 Report*, 1; *1936 Eight Meeting of the Seventeenth Session of the Fifth Committee*, 43–45; Letter van der Aa, Nov. 30, 1936, Box 48, File 7; Replies to Questionnaire Relating to the SMR Revision, 1937, Box 26, File 3, 1.
30. Letter van der Aa to the Foreign Ministers of Afghanistan, Iraq, Liberia & Saudi Arabia, Oct. 5, 1937, Box 49, File 1, 1–2; *Eighth Meeting of the Eighteenth Ordinary Session of the League of Nations Fifth Committee, Sept. 25, 1937*, 174 LN Official J., Special Supp. 47, 49, 51 (1937); John J. Hearne, *Penal and Penitentiary Questions: Report of the Fifth Committee to the Assembly*, 174 LN Official J., Special Supp., 87–88 (1937).
31. Anne Logan, *The Politics of Prison Reform: Margery Fry and the Howard League*, 126 (Routledge, 2018) (quoting a 1938 Fry report).
32. *Eighth Meeting of the Eighteenth Ordinary Session of the League of Nations Fifth Committee, Sept. 24, 1938*, 188 LN Official J. Special Supp., 30–35 (1938); Enquiry into the Number of Prisoners and the Measures Taken to Reduce It: Report by the International Penal and Penitentiary Commission, 1938, Box 48, File 7; Société des Nations: Questions Pénales et Pénitentiaires. Réunion des Organisations Techniques Pour Discuter la Question du Traitement des Témoins et des Prévenus, June 22, 1939, Box 49, File 5; Letter Fry to Ernest Delaquis, Aug. 1, 1939, Box 49, File 6.
33. Letter Delaquis to Paterson, May 2, 1939, Box 62, File 5.

34. *Jews Are Ordered to Leave Munich*, NY Times, 3, Nov. 11, 1938; *A Black Day for Germany*, London Times, 15, Nov. 11, 1938. *No Regrets Voiced: Goebbels Declares the Nation Followed its "Healthy Instincts,"* NY Times, 1, Nov. 12, 1938; Alan E. Steinweis, *Kristallnacht 1938* (Belknap Press of Harvard U. Press, 2009); Kyle Jantzen & Jonathan Durance, *Our Jewish Brethren: Christian Responses to* Kristallnacht *in Canadian Mass Media*, 46 J. Econ. Stud. 537 (2011).

35. *Liberté, Droit, Paix Détruits Pendants 5 Ans de Régime Hitlérien*, Centre International Pour le Droit et la Liberté en Allemagne, Paris, France, Jan. 30, 1938 ("Liberty, Rights, and Peace Destroyed Throughout 5 Years of Hitler's Regime," International Center for Rights and Liberty in Germany), and Annex I, IPPC/UN Archives S-0915, Box 55, File 5. Figure 7.3 is reproduced courtesy of the UN Archives. The cover letter from Andrée Marty-Capgras asked van der Aa to submit the materials to the Commission. Its folder labeled "various questions, November 9, 1935 to 1950" did not include responses. This French memorandum may reside in archives of other organizations; thus far, I have not found discussions of it in English or French. Thanks to French historians Alice Kaplan and Patrick Weil, who identified references to prominent participants in the French Communist Party; their guidance enabled me to locate a 1937 European conference held in Paris at which 169 delegates joined to create the Center, composed of eighty-four parties, unions, and religious organizations. *Le Conférence pour le Droit et la Liberté en Allemagne a Terminé ses Travaux*, L'Œuvre, 3, Nov. 15, 1937. The Center published articles in the "Correspondence Internationale," and some members wrote pamphlets calling for efforts to stop the Nazis. *La Nouvelle Année dans les Geôles Hitlériennes*, Correspondance Internationale, 19, Jan. 1, 1938; *La Gestapo Veut Faire Croire à une Amnistie*, Correspondance Internationale, 38, Jan. 8, 1938; N. N. Marceau, *Cinq Ans de Dictature Hitlérienne*, 44 (1938).

36. *1938 Régime Hitlérien*, 1–23.

37. *1938 Régime Hitlérien*, 19–24; *Le 16 avril: Ernst Thälmann a eu 53 ans*, Le Cri des travailleurs des A.M.: organe de la région communiste du Sud-Est, 3, Apr. 22, 1939.

38. Memorandum on the Vocational Training of Penitentiary Officials, July 7, 1938, Box 19, File 6; Letter van der Aa to Giovanni Novelli, July 30, 1938, Box 35, File 6.

39. Henze, *Crime on the Agenda*, 388–90; Letter Delaquis to Polwarth, Paterson, Bates & Beyers, Oct. 19, 1938, and Dec. 5, 1938, Box 61, File 6; Delaquis to Members of the IPPC, re: Traitement des prévenus et des témoins (Treatment of Persons Awaiting Trial and of Witnesses), Dec. 29, 1938, Box 49, File 8.

40. Enquiry into the Number of Prisoners and the Measures Taken to Reduce It: Report by the International Penal and Penitentiary Commission 1938, Box 48, File 7, 4–40.

41. Annotation for the Report of the International Penal and Penitentiary Commission, Europe, Dec. 1936, Box 48, File 8. Figure 7.4 is reproduced courtesy of the UN Archives.

42. Dear Sir, Form Letter, undated (sent Jan.–Apr. 1939), Box 61, File 6; Liste des rapporteurs belges pour le Congrès de Rome, 1940, undated, Box 4, File 1; Printed Programme of Questions to be Dealt with at the XIIth International Penal and Penitentiary Congress, Rome 1940, Box 67, File 2.
43. Programme of Questions to be Dealt with at the XIIth International Penal and Penitentiary Congress, Rome 1940, Box 61, File 4, 8–14.

CHAPTER 8

1. Letter Sanford Bates to Ernest Delaquis, Sept. 12, 1939, IPPC, UN Archives, NY, S-0915, Box 62, File 4 (all UN/IPPC archival material in this chapter are from S-0915 unless otherwise specified).
2. Letter Delaquis to "His Excellency the Minister of the United States of America" (US State Dept.), responding to a Nov. 20, 1942, request of the State Dept., Dec. 11, 1942, Box 5, File 3, 9.
3. Letter Thorsten Sellin to Bates, May 26, 1950, Box 52, File 8, 2.
4. Letter Alexander Paterson to Delaquis, Aug. 30, 1939, Box 5, File 2.
5. Giovanni Novelli, *The Prison Program of Italy*, 157 Annals of the Am. Acad. Pol. Soc. Sci. 208 (D. Vittorini trans., 1931); Nathaniel Cantor, *New Prison Program of Italy*, 26 J. Crim. L. & Criminology 216, 220–22 (1935); Paul Garfinkel, *Criminal Law in Liberal and Fascist Italy*, 457–69 (Cambridge U. Press, 2017); Patrick Bernhard, *Blueprints of Totalitarianism: How Racist Policies in Fascist Italy Inspired and Informed Nazi Germany*, 6 Fascism 127 (2017); Martina Henze, *Crime on the Agenda: Transnational Organizations*, 1870–1955, 109 Historisk Tidsskrift 369, 390 (2009).
6. Letter Delaquis to Paterson, May 2, 1939, Box 62, File 5; Paterson to Delaquis, May 31, 1939, Box 62, File 5; Delaquis to Novelli, Apr. 15, 1939, Box 49, File 7, 3. Delaquis sent a "confidential" letter to learn about relocation to a Swedish colleague, who replied a 1945 Congress was a possibility, pending approval by the IPPC Commission. Delaquis to Karl Schlyter, Apr. 18, 1939; Schlyter to Delaquis, Apr. 25, 1939, Box 62, File 6.
7. Letter Bates to Delaquis, Sept. 12, 1939.
8. Letter Margery Fry to Delaquis, Sept. 16, 1939, Box 4, File 1.
9. Letter Delaquis to Commissioner re Activity of the Commission during the European Crisis, Sept. 20, 1939, Box 5, File 3; Thorsten Sellin, Lionel Fox and the International Penal and Penitentiary Commission, *Studies in Penology Dedicated to the Memory of Sir Lionel Fox*, 195 (Manuel López-Rey & Charles Germain eds., 1964) (Sellin on Fox); Delaquis to IPPC Commissioners, Dec. 16, 1939, Box 4, File 1; Delaquis to Novelli, Dec. 18, 1939, Box 62, File 4.
10. Delaquis to IPPC Members, Dec. 16, 1940, Box 4, File 1; Letter Delaquis to Novelli, July 1, 1941; Delaquis to Novelli, Oct. 3, 1941, Box 61, File 8. Delaquis had been a professor in Germany and after the war did not condemn Nazis.
11. Delaquis to IPPC Members, Dec. 10, 1941, Box 4, File 1.
12. Karolina Wierczyńska & Grzegorz Wierczyński, Stefan Glaser: Polish Lawyer, Diplomat and Scholar, *The Dawn of a Discipline: International Criminal*

Justice and Its Early Exponents, 306–34 (Frédéric Mégret & Immi Tallgren eds., 2020); Letter Glaser to Delaquis, Dec. 1, 1941, Box 4, File 1, 1; Delaquis to Glaser, Jan. 14, 1942, Box 4, File 1.

13. Delaquis to IPPC Members, Dec. 8, 1945, Box 4, File 1, 1.

14. Sanford Bates, *One World in Penology*, 38 J. Crim. L. & Criminology 565, 575 (1948).

15. Delaquis to IPPC Members, Dec. 16, 1943; Delaquis to IPPC Members, enclosing the "Procès-verbaux" from the Aug. 26–31, 1945, IPPC in Berne, Dec. 27, 1944, Box 4, File 1; Delaquis to IPPC Members, Dec. 8, 1945.

16. Appointed in 1939, Fry left that position in 1948. Anne Logan, *The Politics of Prison Reform: Margery Fry and the Howard League*, 126 (Routledge, 2018).

17. In March 1946, Paterson had written Delaquis that he would be submitting a resolution on "concentration camps and internment." Réunion de Bureau, Berne June 29, 1945–Sept. 1946, Box 7, File 2. Paterson became ill, and Fox replaced him. Letter Fox to Delaquis, Apr. 1, 1946, Box 7, File 2. Fox noted that Paterson was the source of the 1946 resolution, which attested to his "deeply humane sense." Administrative Report by the Executive Committee of the IPPC, Sept. 1946–July 1948, 10. The 1946 resolution echoed concerns that Paterson had raised in 1935, as recounted in the last chapter. Paterson, Memorandum on Extending the Scope and Activities of the International Penal and Prison Commission, May 1935, Box 11, File 1, 6.

18. Relations between IPPC and UNO (date unclear/Apr. 28 or Sept. 28), 1946, Box 11, File 6, 1; Delaquis to IPPC Members, Dec. 27, 1946, 1; IPPC's Confidential 1947 Plan for the Negotiations with UNO, Box 52, File 4, 30–31; Sellin on Fox, 197–200.

19. Sellin on Fox, 199–200.

20. *Sanford Bates, 88, Who Headed Federal Prison System, is Dead*, NY Times, 26, Sept. 9, 1972; Andrew R. Bruce, Editorial, *Appointment of Mr. Bates*, 20 J. Crim. L. & Criminology 165, 166 (1929); *Bates Appointment*, 23 J. Crim. L. & Criminology, 856, 856 (Newman F. Baker ed., 1933); *Bates Resignation*, 27 J. Crim. L. & Criminology 923, 923 (1937); *Encyclopedia of American Prisons*, 52 (Marilyn D. McShane & Frank P. Williams III eds., Garland Publ., 1996).

21. Sanford Bates, *Honor System for Inmates of Prisons and Reformatories*, 13 J. Crim. L & Criminology 109, 110 (1922).

22. Hans von Hentig, *Degrees of Parole Violations and Graded Remedial Measures*, 33 J. Crim. L. & Criminology 363, 363–70 (1943). Refusing to salute Hitler, Hentig was fired from the University of Bonn, fled to the United States, and taught at several universities. Hans von Hentig Papers, U. Colo. Boulder Libraries, Special Collections & Archives; Mabel A. Elliott, *A Comment on the Von Hentig-Bates Parole Controversy*, 34 J. Crim. L & Criminology 96, 97 (1943).

23. Bates, *One World*, 567–69.

24. Letter Fox to Delaquis, Nov. 1, 1946, Box 11, File 6; Bates to Delaquis, Dec. 26, 1946, Box 51, File 1; Administrative Report by the Executive Committee of the IPPC, Sept. 1946–July 1948, Box 8, File 6, 1–2.

25. Address by Sanford Bates to the Hon. Chairman and Gentlemen of the Social Commission ("not for release"), Apr. 9, 1948, Box 19, File 5, 1.

26. Adolphe Delierneux, Action of the United Nations in the Field of Prevention of Crime and Treatment of Offenders, *1949 Proceedings Annual Congress of the American Prison Association*, 270, 277 (1949).

27. "Confidential" Plan for the Negotiations with UNO, Table of Contents, Synoptic Table of the Alternatives, Box 52, File 4; Sessions 1948 de la Commission Internationale Pénale et Pénitentiaire, Berne, Aug. 5, 1948, Box 13, File 4, 9; Letter Bates & Delaquis to Henri Laugier, Feb. 1948, Box 19, File 5. The letter had a thirteen-page attachment, Views of the International Penal and Penitentiary Commission Regarding Those Aspects of the Problem of Prevention of Crime and Treatment of Offenders Which Are Suitable for International Action, and How Such International Action Could Be Carried Out Most Effectively, Feb. 1948, 2–13; Data on Inter-Governmental Organizations, provided to the Division of Co-ordination and Liaison of the United Nations, Apr. 1948, Box 52, File 1, 2.

28. Plan for the Negotiations with the UNO, 22–43; Delaquis to Members of the IPPC, Mar. 31, 1947, Box 11, File 7; Recueil de Documents en Matière Pénale et Pénitentiaire, Mar. 1947, Box 19, File 6; Ensemble de Règles pour le Traitement des Prisonniers, Extrait, Observations préliminaires; Rules 36, 37, IPPC Bulletin, Vol. 12, Mar. 1947, Box 19, File 6.

29. *Criminologists to Get Data from 70 Countries—Social Commission Will Receive Projects Early in 1948*, NY Times, 7, June 21, 1947; Social Commission's "Instructions to Accompany Questionnaire on Prevention of Crime and Treatment of Offenders," Annex B to Preliminary Report on the Prevention of Crime and the Treatment of Offenders, UN, Economic and Social Council, Social Commission, Second Session, Aug. 28–Sept. 13, 1947, E/CN.5/30, Aug. 4, 1947, 14–16; Delierneux, Action of the United Nations, 277; Adolphe Delierneux, *Evolution of the Prison System in Belgium*, 157 Annals of the Am. Acad. Pol. & Soc. Sci. 180 (William Rex Crawford trans., 1931).

30. Letter Fox to Bates, Apr. 23, 1949, Box 52, File 5, 1; Delaquis to Fox Apr. 28, 1949, Box 52, File 5.

31. Memorandum re: International Penal and Penitentiary Commission, Restricted, May 10, 1949, Box 9, File 2, 1. (labeled for the "file" without author or addressee).

32. The IPPC had a house in Berne, "about 90,000 US dollars in investments, and about 20,000 dollars in annual revenue" from dues, of which the United States "accounted for thirty per cent." Letter Fox to Bates, Apr. 23, 1949; Sellin on Fox, 201; Letter Bates to Durward V. Sandifer, Deputy Dir. of the Office UN Affairs, US Dept of State, May 2, 1949, Box 52, File 5; Memorandum re: International Penal and Penitentiary Commission, Restricted, May 10, 1949. Delaquis explained that the "the IPPC alone" had the power to "dissolve itself and dispose of its funds." Letter Delaquis to Bates, May 7, 1949; Bates to Delaquis, May 13, 1949, Box 52, File 5; Walter Kotschnig, Chief, Div. UN Economic and Social Affairs to Bates, May 19, 1949, Box

9, File 2; Position Paper, US Delegation to the General Assembly, International Penal and Penitentiary Commission, Restricted US/A/C. 2&3 /13, Sept. 30, 1950, Box 53, File 2, 1.

33. Report Adopted by the Conference on 16 October 1948, Meeting of International Organizations Concerned with the Problem of the Prevention of Crime and Treatment of Offenders, Box 52, File 1, 7–8; Delaquis to IPPC Executive Committee, Sept. 23, 1949; Letter Fox to Delaquis, Sept. 26, 1949; Dr. E. Stan Rappaport to Delaquis, Oct. 5, 1949; Edgar M. Gerlach to Sellin, Dec. 5, 1949; Sellin to Gerlach, Dec. 14, 1949; Sellin to Gerlach, Feb. 13, 1950; Office of the Educational Adviser, Bielefeld, to Fox (undated), Box 64, File 2; IPPC Session of Aug. 6, 1948, Box 13, File 4, 7, 13.

34. International Penal and Penitentiary Commission: Report of the Sec.-Gen. under Resolution 262 B (IX) of the Economic and Social Council, Eleventh Session, June 19, 1950, Box 52, File 8, 2.

35. Berne 1949 Commission morning meeting minutes, Aug. 5, 1949, meeting, Box 11, File 8, 61–64; Thorsten Sellin, *Pioneering in Penology: The Amsterdam Houses of Correction in the Sixteenth and Seventeenth Centuries* (U. Penn. Press, 1944); Marvin E. Wolfgang, *Thorsten Sellin*, 140 Proc. Am. Phil. Soc. 581, 581–82 (1996); Sellin on Fox, 197; Letter Delaquis to Sellin, Dec. 22, 1949, Box 1, File 13.

36. Berne 1949 transcript excerpts, Aug. 1–6, 1949, meeting, Box 11, File 8, 18–48.

37. Berne 1949 transcript, Aug. 5, 1949, Box 11, File 8, 70–71; Résolution concernant la Révision de L'Ensemble de Règles, adopted Aug. 6, 1949. The IPPC constituted a subcommittee, chaired by Fox, to do so. Delaquis wrote the UN Sec.-Gen. that the IPPC hoped that its revisions would be "brought before the competent organs of the UN" at an appropriate time. Delaquis to UN Sec.-Gen., Aug. 19, 1949, Box 52, File 5; Commission Internationale Pénale et Pénitentiaire, collaboration with the UN, Aug. 5, 1949–Aug. 8, 1950, Box 25, File 5, 1, 3.

38. Lucy Freeman, *Crime Study Group is Proposed to UN*, NY Times, 7, Aug. 6, 1949; Report of the IPPC on its Activities During the Six-Month Period, Apr.-Sept, 1950, Box 53, File 2; Resolution Adopted by the Economic and Social Council, Aug. 10, 1949, Box 52, File 7; The United States, Statement on the International Penal and Penitentiary Commission, undated, 1–2. The United States proposed a "liquidation." On January 27, 1950, Martin Hill, the UN Director of Coordination for Specialized Agencies and Economic and Social Matters, wrote Sellin that several governments had commented on the "eventual integration" of the IPPC with the UN. Letter Hill to Sellin, Jan. 27, 1950; Sellin to Hill, Feb. 8, 1950, Box 52, File 8. The IPPC subcommittee for dissolution included Bates, Fox, and Cornil. They sought to "retain the professional character of the work" and for "precedence" on the agenda of the Social Commission. Suggested Agenda for Preliminary Conversation between Representatives of the United Nations and the Committee of the International Penal and Penitentiary Commission Appointed Aug. 1949, Mar. 21, 1950, Box 52, 1.

Observations Received from Governments on the Resolution of the Economic and Social Council of 10 Aug. 1949 with Respect to the International Penal and Penitentiary Commission, E/Cn.5.205, Feb. 21, 1950, Box 52, File 8. Representatives from France thought the "disappearance of the IPPC would be regrettable," from New Zealand that the IPPC had been "useful" at "small cost" and ought to continue, and from Norway, that IPPC identity should continue "within the framework of the United Nations." A member from Portugal called for "autonomy," and a person from Switzerland (where the IPPC had been sited for decades) argued that the UN should coordinate regional groups with Europe's within the IPPC. The United States' representative reiterated the country's support for full integration and the "termination of the IPPC." UN Economic and Social Council, Report of the Fifth Session of the Social Commission to the Economic and Social Council, E/1568, E/CN. 5/185, 14–15; Box 25, File 7 (6 Aug. 1949–8 Aug 1951). Remarques sur la Résolution du Conseil Économique & Social du 10 Août 1949, Se Rapportant aux Relations avec les Organisations Intergouvernementales, Dec. 1949, Box 52, File 7, 6.

39. Delaquis to IPPC Commissioners, Dec. 24, 1949, Box 5, File 1, 2. Before Sellin arrived in February of 1950, Dr. Hélène Pfander was in charge; I have found no suggestions the commissioners considered appointing her, although they sought to ensure her employment after the IPPC's demise. Administrative Report, Aug. 1949 to date, May 4, 1950, Box 27, File 5, 1.

40. Report of the Sec.-Gen., June 19, 1950; UN Economic and Social Council, Inter-Governmental Organizations, International Penal and Penitentiary Commission: Report by the Sec.-Gen. Under Resolution 262 B (IX) of the Economic and Social Council, E/1735, June 27, 1950, Box 52, File 8. The UN Economic and Social Council approved the final text on July 11, 1950, Letter Sellin to IPPC, July 20, 1950, Box 53, File 1. The General Assembly followed suit. Per the IPPC constitution, "due notification" was provided to all commissioners of the proposed "dissolution." Thorsten to IPPC Members, July 3, 1950; The IPPC commissioners approved, as recorded in a memorandum from Sellin to IPPC members not represented at the August 1950 Hague session, Aug. 17, 1950, Box 53, File 1. The two remaining IPPC staff members were given jobs with the UN By then, planning for a 1955 Congress was underway. J. Altmann-Smythe to Delierneux, Feb. 16, 1950, UN/IPPC, S-0441-0284-21773, 2.

41. Letter Bates to Delaquis, Aug. 22, 1949, Box 52, File 7, 2.

42. Letter Bates to Dean Acheson, Sec. of State, Oct. 24, 1949, Box 26, File 1.

43. Reference: Inquiry on the Penitentiary Aspect of the Problem of the Status of Women, Letter from the UN Acting Sec.-Gen. to the Members of the IPPC, Feb. 3, 1950; Questionnaire on the Penitentiary Aspect of the Problem of the Status of Women, attached to the Feb. 3, 1950; UN Commission on the Status of Women, Fourth Session, Application of Penal Law to Women: Preliminary Report Submitted by the Secretary-General, Apr. 13, 1950, 2–3, E/CN.6/139, I, Box 35, File 1.

44. UN Commission on the Status of Women, Application of Penal Law to Women, 14–15.
45. American Correctional Association, *A Manual of Corrections Standards*, vii–viii, 11, 246–48, 346–61 (1954).
46. Nir Shafir, *The International Congress as Scientific and Diplomatic Technology: Global Intellectual Exchange in the International Prison Congress, 1860–90*, 9 J. Glob. Hist. 72 (2014).

CHAPTER 9

1. Standard Minimum Rules for the Treatment of Prisoners (SMR), Resolution adopted by the First United Nations Congress on the Prevention of Crime and the Treatment of Offenders, held at Geneva, Aug. 30, 1955.
2. *Proceedings of Twelfth International Penal and Penitentiary Congress, The Hague, Aug. 14–19, 1950*, Vol. II, 529–30, 501, 482 (Thorsten Sellin ed., 1951).
3. Reproduction of this photograph was enabled by Dr. Mary Rogin, President of IPPF, and by Vice President Alejo Garcia Basalo.
4. Volume I gave French pride of place; Vol. II was in English. This chapter's quotes are from the English rather than my translations. Vols. III through VI, in French and English, included questions raised, papers presented, and discussions about "pre-sentence examination of the offender," "open institutions," "the problem of short-term imprisonment," and the "penal treatment of juvenile offenders." Hooykaas was a prosecuting attorney at the Netherlands' Cour de cassation and a counselor to its Ministry of Justice. The two women were Hélène Pfander, who had worked for the IPPC for years (and later joined the UN), and Elisabeth Rezelman of the Netherlands' Justice Ministry. The two delegates from Asia were Tomomitsu Ie, Inspector General of the Tokyo Prison Administration, and Senjin Tsuruoka from the Tokyo Prosecutor-General's office. *1950 IPPC Proceedings*, Vol. II, 570, 574, 564; IPPC Hague Conference Bulletin, Aug. 19, 1950, IPPC, UN Archives, NY, S-0915, Box 64, File 5, 2 (all UN/IPPC archival materials in this chapter are from S-0915).
5. *1950 IPPC Proceedings*, Vol. II, 565–80; 579–80; Administrative Report, Aug. 1949 to date, May 4, 1950, Box 27, File 5, 4; Offprint from Select Papers on Penal and Penitentiary Affairs, 15 IPPC Bulletin, Nov. 1950, Box 26, File 5, 348.
6. Charles Richmond Henderson, *Report of the Proceedings of the Eighth International Prison Congress, Wash. DC, Sept. and Oct. 1910*, HR Doc. No. 52, 23 (1913); Thorsten Sellin, Preface to *1950 IPPC Proceedings*, Vol. II, XI, XV.
7. *1950 IPPC Proceedings*, Vol. II, 524–26; photographs with overlays, 530–37.
8. *1950 IPPC Proceedings*, Vol. II, XV, 4.
9. Bulletin of the IPPC, Aug. 19, 1950, 2–5; *1950 IPPC Proceedings*, Vol. II, 591.
10. *1950 IPPC Proceedings*, Vol. II, 488.
11. *1950 IPPC Proceedings*, Vol. II, 503–51; Marc Ancel, *Social Defense: A Modern Approach to Criminal Problems*, 18–26 (Routledge & Kegan Paul, 1965). Sellin, joined by Chicago criminologist Norval Morris, issued a revised edition

describing social defense as a "utilitarian philosophy of punishment . . . deeply respectful of basic human rights and freedoms." Preface to Ancel, *Social Defense: The Future of Penal Reform*, xiii (Fred B. Rothman & Co., 1987).

12. *1950 IPPC Proceedings*, Vol. II, 491–501; Report Prepared by the Secretariat, First United Nations Congress on the Prevention of Crime and the Treatment of Offenders, Geneva, 22 Aug.–3 Sept. 1955, 3 (UN Dept. Econ. & Soc. Aff., NY 1956).

13. *1950 IPPC Proceedings*, Vol. II, 476.

14. *1950 IPPC Proceedings*, Vol. II, 476–85.

15. *1950 IPPC Proceedings*, Vol. II, 481–83, 488–90; Council of Europe Committee of Ministers, *Recommendation Rec (2006) 2-rev of the Committee of Ministers to Members States on the European Prison Rules* (adopted Jan. 11, 2006, amended July 1, 2020). Rule Two stated: "Persons deprived of their liberty retain all rights that are not lawfully taken away by the decision sentencing them or remanding them in custody."

16. *1950 IPPC Proceedings*, Vol. II, 488–90.

17. The report stated Cornil had been involved with a Committee for Assisting Jewish Refugees that, in May of 1940, was to make arrangements for Jewish women, senior citizens, and children when Jewish men were sent to camps. Rudi Van Doorslaer, Emmanuel Debruyne, Frank Seberechts & Nico Wouters, *La Belgique docile: Les autorités belges et la persécution des Juifs en Belgique pendant la Seconde Guerre mondiale*, 158, 700 (2007), quoting Note L.257, Paul Cavyn, s.l., (Oct. 1942), AMAE, dossier 11.573. Also cited was Jacques Mechelynck-Masson, President of the Court of Appeals of Brussels, who noted Cornil's arrival on January 19, 1943 and departure February 17, 1943; he reported that Cornil gave a lecture on "the penal regime" to fellow prisoners. André L. Mechelynck, *Jacques Mechelynck-Masson: Carnets de Campagne (1914–1919 et 1940–1945)*, 6, 196, 199, 204, 201–12 (2019). Another prisoner mentioned the "amusing paradox: among the hostages . . . is also our friend Paul Cornil, Inspector-General of Belgian prisons, now a prisoner himself." Anne S. Somerhausen, *Written in Darkness: A Belgian Woman's Record of the Nazi Occupation, 1940–1945*, 206 (Eumenes Publ., 2019).

18. Memoranda to and from Cornil, 1940–1944, including to Monsieur le Secrétaire Général, Sept. 26, 1941, 7. Cornil recorded concern that German orders did not comply with Belgium prison regulations. Unsigned memoranda of Oct. 3, 1942, and Oct. 10, 1942. Discussion through 1944 was about relieving Cornil of his duties. On Sept. 26, 1941, a Major Schriever relayed regulations from the High Command of the German Army on Belgian citizens sentenced in German courts. Rejecting Cornil's protests, Schriever stated that prisoners were to be treated in accordance with German principles requiring institutional clothing, forced labor of nine to ten hours per day, free movement every half hour, and in some prisons, fifteen-minute visits every two months, letters every four weeks, packages every two weeks of up to six kilograms, and prison commissary purchases every week. Forbidden activities included smoking, radio broadcasts, and

keeping newspapers. Punishments included revoking book privileges, contact with the outside world, free movement, commissary purchases, "hard beds," reduction of food provisions, deprivation of lighted cells, and extending sentences. Memorandum German Commander to Cornil, Sept. 26, 1941, 3–4. Other memoranda added more about German control. Memo Major Schriever to Cornil Regarding the Sentencing of Belgian Residents Convicted by German Courts, Oct. 6, 1941; Memo Cornil to Monsieur le Secrétaire Général, Sept. 26, 1941. Cornil later protested a plan to detain Belgian citizens (possibly members of the resistance) as violating Belgian law. Memo Cornil, Détention de Personnes Suspectes, to Ministère de l'Intérieur, Apr. 26, 1944. Thanks to staff at CEGES-SOMA for locating the archive's PALLAS catalogue and memoranda between 1940 and 1944 and two interviews.

Cornil's post-war work is discussed in Helen Grevers, *Re-education in Times of Transitional Justice: The Case of the Dutch and Belgium Collaborators After the Second World War*, 22 Eur. Rev. Hist. 771, 774 (2015). In his contribution to a 1954 US symposium, Cornil wrote that after the 1945 liberation, Belgium held about 70,000 alleged collaborators, by 1946, 26,000 individuals remained. He reported that "237 men and 4 women were . . . executed," and many sentenced to long terms. Paul Cornil, Prison Reform in Belgium Since the War, *Prisons in Transformation*, 293 Annals Am. Acad. Pol. & Soc. Sci. 130, 133 (Thorsten Sellin ed., 1954).

19. Martin Conway, *Collaboration in Belgium: Lèon Degrelle and the Rexist Movement, 1940–1944, at 286* (Yale U. Press, 1993).

20. Box 26, File 6, 2 of 2.

21. IPPC Sub-Committee on SMR, Second Report of the Chairman, Lionel Fox, Jan. 31, 1951; Travail de Sous Comm. Berne, Jan. 4–July 31, 1951; IPPC Sub-Committee on SMR, Report of Chairman for consideration at the meeting of the Sub-Committee in Paris, May 13–14, 1950, Box 26, File 3, 4; UN Economic and Social Council, Report of the Fifth Session of the Social Commission of the Economic and Social Council, E/1568, E/CN.5/18, Dec. 20, 1949, Box 25, File 7, 13.

22. Fox did a "Draft of an Enquiry to be addressed to each member on the question of revision of the Standard Minimum Rules." Aug. 8, 1949, Box 27, File 2. In addition to IPPC commissioners, letters were sent to prison directors. Letter Ernest Delaquis to Dr. Hans Gautschi, Dir. Cantonal Penitentiary in Saint-Gall, Sept. 7, 1949; Delaquis to IPPC, Sept. 3, 1949, Box 26, Files 1, 2, and 3. Many responses were "no reply" and "no comment." Sellin to Fox, Apr. 6, 1950, App. 2, 1–10.

23. Letter Sellin to Henri Langier, Asst. Sec.-Gen. in charge of the Dept. Soc. Aff., Mar. 6, 1950; Sellin to Fox, Mar. 10, 1950, Box 25, File 7; IPPC Sub-Committee on SMR, Report of Chairman, May 13–14, 1950. Fox totaled seventeen government replies. IPPC Sub-Committee on SMR, Second Report of the Chairman, Jan. 31, 1951, 3; France, Révision de l'ensemble de règles relatives au traitement de détenus, Aug. 6, 1949–Aug. 6, 1951, Box

25, File 6, 1; IPPC Sub-Committee on SMR, Second Report of the Chairman, Jan. 31, 1951, 2; Sellin to Fox, Apr. 6, 1950, Box 26, File 3, 1; Sellin to Fox, Apr. 6, 1950, and attached Appendix 3 (Additional Rules Suggested by the United States), Box 26, File 3; Israel's Answers to the Questionnaire on: the Standard Minimum Rules for the Treatment of Prisoners, Box 25, File 6, 1.

24. SMR Draft, July 1951, printed with hand annotations, Rule 1, 24, 52, Box 26, File 6 (2 of 2).

25. Process verbal, séance de Berne, July 2, 1951, Bandes 20, 4–5, Box 12, File 8. These transcribed tapes (*bande*), labeled by numbers, noted points when the transcriber could not catch what had been said.

26. SMR 1955, Rule 17.1, 17.3.

27. 1951 Process verbal, Bande 19, 8–9; SMR 1955, Rule 21.2, 68.

28. 1951 Process verbal, Bande 21, 1.

29. 1951 Process verbal, Bande 21, 3–4; 1951 IPPC Draft Rule 25, 466.

30. 1951 Process verbal, Bande 21, 3–4; 1951 IPPC Draft Rules, Preliminary Observation 4, 458.

31. Thorsten Sellin, Lionel Fox and the International Penal and Penitentiary Commission, *Studies in Penology Dedicated to the Memory of Sir Lionel Fox*, 195, 206 (Manuel López-Rey & Charles Germain eds., Martinus Nijhoff Publishers, 1964); Resolutions Adopted by the International Penal and Penitentiary Commission at its Last Session on 6 July 1951, 98–99.

32. IPPC's functions were transferred to the UN, which paid "tribute" to the accomplishments. Resolution 415(V), Adopted by the General Assembly at its 314th Plenary Meeting, Dec. 1, 1950, Box 53, File 3; Sellin on Fox, 206. Cornil became the president. Cornil, *Prison Reform in Belgium*, 138. Sellin chaired the IPPF from 1965 until 1971. Martina Henze, *Crime on the Agenda: Transnational Organizations, 1870–1955*, 109 Historisk Tidsskrift 369, 408, 410, 214n (2009).

33. *International Penal and Penitentiary Foundation*, 31 Int'l Rev. Crim. Pol'y 55, 57 (1974); Pierre-Henri Bolle, IPPF: Activities of the International Penal and Penitentiary Foundation, *The Contributions of Specialized Institutes and Non-Governmental Organizations to the UN Criminal Justice Program: A volume in honor of Adolfo Beria di Argentine*, 295, 298–302 (M. Cherif Bassiouni ed., Martinus Nijhoff Publishers, 1995); *Mental Health and Criminal Justice: International and Domestic Perspectives on Defendants and Detainees with Mental Illness*, xix (P. H. P. H. M. C. van Kempen & M. J. M. Krabbe eds., Eleven, 2021).

34. Seven people were appointed initially; the group expanded to ten, fifteen, and then twenty-seven when it became the "Committee on Crime Prevention and Control." Eduardo Vetere, The Work of the United Nations in Crime Prevention and Criminal Justice, *Contributions UN Criminal Justice Program*, 15, 16–17. The connotations of the term "social defense" prompted explanation that it meant no offense. Manuel López-Rey, *The First UN Congress on the Prevention of Crime and the Treatment of Offenders*, 47 J. Crim.

L. Criminology & Police Sci. 526, 527 n.1 (1957); Manuel López-Rey, *International Co-operation by the United Nations in the Prevention of Crime and the Treatment of Offenders*, 5 Br. J. Delinquency 125, 126–27 (1954); William Clifford, *Echoes and Hopes: The United Nations Committee on Crime Prevention and Control* 10 (Australian Inst. Criminology, 1979).

35. Details of the regional discussions of each rule were in the 1955 Observations and Proposals of the Secretariat. Report by the Secretariat, First United Nations Congress on the Prevention of Crime and the Treatment of Offenders, Standard Minimum Rules for the Treatment of Prisoners, Observations and Proposals of the Secretariat, A/Conf. 6/C.1/L.1, Geneva, Feb. 14, 1955. A rule-by-rule analysis, at 7–92, was followed by the Secretariat Draft, at 93–114, and the Human Rights Division discussion, at 49–50.

36. UN Department of Public Information, Press Release: UN Congress on Prevention of Crime Elects Officers, Aug. 22, 1955, SOC/2099, 1–2. The report identified 191 delegates from fifty-one countries, 101 from NGOs, and 234 attending in their personal capacity. *1955 UN Congress Report*, 2–5; Freda Adler & G. O. W. Mueller, A Very Personal and Family History of the United Nations Crime Prevention and Criminal Justice Branch, *Contributions UN Criminal Justice Program*, 3, 6; *1955 UN Congress Report*, 64–66; Negley K. Teeters, *What Have the States Done About Riots?*, 34 Prison J. 3–5 (1954); *1955 UN Congress Report*, 3; Margaret Tilley, *United Nations Congress on the Prevention of Crime and the Treatment of Offenders*, 3 Brit. J. Psychiatric Soc. Work 29 (1956). Fox became the Honorary President of the UN's Second Congress on the Prevention of Crime and Treatment Offenders, held in London in 1960. The membership shifted somewhat in 1976. William Clifford, *The Committee on Crime Prevention and Control*, 34 Int'l Rev. Crim. Pol'y 11, 16 (1978).

37. SMR 1955 Rules 1–3, 4(2); Tilley, 29; López-Rey, *The First UN Congress*, 530.

38. *1955 UN Congress Report*, 8, para. 61. Regional groups favored keeping the word "minimum" as some countries were not complying, and others had gone beyond the Rules. *1955 Secretariat Observations and Proposals*, 7–8, 6, para. 17, 10–12. The 1955 Congress debated the colonial issue; Fox argued that specific exemptions were not necessary as the Rules included a generic acknowledgment of difficulties of application. Those references were deleted, "not due to a lack of interest in the situation of the Trust and Non-Self-Governing Territories," but to avoid establishing distinctions in the "application of the Standard Minimum Rules." *1955 UN Congress Report*, 9–10, para. 75. Rule 2 stated the goal was to "stimulate a constant endeavor to overcome practical difficulties," as these standards were what was "accepted as suitable by the United Nations." Adoption was confirmed in ESC Res. 663 (XXIV) Social Commission Eleventh Session, Recommendations of the First United Nations Congress on the Prevention of Crime and the Treatment of Offenders (1957).

39. SMR 1955 Rule 6(1); UN General Assembly, Universal Declaration of Human Rights, art. II, Dec. 10, 1948; SMR 1955 Rule 45, 7, 38, 35(1), 44(3). The

Middle East regional group noted that many prisoners were not literate, and rules needed to call for information to be conveyed orally. *1955 Secretariat Observations and Proposals*, 46; SMR 1955 Rules 35(2), 45, 39, 55. The Rules provided that access to news (including "wireless transmissions") was to be "controlled by the administration."

40. Paul Cornil, *International Standards for the Treatment of Offenders*, 26 Int'l Rev. Crim. Pol'y 3, 4 (1968).

41. SMR 1955 Rules 9(1), 11(a), 13–14, 20–22. The proposed draft had called for a prisoner to have water "whenever he needs it," but was amended to be less "rigid from the point of view of the administration." *1955 UN Congress Report*, 12, para. 92.

42. Cited in Herman Woltring, The Evolution of the UN Policy Approaches to Crime Prevention and Criminal Justice: From the Committee on Crime Prevention and Control to the Commission on Crime Prevention and Criminal Justice, *Contributions UN Criminal Justice Program*, 65–66 (M. Cherif Bassiouni ed., 1995).

43. SMR 1955 Rules 57, 71, 59, 28(2).

44. SMR 1955 Rules 27–34. The ban on prisoner involvement in discipline came from all four of the regional groups, which "approved the insertion" of that principle, while also hoping to protect some forms of self-government. *1955 Secretariat Observations and Proposals*, 36–37.

45. SMR 1955 Rules 32, 57–58.

46. *1955 UN Congress Report*, 67.

47. Frank Dawtry, *First United Nations Congress on the Prevention of Crime and Treatment of Offenders*, 9 Howard J. 249, 250 (1956).

48. From 1951 until 1999, the UN journal was called the *International Review of Criminal Policy*. In 2001, the name became *Forum on Crime and Society*, which was published twice a year by the Center for International Crime Prevention, Office for Drug Control and Crime Prevention of the UN Secretariat. The six official languages were Arabic, Chinese, English, French, Russian, and Spanish. Antoinette Al-Mulla, *Note from the Managing Editor*, 1 F. Crime & Soc'y, iii (2001). The first issue drew on papers from the Tenth UN Congress on the Prevention of Crime and the Treatment of Offenders, held in April of 2000 in Vienna. Congresses remained the "principal policy-setting bodies" of the UN program on crime prevention and control. Woltring, 65–66.

49. J. Carlos Garcia Basalo, *Obstacles to the Implementation of the Standard Minimum Rules in Latin America*, 26 Int'l Rev. Crim. Pol'y 17 (1968); Jean Graven, *Importance and Scope of Minimum Rules for the Protection of Non-Delinquent Detainees*, 26 Int'l Rev. Crim. Pol'y 56, 64 (1968). By 1970, "more than twenty international conventions in different areas of human rights" had been concluded. The Standard Minimum Rules for the Treatment of Prisoners in the Light of Recent Developments in the Correctional Field, Working Paper prepared by the Secretariat for the Fourth United Nations Congress on the Prevention of Crime and the Treatment of Offenders, Kyoto, Japan, Aug. 17–26, 1970, 14, 25–26, 32.

50. International Covenant on Civil and Political Rights art. 7, Dec. 19, 1966, 999 United Nations Treaty Series 171; Draft Declaration on the Protection of All Persons from Being Subjected to Torture and Other Cruel, Inhuman or Degrading Treatment or Punishment art. I, adopted in 1975 by the UN Fifth Congress on the Prevention of Crime and the Treatment of Offenders and adopted unanimously by the UN General Assembly on Dec. 9, 1975, GA Res. 3452; Convention Against Torture and Other Cruel, Inhuman or Degrading Treatment or Punishment art. 1, Dec. 10, 1984, 1465 United Nations Treaty Series 85.

51. M. Cherif Bassiouni, Preface, *Contributions UN Criminal Justice Program*, xi–xii. Clifford described the lack of authority in 1978 of the "specialists on crime prevention and control," "[t]ucked neatly away in the interstices of the massive edifice of councils, agencies, programmes, funds, and standing conferences." Clifford, *UN Committee*, 11, 18; Clifford, *Echoes and Hopes*, 5–6, 20.

52. López-Rey y Arrojo, *The Quinquennial United Nations Congresses on the Prevention of Crime and the Treatment of Offenders*, 34 Int'l Rev. Crim. Pol'y 3, 10 (1978); López-Rey, *The First UN Congress*, 527.

53. Sanford Bates, *The Prison: Asset or Liability?*, 293 Annals Am. Acad. Pol. & Soc. Sci. 1, 8, 9 (1954).

54. Paul W. Tappan, *The Legal Rights of Prisoners*, 293 Annals Am. Acad. Pol. & Soc. Sci. 99, 100–11 (1954). Tappan relied on a Yale Law School dissertation, *The State Convict* (1952) by Samuel W. Widdifield. That two-volume account detailed gruesome use in the 1940s of corporal punishment in state facilities, overcrowding, and a lack of programs. Tappan called for recognizing prisoners' civil rights to maintain a "legitimate measure of self-respect on the part of the offender."

55. Report prepared by the Secretariat, Third United Nations Congress on the Prevention of Crime and the Treatment of Offenders, A/Conf. 26/7, Stockholm, Aug. 9–Aug. 18, 1965, 45. In the Petition and Brief in Support of Petition for Writ of Certiorari to the Supreme Court of Michigan, 6–7, 28, Sipes v. McGhee, 334 US 1 (1948) (No. 87), the argument was that the "solemn obligations of the United Nations Charter" would become "dead letters" without "protection against such judicial action to implement private agreements." The Michigan *Sipes* decision, 25 NW.2d 638 (Mich. 1947), was reversed by the Supreme Court when consolidated with Shelley v. Kraemer, 334 US 1 (1948). Paul Sayer, *Shelley v. Kraemer and United Nations Law*, 34 Iowa L. Rev. (1948), which invalidated racially restrictive land covenants; Judith Resnik, *Law's Migration: American Exceptionalism, Silent Dialogues, and Federalism's Multiple Ports of Entry*, 115 Yale L. J. 1564 (2006).

56. *1965 UN Congress Report*, 31–32; *The Challenge of Crime in a Free Society: A Report by the President's Commission on Law Enforcement and Administration of Justice* (1967); Elizabeth Hinton, *From the War on Poverty to the War on Crime: The Making of Mass Incarceration in America* (Harvard U. Press, 2016).

57. Kyoto 1970 SMR Working Paper, 32.

CHAPTER 10

1. Vernon C. Sloan v. Dan D. Stephens, Petitioner's Complaint, 2–4, July 14, 1965, filed Aug. 5, 1965; Talley, Hash, and Sloan v. Stephens, PB 65-C-33, ED Ark., Nat'l Archives & Records Admin. (NARA), NAID No. 611128 (all litigation materials are from NARA); Talley v. Stephens, 247 F. Supp. 683 (ED Ark. 1965).

2. *Police Charge Youth with Forgery*, Ark. Democrat, 8, Sept. 13, 1959; *3 Charged with Forgery*, Ark. Gazette, B12, Feb. 24, 1959; *Felony Charges*, Ark. Gazette, B7, June 18, 1959; *Five Given Penitentiary Sentences*, Ark. Democrat, 13, Jan. 4, 1960; *Nine Get Prison Terms for Felonies*, Ark. Gazette, B14, Feb. 2, 1960; *Man Beaten, Robbed at North Little Rock*, Ark. Gazette, 38, June 2, 1961; *Guilty Plea Nets Talley Jail Term*, Ark. Democrat, 9, July 15, 1961; *Sheriff Says Prison Trusties Worked with Burglary Ring*, Ark. Gazette, 4, Nov. 11, 1962; *Convict's Trial Opens*, Ark. Democrat, 3, Oct. 7, 1963; *Convict Gets 7-Year Term*, Ark. Democrat, 13, Oct. 8, 1963; George Douthit, *Stephens to Defend Strap in US Court Appearance*, Ark. Democrat, 1, Oct. 12, 1965.

3. *Brothers Held in 17 Burglaries*, Ark. Democrat, 4, Dec. 11, 1956; *Three Held in 17 Burglaries in Four Arkansas Counties*, Ark. Gazette, 17, Dec. 11, 1956; *Strong Urge to Steal Brings Five-Year Term*, Ark. Democrat, 13, Jan. 15, 1957; *Convict's Brother Get Five Years for Burglaries*, Ark. Gazette, B14, Jan. 16, 1957; *Burglar's Error Was a Ringer*, Ark. Democrat, A14, June 28, 1959; *Larceny Case Bound Over*, Ark. Democrat, 4, July 2, 1959. In 1965, Sloan had been incarcerated for more than five years. Sloan v. Stephens, Consent Judgment, filed Oct. 28, 1965.

4. *Army Enlists 23, Air Force Three*, Lexington Herald, 9, July 29, 1948; *Defendant Makes Bond*, Ark. Democrat, A7, May 6, 1956; *Felony Charges*, B7; *Michigan Man Held in Cycle Theft*, Ark. Democrat, 2, Mar. 24, 1962.

5. Sloan v. Stephens, Petition for a Grand Jury Investigation, 3, July 14, 1965, filed Aug. 5, 1965.

6. *Faubus Unaware of Whip; Head of Pen Defends Use*, Ark. Democrat, 11, Sept. 21, 1965; Jerol Garrison, *Convict Testifies He Was Whipped on 75 Occasions*, Ark. Gazette, A1–2, Oct. 14, 1965; George Douthit, *Prison Whipping Aired by Prisoner at Court Hearing*, Ark. Democrat, 1, Oct. 13, 1965; George Douthit, *Warden, Trusty Describe "Strapping" of Prisoners*, Ark. Democrat, 2, Oct. 14, 1965.

7. William Warren Hash v. Dan D. Stephens, Petition for Writ of Prohibition, filed Aug. 5, 1965.

8. Sloan v. Stephens, Petitioner's Complaint, 2–4.

9. Talley, Hash, and Sloan v. Stephens, Answer, filed Aug. 23, 1965.

10. Act of Mar. 20, 1903, Act 95, 1903 Ark. Acts 160; *Inside Cummins Farm*, Ark. Democrat Sunday Mag., 8–9, Aug. 4, 1963; Campbell Gibson & Kay Jung, Historical Census Statistics on Population Totals by Race, 1790 to 1990, and by Hispanic Origin, 1970 to 1990, for the United States, Regions, Divisions, and States, Working Paper No. 56, US Census Bureau, Sept. 2002, at 46 tbl.18. That acreage figure comes from a stipulation filed Feb. 1, 1967,

in Jackson v. Bishop, para. 2 (ED Ark. Feb. 1, 1967). By then, about 1,800 people were at Cummins and 275 at Tucker.

11. *Inside Cummins Farm*, 8–9. Joe Wirges, *As Lee Henslee Packs, His Prisoners Harvest Biggest Arkansas Crop*, Ark. Gazette, 12, July 2, 1963; Doug Smith, *Stephens Relates How Prison System Boon for Everyone*, Ark. Gazette, A15, Jan. 3, 1965. Decisions holding conditions unconstitutional in Mississippi's Parchment Farms and Alabama's prisons also referenced "free-world" employees. Gates v. Collier, 454 F. Supp. 567, 572 (ND Miss. 1978), aff'd 606 F.2d 115 (5th Cir. 1979); Jones v. Diamond, 594 F.2d 997, 1037 (5th Cir. 1979).

12. In 1942, a referendum amended the Arkansas Constitution to require five-year terms for members of five-person boards "charged with the management or control of all charitable, penal or correctional institutions and institutions of higher learning." Ark. Constitution, Amendment No. 33, § 1., current as of 2023.

13. Douthit, *Prison Whipping*.

14. Jerol Garrison, *Rules Ordered on Use of Whip at Penitentiary*, Ark. Gazette, 1–2, Nov. 16, 1965.

15. Ryan Anthony Smith, *Laura Conner and the Limits of Prison Reform in 1920s Arkansas*, 77 Ark. Hist. Q. 1, 56, 59–62 (2018). A digital compilation of handwritten letters, drafts, and reports includes Conner's pain-filled details as well as press clippings. Report by Laura Conner regarding her investigations into inmate treatment in Arkansas Prisons, *Further Charges by Mrs. Conner*, Ark. Gazette, 6, July 9, 1922; Laura Conner to the Editor of the *Arkansas Democrat*, July 7, 1922, Butler Center for Arkansas Studies, Central Arkansas Library, Laura Cornelius Conner Papers, Box 1, Folder 5; *Mrs. Conner Replies to Recent Attack by Rotary Club Committee*, Ark. Democrat, 5, July 9, 1922; *17 Convicts Are Whipped for Answering Questions Asked by Members of Board*, 1921, Box 1, Folder 9; *Grand Jury Report Surprise, Even to Governor Himself*, 1922, Box 1, Folder 8 (newspaper names not legible); Letter Conner to Governor T. C. McRae, Feb. 3, 1922, Box 1, Folder 3.

16. Woodcock was described as a chiropractor incarcerated in Arkansas in 1953 and released to Oklahoma officials on other theft charges. *Ex-Convict's Book to "Expose" Pen*, Ark. Democrat, 13, Aug. 22, 1958. Woodcock wrote that he hired a lawyer, posted bond, and fled because he had a "great fear" of Arkansas' prisons, about which he had heard "sadistic and brutal stories." Dale Woodcock, *Ruled by the Whip*, 14–16, 28, 34 (Exposition Press, 1958); Colin Woodword, *Ruled by the Whip*, Encyclopedia of Arkansas (Feb. 26, 2020).

17. Woodcock, 28, 34, 69–70, 86, 126, 130. Woodcock dedicated his book to Ben Sanford, whom he described as having died from beatings. Woodcock, 103–04.

18. Woodcock, 129; *Book by Ex-Convict Charges Cummins Is "Devil's Island*," Ark. Gazette, 9, Nov. 16, 1958; Resolution attached to the Minutes of the Penitentiary Commission Meeting, Mar. 7, 1962, submitted in Talley v. Stephens.

19. *Stephens Quits as Prison Chief*, Commercial (Com.) Appeal, Oct. 12, 1965; Carl Crawford, *Prison Lash Embarrassing to Faubus*, Com. Appeal, Oct. 17, 1965,

U. Ark. Little Rock (UALR), Center Arkansas History and Culture, Winthrop Rockefeller Collection, Record Group IV, Box 259, File 5; Smith, *Stephens Relates How Prison System Boon for Everyone.*

20. Jerol Garrison, *State Prisoners Petition US Court to Bar Whippings,* Ark. Gazette, A10, Sept. 21, 1965; *The Resignation . . . and the Reason,* Pine Bluff Com., Oct. 12, 1965, Rockefeller, IV, Box 259, File 5; *Faubus Unaware of Whip: Head of Pen Defends Use,* 11; George Douthit, *Prison Punishment System to Be Aired by Board Oct. 27,* Ark. Democrat, 1, Oct. 19, 1965.

21. *Dan Stephens Will Replace Henslee,* Ark. Democrat, 3, Nov. 1, 1962; George Douthit, *Patronage Decision Made in Washington,* Ark. Democrat, 1, Feb. 23, 1961; Jerol Garrison, *McClellan's Big Task: Find Democrat Who'll Please All, Protect US,* Ark. Gazette, 4, Mar. 26, 1961; *Screeners Rule Judge Miller at 72 Too Old for US Appeals Court Job,* Ark. Gazette, 1, Mar. 30, 1961; *Stephens to Get PSC Job,* Ark. Democrat, 6, Apr. 7, 1961; *Stephens Gets Job Held by Bohlinger,* Ark. Gazette, 13, Sept. 7, 1961; *Independence Not Enhanced,* Ark. Gazette, E5, Sept. 10, 1961; L. D. Kerr, *Legislators on Tour Find Some Institutions in Need,* Ark. Democrat, 4, Nov. 11, 1962.

22. Anne Reeves, *Achievements Mark Henslee's Tenure as State Prison Head,* Ark. Democrat, 2, July 2, 1963; L. D. Kerr, *Audit Committee Gives Best Wishes to Henslee,* Ark. Democrat, 8, June 30, 1963. In October 1965, the press reported 2,500 men confined, thirty-nine salaried employees, income of $1.9 million, expenses $1.7 million, and profits of $243,000. See *Resignation May Spark Prison Issue,* Com. Appeal, Oct. 12, 1965, Rockefeller, IV, Box 259, File 5.

23. *Lee Henslee, Ex-State Prison Head, Found Dead,* Ark. Democrat, 10, Oct. 17, 1963.

24. *Stephens Praises Trusty Plan,* Ark. Democrat, 4, Sept. 24, 1963; George Douthit, *It's a Tough Row to Hoe,* Ark. Democrat, 1–2, Oct. 17, 1965; *Inside Cummins Farm,* 8–9; *Sheriff Bishop New Prison Head,* Ark. Gazette, A11, Dec. 2, 1965.

25. John R. Starr, *Arkansas Convicts to Give Blood for Spending Money,* Ark. Democrat, 22, Sept. 25, 1963; *Prisoners Earn $13,000 by Selling Their Blood,* Ark. Gazette, B7, Nov. 7, 1963. In 1967, the University of Arkansas Medical Center took over the program and redirected revenues to the prison or the Medical Center. George Douthit, *State Prepares to Enter Blood Plasma Business,* Ark. Democrat, 1, Apr. 19, 1967. A nonprofit foundation, Medcor, was formed to operationalize that plan. Memorandum from Governor Winthrop Rockefeller to Arkansas Weekly Newspaper Editors, Aug. 28, 1967, Rockefeller, IV, Box 251, File 3. "Profits" rose. *New Blood-Plasma Program May Net $100,000 at Prison,* Pine Bluff Com., Oct. 20, 1967, Rockefeller, IV, Box 249, File 17; Martha Ann Riley, *Penitentiary Inmates Give Accounts of Early Starts on Road to Crime,* Ark. Democrat, D1, Apr. 18, 1965; Wayman Dunlap, *Convict Panel Gives Advice to Students,* Ark. Democrat, 15, May 5, 1965. Most stories listed the prisoners as A, B, C, and D; one account named Earl Ellis, Lamar House, Bob Scanlon, and Bill Clubb and noted one had been a lawyer. *Warden Stephens,* Ark. Gazette, E3, Aug. 15, 1965.

26. *Stephens Praises Trusty Plan*; Smith, *Stephens Relates How Prison System Boon for Everyone*, A15.

27. Douthit, *Warden, Trusty Describe "Strapping" of Prisoners*; Robert Pearman, *The Whip Pays Off*, Nation, 701, 703, Dec. 26, 1966.

28. Kerr, *Audit Committee Gives Best Wishes to Henslee*, 8; *Prison to Start Cucumber Harvest*, Ark. Gazette, 19, May 26, 1965; *Governor Touches Many Bases in Announcements*, Ark. Democrat, 13, Jan. 30, 1964; Smith, *Stephens Relates How Prison System Boon for Everyone*, A15; *The Faubus Years and the Professionals*, Editorial, Ark. Gazette, A4, Feb. 15, 1965; *Guilty Plea Nets Talley Jail Term*, 9; *Sheriff Says Prison Trusties Worked with Burglary Ring*, 4; *Convict Gets 7-Year Term*, 13; *Two Killed in Shooting at Prison*, Ark. Democrat, 14, Sept. 16, 1965; Douthit, *Stephens to Defend Strap*. Stephens did not take the stand when Talley, other prisoners, and Warden Mose Harmon testified. Douthit, *Warden, Trusty Describe "Strapping" of Prisoners*.

29. *Talley*, 247 F. Supp., 688.

30. An Open Letter to the Editor, signed by William M. Clubb and Hugh White, Oct. 5, 1965, Rockefeller, IV, Box 251, File 5. Clubb, a speaker in "Operation Teenage" program, became Stephens' personal secretary. *Arkansas Convicts Seek to Halt Resignation of Prison Chief*, Com. Appeal, Oct. 16, 1965, Rockefeller, IV, Box 259, File 5; *Stephens Asks to Be Replaced*, Ark. Gazette, A1–2, Oct. 12, 1965; *Resignation May Spark Prison Issue*; *Those Wonderful Porkers and the Prison Strap*, Ark. Gazette, E3, Oct. 24, 1965; Letter Orval E. Faubus to Capt. Dan D. Stephens, Oct. 11, 1965, Rockefeller, IV, Box 252, File 12. Douthit, *Stephens to Defend Strap*. Douthit, *Warden, Trusty Describe "Strapping" of Prisoners*.

CHAPTER 11

1. Frances Ross, Dir., Oral History Program, Interview Judge Jesse Smith Henley in Harrison, Ark. (June 3, 1987), Univ. of Ark. at Little Rock.

2. Patrick Henry, *Judge Who Reformed Prison System Dies*, Ark. Democrat-Gazette, B1, Oct. 20, 1997.

3. Criminal Justice Act 1948, 11 & 12 Geo. 6 s.2 (Eng.); Criminal Justice Act 1967, s.65 (Eng.); Correctional Service Canada, *Abolition of Corporal Punishment 1972* (2015); Ingraham v. Wright, 430 US 651, 659 (1977); GA Res. 44/25, UN Convention on the Rights of the Child (Nov. 20, 1989); Committee on the Rights of the Child, The Right of the Child to Freedom from All Forms of Violence, para. 22a, General comment No. 13 (Apr. 18, 2011); Canadian Foundation for Children, Youth and the Law v. Canada, [2004], 1 SCR 76; Yong Vui Kong v. Public Prosecutor, 2 Sing. L. Rep. 1129 (SGCA, 2015); *Comparative Capital Punishment* (Carol Steiker & Jordan Steiker eds., Edward Elgar Publ., 2019).

4. Talley v. Stephens, 247 F. Supp. 683, 686, 689 (ED Ark. 1965).

5. Jackson v. Bishop, 404 F.2d 571 (8th Cir. 1968); Holt v. Sarver (*Holt I*), 300 F. Supp. 825 (ED Ark. 1969); Holt v. Sarver (*Holt II*), 309 F. Supp. 362, 381 (ED Ark. 1970). Henley was elevated to the Eighth Circuit in 1975 and took

senior status in 1982. Jeffrey B. Morris, Jesse Smith Henley, *Encyclopedia of Ark.*, July 19, 2018.

6. Jack Bass, *Unlikely Heroes* (Simon & Schuster, 1981).

7. *Holt II*, 365.

8. The *Arkansas Gazette's* Pulitzer Prize in 1957 was for its accounts of school desegregation; at that point, the paper had "become so unpopular that the *Arkansas Democrat* did not even report the honor." Elizabeth Jacoway, *Turn Away Thy Son: Little Rock, The Crisis that Shocked the Nation*, 248 (Free Press, 2007).

9. Judicial Circuits Act of July 23, 1866, chap. 210, 14 Stat. 209.

10. Susan Webber Wright, *The Judge from St. Joe, in Tributes to Judge J. Smith Henley*, 52 Ark. L. Rev. 297, 309 (1999); Becker v. Lockhart, 971 F.2d 172, 174, 176 (8th Cir. 1992).

11. Equal Justice Institute, *Lynching in America*, 40 (3d ed., 2023). Mississippi, Georgia, and Louisiana had more lynchings.

12. *Revival of Arkansas Feud Feared in Primary Contest*, St. Louis Post-Dispatch, A10, June 23, 1936.

13. Act of Oct. 13, 2000, Pub. L. 106–296, 114 Stat. 1044.

14. In 2019, Harrison was the postal address for Thomas Robb, the national director of the Knights of the Ku Klux Klan. Harrison Race Riots of 1905 and 1909, *Encyclopedia of Ark.*, Dec. 11, 2020; Bret Schulte, *The Alt-Right of the Ozarks*, Slate, Apr. 3, 2017; Peter Rugh, *The KKK Embraces Diversity in Harrison, Arkansas*, Vice, Mar. 11, 2014.

15. Jack Walter Peltason, *Fifty-Eight Lonely Men: Southern Federal Judges and School Desegregation*, 75 (U. Ill. Press, 1961).

16. Hearing on the Nominations of J. Smith Henley to be US District Judge for the Eastern and Western Districts of Arkansas, and Gordon E. Young to be US District Judge for the Eastern District of Arkansas, Subcommittee of the Senate Committee on the Judiciary, Aug. 26, 1959, 19. Gregory L. Richard, *The Rule of Three: Federal Courts and Prison Farms in the Post-Segregation South*, 19-20 (PhD diss., U. Miss., May 2013) (ProQuest No. 3567622); Sheldon Goldman, *Picking Federal Judges: Lower Court Selection from Roosevelt Through Reagan*, 128–29 (Yale U. Press, 1997); 102 Congressional Record S4459–64 (1956); 102 Congressional Record H4515–16 (1956).

17. Jerry Jones, *City Is Ordered to Desegregate Most Facilities*, Ark. Gazette, 1, Feb. 16, 1963; Heart of Atlanta Motel, Inc. v. US, 379 US 241 (1964); John A. Kirk, *Desegregating the Seat of Arkansas Government, 1964–1965*, 72 Ark. His. Q. 95 (2013); John Kirk, *The Fight to Desegregate the Arkansas Capitol Cafeteria*, Ark. Times, Feb. 14, 2013; Kyles v. Paul, 263 F. Supp. 412, 418 (ED Ark. 1967), aff'd Daniel v. Paul, 395 F.2d 118 (8th Cir. 1968), rev'd Daniel v. Paul, 395 US 298 (1969).

18. Dove v. Parham, 176 F. Supp. 242 (ED Ark. 1959); Parham v. Dove, 271 F.2d 132 (8th Cir. 1959); Dove v. Parham, 181 F. Supp. 504 (ED Ark. 1960); Dove v. Parham, 183 F. Supp. 389 (ED Ark. 1960); Dove v. Parham, 282 F.2d 256 (8th Cir. 1960); Jeffrey Brandon Morris, *Establishing Justice in Middle America: A*

History of the United States Court of Appeals for the Eighth Circuit (U. Minn. Press, 2007), 195–200.

19. Cross v. Bd. Educ. Dollarway, 395 F. Supp. 531 (ED Ark. 1975).
20. John B. Pickhardt, *We Don't Intend to Have a Story: Integration in the Dollarway School District*, 68 Ark. Hist Rev. 357, 360, 387 (2009).
21. Constructed in 1966, the George Howard Jr. Federal Building and US Courthouse, named in 2008 after Howard had died, housed federal agencies. This building, like the facility in Harrison named for Judge Henley, bore the title "courthouse" but is not a site of litigation.
22. Trop v. Dulles, 356 US 86 (1958); Monroe v. Pape, 365 US 167 (1961); Cooper v. Pate 378 US 546 (1964). After Chief Judge Henley issued his November 1965 decision in *Talley*, Thomas Cooper, held in Joliet, Illinois and whose lawsuit (discussed in a later chapter) had established prisoners' eligibility to use §1983, was told he had to pay copying fees of fifty cents per page for the opinion. Letter F. J. Pate re: Thomas Cooper, to the Chief Clerk of the US District Court, Little Rock, Arkansas, Jan. 27, 1966, requesting acknowledgment that the Joliet prison had sent Cooper's mailings; Letter Charles F. Cole, Clerk, to Cooper, Feb. 1, 1966. Talley, Hash, and Sloan v. Stephens, PB 65-C-33, ED Ark., NARA NAID No. 611128. (All unpublished case materials are from NARA.)
23. Talley and Sloan had requested counsel; Hash said he would provide his own but did not. In the appointment letter, Henley told the lawyers that, if conflicts arose, Bullion would represent Talley and Ramsay would represent Sloan. Letter Chief Judge Henley to Bruce T. Bullion & Louis L. Ramsay Jr., Sept. 8, 1965. Talley, Hash, and Sloan v. Stephens, NARA.
24. *Bar Officials Interested*, El Dorado Times, 11, Jan. 18, 1965; *Outstanding Legal Authorities to Participate in Spa Conference to Advise Public On Ways to Help*, El Dorado Times, 12, Sept. 17, 1965; Bruce T. Bullion, *The President's Address: The Judiciary Commission Report of 1965*, 19 Ark. L. Rev. 238, 241 (1965); Mark Newman, *The Arkansas Baptist State Convention and Desegregation, 1954–1968*, 56 Ark. Hist. Q. 294 (1997); Letter Bruce T. Bullion to James O. Eastland, Chair of the Judiciary Comm., Apr. 1, 1959, in Henley/Young 1959 Hearing, 50.
25. Bruce Bullion, *Reflections from 1963: A Letter from Bruce Bullion to Louis Ramsay Jr.*, 39 Ark. L. Rev. 26, 27 (2004); Epperson v. Arkansas, 393 US 97 (1968). After losing a bid in 1966 for the state Supreme Court, Bullion was appointed by Governor David Pryor to the Chancery Court where he served until retiring in 1986. *Little Rock Attorney Tapped to Fill Chancery Court Vacancy*, Courier News, Aug. 14, 1976.
26. Louis L. Ramsay Jr., *The President's Address: A Look in the Mirror*, 18 Ark. L. Rev. 218, 220–22 (1964); Mike Ross, *In Lasting Memory of Louis L. Ramsay Jr.*, Jan. 20, 2004, 150 Congressional Record E2–05, E3, E155–01, E155 (2004); *Celebrating the Life and Contributions, and Mourning the Passing of Louis L. Ramsay*, Ark. Senate Memorial Resolution SMR8 1 (2003).

27. George Douthit, *Prison Whipping Aired by Prisoner at Court Hearing*, Ark. Democrat, 1–2, Oct. 13, 1965; Talley, Hash, and Sloan v. Stephens, Pre-Trial Conference Order, 2–3, para. 3 and 7, Sept. 30, 1965.

28. Douthit, *Prison Whipping Aired*, 1. Wallin later worked as a city attorney for West Memphis, Arkansas; Jackson spent decades as an assistant United States Attorney in Arkansas. B. Ghormley, *Oyez-Oyez!*, 5 Ark. L. Rev. 1, 2 (1971); Obituary, *Earl Fletcher "Bear" Jackson of Little Rock, Ark., 1938–2014*, Ark. Democrat-Gazette, Nov. 23, 2014; *Two Democrats in Arkansas Face a Tough Runoff June 8*, NY Times, 22, May 27, 1982; Jeff Woods, Bruce Bennett (1917–1979), *Encyclopedia of Ark.* (Oct. 24, 2016).

29. Commercial Appeal, Oct. 14, 1965, U. Ark. Little Rock (UALR), Center Arkansas History and Culture, Winthrop Rockefeller Collection, Record Group IV, Box 259, File 5. Unless otherwise noted, Rockefeller archival materials are from Record Group IV. Douthit, *Prison Whipping Aired*, 1; George Douthit, *Warden, Trusty Describe "Strapping" of Prisoners*, Ark. Democrat, 1, Oct. 14, 1965.

30. Bob Lancaster, *Prisoners' Testimony Questions "Humanity" of Beatings with "Bullhide,"* Pine Bluff Com., Oct. 14, 1965, Rockefeller, IV, Box 259, File 5, 1; Jerol Garrison, *Convict Testifies He Was Whipped On 75 Occasions*, Ark. Gazette, Oct. 14, 1965, 1; Douthit, *Warden, Trusty Describe "Strapping" of Prisoners*, 2; John R. Starr, *Convict Testifies to 75 Whippings*, Com. Appeal, Oct. 14, 1965, Rockefeller, IV, Box 259, File 5; J. C. Tillman, *Warden Defends Practice of Whipping Prisoners*, Corpus Christi Times, 12, Oct. 13, 1965.

31. George Douthit, *News Accounts of Strapping Case Hit by Bennett*, Ark. Democrat, 1, Oct. 15, 1965; Editorial, *A Peek Under the Lid of Our State Prisons*, A6, Ark. Gazette, Oct. 15, 1965.

32. Letter Dan Stephens, Superintendent, to Hon. J. Smith Henley, re: Talley vs Stephens, dated Nov. 4, 1965, filed Nov. 8, 1965; George Douthit, *Prisoner Says Whip Applied "For Lying,"* Ark. Democrat, 1, Nov. 3, 1965; Joan Craw, *Federal Judge Not Ready to Prohibit Strap at This Time*, Ark. Democrat, 1, Nov. 1, 1965; Bobbie Forster, *Whip Used On Prisoner Who Testified*, Ark. Democrat, 1, Nov. 8, 1965; Jerol Garrison, *Mose Harmon Says He Whipped Talley After Testimony*, Ark. Gazette, 1, Nov. 9, 1965.

33. *Talley*, 686 n.3.

34. *Talley*, 685 n.2; 687–89.

35. Talley, Hash, and Sloan v. Stephens, Decree, 2, para. 7, filed Nov. 15, 1965; *Talley*, 690–91 n.4; Notice to All Inmates, Arkansas State Penitentiary, filed approx. Sept. 20, 1965.

36. *Attorney General Will Not Oppose Convict Petitions*, Ark. Democrat, 2, Oct. 29, 1965; Jerol Garrison, *State Won't Contest Convicts' Suit*, Ark. Gazette, A12, Oct. 29, 1965; Consent Judgment, Hash v. Stephens, Oct. 28, 1965; Sloan v. Stephens, Consent Judgment, Oct. 28, 1965. Sloan later filed another handwritten "Petition to Reopen," alleging that Superintendent Bishop denied him medical care. Vernon C. Sloan v. State of Arkansas, O. E. Bishop, and Doctor Quinn Atnip, Petition to Re-open, Oct. 31, 1966. The state reported

it had purchased orthopedic shoes for Sloan; he did not respond to the judge's queries. Henley reminded the state not to obstruct access and ruled it was not the court's "function . . . to supervise the day-to-day administration of the prison." Talley, Hash, and Sloan v. O. E. Bishop, Memorandum and Order, 3, Nov. 29, 1966.

37. *Talley*, 687; Decree, 2, para. 5–6.
38. *Talley*, 689.
39. *Trop*, 101–02. Justice Brennan concurred; Justices Frankfurter, Burton, Clark, and Harlan dissented.
40. Weems v. United States, 217 US 349, 377–78 (1910).
41. A major proponent was Antonin Scalia, *Originalism: The Lesser Evil*, 57 U. Cinn. L. Rev. 849, 861 (1989). Justice Neil Gorsuch championed originalism in his book, *A Republic If You Can Keep It* (2019). One scholar has argued that his fellow originalists were not correct when interpreting the words and the reach of the Eighth Amendment. John F. Stinneford, *The Original Meaning of "Cruel,"* 105 Geo. L. J. 441 (2017); John F. Stinneford, *The Original Meaning of "Unusual": The Eighth Amendment as a Bar to Cruel Innovation*, 102 Nw. U. L. Rev. 1739, 1749–51 (2008). Other critiques come from many viewpoints. Sherif Girgis, *Living Traditionalism*, 98 NYU L. Rev. 1477 (2023); Helen Hershkoff & Judith Resnik, *Constraining and Licensing Arbitrariness: The Stakes in Debates about Substantive-Procedural Due Process*, 76 SMU L. Rev. 613 (2023); Melissa Murray & Katherine Shaw, *Dobbs and Democracy*, 137 Harv. L. Rev. 728 (2024); Reva B. Siegel, *The "Levels of Generality" Game, or "History and Tradition" as the Right's Living Constitution*, 47 Harv. J. L. & Pub. Pol'y 1 (2024); Emily Bazelon, *How Will Trump's Supreme Court Remake the Constitution?*, NY Times Mag., Feb. 27, 2020.
42. State v. Cannon, 190 A.2d 514, 516–17 (1963). Public protests followed after a judge imposed lashes for minor offenses. Ben A. Franklin, *Public Flogging Seems Near an End in Delaware*, NY Times, 46, Feb. 2, 1964. In 1970, a new governor ordered the three state whipping posts removed; the revised later read "No punishment by whipping is provided for in this Criminal Code." governor's Committee on Revision of the Criminal Law, Delaware Criminal Code with Commentary, 473 (1973).
43. Bucklew v. Precythe, 587 US 119, 133 (2019), citing Baze v. Rees, 553 US 35, 48 (2008).
44. City of Grants Pass, Oregon v. Johnson, 144 S. Ct. 2202 (2024). At issue was a local ordinance criminalizing homelessness, which the Court, six to three, upheld. Justice Thomas concurring stated the Clause had a "fixed meaning" based on "text and original meaning." Id. at 2226–28.
45. For example, Chief Justice Warren's decision, Miranda v. Arizona, 384 US 436, 488–89 (1966), requiring police to advise people of rights to remain silent, discussed how Scotland, India, and Ceylon treated suspects.
46. Jack M. Balkin, *The New Originalism and the Uses of History*, 82 Fordham L. Rev. 641 (2013); Jack M. Balkin, *Framework Originalism and the Living Constitution*, 103 Nw. U. L. Rev. 549 (2009); Craig S. Lerner, *Justice Scalia's Eighth*

Amendment Jurisprudence: The Failure of Sake-of-Argument Originalism, 42 Harv. J. L. & Pub. Pol'y 91 (2019).

47. Vicki C. Jackson, *Constitutional Engagement in a Transnational Era* (Oxford U. Press 2010).
48. *Talley*, 689.
49. *Talley*, 689; Decree, 2, para. 4.
50. *Restraints on the Whip*, Ark. Democrat, Nov. 18, 1965, Rockefeller, IV, Box 259, File 4. In 1967, Talley was paroled and in 1968, returned to prison after convictions for burglary and grand larceny resulting in a thirty-year sentence. As discussed later, Talley testified in *Holt II* that he gave and received bribes in his role as a trusty. In 1970, he escaped. *Prisoner, 30, in Strap Case, Escapes*, Ark. Gazette, A21, Apr. 5, 1970; *Inmate Seeks to Block Extradition*, Ark. Democrat, 3, June 24, 1970.

CHAPTER 12

1. Talley v. Stephens, 247 F. Supp. 683, 689 (ED Ark. 1965).
2. *Faubus Reverses Board Secrecy About New Prison Rules*, Fort Smith Newspaper, Feb. 2, 1966, U. of Ark. Little Rock (UALR), Center Arkansas History and Culture, Winthrop Rockefeller Collection, Record Group IV, Box 259, File 6; *Strap Finally Official*, Ark. Democrat, D1, Feb. 6, 1966; *No More than 10 Lashes*, Ark. Democrat, 4, Feb. 4, 1966; *New Prison Rules Limit Lashings to 10, Provide for Board of Inquiry*, Ark. Gazette, A1–2, Feb. 3, 1966. Unless otherwise noted, Rockefeller materials are from Record Group IV.
3. Talley v. Stephens, Submission by Bruce Bennett, Attorney General, and Fletcher Jackson, Assistant Attorney General, Feb. 2, 1966, PB 65-C-33, ED Ark., Nat'l Archives & Records Admin. (NARA); Laura Conner, Suggestions for Humanitarian Measures, July 11, 1921, Laura Cornelius Conner Papers, Butler Center for Arkansas Studies, Central Arkansas Library.
4. Associated Press, *Con's Whipping Ruled "Frivolous Excuse,"* Ark. Democrat, 5, Aug. 25, 1966.
5. *Use of Strap Raises Constitutional Questions*, El Dorado Times, 1, Sept. 3, 1966, Rockefeller, IV, Box 252, File 12.
6. Frances Cordell, *Sheriff Bishop: He Fulfilled a Boyhood Yen*, Ark. Gazette, A8, Dec. 26, 1965.
7. *Lawmen Laud Stephens' Aid to Prisoners*, Ark. Gazette, 8, Oct. 20, 1965; *Bishop Offered Stephens' Job*, Ark. Gazette, A26, Nov. 12, 1965; *Sheriff Bishop New Prison Head*, Ark. Gazette, A11, Dec. 2, 1965.
8. *Filling the Prison Job*, Ark. Gazette, 4, Nov. 13, 1965; *Chilling Scandal in Our "Model" Prisons*, Editorial, Ark. Gazette, A4, Sept. 3, 1966; Mike Trimble & Ernest Valachovic, *144 Cummins Inmates Hold Sit-down Strike*, Ark. Gazette, 1, Sept. 3, 1966.
9. *Smuggled Letter Reports Reasons for Prison Strike*, Ark. Gazette, A5, Sept. 17, 1966.
10. George Douthit, *Bishop Says Prison Situation in Hand*, Ark. Democrat, 2, Sept. 7, 1966.

11. George Douthit, *Prison Board Meets on Firings, Strike*, Ark. Democrat, 1, Sept. 3, 1966; *Strap Ends Strike by 146 Prisoners: Tear Gas Is Used*, Ark. Gazette, 1, Sept. 6, 1966.

12. Ernest Valachovic, *Bishop Reports Calm at Prison*, Ark. Gazette, 1, Sept. 7, 1966; Larry J. Fugate, *Strike Was a Rebellion Against Prison Authority, Bishop Says*, Pine Bluff Commercial, Sept. 7, 1966, Rockefeller, IV, Box 251, File 5; Crawford, *New Prison Solitary Cells May Doom Arkansas Strap*, Com. Appeal, 1, Sept. 10, 1966, Rockefeller, IV, Box 252, File 12; Robert Pearman, *The Whip Pays Off*, Nation, 701, Dec. 26, 1966.

13. *Convicts at Cummins Send Out 2 Letters Listing Grievances*, Pine Bluff Com., Sept. 17, 1966, Rockefeller, IV, Box 251, File 5; *"We Deny All That Stuff," Prison Says*, Ark. Gazette, 1, Sept. 19, 1966.

14. H. H. Atkinson, Case Report (undated), Criminal Investigations Division, Arkansas State Police, Little Rock, Arkansas, 1–3, 61, Rockefeller, IV, Box 250, File 8 (referenced as 1966 Ark. State Police); *Chilling Scandal in Our "Model" Prisons*, editorial, Ark. Gazette, A4, Sept. 3, 1966; *Convict Sit-In Greets Faubus*, Com. Appeal, Sept. 3, 1966, Rockefeller, IV, Box 251, File 5; Douthit, *Prison Board Meets On Firings, Strike*; Anne Reeves, *Goodwin Says He Tried Hard in Tucker Job*, Ark. Gazette, 1, Dec. 14, 1966. A portion of the Arkansas State Police report would have been filed in *Jackson v. Bishop* with or soon after an accompanying list of photographs dated August 27, 1966.

15. Inaugural Address, Jan. 10, 1967, Winthrop Rockefeller Institute; *Some Excerpts From the Report on Tucker Prison Farm*, Pine Bluff Com., 11, Jan. 22, 1967; *Investigator Compiles Chronicle of Inhumanity*, Com. Appeal, Jan. 17, 1967; Maurice Moore, *Blue Ribbon Commission Starts Nine Month Investigation of State's Penitentiary System*, Daily Banner-News, Mar. 19, 1967, in Rockefeller, IV, Box 260, File 6, File 2; Doug Smith, *Felony Cases Are Postponed*, Ark. Gazette, 1, Jan. 20, 1967.

16. Michael B. Smith, *Jim Bruton Is Still Recuperating*, Pine Bluff Com., July 23, 1967, Rockefeller, IV, Box 252, File 9.

17. 1966 Ark. State Police 8, 10, 6, 7; *Investigator Compiles Chronicle of Inhumanity*, Com. Appeal, Jan. 17, 1967, Rockefeller, IV, Box 260, File 6.

18. 1966 Ark. State Police, 4, 15, 20–22, 60–63.

19. 1966 Ark. State Police, 11–13, 24.

20. 1966 Ark. State Police, 15, 33–57, 62; Paul N. Schalchlin, "Photographs taken at Tucker Prison Farm"; *20 on Hand to Testify on Prisons*, Ark. Democrat, A16, July 9, 19696.

21. *Jim Bruton Is Charged in Excessive Punishment of Prisoners at Tucker*, Pine Bluff Com., Jan. 27, 1967, Rockefeller, IV, Box 260, File 6; Bill Rutherford, *Prison Torture Charged to 4*, Wash. Post, A6, Jan 28, 1967.

22. Memorandum re: Tucker Prison Farm Investigation Report, Colonel Herman E. Lindsey, Dir. of State Police, to Gov. Winthrop Rockefeller, Feb. 6, 1967; Memorandum Gov. Rockefeller to Members of the Legislative Committee Investigating the State Prison System, Feb. 6, 1967, 2; Letter Nelson A. Rockefeller to Winthrop Rockefeller, Jan. 30, 1967, both Rockefeller,

Record Group III, Box 99, File 5; Moore, *Blue Ribbon Commission Starts Nine Month Investigation of State's Penitentiary System.* Tom Murton & Joe Hyams, *Accomplices to the Crime* (Grove Press, 1969).

23. Jackson, Ernst, and Mask v. Bishop, Brief of Appellants, 1–2 (8th Cir. Nos. 18957, 18958, 18969, filed Sept. 25, 1967).

24. 102 Congressional Record H4515–16 (1956); Wiley Branton Jr., *Reflections on the Commemoration of the 50th Anniversary of the Crisis at Little Rock Central High School,* 30 U. Ark. Little Rock L. Rev. 317 (2008).

25. Matilda Touhey, *Emotional Tributes Mark the Transition Of Harris to the Bench,* Ark. Gazette, B1, Feb. 4, 1966; Sherry Laymon, Oren Harris (1903–1997), *Encyclopedia of Ark.* (Sept. 28, 2015); U. Ark. Libraries, Special Collections, Oren Harris Supplementary Papers; US Food & Drug Admin., *Kefauver-Harris Amendments Revolutionized Drug Development,* Consumer Updates (Mar. 20, 2017); Branton Jr., *Reflections on the Commemoration of the 50th Anniversary of the Crisis at Little Rock Central High School*; Oren Harris, Ark. Congressman, *Telegram to President Eisenhower* (Sept. 26, 1957), Eisenhower Presidential Records, Official File, NARA, Box 615, OF 142-A-5-A (3), NAID No. 17366843. Reversals included Hegler v. Bd. Edu. Bearden Sch. Dist., 447 F.2d 1078, 1080 (8th Cir. 1971); Smith v. Bd. Educ. Morrilton Sch. Dist. No. 32, 365 F.2d 770 (8th Cir. 1966).

26. *"Lawyer's Lawyer" Young Takes Oath as US Judge,* Ark. Gazette, 2, Sept. 26, 1959; David Young, Gordon Elmo Young, 1959–69, *United States District Courts and Judges of Arkansas, 1836–1960,* 170 (Frances Mitchell Ross ed., U. Ark. Press, 2016).

27. Reversals included Mitchell v. Henslee, 332 F.2d 16 (8th Cir. 1964); Maxwell v. Bishop, 398 F.2d 138 (8th Cir. 1968), aff'd 398 US 262 (1970); Yarbrough v. Hulbert-West Memphis Sch Dist. No. 4 of Crittenden Cty., 380 F.2d 962 (8th Cir. 1967). A decision finding for civil rights claimants was Rogers v. Bd. Educ. Little Rock, 281 F. Supp. 39, 41 (ED Ark. 1968), a class action challenge to Arkansas Athletic Association's policy of stripping eligibility from students who transferred schools within the district.

28. *Use Of Strap Raises Constitutional Questions,* 1.

29. Letter Oren Harris to Edward L. Wright & William S. Arnold, Re: Jackson v. Bishop, Sept. 1, 1966; Wright to Harris, Sept. 2, 1966, filed Sept. 6, 1966; Gordon E. Young to William S. Arnold & Wright, Re: Ernst v. Bishop, Sept. 3, 1966.

30. Phil Carroll, *Memorial to William S. Arnold,* 31 Ark. Lawyer 47 (Fall 1996); Natalie Kottke & Erica Sardarian, *Company Town,* 2016.

31. Robert R. Wright, *Old Seeds in the New Land: History and Reminiscences of the Bar of Arkansas,* 107 (M&M Press, 2001); Winslow Drummond, *Edward Wright,* 5 Ark. Lawyer 1, 10–11 (Jan. 1971); *Arkansans Mourn Edward Wright Sr.,* Guardian, Official Publication of the Diocese of Little Rock, 1, Feb. 4, 1977; *National Forum on Presidential Inability Held in Washington, DC, on May 25,* 50 ABA J. 638 (July 1964); Birch Bayh, *One Heartbeat Away: Presidential Disability and Succession,* 46 (Bobbs-Merrill Co. 1968).

32. James M. Altman, *Considering the ABA's 1908 Canons of Ethics*, 71 Fordham L. Rev. 2395 (2003); Edward L. Wright, *Channel Change through Law and Reason*, 24 Okla. L. Rev. 349 (1971); Edward L. Wright, *Sixty Years: We Have Come of Age*, 12 Ark. L. Rev. 260 (1958). Edward L. Wright, *ABA and the Public Interest*, 49 Mich. St. Bar J. 11, 14 (Nov. 1970). Thanks are due to Kate Askew and Jess Askew for trying to locate case files, providing family records, and guidance.

CHAPTER 13

1. William King Jackson, Lyle Edward Ernst Jr., Grady W. Mask v. O. E. Bishop Superintendent of the Arkansas State Penitentiary, Trial Transcript, 6, 9, 84, 138 (referenced below as Transcript), NARA (PB 66-C-64, PB 66-C-74, No. PB 66-C-99, ED Ark. Jan. 26, 1967). Unpublished litigation material related to Jackson, Ernst, and Mask are from NARA; Resnik telephone interview with Linwood Jackson, Apr. 10, 2019.
2. Associated Press, *Whittington Forced into a Runoff*, Hope Star, 3, July 29, 1964; *Talley Trial Rescheduled at Pine Bluff*, Ark. Democrat, 2, Oct. 4, 1967; *To Study Prisons*, Nw. Ark. Times, 2, Feb. 20, 1967.
3. Jackson v. Bishop, Deposition of William King Jackson, 16, 20–22, taken Jan. 23, 1967, filed June 21, 1967; Arkansas v. William Jackson, Transcript of Trial, 74 (No. 5166, Jefferson Cty. Cir. Ct. filed Oct. 10, 1966), Arkansas Supreme Court digital records; Jackson v. State, Abstract and Brief for Appellant (No. 5166) filed Oct. 10, 1966, by Coleman, Gantt, Ramsay & Cox); Jackson v. Stephens, Brief for Appellant (No. 5166 filed Nov. 3, 1965, by Reinberger, Eilbott, Smith & Staten); Jackson v. State, 241 Ark. 850, 851–53 (Ark. 1967).
4. Jackson Deposition, 23; Jackson v. Bishop, Petition for a Writ of Habeas Corpus, 1–5, filed Aug. 29, 1966.
5. *Convict Files Suit on Whip*, Ark. Democrat, 2, Sept. 8, 1966; *Inmate's Suit Seeks Restraint in Use of Strap*, Ark. Gazette, 11, Sept. 8, 1966; Ernst v. Bishop, Amendment to Complaint, para. 3, 1, filed Dec. 22, 1966; Ernst v. Bishop, Deposition of Lyle Edward Ernst Jr., 3–6, taken Jan. 23, 1967, filed June 21, 1967; Mask v. Bishop, Deposition of Grady W. Mask, 4–7, taken Jan. 23, 1967, filed June 21, 1967: Trial Transcript, 84, 135.
6. Ernst Deposition, 7–8; Ernst v. Bishop, Petition for Writ of Mandamus in Forma Pauperis, 2–3, written Aug. 29, 1966; Mask v. Bishop, Petition, filed Nov. 25, 1966; *State Inmate Files Suit Against Strap*, Ark. Gazette, B14, Dec. 1, 1966.
7. Jackson v. Bishop, Amendment to Complaint, para. 3, 1–2, filed Dec. 1, 1967; Ernst v. Bishop, Amendment, para. 3, 1; Mask v. Bishop, Amendment, para. 3, 1–2, filed Jan 14. 1967.
8. Jackson Amendment, para. 7, 2–3; Ernst Amendment, para. 3, 2; Mask Amendment, para. 5, 2–3.
9. E.g., Ernst Amendment, 3–4.

10. Transcript, 4. In 1966, the federal rule governing class actions was amended and required lawyers to ask for certification of a case as a class action after establishing that the named individuals were typical of the group they sought to represent and had enough in common and no conflicts with other class members. Named representatives also needed to show they had lawyering resources sufficient to pursue the claims, that the group was too numerous for individual adjudication; and that the relief sought was appropriately applicable to the whole. The prisoners' lawyers did not request nor did the judge formally certify a class action; defendants understood that the ruling would require them to treat all prisoners in the same way.

11. *Investigator Compiles Chronicle of Inhumanity*, Com. Appeal, Jan. 17, 1967, U. Ark. Little Rock (UALR), Center Arkansas History and Culture, Winthrop Rockefeller Collection, Record Group IV, Box 260, File 6. Unless otherwise noted, Rockefeller archival materials are from Record Group IV.

12. Talley v. Stephens, 247 F. Supp. 683, 689 (ED Ark. 1965).

13. Transcript, 11–26.

14. Transcript, 7, 26–41, 49–55.

15. Transcript, 85–104.

16. Transcript, 115–28.

17. Transcript, 136–37, 140–76. A January 10, 1967, report by a doctor said that Mask could work. Transcript, 184–87.

18. Transcript, 189–204, 215–23.

19. Transcript, 240–46, 199–201, 224–25, 249–50, 254.

20. Transcript, 262–70. Photograph courtesy of the UALR Center Arkansas History and Culture, UALR.MS.0251, Hon. Garnett Thomas Eisele Papers, Box 17, Folder 5, photograph 2.

21. Transcript, 273–80.

22. Transcript, 280–85.

23. Transcript, 286–90.

24. Transcript, 322–23, 331.

25. Transcript, 295–310.

26. Transcript, 326–30.

27. Transcript, 333–42.

28. Transcript, 344–47; 352, 356–57, 361–67.

29. Transcript, 372.

30. Letter Oren Harris to William King Jackson, Re: Jackson v. Bishop, Nov. 17, 1966.

31. Letter Harris to Wright, Re: Jackson v. Bishop, Nov. 21, 1966; Harris to the Hon. Bruce Bennett, Atty. Gen., Re: Nov. 21, 1966.

32. Transcript, 422.

33. Robert Pearman, *The Whip Pays Off*, Nation, 701, Dec. 26, 1966; Transcript, 378–84, 406–07.

34. Transcript, 385–93.

35. Transcript, 388–96.

36. Transcript, 398–404.

37. Transcript, 417–33.
38. Transcript, 412–17.
39. Transcript, 425–31; Anne Reeves, *Goodwin Says He Tried Hard in Tucker Job*, Ark. Gazette, A1–2, Dec. 14, 196.
40. Transcript, 437–51.
41. Transcript, 465.
42. Transcript, 424–31, 453–61, 465–76.
43. Transcript, 474–78, 482–96.
44. Transcript, 506–25, 538; *The Strap for Punishing Prisoners*, Ark. Gazette, A4, Sept. 7, 1966.
45. Transcript, 530–34, 540.

CHAPTER 14

1. *Jackson* Trial Transcript, 560.
2. *Penologists Hear About the Arkansas Prison*, Pine Bluff Com., Feb. 22, 1967, U. Ark. Little Rock (UALR), Center Arkansas History and Culture, Winthrop Rockefeller Collection, Record Group IV, Box 253, File 1. Unless otherwise noted, all Rockefeller archival materials are from Record Group IV.
3. James V. Bennett, interview by Joan-Ellen Marci, Robert Kennedy Oral History Program of the John F. Kennedy Library, *10, Nov. 11, 1974; James V. Bennett, *I Chose Prison*, 190 (Rodney Campbell ed., Alfred A. Knopf, 1970); Transcript, 548–49.
4. Bennett, *I Chose*, 11, 229, 54–59; John W. Roberts & James V. Bennett, *Encyclopedia of American Prisons*, 55 (Marilyn D. McShane & Franklin P. Williams eds., Garland Publ., 1996).
5. Bennett interview, 33; Bureau of Prisons, US DOJ, FY 2024 Performance Budget, Congressional Submission, Federal Prison System, Buildings and Facilities (2024); Data sources for prison population include Bureau of Justice Statistics, *Correctional Populations in the United States, 2022—Statistical Tables*, tbl. 1, US DOJ (2024); Wendy Sawyer & Peter Wagner, *Mass Incarceration: The Whole Pie 2024*, Prison Pol'y Initiative, Mar. 14, 2024.
6. James V. Bennett, *The Federal Penal and Correctional Problem* (1928), Federal Penal and Reformatory Institutions: Hearings before the Special Comm. on Federal Penal and Reformatory Institutions, H. Rep. (1929), 73–93, 173–207; Paul Keve, *Prisons and the American Conscience: A History of US Federal Corrections*, 92 (S. Ill. U. Press, 1991).
7. Bennett, *Federal Penal and Correctional Problem*, 177, 186, 188–89, 107–98, 205; James V. Bennett, *Countdown for Judicial Sentencing*, 25 Fed. Probation 22, 22–25 (Sept. 1961); James V. Bennett, *The Sentence and Treatment of Offenders*, 339 Annals Am. Acad. Pol. & Soc. Sci. 142 (Jan. 1962).
8. Representative George Graham (R-PA) introduced legislation to create the Bureau of Prisons in 71 HR 2832 on Dec. 19, 1929; some credit A. H. Conner, Superintendent prior to Sanford Bates, as the original drafter. Keve, 96, 854–85; Bennett, *I Chose*, 85–88. Authorizations for employment, schooling

in trades, and industries were provided in Act of May 27, 1930, ch. 340, 46
Stat. 391, and Act of June 23, 1934, ch. 737, §§ 1, 2, 48 Stat. 1211; Executive Order 6917 (Dec. 11, 1934); *Sanford Bates, 88, Who Headed Federal Prison System,
Is Dead*, NY Times, 26, Sept. 9, 1972; Sanford Bates, *One World in Penology*,
38 J. Crim. L. & Criminology 565 (1948).

9. Bennett, *I Chose*, 13, 91–94, 205–10; 18 USC § 4082 (1965).

10. Model Penal Code, Official Draft and Explanatory Notes (as adopted at the
1962 Annual Meeting, ALI); Section 1.02.(2), 2.

11. Bennett, *I Chose*, 5–15, 229.

12. Bennett, *I Chose*, 12, 37–39, 219–28.

13. Bennett, *I Chose*, 37.

14. Wright v. McMann, 321 F. Supp. 127, 136, 138–40 (NDNY 1970), aff'd in part
and rev'd in part, 460 F.2d 126 (2d Cir. 1972); as discussed in the next chapter, Judges Harris and Young had relied on the earlier decision, Wright v.
McMann, 257 F. Supp. 739 (NDNY 1966), that was reversed by the Second
Circuit. 387 F.2d 519 (2d Cir. 1967).

15. Inmates of Suffolk County Jail v. Eisenstadt, 360 F. Supp. 676 (D. Mass.
1973), aff'd, 494 F.2d 1196 (1st Cir. 1974). Decades later, in Rufo v. Inmates
of Suffolk County Jail, 502 US 367 (1992), the US Supreme Court, lowering
the standard to modify injunctions, permitted government defendants to
alter its obligations.

16. *Charles Street Jail Called "Museum Piece,"* Bost. Globe, June 6, 1972; *Boston's
Ugly Scar*, Bost. Globe, Nov. 16, 1972; *Inmates of Suffolk County Jail*, 360 F.
Supp. 680. Bennett was also cited in Judge Tuttle's dissent in Novak v. Beto,
453 F.2d 661, 685 (5th Cir. 1971); and in Williams v. Robinson, 432 F.2d 637,
645 n.36 (DC Cir. 1970), and he participated in litigation about Virginia's
prison conditions. Philip J. Hirschkop & Michael A. Millemann, *The Unconstitutionality of Prison Life*, 55 Va. L. Rev. 795, 838 (1969).

17. Burns v. Swenson, 288 F. Supp. 4, 8 (WD Mo. 1968); Burns v. Swenson, 300 F.
Supp. 759, 765 (WD Mo. 1969); Burns v. Swenson, 430 F.2d 771 (8th Cir. 1970).

18. Transcript, 550, 563, quoting American Correctional Association's 1966
Manual of Correctional Standards, 55.

19. Transcript, 550–56.

20. Transcript, 560–67. Wright used a 1958 edition; the UN Congress approved
the Rules in 1955; the UN General Assembly adopted them thereafter. E/
RES/663 C, UN Standard Minimum Rules for the Treatment of Prisoners
(July 31, 1957).

21. Transcript, 577–86.

22. Transcript, 590–94.

23. Transcript, 599–601.

24. Fred T. Wilkinson with Fred DeArmond, *The Realities of Crime and Punishment: A Prison Administrator's Testament*, 15 (Mycroft Press, 1972).

25. Transcript, 605–21; Wilkinson, 224.

26. Warren E. Hearnes, Foreword to Wilkinson, vii–viii; Wilkinson, 98–99, 103–
04, 167, 173; Johnson v. Avery, 393 US 483 (1969).

27. Transcript, 608–15.
28. Transcript, 617–36.
29. Transcript, 570–75.
30. Transcript, 638–39, 641.

CHAPTER 15

1. Jackson v. Bishop, 268 F. Supp. 804, 809–11 (ED Ark. 1967).
2. *Jackson*, 811–14.
3. *Jackson*, 807, 813–15.
4. *Jackson*, 814. The two decisions were *Lee v. Tahash*, 352 F.2d 970 (8th Cir. 1965); and *Carey v. Settle*, 351 F.2d 483 (8th Cir. 1965). Both involved prisoners losing claims that mail or access to books were unconstitutionally limited.
5. Wright v. McMann, 257 F. Supp. 739, 740, 745 (NDNY 1966).
6. Wright v. McMann, 387 F.2d 519, 520–21 (2d Cir. 1967). Wright, listed as "pro se," had attorney Betty D. Friedlander appearing for him. On remand, district court Judge Foley referenced the Eighth Circuit's reversal, Jackson v. Bishop, 404 F.2d 571 (8th Cir. 1968). Wright v. McMann, 321 F. Supp. 127, 131, 140, 144 (NDNY 1970), aff'd, 460 F.2d 126 (2d Cir. 1972). Wright, born in 1939, serving an indeterminate sentence after a 1963 conviction "for certain sexual offenses," was, according to genealogical records, white.
7. Jordan v. Fitzharris, 257 F. Supp. 674 (ND Cal. 1966).
8. *Jackson*, 815–16.
9. *Jackson*, 815–16; Bucklew v. Precythe, 587 US 119 (2019).
10. *Prison Ordered to Bar Strap*, Camden News, 3, June 6, 1967; *Jackson*, 816.
11. Belgian General Observations Concerning the Project's Aims, Fall, 1927, IPPC, UN Archives, NY, S-0915, Box 35, File 4, 2 (my translation).
12. Criminal Justice Act 1948, s.2 (Eng.) ended judges' power to order whipping at sentencing; Criminal Justice Act 1967, s.65 (Eng.) ended authority to order whipping in prisons as discipline; Correctional Service of Canada, Abolition of Corporal Punishment, 1972; Yong Vui Kong v. Public Prosecutor, 2 Sing. L. Rep. 1129 (SGCA 2015). In Australia, corporal punishment was abolished for federal offences in 1914 but remained legal in some of its subdivisions. South Australia ended corporal punishment in 1971. Crimes Act 1914 (Cth), D16; Corporal Punishment Abolition Act 1971 (SA).
13. Ingraham v. Wright, 430 US 651, 656–63 (1977).
14. Brief for Petitioners at 4–11, *Ingraham*, 430 US 651 (No.75–6527); Ingraham v. Wright, 498 F.2d 248 (5th Cir. 1974), rev'd, 525 F.2d 909 (1976) (en banc).
15. Justin Driver, *The Schoolhouse Gate: Public Schools, The Supreme Court, and the Battle for the American Mind*, 168–74 (Pantheon, 2018).
16. Additional Views of Messrs. [Leon] Jaworski, [Ross L]. Malone, [Lewis. F.] Powell & [Robert G.] Storey, *The Challenge of Crime in a Free Society: A Report by the President's Commission on Law Enforcement and Administration of Justice*, 303–08 (US Gov't Printing Office, 1967).

17. Earl M. Maltz, *Portrait of a Man in the Middle—Mr. Justice Powell, Equal Protection, and the Pure Classification Problem*, 40 Ohio St. L. J. 941, 950 (1979); *Ingraham*, 430 US 664, 670–72.

18. Aniya Greene-Santos, *Corporal Punishment in Schools Still Legal in Many States*, NEA Today, May 20, 2024; Elizabeth T. Gershoff & Sarah A. Font, *Corporal Punishment in US Public Schools: Prevalence, Disparities in Use, and Status in State and Federal Policy*, 30 Soc. Pol'y Rep. 1 (2016); Civil Rights Data Collection, *2015–16 State and National Tables—Discipline by Discipline Type: Corporal Punishment*, US Dept. of Educ. (2016); *K-12 Education: Discipline Disparities for Black Students, Boys, and Students with Disabilities*, US Gov't Accountability Office (Mar. 2018).

19. *Jackson*, 808–09.

20. Governor Rockefeller, *Inaugural Address*, Jan. 10, 1967, Winthrop Rockefeller Institute.

21. Meeting Minutes, Arkansas State Penitentiary Board, 1, Aug. 30, 1967; Dr. Ed Barron, Memorandum re: Inspection Made at Cummins Prison Farm to Members of the State Penitentiary Board, Sept. 20–21, 1967, John. H. Haley Papers, Butler Center Arkansas Studies, Series 1, Box 2, File 8, 1–3; *Barron to Leave Soon*, Ark. Gazette, B1, Feb. 7, 1968; *Negro Hired as Warden at Cummins Prison Farm*, Pine Bluff Com., Sept. 18, 1967, U. Ark. Little Rock (UALR), Center Arkansas History and Culture, Winthrop Rockefeller Collection, Record Group IV, Box 251, File 6.

22. Meeting Minutes, Oct. 4, 1967.

23. Meeting Minutes, Nov. 29–30, 1967; Bobbie Forster, *Dope, Filth at Pen Termed "Incredible,"* Ark. Democrat, 1, Oct. 31, 1967; *Cummins Joins Tucker in the Penal Scandal*, Ark. Gazette, A2, Nov. 2, 1967; Editorials, *More Light on the Shame*, Crossett, Ark. Newspaper, Nov. 9, 1967; Editorial, *One More Scandal*, Pine Bluff Com., Rockefeller, IV, Box 252, File 5; *Lincoln Jury Raps Barron, Indicts No One*, Ark. Gazette, A2, Nov. 29, 1967.

24. Meeting Minutes, Nov. 29–30, 1967; Thomas O. Murton, Criminologist, Observations on the Correctional Needs of the State of Arkansas: A Proposal Prepared for the Arkansas Prison Study Commission, Aug. 1, 1967, Rockefeller, IV, Box 251, File 1; Doug Smith, *Bishop, Murton Differ Sharply on Prison Reform Ideas*, Ark. Gazette, A4, Aug. 24, 1967; Governor Rockefeller, Memorandum to Arkansas Weekly Newspaper Editors, Aug. 28, 1967, Rockefeller, IV, Box 251, File 3, 2; George Douthit, *Bishop Resigns, Says His Position Made "Impossible,"* Ark. Democrat, 1, Nov. 1, 1967.

25. John Haley, Arkansas Penitentiary System: A Case for Reform, Rockefeller, IV, Box 258, File 1, 1–6 (undated); Report of the Arkansas State Penitentiary Commission, Jan. 1, 1968, Arkansas State Archives, Prison Records, Box 1, Folder 8, 3.02, 3.05–3.06.

26. Tucker Steinmetz, *3 Prison Board Members Resign*, Pine Bluff Com., Jan. 4, 1968; *4 Appointments Set Saturday*, Ark. Gazette, Jan. 12, 1968; *Rockefeller Gains Prison Control*, Com. Appeal, Jan. 16, 1968; *4 Vacancies Filled On Prison Board: First Negro Named*, Ark. Gazette, A3, Jan. 16, 1968; *Prison Board's*

4 Newcomers: Average Age 43, Pine Bluff Com., Jan. 17, 1968, Rockefeller, IV, Box 250, File 2, 6; *US Joins Move to Halt Faubus on School Plan*, Ark. Gazette, 1, 3, Sept. 25, 1958; *Prison Board Post to Go to John Haley*, Ark. Gazette, A12, Jan. 18, 1967; *Murton Applies to Take Over Bishop's Post*, Ark. Gazette, 13, Dec. 21, 1967; Thomas Murton & Joe Hyams, *Accomplices to the Crime*, 17–21 (Grove Press, 1969).

27. State Commission Report, R.07.

28. Act of Jan. 31, 1967, No. 22, §§ 1–2, 1965–1967 Ark. Acts A25, A25–28; Tucker Steinmetz, *Penologist Offers to Be Free Consultant to Prison Study Panel*, Pine Bluff Com., 5, Mar. 19, 1967; Tucker Steinmetz, *Austin McCormick: The Key Figure in Arkansas Prison Reform*, Pine Bluff Com., Aug. 6, 1967, Rockefeller, IV, Box 260, File 2, 7; Austin MacCormick, *Adult Correctional Institutions in the United States*, 2–3, 48, 53 (1967); W. Wesley Johnson, Austin Harbutt MacCormick, *Encyclopedia of American Prisons* 314 (Marilyn D. McShane & Franklin P. Williams eds., Garland Publ., 1996).

29. State Commission Report, R.7.19, quoting 1966 American Correctional Association's Manual of Correctional Standards, 417; R.7.18; 7.15–7.16, R.01; R.08–09.

30. State Commission Report, R.03, R.09.

31. State Commission Report, R.01, R.03, R.05.

32. Tucker Steinmetz, *Money Bill for Prisons in Works*, Pine Bluff Com., Jan. 23, 1968, Rockefeller, IV, Box 250, File 2.

33. Tucker Steinmetz, *Murton Puts His Job at Prison in Jeopardy*, Pine Bluff Com., Feb. 7, 1968, Rockefeller, IV, Box 250, File 2; Walter Rugaber, *Arkansas Prison Board Approves New Hunt for Bodies and Starting a Formal Burial Plot*, NY Times, Feb. 8, 1968; Walter Rugaber, *Arkansas Prison: Chamber of Horror*, NY Times, 1, 48, Jan. 27, 1968; Arkansas State Police, Investigative Report, Mar. 11, 1968, Prison Records, Box 1, Folder 2, 1.

34. Bill Lewis, *Cummins Inmate Says One Grave Only 7 Years Old*, Ark. Gazette, 1–2, Jan. 31, 1968; *The Prison Investigation: Notes for the News Media*, Mar. 22, 1968, UALR, Eisele Papers, Box 15, File 3; Tucker Steinmetz, *Grand Jury Hears First Testimony*, Pine Bluff Com., Feb. 13, 1968; *Murton Firing is Tied to 3 Causes*, Com. Appeal, 20, Mar. 9, 1968; *Parolees Recount Prison Horrors Under Strap, Astride "Teeter Board,"* Com. Appeal, 1, Feb. 5, 1968; James Phelan, *The Prison Scandal That Won't Stay Buried*, True: The Men's Magazine, Oct. 1968, Rockefeller, IV, Box 253, File 2, 33, 36, 67, 87.

35. *Inmate Finds Protection in Cummins Prison "Hole,"* Com. Appeal, 22, Feb. 5, 1968; Notes Taken at [Penitentiary] Board Meeting, Feb. 11, 1968, Mr. Haley's Office, Haley Papers, 1, Box 2, File 11; *Prison Board Secretly Takes More Power*, Ark. Gazette, A5, Feb. 24, 1968; Memorandum Tom Eisele to Governor Rockefeller, Feb. 28, 1968, Eisele Papers, Box 15, File 5, 2–3.

36. *Penitentiary Reform Bills Meet Opposition in Assembly*, Ark. Gazette, A4, Feb. 14, 1968; Jerol Garrison, *Strap Prohibition in Penitentiary Bill Removed by House*, Ark. Gazette, 1, Feb. 15, 1968; Doug Smith, *Funds to Be Asked for Penitentiary*, Ark. Gazette, A4, Feb. 21, 1968; *Delay Is Proposed on 3 Prison*

Bills, Com. Appeal, 16, Feb. 14, 1968; Doug Smith, *"Brand New" Bill on Prison Reform to Be Introduced*, Ark. Gazette, 1, Feb. 15, 1968.

37. Kelsey Garman, *Days of Brutal Punishment End in Arkansas Prisons*, Ark. Democrat, 3, Oct. 6, 1968; Act of Feb. 21, 1968, No. 50, §§ 2–4, 1968–1969 Ark. Acts 1646, 1648–52; Progress Report, Department of Correction, Sept. 26, 1968, Rockefeller, IV, Box 253, File 2, 1.

38. *Prison Board Bans the Strap*, Ark. Gazette, 2, Mar. 1, 1968; Tucker Steinmetz, *Prison Board Concentrates on Cucumbers*, Pine Bluff Com., Mar. 1, 1968; George Bentley, *3 of 5 on Board Don't Want Murton in Correction Post*, Ark. Gazette, 1, Mar. 3, 1968; Notes Taken Board Meeting, Mar. 2, 1968, Cummins Farm, Haley Papers, 1, Box 2, File 12, 91; Rebecca Rather, *"Profitable Prison" Days Gone*, Ark. Democrat, 1, Jan. 26, 1968.

39. Ernest Dumas, *Board Fires Murton After WR's Urging*, Ark. Gazette, 1, Mar. 8, 1968; George Douthit, *Haley Says Murton Ignored Orders in Insubordinate Way*, Ark. Democrat, 1, Mar. 8, 1968; George Douthit, *Murton's Purchases, Unbending Attitude Criticized by Haley*, Ark. Democrat, 2, Mar. 9, 1968; *Urban to Head Parole Board*, Ark. Gazette, B9, Sept. 30, 1967.

40. *Brutality at Pen in Past, Urban States*, Baxter Bull., 17, Apr. 25, 1968.

41. *Manpower Shortage Delays Harvesting of Crops at Prison*, Ark. Democrat, A6, June 12, 1969; George Douthit, *Rehabilitation, Prison Farming System Collide*, Ark. Democrat, 2, June 13, 1968; *Prison School Faces New Threat: Its Pupils Are Needed in the Fields*, Pine Bluff Com., June 13, 1968, Rockefeller, IV, Box 250, File 1.

42. *Parole Man, Builder Hired at Tucker*, Ark. Gazette, A6, Apr. 8, 1967; *Cummins Is Calm: WR "Takes Pulse of Atmosphere,"* Ark. Gazette, A2, Mar. 9, 1968; *It's What Comes Next That Counts*, Ark. Democrat, 6, Mar. 12, 1968; Victor Urban, Superintendent, Memorandum Re: State Penitentiary Study to Board Members, Sept. 3, 1968, Rockefeller, IV, Box 253, File 2.

43. UPI, *LR Attorney Demands an End to Segregation in Prisons*, Ark. Gazette, 3, Mar. 23, 1968; *Segregation in Penitentiary Called Illegal*, Ark. Gazette, 21, Apr. 17, 1968. *Black Muslims' Meetings Troublefree, Urban Says*, Ark. Gazette, 29, May 31, 1968. Chachkin, who had worked for the NAACP Legal Defense and Education Fund, was a white lawyer at the firm of John W. Walker, "the Negro lawyer who handles many civil rights cases."

44. Progress Report, Department of Correction, Sept. 26, 1968, Rockefeller, IV, Box 253, File 2, 2–5.

45. Garrison, *Increase of 3 Cents in Cigarette Tax Defeated by House*, Ark. Gazette, 2, May 28, 1968; Murton & Hyams, 224–25; Tim Hackler, *Prosecutor Gets Prison Audit*, Ark. Democrat, A3, Nov. 21, 1968; Bob Ferguson, *Gunshots End Rebellion: Work Resumes at Prison*, Ark. Democrat, 8, Oct. 15, 1968.

46. *Inmates Defy Order to Move: 24 Shot*, Ark. Gazette, 1, Oct. 15, 1968; *Shooting at Prison Called Unnecessary*, Ark. Democrat, 3, Nov. 9, 1968; Associated Press, *Controversial Official Quits Post at Cummins*, Ark. Democrat, 1, Nov. 18, 1968; *Rockefeller Confirms Prisoners Chained*, Com. Appeal, 9, Nov. 2, 1968; *Haley Sees a Political Motivation in Photo of Prisoner in Stockade*, Ark. Gazette, 1,

Nov. 2, 1968, 1; ADC Budget 1968–1969, Rockefeller, IV, Box 250, File 2, 4; *"Dog Pen" Use Will Continue*, Com. Appeal, 22, Nov. 3, 1968.

47. *Prison Board Considering W. Virginian*, Ark. Gazette, 24, Oct. 30, 1968; *Corrections Board Takes Up Wounding of 24 Prisoners*, Ark. Democrat, 6, Nov. 8, 1968 George Douthit, *New Prison Chief Goes on the Job*, Ark. Democrat, 2, Nov. 19, 1968; *West Virginia Lawyer Gets Corrections Job*, Ark. Gazette, 5, Nov. 9, 1968. *Sarver: A Biographical Sketch*, Pine Bluff Com., Dec. 29, 1968, Rockefeller, Series IV, Box 250, File 1, 10.

48. Bob Ferguson, *Sarver Offers Budget and Some Philosophy*, Ark. Democrat, 1–2, Nov. 26, 1968; George Douthit, *Sarver Finds Doors Open*, Ark. Democrat, 37, Dec. 1, 1968.

49. C. Robert Sarver, Commissioner, Arkansas Department of Correction, Annual Report to the Governor and the General Assembly, Covering the Period Mar. 1, 1968–Sept. 30, 1970, Prison Records, Box 1, Folder 5.

50. ADC Budget 1968–1969, Rockefeller, IV, Box 250, File 2, 18; Tim Hackler, *Prosecutor Gets Prison Audit*, Ark. Democrat, A3, Nov. 21, 1968.

CHAPTER 16

1. Theodore J. Fetter, *A History of the United States Court of Appeals for the Eighth Circuit*, 86–87 (Judicial Conference of the United States Bicentennial Committee, 1977).

2. Gerald W. Heaney, *Judge Martin Donald Van Oosterhout: The Big Judge from Orange City, Iowa*, 79 Iowa L. Rev. 1, 1–5, 12–16, 20 (1993).

3. Harvey M. Johnsen, Donald P. Lay, Paul W. White, Roman L. Hruska & Carl T. Curtis, *Robert Van Pelt Dedication*, 49 Neb. L. Rev. 503, 503–04 (1970); Robert Van Pelt, Oral History by Richard Shugrue, Eighth Circuit Library, St. Louis, Missouri; Resolution in Memoriam of The Honorable Robert Van Pelt, Adopted at the Eighth Circuit Judicial Conference, St. Louis, Mo., 1–2, July 14, 1988; Associated Press, *Robert Van Pelt; Federal Judge, 90*, NY Times, 11, Apr. 30, 1988.

4. Haynsworth was nominated on August 21, 1969 and Carswell on January 19, 1970. Linda Greenhouse, *Becoming Justice Blackmun: Harry Blackmun's Supreme Court Journey*, 2–13, 82–101 (Times Books, 2005); Roe v. Wade, 410 US 113 (1973), rev'd, Dobbs v. Jackson, 597 US 215 (2022).

5. Memo, Nos. 18,957/9, Jackson v. Bishop, typed, signed H. A. B., Mar. 13, 1968, Library of Congress, Harry A. Blackmun Papers, Box 42, Folder 31, File 696, 5. All references to unpublished materials and correspondence are from Box 42, Folder 31, File 696.

6. The Eighth Circuit heard arguments in St. Louis; at the suggestion of Judge Blackmun, in 1969, the Circuit began also sitting in St. Paul, Minnesota. Fetter, 86–87. *Jackson* was scheduled on April 3, 1968; Edward Wright asked to reschedule because of a bar meeting conflict. He wrote that, as appointed counsel, he served "without compensation" and had "borne all of the expense incident to the litigation." Edward L. Wright to Robert

C. Tucker, Clerk of the US Court of Appeals, Re: Jackson, Ernst and Mask v. Bishop, Mar. 11, 1968. The Chief Judge, noting that "Mr. Wright has devoted a great amount of time and ability to various Bar activities," directed the clerk to check that the other lawyers could switch dates, and the appeal was rescheduled. Martin D. Van Oosterhout to Robert C. Tucker, Mar. 18, 1968; Tucker to Van Oosterhout, Harry A. Blackmun, and Robert Van Pelt, Mar. 19, 1968.

7. Blackmun Memorandum, Mar. 13, 1968, 1, 5.

8. Blackmun Memorandum, Mar. 13, 1968, 1–4.

9. Blackmun Memorandum, Mar. 13, 1968, 5. Judge Blackmun's file also contained two other typed and signed H. A. B. memoranda with the same date—a seven-page summary of the proceedings below in *Jackson v. Bishop* and a five-page account of *Talley v. Stephens*.

10. Jackson v. Bishop, 404 F.2d 571, 573 (8th Cir. 1968).

11. George Douthit, *Prison Whipping Aired by Prisoner at Court Hearing*, Ark. Democrat, 1, Oct. 13, 1965. Examples of Black habeas litigants include Luther Bailey, who argued that race permeated his conviction for raping a white woman. Chief Judge Henley denied that petition on the grounds that Bailey had failed to raise a claim of jury selection bias at trial. Bailey v. Henslee, 168 F. Supp. 314 (ED Ark. 1958), rev'd, 287 F.2d 936 (8th Cir. 1961). In another case, a Black petitioner with a sixth-grade education was convicted of raping a white woman and sentenced to death. After Judge Young denied relief, the Eighth Circuit reversed and held that the petitioner was entitled to present claims about racial discrimination, a coerced confession, and ineffective assistance of counsel. Mitchell v. Henslee, 332 F.2d 16 (8th Cir. 1964). On remand, Young again denied relief, and the Eighth Circuit again reversed. Mitchell v. Stephens, 232 F. Supp. 497 (ED Ark. 1964), rev'd, 353 F.2d 129 (8th Cir. 1965).

12. *Jackson*, 572.

13. *Jackson*, 576 n.5; Blackmun Papers, handwritten notes about the argument by Mr. Langston, Apr. 5, 1968.

14. *Jackson*, 573–75.

15. *Jackson*, 576. Section 2 of the Fourteenth Amendment, which guarantees the right of "male inhabitants" to vote in federal elections, excluded people who had participated "in rebellion, or other crime." Under US constitutional law, felon disenfranchisement (including after release) is unconstitutional only if individuals can establish racial animus. That test was met in 1985; the Court held that a 1901 amendment to Alabama's Constitution that took voting rights away based on "moral turpitude" aimed to disenfranchise Black voters. Hunter v. Underwood, 471 US 222, 223–25 (1985). Millions, disproportionately of color, remained unable to vote. Marc Meredith & Michael Morse, *Discretionary Disenfranchisement: The Case of Legal Financial Obligations*, 46 J. Legal Stud. 309 (June 2017). Outside the United States, several courts have held felon disenfranchisement unlawful. Examples include Sauvé v. Canada (Chief Electoral Officer), 3 SCR 519

(Can. 2002); Minister for Home Affairs v. Nat'l Inst. For Crime Prevention and the Reintegration of Offenders (NICRO) 5 BCLR 445 (CC S. Afr. 2004); Hirst v. United Kingdom (No. 2), 41 Eur. Ct. HR (2005) (App. No. 74025/01). A UK backlash followed, and the ECtHR law shifted somewhat. Judith Resnik, Judicial Methods of Mediating Conflicts: Recognizing and Accommodating Differences in Pluralist Legal Regimes, *Judicial Power: How Constitutional Courts Affect Political Transformations*, 250–89 (Christine Landfried ed., Cambridge U. Press, 2019).

16. *Jackson*, 576–77.
17. *Jackson*, 577, citing Justice Field's dissent in O'Neil v. Vermont, 144 US 323, 340 (1892); *Jackson*, 578, citing Louisiana *ex rel*. Francis v. Resweber, 329 US 459, 463 (1947); Robinson v. California, 370 US 660, 676 (1962) (Douglas, J., concurring); Justices Goldberg, Douglas, and Brennan dissented to the denial of certiorari in Rudolph v. Alabama, 375 US 889, 890 (1963); *Jackson*, 579, citing Trop v. Dulles, 356 US 86, 100–01 (1958).
18. Carey v. Settle, 351 F.2d 483 (8th Cir. 1965); Lee v. Tahash, 352 F.2d 970 (8th Cir. 1965).
19. *Jackson*, 579.
20. *Jackson*, 579–80.
21. *Jackson*, 580–81; Blackmun, oral argument notes, describing Mr. Wright's "forceful" statement, Apr. 5, 1968.
22. American Correctional Association, *Manual of Correctional Standards*, 417 (1966).
23. Hope v. Pelzer, 536 US 730, 739 (2002). Justice Thomas, dissenting, argued that the unconstitutionality of hitching a person to a post had not then been clearly established and therefore no liability existed for damages. *Hope*, 748–64.
24. The "point to be argued" was whether "the court erred in refusing to hold that corporal punishment of prisoners [was] cruel and unusual punishment . . . and in holding that whipping was not unconstitutional per se." Jackson, Ernst, and Mask v. Bishop, Brief of Appellants, 6 (Nos. 18957, 18958, 18968) (8th Cir. filed Sept. 25, 1967).
25. Letter Blackmun to Van Oosterhout and Van Pelt, Re: Jackson, Ernst and Mask v. Bishop, Superintendent, Nov. 22, 1968.
26. Letter Van Pelt to Blackmun, Nov. 25, 1968; Van Oosterhout to Blackmun, Nov. 25, 1968.
27. Letter Pat Mehaffy to Blackmun, Dec. 10, 1968; Jack Erwin, *Blackmun Decision—Use of Whips on Prisoners Banned in Precedent Case*, Rochester Post Bull., Dec. 9, 1968.
28. Letter Oren Harris to Blackmun, Jan. 24, 1969; Gordon E. Young to Blackmun, Dec. 12, 1968; Blackmun to Harris, Jan. 27, 1969; Blackmun to Young, Dec. 16, 1968.
29. Letter Wright to Blackmun, Mar. 4, 1969.
30. Letter James V. Bennett to Blackmun, Jan. 28, 1969; Blackmun to Bennett, Feb. 3, 1969.

31. Letter Hans W. Mattick to Blackmun, Dec. 20, 1968; Blackmun to Mattick, Dec. 30, 1968; Hans Mattick, *The Future of Imprisonment in a Free Society*, 8 Brit. J. Criminology, 450 (1967).
32. Greenhouse, 50–51.
33. Richard G. Kleindienst, Deputy Atty. Gen., to James O. Eastman, Chairman, Comm. on the Judiciary, Nomination of Harry A. Blackmun of Minnesota to be Associate Justice of the Supreme Court of the United States, Hearing before the S. Comm. on the Judiciary, 91st Cong. 14 (1970).
34. Blackmun said so when concurring in *Rhodes v. Chapman*, 452 US 337, 368–69 (1981) and speaking to his law clerks. Pamela S. Karlan, *Bringing Compassion into the Province of Judging: Justice Blackmun and the Outsiders*, 71 ND L. Rev. 173, 175 (1995). More than three dozen circuit opinions relied on Jackson before the US Supreme Court expanded its own discussion of prisoners' rights, such as in *Wolff v. McDonnell*, 418 US 539 (1974).
35. Connie L. Cartledge, *Harry A. Blackmun Papers: A Finding Aid to the Collection in the Library of Congress*, 5 (2019).

CHAPTER 17

1. Garrett Felber, *Those Who Know Don't Say: The Nation of Islam, the Black Freedom Movement, and the Carceral State* (UNC Press, 2020); Dan Berger & Toussaint Losier, *American Social and Political Movements of the 20th Century: Rethinking the American Prison Movement* (Routledge, 2017); Christopher E. Smith, *Black Muslims and the Development of Prisoners' Rights*, 25 J. Black Stud. 131 (1993).
2. Mike Fitzgerald, *Prisoners in Revolt* (Penguin Books, 1977); Dan Berger, *Captive Nation: Black Prison Organizing in the Civil Rights Era* (UNC Press, 2014); Albert Woodfox, *Solitary* (Grove Press, 2019).
3. Cooper v. Pate, Notice of Appeal and Petition to File and Prosecute of Jan. 9, 1963, NARA, Dist. Ct. No. 62-C-1208, US CA No. 14127. All unpublished materials are from this archive.
4. James B. Jacobs, *Stateville: The Penitentiary in Mass Society* (U. Chi. Press, 1977).
5. Gov. Bruce Rauner, *In Name of Justice, I'm Closing Stateville's F House*, Sun-Times, Op-Ed, Oct. 14, 2016.
6. Siegel v. Ragen, Complaint, 11 (No. 49C47 ND Ill); Siegel v. Ragen, 88 F. Supp. 996, 999 (ND Ill. 1949), aff'd, 180 F.2d 785, 788 (7th Cir. 1950). Meyer, a "prominent jailhouse lawyer," assisted many prisoners. Toussaint Losier, *. . . For Strictly Religious Reason[s]*, 15 Souls 19, 24 n.20, 36 (2013).
7. Cooper was one of many skilled in-house litigants. Mumia Abu-Jamal, *Jailhouse Lawyers: Prisoners Defending Prisoners v. the USA* (City Light Books, 2009).
8. *Cooper*, Complaint; Losier, 20–28, NARA, Dist. No. 62-C-1208.
9. Appellant Briefs and Appendix, 5, 7–8, 10; Brief and Argument for Respondents-Appellees, 10–12, 17–46, Cooper v. Pate 324 F.2d, 165, 165–67 (7th Cir. 1963), citing *Siegel*, 180 F.2d, 788.

10. Weisberg had clerked for Justice Tom Clark; the lawyers become counsel "three weeks after the Court of Appeals issued" and did not have access to the record. Application for an Extension of Time in Which to File Petition for Writ of Certiorari of Jan. 22, 1964, Cooper v. Pate, 378 US 546 (1964) (No. 1134); Letter John F. Davis, Clerk at the US Supreme Court's Clerk's Office, to Seymour H. Bucholz, Jan. 23, 1964; Petition for Certiorari and Motion for Leave to Proceed *In Forma Pauperis*, filed March 4, 1964; Foreword to ACLU Ill. Div., *Secret Detention by the Chicago Police: A Report by the American Civil Liberties Union*, 5 (1959).

11. Brief for Petitioners, 4–5, Monroe v. Pape, 365 US 167 (1961) (No. 39), 1960 WL 98617; *Monroe*, 169–72; Myriam Gilles, *Police, Race and Crime in 1950s Chicago*: Monroe v. Pape *as Legal Noir*, Civil Rights Stories, (Myriam E. Gilles & Risa L. Goluboff eds., Foundation Press, 2007).

12. Illinois had to reply by May 4, 1964; Letter US Supreme Court's Clerk's office to William G. Clark, Atty. Gen. of Ill., Apr. 2, 1964; Stipulation of Apr. 2, 1964; Western Union Telegram, Davis, Clerk, to Bucholz, June 23, 1964.

13. *Cooper*, 378 US, 546.

14. Pierce v. LaVallee, 293 F.2d 233 (2d Cir. 1961); Sewell v. Pegelow, 291 F.2d 196 (4th Cir. 1961).

15. *Cooper*, 324 F.2d, 166; Losier, 28.

16. Fulwood v. Clemmer, 206 F. Supp. 370, 378 (DDC 1962).

17. Sostre v. Rockefeller, 312 F. Supp. 863, 866 (SDNY 1970).

18. Sostre v. McGinnis, 442 F.2d 178, 191 (2d Cir. 1971).

19. *Fulwood*, 372–78. Nominated by President Harry Truman in 1949, Matthews died in 1988. Linda Greenhouse, *Burnita S. Matthews Dies at 93; First Woman on US Trial Courts*, NY Times, D27, Apr. 28, 1988; Kathanne W. Greene, *Burnita Shelton Matthews: Suffragist, Feminist, and Judicial Pioneer*, Miss. Hist. Now, Aug. 2017; Interview Robert H. Kapp, Hist. Soc'y of the DC Circuit Court, with E. Barrett Prettyman Jr., Washington, DC (Oct. 3, 1996); Sam Roberts, *E. Barrett Prettyman Jr., Lawyer Who Fortified Desegregation Ruling, Dies at 91*, NY Times, Nov. 8, 2016.

20. *Sewell*, 291 F.2d, 197. Given the District of Columbia's statement of an amended policy to "accommodate the practice of the Muslim faith in the religious program at the reformatory," Sewell lost a subsequent enforcement effort. Sewell v. Pegelow, 304 F.2d 670, 670–72 (4th Cir. 1962).

21. Lawrence O'Kane, *Muslim Negroes Suing the State*, NY Times, 1, 46, Mar. 19, 1961; *Pierce*, 293 F.2d 233; Felber, 50–84; Berger & Losier, 59–61. Jacko, who later became counsel to the Nation of Islam, represented Cooper on remand. Clarence Taylor, *Fight the Power: African Americans and the Long History of Police Brutality in New York City*, 81 (NYU Press, 2019); Malachi D. Crawford, *Black Muslims and the Law: Civil Liberties from Elijah Muhammad to Muhammad Ali*, xi (Lexington Books, 2015).

22. O'Kane, 46, quoting Judge Stephen Brennan; Pierce v. LaVallee, 212 F. Supp. 865 (NDNY 1962); Berger & Losier, 60–61.

23. *Pierce*, 293 F.2d, 234–35; *Pierce*, 212 F. Supp., 867, 869; Pierce v. LaVallee, 319 F.2d 844, 845 (2d Cir. 1963), per curiam, cert. denied, 376 US 918 (1964).

24. Felber, 7–8, 196 n.33; Desmond King, *Separate and Unequal: Black Americans and the US Federal Government*, 166 (Oxford U. Press, 1997).
25. Martin Sostre, *Letters from Prison* (Sostre Defense Committee ed., Philosophical Society of SUNY Buffalo, 1968); Malcolm McLaughlin, *Storefront Revolutionary: Martin Sostre's Afro-Asian Bookshop, Black Liberation Culture, and the New Left, 1964–75*, 7 J. Hist. Pol. Culture 1, 4 (2014); Warren L. Schaich & Dianne S. Hope, *The Prison Letters of Martin Sostre: Documents of Resistance*, 7 J. Black Stud. 281, 281 (1977); Alexandria Symonds, *Overlooked No More: Martin Sostre, Who Reformed American's Prisons from His Cell*, NY Times, Apr. 24, 2019. Sostre died in 2015 at 92.
26. Constance Baker Motley, *Equal Justice . . . under law*, 58–62, 203–27 (Farrar Straus & Giroux, 1998).
27. Tomiko Brown-Nagin, *Civil Rights Queen: Constance Baker Motley and the Struggle for Equality*, 288–92 (Pantheon, 2022); Johnson v. Avery, 393 US 483 (1969).
28. *Sostre*, 312 F. Supp., 868–71, 889; UN Office on Drugs and Crime, *United Nations Standard Minimum Rules for the Treatment of Prisoners*, Rules 43, 44, A/Res/70/175 adopted Dec. 17, 2015 (*2015 Nelson Mandela Rules*).
29. Sostre v. McGinnis, 442 F.2d 178, 186, 191 (2d Cir. 1971), en banc, aff'd and rev'd in part, cert. denied *sub nom.* Sostre v. Oswald, 404 US 1049 (1972). Chief Judge Kaufman later praised the ruling for protecting religious freedom and access to courts while warning about the "unpredictable effects of court intervention in prison affairs." Irving R. Kaufman, *The Judge's Dilemma*, 41 Fordham L. Rev. 495, 505–09 (1973).
30. *Sostre*, 312 F. Supp. 866; Tom Wicker, *Irony of Martin Sostre*, NY Times, 17, Dec. 8, 1974.
31. O'Lone v. Estate of Shabazz, 482 US 342, 345, 353 (1987). Justice Brennan, with Justices Marshall, Blackmun, and Stevens, dissented.
32. Religious Land Use and Institutionalized Persons Act (RLUIPA), 42 USC § 2000cc-1a (2018).
33. Holt v. Hobbs, 574 US 352, 363–66 (2015).
34. Filed February 18, 1966, the complaint alleged it fit the new class action rule, circulated the year before and promulgated by the Supreme Court to become effective July 1, 1966. Documents are available at *Case Profile: Washington v. Lee*, Civil Rights Litigation Clearinghouse at U. Mich.; ACLU lawyer Charles Morgan's materials are in Washington v. Lee, Work File, 1969–1971, c15497, MS Southern Regional ACLU Office Files, Making of Modern Law (MoML) ACLU Papers, Mudd Library, Princeton University. I also draw on Jonathan Bass, *He Calls Me by Lightning: The Life of Caliph Washington and the Forgotten Saga of Jim Crow, Southern Justice, and the Death Penalty*, 236–40 (Liveright, 2017).
35. Holman v. Washington, 364 F.2d 618, 619 (5th Cir. 1966); Bass, xiii, xvi, 270–75.
36. Washington v. State, 269 Ala. 146, 157–59 (1959); Bass, 70, 77–82, 101–05, 116–18, 177–81. That decision rested on wrongfully admitted evidence. 269 Ala.,

157–59. After retrial and reconviction, the court affirmed the conviction. Washington v. State, 274 Ala. 386 (1962). Execution had been set for 1963. On August 8, 1966, the Fifth Circuit upheld in part Judge Johnson's ruling. Washington remained in the Jefferson County jail for years pending retrial.

37. Bass, 216–22. After Judge Johnson issued decisions to end poll taxes and the segregation of buses, police forces, and libraries, and to prevent warehousing people with disabilities and violent prison conditions. Death threats followed, as did acknowledgments of his contributions. In 2019, the University of Alabama inaugurated the Judge Frank M. Johnson Jr. Institute, devoted to constitutional history and law. Judge Frank M. Johnson Jr. Centennial Symposium & Law Clerks Reunion, 71 Ala. L. Rev 601 (2020).

38. Washington v. Lee, 263 F. Supp. 327, 331 (MD Ala. 1966) (three-judge court).

39. Appellants' Jurisdictional Statement, Petition, Motion and Filing, Lee v. Washington, 390 US 333 (1968) (No. 75) 1967 WL 129475; Bass, 248–49. In contrast to that testimony, the press reported three people stabbed in a "six-man cell that was being integrated" at that federal prison. *Desegregated Cells Cited in Stabbings*, Atl. J., March 2, 1966, Morgan File Clippings, 1966–1969, c15492.

40. *Washington*, 263 F. Supp., 329–33.

41. Lee v. Washington, Oral argument, 1, available on Oyez, 1967/75. Nicolas S. Hare, arguing for the state, was a high-profile segregationist in the 1950s. Bass, 257–58.

42. Appellants' Jurisdictional Statement, 4–9; Campbell Gibson & Kay Jung, *Historical Census Statistics on Population Totals by Race, 1790 to 1990, and by Hispanic Origin, 1970 to 1990, for Large Cities and Other Urban Places in the United States* (US Census Bureau, Working Paper No. 76, 2005); Justice Black referred the application to the full Court. The lower court had denied the stay. Bass, 258–61; Letter Davis, Clerk, to R. C. Dobson, MD Ala. Clerk, Mar. 7, 1967; Order of Mar. 9, 1967.

43. Argument, 1–2.

44. Argument, 1, 6, 27–28; Brief for Appellants, 16, 20–21, *Lee*.

45. Argument, 12, 20, 31; Bass, 264.

46. *Dr. King Sings "B'ham Jail" Now*, Anniston Star, 2, Nov. 1, 1967; *Massive Street Mobs Foreseen*, Selma-Times Journal, 2, Oct. 29, 1967; *King Begins Martyrdom*, Selma-Times Journal, 1, Oct. 30, 1967; *Dr. King is Shifted to Safer Jail Cell*, NY Times, 34, Nov. 2, 1967; *Judge Lets King Out Day Early*, Montgomery Advertiser, 7, Nov. 4, 1967; Supplemental Brief of Appellants after Argument, 11–15, and Appellees' Motion to File Reply Brief and Reply Brief to the Supplemental Brief of Appellants after Argument, 4–5, *Lee*.

47. Walker v. City of Birmingham, 388 US 307, 309–13, 321, 339 (1967). The others sentenced to five days in jail included Wyatt Tee Walker, Ralph Abernathy, A. D. King, J. W. Hayes, T. L. Fisher, Fred L. Shuttlesworth & J. T. Porter. *Supreme Court Upholds Contempt Citations for King, 7 Others*, Montgomery Advertiser, 1, June 13, 1967; Martin Luther King Jr., *The Negro Is Your Brother*, 212 Atl. Monthly 78 (1963); Shuttlesworth v. City of Birmingham, 394 US 147 (1969).

48. Earl Warren to Byron White, November 28, 1967, Papers of Chief Justice Earl Warren, Library of Congress, MSS52258, Box 650, Opinions—Per Curiam. I also draw on the papers of Justice Byron White, Library of Congress, MSS77264, Part I, Box 120, File 67–75; Justice Potter Stewart, MS 1367, Box 228, File 2524; and Justice Abe Fortas, MS 858, Box 60, File 1218, at the Sterling Memorial Library, Manuscripts and Archives, Yale University. Memorandum Nov. 13, 1967, signed Hugo L. Black, to Justice White and copied to "Members of the Conference," Justice Fortas Papers; Memorandum Nov. 14, 1967, signed B. R. W., cover memo and 2, Justice Fortas Papers.

49. Memorandum Marshall to White, Nov. 14, 1967, Justice Stewart Papers; Memorandum Marshall to the Conference, Nov. 16, 1967, 1, 2–5, 6, Chief Justice Warren Papers; Memorandum Harlan to Stewart, Nov. 7, 1967, Justice Fortas Papers; Memorandum Fortas to Marshall, Nov. 24, 1967, Justice Fortas Papers; Handwritten Note Brennan on Recirculated Draft, February 2, 1968; Memorandum Warren to White, Nov. 28, 1967, Chief Justice Warren Papers. Justice Brennan underlined the word "still" three times.

50. Memorandum Black to White, Feb. 5, 1968, Chief Justice Warren Papers; Memorandum, Stewart, concurring, undated, Justice Stewart Papers; *Lee*, 390 US, 333–34.

51. *Lee*, 334.

52. Letter Commissioner Frank Lee to Judge Johnson, June 9, 1969; Memo Reber [F. Boult Jr.] to Chuck [Morgan], March 18, 1969; Letter Judge Frank M. Johnson Jr. to Commissioner Lee, June 10, 1969, Morgan/ACLU Work File.

53. Jerry Lee Pugh and Worley James filed individual complaints. Judge Johnson appointed lawyers, consolidated the lawsuits, and held a trial in 1975. Pugh v. Locke, 406 F. Supp. 318, 321 n.1 (MD Ala. 1976), affirmed in part and reversed in part *sub nom.* Newman v. Alabama, 559 F.2d 283, 291 (5th Cir. 1977). The original complaints and their history are in Judith Resnik, *The Puzzles of Prisoners and Rights: An Essay in Honor of Frank Johnson*, 71 Ala. L. Rev. 665, 715–22 (2020); analysis also comes from Larry W. Yackle, *Reform and Regret: The Story of Federal Judicial Involvement in the Alabama Prison System* (Oxford U. Press, 1989).

54. Washington v. Sullivan, Order, 2 (No. 2350-N, MD Ala. Sept. 12, 1975), Civil Rights Litigation Clearinghouse.

55. Bass, 287–91.

56. Bass, 294, 323–37, 354–55; Washington v. State, 46 Ala. App. 539, 542 (Ct. Crim. App. Ala. 1971). The trial court denied quashing the indictment and was reversed in Washington v. State, 46 Ala. App. 539, 542 (Ct. Crim. App. Ala. 1971); the basis was the argument Hood made initially—that Black people were excluded on the 1957 grand jury.

57. Losier, 30, quoting Seventh Circuit archival materials.

58. *Prisoners Strike, Letter to the Editor from Alexander M. Man*, Pittsburgh Courier, 18, Nov. 20, 1943; Felber, 22–24, 199–201, nn.37–61; *Objectors Protest Segregation at Prison: Urge Mates' Release*, Baltimore Afro-Am., 5, Mar. 23,

1943; Paul W. Keve, *Prisons and the American Conscience: A History of US Federal Corrections*, 205–06 (S. Ill. U. Press, 1991).

59. James V. Bennett, interview by Joan-Ellen Marci, Robert Kennedy Oral History Program of the John F. Kennedy Library, *14, Nov. 11, 1974; Bennett, *I Chose Prison*, 13 (Alfred A. Knopf, 1970).

60. King, 150; Keve, 205–06.

61. King, 151–52, 153–55 tbl.5.4; 166; Keve, 207.

62. Title VI of the Civil Rights Act of 1964. 28 CFR § 50.3; *State Penitentiary Leads Move to Desegregate Penal Facilities*, Chattanooga Times Free Press, Jan. 13, 1966, quoting Warden C. Murray Henderson; *US Urges Norfolk to Integrate its Jail*, Richmond News Leader, Apr. 29, 1966, Morgan/ACLU.

63. Elizabeth Hinton, *From the War on Poverty to the War on Crime: The Making of Mass Incarceration in America*, 79–95 (Harvard U. Press, 2016).

64. Johnson v. California, 321 F.3d 791, 797 (9th Cir. 2003).

65. Paul W. Valentine, *Segregation Policy at Lorton Prison Defended in Court*, Wash. Post, A6, Jan. 11, 1966 "[T]wo Negro inmates" invoked Fulwood v. Clemmer, 206 F. Supp. 370 (DDC 1962).

66. Edwards v. Sard, 250 F. Supp. 977, 980–81 (DDC 1966).

67. *Johnson*, 321 F.3d, 794–95.

68. O'Lone v. Estate of Shabazz, 482 US 342 (1987); Turner v. Safley, 482 US 78 (1987).

69. *Johnson*, 321 F.3d, 801–02, 804. Judge Warren Ferguson, joined by Harry Pregerson, Dorothy Nelson, and Stephen Reinhardt, would have granted rehearing. Johnson v. California, 336 F.3d 1117, 1120–23 (9th Cir. 2003).

70. Brief of the States of Utah, Alabama, Alaska, Delaware, Idaho, Nevada, New Hampshire, and North Dakota as Amici Curiae in Support of Respondent, Johnson v. California, 543 US 499 (2005) (No. 03-636), 2004 WL 1776910.

71. Brief of the Nat'l Assn. of Black Law Enforcement Officers, Inc. as Amicus Curiae in Support of Respondents, *3, *Johnson*, 2004 WL 1790882.

72. Brief for the United States as Amicus Curiae Supporting Petitioner, *24–27, *Johnson*, 2004 WL 1261255; Brief of Amici Curiae ACLU and its Three Cal. Affiliates in Support of Petitioner, *Johnson*, 2004 WL 1248855; Brief of Former State Corrections Officials as Amici Curiae in Support of Petitioner, *Johnson*, 2004 WL 1261069. Wanting use of both tests was the position of The Brief Amicus Curiae of Pacific Legal Foundation in Support of Neither Party, *Johnson*, 2004 WL 1148634.

73. *Johnson*, 543 US, 507–12, 514–15; Chad Trulson & James W. Marquart, *The Caged Melting Pot: Toward an Understanding of the Consequences of Desegregation in Prisons*, 36 Law & Soc'y Rev. 743 (2002).

74. *Johnson*, 543 US, 516; 518–19 (Stevens, J., dissenting).

75. *Johnson*, 543 US, 532 (Thomas, J., dissenting, joined by Scalia, J.) Chief Justice Rehnquist did not participate.

76. Rhodes v. Chapman, 452 US 337 (1981).

77. Settlement and Release Agreement, 2, Johnson v. California (9th Cir. 2005), Civil Rights Litigation Clearinghouse. Cal. Code. Regs. tit. 15, § 3269.1; Cal.

Dept. of Corrections and Rehabilitation Operations Manual, Ch. 5, Art. 47, 492 (2021). Pelican Bay State Prison had five racial and ethnic groups: "White," "Black," "Northern Hispanic," "Southern Hispanic," and "Other." Other challenges were Richardson v. Runnels, 594 F.3d 666 (9th Cir. 2010); Grandberry v. Lewis, 569 F. App. 503 (9th Cir. 2014); Figueroa v. Clark, No. 1:19-cv-00968, 2020 WL 4700806 (ED Cal. Aug. 13, 2020), report and recommendation adopted, No. 1:19-cv-00968, 2020 WL 7714261 (ED Cal. Dec. 29, 2020).

78. Wendy Sawyer, *Visualizing the Racial Disparities in Mass Incarceration*, Prison Pol'y Initiative, July 27, 2020.

79. Correctional Leaders Association & Arthur Liman Center Public Interest Law at Yale Law School, *Time-In-Cell 2019: A Snapshot of Restrictive Housing Based on a Nationwide Survey of US Prison Systems*, Sept. 2020, 24–45.

80. Death in Custody Reporting Act of 2013, Pub. L. No. 113–242, 128 Stat. 2860 (2014) (codified at 34 USC § 60105); Bureau of Justice Statistics, *Mortality in Correctional Institutions (MCI), Formerly Deaths in Custody Reporting Program (DCRP)*, US DOJ (2019); Prison Rape Elimination Act of 2003, Pub. L. No. 108–79, 117 Stat. 972 (codified as amended at 34 USC § 30301–9); Bureau of Justice Statistics, *Survey of Sexual Victimization*, US DOJ (2022); Eyal Press, *A Fight to Expose the Hidden Human Costs of Incarceration*, New Yorker, Aug. 16, 2021; *About Us*, Incarceration Transparency, https://www.incarcerationtransparency.org/?page_id=391; Leah Wang & Wendy Sawyer, *New Data: State Prisons are Increasingly Deadly Places*, Prison Pol'y Initiative, June 8, 2021.

CHAPTER 18

1. Holt v. Sarver (*Holt I*), 300 F. Supp. 825 (ED Ark. 1969).

2. *Jim Bruton Indicted for Brutality*, Nw. Ark. Times, 1, July 12, 1969; *Jury Indicts Guards in Ark. Prison Farms*, Greensboro Daily News, A2, July 12, 1969; Jerol Garrison, *15 Are Indicted in Brutality Cases at Prison Farms*, Ark. Gazette, 1–2, July 12, 1969; *Hearings Open on Punishment of Prisoners*, Ark. Gazette, 1, July 8, 1969; Jerol Garrison, *Constitutionality of Trusty System Subject of Inquiry*, Ark. Gazette, A8, Dec. 24, 1969; *More Testimony on "Tucker Telephone,"* El Dorado Times, 15, Nov. 20, 1969; Robert Shaw, *Jury Acquits Jim Bruton*, Courier News, 1, Nov. 22, 1969; *Count Dropped Against Last 5 in Prison Case*, Ark. Gazette, 8, Jan. 29, 1970; *Ex-Arkansas Prison Head Fined for Cruel Treatment of Inmates*, NY Times, 37, Jan. 19, 1970; Tim Hackler, *Ex-wardens Acquitted in Penal Farms Rights Cases*, Ark. Democrat, A11, Oct. 30, 1969; Jerol Garrison, *Two Ex-wardens Acquitted in Death of Curtis Ingram*, Ark. Gazette, A2, Oct. 30, 1969.

3. Holt v. Sarver (*Holt II*), 309 F. Supp. 362, 364 (ED Ark. 1970).

4. Colin Woodward, *"There's a Lot of Things that Need Changin": Johnny Cash, Winthrop Rockefeller, and Prison Reform in Arkansas*, 79 Ark. Hist. Q. 40, 67 (2020). The song's text was printed in Tim Hackler, *Johnny Cash Sings at*

Cummins, Ark. Democrat, A3, Apr. 11, 1969. Cash's *Folsom* lyrics were that "Mister Congressman you can't understand"; the San Quentin song did not mention legislators.

5. Tom Dearmore, *Arkansas Johnny Cash Is Now a National Sensation*, Ark. Gazette, 66, Sept. 28, 1969; Tom Dearmore, *Cash's Hangups—Rails, Indians, Convicts*, Ark. Gazette, E5, Sept. 28, 1969.

6. Daniel Geary, *"The Way I Would Feel about San Quentin": Johnny Cash & the Politics of Country Music*, 10 Daedalus: J. Am. Acad. Arts & Sci. 64, 65 (2013); Martin Luther King, *Where Do We Go from Here: Chaos or Community*, 112 (1967). In 1972, Cash testified in support of more accessible parole. Hearings Before the Subcomm. on Nat'l Penitentiaries of the S. Comm. on the Judiciary, 92d Cong. 71–88 (July 26, 1972).

7. *Hello, Cummins Prison Farm. I'm Johnny Cash*, Ark. Gazette, A12, Sept. 13, 1969.

8. *Manpower Shortage Delays Harvesting of Crops at Prison*, Ark. Democrat, A6, June 12, 1969.

9. *Charges Filed in Arkansas Prison Terror*, LA Times, 14, Jan. 28, 1967.

10. Cathy Kunzinger Urwin, *Agenda for Reform: Winthrop Rockefeller as Governor of Arkansas 1967–1972*, 93–95 (U. Ark. Press, 1991); Lloyd Holbeck, *New Chief at Arkansas Says He Hasn't Used the Whip Yet*, Bost. Globe, 26, Jan. 23, 1967; Crim. Investigation Div., Ark. State Police, Case Report No. 916–166–66, 1–3, 54–61 U. Ark. Little Rock (UALR), Center for Arkansas History and Culture, Winthrop Rockefeller Collection, Record Group IV, Box 250, File 8 (1966); Mike Trimble & Ernest Valachovic, *144 Cummins Inmates Hold Sit-Down Strike*, Ark. Gazette, 1, Sept. 3, 1966; *Tortures at Prison in Arkansas Listed*, NY Times, 26, Jan. 17, 1967; *Some Excerpts from the Report on Tucker Prison Farm*, Pine Bluff Commercial, Jan. 22, 1967; Paul N. Schalchlin, "Photographs taken at Tucker Prison Farm" ("Very Confidential"); *Investigator Compiles Chronicle of Inhumanity*, Com. Appeal, Jan. 17, 1967, Rockefeller, IV, Box 260, File 6. Unless otherwise noted, Rockefeller archival materials are from Record Group IV.

11. Ark. Stat. § 46–158. Arrested in June of 1967, Bruton posted $1,000 for each of the two counts. *Ex-Prison Head Is Arrested*, Baxter Bull., 9, June 22, 1967; *Wider Charge Against Bruton*, Baxter Bull., 10, Apr. 18, 1968.

12. Michael B. Smith, *Jim Bruton Is Still Recuperating*, Pine Bluff Com., July 23, 1967, Rockefeller, IV, Box 252, File 9; *Ex-Tucker Officials Go on Trial Oct. 11*, Nw. Ark. Times, 9, Sept. 13, 1967; *The Tucker Cases*, Ark. Gazette, A6, Oct. 12, 1967; *Arkansas Judge Voids Prison Case*, NY Times, 59, May 14, 1968; *Court Affirms Suit's Dismissal*, El Dorado Times, 1, Mar. 3, 1969; *Ex-Warden at Tucker Fined $100*, Ark. Gazette, 19, Oct. 11, 1967.

13. Loper Bright Enterprises v. Raimondo, Secretary of Commerce, 144 S. Ct. 2244 (2024); Ohio v. Environmental Protection Agency, 144 S. Ct. 2040 (2024).

14. State v. Bruton, 246 Ark. 293, 295 (1969).

15. Risa L. Goluboff, *The Thirteenth Amendment and the Lost Origins of Civil Rights*, 50 Duke L. J. 1609 (2001); David M. Bixby, *The Roosevelt Court, Democratic Ideology, and Minority Right*, 90 Yale L. J. 741 (1981). In the Civil Rights Act of 1957, Congress authorized a Division of DOJ to enforce "all Federal statutes affecting civil rights" and created a US Commission on Civil Rights. Pub. Law No. 85–315, 71 Stat 634 (1957); William P. Rogers, Atty. Gen. of the United States, *Establishment of the Civil Rights Division of the Department of Justice*, Order No. 155–57, Office Atty. Gen. (Dec. 7, 1957). Congress broadened the portfolio through the 1964 Civil Rights Act, the 1965 Voting Rights Act, and the 1968 Fair Housing Act. Brian K. Landsberg, *Enforcing Civil Rights: Race Discrimination and the Department of Justice*, 10–14, 53 (U. Kan. Press, 1997); Wan J. Kim, *The Department of Justice's Civil Rights Division: A Historical Perspective as the Division Nears 50*, DOJ, Mar. 22, 2006, 3–4; John Doar, *Lawyer on Front Lines of Segregation Dies at 92*, NY Times, A25, Nov. 12, 2014; William R. Yeomans, *The Politics of Civil Rights Enforcement*, 53 Washburn L. J. 509 (2014); Ron Grossman, *Fatal Black Panther Raid in Chicago Set off Sizable Aftershocks*, Chi. Tribune, Dec. 4, 2014.

16. Dillahunty was replaced after President Carter took office. Robert Kellet, *Dillahunty Apparently on Way Out after Rebuff by Senators*, Com. Appeal, 3, June 8, 1979.

17. *Skeletons Found at Prison Farm*, NY Times, 1, Jan. 30, 1968; Walter Rugaber, *Arkansas Prison: Chamber of Horror*, NY Times, 1, Jan 28, 1968; *Arkansas Begins Inquiry into Deaths at Prison as Aides Suggest More Bodies May Be Found*, 17, NY Times, Jan. 31, 1968; *Grand Jury Called in LR*, Ark. Gazette, 23, June 26, 1969.

18. Civil Rights Act of 1866, An Act to Protect All Persons in the United States in their Civil Rights, and Furnish the Means of Their Vindication, ch. 31, 14 Stat. 27 (1866). Bruton was prosecuted under 18 USC § 242, which authorizes criminal charges against officials "acting under color of law who willfully deprive a person" of constitutional rights to be a crime. First construed in *United States v. Classic*, 109 US 3 (1883), the Court revisited the statute in *Screws v. United States*, 325 US 91 (1945), and held it applicable to individuals acting under color of state law, as long as the prosecution established they had specifically intended to deprive people of federally protected rights.

19. Tucker Steinmetz, *Grand Jury Begins Its Prison Inquiry as Henley Presides*, Ark. Democrat, A5, July 8, 1968; *Hearings Open on Punishment for Prisoners*, Ark. Gazette, 15, July 8, 1969; *20 on Hand to Testify on Prisons*, Ark. Democrat, A16, July 9, 1969; *Ex-Arkansas Prisoners to Testify*, Hope Star, 10, July 10, 1969; *Prisoners Testify in Cruelty Hearing*, Ark. Gazette, A19, July 10, 1969; *US Jury Indicts Arkansas Jailers*, NY Times, 1, July 12, 1969; *Bruton, Four Others Accused by US in Tucker Brutality Plead Not Guilty*, Ark. Gazette, 8, Aug. 13, 1969. Bruton posted bond of $2,500, as did co-defendants. *Bond is Posted by Accused Men*, Baxter Bull., 9, July 17, 1969.

20. John Kirk, *An "Eyeball-to-Eyeball Kind of Organization": Black United Youth and the Black Power Movement in Arkansas*, 75 Ark. Hist. Q. 206, 213–16

(2016); George Bentley, *Ingram's 1st Arrest Followed Several Complaints*, Ark. Gazette, A6, Aug. 18, 1968; George Bentley, *Mrs. Ingram Explains How She Discovered Son Was at the Farm*, Ark. Gazette, A3, Aug. 11, 1968.

21. *Federal Jury Investigating State Prison*, Ark. Gazette, A2, July 9, 1969; George Bentley, *Mother of Ingram Seeks $100,000 in His Death*, Ark. Gazette, A2, 1, Aug. 16, 1968; Garrison, *Two Ex-wardens Acquitted in Death of Curtis Ingram*; *Beck Named in Suit by Mrs. Ingram*, Nw. Ark. Times, 2, Aug. 16, 1968; *Farm Had History of Incidents*, Ark. Democrat, A2, Aug. 15, 1968.

22. Williams v. Illinois, 399 US 235 (1970).

23. Hamilton v. Love, 328 F. Supp. 1181 (ED Ark. 1971). Judge Thomas Eisele, a former Rockefeller adviser, presided; Philip Kaplan, co-counsel for the prisoners in *Holt II*, was at the helm of this class action. In 1973, the prisoners moved for contempt for noncompliance. Judge Eisele ruled that, if conditions did not improve, he would order the facility closed; two months later, he lifted the contempt and permitted continuing use of the facility. Hamilton v. Love, 358 F. Supp. 338 (ED Ark. 1973); Hamilton v. Love, 361 F. Supp. 235 (ED Ark. 1973). Judge Eisele also presided in the challenge to the Mississippi County Penal Farm. After overseeing two years of negotiations and obtaining stipulations on operating procedures, he awarded costs to the prisoner–plaintiffs and dismissed on the grounds that the defendant county officials "sincerely desire to conform their facilities, operations, and procedures to constitutional standards." Howerton v. Miss. Cty., 361 F. Supp. 356, 358 (ED Ark. 1973).

24. John Kirk, *The 1968 Little Rock Uprising*, Ark. Times, Sept. 10, 2015; *US Jury Indicts Arkansas Jailers*, NY Times, 1, July 12, 1968; *Penal Farm Death Sparks Racial Disorders*, Ark. Democrat, D1, Aug. 18, 1968.

25. George Bentley, *Farm Trusty Gets 3 Years in Ingram Case*, Ark. Gazette, 1, A2, Sept. 25, 1968; Tim Hackler, *Ex-Wardens' Trial Starts*, Ark. Democrat, 8, Oct. 29, 1969; Jewell v. Stebbings, 288 F. Supp. 600 (ED Ark. 1968).

26. John Kirk, *Black United Youth*, 212, 223. The plaintiffs' lawyers included John Walker, whose firm Philip Kaplan joined. *Jewell*, 602–03. In addition to Supreme Court precedent, Henley relied on Bailey v. Henslee, 287 F.2d 936 (8th Cir. 1961), finding an Arkansas petit jury constitutionally defective.

27. Younger v. Harris, 401 US 37 (1971).

28. *Jewell*, 605–08.

29. *Ex-Director of Prison Dies at 62*, Ark. Democrat, 1, July 5, 1975.

30. Jerol Garrison, *Ex-Warden Insists Limit of 10 lashes Wasn't Exceeded*, Ark. Gazette, 5, Oct. 8, 1969.

31. Jerol Garrison, *Ex-Wardens Acquitted of Charges of Violating Inmate's Civil Rights*, Ark. Gazette, 5, Nov. 7, 1969.

32. In 1948, Congress recodified the 1866 statute, June 25, 1948, ch. 645, 62 Stat. 696. In 1968, Congress added that "if death results," a person could be "subject to imprisonment for any term of years or for life." An Act to Prescribe Penalties for Certain Acts of Violence or Intimidation, and for Other Purposes, Pub. L. No. 90–284, § 101, 82 Stat. 73, 74 (1968), codified at 18 USC

§ 245b. In 1986, Congress provided the potential for a sentence of not more than ten years if "bodily injury results." Anti-Drug Abuse Act of 1986, Pub. L. No. 99–570, § 1002, 100 Stat. 3207, 3207–2 (codified at 21 USC § 841(b) (1)). Both the 1968 and 1986 penalty provisions were replaced in 1994 in the Violent Crime Control and Law Enforcement Act of 1994, Pub. L. No. 103–322, § 32010(b)(12)–(5), 108 Stat. 1796, 2109 (codified at 18 USC § 242). If no bodily injury occurred, the one year and an unspecified amount of a fine were permissible penalties. If bodily injury occurred, or the acts included "a dangerous weapon," fines or up to ten years imprisonment could be imposed. If death, kidnapping, or aggravated sexual abuse occurred, then fines, years-to-life prison sentences, or death could be imposed.

33. Jerol Garrison, *15 Are Indicted in Brutality Cases at Prison Farms*, 1; *US Jury Indicts Arkansas Jailers*, NY Times, 1, July 12, 1969; *15 Ark. Prison Aides Indicted in Beatings*, Wash. Post, A3, July 12, 1969; *Arkansas Prison Workers Indicted*, Balt. Sun, A7, July 12, 1969; *15 Indicted in Beatings*, Phila. Inquirer, 1, July 12, 1969; *Prison Beatings Net Indictments*, Indianapolis Star, 1, July 12, 1969; *Arkansas Prison Workers Indicted*, Montreal Gazette, 2, July 12, 1959.

34. *Bruton Loses Bid to Get Dismissal of 19 Indictments*, Ark. Gazette, A20, Aug. 28, 1969; Cliff McIntyre, *Bruton Asks Court to Restrain News Media*, Ark. Democrat, A5, July 22, 1969; *Bruton Requests Court to Prevent "Publicity" on Prison Conditions*, Ark. Gazette, A3, July 23, 1969.

35. *Bruton Trial Set to Start November 18*, Baxter Bull., 7, Oct. 2, 1969; *Never Violated Rules*, Ark. Democrat, 2, Oct. 8, 1969; Jerol Garrison, *Fletcher Hit Him at Least 11 Times, Ex-Inmate Says*, Ark. Gazette, A16, Oct. 7, 1969.

36. Garrison, *Ex-Warden Insists Limit of 10 Lashes Wasn't Exceeded*.

37. *US Jury Acquits Fletcher of Tucker Brutality Charge*, Ark. Gazette, 23, Oct. 9, 1969; *8 charges on Bruton Dismissed*, Ark. Democrat, Oct. 15, 1969, 11.

38. Hackler, *Ex-Wardens' Trial Starts*; *At the Penal Farm*, Editorial, Ark. Gazette, 6, Nov. 3, 1969.

39. Hackler, *Ex-Wardens Acquitted in Penal Farm Rights Case*.

40. *Ex-Penal Farm Employe[e] Trial Testimony Set*, Sentinel-Record, 13, Nov. 5, 1969; Jerol Garrison, *Inmates Say Wardens Beat Phelps with Handle, Hose*, Ark. Gazette, A8, Nov. 5, 1969; *Three Testify They Saw Convict Beaten*, Ark. Democrat, 3, Nov. 6, 1969.

41. Jerol Garrison, *Ex-Wardens Deny Brutality Charge*, Ark. Gazette, A2, Nov. 6, 1969; *Three Testify They Saw Convict Beaten*; *State Rests in Trial of 2 for Beating*, Ark. Democrat, A14, Nov. 6, 1969. *Former Penal Workers Found Not Guilty*, Hope Star, 2, Nov. 7, 1969; *2 Found Innocent after Rights Trial*, Ark. Democrat, 2, Nov. 7, 1969.

42. Robert Shaw, *Jury Acquits Jim Bruton*, Courier News, 11, Nov. 22, 1969.

43. Associated Press, *Witness Accuses Bruton*, Sentinel-Record, 1, 14, Nov. 18, 1969; Tim Hackler, *Inmate Says He Used "Tucker Telephone" on Bruton's Orders*, Ark. Democrat, 1, Nov. 19, 1969; Jerol Garrison, *Ex-Inmate Says He Used Electric "Tucker Telephone" on Three Prisoners*, Ark. Gazette, 13, Nov. 20, 1969; *Former "Inmate-Doctor" Claims Abuses at Tucker*, Sentinel-Record, 8, Nov.

20, 1969; *Links Beating to Visit of Woman*, Hope Star, 1, Nov. 19, 1969; *More Testimony on "Tucker Telephone,"* El Dorado Times, 15, Nov. 20, 1969.

44. *Arkansan Freed in Cruelty Trial*, NY Times, 32, Nov. 23, 1969.

45. Jerol Garrison, *Bruton Cleared on 8 Counts*, Ark. Gazette, 1, A3, Nov. 22, 1969; Robert Shaw, *Jury Acquits Jim Bruton*, Courier News, 1, Nov. 22, 1969. Another reporter recorded Henley saying he could not see how "a person of ordinary intelligence and understanding could have acted other than willfully and wrongfully in inflicting such punishment or commanding them to be inflicted, if that was done." *Arkansan Freed in Cruelty Trial*.

46. Garrison, *Bruton Cleared on 8 Counts*.

47. *Bruton Loses Bid to Get Dismissal of 19 Indictments*.

48. *Trial Today in Shooting of Inmates*, Ark. Gazette, A16, Dec. 16, 1969; Diane Gage, *Shooting at Prison Defended*, Ark. Democrat, 1, Dec. 17, 1969.

49. *Innocent Verdict Directed*, Sentinel-Record, 26, Dec. 18, 1969.

50. *Ex-Arkansas Prison Head Fined for Cruel Treatment of Inmates*, NY Times, 37, Jan. 19, 1970; Marty Dunn, *Bruton Pleads "No Contest,"* Ark. Democrat, 1, Jan 16, 1970.

51. *Holt II*, 368 n.4.

52. *Count Dropped Against Last 5 in Prison Case*, Ark. Gazette, 8, Jan. 29, 1970; *Charges Dismissed against 5 Accused of Prison Abuses*, Ark. Democrat, 6, Jan. 29, 1969.

53. Morgan, an "inmate-doctor," testified at Bruton's trial that he would crank the telephone under Bruton's direction until Bruton was satisfied with answers to his questions. Hackler, *Inmate Says He Used "Tucker Telephone" on Bruton's Orders*, 1, 8.

54. *Bruton, Four Others Accused by US in Tucker Brutality Plead Not Guilty*, Ark. Gazette, A8, Aug. 13, 1969; *No-Contest Plea Entered in Prison Case*, Ark. Democrat, A3, Oct. 1, 1969; *Varner Gets Probation for Safety*, Ark. Gazette, B12, Dec. 26, 1969; *Judge Puts Parolee on Probation*, Ark. Democrat, C4, Dec. 25, 1969.

55. *Ex-director of Prison Dies at 62*, Ark. Democrat, 12, July 5, 1975, 1; *Former Prison Superintendent, Figure in Probe, Dies at Age 62*, Ark. Gazette, 1, July 5, 1975.

56. Jerry Mitchel, *Race Against Time: A Reporter Reopens the Unsolved Murder Cass of the Civil Rights Era* (Simon & Schuster, 2020).

57. Plumhoff v. Rickard, 572 US 765 (2014); Pearson v. Callahan, 555 US 223 (2009); Johanna Schwartz, *How the Police Became Untouchable* (Viking, 2023).

CHAPTER 19

1. *The Prisons*, Ark. Gazette, E3, Dec. 21, 1969 (quoting the Paragould Daily Press).

2. Bill Lewis, *WR Overspent to Force Taxes, McClerkin Says*, Ark. Gazette, 1, Oct. 19, 1969; *Tax Structure and Governor Get Lambasted*, Ark. Democrat,

A7, Oct. 19, 1969; Bill Simmons, *Matthews Says WR's Tours Backfired*, Ark. Democrat, A8, Nov. 30, 1969; Associated Press, *Matthew Contends WR's Popularity Sagging*, Sentinel-Record, 11, Nov. 30, 1969; *Hearings Are Set to Guide WR*, Ark. Gazette, A2, Dec. 2, 1969; Doug Smith, *State Educators Cite Fund Needs at WR Hearings*, Ark. Gazette, A8, Dec. 5, 1969; Doug Smith, *Murderer Example of Wasted Funds, Law Officer Says*, Ark. Gazette, 3, Dec. 6, 1969.

3. *Prison Desegregation Plan Approved by State Board*, Ark. Gazette, A 11, Mar. 6, 1969; *Women's Unit at Cummins Integrated: "All Friendly,"* Ark. Gazette, B1, June 10, 1969; *Prison Integration to Begin with Dining*, Ark. Democrat, A6, June 11, 1969.

4. *The Pea Pickers Picayune*, no. 38, 2, Mar. 1, 1969, U. Ark. Little Rock (UALR), Center for Arkansas History and Culture, Winthrop Rockefeller Collection, Record Group IV, Box 250, File 3; some are also available on JSTOR at https://jstor.org/stable/community.29687096. The subsequent publication, the *Cummins Journal*, also on JSTOR, is at https://jstor.org/stable/community.29686504. *Prison Paper*, Ark. Gazette, E3, Nov. 24, 1968; *Prison Editor Getting More Cheers than Jeers*, Sentinel-Record, 13, Sept. 17, 1968; Tim Hackler, *Kidnapper-Editor Chronicles Life at Cummins Prison*, Ark. Democrat, A3, Nov. 17, 1968; Time Hackler, *Prisoner Editor to Continue News Career after Parole*, Ark. Democrat, 5, May 9, 1969. Another publication, the *Kons-Kite*, started in 1970; one of its editors, Jack Barber, was a named plaintiff in Holt v. Sarver (*Holt II*), 309 F. Supp. 362 (ED Ark. 1970). *Kons-Kite Is Published at Tucker*, Ark. Gazette, 10, July 22, 1970. After a hiatus, the *Cummins Journal* followed. *Cummins Resumes Inmate Journal*, Ark. Gazette, 5, Sept. 11, 1972. Unless otherwise noted, Rockefeller archival materials are from Record Group IV.

5. George Douthit, *Governor Acts to Avert a Sitdown at Cummins*, Ark. Democrat, 1, May 22, 1969; *Letter-Writing Drive on in Prison*, Pine Bluff Com., Oct. 30, 1969, Rockefeller, IV, Box 251, File 8.

6. *571 Respond So Far to Plea for $1 by Sarver, Chaplain to Help Build Prison Chapel*, Ark. Gazette, 91, June 4, 1969; *$4,283 Sent for Chapel at Tucker*, Ark. Gazette, B1, June 6, 1969.

7. *Two Prison Fiscal Men Are Fired*, Ark. Gazette, A11, Mar. 6, 1969; *$100,000 Is Asked to Finance Farm Equipment for Prisons*, Ark. Democrat, A3, Mar. 18, 1969.

8. *Hearing Set on Complaints of Prisoners*, Ark. Gazette, 17, May 25, 1969.

9. *Inmate Writes His Petition on Toilet Paper*, Ark. Gazette, 5, April 18, 1969; *Convict Says Inmates Overcharged on Stamps*, Ark. Democrat, 3, May 1, 1969; *2 at Tucker Say Isolation is "Inhumane,"* Ark. Gazette, 31, Oct. 25, 1968.

10. Holt v. Sarver (*Holt I*), 300 F. Supp. 825, 826 (ED Ark. 1969). Harold Granor, David Monroe Teague, James W. Martin, Carlton J. Carney, Randy Arnold, William Ernest Eaton, James Albert Standridge, Robert Grocke, and Johnny C. Wilson also filed petitions. Fields was arrested in 1972 in Pennsylvania for disorderly conduct, three years after his escape from a one-year term for burglary. *Fugitive Warrant Served Upon Suspect's Release*, Pottsville Republican,

15, Jan. 17, 1973; *Courthouse News*, Evening Herald, 10, Jan 18, 1973. Overton had escaped four times. *Cell Unsanitary, Inmate Asserts*, Ark. Gazette, A14, Nov. 5, 1968. After *Holt I*, a state judge added a year to Overton's twelve-year sentence for robberies. *Escape Costs Inmate a Year*, Ark. Gazette, B8, June 21, 1969. Overton was caught in another attempt; the person with him was shot. *Prisoner Critically Wounded*, Ark. Democrat, 7, Oct. 6, 1969. Overton walked away again and was recaptured. *Cummins Inmate Escapes on Foot*, Ark. Gazette, A5, Apr. 26, 1970; *Two Escapees Are Captured*, Ark. Democrat, A3, Apr. 27, 1970. In 1982, Overton was charged with drunk driving after a collision. *Crash Injures Six Persons in Jacksonville*, Ark. Gazette, A6, Sept. 13, 1982.

11. Wayne Jordan, *Politicians Exploit Fears of Escapes, Prison Head Says*, Ark. Gazette, 5, May 31, 1970.

12. *Holt I*, 827; John Kyle Day, *The Fall of a Southern Moderate Congressman Brooke Hays and the Election of 1958*, 59 Ark. Hist. Q. 241, 248 (2000); Ernest Dumas, Marion Steele Hays (1925–2011), *Encyclopedia of Ark.* (Oct. 14, 2020); *Steele Hays to Fill New Judgeship in Pulaski-Perry Criminal Division*, Ark. Gazette, A4, Apr. 23, 1970.

13. *Hearing Set on Complaints*.

14. *Sarver Says Hearing to Have Good Results*, Ark. Democrat, A2, May 26, 1969.

15. *Convict Asks Judge to Send Full-Time Doctor to Prison*, Ark. Democrat, A2, May 26, 1969; Tucker Steinmetz, *Trusty Asks Return of Strap in Hearing*, Ark. Democrat, A2, May 27, 1969; *Cummins Inmates Call Confinement Cruel Punishment*, Ark. Gazette, A14, May 27, 1969; Tucker Steinmetz, *Convicts End Pleas; Judge Wants Change*, Ark. Democrat, A3, May 28, 1969.

16. *Sarver Says Unit to End Overcrowding*, Ark. Gazette, B10, May 28, 1969; *Cummins Inmates' Petitions Taken under Advisement*, Ark. Gazette, A8, May 29, 1969.

17. *Cummins Inmates' Petitions Taken under Advisement*.

18. *Correction Agency Says It Is Broke*, Ark. Gazette, A3, June 12, 1969.

19. *Sarver Advises Inmates to Work*, Ark. Gazette, A22, June 20, 1969.

20. *Correction Agency Says It Is Broke*.

21. *Manpower Shortage Delays Harvesting of Crops at Prison*, Ark. Democrat, A6, June 12, 1969; George Douthit, *Sarver Seeks Action on Labor Shortage*, Ark. Democrat, A1, June 13, 1969; *Sarver Wants to See Board on Cummins Labor Shortage*, Ark. Gazette, A3, June 14, 1969; *Sarver Delays Call for Meet on Prison Crop*, Ark. Gazette, B1, June 18, 1969.

22. *Correction Agency Says It Is Broke*.

23. Douthit, *Prisoners Told They Must Work*, Ark. Democrat, A2, June 19, 1969; *Sarver Advises Inmates to Work*, Ark. Gazette, A22, June 20, 1969; *103 Inmates Transferred to Field World*, Ark. Gazette, A2, June 21, 1969; *Sarver Offers Inducements in Farm Job*, Ark. Gazette, A2, June 24, 1969; *Help Offered to Prisoners If They Work*, Ark. Democrat, A6, June 24, 1969; *Lawmaker Committee to Tour Prison Farms*, Ark. Democrat, A5, June 25, 1969; *Sarver's Explanation Job Made Harder by Prisoners*, Ark. Democrat, B1, June 27, 1969; *Prison Paper Deplores Food, but Lauds Doctor*, Ark. Democrat, 4, Oct. 8, 1969.

24. *Holt I*, 831.

25. *Isolation Cells at Cummins Declared "Unconstitutional,"* Ark. Gazette, B16, June 21, 1969; *Holt I*, 827.

26. Courtney v. Bishop, 409 F.2d 1185 (8th Cir. 1969). Judge Harris appointed counsel for Courtney, held a hearing in January of 1968, and ruled the placement was not arbitrary and the treatment not cruel and unusual.

27. Jordan v. Fitzharris, 257 F. Supp. 674 (ND Cal. 1966).

28. George Jackson, *Soledad Brother: The Prison Letters of George Jackson* (Lawrence Hill Books, 1994). Jackson died on August 21, 1971 during an escape attempt from San Quentin Prison. His book *Blood in My Eye* was published in 1972.

29. Robert Charles Jordan Jr., born in 1939, was convicted at age nineteen of an assault. He filed the strip-cell case when he was twenty-seven. *Soledad Prison Goes on Trial Tomorrow*, Santa Cruz Sentinel, 4, Aug. 8, 1966. Jordan had been "disciplined 65 times" for allegations related to assaults. *Soledad Prisoner to Serve Time Elsewhere*, Oakland Trib., 17, Aug. 19, 1966. After Jordan's lawsuit was dismissed on August 12, 1965 for not exhausting state remedies, he lost a petition before the California Supreme Court on October 7, 1965 and returned to federal court. Resubmission for Petition for a Writ of Habeas Corpus; Complaint, Jordan v. Fitzharris, No. 43983, (ND Cal. 1965), *Case File: Jordan v. Fitzharris*, Civil Rights Litigation Clearing House; Memorandum in Support of Motion to Dismiss Pursuant to Rule 12(b)(6); Return to Order to Show Cause & Points & Authorities in Opposition to Petition for Writ of Habeas Corpus, 2. Chief Judge Harris appointed San Francisco lawyer Charles B. Cohler to represent Jordan. Tom Hall, *Soledad "Strip Cells" Shock Federal Judge*, SF Exam'r, 1, Sept. 6, 1966; Trial Transcript, 368–422; *Jordan*, 257 F. Supp., 674–82. Jordan later won a challenge to state intrusions into confidential prisoner-attorney exchanges. *In re* Jordan, 500 P.2d 873, 879–80 (Cal. 1972); *In re* Jordan, 526 P.2d 523, 527 (Cal. 1974). In 2020, I corresponded with Jordan, then in a California prison. Jordan, describing himself as a self-taught paralegal affiliated with the "black nationalist" movement, said his lawsuits responded to authorities' denial of prisoners' humanity.

30. *Holt I*, 827 (quoting *Jordan*, 680), and 831–32.

31. *Holt I*, 829–33.

32. *Holt I*, 828–33.

33. *Jordan*, 683–84; *Jordan Is Moved to Quentin*, Californian, 1, Sept. 9, 1966; Jack Welter, *Strip Cells Defended by McGee*, SF Examiner, 1, Sept. 7, 1966.

34. *Holt I*, 830–34; *Holt II*, 373–76.

35. *Slapped Rather Hard, Sarver Says of Ruling*, Ark. Democrat, 2, June 21, 1969; *Prison Scored in Court Decree*, Baxter Bull., 9, June 26, 1969; Bob Qualls, *The Week in Arkansas: Overcrowding of Isolation Cells Hit*, Ark. Democrat, D1, June 29, 1969.

36. *Prison Abuses Again Charged*, Nw. Ark. Times, 1, Sept. 19, 1969; *Inmate Asks Punishment in Field Cut*, Ark. Gazette, A5, Oct 1, 1969. Courtney, who had

pled guilty to grand larceny in 1956 and was given a ten-year sentence, received twenty-one more years in 1963 for escape attempts. In 1970, Judge Harris found Courtney had not been informed of his right to counsel when he pled guilty. *10-Year Term for Courtney Set Aside*, Ark. Gazette, A3, July 23, 1970. Commissioner Sarver reported that Hildebrandt had been placed in isolation on Aug. 13, 1969 "for assaulting an inmate." *Cummins Inmates in Isolation After Suit Filed*, Nw. Ark. Times, 2, Sept. 23, 1969. Hildebrandt had been charged with escape; the Arkansas Supreme Court required a new trial because the state had not proven he was "legally in prison" when attempting escape. *Court Orders New Trials for Inmates*, Ark. Democrat, A7, June 20, 1970; Harding v. State, 455 S.W.2d 695, 700 (Ark. 1970). Hildebrandt later filed a federal habeas petition contesting the timing of the retrial, which Henley rejected. *Requests Denied Cummins Inmates*, Ark. Gazette, A5, Aug. 17, 1971. By then, Hildebrandt was housed in Cummins' maximum-security unit. In 1974, at age twenty-seven, he was shot and killed "when a service station operator surprised two burglars." *Burglars Surprised: One Slain*, El Dorado News-Times, 2, Nov. 28, 1974; *Six File Toilet Paper Petition*, Ark. Democrat, A9, Oct. 3, 1969. Other petitioners included Carlton Carney, Billy E. McCurley, James Townsend, Otis Taylor, Billy Martin, and Andy Anderson.

37. United Press International, *23–25 to Lose Prison Jobs, Sarver Says*, Ark. Gazette, A14, Dec. 2, 1969.
38. Presentation on Department of Correction (before Honorable Winthrop Rockefeller, Governor), Dec. 5, 1969, 2, cover letter J. R. Price to the Governor, sending a "revised copy of the material I presented to you December 4, 1969." Rockefeller, IV, Box 250, File 3.
39. For example, the Texas Public Policy Foundation promoted reinvestment to reduce the economic costs of crime and punishment and to improve community and individual well-being. The federal government explained its support and funding for "data-driven" policies. DOJ, *Bureau of Justice Assistance: Justice Reinvestment Initiative: A Guide for States* (May 2021).
40. Rockefeller Presentation, 6–9.
41. United Press International, *23–25 to Lose Prison Jobs, Sarver Says*; Rockefeller Presentation, 5.
42. Associated Press, *Sarver Stand on Prisons Is Attacked*, Ark. Gazette, B1, Dec. 23, 1969; *The Prisons*.

CHAPTER 20

1. Holt v. Sarver (*Holt II*), 309 F. Supp. 362, 381 (ED Ark. 1970).
2. That analysis is criticized in Gideon Yaffe, *The Norm Shift Theory of Punishment*, 132 Ethics 478 (2022).
3. Frances Ross, Dir., Oral Hist. Program, Interview Judge Jesse Smith Henley in Harrison, Ark., 114 (June 3, 1987), U. of Ark. at Little Rock Oral Hist. Program.

4. Bill Simmons, *What's Wrong with Prisons? Sarver: "What's Right?,"* Courier News, 1, Feb. 5, 1970.

5. Memorandum and Pre-trial Order, Dec. 23, 1969, Docket Sheet, Holt v. Sarver, PB [Pine Bluff] 69-C-25, PB 69-C-2 ED Ark. Apr. 17, 1969, National Archives and Records Administration (NARA), Accession No. 021–74K0713, Box 123, Location No. A2305065; *Complaints by Inmates Due at Hearing*, Ark. Democrat, A3, Dec. 24, 1969; *Holt II*, 363, 368 n.3.

6. *Complaints by Inmates Due at Hearing*; *The Trusty System*, Ark. Gazette, 6, Dec. 31, 1969. Henley referred new petitions to Holt and Kaplan and noted a "full hearing on penitentiary conditions" would be early in 1970. Letter Henley to Bill McCord, Dec. 30, 1969, U. Ark. Little Rock (UALR), Kaplan Papers, Series 1, Box 18A, File 1.

7. Holt v. Sarver, 442 F.2d 384 (8th Cir. 1971); Finney v. Ark. Bd. of Corr., 505 F.2d 194 (8th Cir. 1974); Finney v. Hutto, 548 F.2d 740, 741 (8th Cir. 1977); Hutto v. Finney, 437 US 673 (1978).

8. Finney v. Mabry, 455 F. Supp. 756 (ED Ark. 1978); Finney v. Mabry, 458 F. Supp. 720 (ED Ark. 1978); Finney v. Mabry, 534 F. Supp. 1026 (ED Ark. 1982); Finney v. Mabry, 546 F. Supp. 626, 628 (ED Ark. 1982).

9. By 2021, Kaplan was too ill to read this book's drafts; he died in 2023. Holt reviewed drafts before his death in March of 2023.

10. Letter Morton Gitelman, Pres. of ACLU of Ark. to Charles M. Morgan Jr. in the ACLU Southern Regional Office, Jan. 14, 1970, Kaplan, 1, Box 18A, File 1; *Bill Lewis, Convicts' Lawyers Pleased by Ruling, Raise Few Points*, Ark. Gazette, 1, Feb. 20, 1970; *LDF Mourns the Loss of John W. Walker, Legendary Arkansas Civil Rights Lawyer and LDF Board Member*, (website, Oct. 30, 2019); *Attorney, Civil Rights Icon John Walker Dies at 82*, Nw. Ark. Democrat-Gazette, Oct. 28, 2019.

11. Letter and Enclosure William Bennett Turner to Kaplan, Dec. 31, 1969, with a seven-page outline, "Can Litigation Improve the Quality of Prisons?" from Bennett's presentation to the National Legal Aid and Defender Organization, and Phil Hirschkop & Michael Millemann, *The Unconstitutionality of Prison Life*, 55 Va. L. Rev. 795 (1969). Linda Singer, working with Ronald Goldfarb on a study of corrections funded by the Ford Foundation, reached out to Kaplan and Holt after national news coverage of *Holt II*. Letter Linda R. Singer to Kaplan, Jan. 27, 1970; Kaplan to Singer, Jan. 30, 1970, Edward Wright, the lawyer in *Jackson v. Bishop*, loaned Kaplan transcripts from that hearing. Kaplan to Edward L. Wright, Feb. 23, 1970, and Kaplan struggled to make copies available "free of charge." Kaplan to Norman Chachkin, Feb. 19, 1970. All materials are in Kaplan, 1, Box 18A, File 1.

12. David Rudofsky, *The Rights of Prisoners* (Avon Books, 1973); The National Prison Project Journal (ACLU Foundation, Inc, 1987); Hamilton v. Love, 328 F. Supp. 1182 (ED Ark. 1971); Hamilton v. Love, 358 F. Supp. 338 (ED Ark. 1973); Hamilton v. Love, 361 F. Supp. 1235 (ED Ark. 1973). Kaplan later worked on employment litigation.

13. Ernest Dumas, Interview with Jack W. Holt Jr. (Nov. 1, 2012), Ark. Sup. Ct. Project, Ark. Sup. Ct. Hist. Soc'y, 12; Jacqueline S. Wright Walker, *Three Men Named Holt*, 42 Ark. Lawyer 26 (Fall 2007); Bill Lewis, *Convicts' Lawyers Pleased by Ruling, Raise Few Points*, Ark. Gazette, 1, Feb. 20, 1970; Ernest Dumas, Jack Wilson Holt Sr., 1903–1998, *Encyclopedia Ark.* (Nov. 04, 2021).

14. Dumas/Holt, 14; Ernest Dumas, *The Education of Ernie Dumas: Chronicles of the Arkansas Political Mind* (2019). Dumas was a wonderful resource and connected me to Arkansas publishers who authorized use of many of this book's photographs.

15. Dumas/Holt, 11–14.

16. Dumas/Holt, 16.

17. Dumas/Holt, 15.

18. Dumas/Holt, 15–16; Dala McKinsey, *Prison Trusty Guard Setup Challenged*, Hope Star, 5, Jan. 8, 1970; Associated Press, *Prison Probe Could Change Entire System*, Ark. Gazette, 19, Jan. 8, 1970.

19. *Nation's Prisons "Snake Pits," Sarver Tells Women Lawyers*, Ark. Democrat, A6, Jan. 4, 1970.

20. *Report Fails to Confirm "Staged" Uprising at Prison*, Courier News, Dec. 15, 1970, 3; *Prisons*, Ark. Gazette, E3, Jan. 4, 1970; Editorial, *Penurious Policy for the Prisons*, Ark. Gazette, A4, Dec. 27, 1969.

21. Associated Press, *Sarver Stand on Prisons Is Attacked*, Ark. Gazette, 15, Dec. 23, 1969; *Penurious Policy for the Prisons*; *Sarver Speeding Prisoner Releases*, Sentinel-Record, 3, Dec. 24, 1969.

22. Dala McKinsey, *Those Who Know Say Women Inmates Are Neglected*, Ark. Democrat, A4. Jan. 11, 1970; *Women: Most Neglected Prisoners?*, Sentinel-Record, 6, Jan. 11, 1970; *Prison Protest Very Peaceful, Sarver Reports*, Ark. Gazette, A8, Jan. 14, 1970; *Nonviolent Protests Erupt at Cummins: 40 Sit, Chant*, Ark. Gazette, A2, Jan. 13, 1970; *Two Protests at Cummins: Inmates Complain of Prison Conditions*, Ark. Democrat, A3, Jan. 13, 1970; George Douthit, *Awaits Ruling*, Ark. Democrat, A2, Jan. 9, 1970; George Douthit, *If Trusty System Were Abolished, Cost Would Be $1 Million a Year*, Ark. Democrat, 1, Jan. 13, 1970.

23. *Nation's Prisons "Snake Pits," Sarver Tells Women Lawyers*, Ark. Democrat, A6, Jan. 4, 1970; Wayne Jordan, *Trusty's at Top in Pecking Order: What's He Like?*, Ark. Gazette, 1, A2, Jan. 25, 1970; *Prison Hearing Opens Monday: Could Cause Closing of Tucker, Cummins*, Ark. Gazette, 1, Jan. 25, 1970.

24. *Trusty System Is Challenged by 24 Inmates*, Ark. Gazette, A18, Jan. 15, 1970; *Holt II* Complaint, para. 14, at 5; paragraphs 17–18, at 5; para. 16, at 5; para. 13, at 4–5, Kaplan, 1, Subseries 2, Box 6, File 4, January 1970.

25. Act 50 § 1, 1968 Ark. Acts 1647. *Holt II* Complaint, paragraphs 4–5, at 2–3; paragraphs 3, 8–12, at 2–4; para. 13, at 4–5. The lawyers appear to have invoked the statute to support a violation of federal law. In later cases, institutional litigants had relied on violations of state as well as federal law but, in 1985, in a five-person majority decision by Justice Lewis Powell, the Supreme Court held federal courts did not have the power to enjoin breaches of state law by state actors but could only issue injunctions predicated on

federal law violations. Pennhurst State Sch. & Hosp. v. Halderman, 465 US 89 (1984).

26. *Holt II* Complaint, para. 20, at 5–6; and "Wherefore clause," 6.

27. George Douthit, *More Money Only Solution to Prison Ills*, Ark. Democrat, 19, Jan. 18, 1970.

28. *Correction Lawyers Ask for Dismissal*, Ark. Democrat, 2, Jan. 19, 1970; *Sarver Seeks to Dismiss Prison Suit*, Ark. Gazette, 2, Jan. 20, 1970; *Prison Loses Dismissal Plea*, Ark. Gazette, 27, Jan. 21, 1970. Henley applied then current interpretations of the Eleventh Amendment of the Constitution. Vicki Jackson & Judith Resnik, Sovereignties—Federal, State and Tribal: The Story of Seminole Tribe of Florida v. Florida, *Federal Courts Stories*, 329–58 (Vicki C. Jackson and Judith Resnik eds., Foundation Press, 2010).

29. *Hearing Delayed on Penitentiary*, Ark. Gazette, 24, Jan. 7, 1970; *Henley Resets Prison Case Later in Month*, Ark. Democrat, 3A, Jan. 7, 1970. The lawyers had requested an additional week. Wayne Jordan, *Trusty's at Top in Pecking Order: What's He Like?*, Ark. Gazette, 2, Jan. 25, 1970; *Ex-Arkansas Prison Head Fined for Cruel Treatment of Inmates*, NY Times, 37, Jan. 19, 1970; Cragg Hines, *Hearings to Open on Arkansas Jails*, Long Island Press, Jan. 25, 1970, UALR, Rockefeller, Record Group IV, Box 253, File 5. The copy of this photograph comes from Rockefeller, IV, Box 252, File 1.

30. Simmons, *What's Wrong with Prisons?*; Bill Simmons, *Suit Spotlighted the Prison Dilemma*, Baxter Bull., E4, Feb. 19, 1970.

31. Marty Dunn, *Prison Head Is Critical of Operation*, Ark. Democrat, 2, Jan. 31, 1970; *Many Would Pass Up Chance to Be "Pusher," Inmate Supervisor Says*, Ark. Gazette, 16, Feb. 1, 1970. *Count Dropped Against Last 5 in Prison Case*, Ark. Gazette, A8, Jan. 29, 1970. I focus on press dissemination and, on occasion, draw on transcripts in the Kaplan Papers, especially Remarks of Court at Conclusion of Hearing, Dec. 3, 1971, Kaplan, Box 2, File 1.

32. Bill Simmons, *What's Wrong with Prisons? Sarver: "What's Right?"*, Courier News, 1, Feb. 5, 1970.

33. Kaplan sent Bennett $165 for travel. Letter Kaplan to James V. Bennett, Re: Holt v. Sarver, Feb. 10, 1970, Kaplan, 1, Box 18A, File 1.

34. Bill Simmons, *Ate Rat Rather than Gruel, Inmate Says*, Courier News, 1, Jan. 28, 1970.

35. Marty Dunn, *Trusty System Said to Lead to "Corruption,"* Ark. Democrat, A1, Jan. 26, 1970.

36. Jerol Garrison, *Cummins Inmates Tell of Buying Jobs, Knives*, Ark. Gazette, 5, Jan. 28, 1970; Jerol Garrison, *Youth Described Inmates' Attacks: Others Tell of Rats in Isolation Cells*, Ark. Gazette, A8, Jan. 28, 1970; Marty Dunn, *I'd Rather Eat a Rat*, Ark. Democrat, A6, Jan. 28, 1970; Marty Dunn, *No Pledge of Safety in Prisons*, Ark. Democrat, 1, Jan. 27, 1970; *Sarver Claims Too Few "Free" Guards to Prevent Them*, Sentinel-Record, 1, Jan. 28, 1970. The judge reserved decision on Dunn's contempt; Sarver later said Dunn was a "victim of a money-lending racket at Cummins," where 50 cents on the dollar

was charged as interest. John Bennett, *Isolated Tucker Inmate Tells of Dining on Rat*, Commercial Appeal, Jan. 28, 1970, Rockefeller, IV, Box 253, File 4.

37. Dunn, *Rather Eat a Rat*. Taylor was not depicted in the artist sketches accompanying the article. In a 1972 report on failures to comply with court-ordered improvements, Taylor also testified; he was described as "a black inmate confined in the maximum-security unit." Mike Tremble, *Nine Inmates Testify: Hearings on Prisons Recessed until January*, Ark. Gazette, 18, Dec. 22, 1972.

38. Dunn, *No Pledge of Safety*. Marty Dunn, *Cummins Prisoner Advances Testimony After Death Threat*, Ark. Democrat, 1, Jan. 21, 1970; Jerol Garrison, *Inmate Testifies He Paid for Job at Cummins Farm*, Ark. Gazette, A16, Jan. 22, 1970.

39. Jerol Garrison, *Trusty Use Leads to Corruption, Witness Says: Cummins Inmates Tell of Buying Jobs, Knives*, Ark. Gazette, 5, Jan. 27, 1970; John Bennett, *Inmate Tells of Cummins Extortion, Assaults*, Com. Appeal, 13, Jan. 27, 1970, Rockefeller, IV, Box 252, File 1. One plaintiff, Maurice Sanford from Detroit, was a Black man convicted in Arkansas of joining others in raping a white girl. *Three Charged with Rape*, Hope Star, 8, Aug. 25, 1969. The alleged victim was a "15-year-old white girl"; one co-defendant was said to be "a member of the Memphis black militant group called the Invaders." *Sheriff Charges 5 for Destroying Public Property*, Camden News, 1, Sept. 10, 1969. "An all-male jury of 10 whites and two Negroes deliberated about four hours" and found Sanford and a co-defendant guilty. *A.M. Roundup*, Courier News, 1, Nov. 1, 1969. The two were given life imprisonment; the third who pleaded guilty received a ten-year suspended sentence. *Term Held up in Rape Case*, Ark. Democrat, 2, Apr. 11, 1970. Arkansas' Supreme Court affirmed over objections of racial discrimination in jury selection and noted that, although the alleged crime took place during "racial tensions in Forrest City," no mention of civil unrest was made at trial. *Convictions Are Affirmed*, Ark. Democrat, 6, Feb. 8, 1971. In 1975, Chief Judge Henley set aside the conviction because "blacks had been excluded from the jury." *Convictions Set Aside in 2 Rapes*, El Dorado News-Times, 3, June 5, 1975; *Hutto Seeking to Hold Blacks*, Nw. Ark. Times, 9, June 13, 1975; Sanford v. Hutto, 394 F. Supp. 1278 (ED Ark. 1975). In November of 1975, after the Eighth Circuit affirmed, the two were released. *Retrial Ruling*, Courier News, 4, Oct. 23, 1975; Sanford v. Hutto, 523 F.3d 1383 (8th Cir. 1975). Hutto, who said Sanford had been "disciplined 30 times" and threatened to "kill" a prosecutor, objected but Judge Eisele, presiding, entered the order. *Johnson, Sanford Win Release*, Nw. Ark. Times, 13, Nov. 8, 1975.

Leslie Hill, incarcerated in the 1950s on a murder charge, was accused in 1955 of assault when "another Negro" was shot in an argument over money. *Negro Injured by Rifle Shot in Argument*, Courier News, Feb. 15, 1955. In 1971, Hill was given a life sentence on a murder charge; in 1974 at age forty-nine, Hill became a trusty working at the Arkansas Law Enforcement

Academy in Camden. After he did not return from his merit-based furlough, he was returned to the state from Michigan. *Trusty, 49, Fails to Report Back*, Ark. Gazette, B1, Sept. 10, 1974; *Hearing Set for Arkansan*, Ark. Gazette, 5, Sept. 26, 1974.

Public record searches indicate that another plaintiff, Noah Simmons, was a Black man. Other named plaintiffs were white men, some of whom also challenged the legality of their convictions. For example, Jack Allen Barber, who testified in the *Holt II* hearing and was then "chairman of the inmate's council at Tucker," had been charged in 1957 with robbery and in 1961, along with three others, of an armed robbery of $60,000. *Former Tulsa Officer Is among 4 Charged in $60,000 Store Holdup*, Miami Daily News-Rec., 1, Aug. 23, 1961. A unanimous Supreme Court reversed the conviction; Oklahoma prosecutors had made "absolutely no effort" to obtain the presence of a co-defendant who had testified against Barber at the pretrial hearing and who was held 225 miles away in a federal prison in Texas. Barber v. Page, 390 US 719, 723 (1968). Barber was later arrested after a "brief gun battle" in Arkansas. *Tulsa Trio Facing Gun Fight Charges*, Daily Oklahoman, Feb. 16, 1969, 10. When serving a five-year sentence at Tucker, Barber started the newspaper, *Kons-Kite*, discussed earlier; the first edition was a four-page mimeographed print focused on the new "free-world personnel" in the prison. *Inmates Start Newspaper at Tucker Farm*, Baxter Bull., B6, July 30, 1970.

40. Milton Sullivan, a twenty-two-year-old "Negro" who had attended Arkansas State University on a "basketball scholarship," had been a police officer. He was serving time on burglary and grand larceny charges; he testified that he had been a trusty until he got drunk and broke into the commissary.

41. Jerol Garrison, *Sarver Testified System Permits Wheeling, Dealing*, Ark. Gazette, 3, Jan. 30, 1970. The legislature had established the Arkansas State Farm for Women and authorized imprisonment for up to three years for women convicted of misdemeanors including "habitual intoxication," prostitution, and "conducting a disorderly house." Act 494 of the 42nd General Assembly of 1919 (Mar. 28, 1919); T. D. Crawford & Moses Hamilton, *A Digest of the Statutes of Arkansas: Embracing All Laws of a General Nature*, § 9316 (1919). In 1939, the legislature permitted commitment of women over eighteen to a Training School for Girls and a State Farm for Women. Act 117 (Feb. 22, 1939), Ark. Stats. 1947 § 46–315, later Ark. Stats. 1947 § 46–804 (Repl. 1964). The 1971 repeal stated that "State correctional institutions are not the proper institutions to receive women found guilty of these misdemeanors." Ark. Stats. 1947 §§ 46-804 (Repl. 1977). Thanks to legal historian Elizabeth Katz, Ava Hicks, Director of the Arkansas Supreme Court Library, and Records Supervisor Holli North for unearthing these statutes.

42. *Prison Problems Outlined*, Ark. Democrat, A3, Jan. 29, 1970.

43. Dunn, *Trusty System Said to Lead to "Corruption"*; Simmons, *What's Wrong with Prisons?*; Kathy Gosnell, *Doctor Testifies Against Prison System's Living Arrangements*, Com. Appeal, Jan. 30, 1970, Rockefeller, IV, Box 253, File 4.

44. *Doctor Says Prison Food Often Inedible*, Ark. Democrat, A6, Jan. 30, 1970.

45. Dunn, *Prison Head Is Critical of Operation*. Price had delivered the presentation and the memorandum to the governor; as discussed, he described the state's awful prisons and their underfunding.

46. *Decision on Prisons No Surprise: Need for More Funds Is Indicated*, Ark. Gazette, A11, Feb. 19, 1970; Sylvia Spencer, *Legislators Tour "Clean, Neat" Prisons*, Ark. Gazette, 3, Feb. 7, 1970.

47. *Holt II*, 383; *State's Prison Duty*, Ark. Gazette, 4, Feb. 21, 1970.

48. In 5:5–12 in the Book of Daniel (in the Old Testament's Writings and the New Testament's Prophets, and depicted in a Rembrandt 1636 painting of the *Feast of Belshazzar*), Daniel, a Jew in exile in Babylonia, saw "the writing" on a wall forecasting the death of King Belshazzar, who was overthrown when Persians conquered the area.

49. *Holt II*, 365.

50. Marty Dunn, *Conditions at Prison Held Illegal*, Ark. Democrat, 1, Feb. 19, 1970; Jerol Garrison, *Arkansas Prisons, as Presently Run, Are Declared Illegal*, Ark. Gazette, 1, Feb. 19, 1970; *Ruling Terms Arkansas Prisons "Dark and Evil World,"* Ark. Gazette, A10, Feb. 22, 1970. An editorial spoke of the "shame" on the legislature, the people, and the press for ignoring conditions for far too long. *Cruel and Unusual*, Ark. Democrat, A4, Feb. 20, 1970.

51. The judge also considered a report from Dr. Charles M. Friel, Director of Research, Institute of Contemporary Corrections and the Behavioral Sciences at Sam Houston State University in Texas, given on January 29, 1970 (while the *Holt II* hearing was underway) to the Arkansas Commission on Crime and Law Enforcement; while "not formally introduced in evidence," Henley felt at "liberty to consider it." *Holt II*, 364–65.

52. *Holt II*, 366, 381.

53. *Holt II*, 367, 381.

54. Butler v. Perry, 240 US 328 (1916), quoting 1913 Fla. Laws, ch. 6537, 469, 474–75; United States v. Ballek, 170 F.3d 871 (9th Cir. 1999).

55. James Gray Pope, *Mass Incarceration, Convict Leasing, and the Thirteenth Amendment: A Revisionist Account*, 94 NYU L. Rev. 1465 (2019).

56. *Holt II*, 370–72. The Fifth Circuit relied on Congress' war powers for authorizing Heflin's confinement at the federal penitentiary in Atlanta as punishment for noncompliance. Heflin v. Sanford, 142 F.2d 798 (5th Cir. 1944).

57. *Holt II*, 381.

58. *Holt II*, 372–80.

59. *Holt II*, 369–79, quoting paragraphs from *Holt I*.

60. *Holt II*, 381.

61. Goldberg v. Kelly, 397 US 254 (1970); Charles Reich, *The New Property*, 73 Yale L. J. 733 (1964).

62. Pugh v. Locke, 406 F. Supp. 318, 329 (MD Ala. 1976); Laaman v. Helgemoe, 437 F. Supp. 269, 317 (DNH 1977); Estelle v. Gamble, 429 US 97 (1976).
63. *Holt II*, 368, 379–80.
64. *Holt II*, 383.
65. *Holt II*, 382–83.
66. *Holt II*, 382 (quoting *Holt I*, 833); George Douthit, *Federal Judge in Prison Case Held Whip Hand*, Ark. Democrat, 25, Mar. 15, 1970.
67. *Holt II*, 381–85.
68. *Holt II*, 384–85.

PART 3

1. David Brion Davis, *The Problem of Slavery in the Age of Emancipation* (Alfred A. Knopf, 2014).
2. Holt v. Sarver (*Holt II*), 309 F. Supp. 362, 379 (ED Ark. 1970), aff'd, Holt v. Sarver, 442 F.2d 304, 309–10 (8th Cir. 1971). Other cases include Mississippi: Gates v. Collier, 501 F.2d 1291 (5th Cir. 1974); Alabama: James v. Wallace, 406 F. Supp. 318 (MD Ala. 1976), aff'd in part and rev'd in part *sub nom.*, Newman v. Alabama, 559 F.2d 283 (5th Cir. 1977); New Hampshire: Laaman v. Helgemoe, 437 F. Supp. 269 (DNH 1977); Texas: Ruiz v. Estelle, 503 F. Supp. 1265 (SD Tex. 1980); Rhode Island: Palmigiano v. Garrahy, 443 F. Supp. 956 (DRI 1977). Analyses come from participants, such as Wilbert Rideau and Billy Sinclair, *Prisoner Litigation: How it Began in Louisiana*, 45 La. L. Rev. 1061 (1985); both of whom were editors of the prison's award-winning magazine, *The Angolite*. Another account comes from the presiding judge in the Texas prison litigation. William Wayne Justice, *The Origins of* Ruiz v. Estelle, 43 Stan. L. Rev. 1 (1990). Many academics have explored the genesis and impact of prisoners' litigation. Examples include Malcolm M. Feeley and Edward L. Rubin, *Judicial Policy Making and the Modern State: How the Courts Reformed America's Prisons* (Cambridge U. Press, 1998); Margo Schlanger, *Beyond the Hero Judge: Institutional Reform Litigation as Litigation*, 97 Mich. L. Rev. 1994 (1999); Dan Berger & Toussant Losier, *Rethinking the American Prison Movement* (2017).

CHAPTER 21

1. Warren E. Burger, Chief Justice, Address, *Proceedings of the National Conference on Corrections (NCC), Williamsburg, Va., Dec. 5–8, 1971*, 13.
2. Warren E. Burger, *Paradoxes in the Administration of Criminal Justice*, 58 J. Crim. L. Criminology & Police Sci. 428 (1967); Earl M. Maltz, *The Chief Justiceship of Warren Burger, 1969–1986*, 9 (2000); Warren E. Burger, Foreword, *Privatizing Correctional Institutions*, ix (Gary W. Bowman, Simon Hakim & Paul Seidenstat eds., 1993); Warren E. Burger, *No Man Is an Island*, 56 ABA J. 325, 327–28 (1970); Jerome J. Shestack, Chief Justice Warren E. Burger and the Legal Profession, *The Burger Court: Counter-Revolution or Confirmation*, 189, 193 (Bernard Schwartz ed., 1998); Statement, Ronald Goldfarb,

Oversight Hearings on the Nature and Effectiveness of the Rehabilitation Programs of the US Bureau of Prisons, Hearing before the Subcomm. on National Penitentiaries of the Comm. on the Judiciary, US Senate, 92d Cong. 2d Sess., June 13–14 1971, 157, 139; James B. Jacobs, *The Prisoners' Rights Movement and Its Impacts, 1960–1980*, 2 Crime & Just. 437–39 (1980).

3. Warren E. Burger, *A Proposal: A National Conference on Correctional Problems*, 33 Fed. Prob. 3 (1969); Richard M. Nixon, Memorandum for the Attorney General, *1971 NCC*, 1; William Clifford, Correctional Problems and Programs in Other Nations, *1971 NCC*, 29; Torsten Eriksson, Correctional Problems and Programs in Other Nations, *1971 NCC*, 36–37.

4. Burger Address, *1971 NCC*, 10–12; Lesley Oelsner, *Burger Bids Prison Heads Give Inmates Some Voice*, NY Times, 109, Dec. 8, 1971; John N. Mitchell, New Doors, Not Old Walls, *1971 NCC*, 5–8.

5. Chamber of Commerce of the United States, *Marshaling Citizen Power to Modernize Corrections*, Dec. 6, 1971, Arkansas State Archives, Prison Files Box 2, Folder 1, 1–19.

6. William B. Bryant, Substantive Rights of the Prisoner, *1971 NCC*, 43–44.

7. Eugene N. Barkin, Judicial Impact on the Prison Administrator, *1971 NCC*, 38.

8. Robert J. Kutak, New Directions in Corrections, Summary of Workshop III Reports, *1971 NCC*, 52; Grp. E Report, *1971 NCC*, 128.

9. Eddie M. Harrison, Inside Looking Out, *1971 NCC*, 15–18; Harrison v. United States, 387 F.2d 203 (DC Cir. 1967), rev'd, 392 US 219 (1968).

10. Christopher F. Edley, The Community in Corrections, *1971 NCC*, 24, 27; Norval Morris, Corrections Lurches Forward, *1971 NCC*, 20, 21.

11. *Attica: The Official Report of the New York State Special Commission on Attica*, xii (Bantam Books, 1972).

12. Heather Ann Thompson, *Blood in the Water: The Attica Prison Uprising of 1971 and Its Legacy*, 5–8 (Pantheon, 2016).

13. Thompson, 79–80, 120–26, 153–56; Statement, Herman Badillo, *Corrections: Prisoners' Representation (Part III)*, Hearings Before Subcomm. No. 3 of the HR Comm. of the Judiciary, 92d Cong. 1st Sess., Nov. 10, 11, Dec. 2, 1971, 2–4; Statement, Vincent R. Mancusi, *American Prisons in Turmoil (Part I)*, Hearings Before Select HR Comm. on Crime, 92d Cong. 1st Sess., Nov. 20, 30, Dec. 1, 2, and 3, 1971, 3, 12; Statement, Norman A. Carlson, 291.

14. Douglas J. Besharov & Gerhard O. W. Mueller, *The Demands of the Inmates of Attica State Prison and the United Nations Standard Minimum Rules for the Treatment of Prisoners: A Comparison*, 21 Buffalo L. Rev. 839, 841–54 (1972).

15. *Attica Commission Report*, xix–xxv.

16. Morris, *1971 NCC*, 21–24; Burger's Address, *1971 NCC*, 11; Russell G. Oswald, What Are the Implications for Correction of the Increasing Proportion of Minority Group Persons among Sentenced Prisoners, *1971 NCC*, 162.

17. Spiro T. Agnew, *The "Root Causes" of Attica*, NY Times, 43, Sept. 17, 1971.

18. Roger J. Traynor, *Role of the Law in Protecting the Rights of Prisoners, Lectures Delivered at the Fourth United Nations Congress on the Prevention of Crime and the Treatment of Offenders*, 29 Int'l Rev. Crim. Pol'y 79, 87 (1971).

19. National Council on Crime and Delinquency (NCCD), *A Model Act for the Protection of Rights of Prisoners*, § 1a (1972).

20. Thompson, 560.

21. Traynor, 85–90; Takashi Oka, *UN Group Urges Anticrime Plans*, NY Times, 13, Aug. 30, 1970; Press Release, US Dept. State, No. 235 United States Delegation to the Fourth United Nations Congress on the Prevention of Crime and the Treatment of Offenders, Kyoto, Japan, Aug. 17–26, 1970 (Aug. 10, 1970); Elizabeth Roth, *The Two Voices of Roger Traynor*, 27 Am. J. Legal Hist. 269, 296 (1983); Mathew O. Tobriner, *Chief Justice Roger Traynor*, 83 Harv. L. Rev. 1769, 1772 (1970).

22. The Subcommittee on National Penitentiaries, created in 1949 and extant into the 1970s, made some unannounced site visits and inspections; as one member reported, they "always ask[ed] to see the men in solitary confinement." Investigation of National Penitentiaries, 99 Cong. Rec. Senate 1307–19 (1953); Annual Report of the Subcommittee on National Penitentiaries, S. Rep. 95–86, 95th Cong. 1st Sess., Apr. 6, 1977.

23. HR 11605, Prisoner Treatment Act of 1971, 92d Cong. 1st Sess., Nov. 5, 1971; HR 12758, Prisoner Treatment Act of 1972, 92d Cong. 2d Sess., Jan. 31, 1972; HR 36901, Prisoner Treatment Act of 1873, 93d Cong. 1st Sess., Feb. 7, 1973; HR 4097, 94th Cong. 1st Sess., Mar. 3, 1975. Representative Ron Dellums made a similar proposal, the Omnibus Penal Reform Act of 1972, which included "minimum standards," reform of parole, and re-enfranchisement provisions. HR 14327, 92d Cong. 2d Sess., Apr. 12, 1972. The text of some provisions, including a ban on "corporal punishment" and "dark cells," paralleled the 1955 UN Rules.

24. HR 16632, Prisoner Rights Act, 92d Cong. 2d Sess., Sept. 13, 1972; HR 16849, 92d Cong. 2d Sess., Sept. 27, 1972 (resubmitted, joined by twenty members of the House); HR 4188, 93d Cong. 1st Sess., Feb. 8, 1973; HR 5202, 93d Cong. 1st Sess., Mar. 6, 1973 (resubmitted, joined by twenty); HR 3200, Prisoner Rights Act, 94th Cong. 1st Sess., Feb. 19, 1975, and with co-sponsors, HR 6688, 94th Cong. 1st Sess., May 6, 1975.

25. Rep. Kastenmeier, HR 689 (1975); HR 192 (1977); HR 558 (1977).

26. NCCD Model Act, 5. *Federal Prisons Chief*, NY Times, 51, Mar. 26, 1970. The other members were John D. Case, Warden of Bucks County Prison, Doylestown, Pennsylvania; Joseph S. Coughlin, Assistant Director of Illinois' Department of Correction; Walter W. Finke, Chair of the Board of Dictaphone Corporation and an NCCD trustee; Peter Lejins, Director of the Institute on Criminal Justice and Criminology at the University of Maryland; Richard A. McGee, President of the American Justice Institute; Karl Menninger, a psychiatrist heading the Menninger Foundation; Elmer K. Nelson, directing USC's School of Public Administration; and George H. Revelle, a judge on the Superior Court in Seattle, Washington. NCCD

was renamed "Evident Change." Barry Krisberg, Carolina Guzman & Linh Vuong, *Crime and Economic Hard Times: NCCD Special Report*, 2 (Feb. 2009).

27. NCCD Model Act § 1b; Sol Rubin, Henry Weihofen, George Edwards & Simon Rosenzweig, *The Law of Criminal Correction* (West Publ. Co., 1963); Norval Morris, Book Review, *The Law of Criminal Corrections*, 32 U. Chi. L. Rev. 605 (1965). Sol Rubin, *Introduction: A Model Act for the Protection of the Rights of Prisoners*, 1973 Wash. U. L. Q. 553, 556; NCCD Model Act § 1a, § 1b, § 6; James W. L. Park, *On Being Medium Nice to Prisoners*, 1973 Wash. U. L. Q. 607; Fred Cohen, *In Search of a Model Act for Prisoners' Rights*, 1973 Wash U. L. Q. 621; James A. Jablonski, *Controlling Discretionary Power in Prison Organizations: A Review of the Model Act*, 1973 Wash. U. L. Q. 563, 563; Myron Gochnauer, *Necessity and Prisoners' Rights*, 10 New Eng. J. Crim. & Civ. Confinement 27–28 (1984).

28. In 1972, corrections departments in Kansas and New Mexico adopted aspects. Rubin, *Introduction*, 553 n.2. The ABA approved fifty-eight standards in ten parts, ABA, *Standards: The Legal Status of Prisoners*, 14 Am. Crim. L. Rev. 387, 387–416 (1977); it issued revisions in 2011, *ABA Standards for Criminal Justice: Treatment of Prisoners* (ABA, 3d ed. 2011); Richard G. Singer, *Privacy, Autonomy, and Dignity in Prison: A Preliminary Inquiry Concerning Constitutional Aspects of the Degradation Process in Our Prisons*, 21 Buffalo L. Rev. 669 (1972).

29. Statement, Richard W. Velde, Hearings Before the Subcomm. on National Penitentiaries of the S. Comm. on the Judiciary, 92d Cong. 1st Sess., May 13, 18, 19, 20, 1971, 204.

30. Statement, Sen. Jacob K. Javits, S.3049 National Correctional Standards Act, Hearing before the S. Subcomm. on National Penitentiaries of the Comm. on the Judiciary, 92d Cong. 2d Sess., June 2, 22 1972, 4.

31. Prison Reform Legislation, 92d Cong., Cong. Rsch. Serv., Jean Wolf, Education and Public Welfare Division, HV 8442, 723–90 ED, Apr. 6, 1973, I; S. Hearing on S.3049, 1, 3.

32. *Corrections: Prisons, Prison Reform and Prisoners' Rights: Michigan (Part VIII)*, Hearings Before the Subcomm. No. 3 of the H. Comm. on the Judiciary, 92d Cong. 2d Sess., Mar. 21, 1972; *Corrections: Prisons, Prison Reform and Prisoners' Rights: California (Part II)*, Hearings Before the Subcomm. No. 3 of the H. Comm. on the Judiciary, 92d Cong. 2d Sess., Oct. 27, 1971.

33. Statement, Ronald Goldfarb, 1971 S. Oversight Hearings on the Nature and Effectiveness of the Rehabilitation Programs of the US Bureau of Prisons, 157, 160; Statement, Sen. Quentin Burdick, S.662, May 1971 Hearings Before the Subcomm. on National Penitentiaries of the S. Comm. on the Judiciary, 25–28; Prepared Statement, Richard J. Hughes, Chairman, ABA Commission, May 1971 S. Hearings on Priorities for Correctional Reform and S.662, 334–45; Prepared Statement, William D. Leeke, Dir., SC Dept. of Corrections, May 1971 S. Hearings on Priorities for Correctional Reform and S.662, 75, 78–79; Statement, Raymond K. Procunier, Dir., Cal. Dept. of Corrections, 122–29; Statement, Barney Apfel, Sec. Treasurer, International

Brotherhood of Teamsters, Local 960, SF, 59–61 both from 1971 HR Hearings, Part II, Prisons, Prison Reform and Prisoners' Rights: California.

34. S.3049 National Corrections Standards Act, 92d Cong. 2d Sess., Jan. 21, 1972; to amend the Omnibus Crime Control and Safe Streets Act of 1968; Statement, Sen. Javits, S.3049, 4; 1972 National Corrections Standards Act §§ 2a, 3.

35. Statement, James V. Bennett, S.3049, 11, 12, 21–23; Statement, Norval Morris, S.3049, 75–76; Statement, Richard G. Singer, School of Law, U. Cinn., S. 3049, 85–110.

36. S.3309, The Community Supervision and Services Act, Hearing before the Subcomm. on National Penitentiaries of the S. Comm. on the Judiciary, 92d Cong. 2d Sess., July 19, 20, 1972; Statement, Whitney North Seymour Jr., 34–35; Letter to Senator John O. Eastland, Chairman of the Committee on the Judiciary, from Ralph Erickson, Deputy Atty. Gen., 138–39; Statement, Norman Carlson, May 1971 S. Hearings on Priorities for Correctional Reform and S. 662, 199–201; Elizabeth Hinton, *From the War on Poverty to the War on Crime: The Making of Mass Incarceration in America*, 162–74 (Harvard U. Press, 2016); National Research Council, *The Growth of Incarceration in the United States*, 104–28 (2014).

37. Justice Stewart, noting the case was to be discussed on February 26, attached a memorandum from his law clerk Duncan Kennedy (later a high-profile Harvard law professor) and said the case "merits Conference discussion." Memorandum Justice Potter Stewart to the Conference, No. 5940, Haines v. Kerner, Feb. 23, 1971, Library of Congress, Harry A. Blackmun Papers, Series 3, Box 143; Transcript, Oral Argument of Warren Smoot, on behalf of Illinois, 35, Haines v. Kerner, 404 US 519 (1972); Brief for Petitioner, 6–18, 18–24, *Haines*, 1971 WL 133427.

38. Haines v. Kerner, No. 70–5025 H. A. B., Nov. 22, 1971, Blackmun Papers, 2–3.

39. *Haines*, 404 US 519. Neither Justices Powell nor Rehnquist participated. *Justices Direct Federal Hearing on Prison Rights*, Ark. Democrat, 24, Jan 14, 1972; Cruz v. Beto, 405 US 319 (1972).

40. Haines v. Kerner, 492 F.2d 937, 942–43 (7th Cir. 1974).

41. Novak v. Beto, 453 F.2d 661 (5th Cir. 1971); Cruz v. Beto, 329 F. Supp. 443 (SD Tex. 1970), aff'd, 445 F.2d 801 (5th Cir. 1971), vacated, 405 US 319 (1972), rev'd *sub nom.* Cruz v. Estelle, 497 F.2d 496, 498 (5th Cir. 1974); Novak v. Beto, 456 F.2d 1303 (5th Cir. 1972), cert. denied *sub nom.* Sellars v. Beto, 409 US 968 (1972). Justice Douglas, joined by Justices Brennan and Marshall, dissented and called the conditions "considered inhuman in the time of Charles Dickens." *Sellars*, 969; Cruz v. Beto, 453 F. Supp. 905, 906 (SD Tex. 1977), referencing the 1976 order, aff'd, 603 F.2d 1178 (5th Cir. 1979). The lawyer, Frances Jalet, also a plaintiff, married Cruz, whom she met while he was incarcerated. Jalet, a graduate of Columbia Law School, was one of the first in 1967 to receive a federally funded Reginald Heber Smith Fellowships; at age fifty-six, she went to the Legal Aid and Defender Society in

Travis County, Texas. Ethan Watters, *The Love Story that Upended the Texas Prison System*, Tex. Monthly, Oct. 11, 2018.

42. Brief of the Petitioners, *17, Wolff v. McDonnell, 418 US 539 (1974), 1974 WL 187450.

43. Meachum v. Fano, 427 US 215, 233 (1976). Justices Brennan and Marshall joined the dissent.

44. McDonnell v. Wolff, 342 F. Supp. 616, 644–45 (D. Neb. 1972), aff'd in part, rev'd in part, 483 F.2d 1059 (8th Cir. 1973).

45. *Wolff*, 418 US 542. The Court affirmed the need to ensure access to legal assistance from other prisoners for civil rights and habeas corpus petitions. *Wolff*, 576–79. The Court revised the lower court's ruling on control of mail; Nebraska could require lawyers to identify letters as privileged, and staff could open them in front of the prisoner but not read the contents; Brief of Inmates of the District of Columbia Correctional Complex at Lorton, Virginia, Amici Curiae, *34–15, 1974 WL 185775; Brief of the National Council on Crime & Delinquency as Amicus Curiae, *3–4, 9–11, 14–16, 21–26, 1974 WL 185767; Brief of the Legal Aid Society of New York as Amicus Curiae, *2, 1974 WL 185769; Brief for the Respondent, *14, 26 n.22, 27 n.24, 28, 25, 27, 30 nn.29–31, app. at 4a–7a, 11a, 1974 WL 185771. The ABA report, issued before *Wolff*, was revised to include an "analysis" of its impact. Melvin T. Axilbund, Preface, *Am. Bar Assn. Survey of Prison Disciplinary Practices and Procedures: With an Analysis of the Impact of* Wolff v. McDonnell, Res. Ctr. on Corrections Law & Legal Services (1974).

46. Brief for the United States as Amicus Curiae, *5–11, 1974 WL 185774; Transcript of Oral Argument of Robert H. Bork for the United States, as Amicus Curiae, Supporting Petitioner, *11.

47. Transcript of Oral Argument of Melvin Kent Kammerlohr for Petitioner Nebraska, 40, 2, 3, 7; Brief of the Petitioners, *17.

48. *Wolff*, 547, 557–58.

49. *Wolff*, 552–71.

50. *Wolff*, 552–70.

51. *Wolff*, 581–89.

52. *Wolff*, 594–99, 571–72.

53. *Meachum*, 233–35.

54. Sandin v. Conner, 515 US 472, 491–92 (1995).

55. Brief for the United States as Amicus Curiae, *2–3; Brief of Evelle J. Younger, Attorney General of the State of California as Amicus Curiae, *10 n.9, 1974 WL 185773.

56. Telephone Interview and email with Melissa D. Nofziger, Assistant Inspector Gen. for Hearings, Or. Dept. of Corr., Nov. 15 and 18, 2019.

57. Gamble v. Estelle, 516 F.2d 937, 940 (5th Cir. 1975).

58. Estelle v. Gamble, 429 US 97, 102, 104 (1976).

59. Gamble v. Estelle, 554 F.2d 653, 654 (5th Cir. 1977).

60. Examples include the Community Oriented Correctional Health Services, the National Commission on Correctional Healthcare, and the American

College of Correctional Physicians. Failings were detailed in US Department of Justice, Office of the Inspector General, Review of the Federal Bureau of Prisons' Medical Staffing Challenges (Mar. 2016); Braggs v. Dunn, 257 F. Supp. 3d 1171, 1267–68 (MD Ala. 2017); Braggs v. Dunn, 367 F. Supp. 3d 1340 (MD Ala. 2019).

61. Brown v. Plata, 563 US 493 (2011).
62. Civil Rights of Institutionalized Persons Act, Pub. L. No. 96–247, 94 Stat. 3449 (1980), codified at 42 USC § 1997 *et seq.*
63. Brief of the Petitioners, *20.
64. William F. Swindler, *The Chief Justice and Law Reform, 1921–1971*, 1971 Sup. Ct. Rev. 241, 245; Edward B. McConnell, *The National Center for State Courts—A Progress Report*, 60 Judicature 39 (1976).
65. *Interview with National Institute of Corrections Director Allen F. Breed*, 13 The Third Branch 1, 6 (1981); Palmigiano v. Garrahy, 443 F. Supp. 956 (DRI 1977); 448 F. Supp. 659 (DRI 1979); Susan Sturm, *Mastering Intervention in Prisons*, 88 Yale L. J. 1062 (1979); Allen F. Breed, *The Power of Prisons*, 19 Judges J. 20, 20, 23 (1980).
66. Warren E. Burger, *Our Options Are Limited*, 18 Vill. L. Rev. 165, 167–69 (1972); When on the DC Court of Appeals, Burger had admonished a trial judge for not requiring a response from jailors when prisoners complained of horrid heat and rotten food. Brooks v. Anderson, 317 F.2d 179 (DC Cir. 1963); Smith v. Anderson, 317 F.2d 172 (DC Cir. 1963); Warren E. Burger, *Prison Industries: Turning Warehouses into Factories with Fences*, 45 Pub. Admin. Rev. 754, 754 (1985): William Raspberry, *Burger's Prison Dream*, Wash. Post, June 28, 1995.
67. Burger, *Our Options*, 170; Michael Graetz & Linda Greenhouse, *The Burger Court and the Rise of the Judicial Right* (Simon & Schuster, 2016).
68. Matthew L. Myers, *The Alabama Case: 12 Years After* James v. Wallace, 13 J. Nat'l Prison Project, 8-9, Fall 1987.

CHAPTER 22

1. *State's Prison Duty*, Ark. Gazette, 4, Feb. 21, 1970.
2. Wayne Jordan, *Politicians Exploit Fears of Escapes, Prison Head Says*, Ark. Gazette, 5, May 31, 1970.
3. Bill Lancaster, *Black and White Inmates Clash at Cummins Prison*, Pine Bluff Commercial (Com.), Nov. 21, 1970, U. Ark. Little Rock (UALR), Rockefeller Collection, Record Group IV, Box 252, File 1; *The Uprising at Cummins*, Ark. Gazette, A6, Nov. 4, 1970. Unless otherwise noted, all Rockefeller references are to Group IV.
4. Holt v. Sarver, 442 F.2d 304, 310 (8th Cir. 1971).
5. Holt v. Sarver (*Holt II*), 309 F. Supp. 362, 381, 385 (ED Ark. 1970); *Prison Edict Fails as Grounds to Free 2 Cummins Convicts*, Ark. Democrat, 6, Mar. 13, 1970.
6. 442 F.2d, 305.
7. Doug Smith, *Legislature Passes $2.3 Million Plan for State Prisons*, Ark. Gazette, A10, Mar. 7, 1970; *McClerkin: Trim "Fat" From Budget*, Ark. Democrat,

8, Mar. 14, 1970; George Douthit, *Federal Judge in Prison Case Held Whip Hand*, Ark. Democrat, 25, Mar. 15, 1970; Bob Stover, *Campaigns "Open Officially" at Pink Tomato Festival*, Ark. Gazette, 3, June 14, 1970.

8. *Purcell to Appeal Order to Reform Arkansas Prisons*, Ark. Gazette, 21, Mar. 6, 1970.

9. John Bennett, *Prisons Appeal Termed "Must,"* Com. Appeal, Feb. 25, 1970, Rockefeller, IV, Box 253, File 5.

10. *Inaugural Address*, Jan. 10, 1967, Winthrop Rockefeller Institute; Ernest Dumas, *Prison Ruling Delights WR, Aides, But the Question Is: What About Money?*, Ark. Gazette, A4, Feb. 20, 1970.

11. *Legislators Want Ruling Appealed*, Ark. Gazette, 1, Feb. 20, 1970; Doug Smith, *Legislative Panel Asks Prison Board to Back Appeal*, Ark. Gazette, 11, Feb. 26, 1970; 1970; Editorial: *Appeal at Last*, Ark. Democrat, 48. Mar. 8, 1970, quoting Warren E. Burger, *No Man Is an Island*, 56 ABA J., 325, 328 (1970). The prisoners' lawyers cross-appealed to reverse Henley's Thirteenth Amendment ruling but then stuck to defending what Henley had done. *Prisoners Can Appeal as Paupers*, Ark. Democrat, 9, Mar. 21, 1970; Hutto v. Finney, 437 US 678 (1978).

12. *Funds for Prison Squeak by Senate, Slashed in House*, Ark. Gazette, 1, Mar. 6, 1970; Doug Smith, *Legislature Passes $2.3 Million Plan for State Prisons*, Ark. Gazette, A10, Mar. 7, 1970; *Prison Unit Contract is Delayed*, Ark. Gazette, 10, Mar. 15, 1970; *WR Authorizes Prison Project*, Ark. Gazette, 8, Mar. 27, 1970; *Prison Contract Is Signed*, Ark. Democrat, 8, Mar. 28, 1970; *Prisons Face July 1 Deficit of $104,993*, Ark. Democrat, 8, Mar. 28, 1970; *Sarver in Hospital for Tests*, Ark. Democrat, 8, Mar. 25, 1970; Charles Robert Sarver, Resume, Rockefeller, Record Group I, Box 486, File 1, 2.

13. *Trusties in Critical Jobs to Be Replaced at Prisons, Report for Henley Asserts*, Ark. Gazette, 35, Apr. 1, 1970; *Prison Document Submitted*, Ark. Democrat, 3, Apr. 1, 1970.

14. *Prison Assaults Must Be Curbed, Judge Henley Says*, Ark. Gazette, 22, Apr. 16, 1970; *No More Nonsense in Penal Reform*, Ark. Gazette, 60, Apr. 19, 1970.

15. *Sarver Reports on Steps Taken to Reduce Assaults in Prison*, Ark. Democrat, 2, May 11, 1970; *Weapons Seized, Henley Is Told*, Ark. Gazette, B14, May 12, 1970; *Judge Still Not Satisfied with Prisons*, Ark. Gazette, 12, May 29, 1970; *Prison Plan Leaves Henley Dissatisfied*, Ark. Gazette, 44, May 29, 1970; *Trusties Lose Power over Other Convicts, Board Tells Henley*, Ark. Democrat, 1, July 10, 1970; Jimmy Jones, *Ball Field "Cruel": Harris Order Cummins to Quit Punishment of Prisoner*, Ark. Democrat, 3, July 24, 1970; Fred Petrucelli, *From: Bill Conley, Governor's Office, For Immediate Release*, July 6, 1970, "To WR from John Ward re Maximum Security United at Cummins," Aug. 5, 1970, both Rockefeller, IV, Box 252, File 3.

16. *ALC Tours State's Prisons*, Sentinel-Record, 7, July 17, 1969; George Douthit, *Haley Sees Partisan Salvo on the Prisons*, Ark. Democrat, B7, July 26, 1970; Jerol Garrison, *3 Inmates Tell Judge Henley of Supervisor Selling Vodka*, Ark. Gazette, A19, Aug. 6, 1970.

17. ADC, Annual Report March 1, 1968–Sept. 30, 1970 [with Revisions], Arkansas State Library, Ark Doc CR 1.3: 970 copy 2, at 31.
18. ADC 1968–1970, iii, 30.
19. ADC 1968–1970, 12.
20. ADC 1968–1970, 2–12; ii.
21. Dale Bumpers, *The Best Lawyer in a One-Lawyer Town*, 176–88 (Random House, 2003).
22. *WR70 Fact Sheet: Accomplishments During the Rockefeller Administration in the Area of Prison Reform*, Rockefeller, IV, Box 250, File 6.
23. Arkansas Heritage, *Arkansas Politics in the 20th Century: Twelve Elections That Shaped a Century*, 53; Doug Smith, *Style as a Political Asset in Arkansas*, Ark. Gazette, E3, Sept. 13, 1970; *Let's Talk About the Issues: Prisoners Regularly Escape from Arkansas' Prisons*, Ark. Gazette, A10, Oct. 28, 1970.
24. *Tide of Reform*, Ark. Democrat, A6, Sept. 9, 1970; Bumpers, 212–15; Diane D. Blair, *The Big Three of Late Twentieth-Century Arkansas Politics: Dale Bumpers, Bill Clinton, and David Pryor*, 54 Ark. Hist. Q. 53, 58 (1995).
25. *Inmate Was Hit by a Ricochet, Sarver Says*, Ark. Gazette, A3, Sept. 19, 1970; *Inmate Shot: 200 on Strike: Prisoners Sitting on Cummins Field*, Ark. Gazette, 1, Sept. 17, 1970; *60 Inmates Still on Strike Against Armed Trusties*, Ark. Democrat, A2, Sept. 18, 1970; Kathy Gosnell, *Cummins Inmates Free Hostages: No Promises Offered for Release*, Pine Bluff Com., 1, Nov. 3, 1970; *Arkansas Prisoners Release 4 Hostages*, NY Times, 24, Nov. 3, 1970; Martin Kirby, *Prison Rebellion Ends*, Ark. Democrat, 1, Nov. 3, 1970; *The Uprising at Cummins*, Ark. Gazette, A6, Nov. 4, 1970.
26. Bill Lancaster, *Black and White Inmates Clash at Cummins Prison*, Pine Bluff Com., Nov. 21, 1970, Rockefeller, IV, Box 252, File 1; *Armed State Police Move into Prison as Fighting Flares*, Ark. Gazette, 1, Nov. 22, 1970; *Prison Is Quiet as Convicts Go Back to Work*, Ark. Democrat, 1, Nov. 23, 1970; Kathy Gosnell, *Cummins Calm After Riot: State Police on Standby*, Pine Bluff Com., 1, Nov. 23, 1970, Rockefeller, IV, Box 252, File 1; *State Police Display Objects Called Potential Weapons Taken at Prison*, Ark. Gazette, 1, Nov. 25, 1970.
27. Memorandum Anthony G. Amsterdam to the Hon. Winthrop Rockefeller, re Commutation of the Sentences of the Fifteen Men Currently Under Sentence of Death, Dec. 22, 1970, Rockefeller, IV, Box 249, File 14; John L. Ward, *The Arkansas Rockefeller*, 194–95 (La. State U. Press, 2011); Tom Parsons, *Governor Visits Prisons*, Ark. Democrat, 1, Jan. 1, 1971.
28. Ernest Dumas, *Bumpers Gives Prison Reform High Priority*, Ark. Gazette, 1, Dec. 11, 1970.
29. *Caving in With Dignity*, Pine Bluff Com., Apr. 7, 1971, Rockefeller, IV, Box 250, File 5.
30. *Where from Here? Alternatives for a Ten-Year Action Plan for Arkansas Corrections*, Ark. Comm. on Crime and Law Enforcement, Nov. 30, 1970, Arkansas State Archives, Prison Records, Box 1, Folder 12, 1–2.
31. *Bell Vows Move to Dismiss Sarver Despite Bumpers*, Ark. Gazette, 3, Nov. 25, 1970; *Haley Asks $12 Million Prison Operating Budget*, Sentinel-Record, 6,

Dec. 8, 1970; *Prisons' Budget Tentatively Set, Bumpers Says*, Ark. Democrat, A7, Jan. 5, 1971.

32. *Pulaski Jail Inmates Charge "Cruel Punishment,"* Ark. Democrat, A9, Oct. 1, 1970; Jerol Garrison, *Use of Isolation Cell Barred for Teen-agers, US Inmates*, Ark. Gazette, B20, Oct. 23, 1970; *US Avoids Using Jail in Pulaski*, Ark. Democrat, 10, Apr. 7, 1971; *Jail Report Is Presented to Tucker*, Ark. Gazette, 32, Apr. 28, 1971; *Parties Agree in Penal Farm Investigation*, Ark. Gazette, 3, Oct. 1, 1971; *New Pleading Filed in Death Case*, Ark. Democrat, 3, Oct. 13, 1971; *Inmate Forced into Ditch, Suit Charges*, Ark. Gazette, 15, Oct 13, 1971; *Jury Says "No Foul Play" in Death*, Ark. Democrat, 8, Oct. 21, 1971; *Plaintiff in Case to Close Penal Farm Receives Sentence*, Ark. Democrat, 1, Nov. 3, 1971; Williams v. Illinois, 399 US 235 (1970); *Ruling Says Prison, Jail are Different*, Ark. Gazette, 29, Feb. 26, 1971; Hamilton v. Love, 358 F. Supp. 338 (ED Ark. 1973).

33. *Prison Budget Compromise Is Worked Out*, Ark. Gazette, 4, Jan. 5, 1971; *Bumpers Noncommittal on Prison Budget Proposal*, Sentinel-Record, 3, Jan. 5, 1971; *Prisons' Budget Clears Hurdle: Compromise Keeps Bumpers' Proposals*, Ark. Democrat, 1, Jan. 6, 1971; *Compromise Corrections Budget Approved by ALC: Bumpers, Sarver Pleased*, Ark. Gazette, A5, Jan 6. 1971; *Try to Fire Sarver Seen by Senator*, Ark. Gazette, 1, Jan. 10, 1971; *Priority to Pettiness*, Ark. Gazette, 6, Jan. 13, 1971; *Hendrix Wants Sarver to Shut Up*, Ark. Gazette, 25, Jan. 15, 1971; Editorial, *Hendrix and Sarver*, Ark. Gazette, 6, Jan. 19, 1971; *Prison Obstruction Rears Its Ugly Head*, Ark. Gazette, 6, Feb. 24, 1971; *Bumpers Defends Sarver*, Ark. Democrat, 8, Feb. 25, 1971; *Foes of Sarver Irk Bumpers*, Ark. Gazette, 1, Feb. 25, 1971.

34. Dennis Hevesi, *Donald P. Lay, 80, Federal Judge Notable in Rights Cases, Dies*, NY Times, C17, May 2, 2007; *Prison Ruling Arguments Set for Wednesday*, Ark. Gazette, 2, Mar. 9, 1971; Barlow Merget, *Attorneys Debate Control of State's Prisons in Federal Appeals Court*, Ark. Democrat, A9, Mar. 11, 1971; *Appeals Court Considering State Prisons*, Ark. Gazette, 10, Mar. 12, 1971; *Case Involving Arkansas May Open Door to Nationwide Prison Reform*, Ark. Democrat, A4, Mar. 14, 1971.

35. David Kotok, *Not Fully Satisfied, Sarver Looks at Funds for Women's Unit*, Ark. Democrat, 8, Mar. 25, 1971; *$1.1 Million in Prison Work Approved by Budget Group*, Ark. Gazette, A8, Mar. 24, 1971; *Why Are the State Legislators Critical of Sarver?*, Ark. Democrat, A4, Mar. 28, 1971; *Sarver Bristles After Governor Says He Should Quit*, Sentinel-Record, 1, Mar. 30, 1971; *Board Fires Sarver: Haley Cites Clash with Legislators*, Ark. Gazette, 1, Mar. 30, 1971; David Kotok, *Sarver Out as Director of Prisons*, Ark. Democrat, 1, Mar. 30, 1971; Martin Kirby, *Sarver's Aides Stunned*, Ark. Democrat, A2, Mar. 30, 1971. In addition to a law degree, Sarver had done graduate work in law and sociology at Indiana University, Bloomington. Sarver, Resume, 1, 3.

36. *Prison Board Decides to Back Reformatory Bill*, Ark. Gazette, B10, Feb. 22, 1971; *Bumpers' Prison Bills*, Ark. Gazette, A6, Feb. 16, 1971; *Four Prison-Reform Bills Are Introduced in the Senate*, Ark. Democrat, 2, Feb. 13, 1971; *With Sarver Gone,*

Prison Funding Passes in Breeze, Ark. Gazette, 3, Mar. 31, 1971; Jerol Garrison, *$28 Million in New Taxes Sets Record for State*, Ark. Gazette, A19, Apr. 11, 1971; Ernest Dumas & Doug Smith, *In Sheer Volume, It Was a Session to Remember*, Ark. Gazette, A4, Apr. 18, 1971. The "Extraordinary Session" (a special meeting) provided $300,000 for farm mechanization, $150,000 to replace obsolete equipment, $176,000 for barrack renovation, and $174,000 to improve kitchen and sanitation. Respondents' Report, 2, *Holt II* (PB 69-C-24), Arkansas State Prison Records, Arkansas State Archives, Box 2, Folder 10.

37. Holt v. Sarver, 442 F.2d, 304, 305–08 (8th Cir. 1971).

38. 442 F.2d, 308–09.

39. 442 F.2d, 309–10, 310 n.1.

40. Donald P. Lay, *A Judicial Mandate*, 7 Trial Mag. 14, 15 (1971); Donald P. Lay, *The Writ of Habeas Corpus: A Complex Procedure for a Simple Process*, 77 Minn. L. Rev. 1015 (1993); Press release, Oct. 16, 1991, quoted in Hon. Myron H. Bright, *In Memoriam: Judge Donald P. Lay*, 92 Iowa L. Rev. 1555, 1557 (2007); Richard S. Arnold, *A Tribute to Judge Donald P. Lay*, 18 William Mitchell L. Rev. 561, 565 (1992).

41. *Arkansas Prisons Unconstitutional, 3 Judges Agree*, Ark. Gazette, 1, May 7, 1971; *Prisons Chief Will Be Named on May 15*, Ark. Gazette, A3, May 6, 1971; *Hutto Likely to Be Named Prison Chief*, Ark. Gazette, A8, May 13, 1971; Tucker Steinmetz, *For Unity, Bumpers Was Asked to Offer Job to Hutto*, Ark. Democrat, 1, May 16, 1971; *Texan Gets Prison Post in Arkansas*, Corpus Christi Caller-Times, A3, May 16, 1971; Tucker Steinmetz, *A Visit with the New Prison Chief in His Sophisticated Institution in Texas*, Ark. Democrat, 1, May 19, 1971; Tucker Steinmetz, *Quiet Prison Chief "Intrigued" by Arkansas*, Ark. Democrat, 1, May 20, 1971. The pay was $22,500 with benefits.

42. Women's Commission for Refugee Women and Children, Lutheran Immigration and Refugee Service, *Locking Up Family Values: The Detention of Immigrant Families*, Feb. 2007; *The Least of These* (La Sonrisa Productions Inc. 2009); *Remembering T. Don. Hutto, Champion for High Standards of Care*, CoreCivic, Nov. 4, 2021.

43. *Sen. Fletcher Was Right About State Prisons*, Ark. Democrat, 5, May 9, 1971; *Hutto Is Ordered to Produce Report*, Ark. Gazette, 3, June 17, 1971; *Holt* Docket, 7; *Trusties Still Act as Guards, Powers Cut, Board Says*, Ark. Gazette, A13, July 20, 1971.

44. Mike Trimble, *Allow "Hair" at LR for Six-Day Run, Judge Eisele Orders*, Ark. Gazette, 1, Aug. 12, 1971; Southwest Productions Inc. v. Freeman, Civ. No. LR-71-C-137 (ED Ark. Aug. 13, 1971).

45. Hamilton v. Love, 328 F. Supp. 1182, 1191–94 (ED Ark. 1971); *Improve Jail by September or Else Close It, Eisele Says*, Ark. Gazette, 1, June 3, 1971; *Jail Hearing Scheduled*, Hope Star, 1, Jan. 12, 1971; *Eisele Issues Jail Standards*, Nw. Ark. Times, 11, June 23, 1971.

46. Letter and Attachments Michele Hermann, Assoc. Dir., Prisoners' Rights Project of the American Civil Liberties Union, to Philip Kaplan, Oct. 27, 1971, UALR, Kaplan Papers, Series 1, Box 18A, Folder 2.

47. *Riot Unlikely in Arkansas, Hutto Says*, Ark. Gazette, B10, Sept. 15, 1971.

48. Robert Shaw, *Arkansas Holds Promise for Model Prison System: Hutto Points with Pride to Farm-Based Correction Institution*, Ark. Democrat, A3, Oct. 7, 1971; *Discusses His General Philosophy of Prison Security, Discipline*, Ark. Democrat, A4, Nov. 25, 1971; ADC, Inmate Handbook, Dec. 1, 1971, Prison Records, Box 2, Folder 15, vi, 16–22, 57–58; Martin Kirby, *A Handbook for Reform: Correction Department Publication Cites Guidelines for Inmates*, Ark. Democrat, A4, Dec. 5, 1971.

49. *Requests Denied Cummings Inmates*, Ark. Gazette, 5, Aug. 17, 1971; *"Texas TV" Abolished, Quiet Cell Used Less, Hutto Tells US Court*, Ark. Gazette, 10, Dec. 2, 1971.

50. Mike Trimble, *Confined 6 Days for "Peace Sign," Inmate Says*, Ark. Gazette, A2, Nov. 18, 1971.

51. Leslie Mitchell, *Inmates Testify on Prison*, Ark. Democrat, 1, Nov. 16, 1971; Martin Kirby, *Bumpers Defends Prisons*, Ark. Democrat, 1, Nov. 19, 1971; *Prisoner Says Religious Rights Were Violated*, Ark. Democrat, A11, Nov. 17, 1971; Kathy Gosnell, *Hutto Takes Stand to Defend Prisons, Deny Mistreatment Charges*, Pine Bluff Com., Dec. 2, 1971, Rockefeller, IV, Box 254, File 8.

52. Mike Trimble, *Cummins Uses Cold "Quiet Cells," Inmates Say*, Ark. Gazette, 5, Nov. 17, 1971; *Progress Made at Prisons Told Before Hearing*, Camden News, 1, Nov. 17, 1971; Leslie Mitchell, *Tucker Inmate Tells US Court of Beatings*, Ark. Gazette, A6, Nov. 18, 1971; *Assistant at Texas Unit Hired to Replace Steed*, Ark. Democrat, 13, June 24, 1971.

53. *Cummins Punishment to Be Modified, Hutto Tells Court Hearing*, Ark. Democrat, 7, Dec. 2, 1971; United Press International, *Hutto Confirms Chaplain Resigns*, Ark. Gazette, A10, Nov. 20, 1971; *Cooley Pleads for Inmates*, Ark. Democrat, A3, Dec. 7, 1971.

54. Leslie Mitchell, *Tucker Inmate Tells US Court of Beatings*; Cruz v. Beto, 405 US 319 (1972).

55. Trimble, *Confined 6 Days for "Peace Sign"*; Mitchell, *Tucker Inmate Tells US Court of Beatings*.

56. *1-Day Prison Sentence of LR Youth, 17, Ends in Death at Cummins*, Ark. Gazette, B1, Dec. 1, 1971; Mike Trimble, *Unconscious Youth Dragged by Prison Guards, Court Told*, Ark. Gazette, A10, Dec. 2, 1970; *"Disgruntled" Man Made Death Report, Hutto Testifies*, Ark. Democrat, A9, Dec. 2, 1971; Mike Trimble, *Ordered to Fire at Feet of Youth, Guard Testifies*, Ark. Gazette, 1, Dec 3, 1971; *Bumpers Hit, Study Urged on Prisons*, Ark. Gazette, B16, Jan. 15, 1972; *Arkansas Easing One-Day Prison Hazing of Youths After Death of a Black Teen-Ager*, NY Times, 83, Dec. 12, 1971.

57. *Disclosures about Life in the "Pea Patch,"* Ark. Gazette, 6, Nov. 26, 1971.

58. Leslie Mitchell, *Penal Farm Called Segregated: Official Admits "Switching" Convicts*, Ark. Democrat, 1, Nov. 19, 1971; Mike Trimble, *Pulaski Penal Farm Inmates Whipped for Discipline, Superintendent Says*, Ark. Gazette, 11, Nov. 20, 1971; Leslie Mitchell, *Judge Tours Penal Farm*, Ark. Democrat, 1, Dec. 10, 1971; Mike Trimble, *One-Legged Inmate Put in Fields, Hearing Told*,

Ark. Gazette, 8, Dec. 10, 1971; *Now the Penal Farms*, Ark. Gazette, 6, Dec. 16, 1971; Mike Trimble, *Conditions at Penal Farm Ruled Unconstitutional*, Ark. Gazette, 1, Dec. 11, 1971.

59. *What Penal Farm Must Do*, Ark. Democrat, 3, Dec. 31, 1971; *Henley Says Pulaski Penal Farm Not Following His Guidelines*, Ark. Democrat, A5, Nov. 30, 1972. In 1974, the judge ordered the facility closed. *County Officials Disobey Order, Plaintiffs Charge*, Ark. Gazette, B1, July 17, 1974.

60. Doug Smith, *Bumpers Disturbed Inmate Spent Month Inside "Quiet Cell,"* Ark. Gazette, 1, Nov. 20, 1971; Remarks of the Court at Conclusion of Hearing, 2–5, *Holt v. Hutto*, No. PB-69-C-24, Dec. 3, 1971, Kaplan, 1, Box 2, Folder 1; Mark Trimble, *Judge Praises Reforms at Prisons, Condemns Intimidation, Retaliation*, Ark. Gazette, 3, Dec. 4, 1971.

61. 1971 Remarks, 6–19; *1-Day Sentences for Youths Defended by Judge*, Ark. Gazette, 3, Dec. 4, 1971; Mike Trimble, *FBI Investigates Death of Steward for Rights Violations*, Ark. Gazette, 15, Jan. 11, 1972. The state settled, paying the family $25,000. *Settlement Is Made in Prisoner's Death*, Ark. Democrat, 5, Mar. 8, 1974.

62. 1971 Remarks, 10–19.

63. Doug Smith, *Bumpers Lists Reform Ideas for 2 Prisons: End of Race Slurs, All Harassment among Demands*, Ark. Gazette, A8, Dec. 10, 1971.

64. Ernest Dumas, *The Prison Issue Just Won't Go Away*, Ark. Gazette, E3, Dec. 5, 1971; *Prison Panel to Get Ideas of Bumpers*, Ark. Gazette, B11, Dec. 8, 1971; Tucker Steinmetz, *Board Orders End to Abuse of Prisoners*, Ark. Gazette, 1, Dec. 13, 1971.

65. *Decrees Issued on Conditions at Prisons*, Ark. Gazette, A3, Dec. 31, 1971; Letter Elijah Coleman, Exec. Dir. of Council on Human Relations, to Gov.'s Office, Dec. 13, 1971, attaching Cummins Prison Farm Preliminary Report, Nov. 18, 1971, Prison Records, Box 2, Folder 11, 1–3.

66. *Inmate Stabbed as State Board Tours Cummins*, Ark. Gazette, A2, Dec. 13, 1971; Tucker Steinmetz, *Parole Decrease, Rise in Arrivals Overcrowd Prisons*, Ark. Gazette, B1, Dec. 16, 1971; *"Near Riot" Revealed at Mississippi Country Penal Farm*, Ark. Gazette, 6, Oct. 21, 1971; *Defendants Ask Dismissal of Suit over Penal Farms*, Ark. Democrat, 6, Oct. 22, 1971; Mike Trimble, *Mississippi County Officials Agree Farm Substandard*, Ark. Gazette, A7, Dec. 16, 1971; *May Trial Set for Challenge on Prison Farm*, Ark. Gazette, 29, Dec. 22, 1971.

CHAPTER 23

1. Excerpted in *Reform Program for the State's Prisons*, Ark. Gazette, 75, Dec. 19, 1971.

2. Holt v. Hutto (*Holt III*), 363 F. Supp. 194, 198 (ED Ark. 1973).

3. *Holt* Docket, 8, Dec. 30, 1971. The judge held hearings in November and December of 1972 and January of 1973. *Holt III*, 198, 216–17.

4. Johnson v. Glick, 481 F.2d 1028, 1030–33 (2d Cir. 1973); Robert Plotkin, *Surviving Justice: Prisoners' Rights to be Free from Physical Assaults*, 23 Clev. St. L. Rev. 387 (1974).

5. Whitley v. Albers, 475 US 312, 314, 319 (1986); Hudson v. McMillian, 503 US 1 (1992); Farmer v. Brennan, 511 US 825 (1994). The Supreme Court later explained that pretrial detainees, protected by the liberty guarantees of the Due Process Clause, did not have to demonstrate subjective intent when force was objectively unreasonable. Kingsley v. Hendrickson, 576 US 389 (2015); Margo Schlanger, *The Constitutional Law of Incarceration, Reconfigured*, 103 Cornell L. Rev. 357 (2018).

6. Finney v. Ark. Bd. of Corr. (*Finney I*), 505 F.2d 194, 200, 215 (8th Cir. 1974).

7. *Holt* Docket, 8, Dec. 30, 1971; *Judge Increases the "Defendants" in Prison Case*, Ark. Democrat, 6, Dec. 30, 1971; Mary L. Parker, *Judicial Intervention in Correctional Institutions: The Arkansas Odyssey*, 345 (PhD diss., Sam Houston State University, 1982), U. Mich. microfiche DA8603308.

8. Martin Kirby, *"Penal Reform Movement" Continues: Visible Changes at Cummins Are Easy to Spot*, Ark. Democrat, A1, Aug. 15, 1971; David Kotok, *Prisons Impress Council*, Ark. Democrat, A7, Sept. 8, 1971; *Legislators Praise Cummins and Hutto*, Ark. Democrat, A8, Sept. 2, 1971; *Hutto Says Penal Reforms to Meet Order*, Ark. Gazette, B22, Oct. 29, 1971; *Arkansas Prisons "Suffering From Neglect," Hutto Says*, Ark. Gazette, 16, Jan. 13, 1972; *Arkansas Prisons Clear the Fields*, Ark. Democrat, A1, Jan. 5, 1972; *Hutto Manages to Make Several Improvements at Prisons During First Year*, Ark. Gazette, A20, July 7, 1972; *Escape Rate Lower Now, Hutto Says*, Ark. Gazette, 8, Aug. 29, 1971; Bill Lancaster, *Progress in Arkansas Prisons: Education for Inmates*, Ark. Gazette, E1, Oct. 8, 1972; *Hutto Appoints Two Officials for Prisons*, Ark. Gazette, A5, July 10, 1971. Carruthers, a graduate of Chicago's Roosevelt University, spent twelve years in the Women's Army Corps and more than a decade in Arkansas. *Warden of Women's Unit Sworn in as Commissioner on Federal Parole Panel*, Ark. Gazette, A4, Dec. 2, 1983.

9. *Youth Claims Cummins "Torture,"* Sentinel-Record, 11, Jan. 16, 1972; *Demotions Set at Tucker, Hutto Reports*, Ark. Gazette, B13, Mar. 15, 1972; *Cummins Inmate Lists Complaints*, Ark. Democrat, A10, July 12, 1972; *Was Starved at Cummins, Inmate Writes*, Ark. Gazette, A5, July 12, 1972; *Investment Bill Could Pay for Session, Bumpers Says*, Ark. Gazette, A14, Jan. 2, 1972; Doug Smith, *1971 Farm Income at State Prison is $1,793,449.46*, Ark. Gazette, 25, Jan. 6, 1972.

10. *Haley Points Out 3 Major Goals of Prison System*, Ark. Democrat, A2, Jan. 19, 1972; Tucker Steinmetz, *Parole Decrease, Rise in Arrivals Overcrowd Prisons*, Ark. Gazette, B1, Dec. 16, 1971; *Crime Commission Approves Funds for Cummins Unit*, Ark. Gazette, A12, Feb. 19, 1972. *Bill Lancaster, Prison Board Chairman Sees Women's Facility as Pressing Need*, Ark. Gazette, A19, Mar. 26, 1972; Martin Kirby, *Schooling for Arkansas Inmates: Hutto Asks for "Nongeographical" District*, Ark. Democrat, A4, Mar. 19, 1972; *1st Annual Cummins Rodeo Set for August by Board*, Ark. Gazette, A3, May 21, 1972; *Inmates Plan for Annual Rodeo*, Pea Pickers Picayune, 1, May 28, 1971; Martin Kirby, *Sanatorium Is Treating Nine from Cummins Prison Farm*, Ark. Democrat, A1, Mar. 16, 1972; *Corrections Panel Backs Firing of Commander for Field Security*, Ark. Democrat, A8, Mar. 17, 1972.

11. Glenn Smith, *Arkansas Prison "Reforms" Given Praise by ABA Chief*, Sentinel-Record, 1, June 2, 1972; *Lawyer Chairman Terms State Prisons "Progressive,"* A3, Ark. Democrat, June 2, 1972; *Prison Budget of $4 Million Gets Approval*, Ark. Gazette, A11, June 25, 1972; *Correction Department Seeks Bigger Budget: New Employees Planned*, Ark. Gazette, B1, Nov. 22, 1972.

12. Letter Philip Kaplan to The Hon. J. Smith Henley, re Holt v. Hutto, 3–4, Dec. 1, 1972, U. Ark. Little Rock (UALR), Kaplan Papers, Series 1, Box 18A, Folder 2.

13. *No Serious Threat for Incumbents*, Ark. Gazette, A6, Oct. 19, 1972; Brenda Tirey, *Bumpers Speaks at Russellville on a Positive Theme*, Ark. Democrat, A8, May 25, 1972.

14. Letter J. Smith Henley to The Hon. Oren Harris and The Honorable Garnett Thomas Eisele, Sept. 28, 1972; J. Smith Henley to Milton Lueken, Asst. Atty. Gen., Oct. 10, 1972, both in Kaplan, 1, Box 18A, Folder 2; J. Smith Henley to Philip Kaplan, re Complaint of Ray Burchell, Nov. 6, 1972, and other complaints, Letters and witness interview sheets, Kaplan, 1, Subseries 1, Box 12, Folders 1 and 2; and Subseries 1.4, Box 10, Folder 1.

15. Rik O'Neal, *Abuse Called "Deliberate": Minister Says Muslim Literature Was Burned at Prison*, Ark. Democrat, 1, Nov. 14, 1972; *Requests Denied Cummins Inmate*, Ark. Gazette, A5, Aug. 17, 1971; Letter Dudley P. Spiller Jr. to Robert Sarver, Oct. 23, 1976, UALR, C. Robert Sarver Papers, Series I, Box 6, File 4; *Testimony on Conditions in Arkansas Prisons to Resume*, Nw. Ark. Times, 8, Dec. 20 1972; *Workers Collapsed, Prison Law Library is Off Limits, Inmate Contends*, Ark. Democrat, 9, Dec. 20, 1972; Bill Husted, *Judge to Rule on State Prison Conditions*, Ark. Democrat, A10, Jan. 11, 1973. *Finney I*, 505 F.2d, 199.

16. Mike Trimble, *Nine Inmates Testify: Hearings on Prisons Recessed Until January*, Ark. Gazette, 31, Dec. 22, 1972; Letter Ervin X Lacy, Acting Coordinator, to A. L. Lockhart, July 19, 1972, Kaplan, 1, Box 12, Folder 1; Petition for Writ of Habeas Corpus, 1–5, Ervin X Lacy, et al. v. Terrel Don Hutto, attached to letter Lacy to Kaplan, Oct. 2, 1972. Kaplan, 1, Box 12, Folder 2.

17. Jerry Dean, *Testimony of Inmates Is Disputed*, Ark. Democrat, 6, Jan 5, 1973; *Allegations of Prisons Are Disputed*, Ark. Gazette, 30, Jan 7, 1973; Bill Husted, *Official Denies Remodeling Homes with Prison Funds*, Ark. Democrat, 5, Jan 10, 1973; *Prison Roommate Policy*, Ark. Democrat, 10, Jan. 9, 1973; *Cummins Officer Fears Race Mixing May Bring Trouble*, Ark. Gazette, 4, Jan 9, 1973.

18. Letter Kaplan to Henley, Kaplan 1, Subseries I, Box 12, Dec. 1, 1972, 1–4.

19. *Correction Panel Seeks Enlargement of Budget, Staff*, Ark. Democrat, A12, Nov. 22, 1972; *Funds to Plan Prison Hospital Are Approved*, Ark. Gazette, 5, Mar. 9, 1973.

20. Editorial, *A Significant Step*, Cummins J., 4, Apr. 1972; Herman Ewing, *A Land Without Prisons?*, Cummins J., 19, June–July 1973.

21. Chuck Dulyea, *Inmate Council*, Cummins J., 33, July–Aug. 1972. A council had existed under Commissioner Sarver. *What Is the Inmate Council*, Pea Pickers Picayune, 2–3, Mar. 29, 1970; Ronny Barber, *Dear Mom: This Is Our Kitchen*, Cummins J., 14–15, Sept. 1972. *Prisons to Ask for Extra $1 Million*,

Cummins J., 13, Sept. 1972; *Hutto Says Attorney to be Employed Soon*, Ark. Democrat, B6, July 4, 1972. *Prisons to Ask for Extra $1 Million*, Cummins J., 13, Sept. 1972; Cummins J., 13–17, Sept. 1972; Robert A. Newcomb, *Law Report*, Cummins J., 9, Nov.–Dec. 1972.

22. Cummins J., 10, 17, Apr. 1972. The Jaycee chapter began in 1971. Cummins J., 15, June 1972; Cummins J., 15, July–Aug. 1972; *Jaycees*, Cummins J., 16, Apr. 1974; Robert J. Trotter, *Stout Walls and Bars Do Not a Prison Make*, Cummins J., 8–12, Sept. 1972.

23. Cummins J., 12, Sept. 1972. A fellowship from Harvard University enabled Jackson to gather prison work songs, which led him to documentary films, photography, and a professorship at SUNY Buffalo. Bruce Jackson, *Prison Folklore*, 78 J. Am. Folklore 317 (1965); Bruce Jackson, *Texas Death Row and the Cummins Prison Farm in Arkansas*, 13 Southern Cultures 112 (2007); Brian Wallis, *Bruce Jackson on the Inside*, Aperture (Spring 2018); Bruce Jackson, *Killing Time: Life in the Arkansas Penitentiary* (Cornell U. Press, 1977); Bruce Jackson, *Inside the Wire: Photographs from Texas and Arkansas Prisons* (U. Tex. Press, 2013). Museums showed his work, including at the Albright-Knox Museum in Buffalo, New York, and in Arkansas. Ellis Widner, *Photos of Cummins a Window into Arkansas History*, Ark. Democrat-Gazette, May 17, 2009; Ellis Widner, *Japanese Internees, Prisoners Subjects of Two Butler Exhibits*, Ark. Democrat-Gazette, Apr. 9, 2017.

24. *Holt III*, 198, 201; Jess Henderson, *Legal Corner*, Cummins J., 4–5, Apr. 1974.

25. Malcolm M. Feeley & Edward L. Rubin, *Judicial Policy Making and the Modern State: How the Courts Reformed America's Prisons* 71 (Cambridge U. Press, 1998); *Holt III*, 216.

26. *Holt III*, 198–99 & n.2.

27. *Holt III*, 199–201, 210, 216.

28. *Holt III*, 200.

29. *Holt III*, 200. A doctor was hired before the opinion was issued. Jerry Dean, *First Full-time Physician Is Hired by State Board of Correction*, Ark. Democrat, A12, Jan. 21, 1973.

30. George Bentley, *2 Officials Admit Prison Health Care "Unsatisfactory,"* Ark. Gazette, 11, Jan 7, 1973; Jerry Dean, *Medical Care in Prisons is Inadequate, Inmates and Officials Agree*, Ark. Democrat, A6, Jan. 14, 1973; *Holt III*, 200.

31. Estelle v. Gamble, 429 US 97, 104 (1976). A few circuits had earlier focused on "deliberate indifference" or "willful refusal" to provide essential treatment. Martinez v. Mancusi, 443 F.2d 921 (2d Cir. 1970), cert. denied, 401 US 983 (1971); Landman v. Royster, 333 F. Supp. 621 (ED Va. 1971), supplemented, 354 F. Supp. 1302 (ED Va. 1973); Collins v. Schoonfield, 344 F. Supp. 257 (D. Md. 1972), supplemented, 363 F. Supp. 1152 (D. Md. 1973).

32. Cates v. Ciccone, 422 F.3d 926, 928 (8th Cir. 1970). Henley was also reversed for dismissing an individual's complaint of permanent eye damage from exposure to tuberculosis; if substantiated, the lack of treatment had "so endanger[ed] the prisoner's physical well-being that his Fourteenth

Amendment right to life [was] violated." Freeman v. Lockhart, 503 F.2d 1016, 1017 (8th Cir. 1974). On remand, with representation by Holt Jr. and Kaplan, Sam Freeman lost; the Eighth Circuit affirmed that the record did not establish "deliberate indifference to serious medical needs." Freeman v. Lockhart, 561 F.2d 728, 730 (8th Cir. 1977).

33. Newman v. Alabama, 349 F. Supp. 278 (MD Ala. 1972), aff'd in part, 503 F.3d 1320 (5th Cir. 1974).

34. *Holt III*, 215, 201.

35. *Holt III*, 212–16.

36. *Holt III*, 201–03.

37. *Holt III*, 202–03; Washington v. Davis, 426 US 229 (1976).

38. *Holt III*, 203–04.

39. Mahzarin R. Banaji & Anthony G. Greenwald, *Blindspot: Hidden Biases of Good People* (Delacorte Press, 2013); *Holt III*, 204.

40. *Holt III*, 204–05.

41. *Holt III*, 217, 205.

42. *Holt III*, 208–09.

43. *Holt* Docket, 10–11, Aug. 13, 1973. Steele Hayes and Jerry T. Jackson, the lawyers Henley enlisted for *Holt I* , had not requested fees; *Holt III*, 217–18.

44. Bill Lancaster, *Prison Abuses Are Alleged by Ex-employe[e]s*, Ark. Gazette, 23, Mar. 22, 1974.

45. Bill Lancaster, *Cummins Inmate Fight at Christmas Revealed During Board Meeting*, Ark. Gazette, 5, Jan. 20, 1974; *Cummins Unrest Causes No Injury*, Sentinel-Record, 5, Jan. 20, 1974. Henley later declined to award damages. Docket Entries, Graves v. Lockhart from Appendix of Opinions, Decrees, Orders, and Pleadings, 19–21, Hutto v. Finney, 437 US 678 (1978). *Nelson Will Ask Council to Probe Prison Agency*, Ark. Gazette, 21, Jan. 11, 1974; *Boren Hires Kaplan to Aid in Campaign*, Ark. Gazette, 37, Jan. 13, 1974; Tom Jordan, *Bumpers Backs Hutto's Work*, Ark. Democrat, 11, Jan. 16, 1974; *Legislative Council Votes to Investigate the Correction Department*, Ark. Democrat, 3, Jan. 19, 1974; Tom Jordan, *Many of 16 Ex-employe[e]s Cite a "Termination List,"* Ark. Democrat, 1, Mar. 3, 1973; *Prison Board to Alter Policy, Rush Reports*, Ark. Gazette, 1, Feb. 11, 1972; *Boren is Disappointed with Probe at Cummins*, Ark. Gazette, B1, Feb. 13, 1974.

46. *Prison Farming Hits $3 Million in Gross Profits*, Ark. Gazette, 3, Feb. 21, 1974.

47. Tom Jordan, *Ex-guard Tells of "Kill" Request*, Ark. Democrat, 3, Mar. 22, 1974; *Legislative Panel Schedules Hearing for Prison Employe[e]s*, Ark. Gazette, A25, Mar. 15, 1974; *Correction Agency Gets Diagnostic Center Funds*, Ark. Gazette, A5, June 6, 1974.

48. Leslie Mitchell, *Guards, Inmates Asked to Keep Unit Peaceful*, Ark. Gazette, B7, July 18, 1974; Dudley P. Spiller, *After Decision: Implementation of Judicial Decrees in Correctional Settings: A Case Study of* Holt v. Sarver *(Draft Report)*, Oct. 23, 1976, UALR Center for History and Culture, C. Robert Sarver Papers, Series I, Box 6, File 4, 49–69.

CHAPTER 24

1. *I Pray of Thee, Just Let Me Flee*, Ark. Democrat, A1, Sept. 15, 1972. Public records indicate that Finney was white.
2. Finney v. Ark. Bd. of Corr. (*Finney I*), 505 F.2d 194, 200 (8th Cir. 1974).
3. Leslie Mitchell, *Henley Overruled: Changes Ordered in Prison System, Quick Action Is Necessary State Is Told*, Ark. Gazette, 1, Oct. 12, 1974; *Finney I*, 200–01, 210–15.
4. *Finney I*, 200–01.
5. Holt v. Sarver (*Holt II*), 309 F. Supp. 362, 379 (ED Ark. 1970); William B. Bryant, Substantive Rights of the Prisoner, *US DOJ, Proceedings of the National Conference on Corrections, Williamsburg, Va., Dec. 5–8, 1971*, 42–43; "The purpose of involuntary hospitalization for treatment purposes is treatment and not mere custodial care or punishment." Wyatt v. Stickney, 325 F. Supp. 781, 784 (MD Ala. 1971); 344 F. Supp. 387 (MD Ala. 1972); Pugh v. Locke, 406 F. Supp. 318, 330 (MD Ala. 1976), citing *Holt II*.
6. *Finney I*, 208–09, quoting Jackson v. Indiana, 406 US 715, 717–18, 738 (1972); 208, discussing Procunier v. Martinez, 416 US 396, 412–13 (1974).
7. *Finney I*, 201–02; Ark. Division of Correction, Board Report 1 (April 2024).
8. *Finney I*, 202–04; *Thomas Wortham, Jan. 12, 1927–Jan. 20, 2015*, Smith Family Funeral Homes, obituaries.
9. *Finney I*, 204–06.
10. *Finney I*, 208–10; Wolff v. McDonnell, 418 US 539 (1974), aff'g in part, rev'g in part McDonnell v. Wolff, 483 F.2d 1059 (8th Cir. 1973).
11. *Finney I*, 207–08 n.9.
12. *Finney I*, 211–15.
13. Letter and draft, Dudley P. Spiller Jr. to Robert Sarver, Oct. 23, 1976, U. Ark. Little Rock (UALR), C. Robert Sarver Papers, Series I, Box 6, File 4. The quote is from Spiller's 1976 Draft, ii, and v, and was removed before publication. Coauthored by M. Kay Harris, the book was supported by the National Institute of Law Enforcement and Criminal Justice, the Law Enforcement Assistance Administration, and the US DOJ. *After Decision: Implementation of Correctional Decrees in Correctional Settings*, vii (Oct. 1977). The project looked at "four recent, significant correctional law cases": the Arkansas litigation, decisions on Jefferson and at Orleans Parish Jails in Louisiana, and another related to the Baltimore City Jail. Spiller, an LSU law graduate, had appeared before Judge Eisele to challenge treatment of juveniles in Pulaski County. Jerry Dean, *Juvenile Center Lawsuit*, Ark. Democrat, 10, Mar. 10, 1973. Harris, a University of Chicago social work school graduate, served as Assistant Director of the ABA's Resource Center on Correctional Law and Legal Services. M. Kay Harris, *Disquisition on the Need for a New Model of Criminal Sanctioning Systems*, 77 W. Va. L. Rev. 263 (1975). Many other analyses of the impact of prison litigation followed. Susan Strum, *The Legacy and Future of Corrections Litigation*, 142 U. Penn. L. Rev. 639 (1993).

14. *After Decision*, 33, 68–69; Spiller 1976 Draft, i–ii, 33–34.
15. *After Decision*, 113; Spiller 1976 Draft, i–ii, 32, 52–59, 67–76.
16. Bill Husted, *Prison Rehearing Sought: Board Admits Only Overcrowding*, Ark. Democrat, 1, Oct. 19, 1974; ADC, Inmate Handbook, 3, 12–14, 23–30 (Ark. State Library, 4th rev. ed. Jan. 1975).
17. David Terrell, *Prison Inmate Tells of Beatings*, Ark. Democrat, A10, Mar. 27, 1975; David Terrell, *Tucker Inmate Testifies of Homosexual Assaults*, Ark. Democrat, B8, Mar. 26, 1975; Order Holt v. Hutto, *Holt* Docket 12, (Apr. 17, 1975). Twelve cases, some seeking monetary damages, were listed. Order of Consolidation and Reference of the District Court in Holt v. Hutto and related cases, Apr. 15, 1975, *Hutto v. Finney*, Appendix of Opinions, Decrees, Orders, and Pleadings, 135–39.
18. Orders of Apr. 17, July 11, and Oct. 29, 1975, *Holt* Docket, 12–13; Finney v. Hutto, 410 F. Supp. 251, 255 (ED Ark. 1976).
19. Editorial, *Many Kinds of Violence*, Ark. Democrat, A4, Oct. 17, 1975; *Inmate at Tucker Found Hanged in Isolation Cell*, Sentinel-Record, 3, Feb. 21, 1976; *Pryor Predicts Prison Will Open by Deadline*, Ark. Democrat, A7, Feb. 20, 1976; Order of Feb. 19, 1976, and Memorandum, *Holt* Docket, 13; *Finney*, 254.
20. *Finney*, 410 F. Supp., 264.
21. *Finney*, 410 F. Supp., 254, citing Kelly v. Brewer, 525 F.2d 394 (8th Cir. 1975).
22. *Finney*, 410 F. Supp., 257, 263–65, 271–72.
23. *Finney I*, 201; *Finney*, 410 F. Supp., 254–57.
24. *Finney*, 410 F. Supp., 258.
25. *Finney*, 410 F. Supp., 276.
26. *Finney*, 410 F. Supp., 274–76.
27. *Finney*, 410 F. Supp., 276–80.
28. *Finney*, 410 F. Supp., 276–78.
29. *Finney*, 410 F. Supp., 277–81.
30. *Finney*, 410 F. Supp., 278.
31. *Finney*, 410 F. Supp., 272.
32. *Finney*, 410 F. Supp., 263, 272. The habeas cases involved petitioners, Maurice Sanford and Jim Johnson, who were also plaintiffs in *Holt II*. Bumgarner v. Lockhart, 361 F. Supp. 829 (ED Ark. 1973); Sanford v. Hutto, 394 F. Supp. 1278, 1279 (ED Ark. 1975), aff'd, 523 F.2d 1383 (8th Cir. 1975).
33. *Finney*, 410 F. Supp., 258–60.
34. Thereafter, lower court judges held that the lack of parity for women and men prisoners in Michigan and Kentucky was unconstitutional. Glover v. Johnson, 478 F. Supp. 1075 (ED Mich. 1979), modified, 659 F. Supp. 621 (ED Mich. 1987), vacated, 855 F.2d 277 (6th Cir. 1988), remanded to 721 F. Supp. 808 (ED Mich. 1989); Canterino v. Wilson, 546 F. Supp. 174 (WD Ky. 1982), rev'd, 869 F.2d 948 (6th Cir. 1989).
35. *Finney*, 410 F. Supp., 262, 269–70; *Board Backs Creation of District*, Ark. Gazette, C6, Dec. 17, 1972; *His Headache Is No Excuse Prisoner Told*, Ark. Gazette, A8, June 21, 1974; Rutherford v. Hutto, 377 F. Supp. 268, 271 (ED Ark. 1974).
36. *Finney*, 410 F. Supp., 265, 270, 280–81.

37. *Finney*, 410 F. Supp., 255, 266–69.
38. *Finney*, 410 F. Supp., 272.
39. *Finney*, 410 F. Supp., 284.
40. Clayton Act § 4 (1914), codified at 15 USC § 15 (2018); Armand Derfner, *Background and Origin of the Civil Rights Attorney's Fee Awards Act of 1976*, 37 Urb. Lawyer 653, 654 (2005); 42 USC § 2000a-3b (2018); 42 USC § 2000e-5k (2018); Judith Resnik, *Money Matters: Judicial Market Interventions Creating Subsidies and Awarding Fees and Costs in Individual and Aggregate Litigation*, 148 U. Penn. L. Rev. 2119 (2000); Sean Farhang, *The Litigation State: Public Regulation and Private Lawsuits in the US*, 59 (Princeton U. Press, 2010).
41. Newman v. Piggie Park Enterprises, Inc., 390 US 400, 402 (1968); Edelman v. Jordan, 415 US 651, 667 (1974); *Finney*, 283.
42. Wilderness Soc. v. Morton, 479 F.2d 842, 891–93 (DC Cir. 1973) (en banc); 495 F.2d 1026, 1032 (DC Cir. 1974) (en banc); Alyeska Pipeline Serv. Co. v. Wilderness Soc., 421 US 240, 259 (1975).
43. *Finney*, 410 F. Supp., 269, 283–85.
44. *Finney*, 410 F. Supp., 282, 285–86. By then, Phil McMath had joined Holt Jr. and Kaplan; *Texan Gets Prison Post in Arkansas*, Corpus Christie, Caller-Times, A8, May 16, 1971.
45. Motion to Vacate and Alter the Judgment of Mar. 19, 1976, *Holt* Docket, 15, filed Mar. 29, 1976; Clarifying Memorandum Opinion, *Holt* Docket, 13–14, Apr. 2, 1976, both in Hutto v. Finney Sup. Ct. App., 188–93, 232–34.
46. Clarifying Memorandum, 2–4.
47. Leslie Mitchell, *Henley Orders Probe of Report Inmates Beaten*, Ark. Gazette, B1, May 13, 1976; Memorandum Opinion, 4–5, Graves v. Lockhart, PB-74-C-107, Sept. 29, 1977, in Hutto v. Finney Sup. Ct. App., 198–204.
48. Memorandum Opinion, Sept. 29, 1977, 4–5; Answers to Interrogatories Propounded to Defendants, 3–4, *Graves v. Lockhart*, Mar. 29, 1976; Defendants' Response to Request for Admission of Fact, 1–2, *Graves v. Lockhart*, June 14, 1974, in Hutto v. Finney Sup. Ct. App., 222–24; 217–18.

CHAPTER 25

1. A. L. May, *Management, Money Part of Prisons' Problem, Hutto Says*, Ark. Democrat, A12, Oct. 28, 1976.
2. Marvin E. Frankel, *Criminal Sentences: Law Without Order* (Hill & Wang, 1973); Dennis Curtis, Pierce O'Donnell & Michael Churgin, *Toward a Just and Effective Sentencing System: Agenda for Legislative Reform* (Praeger, 1977).
3. Stone v. Powell, 428 US 465 (1976); Rhodes v. Chapman, 452 US 337 (1981).
4. Richard Harnsberger, Roman L. Hruska & Richard G. Kopf, *Dedication* [to Donald Roe Ross], 66 Neb. L. Rev. 627 (1987); Martin v. White, 742 F.2d 469, 472–73 (8th Cir. 1984).
5. Finney v. Hutto (*Finney II*), 548 F.2d 740, 741–42 (8th Cir. 1977); *Award Upheld for Attorneys in Prison Suit*, Ark. Gazette, A4, Jan. 7, 1977. Thereafter Congress made Section 1988 applicable to lawsuits enforcing the Religious

Freedom Restoration Act of 1993 and the Religious Land Use and Institutionalized Person Act of 2000, on which prisoners can rely. The Court
also narrowed Section 1988's reach by concluding that plaintiffs had to
prevail through a court ruling as contrasted with being a "catalyst" for a
settlement. Buckhannon Bd. & Care Home Inc. v. West Virginia Dept. of
Health & Human Resources, 532 US 598 (2001). In 1996, Congress limited
prisoner lawyers' hourly rate to no more than 150 percent of what Congress
provided for federally appointed criminal defense lawyers. Prison Litigation Reform Act, 42 USC § 1997e(d). In 2018, the Court ruled judges had to
enforce a provision that the first 25 percent of fees be paid from damages
awarded to the prisoner. Murphy v. Smith, 583 US 220 (2018).

6. *Finney II*, 742–43, citing Fitzpatrick v. Bitzer, 427 US 445, 457 (1976); Fair-
mont Creamery Co. v. Minnesota, 275 US 70, 77 (1927); Johnson v. Georgia
Highway Express, Inc., 488 F.2d 714, 717–19 (5th Cir. 1974); Entry of Notice,
Holt Docket, Apr. 26, 1977, 16.

7. Brenda Tirey, *Three Young "Names" Vie for Attorney Generalship*, Ark. Democrat, A14, May 23, 1976; Mark Oswald, *Hutto Quits Position as Correction
Chief*, Ark. Democrat, A1, Sept. 24, 1976.

8. *Bill to Expand Prison Assured, Munson Declares*, Ark. Gazette, A3, May 1,
1976; Wayne Jordan, *Panels Resolve to Tighten Up "Good-Time" Law*, Ark. Gazette, B1, May 6, 1976; Ernest Dumas, *Toughening of Laws for Parole Endorsed
by Legislative Panels*, Ark. Gazette, A2, June 11, 1976; Diane D. Blair, *The Big
Three of Late Twentieth-Century Arkansas Politics: Dale Bumpers, Bill Clinton,
and David Pryor*, 54 Ark. Hist. Q. 53 (1995).

9. *Put "Safe" Inmates in Work Centers, Committee Is Told*, Ark. Gazette, A10,
Sept. 24, 1976; *Pay $50,000 for Sarver, Hutto Pleads Before ALC*, Ark. Gazette,
B1, Oct. 28, 1976; Mark Oswald, *Prison Head May be Hard to Find*, Ark. Dem-
ocrat, A8, Oct. 29, 1976.

10. *Housing No. 1 of Problems Facing Prison*, Ark. Gazette, A21, Mar. 14, 1976.

11. *Pryor: Prisons Lack Needed Funds*, Ark. Democrat, 1, Feb. 25, 1976; *Housing
No. 1 of Problems Facing Prison*, A21; Carol Griffee, *Legislators Awed by Costs
on Jails, Seek "Imperatives,"* Ark. Gazette, A3, Apr. 30, 1976.

12. Editorial, *Crime Consensus*, Ark. Democrat, A14, Jan. 23, 1977.

13. *State Senate Approves New Parole Bill, 34–1*, Sentinel-Record, 5, Jan. 27, 1977.

14. *Limit is Placed on Population in State Prisons*, Ark. Gazette, A2, Feb. 27, 1977;
Bill Clinton Promises New Prison Plan, Camden News, 9, Apr. 11, 1977; A. L.
May, *Officials Devise Plan to End Prison Overcrowding*, Ark. Democrat, A12,
Apr. 13, 1977; A. L. May, *Pryor: County Work Release Centers Can Aid Jail Crisis*,
Ark. Democrat, A12, May 12, 1977; Eric Black, *Inmates Have Right to Serve
Time in Prison, Lawyers Agree*, Ark. Gazette, 1, June 1, 1977; Bill Simmons,
Prison or Freedom: Hearing Focuses on Convicts' Rights, Ark. Democrat, 8,
June 8, 1977; Janet Kolodzy, *Prison Problems Further Complicated by Hospi-
tal Board*, Ark. Democrat, 8, Sept. 30, 1978. A decade thereafter, Governor
Clinton again proposed "steps to reduce prison crowding"—including early

releases for first offenders and building. Bill Simmons, *Clinton Proposes Steps to Reduce Prison Crowding*, Baxter Bull., B1, June 2, 1989.

15. ADC Annual Report 1977, Arkansas State Library, CR1.3, 16, 21.

16. 1977 Arkansas Prison Study Commission Report, U. Ark. Little Rock (UALR), Center for Arkansas History and Culture, Kaplan Papers, Series 1, Subseries 10, Box 25, Folder 7, 18, 33, 77. Unless otherwise noted, all Kaplan archival material are from Series 1.

17. A. L. May, *Pryor Tours Prisons to Check Conditions*, Ark. Democrat, 1, Apr. 21, 1977; Bill Simmons, *Prison Study Commission Approves Report*, Ark. Democrat, A10, Mar. 1, 1978; David Pryor, *A Pryor Commitment: The Autobiography of David Pryor*, 124, 148, 233 (Butler Ctr. Arkansas Studies, 2008).

18. *Pryor Appoints 15 For Prison Study*, Courier News, 9, Apr. 21, 1977; *Former Inmate Is On Prison Study Committee*, Camden News, 2, Apr. 21, 1977; *Corrections Department Will Draw Up 5–10 Year Master Plans, Mabry Says*, Courier News, 8, Mar. 28, 1977; *Board of Correction Adopts Plan for Prisons*, Camden News, 20, Oct. 27, 1977; Brenda Tirey, *Correction Board Approves Outline for 10-year Plan*, Ark. Gazette, A10, Oct. 27, 1977.

19. 1977 Arkansas Prison Study Commission, Preface, 2–18.

20. A. L. May, *Correction Department Gets Criticism, Advice*, Ark. Democrat, A13, Oct. 19, 1977; 1977 Arkansas Prison Study Commission, 10–23, 33.

21. 1977 Arkansas Prison Study Commission, 36–38, 47–51, 77–78.

22. 1977 Arkansas Prison Study Commission, 57; *2 Prison Officials Defend "Hoe Squads,"* Hope Star, 14, Nov. 21, 1977.

23. 1977 Arkansas Prison Study Commission, 85; Letter Judge Eisele to Philip Kaplan, Jack Holt Jr. & Phil McMath Re: Finney v. Hutto, June 14, 1977, Kaplan, 1, Subseries 1.6, Box 18A, Folder 4. The last order from Judge Henley on the *Holt* docket was dated Sept. 24, 1976.

24. *Lack of Due Process at Prison Affirmed*, Ark. Democrat, A21, May 28, 1978.

25. Finney v. Mabry, 455 F. Supp. 756, 777 (ED Ark. 1978).

26. John McAnulty, *Prison Officials Stunned by Ruling*, Ark. Democrat, B10, Feb. 18, 1979.

27. Gary Delsohn, *Prison Farm Fight Continues*, Ark. Democrat, A3, Jan. 8, 1978; *Pryor Says Good Warning Was Given*, Sentinel-Record, 3, June 9, 1977; Wayne Jordan, *Inmate's Death in Escape Raises Questions for Jury*, Ark. Gazette, 1, Dec. 18, 1977; Finney v. Mabry, Amendment to Third Consolidated Amended Substituted Complaint, *Holt* Docket, 19 (Jan. 10, 1978).

28. Gary Delsohn, *Abused, Beaten in Prison, Cummins Inmates Testify*, Ark. Democrat, 1, Jan. 10, 1978. Hearings took place that month; most of the prisoner evidence was in by February 2, 1978; the state presented evidence in April. *Holt* Docket, 20–21; *Eisele plans 1½-day Meet on Inmate Case*, A13, Apr. 6, 1978.

29. *Finney*, 455 F. Supp., 758–65, 777–78.

30. Transcript, Oral Argument, 24, Hutto v. Finney, 437 US 678 (1978), No. 76–1660.

31. Memorandum Justice Blackmun to Justice Stevens re No. 76–1660 Hutto v. Finney, June 15, 1978, Library of Congress, John Paul Stevens Papers, Box 89, Folder 4, 25. Justice Stevens, who retired from the Court in 2010, died in 2019; his papers until 1983 became public in October 2020, with later terms released thereafter. Blackmun's papers became available in March 4, 2004. *Papers of Supreme Court Justice Harry A. Blackmun Opened for Research at Library of Congress*, Library of Congress (Mar. 4, 2004).

32. Jane Blotzer, *Arkansas Loses 2 Cases*, Ark. Democrat, 1, June 23, 1978.

33. Petition for Writ of Certiorari, 1977 WL 189244; *State Attorney Before High Court*, Ark. Democrat, 1, Feb. 21, 1978; Tom Hamburger, *Legal Fees of Inmates Debated*, Ark. Gazette, 1, Feb. 22, 1978. Brief of the State of California as Amicus Curiae Supporting Petitioners, 3, 1977 WL 189243; Brief of the State of Iowa as Amicus Curiae Supporting Petitioners, 7, 1977 WL 205329; Brief of the State of Mississippi as Amicus Curiae Supporting Petitioners, 14, 1977 WL 189241; Brief of the Commonwealth of Pennsylvania as Amicus Curiae Supporting Petitioners, 12, 1977 WL 189242. California noted it employed more than 130,000 people and was obliged to defend them; attorney fee awards, even in small numbers, would have "direct and significant impact" on state finances. Texas reported it had been "assessed over $180,000 in attorneys' fees," and attached orders from three district court judges. Brief of the State of Texas as Amicus Curiae, 5 and Appendix C, 1977 WL 189245. After the Court's *Hutto* decision, the Fifth Circuit upheld the fee award, Guajardo v. Estelle, 580 F.2d 748 (5th Cir. 1978); Cruz v. Beto, 603 F.2d 1178 (5th Cir. 1979). Brief for the United States as Amicus Curiae, 1978 WL 206587; Brief for Lawyers' Committee for Civil Rights Under Law as Amicus Curiae, 1978 WL 206588; Brief for the American Civil Liberties Union, et al., 1977 WL 189240, all briefs from *Hutto*.

34. Jan. 13, 1978, Conference, Motion to Dismiss Writ as Improvidently Granted, 1–2, citing Ark. Act 543 of 1977; Dec. 2, 1977, Conference, Motion to Dispense with Printing Appendix both in Stevens Papers, Box 89, Folder 8, 188–89.

35. Hutto v. Finney, Stevens Memo, Stevens Papers, Box 89, Folder 4, 25. Summer List, Sheet 2, 1, 7. Certiorari was granted on Oct. 17, 1977. Handwritten was "grant" with initials of Rehnquist, Powell, White, and Burger; under "deny" were Stevens, Blackmun, Marshall, Stewart and Brennan.

36. *Big Change in Prisons: Punish-Not Reform*, US News & World Report, 1, Aug. 26, 1975. A law clerk signing SAB advised Justice Stevens that the lower courts were "probably wrong." SAB to Justice Stevens re Hutto v. Finney, undated, with hand note, Oct. 14, 1977, 2–4. SAB's Supplemental memo argued for reversal. SAB to Justice Stevens on Hutto v. Finney, 1–3, Stevens Papers, Box 89, Folder 8, 184–85. Stuart A. Baker, who clerked for Justice Stevens during that term, later served in the Administration of George W. Bush as Under Secretary for Policy in the Department of Homeland Security. Justice Blackmun's law clerk Keith Ellison wrote a long memorandum questioning the rehabilitation rationale. Noting that

lower courts had "intimated that a rehabilitation purpose was necessary to justify punitive isolation beyond a certain period of time," the memo found "no support for such a view in any of this Court's precedents interpreting the cruel and unusual punishment clause." Blackmun Clerk Memo, Feb. 14, 1978, Library of Congress, 31. He noted that Justice Blackmun could affirm the merits without agreeing about rehabilitation. Ellison later became a federal district court judge in Texas and ruled on several cases involving prisoners, including requiring protection from dangerously overheated jails and in 2020 from the risk of COVID, later overturned on appeal. See, e.g., Cole v. Collier, No. 4:14-cv-1698, 2018 WL 2766028 (SD Tex 2018); Valentine v. Collier, 455 F. Supp. 3d 308 (SD Tex. 2020), and its subsequent history.

37. *Hutto*, 437 US, 681 & n.3; Blackmun, Memorandum to the Conference, June 14, 1978, Stevens Papers, Box 89, Folder 4, 2; Blackmun to Stevens, June 15, 1978.
38. *Hutto*, 681–83 & n.3–5, 8.
39. *Hutto*, 683–85.
40. *Hutto*, 686 n.8.
41. *Hutto*, 711.
42. *Hutto*, 685, quoting Estelle v. Gamble, 429 US 97, 102 (1976); 687; Claudia Angelos & James B. Jacobs, *Prison Overcrowding and the Law*, 478 Annals Am. Acad. Pol. & Soc. Sci. 100 (1985).
43. *Finney*, 410 F. Supp., 277.
44. *Hutto*, 687, 686 n.8.
45. *Hutto*, 686–87, n.8.
46. Brief for Petitioners, 20, *Hutto*, 1977 WL 189239, citing Newton v. Alabama, 559 F.2d 283, 291 (5th Cir. 1977).
47. Milliken v. Bradley, 418 US 717, 725, 733–35 (1974); Owen M. Fiss, *The Supreme Court, 1978 Term, Foreword: The Forms of Justice*, 93 Harv. L. Rev. 1, 49–50 (1979).
48. *Hutto*, 711–14; Sandin v. Conner, 515 US 472, 478 (1995).
49. *Hutto*, 687–88.
50. *Hutto*, 690–97. The Court had affirmed its power to charge costs to states in *Fairmont Creamery*, 77. The Court had found that Minnesota's regulation of butter fat pricing violated the Creamery's liberty of contract that the Fourteenth Amendment protected. After *Hutto*, Congress understood the need for symmetry, in that states would be liable for attorneys' fees when the federal government was not. In 1980, Congress authorized fee-shifting against the US government in the Equal Access to Justice Act (EAJA), waiving federal sovereign immunity for fees to prevailing parties in some civil litigation. Pub. L. No. 96–481, 94 Stat. 2325 (1980), codified at 5 USC § 504, 28 USC § 2412d; Gregory C. Sisk, *The Essentials of the Equal Access to Justice Act: Court Awards of Attorney's Fees for Unreasonable Government Conduct (Part One)*, 55 La. L. Rev. 217, 220 (1994).
51. *Hutto*, 704–05.

52. Memorandum William Brennan to Lewis Powell, June 13, 1978, 1–2, Stevens Papers, Box 89, Folder 6, 73; *Hutto*, 704, 710, 716; Will v. Michigan Dept. of State Police, 491 US 58, 71 (1989); Atascadero State Hosp. v. Scanlon, 473 US 234 (1985); Seminole Tribe of Fla. v. Florida, 517 US 44 (1996); Torres v. Tex. Dept. of Pub. Safety, 597 US 580 (2022).

53. Janet Kolodzy, *Legislators Approve Plan on Prison Suit*, Ark. Democrat, A10, Sept. 2, 1978.

54. *Prison Panel Hears Consent Decree*, Ark. Democrat, A10, Aug. 8, 1978.

55. Letter Stanley A. Bass, LDF to Kaplan, Jan. 27, 1978, Kaplan, 1, Box 18A, Folder 5, 3–4.

56. *Prison Decree Not Accepted, Attorneys Say*, Ark. Gazette, 5, Sept. 1, 1978; *Eisele Backs Coordinator Concept*, Ark. Democrat, Sept. 6, 1978, B7; Susan Sturm, Note, *Mastering Intervention in Prisons*, 88 Yale L. J. 1062 (1979); Allan F. Breed, *Special Masters Ease Prison Reform*, 41 Corrections Today, 16 (1979); Tirey, *ALC Supports Proposal to End Inmates Suit*, Ark. Gazette, 1, Sept. 2, 1978; Stephen LaPlante, *An Alternative to the Special Master: Institutional Planning with a Compliance Coordinator*, delivered for a workshop at the 110th Congress of the American Correctional Association, Aug. 17–21, 1980, Kaplan, 1, Box 19A, Folder 11.

57. In addition to this photograph from the Arkansas Gazette, the Arkansas Democrat ran a similar photograph by Gary Fountain, under the caption "Sign Decree," A1, Oct. 6, 1978.

58. Finney v. Mabry, 458 F. Supp. 720, 721 (ED Ark. 1978).

59. *Finney*, 458 F. Supp., 721–26; Finney 1978 Consent Decree, para. IV at 1, 11–12, Kaplan, Series 5, Box 7A, Folder 6; Steele Hays, *State's Board of Correction Backs Decree*, Ark. Gazette, 1, Aug. 27, 1978; *State May be Assuming Control of Prison System From Court*, Sentinel-Record, 2, Sept. 7, 1978; Letter Eisele to Honorable George N Leighton, US District Judge, ND Ill., Nov. 15, 1978, UALR, Center for Arkansas History and Culture, Eisele Papers, Box 4, Folder 14.

60. *Finney*, 458 F. Supp., 721–23.

61. *Finney*, 458 F. Supp., 724; Janet Kolodzy, *Inmates Rights Case Ends After 10 Years of Litigation*, Ark. Democrat, A10, Oct. 5, 1978.

62. *Finney*, 458 F. Supp., 725; Addendum to Consent Decree of Feb. 2, 1979; Addendum to Consent Decree of June 7, 1980, both in Kaplan, 1, Subseries 2, Box 7A, Folder 6, 71, 73 and Folder 5, 57.

63. Associated Press, *Law May Complicate Prison Reform*, Ark. Democrat, A18, May 25, 1980.

64. Petition for Attorneys' Fees, Philip E. Kaplan Hours and Expenses, Affidavit in Support of Application for Award of Attorneys' Fees, Oct. 26, 1978; Jack Holt Jr. Hours and Expenses; Affidavit of Eric Schnapper, assistant counsel of the NAACP Legal Defense and Educational Fund, Sept. 12, 1978, Kaplan, 1, Subseries 2, Box 7A, Folder 5, 31–45; Brief in Opposition to Petition for Award of Attorneys' Fees, filed Nov. 27, 1978, Memorandum and Order, Mar. 5, 1979, *Finney*, Kaplan, 1, Subseries 2, Box 7A, Folder 5, 48, 68–71.

CHAPTER 26

1. Janet Kolodzy, *Legislators Approve Plan on Prison Suit*, Ark. Democrat, A10, Sept. 2, 1978.
2. Bill Grady, *New Prisons No Solution: Ex-Warden*, Chi. Tribune, 4, Dec. 17, 1980.
3. *Big Change in Prisons: Punish-Not Reform*, US News & World Report, 1, Aug. 26, 1975.
4. Stephen LaPlante, Second Report of the Prison Compliance Coordinator on the Defendants' State of Compliance, 6, Finney v. Mabry, No. PB-69-C-24, June 29, 1979, Arkansas State Library, Ark Doc CR 178.7, R 4/No. 2d Copy 1.
5. *Californian Selected to Check Compliance with Prison Decree*, Ark. Gazette, A10, Nov. 8, 1978; John Brummett, *Court-Appointed State Prison Ombudsman Retains His Feel for Involvement*, Ark. Gazette, A4, Mar. 12, 1979; Stephen LaPlante, *An Alternative to the Special Master: Institutional Planning with a Compliance Coordinator*, delivered for a workshop at the 110th ACA Congress, Aug. 17–21, 1980, U. Ark. Little Rock (UALR), Kaplan Papers, Series 1, Box 19A, Folder 11.
6. John McAnulty, *Prison Conditions Faulted*, Ark. Democrat, A1, July 10, 1979; George Wells, *Parts of LaPlante Compliance Reports Admitted*, Ark. Gazette, A10, Aug. 13, 1981.
7. ADC, 1979 Annual Report, 13, 30, Ark. Doc CR 1.3: 979 Copy 1; Wayne Jordan, *Charges Excessive Force Used Overshadow Board's Tour of Wrightsville*, Ark. Gazette, A7, Mar. 1, 1979; James R. Taylor, *Prison Violated Order of Court, Report Asserts*, Ark. Democrat, A11, Apr. 5, 1979; *Lawyer Dissatisfied, Will Release Report on Cummins Beatings*, Ark. Gazette, A4, Apr. 4, 1979; James R. Taylor, *Official Named in Beatings: Lockhart Allegedly Struck Prisoner*, Ark. Democrat, 1, Mar. 8, 1979.
8. Letter LaPlante to Philip Kaplan & Richard Earl Griffin, Re: Clarification and Additions to the First Compliance Report, Apr. 3, 1979, 116; First Report of the Prison Compliance Coordinator on the Defendants' State of Compliance, Mar. 23, 1979, 116 Ark Doc CR. 178.7 R.4/No. 1st Copy 1; Taylor, *Prison Violated Order of Court, Report Asserts*; Jerry Dean, *Griffin Says Mabry Resignation Mutual Decision*, Ark. Democrat, A3, Mar. 2, 1979; *Griffin Defends Board's Vote on Lockhart*, Ark. Gazette, A5, Apr. 5, 1979.
9. McAnulty, *Prison Conditions Faulted*. Larry Ault, *Eisele Orders Work Done at Cummins Unit*, Ark. Democrat, 11, Sept. 29, 1981; *LaPlante Faults Mental Facilities*, Ark. Democrat, B10, Sept. 27, 1979; Stephen LaPlante, Third Report, Supplementary Report of the Prison Compliance Coordinator on the Departments' State of Compliance Regarding Mental Health Care, 1–3, 20, Aug. 10, 1979, Ark Doc CR 178.8, S 9, Copy 1.
10. *New Facility Will Get 170 Inmates*, Ark. Gazette, A12, Sept. 7, 1979; LaPlante, Third Report of the Prison Compliance Coordinator on the Defendants' State of Compliance, Vol. 1, 2, June 20, 1980, Ark Doc CR 178.7, R 4/No. 3d v. 1, Copy 1.
11. 1980 Third Report, I, 2–4, 23, 87; Mary L. Parker, *Judicial Intervention in Correctional Institutions: The Arkansas Odyssey*, 256–67 (PhD diss., Sam Houston State University, 1982), U. Mich. microfiche DA8603308.

12. 1980 Third Report, I, 22–24, 88, 94–96, 103–15, 172, 204.
13. 1980 Third Report, II, 262–66.
14. LaPlante, *An Alternative to the Special Master*, 7–11.
15. Robert D. Reid, *A Matter of Trust*, Southern Illinoisan, 4, Apr. 13, 1971.
16. John McAnulty, *Eisele Ruling Allows LaPlante Contract Cutoff*, Ark. Democrat, B2, Mar. 31, 1981.
17. John McAnulty, *Lack of Funds Spurred Resignation, Housewright Testifies*, Ark. Democrat, A23, Aug. 26, 1981.
18. Robert W. Sink, *A Man Makes His Own Decisions: Reality is Keystone to Prison Operations*, Edwardsville Intelligencer, 2, Apr. 24, 1971; Dorothy Collin, *Vienna—It's a Jewel among Prisons*, Chi. Tribune, 11, July 17, 1979; James R. Taylor, *Board Names Prison Head*, Ark. Democrat, 1, Aug. 6, 1979; James R. Taylor, *Prison Director Faces Problems in Hiring Guards*, Ark. Democrat, B2, Aug. 9, 1979; James R. Taylor, *Housewright Sees Challenge in Arkansas*, Ark. Democrat, A10, Aug. 30, 1979; John McAnulty, *Housewright's Philosophy Herald "New Era" in Prisons*, Ark. Democrat, E5, Nov. 4, 1979; Bill Simmons, *White's Prison Budget Draws More Fire*, Ark. Democrat, A21, Dec. 12, 1980; Grady, *New Prisons No Solution: Ex-Warden*.
19. ADC, 1980 Annual Report, front page, 1–2, 19, 29, Ark. Doc CR 1.3: 980, Copy 4.
20. Fred Barbash, *Arkansas Lets the Light into "Brubaker's" Dark Age Prisons*, Wash. Post, A2, Sept. 21, 1980.
21. Jo Ann Pryor, *Prisons Not "At Bottom," Official Says*, Ark. Democrat, B1, Sept. 18, 1979; *Visitors Focus on Classifying Prison Inmates*, Ark. Democrat, B2, Jan. 10, 1980; RI Prison Isolates 30, Bost. Herald, 6, July 3, 1973; Morris v. Travisono, 373 F. Supp. 177 (DRI 1974), aff'd, 509 F.2d 1358 (1st Cir. 1975); Morris v. Travisono, 528 F.2d 856 (1st Cir. 1976); Gomes v. Travisono, 490 F.2d 1209, 1216 (1st Cir. 1973), vacated, 418 US 909, 94 (1974); Gomes v. Travisono, 510 F.2d 537, 541 (1st Cir. 1974); Palmigiano v. Garrahy, 443 F. Supp. 956, 964, 966 (DRI 1977).
22. Pub. L. No. 96–247, 94 Stat. 349, codified at 42 USC § 1997 et seq. (eff. May 23, 1980); *Law Allowing US to Sue on Behalf of Inmates in State Worries Officials*, Ark. Gazette, A12, May 24, 1980.
23. Bill Simmons, *Prison Director Says Budget Too Low to Make Prison Manageable*, Baxter Bull., C3, Dec. 18, 1980; Mike Mansur, *Funds Cut Hurts Compliance Timetable*, Ark. Democrat, B2, Mar. 21, 1981.
24. Mike Mansur, *Correction Board Tables Plan to Name Lockhart Director*, Ark. Democrat, B2, Feb. 25, 1981; Mike Mansur, *Prisons: LaPlante "Shocked" at Intent to Oust Him*, Ark. Democrat, B2, Feb. 28, 1981; Michael Arnold, *Reputation as Bully Undeserved, Acting Prison Director Asserts*, Ark. Gazette, 1, Apr. 5, 1981; Michael Arnold, *Griffin, Waters Fuel Controversy on Naming Lockhart Prison Chief*, Ark. Gazette, 1, Mar. 29, 1981; Bob Wells, *"New" Lockhart for Real? Support of TV Executions Invoke Old Image*, Ark. Democrat, B3, May 22, 1983; Wes Zeigler, *Former Prison Official Has No Regrets*, Ark. Magazine, Ark. Democrat, 7, Aug. 10, 1986.

25. Michael Arnold, *Correction Board Agrees to Press for Ouster of La Plante*, Ark. Gazette, A10, Feb. 27, 1981; McAnulty, *Eisele Ruling Allows LaPlante Contract Cutoff*; *Holt* Docket (Mar. 31, 1981), 27–30; John McAnulty, *LaPlante Says Politics Impede Reform*, Ark. Democrat, 1, June 7, 1981; *LaPlante Unsurprised by Council's Decision*, Ark. Democrat, A13, June 19, 1981.

26. Renee Haines-Saine, *Shortage of Beds May Force Use of Prison Alternatives*, Ark. Democrat, A9, Mar. 20, 1981; *Holt* Docket, Mar. 21, 1981, 27; Aug. 11, 1981, 31; Oct. 5, 1981, 32.

27. Mike Mansur, *Mental Health Care Funds for Inmates Lacking*, Ark. Democrat, B2, Mar. 19, 1981; John McAnulty, *State's Prison System Needs Millions to Reach Standards, LaPlante Reports*, Ark. Democrat, A7, June 20, 1981; Ted Jackovics, *Prison System Has Trouble with Retaining Prison Guards*, Ark. Democrat, B5, Sept. 29, 1981.

28. McAnulty, *State's Prison System Needs Millions*; *Prison System Gets $175,000 from Governor*, Ark. Democrat, B3, Aug. 5, 1981; *Governor Says $7.5 Million Spent on Prison*, Ark. Democrat, B12, Sept. 3, 1981; *Conditions Can Be "Harsh," Still Be Legal*, Ark. Gazette, A2, June 16, 1981.

29. Brief of Petitioners, *35, Rhodes v. Chapman, 452 US 337 (1981) (No. 80–332), 1980 WL 339863 (filed Dec. 22, 1980).

30. *Ruling Restricts US Court Role in State Prisons*, Ark. Gazette, 1, June 16, 1981.

31. Memorandum Opinion, Chapman v. Rhodes, No. C-1-75–251 (SD Ohio Dec. 14, 1976); *Rhodes Plans to Reopen Old Ohio Penitentiary*, Daily Jefferson, 13, July 1, 1977.

32. Chapman v. Rhodes, 434 F. Supp. 1007, 1010–17 (SD Ohio 1977).

33. *Chapman*, 1018; Brief of Respondents, *Rhodes*, 1980 WL 339864 (filed Oct. 1980).

34. Anne Willette, *Lucasville's Legacy: 20 Years of Turmoil*, Cinn. Enquirer, 6, Apr. 22, 1993; David Lore, *Legislative Panel Hears Pen Gripes*, Columbus Dispatch, A3, May 13, 1976; David Lore, *Prisoners Claim Lawyers Aiding Jail Extortionists*, Columbus Dispatch, 1, May 14, 1976; David Lore, *Penitentiary Improvements Cited*, Columbus Dispatch, B10, May 16, 1976; *"Kingdom of the Wild" Exists at Lucasville*, Canton Repository, 43, June 6, 1976.

35. David Lore, *Unemployment Tops 40% Inside Lucasville Facility*, Columbus Dispatch, A8, Apr. 13, 1976; *Lucasville Overcrowding is Called Cruel, Unusual*, Alliance Rev., 5, May 24, 1977; *Expert Hits Ohio Pen Conditions*, Canton Repository, 15, May 24, 1977; *Lucasville Praise Disputed by Several Ex-Employees*, Plain Dealer, A4, May 26, 1977.

36. *Lucasville Praise Disputed by Several Ex-Employees*, A4.

37. *Chapman*, 1007, 1011, 1015–16, 1020.

38. *Chapman*, 1011–21.

39. *Chapman*, 1020–21; Bell v. Wolfish, 441 US 520, 543 (1979).

40. Joseph N. Ulman, *A National Program to Develop Probation and Parole*, 29 J. Crim. L. & Criminology 517, 524–25 (1938). Ulman's comment has been cited as the first published US reference to "mass incarceration." Benjamin

Levin, *The Consensus Myth of Criminal Justice Reform*, 117 U. Mich. L. Rev. 269, 274 n.61 (2018).

41. ACA, *Manual of Correctional Standards*, 49 (1966).

42. James V. Bennett, *The Federal Penal and Correctional Problem*, 177–78 (1929). Am. Prison Association, *Manual of Suggested Standards for a State Correctional System*, 67–68, 85 (Oct. 1946); ACA, *Manual of Correctional Standards*, 102, 172 (1954); Rule 9.1, Standard Minimum Rules for the Treatment of Prisoners, 1955; ACA, *1966 Manual*; ACA, *Manual of Standards for Adult Correctional Institutions*, 27 (1977).

43. Richard S. Allinson, *The Politics of Prison Standards*, Corrections Mag., 54, Mar. 1979; Inmates of Suffolk County Jail, 360 Supp. 676, 684–87 (D. Mass. 1973), aff'd on other grounds, 494 F.2d 1196 (1st Cir. 1974), cert. denied, 419 US 977 (1974), on remand, 518 F.2d 1241 (1st Cir. 1975).

44. *Chapman*, 1022; Ohio Const. art. VIII, § 1; Lee Leonard, *State Issue 4 Calls for Flexible Debt Limit*, Daily Jeffersonian, 9, Oct. 28, 1977; *Judge Grants Delay in Double-Celling Plan*, Columbus Dispatch, D11, Oct. 5, 1977; Alternative Plans in Compliance with the Court's Order of June 29, 1977, filed Nov. 11, 1977; David Lore, *Penal Authorities Urge 2-Man Cells*, Columbus Dispatch, 1, Nov. 14, 1977; *State Submits Plans to End Overcrowding at Lucasville*, Daily Jeffersonian, 13, Nov. 15, 1977; Brief of Respondents, *5, *Rhodes*, 1980 WL 339864; Brief of Petitioners, *12, *Rhodes*, 1980 WL 339863; *Rhodes Plans to Reopen Old Ohio Penitentiary*; *Inmates Transferred into Ohio Penitentiary*, A3, Columbus Dispatch, July 1, 1977.

45. National Institute of Justice, *The Effect of Prison Crowding on Inmate Behavior*, iv (Dec. 1980), with principal investigators Gavin McCain, Verne C. Cox, and Paul B. Paulus.

46. Petition for Certiorari, 1, *Rhodes*, Sept. 2, 1980; certiorari granted November 3, 1980. *Rhodes*, 449 US 951 (1980).

47. *The Effect of Prison Crowding*, 1, 137–39.

48. Brief of Petitioners, *17–19; Brief of Respondents, *10–11, 32–33, *Rhodes*; Chapman v. Rhodes, 624 F.2d 1099, table (6th Cir. 1980).

49. Eighth Circuit Chief Judge Richard Arnold concluded that federal judges did not have the power to say, in essence, that their ruling applied to a single case. Anastasoff v. United States, 223 F.3d 898, 899–900 (8th Cir. 2000), vacated as moot by 235 F.3d 1054 (8th Cir. 2000). As of 2018, 85 percent of decisions by the US courts of appeals have that caveat. Merritt E. McAlister, *"Downright Indifference": Examining Unpublished Decisions in the Federal Courts of Appeals*, 118 Mich. L. Rev. 533 (2020); Rachel Brown, Jade Ford, Sahrula Kubie, Katrin Marquez, Bennett Ostdiek & Abbe R. Gluck, *Is Unpublished Unequal? An Empirical Examination of the 87% Nonpublication Rate in Federal Appeals*, 107 Cornell L. Rev. 1, 37–39 (2021). Between 2019 and 2021, about 14 percent of cert grants came from "not for publication" decisions. Judith Resnik, Testimony for the Presidential Commission on the Supreme Court of the United States; Equity, Access to Justice, and Transparency in the Operation of the Supreme Court, 17 (June 23, 2021).

50. Reply Brief of Petitioners, *9, *Rhodes*, 1980 WL 339865.

51. Brief of Amicus Curiae State of Texas in Support of the Petitioners, *1–3, *Rhodes*, 1980 WL 339869; Brief of the States of Alaska et al. in Support of Petitioners, Amici Curiae, *2–3, *5–6, 15, *Rhodes*, 1980 WL 339866.

52. States of Alaska et al. Amicus, *6, 14–25.

53. Elaine Scarry, *The Body in Pain: The Making and Unmaking of the World*, 2–3 (Oxford U. Press, 1985).

54. Bucklew v. Precythe, 587 US 119, 143 (2019); City of Grants Pass, Oregon v. Johnson, 144 S. Ct. 2202, 2215–2216 (2024). His reference was to the Court's prior case law, quoting Blackstone.

55. Brief of Amicus Curiae United States, *2, *Rhodes*, 1981 WL 390389.

56. Motion for Leave to File Brief Amicus Curiae and Brief of the American Medical Association and the American Public Health Association, *8, *Rhodes*, 1980 WL 339867.

57. AMA/APHA Amicus, *4–5, 5 n.3, quoting Comm. on Accreditation for Corrections, Manual of Standards for Adult Correctional Institutions § 4142 (1977).

58. US Amicus, *1–7, citing *Federal Standards for Prisons and Jails* §§ 2.04, 2.02, US DOJ (Dec. 16, 1980).

59. AMA/APHA Amicus, *1–5, 7–24.; American Public Health Association, Standards for Health Services in Correctional Institutions, 62 (1976); Judith Resnik & Nancy Shaw, *Prisoners of Their Sex: Health Problems of Incarcerated Women*, *in* 2 Prisoners' Rights Sourcebook: Theory, Practice, and Litigation, 319–413 (Ira Robbins ed., Clark Boardman, 1980).

60. Motion for Leave to File Brief Amicus Curiae and Brief Amicus Curiae of the State Public Defender of California in Support of Respondents, *Rhodes*, 1980 WL 339868, *1, 11–12.

61. Transcript, 14, *Rhodes*, available on Supreme Court Argument Transcripts.

62. *Rhodes*, 353.

63. *Rhodes*, 344–45.

64. *Rhodes*, 345–46; Trop v. Dulles, 356 US 86, 101 (1958).

65. Letter Lewis Powell to Chief Justice Burger, Re: 80–332 Rhodes v. Chapman, May 14, 1981, Washington & Lee University School of Law Scholarly Commons, Supreme Court Case Files: Lewis F. Powell Jr. Papers, Box 79. Chief Justice Burger's request was a handwritten as a P.P.S. Letter Burger to Powell, May 13, 1981; Letter Powell to Burger, May 14, 1981; Letter Burger to Powell, May 15, 1981. The two cases were Ingraham v. Wright, 430 US 651 (1977), which Powell wrote, and Estelle v. Gamble, 429 US 97 (1976) written by Marshall.

66. *Rhodes*, 346–47, 352.

67. *Rhodes*, 357, 367 n.15; Linda Greenhouse, *High Court Rules Two May Be Put in a Cell for One*, NY Times, A1, June 16, 1981; *Rhodes*, 340, 349–52; Brief of Petitioners, *11, *13, *19–20.

68. Letter Bill Brennan to Powell, Apr. 23, 1981, Powell Papers; *Rhodes*, 353–55, 360–67; Stewart v. Rhodes, 473 F. Supp. 1185 (SD Ohio 1979). A conditions

lawsuit at Ohio's "Old Penitentiary" ended with a "comprehensive consent decree." In 1986, the state contested attorney's fees and in an "unpublished disposition," the Sixth Circuit affirmed the $107,000 award. Stewart v. Rhodes, 785 F.2d 210 (6th Cir. 1986) (per curiam).

69. *Rhodes*, 368–69.

70. *Rhodes*, 370.

71. Wilkinson v. Austin, 545 US 209 (2005).

CHAPTER 27

1. Dale Bumpers, *Keeping in Touch: Building More Prisons*, Baxter Bull., 23, Feb. 26, 1981; Criminal Justice Construction Reform Act, S.186, 97th Cong. § 201 (1981).

2. Joan Mullen, Kenneth Carlson & Bradford Smith, *American Prisons and Jails, Volume I: Summary and Policy Implications of a National Survey*, Nat'l Inst. Justice (NIJ), 126–27, 139–40 (US DOJ, Oct. 1980).

3. Dan Berger & Toussaint Losier, *Rethinking the American Prison Movement*, 6 (Routledge, 2018). They contrasted warehousing with the "workhouse," using prison labor for profit, and the "big house," that included programming "for rehabilitative purposes."

4. Allen F. Breed, *The Power of Prisons*, 19 Judges J. 20, 24 (1980).

5. *Prisons Ordered to Revise Housing for Isolation Cases*, Ark. Gazette, 13, Dec. 16, 1981.

6. Barri Marsh & Joe Holmes, *Sheriff Dumps 18 Prisoners on State in Bizarre Incident*, Ark. Democrat, 1, July 16, 1981; Larry Ault & Ed Phillips, *Robinson Apparently Wins Power Struggle Over Inmates*, Ark. Democrat, 1, July 17, 1981; George Bentley, *Suit Requests Injunction on Deliveries*, Ark. Gazette, 1, July 18, 1981; George Bentley, *Sheriff Ordered to Transfer Inmates in "Orderly Manner,"* Ark. Gazette, 1, July 21, 1981.

7. Cary Bradburn, *Robinson Spins Web of Controversy*, Ark. Democrat, E10, Dec. 27, 1981; Alyson LaGrossa, *Correction Department Starts Prisoner Shuffle*, Ark. Democrat, 1, July 28, 1981.

8. *Robinson to Request Penal Farm Reopening or New Construction*, Ark. Gazette, A11, Aug. 5, 1981; C. S. Heinbockel, *County Jail in Compliance, Robinson Says*, Ark. Gazette, 2, Sept. 2, 1981; Bob Stover, *In Role Reversal, County Jail Refuses 3 Prisoners, but City Doesn't Force Issue*, Ark. Gazette, 10, Aug. 13, 1981; Jeff Waggoner, *City Officials Unconcerned by Jail Space*, Ark. Democrat, 16, May 5, 1982.

9. Omar Greene, *State Needs New Prisons, Official Says*, Ark. Democrat, 1, Feb. 18, 1982; Marla Dorfman, *Prison Rolls Grow: Official Seeks Relief*, Ark. Democrat, 11, June 11, 1982; Larry Sullivan, *State's Prisons Currently "Full to Brim,"* Lawyer Says, Ark. Democrat, B2, Aug. 7, 1982.

10. Finney v. Mabry, 534 F. Supp. 1026, 1041, 1036 (ED Ark. 1982).

11. *Testimony of Inmates Ends: State to Present Witnesses*, Ark. Gazette, 7, Sept. 2, 1981; Wes Zeigler, *Former Prison Official Has No Regrets*, Ark. Democrat, 7,

Aug. 10, 1986; George Wells, *Not Enough Done for Prison Reform, Former Head Says*, Ark. Gazette, A5, Aug. 26, 1981; John McAnulty, *Lack of Funds Spurred Resignation*, Ark. Democrat, A23, Aug. 26, 1981; John McAnulty, *Bribes Open Doors to Cummins Areas, Inmate Tells Court*, Ark. Democrat, B3, Sept. 1, 1981.

12. Larry Morse, *Week of Testimony Concludes on State Prison*, Ark. Democrat, 5, Sept. 5, 1981; George Wells, *Prison Suit May Be Ended Within a Year: Judge Eisele Concludes Hearing with "Optimism,"* Ark. Gazette, A3, Sept. 12, 1981; Larry Ault, *Eisele Says Prison System Compliance Possible*, Ark. Democrat, B5, Oct. 6, 1981.

13. *Prisons Ordered to Revise Housing for Isolation Cases; Segregated Housing Ordered for Inmates*, Ark. Democrat, B5, Dec. 17, 1981.

14. *Finney*, 534 F. Supp., 1029–42; Finney v. Mabry, 546 F. Supp. 626, 627 (ED Ark. 1982); George Wells, *Parts of LaPlante Compliance Reports Admitted*, Ark. Gazette, A10, Aug. 13, 1981; George Wells, *Security in Barracks Has Improved, State Says*, Ark. Gazette, A4, Dec. 30, 1981.

15. *Finney*, 534 F. Supp., 1036–38.

16. Michael Arnold, *300 at Cummins Are Segregated*, Ark. Gazette, B1, 6, Mar. 4, 1982; George Wells, *Judge Says Integration in Prison Wing Not Required if Inmates Put in Danger*, Ark. Gazette, B1, Mar. 4, 1982; Larry Ault, *Cummins Inmate Warns of Potential Bloodbath*, Ark. Democrat, D10, Mar. 7, 1982; *Finney*, 534 F. Supp., 1043; *Finney*, 546 F. Supp. 626, 627 (ED Ark. 1982).

17. George Wells, *17 Reports Delivered to Eisele by Prisons on Compliance Efforts*, Ark. Gazette, B1, May 8, 1982; Larry Ault, *Judge Asked to Keep Eye on Issues in Prison Lawsuit*, Ark. Democrat, B3, June 29, 1982; *White Pushes Work Centers for Prisoners*, Ark. Democrat, 11, May 21, 1982; Larry Ault, *Judge Rules Prisons in Full Compliance*, Ark. Democrat, 1, Aug. 10, 1982.

18. *Finney*, 546 F. Supp. 628, 641, 642.

19. George Wells, *Continued Monitoring of Prisons Needed, Kaplan Asserts*, Ark. Gazette, 5, Aug. 14, 1982; *Finney* 546 F. Supp. 628, 641–43.

20. *Finney*, 546 F. Supp. 628, 630, 637–42.

21. Edward L. Rubin & Malcolm M. Feeley, *Judicial Policy Making and Litigation Against the Government*, 5 U. Pa. J. Const. L. 617, 656 (2003).

22. *Finney*, 546 F. Supp., 628, 643.

23. *Old Problem of Witness Credibility Affects Prison Hearing*, Ark. Democrat, A12, Aug. 16, 1981.

24. Hunter Field, *G. Thomas Eisele, Longtime Federal Judge in Little Rock, Dies at 94*, Ark. Democrat-Gazette, 1, Nov. 27, 2017; G. Thomas Eisele, *The Case Against Mandatory Court-Annexed ADR Programs*, 75 Judicature 34 (1991); Oral History of G. Thomas Eisele by Frances Ross, Ark. Fed. Jud. Hist. Project, Jan. 19, 1988, 12–15 (tape transcriptions provided by the Eighth Circuit).

25. *Court Candidates Contrast Sharply*, Baxter Bull., 47, Nov. 2, 1984; Mark Albright, *Justices Kill Youth Court: Juvenile Matters Removed from County*

Court Systems, Ark. Democrat, 1, Jan. 21, 1987; Ernest Dumas, *Arkansas Legal Legend Jack Holt Jr. Dies at 93*, Ark. Times, Mar. 6, 2023.

26. William J. Clinton, Governor of Ark., Hard Times and the Promise of Our Tomorrows, Second Inaugural Address (Jan. 11, 1983), *Preface to the Presidency: Selected Speeches of Bill Clinton 1974–1992*, 30 (Stephen Smith ed., 1996).

27. Lisa Fowler, *Prison Board Chief Pushes Alternatives to Incarceration*, Ark. Democrat, E13, Mar. 25, 1987.

28. Karl Cates, *"Dark and Evil World" Gone, but Space Limits Reforms*, Ark. Democrat, 6, Aug. 12, 1991.

29. *Purcell and Clinton: Views on Top Issues*, Ark. Democrat, A7, June 5, 1982; Clinton 1983 Inaugural Address, 30.

30. David F. Kern, *Measure to Relieve Prison Overcrowding Gains Steam*, Ark. Democrat, 21, Jan. 30, 1991; Adam Weintraub, *Sheriffs Doubt State Will Pay Bills*, Ark. Gazette, 2H, Feb. 13, 1991.

31. Tyler Tucker, *Clinton Evaluating 3 Possible Solutions to Ease Full Prisons*, Ark. Democrat, B6, Jan. 30, 1986; Dan Bailey, *Clinton to Seek Funds to Compensate Counties for Sheltering Inmates*, Ark. Democrat, A5, Apr. 22, 1986; Weintraub, *Sheriffs Doubt State Will Pay Bills*; Tom Hayes, *State Prisoners Kept in County Jail Impetus for Suit*, Ark. Democrat, B2, Mar. 26, 1991; Max Parker, *Bill for Prisoners Mounting: Despite Additional $3.4 Million, State Still in Red*, Ark. Democrat, 1, 4, Feb. 6, 1991.

32. John Hofheimer, *Prisoners to Be Freed Under Crowding Act*, Ark. Gazette, 1, Mar. 29, 1988; Paul Barton, *Correction Board to Consider Early Release of State Inmates*, Ark. Democrat, 1, Apr. 7, 1987; *Act Eases Overcrowding*, Sentinel-Record, 1, Aug. 29, 1991.

33. Ernest Megginson, *Sheriffs Warn State Prison System: No Pay, No Jail*, Ark. Democrat, B7, May 28, 1987; Laurie Nelms Crawford, *City Facing Uphill Battle for $80,950*, Ark. Democrat, A20, May 31, 1987, A20; Beth Dempsey, *Gravett Agrees to Pay $22,500 in Settlement of Chained Felons' Suit*, Ark. Democrat, B2, July 22, 1988.

34. Lisa Fowler, *Will Prison Crunch Put "Bars" on Arkansas Homes?*, Ark. Democrat, B1, June 7, 1987; Dan Bailey, *Day After Transfers, County Jail Full*, Ark. Democrat, A9, July 29, 1987; Mark Albright, *Clinton, Gravett Join to Battle Prison Jams*, Ark. Democrat, 1, Aug. 1, 1987; *Lockhart: Prison Jam Here Till '90s*, Ark. Democrat, B1, Nov. 14, 1987; Stephen Steed, *Despite New 700-Bed Facility, Prisons Remain Overcrowded*, Ark. Gazette, 7, Dec. 28, 1987.

35. Max Parker, *Early Release of Inmates Possible After April Meet*, Ark. Democrat, B1, Mar. 29, 1988; Adam Weintraub, *Officials Uncertain on Use of Basement to House Prisoners*, Ark. Gazette, B5, July 31, 1989; Lamar James, *Prisons Cost Every Arkansan Nickel a Day*, Ark. Gazette, A10, Apr. 23, 1989; Tamara Mohawk, *Lawsuits by Inmates Cost State Thousands*, Ark. Gazette, 61, Nov. 20, 1989; Adam Weintraub, *Public a Victim of "Flood,"* Ark. Gazette, 1, Apr. 23, 1989; *Special Report: No Room for Justice*, Ark. Gazette, A9–13, Feb. 4, 1990.

36. Weintraub, *Public a Victim of "Flood"*; James, *Prisons Cost Every Arkansan Nickel a Day*.
37. Adam Weintraub, *Pulaski County to Sue Agency for Prisoner Costs*, Ark. Gazette, B1, Nov. 20, 1990; Noel Oman & Judy Gallman, *Cities Seek $1.4 Million from County in Jail Suit*, Ark. Democrat, 1, July 15, 1989; Noel Oman, *County Says It Doesn't Owe Cities a Dime*, Ark. Democrat, B2, Aug. 17, 1989; John Hoogesteger & John Reed, *Sheriffs Plan Suit on Jails*, Ark. Gazette, B1, Jan. 25, 1990; James Merriweather, *Legislative Panel Supports $8.7 Million for Prison Needs*, Ark. Gazette, B6, Oct. 13, 1989; Tamara Mohawk, *No Relief in Sight for Prisons*, Ark. Gazette, 1, Nov. 20, 1989; Joe Farmer, *Prison Request Includes $5.3 Million to Pay Bill for Inmate Backlog*, Ark. Democrat, A8, Dec. 12, 1990.
38. Judith Palmer, *Jail Plans in the Works Day After OK*, Ark. Democrat, B12, Feb. 22, 1990.
39. *Judge: State Can Seize Felon's Assets for Care*, Sentinel-Record, A6, July 15, 1989; Bennett v. Arkansas, 485 US 395 (1988) (per curiam).
40. Conn. Gen. Stat. § 18–85a, as amended 2021, directed the Corrections Department to adopt regulations "concerning the assessment of inmates . . . for the costs of their incarceration." An Act Concerning Payment of the Cost of Incarceration: Hearing on PA 235 Before the Conn. Judiciary Comm., 1995; Patrick Irving, Opinion, *Prisoners Like Me Are Being Held Hostage to Price Hikes*, NY Times, 4, Nov. 6, 2022; Brittany Friedman, April D. Fernandes & Gabriela Kirk, *"Like If You Get a Hotel Bill": Consumer Logic, Pay-to-Stay, and the Production of Incarceration as a Public Commodity*, 36 Socio. Forum 735 (2021); Brennan Ctr., *Is Charging Inmates to Stay in Prison Smart Policy?* (Sept. 9, 2019); Alan Mills, *Pay to Stay*, Uptown's People L. Ctr. (Aug. 22, 2016); Alexes Harris, *A Pound of Flesh: Monetary Sanctions as Punishment for the Poor* (2016); Jordan Nathaniel Fenster, *Daily Cost to House Inmates Likely to Rise*, New Haven Register, A1, May 29, 2023; Inmate Financial Responsibility Program: Procedures, 88 Fed. Reg. 1331 (Jan. 10, 2023), proposing to amend 28 CFR § 545.
41. *Governor Outlines Prison Reform Package*, Baxter Bull., 6, Feb. 16, 1993; *Governor Says Prison Director Was Forced to Resign His Post*, Baxter Bull., 1, May 1, 1993; *New Prison Chief Is 22-Year Veteran*, Baxter Bull., 2, Dec. 18, 1993.
42. An Act to Amend the Powers of the Department of Correction; to Create the Department of Community Punishment; to Merge the Board of Corrections and the Adult Probation Commission to Create the Board of Corrections and Community Punishment; and for Other Purposes, 1993 Ark. Act 549 (SB 362), §§ 1–2, 4, 5, 7. An Act to Rename the Department of Community Punishment as the Department of Community Correction; To Rename the Board of Correction and Community Punishment as the Board of Corrections; To Rename the Community Punishment Revolving Fund as the Community Correction Revolving Fund; And for Other Purposes, Acts of 2001, Act 323., § 1; Transformation and Efficiencies Act of 2019, Arkansas Code Annotated § 25–43–403, Act 910, § 644. As noted, in 1968, the first statute creating a Department of Correction called its head a "Commissioner,"

I have used that nomenclature throughout, although the 1993 legislation termed the ADC head "Director."

43. Violent Crime Control and Law Enforcement Act of 1994, Pub. L. 103–323 § 20102, 108 Stat. 1798, 1816 (Sept. 13, 1994) (codified at 42 USC § 13702); and at § 20406 (codified at 42 USC § 13721; reclassified to title 34); Susan Turner, Terry Fain, Peter W. Greenwood, Elsa Y. Chen & James R. Chiesa, *National Evaluation of the Violent Offender Incarceration/Truth-in-Sentencing Incentive Grant Program*, NIJ (Oct. 17, 2001); Margo Schlanger, *Trends in Prisoner Litigation as the PLRA Enters Adulthood*, 5 UC Irvine L. Rev. 153 (2015).

44. Cary Bradburn, *Jail Crisis a Vicious Cycle*, Ark. Gazette, A1, Apr. 24, 1989.

45. Arkansas Department of Correction, *Inmate Handbook*, 1 (9th ed. 1986), Arkansas State Library, Ark Doc CR 1.5:I5/986 Copy 1.

46. Jim Nichols, *Director Hopes Task-Force Report Makes Difference*, Ark. Democrat, B2, June 26, 1986.

47. One report described $90,000 to $120,000 missing. *State Police Investigate Missing Funds*, Ark. Democrat, B12, Jan. 7, 1982; Jim Lovel, *Meeting Reviews Prison Charges*, Ark. Democrat, 1, Apr. 2, 1986; Bill Simmons, *State, Private Interests Raise Many Questions*, Baxter Bull., 4, June 16, 1986; Scott Morris, *Inmate Aiding in Investigation Is in Danger, Glover Charges*, Ark. Gazette, A7, July 11, 1986; *Lockhart Comes Up Clean Through State Prison Probe*, Baxter Bull., A1, July 31, 1986. *Cuevas v. Lockhart* was assigned to Judge William R. Overton. George Wells, *Female Inmates File Bias Suit*, Ark. Gazette, A1, Apr. 21, 1984; David Davies, *Inmates' Suit Charges Bias Against Women*, Ark. Democrat, A16, Apr. 21, 1984; Larry Ault, *Judge OKs Women Inmates' Civil Rights Settlement*, Ark. Democrat, A14, June 19, 1986.

48. Teresa Andrews & Mark Albright, *ACLU Files $10 Million Lawsuit Against Maximum Security Prison*, Ark. Democrat, 1, A4, Aug. 17, 1985; Brenda Blagg, *Between the Lines*, Madison County Record, 2, Aug. 29, 1985; Nichols, *Director Hopes Task-Force Report Makes Difference*; Stephen Steed, *$5.2 Million Tag Put on Prison Changes*, Ark. Gazette, 1, Oct. 4, 1986.

49. *Lockhart Says Complaints Part of Job*, Ark. Democrat, B4, July 22, 1986; Tanuja Kanwar, *Inmate Crew Used to Help State Senator*, Ark. Democrat, B1, Dec. 14, 1989; *Ark. Lawmaker Is Facing Fraud Trial by Himself*, Com. Appeal, A14, Aug. 30, 1997; Jeffrey St. Clair, *Tainted Plasma Traced to Arkansas Prison: Bill Clinton's Blood Trails*, Prison Legal News, 1, May 15, 1999.

50. ADC, *Inmate Handbook*, 1 (Feb. 1994), Ark Doc CR 1.5:I5/994 Copy 1; ADC, *Inmate Handbook*, 1 (2001), Ark Doc CR 1.5:I5/2001 Copy 1; ADC, *Inmate Handbook*, 1 (2006), Ark Doc CR 1.5:I5/2006 Copy 1; ADC *Inmate Handbook*, 1 (2013), Ark Doc CR 1.5:I5/2013 Copy 4; *Prison Director Apologizes to Lawmakers*, Sentinel-Record, B1, July 12, 1995; Dennis A. Byrd, *Sample Shows Gas Bought by Prison Was Substandard*, Pine Bluff Com., A1, Sept. 11, 1996; Bruce Roberts & Josh Dooley, *Allegations Arise at Calico Rock Prison*, Baxter Bull., 1, Oct. 28, 1997.

51. Scott Liles, *Space is Running Out, Time to Expand Jail, Says Sheriff*, Baxter Bull., A1, May 3, 2017.

52. *Bond Issue Approved for Private Prisons*, Baxter Bull., A11, Dec. 19, 1996; James Jefferson, *Prisoners to Head for Texas Lockup*, Pine Bluff Com., A1, Jan. 26, 1996; Mark Friedman, *Board of Correction Approves Early Release of 500 Inmates*, Pine Bluff Com., A2, Nov. 20, 1997; David A. Lieb, *Prisons Filling up at Rapid Rate*, Baxter Bull., A8, Jan. 24, 1998.

53. Marie Gottschalk, *Caught: The Prison State and the Lockdown of American Politics*, rev. ed. (Princeton U. Press, 2016); *Officials Narrow Down Potential Prison Sites*, Baxter Bull., 17, July 31, 1999; *Correction Board Takes Steps to Relieve Prison Crowding*, Baxter Bull., A3, Feb. 26, 2000; *Full Prisons to Release Some Inmates Early*, Sentinel-Record, A5, Aug. 26, 2000; Committee on Architecture for Justice, *Justice Facilities Review 1999–2001*, AIA, vii.

54. Frank Wallis, *Cummins Prison: After 100 Years, Still a Foreboding Place*, Baxter Bull., A1, July 16, 2003; James Jefferson, *Prison Board OKs Expansion of Programs*, Sentinel-Record, A3, July 12, 2002; *Legislators Respond Well to Huckabee Prison Plan*, Baxter Bull., A3, Jan. 23, 2003; Frank Wallis, *Prisons Filling Up with Meth-Makers*, Baxter Bull., A1, June 18, 2003. The Corrections Board's Chair was Mary Parker, whose dissertation about the Arkansas prison litigation I cited earlier.

55. ADC July 1, 2005–June 30, 2006, Annual Report 1, 3, 29, Ark Doc CR 1.3, 2006, Copy 4; Senator Randy Laverty, *State Capital Week in Review*, Madison County Record, 4, Jan. 11, 2007; Jan. 27, 2027; June 14, 2007, July 31, 2008, July 8, 2010 (a weekly column). *Beebe Urges Sheriffs to Lobby for Payments*, Baxter Bull., A3, Jan. 27, 2010; *Washington County to Seek More Funds for State Inmates*, Baxter Bull., A2, July 13, 2016; Andrew DeMillo, *Prison Overhaul on Agenda for 2011*, Baxter Bull., 4, Dec. 16, 2010.

56. *Reimbursement Rate for Inmate Overflow Decreases*, Baxter Bull., A2, Jan. 31, 2017; *Arkansas Senate Passes Legislation to Ease Prison Overcrowding*, Baxter Bull., A1, Mar. 1, 2017; Josh Dooley, *Plea Bargains, Overcrowding Result in Jail Time Shaved Off*, Baxter Bull., A1, Mar. 10, 2017; Ark. Code Ann. § 12-41-503b (2021); Ark. Op. Atty. Gen. No. 2011–164 (2012), 2012 WL 424323 *1, n.1; Tom Sisson, *State Report Shows Many Jails Overcrowded*, Ark. News, Oct. 28, 2019; *State Prison Director Says Policy Slips Caused Flare-Ups*, Baxter Bull., A2, Dec. 11, 2017; *Prisons Could See Jump in Restricted Housing*, Baxter Bull., A2, Oct. 17, 2017; Andrew Demillo, *Official: 5 Inmate Deaths Not Acceptable*, Baxter Bull., A1, Sept. 5, 2018. The lack of safety in jails and the power of sheriffs is explored in Aaron Littman, *Jails, Sheriffs, and Carceral Policymaking*, 74 Vand. L. Rev. 861 (2021).

57. *Ark. Prisons Defend Commissions Charged on Inmate Phone Calls*, Baxter Bull., A1, Aug. 17, 2007; *Arkansas Jail to End Free In-Person Visits*, Baxter Bull., A2, July 24, 2018.

58. Mississippi Cty. v. City of Blytheville, 538 S.W.3d 822, 832 (2018); *Crawford County Increases Inmate Housing Fees on Cities*, Baxter Bull., A2, Oct. 19, 2018; *Quorum Court Moves $85,000 to Pay Toward Inmate Housing*, Madison County Record, A11, Nov. 22, 2018; Scott Liles, *Cities Presently Charged $50 Per Day*

for Each Prisoner, Baxter Bull., A1, Aug. 8, 2019; Scott Liles, *Jail's Per-Day Fee Waived for Local Cities*, Baxter Bull., A2, Oct. 3, 2019.

59. Arkansas Division of Correction Board Report, 1, April 2024; Matthew Moore, Arkansas Launches Justice Reinvestment Initiative to Better Understand and Address Recidivism Drivers and Reentry Barriers, Council of State Governments, Justice Ctr. (May 21, 2024).

60. *Authorities: Inmate Attacked and Killed at Prison*, Baxter Bull., A3, Jan. 14, 2020; *Inmate Dies after Being Found Hanging in Cell*, Baxter Bull., A5, Jan. 20, 2020; Scott Liles, *State's COVID-19 Cases Top 800 Mark, Found in Federal Prison*, Baxter Bull., A1, Apr. 6, 2020; Scott Liles, *Cummins Inmates Swell Number of States Infected*, Baxter Bull., A1, Apr. 22, 2020; Scott Liles, *State's COVID-19 Cases Jump to 2,741*, Baxter Bull., A1, Apr. 25, 2020; *Coronavirus in the US: Latest Map and Case Count*, NY Times, updated Mar. 23, 2023; Rachel Aviv, *Punishment by Pandemic*, New Yorker, 56, June 22, 2020; *Judge Rejects Arkansas Inmates' Bid for More Virus Steps*, Baxter Bull., A3, May 20, 2020; Frazier v. Kelley, 460 F. Supp. 3d 799 (ED Ark. 2020); Frazier v. Graves, No. 4:20-CV-00434-KGB, 2021 WL 1236990 (ED Ark. Mar. 31, 2021); Molly Minta, *Inside the Cummins Prison Outbreak*, Baxter Bull., A1, June 19, 2020; Brendan Saloner, Kalind Parish & Julie Ward, *COVID-19 Cases and Deaths in Federal and State Prisons*, 6 JAMA 602 (2020); Julie A. Ward, Kalind Parish, Grace DiLaura, Sharon Dolovich & Brendan Saloner, *COVID-19 Cases among Employees of US Federal and State Prisons*, 60 Am. J. Preventive Med. 840, 841 (2021); Beth Schwartzapfel, Katie Park & Andrew DeMillo, *1 in 5 Prisoners in US has had COVID-19: 1,700 Died*, Baxter Bull., A4, Dec. 19, 2020; Jaimie Meyer, Marisol Orihuela & Judith Resnik, Tolerating the Harms of Detention, With and Without COVID-19, *COVID-19 and the Law: Disruption, Impact and Legacy*, 91–104 (Glenn Cohen, Abbe R. Gluck, Katherine Kraschel & Carmel Shachar eds., Cambridge U. Press, 2023).

61. The years refer to the fiscal year running from July 1, 1965, to June 30, 1966. Until 2009, Arkansas' legislature met only in odd-numbered years, when it enacted a biannual budget. Special sessions were, at times, called. Beginning in 2010, after the enactment of Amendment 86 to the Arkansas Constitution, the legislature met for a limited fiscal session in even-numbered years as well and authorized spending on an annual basis instead. *Five Facts About Fiscal*, Ark. House of Reps. (Feb. 6, 2014); *Biannual Budget Request Manuals*, Ark. Dept. of Fin. & Admin. The budgeting methods were governed by the state's Revenue Stabilization Act, adopted in 1945. Overall funding levels were based on revenue projections; hence the figures do not necessarily represent the amount spent. Fiscal Services Division, *Arkansas Budget and Appropriation Process*, Bureau of Legis. Rsch.

As the table reflects, between 1965 and 1967, the Arkansas State Legislature allocated ad hoc funds to the State Penitentiary System from sources including the State Penitentiary Fund (which was money from the prisons' farming operations dependent on prisoners' labor), the State Penitentiary Employees' Retirement Fund, and the General Improvement

Fund. In 1968, during a special session, the legislature enacted Act 50, which established Arkansas' Department of Correction and amended the state's budget to direct $700,000 from the Governor's Contingency Fund for the new department. In the same session, the legislature authorized $2,714,410.00 for salaries and operating expenses. The moneys spent may have been from "profits" generated by the prison system; the legislature specified that "total expenditures . . . under the provisions of this Act, for the 1968–1969 fiscal year, other than from Federal funds, shall not exceed the aggregate of . . . any unexpended and unencumbered balances that may be on hand to the credit of the Department of Correction fund . . . plus income derived by the Department of Correction from operations of the Department during the 1968–1969 fiscal year . . . plus such amount which may be made available . . . by transfers thereto from savings of funds . . . and upon transfers of moneys under the provisions of the Governor's Contingency Fund." Act 13 § 7, 1968 Acts of Ark. 1784 (June 15, 1968). Thus, aside from the $700,000 allocated from the Contingency Fund, taxpayer dollars did not go into the ADC, which appeared as a line item in the budget for the first time in 1969.

The information on the number of imprisoned individuals for 1971 and thereafter comes from Bureau of Justice Statistics (BJS). Arkansas had not reported information to BJS before then, and the 1968 number comes from the Department of Correction Population Analysis 1963–1968 at 887, 894, U. Ark. Little Rock, Rockefeller Collection, Series IV, Box 251, File 7. The number for 1969 is an estimate from "Where from Here? Alternatives for a Ten-Year Action Plan for Arkansas Corrections," *Ark. Comm. on Crime & Law Enforcement*, 19 (1970), Arkansas State Archives, Prison Records, Box 1, Folder 12. The 1970 number comes from *Holt v. Sarver*, 309 F. Supp. 362, 366 n.1 (ED Ark. 1970). The ranges indicate various numbers reported. The budget dates from National Association of State Budget Officers begins in 1984; Arkansas' records were the sources for the years before then.

62. Act 16, § 1, 1968 Acts of Ark. 1794 (May 29, 1968); *State of Arkansas, Funded Budget, Fiscal Year 2022*, Ark. Dept. of Fin. & Admin.

63. *State Expenditure Report*, Nat'l Assn. of Budget Offs., 6, 11 (2021); Chris Mai, Mikelina Belaineh, Ram Subramanian & Jacob Kang-Brown, *Broken Ground: Why America Keeps Building More Jails and What it Can Do Instead* (Vera Institute of Justice, 2019); Peter Wagner & Bernadette Rabuy, *Following the Money of Mass Incarceration*, Prison Policy Initiative, Jan. 25, 2017.

64. Robert T. Chase, *We Are Not Slaves: State Violence, Coerced Labor, and Prisoners' Rights in Postwar America* (UNC Press, 2020); American Civil Liberties Union and The University of Chicago Law School Global Human Rights Clinic, *Captive Labor: Exploitation of Incarcerated Workers*, 6–8, June 15, 2022.

65. Aaron Littman, *Free-World Law Behind Bars*, 131 Yale L. J. 1385, 1437 (2022). Prisoners have been unsuccessful in changing interpretations limiting the application of statutes and regulations. Vanskike v. Peters, 974 F.2d 806 (7th Cir. 1992); Hale v. State of Ariz., 993 F.2d 1387 (9th Cir. 1993); Ark. Div. of Corr.,

Annual Report: Fiscal Year 2020, Mar. 2021, 38,75, 94; Pat Eaton-Robb, *At $249 Per Day, Prison Stays Leave Ex-Inmates Deep in Debt*, Assoc. Press (Aug. 27, 2022); April D. Fernandes, Brittany Friedman & Gabriela Kirk, *Forcing People to Pay for Being Locked up Remains Common*, Wash. Post, May 2, 2022.

66. Karen M. Benker & Marcia A. Howard, The State Expenditure Report, National Association of State Budget Officers, 14–16, 47, 66, 75 (July 1987) (excluded were Alabama, Georgia, Mississippi, New Hampshire, New Mexico, Nevada, North Carolina, Oklahoma, Texas, West Virginia, and Wyoming, for which NASBO did not report corrections expenditures for 1985); 2021 State Expenditure Report, 5–6, 66, NASBO 2021. The total reported was $63.2 billion, of which $531 million were federal funds during the 2019 fiscal year. As of 2023, the Bureau of Justice Statistics hosted a dashboard, the Justice Expenditure and Employment Tool (JEET), to provide historical and comparative state expenditures on corrections, policing, and judicial services at the national, state, county, and municipal level. The dashboard information did not disaggregate spending within categories and aimed to include data from 1982 onward and, as of 2023, had information from 2016 to 2019. Bureau of Justice Statistics, *Justice Expenditure and Employment Tool*, Office of Just. Progs., US DOJ.

67. 1987 NASBO Expenditure Report, 33. These figures do not include Alabama, Mississippi, New Hampshire, New Mexico, Nevada, North Carolina, Oklahoma, Texas, West Virginia, and Wyoming, for which NASBO did not report higher education expenditures in the 1985 fiscal year. 2021 NASBO Expenditure Report, 11–12, 30, 34.

68. Carol Rosenberg, *The Cost of Running Guantánamo Bay: $13 Million per Prisoner*, NY Times, Sept. 16, 2019, updated Feb. 20, 2021. Office of the New York City Comptroller, *Cost of Incarceration per Person in New York City Skyrockets to All Time High*, Dec. 6, 2021; David Garland, *Punishment and Welfare: A History of Penal Strategies* (Gower, 1985); David Garland, *The Culture of Control: Crime and Social Order in Contemporary Society* (U. Chi. Press, 2001).

CHAPTER 28

1. Joan Mullen, Kenneth Carlson & Bradford Smith, *American Prisons and Jails, Volume I: Summary and Policy Implications of a National Survey*, 27–28 (Nat'l Inst. Just. US DOJ, Oct. 1980); Andrew Rutherford, Kenneth Carlson, Patricia Evans, John Flanagan, David Fogel, Ilene Greenberg, Richard Ku, Karen Ludington, William A. Shaffer, Michael Sherman, Bradford Smith & Franklin Zimring, *Prison Population and Policy Choices: Preliminary Report to Congress* (Nat'l Inst. Law Enforcement & Crim. Just., Sept. 1977).

2. US General Accounting Office, *Prison Costs: Opportunities Exist to Lower the Cost of Building Federal Prisons*, GGD-92-3, B-24494 3 (Oct. 25, 1991). In 2004, that office was renamed the Government Accountability Office (GAO).

3. Wilkinson v. Austin, 545 US 209, 214–15 (2005).

4. James Forman Jr., *Locking Up Our Own: Crime and Punishment in Black America* (Farrar, Straus & Giroux, 2017).
5. Jaimie Meyer, Marisol Orihuela & Judith Resnik, Tolerating the Harms of Detention, With and Without COVID-19, *COVID-19 and the Law: Disruption, Impact, and Legacy* (I. Glenn Cohen, Abbe R. Gluck, Katherine L. Kraschel & Carmel Shachar eds., Cambridge U. Press, 2023).
6. Rachel E. Barkow, *Promise or Peril?: The Political Path of Prison Abolition in America*, 58 Wake Forest L. Rev. 245 (2023).
7. Omnibus Crime Control and Safe Streets Act of 1968, Pub. L. 90–351, 82 Stat. 197, amended by the Omnibus Crime Control Act of 1970, Pub. L. 91–644, 84 Stat. 1880; Letter Jerris Leonard, Administrator, to the President and Congress 1–2, LEAA: 3rd Annual Report of the Law Enforcement Assistance Administration Fiscal Year 1971 (US DOJ, Dec. 31, 1971).
8. Judith Resnik & Robert Schack, Undelivered Care: The Incapacitated and the Mentally Ill New York City Defendant: A Report to the Mayor's Criminal Justice Coordinating Council (New York City, 1973); Eighth Annual Report of LEAA for Fiscal Year 1976, 10 (US DOJ, Dec. 31, 1976); Crime Control Act of 1976, Pub. L. 94–503, 90 Stat. 2407, § 117(a)(5) (codified at USC § 3742); *1980 NIJ American Prisons*, I, overview, 11, 27–28, 134.
9. *1980 NIJ American Prisons*, I, 27–28; Garvin McCain, Verne C. Cox & Paul B. Paulus, *The Effect of Prison Crowding on Inmate Behavior*, 1–4 (NIJ, US DOJ, Dec. 1980); Edna McConnell Clark Foundation, *Overcrowded Time: Why Prisons Are So Crowded and What Can Be Done* (1982).
10. Letter Richard W. Velde, Administrator, to the President and Congress of the United States, in 1976 Eighth Annual LEAA Report, i–ii; Elizabeth Hinton, *From the War on Poverty to the War on Crime: The Making of Mass Incarceration in America*, 2 (Harvard U. Press, 2016); Leonard, *1971 3rd LEAA Report*, 1, 118.
11. *Federal Prisons: Revised Design Standards Could Save Expansion Funds*, GAO, GGD 91–54, 8 (Mar. 1991); Richard S. Allinson, *The Politics of Prison Standards*, Corrections Mag., 54–58, Mar. 1979; Wendell Rawls Jr., *Judge Quits Panel on Prison Ratings*, NY Times, 20, Aug. 8, 1982; Memorandum of Resignation to the Commission on Accreditation for Corrections, Aug. 9, 1982, Biddle Law Library, U. Penn., David L. Bazelon Papers, MMS.03 Box 112, Folder 16.
12. Frank Wallis, *Cummins Prison: After 100 Years, Still a Foreboding Place*, Baxter Bull., 1, June 17, 2003; The Accreditation Con: A Broken Prison and Detention Facility Accreditation System that Puts Profits over People, Office of Sen. Elizabeth Warren, 1 (Dec. 2020).
13. Robert F. Diegelman, *Federal Financial Assistance for Crime Control: Lessons of the LEAA Experience*, 73 J. Crim. L. & Criminology 994, 999–1001 (1982); Marie Gottschalk, *The Prison and the Gallows: The Politics of Mass Incarceration in America*, 86 (Cambridge U. Press, 2006); Justice System Improvement Act of 1979, Pub. L. No. 96–157, 93 Stat. 1167, codified at 42 USC § 3701 (Supp. IV 1980), and at § 302; Richard Friedman & Sally Hamilton, *Criminal*

Justice: Policy Coordination, 9 Md. L. F. 10 (1981); Justice Assistance Act of 1984, Pub. L. Stat. 98–473, § 401, 98 Stat. 2077, 2080, codified at 42 USC § 10141.

14. Jay Farbstein & Melissa Farling, *Understanding Cognitive Processes in Correctional Settings, Workshop Report*, 4–9, 58 (Nat'l Inst. of Corrections, US DOJ, Oct. 2006).

15. James K. Stewart, Director, NIJ, quoted by Charles B. DeWitt, *Ohio's New Approach to Prison and Jail Financing*, 1 (NIJ, No. 102093, US DOJ, July 1986).

16. Letter Governor William P. Clements Jr. to Members of the Legislature (July 2, 1987), in William P. Clements Jr., *Prison Financing and Construction Plan*, 2 (NIJ, No. 112057, US DOJ, July 1987).

17. Stewart, quoted in DeWitt, *Ohio's New Approach*, 1.

18. E. Herrick, *Prison Construction Approaches $4 Billion*, Office of Justice Programs, 12 Corrections Compendium 8 (US DOJ, Feb. 1988); as of 2015, 40 states had limits on state-authorized debt, albeit with some exceptions. Kim Reuben & Megan Randall, *Debt Limits: How States Restrict Borrowing*, 2 (Urb. Inst., Nov. 2017).

19. DeWitt, *Ohio's News Approach*, 2–4, 9. Third parties could be a "public agency, a nonprofit firm, or financial institution," and Ohio's use circumvented otherwise applicable debt limits, as special obligation debt did not provide "holders . . . the right to have excises or taxes levied by the general assembly" for repayment. Ohio Const. art. VIII, § 2i; James K. Stewart, *Foreword*, in Jan Chaiken & Stephen Mennemeyer, *Lease-Purchase Financing of Prison and Jail Construction*, iii–iv (NIJ, US DOJ, Nov. 1987); Ruth Wilson Gilmore, *Golden Gulag: Prisons, Surplus, Crisis, and Opposition in Globalizing California*, 7, 98–102 (U. Cal. Press, 2007); Cal. Gov't Code § 15819 (2021).

20. Clements, *1987 Prison Financing and Construction Plan*, ii–iv; 1–7; Steve J. Martin & Sheldon Ekland-Olson, *Texas Prisons: The Walls Came Tumbling Down* (Tex. Monthly Press, 1987).

21. National Prison Project, *ACLU Status Report: State Prison and the Courts*, 1 (1995); Heather Schoenfeld, *Building the Prison State: Race and the Politics of Mass Incarceration*, 4 (U. Chi. Press, 2018).

22. Jonathan Brinckman, *Riot Shows Violence of Prison Gangs' Ways*, Dayton Daily News, 9, May 2, 1993.

23. Dick Kimmins, *Cost of Riot Could Exceed $10 Million*, Cinn. Enquirer, 37, May 1, 1993.

24. Bazelon, 1982 Memorandum of Resignation, 20; Jonathan Simon, *The New Overcrowding*, 48 Conn. L. Rev. 1191, 1202 (2016); *Report Says Inmates Warned Guard the Day Lucasville Riot Started*, Galion Inquirer, 1, Apr. 26, 1993; Anne Willette, *Lucasville's Legacy: 20 Years of Turmoil*, Cinn. Enquirer, A6, Apr. 22, 1993.

25. Sandy Theis & Tim Miller, *Racial Issues May Be Behind Lucasville Riot*, Dayton Daily News, 1, 6, Apr. 15, 1993, accompanied with text added to the drawing, "Life in an L Block Cell," based on a layout depicted by the Ohio Department of Rehabilitation & Corrections; Jonathan Brinckman, *Racial*

Fears Permeate All-White Lucasville, Dayton Daily News, 3, Apr. 15, 1993; *Riot at Lucasville Prison Preceded by Transfers*, Springfield Sun, A3, May 2, 1993; Jonathan Brinckman, *Big Prisons and Rural Areas Don't Mix*, Casper Star-Tribune, 8, May 3, 1993; Jane Schroeder, *What We Learned from the Lucasville Uprising*, Dayton Daily News, 9, May 10, 1993; *Riot-Torn Prison May Lose Some Inmates*, Pittsburgh Post-Gazette, 40, May 3, 1992.

26. State v. Were, 118 Ohio St.3d 448, 449 (2008); Staughton Lynd, *Lucasville: The Untold Story of a Prison Uprising*, 24 (2d ed., PM Press, 2011). Kristen Delguzzi, *State Prison Officials Review Inmates Demands*, Cinn. Enquirer, 11, May 30, 1993; Jack A. Goldstone & Bert Useem, *Prison Riots as Micro Revolutions: An Extension of State-Centered Theories of Revolution*, 104 Am. J. Sociology 985, 1007–08 (1999). Lynd was one of the lawyers in *Wilkinson v. Austin*, discussed later in this chapter. As of 2023, none of the "Lucasville Five" had been executed.

27. *Riot at Lucasville Prison*; Kimmins, *Cost of Riot*.

28. GAO, *Prisons Costs*, 4.

29. ACA, *Standards for Adult Correctional Institutions*, 32, 38 (2d ed., 1981); Housing Inventory & Population Impact Task Force, Cal. Dept. of Corrections, *Prison Overcrowding: A Plan for Housing Felons Through FY 1986/87*, iv (1979)), quoted in Craig Haney, *The Wages of Prison Overcrowding: Harmful Psychological Consequences and Dysfunctional Correctional Reactions*, 22 Wash. U. J. L. & Pol'y 265, 267 (2006); Gerald G. Gaes & William J. McGuire, *Prison Violence: The Contribution of Crowding Versus Other Determinants of Prison Assault Rates*, 22 J. Rsch. Crime & Delinq. 41, 41, 62 (1985).

30. GAO, *Prison Costs*, 2, 12.

31. ACA, *Standards for Adult Correctional Institutions*, 43 (3d ed., 1990); ACA, *Standards for Adult Correctional Institutions*, 36–37 (4th ed., 2003). The 2003 single-cell requirement for people "assigned to maximum custody" was deleted in 2005. ACA, *Performance-Based Standards and Expected Practices for Adult Correctional Institutions*, 55, 246 (5th ed., 2021).

32. GAO, *1991 Prison Costs*, 3, 4, 32. GAO, *Revised Design Standards*; GAO, *Federal Jail Bedspace: Cost Savings and Greater Accuracy Possible in the Capacity Expansion Plan*, GGD 92–141 (Sept. 1992).

33. GAO, *Prison Costs*, 3–4, 27, 32, 37, 43–51; Gilmore, 105, 107.

34. Letter Harry H. Flickinger, Asst. Atty. Gen. for Administration, US DOJ, to Richard L. Fogel, Asst. Comptroller Gen., July 29, 1991, reprinted in GAO, Opportunities Exist to Lower the Cost of Building Federal Prisons, 66–69; GAO, *Revised Design Standards*, 5; GAO, *Prison Costs*, 45–51.

35. GAO, *Federal Prison Expansion, Overcrowding Reduced by Inmate Population Growth May Raise Issue Again*, GGD 94–48, 8 (Dec. 1993); Rated Capacities for Bureau Facilities, Program Statement Number 1060.11, June 30, 1997, revised Oct. 30, 2017, 1, 3, 4–7; Conditions of Confinement in the SHU, 28 CFR § 541.31 (2017).

36. GAO, *Bureau of Prisons: Growing Inmate Crowding Negatively Affects Inmates, Staff, and Infrastructure*, GAO 12–743, preface, 1, 11 (Sept. 2012).

37. Sandin v. Conner, 515 US 472, 484 (1995).

38. Haney, *Wages of Prison Overcrowding*, 272.

39. Atul Gawande, *Hellhole*, New Yorker, 36, Mar. 30, 2009; Keramet Reiter, *23/7: Pelican Bay Prison and the Rise of Long-Term Solitary Confinement* (Yale U. Press, 2016); Daniel P. Mears, *Evaluating the Effectiveness of Supermax Prisons* (Urb. Inst. Just. Pol'y Ctr., 2006); Ryan T. Sakoda & Jessica T. Simes, *Solitary Confinement and the US Prison Boom*, 32 Crim. Just. Pol'y Rev. 1, 14–15 (2019).

40. *In re* Medley, 134 US 160, 168 (1890). At issue was decision-making about an execution in a federal territory and not the legality of isolation.

41. Reginald Dwayne Betts, *Only Once I Thought About Suicide*, 125 Yale L. J. F. 222 (2016); Pennsylvania Senate Democratic Policy Committee, *Hearing on Solitary Confinement in Pennsylvania*, 27:10 (Aug. 10, 2021); Albert Woodfox, *Solitary: Unbroken by Four Decades in Solitary Confinement. My Story of Transformation and Hope*, 168–423 (2019); Johnson v. Wetzel, 209 F. Supp. 3d 766, 770, 782 (MD Pa. 2016).

42. Madrid v. Gomez, 889 F. Supp. 1146, 1265–66 (ND Cal. 1995).

43. Charles A. Reich, *The New Property*, 73 Yale L. J. 733 (1964).

44. Wolff v. McDonnell, 418 US 539 (1974); Conner v. Sakai, 15 F.3d 1463, 1466 (9th Cir. 1993).

45. *Sandin*, 484, majority opinion; Ginsburg, J. at 490; Breyer, J. at 494.

46. Austin v. Wilkinson, 189 F. Supp. 2d 719, 723 (ND Ohio 2002). Jason Robb, a member of the "Lucasville 5" held at OSP, was one of the plaintiffs. Complaint, 14, *Austin*, 2001 WL 34903823; Transcript of Oral Argument, *4–6, *20–21, Wilkinson v. Austin, 545 US 209 (2005) (No. 04–495), 2005 WL 840885; Brief for the United States as Amicus Curiae Supporting Petitioners, *10, *Wilkinson*, 2005 WL 273649. The radical confinement of ADX Florence is analyzed in Ian O'Donnell, *Prison Life: Pain, Resistance, and Purpose* (NYU Press, 2023); *Wilkinson*, 545 US, 227, 229.

47. Brief of Professors & Practitioners of Psychology & Psychiatry as Amicus Curiae in Support of Respondent, *4, *Wilkinson*, 2005 WL 539137; *Wilkinson*, 545 US, 223–24.

48. Keramet Reiter, *The Pelican Bay Hunger Strike: Resistance Within the Structural Constraints of a US Supermax Prison*, 113 S. Atlantic Q. 579 (2014); Jennifer Medina, *Hunger Strike by California Inmates, Already Large, Is Expected to Be Long*, NY Times (July 10, 2013); Benjamin Wallace-Wells, *The Plot from Solitary*, NY Mag. (Feb. 21, 2014); Michael Schwirtz & Michael Winerip, *Man Held at Rikers Jail for 3 Years Without Trial Commits Suicide at 22*, NY Times, A20, June 9, 2015.

49. Sealey v. Giltner, 197 F.3d 578, 580, 589–90 (2d Cir. 1999); Colon v. Howard, 215 F.3d 227, 229, 231 (2d Cir. 2000); Smith v. Arnone, 700 F. App'x 55, 56 (2d Cir. 2017), quoting Davis v. Barrett, 576 F.3d 129, 133 (2d Cir. 2009) (per curiam).

50. Rezaq v. Nalley, 677 F.3d 1001, 1007, 1016 (10th Cir. 2012); Grissom v. Werholtz, 524 F. App'x 467, 469, 474 (10th Cir. 2013); Grissom v. Roberts, 902 F.3d 1162, 1166, 1166, 1170–72 (10th Cir. 2018).

51. Jones v. Baker, 155 F.3d 810, 812–13 (6th Cir. 1998).

52. Wilkerson v. Goodwin, 774 F.3d 845, 856 (5th Cir. 2014).

53. UN Office on Drugs and Crime, *The United Nations Standard Minimum Rules for the Treatment of Prisoners*, Rules 43–44, A/Res/70/175 adopted Dec. 17, 2015 (*2015 Nelson Mandela Rules*). Rule 43 states that "[i]n no circumstances may restrictions or disciplinary sanctions amount to torture or other cruel, inhuman or degrading treatment or punishment"; both "indefinite" and "prolonged" solitary confinement are "prohibited," as well as placement in a constantly lit or dark cell, corporal punishment, food and drinking water reductions, collective punishments, punitive chaining and shackling, and prohibiting contact with family as a punishment.

54. ACA, *Restrictive Housing Performance Based Standards*, 32, 36, 38, 40 (ACA Standards 4-RH-0027, -0031, -0033, -0035 for prisons); 62, 65, 68, 69 (ACA Standards 4-ALDF-RH-021, -024, -027, -028 for local detention facilities); 39 (ACA Standard 4-RH-0034 for under age eighteen in prisons); 66 (ACA Standard 4-ALDF-RH-025 for local detention facilities) (2016).

55. Emma Kaufman & Justin Driver, *The Incoherence of Prison Law*, 135 Harv. L. Rev. 515 (2021); Sharon Dolovich, *The Coherence of Prison Law*, 135 Harv. L. Rev. F. 302 (2022).

56. Davis v. Ayala, 576 US 257, 288 (2015).

57. *Davis*, 576 US, 287–90. Justice Kennedy's references were: "Simon & Sparks, Punishment and Society: The Emergence of an Academic Field, in *The SAGE Handbook of Punishment and Society* (2013); Homer Venters, *Solitary Confinement and Risk of Self-Harm among Jail Inmates*, 104 Am. J. Pub. Health 442 (Mar. 2014); Metzner & Fellner, *Solitary Confinement and Mental Illness in US Prisons: A Challenge for Medical Ethics*, 38 J. Am. Academy Psychiatry and Law 104–08 (2010)" and "Grassian, *Psychiatric Effects of Solitary Confinement*, 22 Wash. U. J. L. & Poly 325 (2006) (common side-effects of solitary confinement include anxiety, panic, withdrawal, hallucinations, self-mutilation, and suicidal thoughts and behaviors)."

58. Brown v. Plata, 563 US 493, 510–11, 505 n.3.

59. Glossip v. Gross, 576 US 863, 926 (2015), Breyer, J., dissenting, joined by Ginsburg, J., quoting Craig Haney, *Mental Health Issues in Long-Term Solitary and "Supermax" Confinement*, 49 Crime & Delinq. 124, 130 (2003). Justice Breyer did so again in dissents in Jordan v. Mississippi, 138 S. Ct. 2567, 2568 (2018) and Ruiz v. Texas, 580 US 1191 (2022).

60. Apodaca v. Raemisch, 586 US 931, 937 (2018), statement of Sotomayor, J., respecting the denial of certiorari.

61. *Davis*, 576 US, 290; *Plata*, 550. Justice Scalia, joined by Justice Thomas, dissented.

62. Bucklew v. Precythe, 587 US 119 (2019); New York State Rifle & Pistol Assn., Inc. v. Bruen, 597 US 1 (2022); Dobbs v. Jackson Women's Health Org., 597 US 215 (2022); City of Grants Pass Oregon v. Johnson, 144 S. Ct. 2202 (2024). Disagreement within the Court about constitutional method was evident in United States v. Rahimi,144 S. Ct. 1889 (2024). Over a sole dissent by Justice

Thomas, all justices agreed that the government could temporarily refuse to permit a person, demonstrably violent, to carry a gun. That judgment produced six opinions debating how and why to reach that conclusion.

63. Jules Lobel, *Participatory Litigation: A New Framework for Impact Lawyering*, 72 Stan. L. Rev. 87 (2022); Settlement Agreement, Ashker v. Governor of the State of California, No. C 09–05796 CW, 2016 WL 4770013 (ND Cal. Sept. 14, 2016); Paige St. John, *California Agrees to Move Thousands of Inmates out of Solitary Confinement*, LA Times, Sept. 1, 2015.

64. Peoples v. Annucci, 180 F. Supp. 3d 294 (SDNY 2016); Davis v. Baldwin, No. 3:16-cv-00600, 2017 WL 951406 (SD Ill. Mar. 10, 2017); Parsons v. Ryan, 912 F.3d 486 (9th Cir. 2018); Settlement Agreement and General Release, Disability Rights Network of Pa. v. Wetzel, No. 1:13-cv-00635-JEJ (MD Pa. 2015); Elizabeth Alexander, *This Experiment, So Fatal: Some Initial Thoughts on Strategic Choices in the Campaign Against Solitary Confinement*, 5 UC Irvine L. Rev. 1 (2015).

65. Order Granting Motion to Extend Settlement Agreement, Ashker v. Governor of California, No. 09-cv-05796-CW (ND Cal. Jan. 25, 2019), appeals dismissed and remanded, 968 F.3d 975 (9th Cir. 2020); Order Extending the Settlement Agreement, *Ashker*, (ND Cal. Apr. 9, 2021); Order Extending the Settlement Agreement for a Second Twelve-Month Period, *Ashker*, (ND Cal. Feb. 2, 2022), reversed, vacated, and dismissed, 81 F.4th 863, 872 (9th Cir. 2023).

66. Porter v. Clarke, 923 F.3d 348, 353–57, 368 (4th Cir. 2019), aff'd 290 F. Supp. 3d 518, 537–38 (ED Va. 2018); Mary Marshall, *The Promise of* Porter? Porter v. Clarke *and Its Potential Impact on Solitary Confinement Litigation*, 120 Colum. L. Rev. F. 67 (2020).

67. Greenhill v. Clarke, 944 F.3d. 243, 251–52 (4th Cir. 2019).

68. Rick Raemisch, *My Night in Solitary*, NY Times (Feb. 20, 2014); Rick Raemisch, *Why We Ended Long-Term Solitary Confinement in Colorado*, NY Times (Oct. 12, 2017).

69. Hope Metcalf, Jamelia Morgan, Samuel Oliker-Friedland, Judith Resnik, Julia Spiegel, Haran Tae, Alyssa Work & Brian Holbrook, *Administrative Segregation, Degrees of Isolation, and Incarceration: A National Overview of State and Federal Correctional Policies*, 5–8 (2013).

70. The Liman Program & Association of State Correctional Administrators, *Time-In-Cell: The ASCA-Liman 2014 National Survey of Administrative Segregation in Prison*, 10 (Aug. 2015).

71. Correctional Leaders Assn. & Arthur Liman Ctr. Public Interest L. Yale L. School, *Time-In-Cell: A 2021 Snapshot of Restrictive Housing Based on a Nationwide Survey of US Prison Systems*, viii, xi, 5 (Aug. 2022).

72. *Calculating Torture: Analysis of Federal, State, and Local Data Showing More than 122,000 People in Solitary Confinement in US Prisons and Jails*, 3–13 (Solitary Watch and the Unlock the Box Campaign, May 2023).

73. Arianna Zoghi, Alexandra Harrington, Judith Resnik & Anna VanCleave, The Liman Ctr. at Yale Law School, *Regulating Restrictive Housing: State and*

Federal Legislation on Solitary Confinement as of July 1, 2019 (2019); Judith Resnik, Jenny E. Carroll, Skylar Albertson, Sarita Benesch & Wynne Muscatine Graham, *Legislative Regulation of Isolation in Prison: 2018–2021*, available on Liman Ctr. website.

74. Colo. Dept. of Corrections, Reg. No. 650–03, § IV.A.2.a, at 2 (2017, in effect July 1, 2022); An Act Concerning Restrictive Housing in Local Jails, 2021 Colo. Sess. Laws 1974 (codified at Colo. Rev. Stat. § 17–26–301 et seq.); Mass. Gen. Laws Ann. ch. 127, § 39E (West 2018); NJSA §§ 30:4–82.8a9 (West, 2020); Humane Alternatives to Long-Term Solitary Confinement Act (HALT), SB S2836, 2021S, 2021–2022 Reg. Sess. (NY 2021); An Act Promoting Responsible Oversight, Treatment, and Effective Correctional Transparency (PROTECT), Pub. Act 22–18, Substitute for Raised SB 459, 2022 Leg. Sess. (Conn. 2022); US DOJ, Bureau of Justice Statistics, Federal Prisoner Statistics Collected Under the First Step Act, 2022 (NCJ 304953, Dec. 2022). End Solitary Confinement Act, HR 4972, 118th Cong. 1st Sess., introduced July 27, 2023; Solitary Confinement Reform Act, S. 4121, introduced April 15, 2024.

75. Sara Sullivan, Vedan Anthony-North, David Cloud, Léon Digard, Laruen Galarza, Allison Hastings, Jacob Kang-Brown, Byron Kline, Jessi LaChance, Stephen Roberts, Lionel Smith, Elena Vanko & Jessica Wilcox, *Safe Alternatives to Segregation Initiative* (Vera Inst., May 2019); Léon Digard, Elena Vanko & Sara Sullivan, *Rethinking Restrictive Housing: Lessons from Five US Jail and Prison Systems* (Vera Inst., May 2018); American Public Health Association, Solitary Confinement as a Public Health Issue, Policy Number 201310, Nov. 5, 2013; Society of Correctional Physicians, Restricted Housing of Mentally Ill Inmates, Position Statement, Feb. 4, 2014; *Architects/Designers/Planners for Social Responsibility*, https://www.adpsr.org/; Tings Chak, *Alternatives to Incarceration: Raphael Sperry in Conversation with Tings Chak*, 5 Scapegoat J. 394 (2013); *Press Release: AIA Board of Directors Commits to Advancing Justice Through Design*, AIA (Dec. 11, 2020); Julia Jacobs, *Prominent Architects Group Prohibits Design of Death Chambers*, NY Times, Dec. 11, 2020; Tim Nelson, *The AIA Moves to Prohibit Members from Designing Death Chambers*, Architectural Digest, Dec. 14, 2020.

76. *Plata*, 501–02.

77. *Plata*, 565.

78. Simon, *The New Overcrowding*, 1191–97, 1200–02; Ruth Wilson Gilmore, *Golden Gulag: Prisons, Surplus, Crisis, and Opposition in Globalizing California*, 20–29, 55–86, 125–27 (U. of Calif. Press, 2007); Michelle Alexander, *The New Jim Crow: Mass Incarceration in the Age of Colorblindness*, 178–220 (New Press, 2012); Emily Widra, *Since You Asked: Just How Overcrowded Were Prisons before the Pandemic, and at this Time of Social Distancing, How Overcrowded Are They Now?* (Prison Policy Initiative, Dec. 21, 2020).

79. *Plata*, 548–49; 502, 503.

80. *Plata*, Appendix B, 548; Appendix C, 549.

81. Gilmore, 7, 108–18; Jonathan Simon, *Mass Incarceration on Trial: A Remark-able Court Decision and the Future of Prisons in America* (New Press, 2014); *Plata*, 506, 519.

82. *Plata*, 506–08, 520.

83. Prison Reform: Enhancing the Effectiveness of Incarceration, Hearing on S. 3, S. 38, S. 400, S. 8666, S. 930, and HR. 667, Before the Senate Comm. on the Judiciary, 104th Cong. 38 (1995); 18 USC § 3626a1A; *Plata*, 510–11.

84. *Plata*, 510–11, citing *Estelle*; Atkins v. Virginia, 536 US 304, 311 (2002), Trop v. Dulles, 356 US 86, 100 (1958).

85. *Plata*, 501–02, 507, 517–18, 522.

86. *Plata*, 511, 525.

87. *Plata*, 550–53, 563.

88. Judith Resnik, *Diffusing Disputes: The Public in the Private of Arbitration, the Private in Courts, and the Erasure of Rights*, 124 Yale L. J. 2804 (2015).

89. *Plata*, 570–72, 565–66, 580–81, Scalia, J., dissenting, joined by Thomas, J.

90. Holt v. Hobbs, 574 US 352 (2015).

91. Thomas P. Bonczar & Allen J. Beck, US DOJ, *Bureau of Justice Statistics: Special Report: Lifetime Likelihood of Going to State or Federal Prison*, 1 (Mar. 1997) (NCJ-160092); Thomas P. Bonczar, US DOJ, *Bureau of Justice Statistics: Special Report: Prevalence of Imprisonment in the US Population, 1974–2001*, 1 (Aug. 2003) (NCJ 197976); Pew Ctr. on the States, *One in 100: Behind Bars in American 2008*, Pew Charitable Trusts, 3 (Feb. 2008).

92. Benjamin Justice & Tracey L. Meares, *How the Criminal Justice System Educates Citizens*, 651 Annals Am. Acad. Pol. & Soc. Science 159, 157 (2014); Reuben Jonathan Miller & Amanda Alexander, *The Price of Carceral Citizenship: Punishment, Surveillance, and Social Welfare Policy in an Age of Carceral Expansion*, 21 Mich. J. Race & L. 291 (2016); Monica C. Bell, *Police Reform and the Dismantling of Legal Estrangement*, 126 Yale L. J. 2054 (2017).

93. Inimai Chettiar, Lauren-Brooke Eisen & Nicole Fortier with Timothy Ross, *Reforming Funding to Reduce Mass Incarceration* (Brennan Ctr., 2013); Benjamin Levin, *The Consensus Myth in Criminal Justice Reform*, 117 Mich. L. Rev. 259, 262–64 (2018); Marie Gottschalk, *Caught: The Prison State and the Lockdown of American Politics* (Princeton U. Press, 2016).

94. Prison Rape Elimination Act of 2003, Pub. L. 108–79 (codified at 34 USC §§30301–4); Bureau of Justice Statistics: The National Reentry Resource Ctr., *The Second Chance Act* (April 2018); First Step Act of 2018, Pub. L. 115–391, amending several sections of 18 USC including Sections 3582, 3624b, and 4042a.

95. Civil Rights Division, US Dept. Just., *Investigation of the Ferguson Police Dept.* (Mar. 4, 2015); Civil Rights Division, Office of Justice Programs & Office for Access to Justice, US DOJ, *Dear Colleague Letter to Courts Regarding Fines and Fees for Youth and Adults* (Apr. 20, 2023).

96. Vera Institute for Justice, *The Price of Prisons* (2017).

97. Andrea Armstrong, *Louisiana Deaths Behind Bars, 2015–2021*, 2–3, 20 (Loyola U. New Orleans College of Law Research Paper No. 2024-01, Incarceration Transparency, June 2023).
98. Office of the Inspector General, *Audit of the Federal Bureau of Prisons' Efforts to Maintain and Construct Institutions*, US DOJ (redacted for public release, May 2023).
99. *Alabama Question Election Results: Ratify the Recompiled State Constitution*, NY Times, Nov. 8, 2022; Official Vermont General Election Ballot Nov. 8, 2022, Burlington Vt.; *Vermont Proposal 2 Election Results: Prohibit Slavery in State Constitution*, NY Times, Nov. 8, 2022; Oregon Secretary of State, Online Voters' Guide: 2022 General Election, Measure 112; *Election Results: Remove Constitutional Language Allowing Slavery as Punishment*, NY Times, Nov. 8, 2022; Election Results, Tenn. Sec. of State, Nov. 8, 2022; Paige Pfleger, *Slavery Is Still Allowed as a Punishment for Crime in Tennessee's Constitution. Amendment 3 Seeks to Change That*, WPLN, Oct. 31, 2022; Max Matza, *Four States Voted to Abolish Slavery, But Not Louisiana. Here's Why*, BBC, Nov. 10, 2022. An overview of statutory rights comes from Aaron Littman, *Free-World Law Behind Bars*, 131 Yale L. J. 1385 (2022).

CHAPTER 29

1. Jeremy Bentham, Panopticon; Postscript, Part II: Principles and Plan of Management, 1787, published 1791, reprinted in *The Works of Jeremy Bentham* vol. 4, 121–22 (John Bowring ed. 1843).
2. Edwards v. Sard, 250 F. Supp. 977, 981 (DDC 1966).
3. Brief of the States of Alaska et al. in Support of Petitioners, Amici Curiae, *15, Rhodes v. Chapman, 452 US 337 (1981) (No. 80–332), 1980 WL 339866.
4. Morales v. Schmidt, 340 F. Supp. 544, 548 (WD Wis. 1972). The appellate court reversed, rejecting burdening the government to justify differential treatment of incarcerated and free individuals. Morales v. Schmidt, 489 F.2d 1335 (7th Cir. 1973), rehearing en banc, 494 F.2d 85 (7th Cir. 1974).
5. H. L. A. Hart, *Punishment and Responsibility*, 234–35 (Clarendon Press, 1968); Leora Dahan Katz, *Response Retributivism: Defending the Duty to Punish*, 40 L. & Phil. 585 (2021); Dahan Katz, *The Dogma of Opposing Welfare and Retributivism*, 29 Legal Theory 1 (2023); Didier Fassin, *The Will to Punish* (Oxford U. Press, 2018); Baze v. Rees, 553 US 35 (2008); Glossip v. Gross, 576 US 863 (2015); David Garland, *The Problem of the Body in Modern State Punishment*, 78 Soc. Rsch. 767 (2011).
6. *Morales*, 340 F. Supp., 553–54.
7. Payne v. Tennessee, 501 US 808 (1991); Kristen N. Henning, *What's Wrong with Victims' Rights in Juvenile Court? Retributive v. Rehabilitative Systems of Justice*, 97 Cal. L. Rev. 1107 (2009); John Braithwaite, *Restorative Justice & Responsive Regulation* (Oxford U. Press, 2002); Annalise Acorn, Compulsory Compassion: A Critique of Restorative Justice, *The Seductive Vision of*

Restorative Justice: Right-Relation, Reciprocity, Healing, and Repair, 1–26 (UBC Press, 2003).

8. Norval Morris & Michael Tonry, *Between Prison and Probation: Intermediate Punishments in a Rational Sentencing System* (Oxford U. Press, 1990).

9. Caleb Smith, *The Prison and the American Imagination*, 199 (Yale U. Press, 2009); Emily A. Wang, Clemens S. Hong, Liz Samuels, Shira Shavit, Ronald Sanders & Margot Kushel, *Transitions Clinic: Creating a Community-Based Model of Health Care for Recently Released California Prisoners*, 125 Pub. Health Rep. 171 (2010).

10. Hendrik Hartog, *The Constitution of Aspiration and "The Rights That Belong to Us All,"* 74 J. Am. Hist. 1013 (1987).

11. Leah Wang & Wendy Sawyer, *New Data: State Prisons Are Increasingly Deadly Places*, Prison Pol'y Initiative, June 8, 2021; Andrea Armstrong, *Louisiana Deaths Behind Bars, 2015–2021*, 2–3, 20 (Loyola U. New Orleans College of Law Research Paper No. 2024–01, Incarceration Transparency, June 2023).

12. Antonin Scalia, *Originalism: The Lesser Evil*, 57 U. Cinn. L. Rev. 849, 864 (1988). Scalia later "repudiate[d]" his self-description and said that "flogging" was "stupid" but not unconstitutional. Jennifer Senior, *In Conversation: Antonin Scalia*, NY Mag., Oct. 4, 2013.

13. International Covenant on Civil and Political Rights, adopted Dec. 19, 1966, 999 United Nations Treaty Series 171, No. 14668; The Istanbul Statement on the Use and Effects of Solitary Confinement, adopted Dec. 9, 2007, International Psychological Trauma Symposium, Istanbul; Peter Scharff Smith, *Solitary Confinement: An Introduction to the Istanbul Statement on the Use and Effects of Solitary Confinement*, 18 Torture 56 (2008); United Nations Rules for the Treatment of Women Prisoners and Non-Custodial Measures for Women Offenders, adopted Dec. 21, 2010, General Assembly Resolution A/RES/65/229, New York; Sharon Shalev, *Mapping Solitary Confinement*, SolitaryConfinement.org; Juan Mendez, Special Rapporteur on Torture, Address to the UN General Assembly (Oct. 22, 2013); *Solitary Confinement: Effects, Practices, and Pathways to Reform* (Jules Lobel & Peter Scharff Smith eds., Oxford U. Press, 2019).

14. Penal Reform International, Annual Report 2022, 6; Matti Joutsen, *International Standards and Norms as Guidance in the Criminal Justice System*, 54, 55–65, Resource Material Series no. 98, United Nations Asia and Far East Institute for the Prevention of Crime and the Treatment of Offenders (2016); Annabel Jackson Associates Ltd, *Case Study of the Review of the Standard Minimum Rules for PRI and DFID*, 5–21 (Oct. 2015); Jennifer Peirce, *Making the Mandela Rules: Evidence, Expertise, and Politics in the Development of Soft Law International Prison Standards*, 43 Queens L. J. 263, 267–78 (2018); Penal Reform International, *Essex Paper 3, Initial Guidance on the Interpretation and Implementation of the UN Nelson Mandela Rules*, 5 (2016).

15. Peirce, *Making the Mandela Rules*, 289–91; UN Office on Drugs and Crime (UNODC), *United Nations Standard Minimum Rules for the Treatment of Prisoners*, A/Res/70/175 adopted Dec. 17, 2015 (*2015 Nelson Mandela Rules*).

16. SMR 2015 Preliminary Observation 2; Rules, 43, 44, 51, 52, 60; Katrin Tiroch, *Modernizing the Standard Minimum Rules for the Treatment of Prisoners: A Human Rights Perspective*, 293, 19 Max Planck Yearbook of United Nations Law 278 (Frauke Lachenmann, Tilmann Röder & Rudiger Wolfrum eds., Leiden: Koninklijke Brill, 2016); Walter Suntinger & Philipp Meissner, UNODC, *Assessing Compliance with the Nelson Mandela Rules: A Checklist for Internal Inspection Mechanisms* (2017); Dirk van Zyl Smit, UNODC, *Incorporating the Nelson Mandela Rules into National Prison Legislation: A Model Prison Act and Related Commentary* (2022).

17. Dirk van Zyl Smit, International Prison Standards and Transnational Criminal Justice, *Transnational Legal Ordering of Criminal Justice*, 261 (Gregory Shaffer & Ely Aaronson eds., Oxford U. Press, 2020); Hirst v. United Kingdom (no. 2), Grand Chamber-2005 Eur. Ct. HR (2005); limited in Scoppola v. Italy (no. 3), Grand Chamber-2012 Eur. Ct. HR (2012); Torreggiani and Others v. Italy, II-2013 Eur. Ct. HR, (Jan. 8, 2013); Orchowski v. Poland, IV-2009 Eur. Ct. HR, (Oct. 22, 2009); Sikorski v. Poland, IV-2010 Eur. Ct. HR, (Oct. 22, 2009); Öcalan v. Turkey, I-2003 Eur. Ct. HR, App. No. 46221/99 (Mar. 12, 2003); Öcalan v. Turkey, Grand Chamber-2005 Eur. Ct. HR, App. No. 46221/99 (May 12, 2005); Kungurov v. Russia, III-2020 Eur. Ct. HR, App. No. 70468/17, paragraphs 18–20 (Feb. 18, 2020). Dirk van Zyl Smit, *Regulation of Prison Conditions*, 39 Crime & Justice 503 (2010).

18. First United Nations Congress on the Prevention of Crime and the Treatment of Offenders, *Standard Minimum Rules for the Treatment of Prisoners* (Rule 57) (Geneva, 1955, amended 1977).

19. Van Zyl Smit, *Incorporating the Nelson Mandela Rules*, 13–14, art. 3, 1; *Essex Paper 3, Initial Guidance*, 9.

20. HM Chief Inspector of Prisons for England and Wales, Annual Report 2022–2023, July 5, 2023 (Crown Copyright, 2023); Ruth Marin, Fiora Fitzalan Howard & Jenny Tew, *What is a Rehabilitative Prison*, 235 Prison Service J. 3 (2018); Handout, HMP Brixton 2018.

21. HM Chief Inspector, Annual Report 2022–23; Bill Keller, *The Alarming Americanisation of British Prisons*, Prospect, July 19, 2023; Bill Keller, *What's Prison For? Punishment and Rehabilitation in the Age of Mass Incarceration* (Columbia Glob. Reports, 2022); Sharon Dolovich, *The Failed Regulation and Oversight of American Prisons*, 5 Ann. Rev. of Criminology 153 (2021).

22. B. M. and Others v. France, V-2023 Eur. Ct. HR, App. No. 84187/17 (July 2023); Observatoire International des Prisons, Rapport D'Enquête: Au Coeur de La Prison: La Machine Disciplinaire (Jan. 2024); Paule Gonzalès, Le monde pénitentiaire au bord de la rupture, Le Figaro, May 29, 2024.

23. US DOJ, *Investigation of Alabama's State Prisons for Men*, Apr. 2, 2019; US DOJ, *Investigation of Mississippi State Penitentiary (Parchman)*, Apr. 20, 2022; Eduardo Medina, *Alabama Inmates Go on Strike, Citing Prison Conditions*, NY Times, A17, Sept. 29, 2022.

24. Oona Hathaway, *Do Human Rights Treaties Make a Difference?*, 111 Yale L. J. 1935 (2002); Cosette D. Creamer & Beth A. Simmons, *The Dynamic Impact*

of Periodic Review on Women's Rights, 81 L. & Contemp. Probs. 31 (2018); Gráinee de Búrca, *Reframing Human Rights in a Turbulent Era* (2021); Cheryl Corley, *North Dakota Prison Officials Think Outside the Box to Revamp Solitary Confinement*, NPR, July 31, 2018.

25. Seyla Benhabib, Democratic Iterations: The Local, the National, and the Global, *Another Cosmopolitanism*, 45–80 (Robert Post ed., Oxford U. Press, 2006).

26. Van Zyl Smit, *International Prison Standards*, 261–62; Sarah Armstrong, *Securing Prison Through Human Rights: Unanticipated Implications of Rights-Based Penal Governance*, 57 Howard J. Crime & Just. 401 (2018); *European Penology?* (Tom Daems, Dirk van Zyl Smith & Sonja Snacken eds., Oxford U. Press, 2013).

27. Judith Resnik, *Globalization(s), Privatization(s), Constitutional-ization, and Stat-ization: Icons and Experiences of Sovereignty in the 21st Century*, 11 Int'l J. Const. L. 162 (2013); Saskia Sassen, *Territory, Authority, Rights: From Medieval to Global Assemblages* (Princeton U. Press, 2006); Catherine M. Donnelly, *Delegation of Governmental Power to Private Parties: A Comparative Perspective* (Oxford U. Press, 2007); Ben Crewe, Alison Liebling & Susie Hulley, *Staff-Prisoner Relationships, Staff Professionalism, and the Use of Authority in Public- and Private Sector Prisons*, 40 L. & Soc. Inquiry 309 (2013).

28. GEO Group, *2011 Annual Report*, 3, 24; GEO Group, *The GEO Group Reports Fourth Quarter and Full Year 2022 Results*, Feb. 14, 2023; GEO Group, *Answers to the Most Common Criticisms of Contract Detention/Correctional Service Providers*, June 2019.

29. International Corrections & Prisons Association, *About ICPA: For the Advancement of Professional Corrections: Membership*; Gary Hill, *Coming of Age: The International Corrections and Prisons* Association, Corrections Compendium (Mar. 22, 2009); International Corrections & Prisons Association, *Advancing Corrections Journal*.

30. Amy E. Lerman, *Officer Health and Wellness: Results from the California Correctional Officer Survey* 4 (Nov. 2017); Caterina Spinaris and Nicole Brocato, *Descriptive Study of Michigan Department of Corrections Staff Well-being: Contributing Factors, Outcomes, and Actionable Solutions* (July 1, 2019); Frank Valentino Ferdik & Hayden P. Smith, *Correctional Officer Safety and Wellness Literature Synthesis*, 2 (US Dept. Justice, Nat'l Inst. Just., July 2017); Bureau of Labor Statistics, US Dept. of Labor, *Occupational Outlook Handbook, Correctional Officers and Bailiffs* (2021); Mazen El Ghaziri, Lisa A. Jaegers, Carlos E. Monteiro, Paulo L. Grubb & Martin G. Cherniack, *Progress in Corrections Workers Health: The National Corrections Collaborative Utilizing a Total Worker Health Strategy*, 62 J. Occupational & Env't Med. 965 (2020).

31. Lars Trautman, *Addressing Staffing Challenges in Federal Prisons* 3–8, Right on Crime, Tex. Pub. Pol'y Foundation, (2022); ADC Annual Report FY 2022, 15; Homer Venters, *Life and Death at Rikers Island* (Johns Hopkins U. Press, 2019); Mario Koran, *Inside a "Nightmare" Lockdown at a Wisconsin Prison*, NY Times, A1, Aug. 19, 2023; Office of the Inspector General, *Audit of the*

Federal Bureau of Prisons' Efforts to Maintain and Construct Institutions, (US DOJ Report No. 23–064, May 2023).

32. Shane Bauer, *American Prison: A Reporter's Undercover Journey into the Business of Punishment* 226–73 (Penguin, 2018); Ted Conover, *Newjack: A Year as a Prison Guard in New York's Most Infamous Maximum Security Jail* (Ebury Press, 2011).

33. Cyrus Ahalt, Colette S. Peters, Heidi Steward & Brie Williams, *Transforming Prison Culture to Improve Correctional Staff Wellness and Outcomes for Adults in Custody "the Oregon Way,"* 8 Advancing Corr. J. 130 (2019); Cyrus Ahalt, Craig Haney, Kim Ekhaugen & Brie Williams, *Role of a US–Norway Exchange in Placing Health and Well-Being at the Center of US Prison Reform*, 110 Am. J. Pub. Health S27 (2020); Veronica Horowitz, Emily R. Greberman, Patrick E. Nolan, Jordan M. Hyatt, Chris Uggen, Synøve N. Andersen & Steven L. Chanenson, *A Comparative Perspective on Officer Wellness: American Reflections from Norwegian Prisons*, 10 Crim. Just. Stud. 1080 (2021); Brief of Appellee-Intervenor California Correctional Peace Officers' Association, Brown v. Plata, 563 US 493 (2011) (No. 09–1233), 2010 WL 4253495.

34. HMP Grendon began in the 1960s as a "psychiatric prison" and as of 2021 was one of two facilities in England and Wales designed to involve its members in intensive therapeutic efforts. HM Chief Inspector of Prisons, *Report on a Scrutiny Visit to HMP Grendon* (March 2021); Caroline McClatchey, *HMP Grendon: Therapy for Dangerous Prisoners*, BBC News, June 11, 2018; H. P. Tollinton, *Grendon Prison*, 6 Brit. J. Criminology 39 (1966); Jamie Bennett, *Race and Power: The Potential and Limitations of Prison-Based Democratic Therapeutic Communities*, 3 Race & Just. 130 (2013).

35. David Garland, *Punishment and Welfare* (Gower, 1985); Elaine Genders & Elaine Player, *Therapy in Prison: Revisiting Grendon 20 Years On*, 49 Howard J. Crim. Just. 431 (2010); David H. Cloud, Ilana R. Garcia-Grossman, Andrea Armstrong & Brie Williams, *Public Health and Prisons: Priorities in the Age of Mass Incarceration*, 44 Ann. Rev. Pub. Health 407 (2022).

36. Mansoor Malik, Samar Padder, Suneeta Kumari & Haroon Burhanullah, Mental Health Burden and Burnout in Correctional Workers, *Correctional Facilities and Correctional Treatment: International Perspectives*, 93–124 (Rui Abrunhosa Gonçalves ed., IntechOpen, 2023); Andrew Montoya-Barthelemy and fourteen other authors, *Occupational and Environmental Hazards of Correctional Settings*, 64 J. Occupational & Env't Med., 172 (March, 2022); Nina Fusco & six coauthors, *When Our Work Hits Home: Trauma and Mental Disorders in Correctional Officers and Other Correctional Workers*, 11 Frontiers in Psychiatry 493391 (Feb. 2021); David H. Cloud, Cyrus Ahalt, Dallas Augustine, David Sears & Brie Williams, *Medical Isolation and Solitary Confinement: Balancing Health and Humanity in US Jails and Prisons During COVID-19*, 35 J. Gen. Internal Med. 2738 (2020); Wang & Sawyer, *New Data: State Prisons Are Increasingly Deadly Places*; Brendan Saloner, Kalind Parish, Julie A. Ward, Grace DiLaura & Sharon Dolovich, *COVID-19 Cases and Deaths in Federal and State Prisons*, 324 JAMA 602 (2020).

37. Hans W. Mattick, *The Future of Imprisonment in a Free Society*, 17 British J. Criminology 450, 450–52 (1967); Erving Goffman, On the Characteristics of Total Institutions: The Inmate World, *The Prison: Studies in Institutional Organization and Change*, 15–67 (Donald R. Cressey ed., Holt Rinehart & Winston, 1961); David Rothman, *The Discovery of the Asylum: Social Order and Disorder in the New Republic* 295 (Little Brown, 1971).

38. Angela Y. Davis, *Are Prisons Obsolete?* (Seven Stories, 2003); Jessica Mitford, *Kind and Usual Punishment* (Alfred A. Knopf, 1974); Allegra M. McLeod, *Envisioning Abolition Democracy*, 132 Harv. L. Rev. 1613 (2019); Dorothy E. Roberts, *Abolition Constitutionalism*, 133 Harv. L. Rev. 1 (2019); Bernard Harcourt, *Abolition Democracy 13/13*, Columbia Ctr. Contemporary Critical Thought (2020–2021); Mariame Kaba, *We Do This 'til We Free Us: Abolition Organizing and Transforming Justice* (Tamara Nopper ed., Haymarket Books, 2021); Kay Gabriel, *Abolition as Method: Ruth Wilson Gilmore's* Abolition Geography *is Written to be Used*, Dissent Magazine, Fall 2022; Rachel Kushner, *Is Prison Necessary? Ruth Wilson Gilmore Might Change Your Mind*, NY Times Mag., Apr. 17, 2019; Ruth Gilmore, *Abolition Geography: Essays Towards Liberation* (Verso, 2022).

CHAPTER 30

1. Michel Foucault, *The Punitive Society: Lectures at the Collège de France 1972-1973*, 225 (Bernard E. Harcourt ed., Graham Burchell trans., Palgrave MacMillan, 2015).

2. Timbs v. Indiana, 586 US 146, 151–54; 162–70 (2019). The majority, written by Justice Ginsburg, relied on the "incorporation" of this provision through the Fourteenth Amendment that uses the term "person." Justice Thomas invoked the narrower route of the "privileges and immunities of citizenship."

3. Nicholas M. McLean, *Livelihood, Ability to Pay, and the Original Meaning of the Excessive Fines Clause*, 40 Hastings Const. L. Q. 833, 854–57, 869, 884 (2013). McLean cited the Letter from Benjamin Franklin to Robert Morris (Dec. 25, 1783), Benjamin Franklin's Writings 1079, 1082 (Library of America, 1987).

4. Laaman v. Helgemoe, 437 F. Supp. 269, 315–16 (DNH 1977). Judge Bownes explained he was not relying on any "constitutional right to rehabilitation" but on the right to "avoid physical, mental or social degeneration."

5. Willowbrook State School for the Mentally Retarded was at issue in NY State Association for Retarded Children v. Rockefeller, 357 F. Supp. 752 (EDNY 1973). The US Department of Justice joined on behalf of the children, and the parties negotiated a consent decree. NY State Association for Retarded Children v. Carey, 596 F.2d 27 (1979). Alabama's facility was at issue in Wyatt v. Stickney, 325 F. Supp. 781, 785 (MD Ala. 1971), aff'd in part, rev'd in part *sub nom*. Wyatt v. Aderholt, 503 F.2d 1305 (5th Cir. 1974). Related was Youngberg v. Romeo, 457 US 326, 325, 327 (1982).

6. Monica C. Bell, Katherine Beckett & Forrest Stuart, *Investing in Alternatives: Three Logics of Criminal System Replacement*, 11 UC Irvine L. Rev. 1291

(2021); Monica C. Bell, *Next Generation Policing Research: Three Propositions*, 35 J. Econ. Persp. 29 (2021).

7. Ben Crewe, *Depth, Weight, Tightness: Revisiting the Pains of Imprisonment*, 13 Punishment & Soc'y 509 (2011).

8. Council of Europe, Recommendation of the Committee of Ministers on the European Prison Rules, Rec (2006) 2-rev (Jan. 11, 2006, rev'd July 1, 2020); *United Nations Standard Minimum Rules for the Treatment of Prisoners*, 5.1, A/Res/70/175 adopted Dec. 17, 2015 (*2015 Nelson Mandela Rules*).

9. Jeremy Bentham, Panopticon; Postscript, Part II: Principles and Plan of Management, 1787, published 1791, reprinted in *The Works of Jeremy Bentham* vol. 4, 122–25 (John Bowring ed., 1843).

10. Philip Schofield, *Bentham: A Guide for the Perplexed*, 77 (Bloomsbury Publishing, 2009).

11. Bentham, Panopticon; Postscript, 122–23.

12. Lamar James, *Prisons Cost Every Arkansan Nickel a Day*, 10, Ark. Gazette, Apr. 23, 1989.

13. 2006 European Prison Rules Rule 5. French prisons also provided some Euros as grants, albeit conditional on behavior, to assist poor prisoners. Didier Fassin, *Prison Worlds: An Ethnography of the Carceral Condition*, 207–10 (Rachel Gomme trans., Polity Press, 2017).

14. National Research Council, *The Growth of Incarceration in the United States: Exploring Causes and Consequences*, 326 (Jeremy Travis, Bruce Western & Stephen Redburn eds., The National Academies Press, 2014).

15. Bruce Western, *Recent Trends in Punitive Criminal Justice in the United States*, Mar. 2015 (unpublished manuscript) (presented at the Interdisciplinary Roundtable on Punitiveness in America, John Jay College of Criminal Justice, Apr. 2–3, 2015); Michael Tonry, *Equality and Dignity: The Missing Ingredients in American Sentencing*, 45 Crime & Just. 459 (2016).

16. Fassin, *Prison Worlds: An Ethnography of the Carceral Condition*, x–xvi, 206, 285; (Rachel Comme, trans. Polity Press, 2017); Loïc Wacquant, *Deadly Symbiosis: When the Ghetto and the Prison Meet and Mesh*, 3 Punishment & Soc'y 95 (2001); Mary Bosworth, *Theorizing Race and Imprisonment: Towards a New Penalty*, 12 Critical Criminology 221 (2004); Emma Kaufman, *Punish and Expel: Border Control, Nationalism, and the New Purpose of the Prison* (Oxford U. Press, 2015); Mary Bosworth, *Inside Immigration Detention* (Oxford U. Press, 2017); Olivia J. Hull, Olivia D. Breckler & Lisa A. Jaegers, *Integrated Safety and Health Promotion among Correctional Works and People Incarcerated: A Scoping Review*, 20 Int'l J. of Env't Research & Pub. Health 6104, 1 (2023).

17. Nicola Lacey, *The Prisoners' Dilemma: Political Economy and Punishment in Contemporary Democracies*, xvi (Cambridge U. Press, 2008); Nicola Lacey & Hanna Pickard, *The Chimera of Proportionality: Institutionalizing Limits on Punishment in Contemporary Social and Political Systems*, 78 Modern L. Rev. 216 (2015); Nicola Lacey, David Soskice & David Hope, *Understanding the Determinants of Penal Policy: Crime, Culture, and Comparative Political Economy*, 1 Ann. Rev. Criminology 195 (2018).

INDEX

Page numbers in italics indicate figures and tables.

Cornil, Paul: Attica Commission report paralleling Hague proposals of, 371; compared to James Bennett, 230; compared to Margery Fry, 143; degrading punishment objecting to country-specific determinations, 147; Hague 1950 IPPC Congress and, 139, *140*, 143; as IPPC treasurer, 131, 143; as Nazi prisoner, 140, 143, 144, 650n17; Nazi regime in Belgium and, 143, 650–51nn17–18; on prisoners' rights, 140, 143–44, 157, 371, 604; prisons' destruction of autonomy, 143–44, 160, 457, 597; proposing imprisonment's end, 142–45, 157, 230, 597; as rapporteur for Ad Hoc Experts' Advisory Committee, 149; UN 1955 Standard Minimum Rules and, 151

corporal punishment: ACA's *Manual of Correctional Standards* on, 135–36, 222–23, 6225, 232–33, 250; Bates suggesting UN study, 130; domestic punishment of women and children, 21; federal system not permitting, 143; German rejection in early 1900s, 86; Howard League on, 84, 91, 99, 101; IPPC Draft Revisions (1951) and, 147; League of Nations' minimum standards and, 5; religious use of, 21; solitary confinement as, 270–71; threat of, to maintain obedience, 44; UN 1955 Standard Minimum Rules and, 152, 586; US claiming as almost unknown in 1930s, 100. *See also* Arkansas prison cases; flogging; *Jackson v. Bishop* cases; *Talley* Rules; *Talley v. Stephens*; whipping

Correctional Leaders Association (CLA) (formerly Association of State Correctional Administrators), 560

corrections, 48–62; contemporary mission of "care" and respecting "rights," 586; exceptionalism, US claims of, 19, 607; micro-control and, 17, 144, 152, 156, 603; Model Penal Code, 229–30; philanthropic societies for prison reform, 49–51; professionalization of, 2, 9, 48, 59, 65, 149, 228, 368, 465, 579; "safety" and "security" as bywords for, 584. *See also* American Correctional Association; penology; rules for the treatment of prisoners (chronological list of standards)

corruption, 23, 168, 197, 246–47, 345, 358, 463, 464, 485, 489, 524, 525; bribes, 169, 197, 198, 356, 512, 524, 525; extortion, 194, 197, 301, 304, 326, 356, 359, 414, 493; graft, 464, 490; misuse of state funds, 522

costs of incarceration, 11; Arkansas, 520, 521, 526, *527*, 529–33, *530–31*; Auburn prison (NY), 42, 51; Eastern State Penitentiary (Philadelphia), 42; equal eligibility or equal-plus as price tag, 607; Guantánamo detainees, 536; Hutto on, 460; "minimal civilized measure of life's necessities" and, 534; other states (not Arkansas), 534–36, *535*; pay-to-stay approach, 354, 521–22, 528–29, 533–34, 573; per prisoner, 520, 522, 532, 536, 574; prisoner labor to offset (*see* forced farm labor); Rikers Island (NYC), 536; social costs, 13, 509, 522, 571, 581, 597;

See also Arkansas Board of
Correction
halfway houses, 539
Hamilton v. Love (ED Ark. 1973), 403,
408–9, 413
Hampton, Fred, 307
Haney, Craig, 551
hanging and lynchings, 72, 80, 175,
213, 306, 318
Harcourt, Bernard, 597, 624n39,
627n48, 639n31, 752n1, 752n38
Hare, Nicolas S., 681n41
Harlan, John Marshall: *Lee v.
Washington* (1968) memoran-
da, 290–91; *Lee v. Washington*
concurrence, 254
Harmon, Mose, 163, 182, 183–84,
208, 213, 218, 222
harm reduction, 14, 602
Harp, Robert, 275–76
Harper's Weekly's exposé of "shower
bath" (1858), 61. *See also* torture
Harris, George, 328
Harris, M. Kay, 717n13
Harris, Oren: Bennett and, 226; in
Congress, 200–201; letter to
Blackmun on 8th Cir. decision,
270–71; as trial judge in *Jackson
v. Bishop*, 200, 205. See also
Jackson v. Bishop (ED Ark. 1967)
Harrison, Eddie M., 369
Hart, H. L. A., 576
Hartog, Hendrik, 748n10
Hash, William (in *Talley v. Stevens*),
161, 162, 163, 172, 184
Haydis, Gary, on trial for firing bird-
shot at prisoners, 255, 316
Hayes, Rutherford B., 3–4, 55, 58, 59,
64, 65, 629n31
Hays, Brooke, 323
Hays, Steele, 323–24; as lawyer in
Holt I, 323–24
health of prisoners: American Pris-
on Association's 1930 principles
and, 62; Bentham on, 17, 34,
604–5; Cincinnati Principles

(1870) and, 57; deliberate
indifference to serious medical
needs, 505; Eighth Amendment
and, 601; food deprivation's
effect on, 247; Frankfurt 1846 &
1857 International Penitentiary
Congress and, 51, 57; Howard
League seeking to end crowding and diseases in prisons, 75;
inadequate medical delivery
system in California prisons,
568; involuntary hospitalization, 717n5; IPPC proposed
standards and, 92, 94, 97;
League of Nations' minimum
standards and, 100; medical
officer's consultation (*see*
medical officer's consultation
on punishment); prisoners'
copay for, 534; provision of, 7,
16, 223, 247, 303, 305, 325, 349,
351, 386–87, 422, 426–29, 440,
449, 479, 491, 505, 705–6n60;
sanitation risks to, 111, 153,
241, 247, 324, 329–30, 349, 357,
396, 472, 489; UN 1955 Standard
Minimum Rules and, 587. See
also *Brown v. Plata*; *Estelle v.
Gamble*
Heaney, Gerald, 259; as judge in
Finney I, 436; as judge in *Finney
II*, 459
Hearne, John J., 115
Henderson, Charles, 70, 73, 141
Henderson, Thelton, 553
Henley, J. Smith, 1–2, 8, 9, 162, 175,
348; assistance from Faulkner on Penitentiary Cases,
444; as Belk and Emmerling
trial judge, 312–13; as Bruton
trial judge, 314–17, 689n53; as
Eighth Circuit judge, 337, 444;
as federal district court judge,
174, 175–76, 201; grand jury
empaneled by (1969), 307–10;
as Haydis trial judge, 316; *Holt*

Miranda v. Arizona (1966), 245, 663n45
Miřička, August, 96
Mississippi County Penal Farm (Ark.), 403
Mississippi prisons: budget for, 534, *535*; prison-as-plantation, 164; prisoner labor as revenue source, 534; whipping and, 233
Missouri, "Ferguson" communities exploited by monetary sanctions, 573
Mitchell, John, 310–11, 366; speech at 1971 National Conference on Corrections, 367
Model Act for the Protection of Rights of Prisoners (1972), 373, 374–75
Model Penal Code (ALI), 229–30
Monroe v. Pape (1961), 179, 277
Morgan, Charles, Jr. (Chuck), 285, 288–89, 338
Morgan, William James, 317
Morris, Norval, 369, 372, 377
motion pictures, as corrupting influence, 80, 141
Motley, Constance Baker: as first Black woman on federal bench, 281; on solitary confinement and racial and religious discrimination, 279, 281–82. See also *Sostre v. McGinnis*
Muhammad, Abdul Maalik, as plaintiff in *Holt v. Hobbs* (2015), 283
Murton, Thomas (Tom), 199, 246, 248–49, 251–53, 255, 256, 307, 488
Muslims, 7; in Arkansas prison system, 410, 411–12, 421, 423, 450, 456, 479; Beto on, 412; *Cooper v. Pate* and, 179, 273, 275–79, 582; described as pretextual religion, 277; *Fulwood v. Clemmer* and, 279–80; Henley and, 421, 430, 432; Kaplan and, 421; law-

yers for Nation of Islam, 363, 679n21; in Lorton Reformatory (Va.), 279–80, 296; in Lucasville (Ohio), 546; prejudice against, 274–75, 281, 479; Quran in prisons, 277, 278, 280; religious mandates not respected, 283, 416, 430, 450, 484; *Sewell v. Peglow* and, 279–80; *Pierce v. LaVallee, Sostre v. McGinnis* and, 279, 280, 282, 680n29; Traynor on, 373; Urban on, 254
Mussolini, Benito, 110, 115–16, 125

NAACP: Legal Defense Fund/Legal Defense and Education Fund, 7, 262, 338, 363, 378, 481; Marshall and, 155; Walker and, 338
National Association of Black Law Enforcement Officers, 298
National Association of State Budget Officers (NASBO), 533, 534–36, 737n61; *Budgeting for Prisoners*, *530–31*
National Center for State Courts, 388
National Conference of Charities and Corrections (later National Conference for Social Welfare), 62, 76
National Conference on Corrections, 366; 1971 (Williamsburg), 365–67, 368, 438
National Correctional Standards Act (proposed), 377
National Council on Crime and Delinquency (NCCD): compensation for prisoner labor, 424; procedural safeguards for prisoners and, 381; rehabilitation and, 483. See also Model Act for the Protection of Rights of Prisoners
National Education Association on school paddling, 245–46

Prison Litigation Reform Act of 1996 (PLRA), 523, 553, 567–68, 608, 720n5

prison newspapers, 423–24. *See also The Pea Pickers Picayune/Cummins Journal*

Prison Policy Initiative, 300

Prison Policy Institute, 533

Prison Rape Elimination Act of 2003, 300

prison tourism, 46, 353, 580

prison violence. *See* death in custody; violence in prisons

prison workforce: health of, 578, 593–94, 596; number of (2023), 593; prisoners used as security personnel, 446, 513–15; redeployment in prison abolition scenario, 598; staff shortages in the United States and other countries, 578, 593–94 (*see also* Arkansas corrections officials and workforce); training of, 57, 97, 106, 296, 373, 465, 587; unionization of, 593; work-related health problems, 578, 593–94, 596. *See also* AMEND; Arkansas corrections officials and workforce; International Corrections and Prisons Association

privacy as right, 335, 375, 494, 498

privatization, 14, 526, 591–98

probation, 4, 12; as alternative to prison, 596; Ancel and, 142; Bill Clinton and, 462; as feeder of prison population, 13; Joynson-Hicks and, 79

procedural protections. *See* due process, procedural and substantive

Procunier v. Martinez (1974), 439

professionalization of corrections, 2, 9, 48, 59, 62, 65, 149, 368, 465, 579

proportionality in punishment, 4, 25; Beccaria on, 30, 186; Bentham on, 32, 186, 605; Blackmun in *Jackson v. Bishop* on, 265; *Holt I* and, 327; *Hutto v. Finney* and, 473; *Trop v. Dulles* and, 186; *Weems v. United States* and, 186

prostitution, 135, 629n28, 698n41

Pryor, David: appropriations and budgets, 461; as governor, 444, 460–61; parole and, 462; as US senator, 461

Pulaski County Jail (Ark.): ACLU settlement with (1988), 520; funding from sales tax, 521; *Hamilton v. Love*, 403, 408–9; Little Rock City Jail's relations with, 520; state prisoners dumped to reduce crowding, 511, *510*, 518, 520, 521

Pulaski County Penal Farm (Ark.), 302, 307, 308, 403; Henley ruling on conditions and ordering changes, 413–15; whipping and, 413

Purcell, Joe, 393–94

Quakers, 42, 83

quiet cells. *See* solitary confinement/ isolation

Rabinowitz, Victor, 281

race, racism, and racial discrimination, 7; in Arkansas, 175, 176, 261–62; Arkansas prison system and, 250–51, 257, 349, 415, 430–31, 433, 463, 486, 512, 527; Bennett on, 146; Black Codes, 14, 52, 601; colonial prison systems and, 148; death while in custody and, 574; evolving standards vs. originalism in recognition of right to be free from, 188; as factor related to issues of security, discipline,

Prisoners, 148–56 (*see also* UN Standard Minimum Rules for the Treatment of Prisoners)

1977 UN Standard Minimum Rules for the Treatment of Prisoners (revision), 587

2015 Nelson Mandela Rules (UN Standard Minimum Rules for the Treatment of Prisoners, revision) (*see* Nelson Mandela Rules)

Russia, 32, 68, 76, 139

Ryder, Thomas: *The Captive*, *37*, 39

sales tax for county and municipal jails, 521, 528, 529, 543

Salk, Jonas, 542

SaMarion, William (in *Pierce v. LaVallee*), 280

Sandifer, Jawn, 280

Sandin v. Conner (1995): Breyer dissent (joined by Souter), 554; Ginsburg dissent (joined by Stevens), 554; isolation not "atypical and significant" hardship but part of the "ordinary incidents of prison life," 551, 554–57, 585; Rehnquist majority opinion, 551, 554, 557, 585

Sanford v. Hutto (ED Ark. 1975), 697n39

Sarver, Robert, 256, *331*, *346*, 709n35; Bumpers and, 404–5; on Cash's Cummins Concert, 303; damage award against, 461; as doubling as Cummins superintendent due to lack of funding, 322, 326, 341–42; fired and replaced by Hutto, 256, 397, 402, 517; as first Arkansas Commissioner of Correction, 160, 256–57; free-world staff and, 332, 333; funding issues and, 322, 325, 326, 391, 392, 404; helping plaintiffs' lawyers in *Holt* cases, 256, 325, 332,

340–41, 345, 349; as hostage during prisoner uprising, 341, 350, 371; legislature's relations with, 342, 404; Muslims and, 412; prisoner farm labor and, 327, 396; reform efforts of, 256, 319–20, 321–22, 404, 426, 571; report to governor and legislature (1970), 396–97; Spiller and, 442; trustys and, 333, 341–42, 350, 396. See also *Holt v. Sarver* cases

Scalia, Antonin, 586, 748n12; *Brown v. Plata* dissent, 565, 569; *Johnson v. California* dissent, 299

Scanlon, Bob, 162–63, 169, 182, 658n25

Scarry, Elaine: *The Body in Pain: The Making and the Unmaking of the World*, 501

Schlanger, Margo, 700n2, 713n5, 734n43

Schoenfeld, Heather, 544

Schofield, Philip, 32, 605

schools: Arkansas desegregation, 173, 176–78, 306; *Milliken v. Bradley* requirements for school busing, 474–75; paddling in US, 20, 172, 238, 244–46, 335, 729n65; segregation, 10, 155; structural reform litigation in civil rights cases, 177

Schouten, Hendrick P., 621n3

Schwartz, Herman, 409

Schwarzenegger, Arnold, 567

Screws v. United States (1945), 686n18

Second Chance Act of 2008, 573

Section 1983 claims, 207, 276–78, 344, 476

Section 1988 claims, 719–20n5

security and order: as corrections' rationale, 7, 388; "dynamic security," 595; as excuse for radical isolation, 105, 109; Hutto and, 409; obedience ensured by threat of corporal

physical condition, 185; Harmon's testimony, 183–84, 224; Henley appointing Bullion and Ramsay as attorneys in, 179–80, 207, 661n23; *Holt I* citing, 327; *Holt II* citing, 415; *Holt III* citing, 426; impact of, 464, 488, 497–98, 582; pretrial order outlining issues, 180–83; prisoners as witnesses, 181, *181*; proportionality of punishment and, 186, 189; Talley and Stephens at initial hearing, 180–81; Talley's testimony, 183–84; Talley whipped for testifying, 6, 182

Tappen, Paul: *The Legal Rights of Prisoners*, 155, 655n54

Taylor, Otis, 345, 349, 697n37

teeter board as torture, 199, 210, 214, 217, 239, 242, 251–52

Teeters, Negley, 108–9, 641n16

Texas prisons: attorney fee awards and, 722n33; barring specific lawyer from representing prisoner, 380; budget for, 534, *535*; crowding violations and other unconstitutional conditions, 544; depopulation of facilities via consent decree, 544; due process owed to prisoner prior to solitary confinement (*Cruz v. Beto*), 379, 380; prison-as-plantation, 164; prisoner labor, 533, 534; prisoner-to-prisoner help with court filings, 380; *Rhodes v. Chapman* amicus brief, 500; *Ruiz v. Estelle* (SD Tex. 1980), 494, 502

Texas Public Policy Foundation, 572, 693n39

Texas TV used to torture prisoners, 407, 410, 412, 415, 423

Thälmann, Ernst, 118

Thatcher, Margaret, 591–92

Thirteenth Amendment: constitutional interpretation and, 188; prisoner as "slave of the state" and, 8, 141, 368, 385, 388, 516, 578, 585; Punishment Clause and prisoner labor, 8, 51–52, 211, 344, 353, 354, 361; state constitutional protections in lieu of, 574. *See also* enslavement

Thomas, Clarence: *Davis v. Ayala* concurrence, 558; *Hope v. Pelzer* dissent, 677n23; *Johnson v. California* dissent, 299; *Rahimi* dissent, 743–44n62; *Timbs v. Indiana* concurrence, 601, 752n2

Thompson, G. W. (Haydis codefendant), 317

Thompson, Heather: *Blood in the Water*, 370, 371

Timbs v. Indiana (2019), 301, 752n2

Time-In-Cell series (Arthur Liman Center for Public Interest Law), 300, 301, 561

Tocqueville, Alexis de, 3, 38–47, 48; as advocate for the incarcerated, 46, 50, 578, 580; on despotic control of prisons, 41–42, 46–47, 49; inspection of prisons in New York and Pennsylvania (with Beaumont), 39, 42–46, *42*, 47, 51, 54; Lieber as English translator for, 40–41; on New Orleans prison, 39; on obedience through threat of corporal punishment, 44–46; *On the Penitentiary System in the United States and Its Application in France* (with Beaumont), 39–47, *42*, 49, 57; on prisoners outside of rights of man, 47; on prisons as "schools for crime," 571; relevance to contemporary French prisons, 590; as slavery abolitionist, 40, 625n11. *See also*

Cir. appeal, 258. See also *Jackson v. Bishop* (8th Cir. 1968)

van Zyl Smit, Dirk, 591

Varner, Ray Vern, 317

Velde, Richard W., 375

Vera Institute for Justice, 533, 562, 574

victims' rights, 579–80

violence in prisons: Congress acknowledging, 573; creepers attacking sleeping prisoners, 324, 325, 327, 330, 335, 356, 471; duty to protect prisoner safety, 445–46; physical abuse by corrections staff, 185, 266, 335, 411, 414, 466, 512 (*see also* trustys of Arkansas prisons; whipping); rape, 252, 343, 345, 493, 513, 525; statistics collected under Prison Rape Elimination Act, 300; US DOJ reports (2019 & 2021) on Alabama and Mississippi prisons, 590. *See also* Arkansas prison cases; death in custody; excessive force

Violent Crime Control and Law Enforcement Act of 1994, 688n32

Virginia: compulsory sterilization law, 72. *See also* eugenics and Eugenics Movement; Lorton Reformatory

vocational programs. *See* rehabilitation

voting rights, loss of, 13, 58, 264, 573, 676n15; restoration of voting rights in other countries, 588, 606, *606*, 676–77n15; restoration of voting rights movements, 264, 424, 676–77n15

Voting Rights Act of 1965, 686n15

Wackenhut Corrections Corporation, 592

wages: first recognition of prisoner's right to, 63, 533; prisoner labor

without, 8, 97, 141, 372, 534; UN 1955 Standard Minimum Rules and, 151

Walker, John, 338, 687n26

Walker, Woodson, 518

Walker v. City of Birmingham (1967), 289, 681n47

Waller, Maurice, 85; draft of IPPC minimum standards by, 89–94, 96; Fry's acknowledgment of, 98

Wallin, R. E., 181, 662n28

"war": on crime, 156, 230, 295, 364, 458, 502; on "drugs," 408, 502, 520, 521; on "poverty," 10

wardens. *See* Arkansas corrections officials and workforce

warehousing, 49, 366, 463, 465, 493, 509, 540, 578, 585, 602, 730n3

Warren, Earl: *Lee v. Washington* oral argument and memoranda, 288–90; *Miranda v. Arizona* opinion, 663n45; *Trop v. Dulles* plurality opinion, 178, 185–86, 188, 265, 504–5, 506, 568, 582

Warren, Elizabeth: "The Accreditation Con," 541

Warren Court, 235, 245, 364

Warrington, Howard, 219

Washington, Caliph (in *Lee v. Washington*), 7, 284–85, 292, *293*, 681n36, 682n56

Washington Post: on *Brubaker* movie and Arkansas prison conditions (1980), 488; on whippings at Arkansas prison farm (1967), 199

water torture, 60, *61*

Weems v. United States (1910), 186

Weisberg, Bernard, 277, 679n10; *Secret Detention by the Chicago Police* (ACLU report 1959), 277

whipping: ACA on whipping and violent punishments, 60–62, *61*, 6225, 232–33, 268; Amsterdam Men's House of Correction, 22–24, *24*, 38; in Arkansas prison

816   INDEX